A Short
History
of the
Movies

A Short History of the Movies

3rd Edition

GERALD MAST

Bobbs-Merrill Educational Publishing   Indianapolis

The Bobbs-Merrill Company, Inc.
4300 West 62nd Street
Indianapolis, Indiana 46268

Third Edition
Second Printing 1981
Cover design by David Stahl
Cover illustration by Charlie Largent

Library of Congress Cataloguing in Publication Data

Mast, Gerald   1940–
    A short history of the movies.
    Includes bibliographical references and index.
    1. Moving-pictures—History.   I. Title.

PN1993.5.A1M39   1981   791.43'09   80-1802
ISBN 0-672-61521-5

Contents

Preface to the Third Edition

Once again five years has passed, and once again I'm writing the preface to a new edition of *A Short History of the Movies*. This newest *"Short History"* reflects many of the changes and developments that have shaped the history of the movies through the late 1970s and into the 1980s. First, two new major sections have been devoted to the two most important new cinema movements of the last decade: the "Neue Kino" of West Germany and the political films of the Third World. Let me express my gratitude to New Yorker Films and Unifilm, the primary distributors of these films in America, for making the essential texts available to me for study. Second, the book performs the inevitable evaluation of the most significant developments of the past half-decade in the art and commerce of the American and international cinema—particularly a re-evaluation of those directors whose work seems either more or less interesting than it did five years ago. There are revisions in the discussions of the European "New Masters" who have now become "Old Masters"—such as François Truffaut, Jean-Luc Godard, Bernardo Bertolucci, Pier-Paolo Pasolini, and others of their generation—as well as more extensive discussions of the new generation of European and American "Maybe Masters"—such as Woody Allen, Robert Altman, and Alain Tanner. Third, the new edition pays far more attention to the social history of film in its earlier periods—supplementing the discussions of the evolution of film art with a fuller treatment of film as a major shaping force in American and international social, political, and cultural life. This interest in film as cultural force itself reflects some of the most recent scholarly thinking about the historical importance of the movies in twentieth-century life.

These changes in the text have been accompanied by improvements and expansions in the photographs and the Appendix. The stills have been reintegrated with the text, making it easier for the photograph to illustrate the discussion. The number of stills has been increased, and, perhaps even more important, I have chosen to use frame blow-ups rather than production stills as much as possible. Although the use of frame blow-ups results in poorer reproduction than the perfectly composed production still, the blow-up precisely reproduces an actual frame from the film, which the production still most certainly does not. I am quite pleased, however, with the photographic quality of these new blow-ups (I have even replaced many illustrations from previous editions with a sharper still of the same frame), for which I am indebted to the apparatus that made them. Of all the methods I have used for making photographic stills of movie frames, the Bowen Illumitrans seems both to be the simplest and to produce the best results. Finally, I have overhauled the Appendix so that it accurately reflects the 16mm distributors of the key films in America, as stated in their 1980 catalogues. Given the radical changes in the 16mm distribution market over the past five years, the Appendix should be a very reliable guide to finding the films you may want to see.

Of course this new *"Short History"* is even more laughably not-short than the very not-short second edition. But I've become awfully attached to my original title. And so, I think, have many of my readers, who refer to the volume, as I do, as "Short History"—for short. I would also like to preserve the modest claim implied by the book's title: that however long the book may be, it still represents a mere fraction of the length that would be required if the book were to be "A Truly Complete and Encyclopedic History of the Movies."

I wish to thank all those people who helped these three editions to exist—and to exist so felicitously. First, let me thank once again all who added their judgment and knowledge to the creation or re-creation of the manuscript: Joe Adamson, Richard Meran Barsam, Jeanne Eichenseer, Antonin J. Liehm, Steven

Jack, Richard Dyer MacCann, John Matthew, Ned McLeroy, John Mong, Leonard Quart, William Reiter, and Burnell Y. Sitterly. Let me also thank all of you who considerately sent me your constructive suggestions, especially those anonymous readers who so conscientiously detailed their suggestions, corrections, and opinions at the request of the publisher. The revisions in this edition are the surest sign of my respect for the validity of those ideas.

Next, I would like to thank all those commercial film exchanges who lent their aid and their prints to my research for the first two editions: to Walter J. Dauler of Audio-Brandon Films (and where would film teaching and viewing be without this magnificent collection?); to Murray Glass of Em Gee Films (surely the best rental resource of pre-1920 films in America); to Bill Franz and Peter Meyer of Janus Films (one of the great pioneers of the "art film" movement of the 1950s); and to Darrell Flugg and Adam Reilly, who both served so ably and helpfully with Contemporary Films/McGraw-Hill.

Finally, I must express my gratitude to the Museum of Modern Art, although it is simply not possible to thank it sufficiently. I am indebted to Mary Corliss, Charles Silver, Emily Sieger, and Steven Harvey of the Museum's Film Department for their perpetual aid, encouragement, efficiency, courtesy, and patience. Without people like them and a research resource of this kind, there simply would be no scholarly film writing at all in America. It seems time for the various foundations and granting organizations to recognize the indispensable contribution of the Museum to American film study, a resource that has done its very best with inadequate funding and facilities.

1 Introductory Assumptions

The first audience watched a motion picture flicker on a screen in 1895, only some eighty-five years ago. In those eighty-five years the movies have developed from a simple recording device—the first films merely captured a scenic or not-so-scenic view—to a complex art and business. The first movie audiences were delighted to see that it was possible to record a moving scene on film; today we debate the desirability rather than the possibility of capturing an image. The important question for the first film audiences was, "Is the image discernible?" rather than, "Is the image meaningful?" From the simple beginning of turning a camera on to record a scene, filmmakers have learned that their art depends on the way their cameras shape the scene they are recording. Analogous to the novel, the finished movie is not just a story, but a story told in a certain way, and it is impossible to separate what is told from how it is told. Just as novelists discovered that narrative technique can either be subtly invisible—as in Dickens or Hemingway—or intrusively self-conscious—as in Joyce or Faulkner—so too the filmmaker can

construct a lucid, apparently artless story or a complex, almost chaotic maze for traveling to the story. The wonder is that while the evolution of narrative fiction can be traced back to Homer, the movies have evolved such complex techniques in only eighty-five years.

No one takes the movies more for granted than the present generation of moviegoers. For these "third-generation" audiences, who grew up with the polished, technically perfect sound, color, wide-screen films of the last thirty years, there is no consciousness of the way an entertainment novelty evolved into an art. Although the current "film generation" prefers seeing movies to reading novels, prefers making movies to writing poetry, and has pushed the movies into university curricula, it is surprisingly ignorant of the cumulative progress of the movie art—especially surprising since each student filmmaker lives through the identical historical evolution of film in learning the craft. The student begins by trying to record technically correct pictures on film, perfecting the ability to obtain clearly focused, properly exposed images. The student then realizes the

1

power of different pictorial compositions, the strategies of long shots and close-ups, the effects of different lenses and filters, the power of editing in creating a film's meaning and tone. The student's first film is usually a black-and-white silent film with musical accompaniment: precisely the kind of film that evolved during the first thirty-five years of film history. Only after gaining some confidence with this kind of film does the new filmmaker experiment with color and synchronized sound.

The history of the movies is, first of all, the history of a new art. Though it has affinities with the novel, the drama, the dance, painting, photography, and music, like each of these kindred arts it has a "poetics" of its own. When the early films turned from scenic views to fictional stories, directors suspected that the "poetics" of the film was the same as for the stage. Stage acting, stage movement, stage stories, stage players, and stage perspectives dominated the first story films. The camera was assumed to be a spectator in a theatre audience, and just as the spectator has only one seat, the camera had only one position from which to shoot a scene.

Time and experimentation revealed that the camera was anchored by analogy alone—and that the analogy was false. The scene—the locale—is the basic unit of the stage because space in the theatre is so concrete. The audience sits here, the characters play there, the scenery is fixed in space behind the action. But space in the film is completely elastic; only the screen is fixed, not the action on it. Directors discovered that the unit of a film is the shot, not the scene, that shots can be joined together in any number of combinations to produce whole scenes and that scenes can be varied and juxtaposed and paralleled in any number of ways. Unity of place, a rather basic and practical principle of the stage, does not apply to the movie. More applicable is a principle of an appropriate succession

of images that produces the desired narrative continuity, the intended meaning, and the appropriate emotional tension of the film as a whole. By the end of the silent era this principle had not only been discovered but demonstrated.

The discovery of sound raised doubts about the discoveries of the preceding thirty years. Once again the analogy with the stage was suspected; once again stage actors, stage writers, stage directors, and stage techniques flooded the movies. And once again, the analogy was found to be false. Just as the stage is anchored visually in space, so too is it anchored by sound. Sounds come from the speaker's mouth; you see both speaker and mouth. But movies were free to show any kind of picture while the words came from the speaker's mouth. Synchronization of picture and sound also allowed for the disjunction of picture and sound. Further, the freedom of the movies from spatial confinement allowed a greater freedom in the kinds of sounds they could use: natural sound effects, musical underscoring, distortion effects, subjective thoughts, and so forth. Whereas the history of the silent film could be summarized as the discovery of the different means of producing an evocative *succession* of visual images, the history of the sound film is the discovery of the different means of producing an evocative *integration* of visual images and sound.

Just as the history of the novel is, to some extent, a catalogue of important novels and the history of drama a catalogue of important plays, the history of film as an art centers on important films. In film history, a discussion of the significant films is especially relevant, for the individual films are not only milestones on an historical path but also significant artistic discoveries that immediately influenced directors of other films. Although Shakespeare drew from Seneca, and Brecht from Shakespeare, even more immediate was the influence of Griffith on Ford or Ford on Bergman or Bergman on Allen. Without years of stage tradition to draw on, film artists have drawn on the exciting discoveries of their contemporaries. The internationalism of film distribution has always guaranteed the rapid dispersal of any significant discovery.

A study of eighty-five years of film history has led me to make one basic assumption: no truly great film has ever been made without the vision and unifying intelligence of a single mind to create and control the whole film. Just as there is only one poet per pen, one painter per canvas, there can be only one creator of a movie. The *"auteur" theory* is as valid for film as for any other art. Whether the *auteur* improvises the whole film as it goes along—as Griffith did—or whether the filmmaker works according to a preconceived and scripted plan, a single mind must shape and control the work of art. The difficulty with movies, however, is that their very massiveness and complexity work against their having such an *auteur*. The director is often no more than a mechanic, bolting together a machine (often infernal) that someone else has designed.

Those who view the film as an inferior artistic medium most frequently argue that the conditions of making a commercial film nullify its chances for artistic success. The great work of film art is the exception, the mediocre factory product the rule. To see the history of films as several dozen great movies is to simplify the history. All movies, great or small, have been made in the context of the entire film industry. Any film history that intends to reveal the genesis of today's film world must, in addition to discussing the film as art, discuss three related problems that have always influenced the artistic product—and continue to influence it today: the film as business, the film as cultural product and commodity, and the film as machinery.

Movies today are a billion-dollar business. The choice of directors, stars, and scripts is often in the hands of businessmen, not in the heads of artists. The company that invests $20,000,000 in a picture ought to be able to insure the safety of its investment. Commerical values outweigh artistic ones. The name Hollywood, for some synonymous with glamor, is for others synonymous with selling out. For decades Hollywood's commercial crassness has served American novelists—from F. Scott Fitzgerald and Nathaniel West to Gore Vidal—as a metaphor for the vulgar emptiness of the "American Dream." If the gifted young director today seems to face a distasteful dilemma—sell out or get out—directors have faced the same dilemma for sixty years.

The awesome financial pressures of Hollywood are partly responsible for the growing number of independent and underground films—just as Broadway production demands are responsible for the Off-Broadway and Off-Off-Broadway theatres. Young filmmakers often prefer to work alone with the life and life-styles around them; their sole expense is equipment and film. These filmmakers are, in a sense, regressing to the earliest period of film history. But every artistic innovation since then has ironically necessitated spending more money. If lighting was a step forward in film toning, it also required spending money on lighting equipment and on people who knew how to control it. If acting was to be improved, proven actors had to be retained. And as actors supplied greater and greater proofs, they demanded higher and higher salaries. Longer films required more film, more actors, more story material, and more publicity to insure a financial return on the greater investment. It took only twenty-five years for the movies to progress from cheap entertainment novelty to big business.

Making a film is such a massive and complex task it is a wonder that an artistically whole movie can be made at all. The huge sums of money required to make a movie merely reflect the hugeness of the task of taking a movie from story idea to final print. Shooting is painfully slow. It takes time to perfect each setup: lights must be carefully focused and toned, the shot's composition must be attractive and appropriate, the set must be dressed, background action (extras) must be coordinated with the action of the principals, actors must have mastered their interpretations of lines so that a single shot fits into the dramatic fabric of the whole film, make-up must be correct, costumes coordinated, the positions of the players must match those in the preceding shot. And so forth. Because it takes so much time to set up a shot, producers economize by shooting all scenes together that require the same location or setup, regardless of their position in the film's continuity. But even with such economies, to get five minutes of screen time "in the can" is a healthy day's work. Sometimes, on location with mammoth spectacle pictures, a whole day can be devoted to a fifteen-second piece of the finished film—the sun, the caravans, the camels, the soldiers, and the gypsy maidens must be caught just as they reach their proper places. The devastating effect of accomplishing so little each shooting day is that a film's budget is calculated on the number of days it will take to shoot, the average expense for a color film being in excess of $100,000 per day. Whereas the novelist or poet or painter can sit alone and work with a minimum of expense (and waste), the film artist is the servant of an uneconomical master. Even the ten-minute student film can cost over $1,000 for film stock and laboratory costs alone—exclusive of the original cost of the equipment.

Because movies cost so much to make, the companies that spend that money are understandably concerned about getting it back again. The only way to retrieve expenses is with ticket receipts. The film artist not only is at the mercy of expensive machines and services but also is dependent on the consent of the entertained. The history of the movies as a business is inextricably linked with the history of the movies as a mass entertainment medium. To get the public to spend its dollars at the box office— whether it be a theatre box office, the home box office, or a store selling video cassettes or discs— the producer must give the public what it wants, or make the public want what it gets. History indicates that the public has gotten some of both. The crassest movie maxim is the famous, "The box office is never wrong." The validity of the maxim depends on the kinds of questions you ask the box office to answer.

Just as film art has changed radically in the course of its eighty-five year history, so too film audiences have changed. The first movie patrons in America were also patrons of vaudeville houses and variety shows. When those audiences tired of the same kinds of film programs, the movies found a home with lower- and working-class patrons. Small theatres sprang up in poor sections of cities; admission was a nickel or dime. The rich and educated saw movies only on an evening of slumming. As film art and craft improved, larger and more expensive movie theatres opened in respectable and central areas of the cities. Films tried to appeal to a wide range of tastes and interests, much like television today. In this period there was little consciousness of movies as an art; they were mass entertainment. And as with today's network television, the educated, the literati, and the serious shunned them. H. L. Mencken sardonically lauded the movies as the appropriate artistic attainment of the American "booboisie." Similes linking movies with tastelessness and movie patrons with morons continually popped up in fiction and articles of the 1920s and 1930s. Only

The movies as mirror of American social history: social institutions responsive to human needs and challenges (Jean Arthur in the U.S. Senate of Mr. Smith Goes to Washington, *1938); three returning servicemen joyfully view the land they fought to save (Dana Andrews, Fredric March, and Harold Russell in* The Best Years of Our Lives, *1946)*

recent American audiences, the third generation of movie-goers, expect the film to be art and not formulaic entertainment. Current audience surveys indicate that the overwhelming majority of steady movie patrons are between seventeen and twenty-nine with bachelor's degrees either in sight or in hand. The present movie audience takes its movies as seriously as it does the products of the novelist and poet. The new influence of the intellectual movie critics, who now exert more power and attract more attention than the critics of any other art, is merely a symptom of these new expectations. As usual, producers are giving the public what it wants.

This discussion of the evolving audiences for movies indicates the close connection between the movies as an art and conditions in American culture as a whole. Particular cultural conditions influence, if not dictate, the particular qualities and quantities of films in any given era. For a specific movie to become a major hit at a specific time indicates, at least partially, the cultural fact that a sufficient number of people wanted or needed or demanded or responded to just that film then. To compare *Mr. Smith Goes to Washington* of 1938, with *The Best Years of Our Lives* of 1946, with *Rebel Without a Cause* of 1955, with *The Graduate* of 1968, and with *Saturday Night Fever* of 1977 is to write a history of American culture over the past five decades. Any history of the movies must both take account of and account for these cultural shifts and conditions.

A final influence on the movies important to any discussion of their history is the dependence of film art on machines. Appropriately enough, our technological century has produced an art that depends on technology. The first filmmakers were not artists but tinkerers. The same spirit that produced a light bulb and a telephone produced a movie camera and projector. The goal in making a movie was not to create beauty but to display a scientific curiosity. The invention of the first cameras and projectors set a trend that was to repeat itself with the introduction of every new movie invention: the invention was first exploited as a novelty in itself and only later integrated as one tool in making the whole film. The first camera merely exploited its ability to capture images of moving things. The first synchronized-sound films exploited the audience's excitement at hearing the words that the actor's lips were mouthing. Most of the first color films were merely colorful, many of the first wide-screen films merely wide.

Perhaps no invention so clearly demonstrated the ephemerality of pure gimmickry than the short-lived 3-D movie. There were obvious limits to the number of knives, spears, arrows, hatchets, and swords that could be thrown at an audience before it would begin to take itself elsewhere. The technical gimmickry of 3-D was so pervasive that the innovation could rarely be assimilated into a greater artistic whole. The same extinction seemed to threaten Cinerama, with its inevitable rides on roller coasters, hydrofoils, stagecoaches, dogsleds, and anything else that moved, until Stanley Kubrick made a lady of her with *2001* in 1968. Novelty became an artistic tool; rather than exploiting movement for its own sake, Kubrick used movement to echo the subjective impressions of his characters. However, *2001* may have indeed been the ultimate Cinerama film, for there have been no other films made in the process in over a decade.

No other art is so tied to machines. Some of the most striking artistic effects are the products of expanding film technology. For example, the awesome compositions in depth and shadow of Welles's *Citizen Kane* are partially the result of the conversion from carbon-arc lamps to incandescent lighting in the studies and the development of high-speed panchromatic film, which allowed much greater depth-of-field. Research has converted the camera from an erratic, hand-cranked film grinder to a smooth, precise clockworks. Research has silenced the camera's noise without using clumsy, bulky devices to baffle the clatter. Research has developed faster and faster black-and-white stocks, enabling greater flexibility in lighting, composition, and shooting conditions. Research has developed color film stocks that are not only accurate in recording color but also can provide different effects for different artistic purposes. Research has improved sound recording and sound reproduction, has developed huge cranes and dollies, has perfected a wide assortment of laboratory processes and effects, has invented special lenses and special projectors and special filters. Film equipment is so sophisticated that no film artist can master all of it; filmmakers are dependent on mechanics as well as machines.

Because they are mechanical, because they are big business, because they pander to audience tastes, movies have never before been ushered into the temple of high art by those who guard the doors. Throughout their history the movies have carried on a parasitic flirtation with the stage. Conceding the cultural superiority of the older art, movie producers and artists borrowed properties and people from Broadway. The typical route to Hollywood for a story idea was from fiction to Broadway to sound stage. But in the 1970s a significant detour on this route is a sign of the changing times; Broadway now regularly adapts screenplays into stage plays. Despite the difficulties of money and machine, the movies have become the dominant and the liveliest living art.

This short history will follow the road the movies have traveled to get here. To keep a short history even this "short" has required several decisions. First, this history aims at revealing significant trends and turns along the road rather than detailing exhaustive lists of titles, directors, and dates. For further reading in any particular period, the reader should consult the bibliography. Second, because the history of the American film is most relevant to American readers, this short history allots more space to a discussion of American movie practices. But although American films are the dominant force in the film world, to write a history of the art that neglects the influences of non-American films is impossible. Third, the particular films that have been singled out for detailed discussion are not only significant contributions to film art but are readily available in 16mm prints for rental and viewing. A list of these films and their distributors appears in the Appendix. Finally, this history concentrates on the fictional film almost exclusively. The aesthetic principles of the nonfiction (documentary) film are different enough from those of the fictional (or story) film that the documentary or factual film deserves a separate study of its own.

2 Birth

Although some film historians trace the origin of movies back to cave paintings or Plato's Cave of the Shadows, the history of the movies proper begins with the steps leading to the invention of the movie camera and projector. This era in movie prehistory is the province of inventors, not artists. The nineteenth-century mechanical mind created machines for travel, machines for work, machines for the home, and, in the process, machines for entertainment. In the second third of the nineteenth century, three kinds of mechanical experimentation began that, by the end of the century, had combined to create the motion picture: research in the phenomenon of persistence of vision, research in still photography, and research in mechanized audience entertainments.

Persistence of Vision

Movies are an optical illusion. We believe we are watching completely continuous, fluid motion on the screen. In fact, we watch short, jerky, discontinuous bits of

the motion, which the eye sees as continuous because of the way the eye sees and the way the brain interprets that information. The brain retains the images of the eye for a fraction of a second longer than the eye actually records them. If it did not, we would be conscious of the hundreds of times a day that the eyelids blink. The mind has no consciousness of blinking because, although the lids cover the eyeball for a fraction of a second, the mind retains the preblink image. A variation of the same principle, known as the "Phi Effect," accounts for the way that a flashlight rotated in a circle in the darkness appears to produce a circle of light. The brain blurs the individual points of light into a circular figure. If the eye saw sixteen individual but related figures of a moving object in rapid succession, the brain would connect the pieces to make a single, fluid sequence out of them. This optical phenomenon is known as persistence of vision.

Persistence of vision makes movie action seem as fluid and continuous as live action. It cancels out the differences between the event and the recording of the event. The genuine difference between the two can easily be grasped by understanding how motion pictures record movement. The movie camera exposes a single frame at a time; each frame is a single, fixed, still photograph. The succession of frames produces the appearance of movement. To record an image on film, the camera's shutter remains open about one-thirtieth of a second. The shutter exposes, say, sixteen (the approximate, although not standard, silent speed) of these images each second. Simple mathematics indicates that one second of film thus exposed contains only 16/30ths of a second of exposed action and 14/30ths of a second of darkness (of blinking) between the frames. Whereas, in viewing, a second of film appears to be a continuous line, —————————————, it is really a discontinuous one, ---------------------------------------. The eye's persistence of vision fills in the blank spaces.

Persistence of vision, known by the ancients, was investigated and demonstrated by European thinkers and tinkerers between 1820 and 1835. One of the early discussions of the phenomenon was by Peter Mark Rôget, author of the famous thesaurus. Another English scientist, Sir John Herschel, bet a friend that he could show the head and tail of a shilling at the same time. And then Sir John spun the coin. The eye blurred the spinning sides of the coin into a single image. In 1825, Dr. John Ayrton Paris had developed a little toy based on this same spinning-coin principle. On one side of a circular board was a parrot, on the other an empty cage. By holding the board by two attached straps and then spinning it, the viewer saw the parrot inside the cage. Again, two images had melted into one. Paris called his little toy the Thaumatrope.

Four years later, in 1829, Joseph Antoine Ferdinand Plateau published his investigations on persistence of vision, and three years after that (1832) he marketed

his own toy to demonstrate his theoretical research. Painted on a flat, circular piece of board were individual designs in slightly varying positions. When the board was grasped by a handle, held up in front of a mirror, and then spun, the individual designs became a continuous, animated sequence. In order to see the designs moving (rather than as a blur), the viewer looked into the mirror through little slits cut into the circular board of the toy. Plateau called his toy the Phenakistiscope. Plateau's researches were important, for in the course of them he discovered that sixteen images per second were an optimal number for producing continuous movement. The early filmmakers would also discover the utility of sixteen frames per second. In addition, Plateau's machine required moments of darkness, of nonimage, in order to make the images appear to move. The eye needed momentary resting time to soak in the images. A successful projector would not be invented until an analogy to Plateau's slits was discovered.

A German inventor, Simon Ritter von Stampfer, developed the same machine as Plateau's Phenakistiscope in the same year; he called it the Stroboscope. Based on the same principle as the Phenakistiscope and Stroboscope, many refined versions of this toy appeared throughout the nineteenth century. In 1834, William George Horner created a stroboscopic machine that used a circular drum rather than a flat circular board. Exchangeable paper strips would fit inside the circular drum. When the viewer looked through the slits in the drum, which allowed moments of darkness, the pictures on the spinning paper strips appeared in delightfully sequential motion. Horner called his toy the Zootrope (or Zoetrope).

Also in 1834, Baron Franz von Uchatius began combining stroboscopic toys with the magic lantern—a candle-powered slide projector. Uchatius lined up a series of projectors side by side

Early persistence of vision toys: the Thaumatrope, a Zoetrope wheel with paper strip, and a primitive version of what would become a Mutoscope.

and focused them on the same screen. In each lantern was a slide with a slightly different phase of movement. By running with a torch from lantern to lantern, Uchatius threw an apparent sequence of movement on the screen. The result was the progenitor of the animated cartoon. Uchatius's experiments with lanterns continued, and by 1853 he had developed a Projecting Phenakistiscope, combining a phenakistiscopic disc with a single magic lantern. When the operator spun the disc, the lantern threw the sequential animated movement on the screen.

By the end of the nineteenth century, hundreds of variations on these toys abounded, each with its own name, either simple or ornate: Praxinoscope, Choreutoscope, Wheel of Life. All of these stroboscopic toys shared, in addition to the common use of persistence of vision, several traits that were to continue

as trends in later movie history. Most striking was the inventors' passion for fancy Greek and Latin names to dignify their dabblings: Thaumatrope, Phenakistiscope, Viviscope, Zootrope. This passion for nominal embroidery would later dominate the first era of motion pictures—Kinetoscope, Bioscope, Vitascope, Cinématographe—and beyond it—Vitaphone, Technicolor, CinemaScope, television, stereophonic. Also striking is the simultaneity of discoveries by different men in different countries. Many different heads and hands applied themselves to the same problems, primarily in France, England, Germany, and the United States. Such simultaneous experimenting produced a confusion that would continue throughout the century, so that even today these four countries all claim to have invented the motion picture. The claim of each chauvinistic historian can be supported with solid evidence. The validity of each claim is contingent upon whether one defines the motion picture as invented when it was conceived, when it was patented, when it was photographed on film, or when it was projected in public.

All the stroboscopic experiments and toys used drawn figures. Before the movies could progress from stroboscopic toy to motion pictures of the natural world, the means to record the natural world had to be discovered. Simultaneous with the scientific dabblings in persistence of vision were scientific dabblings with photography.

Photography

Before there could be motion pictures, there had to be pictures. A moving picture was born from the union of the stroboscopic toys and the still photograph. The principle of photography dates back to the Renaissance and Leonardo da Vinci's plan for a *camera obscura*. This device—literally translated as dark room or chamber—was a completely dark enclosure that admitted light only through a small hole. The *camera* projected an inverted reproduction of the scene facing it on the wall opposite. After a lens was introduced to brighten and sharpen the image, all the *camera obscura* needed to become a camera was a photographic plate to replace the wall. Nineteenth-century scientists set out in pursuit of this plate that could fix the inverted image permanently.

As early as 1816, Nicéphore Niepce, a Frenchman, used metal plates to capture rather fuzzy and temporary images, which he called Heliographs. But it was another Frenchman, Louis Jacques Mandé Daguerre, who in 1839 determined the future of photography by making clear, sharp, permanent images on silvered copperplate. The exposure time required for an image was fifteen minutes, and the first sitters for Daguerreotypes (the first photos were named after their father) had to sit motionless for fifteen minutes, their heads propped up to keep from wiggling. Before photography could become more practical, exposure time would have to be cut. There obviously could be no motion pictures, which require multiple exposures per second, until the photographic material was sensitive enough to permit such shutter speeds. (Indeed, the first still cameras did not even use a shutter.) After Daguerre's original perfecting of the basic principle, photographic stocks became faster and faster, permitting a three-minute exposure by 1841. Before thirty years had passed, the shutter had been invented and faster photographic plate allowed for exposures of minute fractions of a second.

The first attempts at motion photography were posed stills that simulated continuous action. The stills were then projected with a Projecting Phenakistiscope to give the appearance of movement. But a real motion picture required a continuous action to be first analyzed into its component units and then resynthesized, rather than a simple synthesis of static, posed bits of action. The first man to break a single process into discrete photographic units was an Englishman transplanted to California, Eadweard Muybridge. Muybridge, whose career was as bizarre as the spelling of his first name, was a vagabond photographer and inventor, who had been entangled in a divorce and murder scandal over his wife. In 1872, he was hired by the governor of California, Leland Stanford, to help win a $25,000 bet. Stanford, an avid horse breeder and racer, bet a friend that at some point in the racehorse's stride all four hooves left the ground. In 1877, after five years of unsuccessful research, Muybridge set up twelve cameras in a row along the racing track. He attached a string to each camera shutter and stretched the string across the track. He chalked numerals and lines on a board behind the track to measure the horse's progress. Stanford's horse then galloped down the track, tripping the wires, and Mr. Stanford won $25,000 that had cost him only $100,000 to win.

For the next twenty years, Muybridge perfected his multiple-camera technique. He increased his battery of cameras from twelve to forty. He used faster, more sensitive film. He added white horizontal and vertical lines on a black background to increase the impression of motion. He shot motion sequences of horses and elephants and tigers, of nude ladies and wrestling men and dancing couples. He mounted his photographs on a Phenakistiscope wheel and combined the wheel with the magic lantern for public projections of his work. He called his invention—really just a variation on Uchatius's Projecting Phenakistiscope—the Zoopraxiscope, another very fancy name for a not-so-fancy machine. Muybridge traveled to Europe where he gave special showings of his Zoopraxiscope to admiring scientists and photographers. Despite Muybridge's imitators, and despite

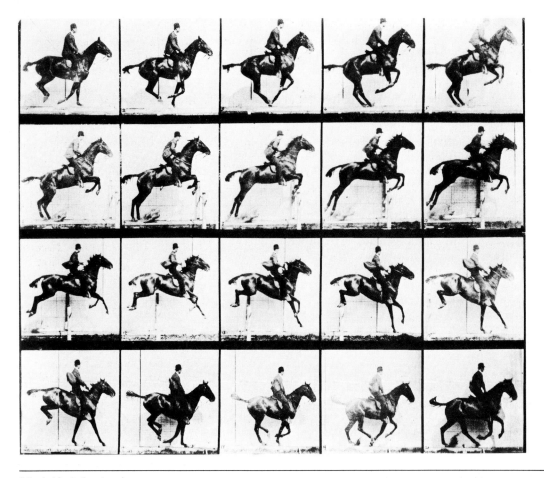

Muybridge's leaping horse

his international honors, his discovery was obviously a dead end. There were limits on the number of animals in motion that one could find interesting. Muybridge's later refinements never surpassed the importance of his first set of motion photographs. Continuous motion had been divided into distinct frames, but it had not yet been photographed by a single camera.

One of Muybridge's hosts in Paris was another scientist, Étienne-Jules Marey, who was experimenting with motion photography. In 1882, Marey was to shoot the first motion pictures with a single camera. "Shoot" quite literally applies to Marey's experiment, for his camera looked like a shotgun. Marey's photographic gun is probably the etymological source of our present "shooting," which we use synonymously with photographing. The photographic gun used a long barrel for its lens and a circular chamber containing a single glass photographic plate. The circular plate rotated twelve times in the chamber during a single second of shooting, leaving all twelve exposures arranged in a ring around the glass plate. Like Muybridge, Marey photographed men and animals: runners, jumpers, fencers, trotting horses, falling cats, flying gulls. But Marey's Chronophotographs produced a much more fluid analysis of motion, the finished print resembling a surreal multiple exposure. In 1888, Marey replaced the glass plate with paper roll film, allowing more and faster exposures. Photography had reached the threshold of motion pictures.

To produce a motion picture that was more than a one- or two-second snippet of activity, a material had to be developed that could accommodate not twelve or forty or one hundred images, as Marey's eventually did, but thousands of images. In 1884, George Eastman began his experiments with celluloid roll film, which he intended to use in his Kodak still camera. By 1888 the camera and film were ready; photography, which had been the sole property of professionals, was now any man's hobby. Eastman's celluloid film became the natural material for further experiments in motion photography. This American discovery of celluloid film shifts the history of the movies back across the Atlantic from France.

Thomas Edison

Appropriately enough, the American father of the movies is the ultimate representative of the ingenious, pragmatic American inventor-businessman—Thomas Edison. The supreme tinkerer threw his support behind the new tinker's craze of motion photography. But Edison gave the motion picture little more than support. Although he assigned employees and laboratory space to the photographic project, he himself gave motion pictures little thought, an oversight that was later to cost him both prestige and money. Edison's real interest in motion pictures was to provide visual accompaniment for the phonograph he had invented earlier. Pictures were not important in themselves but were merely to make the phonographic experience fuller. His original idea was to etch tiny photographs on a wax cylinder in much the same way that sound was recorded on his phonograph cylinders. The same cylinder would contain both sound and picture and could be reproduced by a single machine. The idea was theoretically good enough, but the practical problem of reducing photographic images to pin points was unsolvable. Reproduction of the images was poor and the cylinder was too small to hold a long enough segment of pictorial action. After Eastman perfected celluloid film, Edison's director of the motion picture project, William Kennedy Laurie Dickson, persuaded the "Wizard" to give up cylinders for celluloid. Dickson soon sent his first order to Eastman.

Success did not come quickly. Edison traveled to Europe in 1889, leaving Dickson in charge of perfecting the motion picture apparatus. On Edison's return in October, Dickson claims to have greeted his boss with a projected film on a screen, roughly synchronized with sound. Dickson called the machine the Kinetophonograph. Unfortunately, no evidence other than Dickson's claim exists for this amazingly early synchronization of projection and sound. The earliest pieces of existing film can be traced to no earlier than 1890, and the earliest whole film on record at the Library of Congress is *Fred Ott's Sneeze*, which a contemporary magazine article describes as being shot in 1891. According to legend, one of Edison's mechanics, Fred Ott, was a very comical fellow. Dickson selected Fred as the subject for one of his first strips on celluloid. Of course, Fred froze in front of the camera for the first few takes, but he eventually sneezed his comical sneeze and the first celluloid close-up was in the can.

The problem now confronting Dickson was how to share that sneeze with the public. Edison, worried about the poor

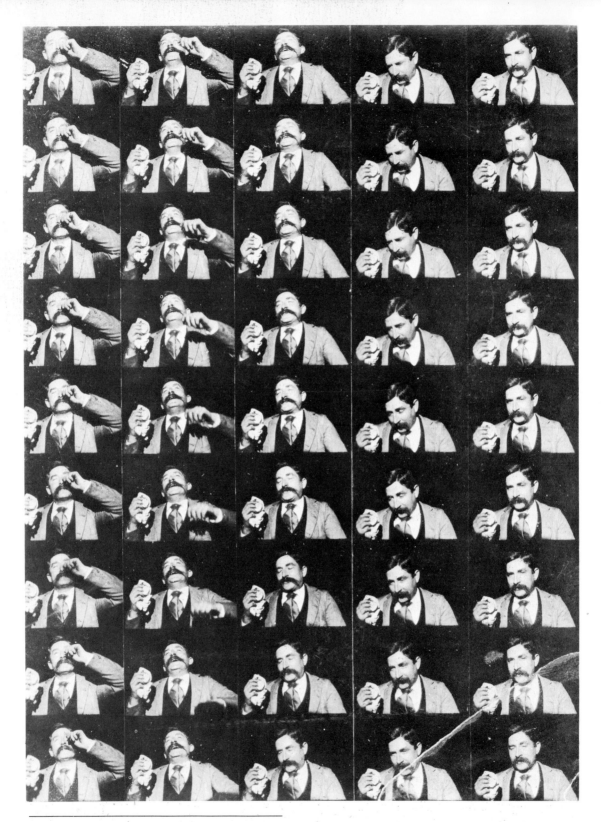

Fred Ott's Sneeze

A Kinetoscope Parlor: phonographs at the left (complete with handkerchiefs for wiping the earpieces), Kinetoscopes on the right.

reproduction of the projected images, decided on direct viewing. Rather than seeing an image projected for large groups, the individual customer would put an eye to the hole of a machine and view a single filmstrip inside it. Edison's decision was based partly on his integrity as an inventor and partly on his greed as a businessman. He saw the greater clarity of reproduction in the little peephole machine; and he was sure he would make more money from the novelty if it were displayed to one person at a time rather than a hall full of people who would quickly tire of a silly novelty. Edison so underestimated the potential of moving pictures that he refused to spend $150 to extend his American patent rights to England and Europe. His shortsightedness would prove expensive.

In 1891, Edison applied for patents on his camera, the Kinetograph, and his peephole viewer, the Kinetoscope. Slowness of manufacture and distribution retarded the popularity of the invention, but within three or four years Kinetoscope Parlors, showing Fred's

sneeze and other items, had sprung up all over the United States. Rows of Kinetoscope machines beckoned the customer to peek at the new marvel of mechanically recorded life.

The requirements and design of this Kinetoscope machine strongly influenced the films that Dickson shot for them. Wound around spools inside the Kinetoscope, the film's ending led continuously into its beginning, exactly as the Phenakistiscope wheels or Zootrope strips had done. The space inside the Kinetoscope box limited the length of a filmstrip to fifty feet, and since Edison's cameras and viewers ran at forty frames per second, the Kinetoscope contained less than a half-minute of action. The films for these machines were not edited; whatever Dickson shot became the finished film. The films had no stories, just a simple bit of action or movement. The most popular filmstrips were bits of dancing, juggling, or clowning, of natural wonders from all over the world, and even of staged historical events.

Despite the crudeness of the first

Edison films—and despite his blunder about projection—Edison left his mark on the future of film. His most important contribution was the decision to use perforations on the side of the film to help it roll smoothly past the shutter. The Edison-Dickson perforations quickly became the standard throughout the world and were known as the American Perforation. Edison was also the father of the movie studio. In order to produce filmstrips for the Kinetoscope Parlors, Dickson built a small room especially for motion pictures adjacent to the Edison laboratories. Because the outside of the studio was protected with black tar-paper, the room quickly became known as the Black Maria, at that time slang for paddy wagon. Dickson mounted his camera on a trolley inside the Black Maria so that it could move closer or further away, depending on the subject of the film. The camera, however, never changed position during the shooting. To light the action, the Black Maria's roof opened to catch the sunlight. The whole studio could be rotated to catch the sun, so that the scene would always be sufficiently lit.

The disadvantages of the Black Maria are obvious. The room was really a small sunlit theatre with the camera as single spectator. There was even a specified stage area where the juggler, dancer, comic, or animal performed. Mobility was further curtailed by the bulky heaviness of Dickson's camera and by Edison's insistence on using electricity rather than a hand crank to run it, so that the machine remained perpetually indoors and inert.

Freeing the camera from its cage and freeing the filmstrip from its peephole box were the final steps in the evolution of the movie machine. For these steps the history of film travels back across the Atlantic.

Projection

The problem of projecting motion pictures was surprisingly difficult to solve. After the principles of motion photography had been discovered and a camera developed to demonstrate the principles, one would have thought that

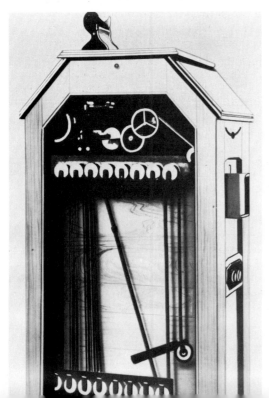

The Kinetoscope mechanism (left); *The first movie studio: Edison's Black Maria* (above)

projecting the images would come easily. In fact, early projection attempts produced blurry images, ripped film, and a great deal of noise. Edison's decision to shelve projection was as much a realization of difficulties as a business blunder. On the other hand, it should have been clear to Edison, as it was to other inventors, that a projected motion picture was the next evolutionary step. For hundreds of years audiences had delighted in mechanically projected shows. Even before photography, audiences had sat in darkened rooms and watched projected images on a screen.

The invention of the magic lantern is attributed to Father Athanasius Kircher, who, in 1646, made drawings of a box that could reproduce images by means of a light passing through a lens. That box was the ancestor of today's slide projector. In the eighteenth century, showmen trooped across Europe giving magic-lantern shows, projecting drawings and, much later, photographs for paying customers. From the beginning, the magic lanternists sought to make their static images move. They developed lantern slides with moving parts and moving patterns. They used multiple lanterns to give the impression of depth and sequence. The most famous of these multiple-lantern shows was the Phantasmagoria, in which ghosts and spirits were made to move, appear, and disappear with the aid of moving lanterns and mirrors. The stroboscopic toys of the nineteenth century further enlarged the lanternist's bag of motion tricks.

The last in this string of premovie projection entertainments was the movie's closest ancestor—the photo play. In the late nineteenth century, Alexander Black, an American author and lecturer, combined the magic-lantern slide, photography, and narrative to produce a complete play with live narrator, live actors, and pictorial slides. Unlike the stroboscopic lantern shows, the goal of these entertainments was not the visual novelty of reproduced motion but the realization of the same stories and dramas that drew audiences to the live theatre. Some of these photo plays lasted a full two hours and contained as many as four slides a minute. A striking connection between the photo play and the early movies is that both used the same melodramatic plots and stereotyped characters.

Such predecessors clearly indicated the potential popularity of projected movie shows. The problem was to develop a machine that could project the filmstrips. There were two specific difficulties, which Edison himself had faced and forgotten: the projector needed a powerful enough light source to make the projected image clear and distinct, and the film needed to run smoothly and regularly past that light source without ripping, rattling, or burning. One of the first successful projections was made by a Virginia family of adventurer-inventors, the Lathams. Major Woodville Latham, former officer in the Confederate Army and former chemistry instructor, together with his two dashing sons, Gray and Otway, invented a camera and projecting machine in 1895 (called either the Panoptikon or the Eidoloscope) that produced better results than Edison's. The Lathams doubled the size of Edison's film to approximately 70mm. The bigger film produced a clearer, brighter, sharper picture. Although the Lathams gave a few showings in southern cities and in New York, their stay in the big city converted the two Latham boys from scientists to playboys. The Lathams and their invention ended in the obscurity of financial disaster.

A successful projector had to do more than just enlarge the film. It required a totally new principle of moving the film past the gate. The new principle, discovered and developed in Europe rather than America, used an intermittent movement of the film rather than a continuous one. Each frame stopped momentarily in front of the lamp and was then succeeded by the next frame, which stopped, and then the next, which stopped, and so forth. The intermittent movement allowed a clear, sharp image, for the stationary frame used the available light more economically. The intermittent motion was, in principle, precisely the same as the slits in the Phenakistiscope; rather than a continuous succession of whirring images, each image was separated from the others into an individual piece of the whole. The intermittent movement solved the problem of ripping film as well as of insufficient illumination. The moments of pause allowed the tension on the take-up reel to ease; the film did not rip as it did with continuous-motion projectors. The single problem caused by intermittent motion was the possibility of burning the film that remained momentarily stationary in the gate. To solve this problem, the intermittent-motion projector required some kind of cooling system to protect the film. Today, despite all the changes and improvements in movie equipment, our projectors are the same in principle as those invented in the final years of the nineteenth century.

As early as 1888, a Frenchman working in England, Louis Augustin Le Prince, patented machines that both shot and projected motion pictures, using intermittent motion in both processes. He also shot several filmstrips with a machine that used perforated film and a much slower film speed than Edison's (twenty frames per second). Le Prince's influence on the history of film is minor, however, for in 1890 he mysteriously disappeared from a train between Dijon and Paris; he was never found. In 1893, an Englishman, William Friese-Greene, patented a combination camera-projector. Because the same machine that shot the films also projected them, and because cameras had always used intermittent motion, intermittent motion for projection was guaranteed by the use of the identical

mechanism. Unfortunately, there is no evidence that this early machine ever successfully photographed or projected any films. The two most significant projectors were developed by men who began, ironically, by buying Edison Kinetographs and analyzing them. Edison's oversight in neglecting European rights allowed an Englishman, R. W. Paul, and, more important, two Frenchmen, appropriately named Lumière, to invent a functional projector and build a more functional camera.

Auguste Marie Louis Nicolas Lumière, the elder, and Louis Jean Lumière, the younger and more important of the two inventor brothers, started dabbling with Edison's Kinetoscope and Kinetograph in 1894. Their father, an avid photographer, had founded a factory in Lyon for manufacturing photographic plates and, later, celluloid film. Interested by the new motion photography, these scientist-industrialist-mechanic brothers developed their own machine within a year. Unlike Edison's bulky indoor camera, the Lumière camera was portable; it could be carried anywhere. The operator turned a hand crank rather than pushed an electric button. In addition, like the invention of Friese-Greene, the same machine that shot the pictures also printed and projected them. While the machine admitted light through its lens during filming, it projected light through its lens during projection. Intermittent motion was guaranteed for projection.

Early in 1895 the Lumière brothers shot their first film, *Workers Leaving the Lumière Factory*. Beginning in March of the same year, the Lumières showed this film and several others to private, specially invited audiences of scientists and friends throughout Europe. The first movie theatre was opened to the paying public on December 28, 1895, in the basement room of the Grand Cafe in Paris. The Lumières showed several films, among them *Workers Leaving the Lumière*

Factory, a Lumière baby's meal (*Le Repas de bébé*), a comical incident of a gardener getting his faced doused by a boy's prank (*L'Arroseur arrosée*), and a train rushing into a railway station (*L'Arrivé d'un train en gare*). The last film provoked the most reaction, as the audience shrieked and ducked when it saw the train hurtling toward them. In Jean-Luc Godard's *Les Carabiniers*—Godard's films are filled with historical tidbits—a farm boy watches his first movie, which is also a train arriving at a station, using the same camera angle as Lumières'. The boy shrieks and ducks, just as the first movie audiences did in the café theatre. Audiences would have to learn how to watch movies.

The Lumiére discovery of 1895 established the brothers as the most influential and important men in motion pictures in the world, eclipsing the power and prestige of Edison's Kinetograph and Kinetoscope. Within five years, the light of the Lumières would also fade. The brothers were more interested in the scientific curiosity of their discovery than the art or business of it, although eventually their film catalogue included over one thousand filmstrips for purchase. The Lumières sent the first camera crews all over the globe, recording the most interesting scenes and cities of the earth for the delight and instruction of a public who would never be able to travel to such places on their own. Despite their brief importance, the Lumière discoveries established several patterns and practices that have remained standard throughout the history of film. The Lumières set the film width at 35mm, still a standard width of film today. The Lumières established the film speed of sixteen frames per second, the approximate standard speed until the invention of sound required a faster one for better sound reproduction. The slower film speed allowed their projector to run more quietly and dependably. Edison, maintaining the visual superiority of forty frames per second, scoffed that the Lumière speed would destroy the sensation of continuous movement; only a year later Edison himself adopted the Lumière speed. And a final Lumière contribution was the fancy name they coined for their invention—the Cinématographe; it is one of the few Greco-Latin names to survive the first era of invention. In many countries today, as well as in the columns of many sophisticated film reviewers, the movies are the cinema.

Almost simultaneously with the Lumières, experimenters in England,

Germany, and America were making progress on their own machines. In England, R. W. Paul and Birt Acres also borrowed Edison's unpatented machines as a basis for their own discoveries. In Berlin, Max and Emil Skladanowsky entertained audiences with their Bioscope, a camera and projector they had developed independently of any other invention. In America, a young inventor named Thomas Armat independently discovered the Lumière principle that the film movement must be intermittent. In addition, Armat discovered that the film ran more smoothly with a small loop to relax the film tension just before and behind the film gate. This loop was quickly adopted around the world and called the American or "Latham" loop, which all projectors still use today. The loop also proved the legal loophole that Edison dragged into the courts for the next ten years in an attempt to get back the money he had lost from his initial mistake. But the story of the lawsuits comes later. Early in 1896, Thomas Armat and Thomas Edison came to a business agreement. Edison would sell Armat's projector as his own invention, enhancing the prestige and sales potential of the machine. Armat would silently receive a handsome percentage of the sales. The Edison company announced its latest invention, the Vitascope, a projecting version of the "Wizard's" Kinetoscope.

The first public showing of a projected motion picture in the United States is difficult to fix. The Lathams projected films in a store in 1895. Thomas Armat demonstrated his projector in Richmond, Virginia, before selling it to Edison. Several other American inventors—Jean-Aimé le Roy, Eugene Lauste, Herman Casler, Francis Jenkins—also demonstrated projection machines to limited audiences. But the first official public showing for a paying audience was on April 23, 1896, at Koster and Bial's Music Hall, on 34th Street and Broadway in New York City—the present site of Macy's. The "amazing Vitascope" was only one act in a vaudeville bill; movies were typically part of vaudeville shows in the United States until they started filling their own theatres shortly after the turn of the century.

For the first Vitascope program, Edison converted several of his Kinetoscope strips for the projector; he also pirated a few of the R. W. Paul films from England. One good piracy deserved another. As with Lumières' first showings, the most exciting films were those with action that came straight out at the audience. During the showing of a filmstrip of *The Beach at Dover* patrons in the front rows ran screaming from their seats, afraid they were about to be drenched. Those cynics who were unimpressed were sure that the film had been shot in New Jersey.

The First Films

The first film audiences were amazed to see that living, moving action could be projected on an inert screen by an inanimate machine. The first films merely exploited their amazement. The films that Louis Lumière shot for his Cinématographe and that Dickson and others shot for the Vitascope were similar. A film lasted between fifteen and ninety seconds. The camera was stationed in a single spot, turned on to record the action, and then turned off when the action had finished. These films were really "home movies"—unedited scenery, family activity, or posed action—that depended for their effect on the same source as today's home movies—the wonder of seeing something familiar and transitory reproduced in an unfamiliar and permanent way. Nowhere is the home-movie-like quality of the first films more obvious than in Lumières' *Le Repas de bébé*, which has been duplicated uncounted times in later 8mm versions. A major difference between the first Edison

A *"home movie"*: Lumières' Feeding Baby

The freedom of the outdoors and the excitement of motion: Lumières' Boat Leaving the Port

films and the first Lumière films is that Lumières' have more of this home-movie quality of merely turning the camera on to record the events that happened to occur around it. The Edison films, despite their lack of editing and plot, were gropings toward a fictional, theatrical film; they were indoor films. The Lumière films took advantage of the outdoors—they were freer, less stilted, better composed, more active.

The categories of the Lumières' catalogue indicate their conception of what the filmstrip would provide its audience. The catalogue breaks its filmstrips into different kinds of "views"—mere visual actualities—General Views, Comic Views, Military Views, Views of Diverse Countries. The most interesting views are those containing the most interesting patterns of movement: a boat struggling out to sea against the waves, a cavalryman mounting and dismounting from his horse in the accepted military style, the charge of a line of cavalry horses, the crumbling of a demolished wall.

The most celebrated of the Lumière films is the comic jest, *L'Arroseur arrosée*. This incident, staged, but shot outdoors, contains the seeds of what was to blossom into one of the most important contributions of the silent film—physical comedy. While a gardener waters a lawn, a boy sneaks behind him and steps on the hose. Seeing the hose is dry, the gardener picks up the nozzle and stares at it. The boy steps off the hose; water gushes out of the nozzle into the gardener's unsuspecting face. The boy laughs. The gardener catches the boy and spanks him (although the camera's refusal to pan with the action makes the final action more difficult to catch than the boy).

This little film contains many elements of a comic art that would one day mature: the gag is completely physical; despite the improbability of the result, the causes are clear and credible; the butt of the joke is unjustly and unwittingly the victim of circumstances of which he is unaware; despite the victim's ignorance, the audience participates in the joke with the boy; the comic punishment is more a

John Rice and May Irwin do their Kiss

blow to the ego than to the body; the comic participants have obvious one-dimensional traits and roles so that complexity of character cannot interfere with the force of the jest.

The early Edison films lack the freshness and freedom of Lumières', failing to understand and exploit the wonder and beauty of watching the world at work and at play, at rest and in motion. Typical is the staged heaviness of *The Execution of Mary, Queen of Scots* (1895). In less than a half-minute of film, besheeted guards lead Mary to the block, push her on it, and whack off her head. The audience then gets the thrill of seeing Mary's head bound off like a basketball. Despite the clumsiness of the

film, two elements of it are worth some attention. First, the camera clearly thinks of itself as a spectator in the theatre. The characters move left and right in a single plane, rather than using the full depth that films were later to discover. Further, the film has a strong sense of entrance and exit, two more stage devices the mature film would discard. This stage mentality would continue to dominate the movies for over fifteen years. Second, the film shows one clear realization of the potential of the film medium. After Mary sets her head on the block, the camera stops to allow a dummy head to substitute for Mary's real one. The ability to stop the action and start it again is one of the advantages that the camera enjoys over the stage. Within a very few years, the Frenchman, Georges Méliès, would make much out of this camera advantage.

A second interesting Edison film, and certainly the most famous, is the *John Rice–May Irwin Kiss*. Shot originally for the Kinetoscope in 1896, this kiss, when projected on the large screen, excited the first wave of moralistic reaction to movie romance, which has remained a constant in film history. John Rice and May Irwin were the romantic leads in a current Broadway stage success; Edison got them to enact their climactic kiss in his Black Maria. When moralists and reformers saw their large, projected mouths meet in lascivious embrace, they showered the local newspapers with letters and the local politicians with petitions. Upon seeing *The Kiss* today, the viewer would probably find more obscenity in the dumpy unattractiveness of the two bussers than in their "torrid" kiss, which seems a quarter-second peck. The players spend more time coyly and clumsily puckering up than they do in physical contact.

Although Lumière specialized in actualities and Edison in theatrical and staged scenes, the success of each in his particular genre led to imitations by the other. Edison's *Washday Troubles* (1898) is a clear descendant of Lumières' gardener film, as a tub of washing douses those who are tending it because of a boy's prank. After seeing Edison's success with historical scenes, Lumière began staging those such as *Marat* and *Robespierre* in 1897. In addition to borrowing successful formulas—a practice that would continue throughout movie history and even into today's television programming—the two companies literally stole each other's films, made up duplicate prints (dupes), and sold them as their own. In addition to competing with and stealing from each other, Edison and Lumière faced both competition and thievery from rivals who were springing up in England, America, and France. The next ten years of film history would be a decade of commercial lawlessness as well as aesthetic discovery.

3 Film Narrative, Commercial Expansion

The two film rulers of 1895, Lumière and Edison, would encounter crafty and powerful competitors within a year. In France, the Lumière superiority was attacked by an artist on one side and by industrialists on the other. Georges Méliès, owner-prestidigitator of the Théâtre Robert-Houdin, saw the movies as a means of inflating his bag of magical tricks. He immediately recognized the cinematic possibilities for fantasy and illusion. In 1896 he asked the Frères Lumières to sell him a camera and projector. When the Lumières refused to sell a Cinématographe, he bought one of R. W. Paul's Theatrographs in London. Méliès shot his first film of illusory tricks, *A Game of Cards*, in the spring of 1896. By 1900, Méliès was supplying the world with films and the Frères Lumières had almost ceased production.

Two other Frenchmen, Charles Pathé and Léon Gaumont, also began building their huge film empires in 1896, several colonies of which still exist today. Charles Pathé and his three brothers formed Pathé Frères, which began by copying the successful Lumière formulas of "views" and "actualities." But the Pathé goal was not entertainment but conquest: to control all branches of the French film industry. Within a very few years the Pathé factory embraced everything to do with motion pictures. Their company manufactured cameras and projectors, it manufactured the raw film stock (after acquiring George Eastman's European patent rights), it produced the filmstrips, and it owned a chain of theatres for showing them. The American film industry would grope hesitatingly toward this monolithic vertical integration that the Pathés quickly realized. Léon Gaumont's perceptions were similar; he founded a second French film empire whose activities ranged from manufacturing machine parts to collecting receipts at the theatre door.

The English film between 1896 and 1906 was perhaps the most innovative in the world. R. W. Paul, who had been displaying the products of his Theatrograph for almost a year, began attracting other inventor-photographers to experiment with moving pictures. This group, which has become known as the "school of Brighton," produced the first original ideas to take cinematic form.

G. A. Smith, James Williamson, and Cecil Hepworth made significant and rapid progress with the principles of editing and composition, realizing that the effect of a filmed story was a function of the way the individual shots were composed and stitched together. Until the emergence of D. W. Griffith some ten years later, the films of these British directors were the slickest on the screen, precisely because they had discovered the importance of editing for both building a story and driving its rhythms.

An American, Charles Urban, joined the native Englishmen to enrich the British film further in this period. Urban, who had tried unsuccessfully to peddle his Edison-imitation camera (called the Bioscope) in America, journeyed to London to try his luck there. Fearing the stigma of Americanism, Urban christened his London concern the Warwick Trading Company. Despite the name, the Urban company pioneered in its production of scientific films using micro-cinematography and in its development of the first successful color process, which Urban called Kinemacolor. These British pioneers discovered the elements of film construction that Griffith would later fuse into more powerful movie chemistry: the close-up, the cross-cut, superimposition, the traveling shot, and the pan shot.

In the United States, artistic and industrial progress was much slower than in England or France. The era of tinkering, piracy, and imitation lasted until after the turn of the twentieth century. By 1897, however, the two companies that would share the power with Edison had begun making and showing films. The American Mutoscope and Biograph Company manufactured both a peepshow machine and a projecting machine that outperformed Edison's. The inventive intelligence behind "Biograph," as the company was to be called, was Edison's own film pioneer, W. K. L. Dickson. Dickson had left Edison because of tensions and

dissatisfaction to go to work for the Lathams; when he found the Lathams to be too "fast," he went on to become the "D" of the K.M.C.D. syndicate. The early film companies often took their names from the initials of their owners; Dickson's initial joined Eugene Koopman's, Henry Marvin's, and Herman Casler's.

The K.M.C.D.'s first project was the Mutoscope, their peephole machine, whose effectiveness put the Kinetoscope out of business. Like the Kinetoscope, the Mutoscope offered a series of moving photographs to the eyes of a single viewer. Unlike the Kinetoscope, however, the Mutoscope pictures were large photographs mounted on individual

The Mutoscope

cards. The viewer flipped the series of cards with a hand crank, persistence of vision blurring each card into the other to produce the same appearance of movement as a motion picture. The large picture cards made the Mutoscope pictures clearer, more detailed, and more lifelike than the Kinetoscope's. The hand crank added to the viewer's pleasure by allowing the motion to go either forward or back, to go slower, faster, or stop altogether. The ultimate testimony to the Mutoscope is that of all the archaic and outdated machines of the invention era, it alone survives today—in penny arcades, amusement parks—delighting children with some of the same photographs that their great-grandparents flicked through nearly ninety years ago. The machine has also survived in "adult" book stores, engaging patrons with a type of photographic entertainment that could not have been envisioned by the Messrs. K.M.C.D.

The K.M.C.D. motion picture machine also bested its Edison opponent. Like the Latham projector, the Biograph used much larger film than Edison's or Lumières'. The similarity of the oversized film implies that Dickson may have developed the Latham machine as well as the Biograph. The Biograph camera's huge pictures could either be mounted on Mutoscope cards or, when combined with its intermittent-motion projector, throw the sharpest, clearest images that had yet been seen on a screen. Dickson's films were also more interesting, more active than Edison's: the Empire State Express (yet another thrilling train shot), President McKinley receiving a letter at home, the parade honoring the Japanese ambassador, the actor Joseph Jefferson performing scenes from his famous *Rip van Winkle*.

As he had done at Edison's West Orange laboratories, Dickson built a special studio for shooting staged scenes. The first Biograph studio was outdoors,

on the roof of the Biograph offices near Broadway and 14th Street. As in the Black Maria, the stage of Dickson's roof theatre rotated to keep the sun at the best lighting angle. From this nuts-and-bolts beginning the company evolved that was to give its name to moving pictures in some parts of the world (in South Africa today the movies are still called the biograph; both Chicago and London still have theatres called the Biograph) and that was to launch the careers of D. W. Griffith, Mack Sennett, Mary Pickford, the Gish sisters, and many others.

Edison's second major competitor was the Vitagraph Company, which had a less spectacular career than Biograph but a longer one. Vitagraph's founder and director of production was J. Stuart Blackton, another Americanized Englishman, who began as a reporter and cartoonist for the *New York World*. Blackton first became interested in moving pictures when he visited Edison at the Black Maria; he even performed his sketching act for Edison's Kinetograph. Edison soon leased Blackton a Vitascope franchise. Blackton repaid Edison's kindnesses by copying Edison's machine and making pictures on his own. Realizing the appeal of the Edison company, Blackton and his partners, William "Pop" Rock and Albert E. Smith, chose a name for their company that was as close to Edison's as the law would allow. Vitagraph's first film, *Burglar on the Roof* (1897), was appropriately filmed on the rooftop of their office building in Chelsea. For several years Manhattan rooftops doubled as film studios. Another interesting early Vitagraph film was *Tearing Down the Spanish Flag* (1898), an attempt to capitalize on the Spanish-American War. Although the film claimed to have been shot in the heat of battle, Blackton actually staged it in the heat of Manhattan on his friendly rooftop. Blackton had not been a journalist for nothing.

Other men all over the country were catching the movie craze, assembling machines, and capturing images. In Chicago, three men began tinkering independently: George Kleine, George K. Spoor, and "Colonel" Selig. Kleine would one day become the "K" of the Kalem (K.L.M.) Company that produced the first *Ben Hur* in 1907. Spoor would one day become the "S" of Essanay (S&A) who, with his partner, "Broncho Billy" Anderson, would shoot the first series of westerns. In Philadelphia, Sigmund Lubin began several tricky activities, including "duping" (illegally duplicating) the films of others to eliminate the problem of paying for them and re-enacting events like a heavyweight title bout or the Oberammergau Passion Play on his Philadelphia rooftop. Movie projectionists trooped across the country with their filmstrips much as the magic lanternists had trooped across Europe with their slides a century earlier. One of these projectionists toured the Caribbean, drawing audiences and applause with the adopted name of Thomas Edison, Jr.; his real name was Edwin S. Porter.

Narrative

Despite the frenzy of movie activity in the United States, the films did not change much until 1902 or 1903. New films imitated the successes of earlier ones; like television and film producers today, the earliest film producers copied successful formulas. The new films were longer, of course, freed from the fifty-foot limit of the Kinetoscope box. But the same rushing trains, ocean and mountain views, one-joke pranks, and historical vignettes dominated the screen. Audiences began to yawn at these same predictable film subjects. The motion picture, formerly the highlight of a vaudeville bill, became the "chaser," the part of the program that was so dull that it chased the old audience out so that the new one could file in. By 1900 the movies were suffering the first of a series of business crises.

The rope that pulled the movies from the abyss was the development of a new kind of screen entertainment. The rope-abyss metaphor is an apt one, for the new kind of movie, the story film, was to use this and other similar heart-stopping devices to weave its spell. The movies were born into the age of Belasco; they have never quite outgrown that heritage. The Belasco theatre era traded on violent emotional effects— violent tears, violent suspense, violent laughter. The two dominant theatre genres were melodrama and farce; they were to become the two dominant film genres as well. The most respected playwrights were Scribe and Sardou, Jones and Pinero, Dion Boucicault, Bronson Howard, and Augustin Daly. In these plays, good and evil were as clearly distinct as black type on a white page. Though evil triumphed over good for the first two hours of the play, good miraculously won out in the last fifteen minutes. Melodrama was a world of pathos, not of tragedy, of fears and tears, not of ideas. No action was irreversible; no matter what mistake the good-hearted character made, it would eventually be erased by his or her essential goodness. The era's farce was just as extroverted; a series of comic mistakes would arise, entangle, and explode until the denouement put all the pieces of the puzzle together. There was no reason why a film could not tell the same kinds of stories.

The problem was to translate these dramatic stories into film terms. There had been early attempts at screen narrative (Blackton's *Burglar on the Roof*, for example). But these early narrative films were made merely by piecing together the same kinds of static, unedited scenes that were shot for the first Kinetoscope—expanding the

fifty-foot strip to a whole reel. A good example of one of these films is *Pullman Honeymoon* (1898). This Edison product records a series of events that might take place in one of George Pullman's sleeping cars involving porters and passengers, lovers, comics, bandits, and the police. The film is strikingly inert. The movie set is a stage set: the berths line the frame at left and right; the center aisle of the Pullman car serves as the stage-center playing area. Although the film lasts almost ten minutes, the camera never shifts its viewing angle nor its distance from any of the action. As in the earliest Edison strips, the camera is the single spectator at a staged play. The only noticeable participation of the camera in the action is that it stops after each incident and then starts again. But the slight jumps between the scenes indicate that the filmmaker tried (and failed) to make these gaps invisible, to keep the camera from participating in the event, refusing to exploit the cinema's ability to manipulate chronological time. Further, because the film uses only one setup, the effect is ploddingly static; the passive camera never picks out the details or facial reactions that give a film emphasis, empathy, and movement. No action, character, or object is more important than anything else. Despite its length, *Pullman Honeymoon* represents no real improvement over *The Execution of Mary, Queen of Scots.*

The Frenchman, Georges Méliès, was a much better film storyteller, precisely because he exploits the very difference between time in nature and in the cinema that *Pullman Honeymoon* tried to cover up. The Méliès films owe their superiority to the wild imagination and subtle debunking humor of their master. Méliès was by trade a magician; just as earlier magicians had adopted the magic lantern, Méliès adopted moving pictures. He saw that the camera's ability to stop and start again brought the magician's two greatest arts to perfection—disappearance and conversion. Anything could be converted into anything else; anything could vanish. One of Méliès's films, *The Conjuror* (1899), is nothing but a series of vanishings and conversions. The magician (played by Méliès himself) vanishes, his lady assistant vanishes, she turns into snow, he turns into her, and she turns into him. It may not be entirely accidental that one of Ingmar Bergman's striking films uses the same metaphor of the magician's art as a parallel to the filmmaker's.

Méliès's most famous film is *A Trip to the Moon* (1902), which successfully combines his fantasy and his humor into a naively charming film. The film's humorous touches almost outweigh the trick effects. Méliès parodies the intellectual doings of academics in the opening scene as a crazy professor (Méliès again) earnestly demonstrates his points and makes his ideological opponents disappear. Méliès's parody of the intelligentsia continues in his later films: *The Doctor's Secret* (1908) and *The Conquest of the Pole* (1912). Delightfully whimsical in *A Trip to the Moon* are the rocket ship's landing with a splat in the eye of the man in the moon, the lines of chorus girls in their short panties who wave goodbye to the moonship and lend their faces to the seven stars of the Pleiades, and the jerky, jumpy gymnastics of the little moon creatures who go up in puffs of smoke when the scientists whack them with their umbrellas. Méliès was an experienced showman; his plots inevitably required the services of one or more scantily attired ladies. He also made sure that the films used plenty of tricks. In *A Trip to the Moon*, telescopes turn into stools, moon creatures disappear into smoke, stars and planets twirl about the heads of the sleeping scientists, and the explorers gesticulate with delight when they see the earth rise.

For all of his camera trickery, Méliès was still very much a stage creator shaping effects for a passive camera. Méliès's art was one of plaster, pulleys, and paint. The camera remained in its single position—just as in *Pullman Honeymoon*—while the magician pulled wires. The earth's rising was contrived by pulling up the earth and pulling down the rear part of the moon's crust; the ship's landing on the moon was contrived by moving the moon closer to the camera, not by moving the camera closer to the moon. Méliès clearly saw the film as a stageplay, and he referred to his technique as making "artificially arranged scenes." The structure of *A Trip to the Moon* reveals his thinking: though the film shifts locations (*Pullman Honeymoon* did not), each scene is presented in a single, unedited, unchanging shot.

Méliès also composes the scenes as on a stage; he is conscious of right and left, of entrances and exits. This staging is clear in those scenes in which the performers line up in a row across the screen: the row of scientists in the first scene, the row of chorines in the departure scene, the row of moon creatures in the moon court. The staginess of Méliès's technique is especially clear in his Oriental fantasy film, *Palace of the Arabian Nights* (1908), in which we can see the trap doors opening, the wires pulling, and the cardboard scenery sliding. Méliès took great pride in his scenic decor and effects, which he painted and plastered and conceived himself. But his insistence on making active scenery perform for a passive camera reveals his inability to distinguish between cinema space, which is discontinuous and yet three-dimensional, and theatrical space, which is continuous but more two-dimensional. But Méliès's tricks relied completely on his perception of the difference between natural time, which is perfectly continuous, and cinema time, which seems perfectly continuous in projection, even if it was not so in filming.

Despite the limits of Méliès's spatial imagination, he is an important film figure because he was the first to have an imagination of any kind. Film theorists of a later generation—particularly Siegfried Kracauer and André Bazin—observed that Méliès and his contemporary, Lumière, established the two potential

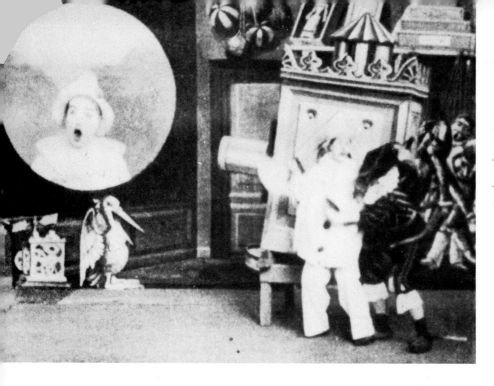

Méliès's The Magic Lantern: *the magic lantern in a two-dimensional toy shop projects a moving image of the clown's face while the clown himself views it—one of film's early references to its own powers*

directions of the cinema in the very infancy of the art: Lumières' realism (the rendering of the world as it is) and Méliès's fantasy (the recreation of the world by the filmmaker's imagination). Interestingly, these theorists find Lumières' realism the more legitimate path. But such a judgment overlooks the fact that in contrast to the impersonal, accidental, soulless filmstrips of Lumière, the Méliès films reveal a wit and mentality behind the camera's lens still capable of producing laughter and delight in an audience that has seen the eighty years of films that followed in Méliès's wake. The Méliès films, abounding in surreal surprises and audacious sight-gags-in-time (unlike the later custard pie, which is a sight-gag-in-space), were the first to prove that a motion picture could be the result of the human act of creation.

Méliès's peak year as a creative artist and as a businessman was probably 1902. His trademark, the star, was seen all over the world. That star steadily declined in the first decade of the century, and by 1914 he had made his last film and disappeared, like one of the moon creatures in his film. Fourteen years later a journalist discovered him selling toys and candy at a kiosk in the Gare Montparnasse. His fame and films (many of which Méliès himself had destroyed out of bitterness) were revived. After receiving a small pension from his cinephile admirers, he died in a sanitarium in 1938.

Méliès had an immense influence on other directors in France and all over the world. The second most imaginative French filmmaker of the decade, Emile Cohl, also delighted in the irrational surprises of a world of tricks. Cohl applied the tricks that Méliès played with the natural world to animated drawings. The surreal illogic of the Cohl cartoons is much closer in spirit to the wildly surreal transpositions of objects in the early Disney cartoons or in the trippy *Yellow Submarine* than to the more realistic later

Disney cartoon. Cohl delighted in converting one kind of drawn figure into another: a stick that becomes a man that becomes a window, an angry woman whose head rolls off and turns into a parrot, a pool cue that becomes a straw. One of Cohl's most delightful films is *The Joyous Microbes* (1909) in which tiny microbic dots flow together to depict the diseases they supposedly cause. In another Cohl film, *The Neo-Impressionist Painter* (1910), a painter tries to sell his very artsy abstract canvases to a buyer (the film is still topical today). As he describes each painting, the events and qualities he discusses come alive in line drawings on the canvas.

Méliès's success also influenced the films of Ferdinand Zecca. Zecca who was director of production at Pathé, made films in all the popular genres: social commentaries, farces, and melodramas. But Zecca also made trick films like *Whence Does He Come?* in which a man leaps out of the sea and begins putting on clothes that also leap out at him. Méliès's influence is also clear in many of Zecca's chase films. The chase was almost obligatory in the first decade of the century; the excitement of people running after other people compensated for the stasis of the camera and the slowness of unedited films. Zecca was one of the masters of the chase, but he added new excitement when he combined the chase with trick shots. In *Slippery Jim* (1905), the police chase a criminal who successfully eludes them because he has the ability to disappear, to appear in two or three places at once, to fly in the air on a bicycle, to unscrew his feet and remove the fetters, to wriggle out of any container or bind. Emile Cohl also made chase-trick films. In *The Pumpkin Race* (1907), the pursuers try to corral some nature-defying pumpkins that persist in rolling all over town, in windows, up steps, up chimneys. Méliès's success accounts for the trick films of G. A.

Smith and Charles Urban in England, for trick films in Denmark and Germany, and for Edwin S. Porter's *The Dream of a Rarebit Fiend* (1906).

One of the most influential French filmmakers in the first decade of the twentieth century was more famous for his performing than for his directing of the films in which he starred. Max Linder was the first internationally famous star of motion pictures and the first film clown. *A Skater's Debut* in 1905, in which a clumsy man meets a pair of iceskates for the first time, was also the debut of a comic character, Max, who was to become the leading figure of hundreds of comic one-reel films over the next decade. By 1910 Linder's yearly salary had jumped to over one million francs, and his face had become one of the most familiar in Europe (few of his films were ever shown in America). Linder, like Chaplin, Keaton, Lloyd, and Langdon who followed him, was a tiny man, and he used his smallness deliberately to contrast with the bigger opponents and obstacles he frequently faced. Linder's dancing moustache and

Cohl's The Joyous Microbes: *the disease of drunkenness*

dandyish mannerisms with hat and cane also set a pattern that Chaplin would follow (and expand). Linder specialized in drunken routines (also a Chaplin specialty) as in *Max and the Quinquina* (1911), in which a woozy Max makes a series of comic mistakes with both people and houses. He also specialized in debunking the intellectual, pretentious, and arty (like Méliès before him and Sennett after) as in *Max Plays at Drama* (c. 1912), which parodies classical tragedy and romantic melodrama, primarily by means of delightful anachronisms.

Because of his European popularity and American anonymity, the Essanay company brought Max over to America in 1917 after Chaplin had left them. Both Max and Essanay soon failed. Although the films he made in America were slick and funny (especially the features, *Seven Years Bad Luck*, 1921, and *The Three Must-Get-Theres*, 1922), they never recaptured the popularity of his earlier, cruder but livelier films in Europe.

The films of Linder, Zecca, and Cohl—like the films of Méliès—had not yet grasped the construction principle of movies. For them, one shot equalled one scene; the finished film was a series of scenes, not of shots. Each scene progressed chronologically, following the central character about. There were no leaps in time or space, no ellipses in the sequence of events. The camera was invariably distant enough from the playing to include the full bodies of all the persons in the shot. The next step in the evolution of film construction was taken by an American. After Edwin S. Porter had returned from the Caribbean, he paid a visit to his "father," Mr. Edison, Sr., and asked for a job. Edison hired him as one of his cameramen; within a few years Porter became director of production for Edison's film company.

Edwin S. Porter shot his two most important films in 1903. *The Life of an American Fireman* begins with the fireman-hero falling asleep, the subject of his reveries appearing, comic-strip style, in a superimposed white space near his head. This convention, known as the "dream balloon," was the only accepted way of presenting a film character's thoughts until Griffith revealed the logic of simply cutting to the character's visions. As the fireman dreams of his wife and child, the film dissolves to a close-up of the fire-alarm box and a hand setting off the alarm. The film dissolves again to the fire station as the men tumble out of their beds and down the pole, and the horses and fire engines charge out of the station house. The scenes of the fire brigade charging out of the firehouse and down the street were bits of stock footage that Porter cut into the narrative. Like the early views of rushing trains, charging engines and horses were favorites with the first film audiences. Here Porter incorporates the delight with movement into a story, just as he would do with the train in *The Great Train Robbery*.

Up to this point in the film, Porter's cutting shows far more fluidity than Méliès's or Zecca's; he cuts freely from place to place, allowing the logic of the story rather than the scene-by-scene progress of the focal characters to determine his cutting. In the film's final scene—the fireman rescuing his own wife and baby from the burning house—Porter took an even more imaginative step. The rescue scene tells its story from two setups: from inside the house (point of view of the wife and child awaiting rescue), and from outside it (point of view of the fireman making the rescue). Porter cuts freely from interior of house to exterior, making the two setups melt into a single sequence. The fireman climbs up the ladder (outside), steps into the room and saves his wife (inside), climbs down the ladder with his wife and then up again (outside), climbs into the house again to save the baby (inside), and then down the ladder again with the child

Porter's Life of an American Fireman: *cutting from inside to outside to depict the sequential rescue process*

(outside). Porter seems to have realized
that the basis of film construction was not
the scene but the sequence of shots that
could be built into a scene. Further, the
final rescue sequence reveals Porter's
perception of what the Soviets later called
"creative geography." The outdoor shots
were clearly shot outside a real house and
the indoor shots just as obviously inside a
studio. Porter seems to have intuited that
the cinema's narrative logic creates a unity
of place where none exists in nature.

Because of its immense popularity and
commercial success, Porter's later film of
1903, *The Great Train Robbery*, receives far
more critical attention. The first series of
shots in the film shows the same kind of
step-by-step, one-shot-one-scene editing of
the Méliès films. The outlaws enter the
telegraph office and tie up the operator,
board the train as it stops for water, rob
the mail car and shoot the railroad man,
seize the locomotive, unhook it from the
rest of the train, rob all the passengers
and shoot one who tries to escape, run to
the locomotive and chug off, get off the
locomotive and run to their horses in the
woods. Up to this point in the film any

director might have made it, except for
the flow and careful detail of the
narrative sequences and the beauty and
vitality of the outdoor shots. The very last
scene of the sequence reveals a new
editing idea. It is clearly an elliptical jump
in time, and it contains a pan shot that
follows the outlaws through the woods.

But the next shot identifies the
director's cinematic imagination more
clearly. He cuts back to the opening shot,
the telegraph office, and shows the
discovery of the assaulted operator.
Although the scene is a backward leap in
time and deserts the spatial focus of the
film (the outlaws), it makes perfect sense
in the story's continuity. It answers the
question which the audience naturally
asks: how will the outlaws be caught?
Porter's next shot reveals yet another
ellipsis. Rather than sticking with the new
focal characters (the operator and,
presumably, his daughter) it jumps to a
barn dance, into which the operator and
the girl eventually enter to tell their tale.
And then another ellipsis. The posse is
tailing the outlaws in the woods. Again,
the audience makes the connecting links

that the director has purposely omitted. Porter was demonstrating a familiar artistic maxim in film form: the most effective way to shape a work is to omit the inessential. Although Porter may have discovered the power of ellipsis accidentally and unconsciously (according to legend, he was running out of film and needed to economize), the finished film demonstrates that power nonetheless.

In the film's final shoot-out, three of the four bandits meet operatic, hands-in-the-air, pirouette-and-fall deaths. The fourth had already fallen off his horse in the chase scene. Ironically, this one gunman who did not know how to ride (he even had trouble mounting up in an earlier scene) later became the world's first cowboy star: "Broncho Billy" Anderson (né Max Aronson). Another irony of the film is that the final close-up of a bandit firing at the audience was intentionally unrelated to the whole film. Like 3-D of later years, the shot merely thrilled customers with a direct assault. The exhibitor could put the shot either at the beginning or end of the film, depending on his personal taste. For the next five years, it became almost obligatory to end a film with a close-up of its major figure (*The Boy Detective* and *Her First Adventure*, two Biograph films of 1908, are good examples)—all because of the success of the device in *The Great Train Robbery*.

Porter's other films do not show the same freshness in cutting as *The Great Train Robbery*. His version of *Uncle Tom's Cabin*, also 1903, is completely bound by the stage and staging. Later films, like *The Dream of a Rarebit Fiend*, despite its comedy and imaginativeness, copied the Méliès formula. Perhaps the freedom of being outdoors influenced Porter's editing plan in *Train Robbery*, the vast spaces being so clearly different from the boundaries of four theatre walls. Indeed, one of the striking characteristics of all American films before 1910 (including

Griffith's) is that their outdoor shots look vital and fresh while the indoor shots look static, flat, and dead. Once outdoors, the accidental attractions of nature compensated for the filmmaker's lack of craft and consciousness. Porter's studio films, like those of his contemporaries, revert to the principles of the first films shot in Edison's Black Maria.

While Porter was developing the tools of continuity and ellipsis in America, the "school of Brighton" was making similar and even more rapid progress in England. Cecil Hepworth's *Rescued by Rover* (1905) is one of the most slickly edited pre-Griffith films, a decided advance over Porter in narrative construction and rhythm. In the first expositional shot, a nurse wheeling a baby carriage insults a gypsy woman, who vows revenge. In the second shot, an ingeniously and carefully blocked pan shot, the gypsy steals the baby as the nurse chats with a beau. Then Hepworth makes a huge elliptical jump. Rather than sticking with nurse, watching her discover the loss and run home to tell baby's parents, the film's third shot begins with nurse bursting into the family living room to tell her news. As she recites her tale, Rover, the family collie, listens intently; he jumps out the window in search of the stolen baby.

Then begins the most remarkable sequence in the film: a series of individual shots showing Rover finding baby, returning to tell his master, and leading master back to baby. The sequence unfolds in the following shots: (1) Rover jumps out of window; (2) runs down the street toward camera; (3) turns corner; (4) swims across stream toward camera (with a delightful moment as Rover shakes himself off after emerging from the water); (5) Rover searches a row of shanty doors; (6) cut to inside shanty where gypsy sits guzzling booze; gypsy exits, Rover enters, nuzzles baby; (7) Rover runs out door of shanty, same setup as 5; (8) Rover swims across stream away from camera, same setup as 4; (9) Rover runs around corner, away from camera, same setup as 3; (10) Rover runs down street away from camera, same setup as 2; (11) Rover jumps into house window, same setup as 1; (12) cut to inside house, Rover "tells" master; (13) Rover and master run down street, same setup as 2 and 10; (14) Rover and master cross stream, same setup as 4 and 8; (15) Rover leads master to door of shanty, same setup as 5 and 7; (16) master finds baby, takes her out of shanty; gypsy returns to find baby gone; she is comforted by baby's clothes and her bottle of booze. In the film's final scene baby, master, mistress, and Rover are happily united in their living room; Hepworth has elliptically omitted the process of returning home, knowing that the sequence was not necessary to the emotional tension of the film.

Hepworth's careful editing of *Rescued by Rover* produced two effects that had not been achieved before, which communicated themselves to the audience by completely cinematic means. His careful use of the same setups to mark Rover's progress both toward and away from baby firmly implanted in the audience's mind exactly where Rover was in relation to the object of the rescue (the gypsy hovel) and the agent of the rescue (the master's house). Without any titles or explanations, the audience had a complete understanding of the rescue process. Second, this technique produced not only awareness but suspense. Because the audience knew where Rover's path was leading, it could participate in the excitement of Rover's finally reaching the end of it. Hepworth increased this excitement with the smooth fluidity of cuts from one setup to the next. Although the locations were undoubtedly far apart, the impression produced by Hepworth's cutting was that Rover ran continuously from one location to the next. Hepworth cut consistently as

Rover was in motion across the frame (Eisenstein and Pabst would later develop the power of cutting on movement), impelling the viewer's eye into the next shot and producing both fluidity and visual energy. The lengths of the shots were perfectly timed to increase the rhythm of excitement. Hepworth did not repeat the shot-by-shot sequence after baby had been rescued because he realized that the effectiveness of the process was dependent on our not knowing how and if baby would be saved.

Perhaps the ultimate testimony to the quality of the primitive British films can be seen in the satirical comedy, *A Suffragette in Spite of Himself*. Produced by the new British branch of the Edison Company in 1912, this little film is the story of an antifeminist male chauvinist who inadvertently carries a profeminist sign on his back all around London, the sign having been stuck there by some pranksterish boys. (The film is a clear extension of the Lumière prank film, effectively complicated by detailed characterization and social satire.) The film's acting is so subtle, its satire so relevant, its plot construction and editing so fluid, its composition so interesting (one shot even uses extreme depth-of-field with both foreground action inside a room and rearground action outside a window that might be said to foreshadow Renoir), its visual texture so consistent between indoor and outdoor shots, that it was far superior to any of the contemporary offerings of the parent Edison Company.

Despite the slower pace of visual and narrative discovery in the American films of the period, the years from 1903 to 1908—in effect between Porter's *Train Robbery* and Griffith's directorial debut—laid the foundation on which Griffith built in the years that followed 1908. Edwin S. Porter cleverly combined live-action comedy and animation in *The Whole Dam Family and the Dam Dog* (1904); he used metaphoric lighting, a firelight's

Rescued by Rover:
*the precise establishment
of locations, the
repetition of set-ups,
and the consistent
direction of movement
within the frame
produce both awareness
of the process and
emotional participation
in the event*

glow, for the final old-age scene of *The Seven Ages* (1905), predating Griffith's famous use of the same visual metaphor in *The Drunkard's Reformation* four years later; and Porter also made some of the earliest American film dramas of social commentary, such as *The Kleptomaniac* (1904), which contrasts the one kind of law that applies to the poor and needy thief and the other kind that applies to a rich, disturbed one.

Even before Griffith, the Biograph company had been producing the most interesting American films on the market. There were frantic serio-comic chases, clearly modeled on Zecca's, like *Personal* (1904), *The Lost Child* (1904), and *Tom, Tom, the Piper's Son* (1907). Within a half decade, two directors at this same studio would refine these chases into their purer but opposite types—D. W. Griffith's last-minute rescues and Mack Sennett's physical farces. Biograph also made films of ingenious thefts, like *The Great Jewel Robbery* (1904), in which the thief hides in a coffin on a train, and *The Silver Wedding* (1906), which concludes with a chase through the city sewers. The bizarre narrative twists and imaginative characterizations of the thieves in these films foreshadow the same sort of narrative imagination in the serials of the French filmmaker, Louis Feuillade, a decade later.

Also in this period at Biograph, Billy Bitzer, the man who was to shoot all of Griffith's most inventive and important films, had begun to master the art of cinematography. In *A Kentucky Feud* (1906), Bitzer's photography creates the appropriate visual setting for a tale of the Hatfields and McCoys; in *The Black Hand* (1906), Bitzer juxtaposes a tale of organized crime with actual location shooting on Seventh Avenue in New York City. (The depiction of organized crime against a background of photographically "real" city life would return seven decades later with films like *On the Waterfront*,

Mean Streets, and *The Godfathers*.) Biograph's *The Paymaster* (1906) may well use available light more creatively and beautifully than any other American film before 1908; especially effective are Bitzer's capturing the reflections of light on the river and his shots inside an old mill, lit entirely by oblique streams of light pouring through its window.

Between 1895 and 1908, the movies had progressed from static, one-shot "views" to increasingly fluid sequences of visually effective shots that produced a continuous if not necessarily complex narrative. The next evolution of narrative would require a master with a firmer and bolder sense, not so much of the individual cinematic elements but of the means to synthesize them into clearer, more credible, and more powerful narrative wholes. D. W. Griffith would display that sense within another year or two.

Business Wars

While movie makers gradually discovered the elements of film construction, American movie exhibitors gradually converted commercial chaos into order. In the last five years of the nineteenth century, the American picture business enjoyed the protection of neither law nor professional ethics. Cameramen and exhibitors blatantly ignored machine patents, pirating and duplicating any instrument that could make them money. Even more vulnerable were the filmstrips themselves, which were not yet protected by copyright laws. The French and English films, especially those of Méliès and Lumiére, were the most vulnerable; although many Méliès films were shown in the United States, his Star Film Company made no money from the prints that had been smuggled out of France and duped in America. A cold war, which on occasion became a very hot one, entangled all producers and exhibitors of motion pictures.

In 1899, for example, Biograph set up a huge battery of hot lights on Coney Island to record the Jeffries-Sharkey fight. The film would be the first to use electricity instead of sunlight. While the Biograph camera was grinding away in the front row, the Vitagraph camera was grinding away twenty rows back. When the Biograph boys discovered the Vitagraph camera, they sent a crew of Pinkerton detectives to seize the machine and film. The fight fans surrounding the Vitagraph camera, unaware of the causes of the attack, manfully protected their neighbor, producing more action outside the ring than in it. Eventually Vitagraph's Albert E. Smith recorded the whole fight, smuggled the film out of the arena, and developed it that night in the Vitagraph lab. The next morning Smith discovered that the pirated film had itself been pirated out of the lab by some late-night delegates from the Edison company. Ironically, although Biograph went to the trouble and expense of lighting the fight, Vitagraph and Edison (both eventually released prints of it) were the only ones to make any money on it.

In December 1897, Thomas Edison served his first legal writ, announcing his intention to eliminate all competitors in motion pictures. Edison, in the next ten years, would bring suit against any company that used a loop of film in either a projection machine or camera, claiming he owned the rights to all loops because of the Armat patent on the "Latham Loop." Ironically, although the Lathams used a loop of film in their patented camera, only Armat used a loop in his projector. But film loops had been identified with the Lathams, and so the "Latham Loop" became the generic name for all loops in all film machines. Edison's private detectives roamed the country searching for shooting companies, serving any they discovered with legal writs or

extralegal wreckage. Edison steadily coerced the smaller companies into accepting his terms, eventually bringing suit against the big ones like Vitagraph.

Then Thomas Armat, dissatisfied with Edison's taking full credit for the Vitascope, took to the courts. Edison had double-crossed Armat commercially by manufacturing his own projecting machine, the Projecting Kinetoscope, just two years after marketing Armat's. Armat, like Edison, brought suit against everyone who used his loop projector; he also sued Edison. Biograph, meanwhile, was preparing its own legal dossiers. With some careful bargaining it bought both the Armat patents and the Latham patents, thereby arming itself with plenty of ammunition to use against Edison. For ten years the motion picture companies busied themselves with suits and countersuits. Some 500 legal actions were taken, over 200 of them making their way into court. The reams of court testimony from this era proved to be valuable for the film historian, if for no one else.

While the company lawyers were busy at each other's legal throats, the movie companies continued making and selling an ever-increasing number of films. Originally, when movies were part of vaudeville bills or amusement arcades, the film company sold the finished picture directly to the exhibitor at between ten and twenty-five cents per foot, depending on the expenses of the film, its potential popularity, whether it was hand-tinted (a common practice of the time), et cetera. The exhibitor then owned the film and could show it until the print wore out. Then he would buy a new one.

But a new exhibiting development, just after the turn of the century, produced a new distributing practice. In 1902, an enterprising Los Angeles showman opened a small theatre in a store specifically for the purpose of showing motion pictures. Thomas L. Tally's Electric Theatre was the first permanent movie theatre in the United States. More and more of these store theatres sprang up, until, in 1905, a Pittsburgh store theatre opened that was a bit plushier, accompanied its showings with a piano, and charged its customers a nickel. It was the first nickelodeon. Within three or four years there were over 5,000 nickelodeons in the United States. So popular were they that in 1908 it was estimated that 80,000,000 Americans patronized them every week (at a time when the entire population of the United States was about 100,000,000).

The permanent movie theatre forced a fundamental change in the relationship of the movie exhibitor and movie producer. The nickelodeon required a large number of films each week; about six films of one reel each (sixty minutes of film) made up a single program, and to keep the customers coming, programs had to change several times a week, if not daily or several times a day. The theatre owner had no use for owning a film outright; after several showings, the regular patrons would not want to see it again. Between the film producer and the film exhibitor stepped a middleman who either bought the film or leased it from the producer and then rented it to the many exhibitors. The exhibitor paid less money for a larger supply of films; the producer was certain of selling films. The three-part structure of the American film industry—the producer who makes the film, the distributor who arranges for its most effective circulation, and the exhibitor who shows it in the theatre—worked out well for all parties. The structure, with some wrinkles, survives today.

Edison would try to use this three-level structure to bring peace and regularity to the chaotic American film world. Pressure, threats, bankruptcy, and collusion led to a combining of the nine leading film companies of 1908: Edison, Biograph, Vitagraph, Essanay, Lubin, Selig, Kalem, Méliès, and Pathé (the latter

two had both begun producing in America). The combine, called the Motion Picture Patents Company, agreed to share the legal rights to the various machine patents, agreed to buttress each other's business procedures, and agreed to keep all other parties and machine parts out of the film business permanently. The Motion Picture Patents Company could make its rules stick because they also agreed not to sell or lease to any distributor that bought a film from any other company. The exchange (distributor) who wanted to handle Patent Company films—the best pictures then on the market—could not handle any other company's films. Further, the Patent Company made an exclusive contract with George Eastman's factory; Eastman would sell raw film stock to the Patent Company and only to the Patent Company. The Patent Company was such a big account that Eastman could not afford to sell to interlopers. After ten years of piracy and bickering, the "War of the Patents" was over. American film production was the exclusive property of nine companies: they leased their films only to those distributors who would accept their terms and pay their fees; and these "licensed" film exchanges, soon to become amalgamated as the General Film Company, rented only to exhibitors who paid a weekly licensing fee ($2.00) and agreed to show Patent Company pictures exclusively. From first shot to final showing, law and order had theoretically come to motion pictures.

Having ended the warfare within the industry, the Motion Picture Patents Company sought to silence the increasing moral clamor outside it. The staggering success and popularity of the nickelodeons, the huge numbers of Americans who had caught the "nickel madness," troubled the moral principles

The beckoning lure of an early nickelodeon

of both amateur advocates and professional politicians. Most states and cities established either censorship boards to assure the cleanliness of film content, licensing boards to assure the cleanliness and safety of motion picture theatres, or both. These boards became commercially troublesome for an increasingly national industry. What if a film were acceptable in New York but not in Chicago? What if a film were acceptable in Pennsylvania but not in Philadelphia? To silence its critics, as well as to insure the commercial health of its product, the infant motion picture industry took the first step of the kind it would take throughout its history when faced with a moral attack that endangered its financial welfare—it established its own censorship board to control film content. The National Board of Censorship, founded in 1908 (in 1916 it changed its name to the more tolerant-sounding National Board of Review), did not put an end to troublesome state and local censorship actions, but it greatly reduced their inconsistencies by establishing standards and principles that most of them could (and did) accept.

Less fortunate for the Motion Picture Patents Company and the General Film Company was the rebellion of some distributors and exhibitors within the industry itself against this monopolistic control. It eliminated bargaining, it eliminated profits from duping, it raised prices. Within months after the peace had been signed in 1908, two distributors, William Swanson of Chicago and Carl Laemmle of New York, decided to "go independent." The two pacesetters urged other film exchanges to follow their example. The Patent War had ended; the Trust War had begun.

The independent distributor faced one problem: obtaining films to distribute that were not made by a Patent Company studio. One of the obvious solutions was for a distributor to turn producer. Carl Laemmle, film exchangeman, became Carl Laemmle, film producer, and gave birth to the organization that would eventually become Universal Pictures. William Fox, distributor and theatre owner, became William Fox, producer, and the organization that would eventually become Twentieth Century–Fox was born. Fox also retaliated against the Patent Company by suing them and their General Film Company as an illegal trust. The lawyers were back in the movie business.

For the next ten years movie companies fought in the courts and fought in the streets. Jeremiah J. Kennedy, a major executive of the Patent Company, sent gangs of gentlemen to visit unlicensed studios, leaving bits of wreckage about for calling cards. Despite the strong-arm tactics of the Trust, the Independents prospered. Adam Kessel and Charles Bauman, two former bookies, formed the Bison Life Motion Picture Company, which eventually founded the film careers of Thomas Ince, Mack Sennett, and Charles Chaplin. Edwin S. Porter left Edison to go independent, making films for his own Rex Company; it would one day be swallowed by Paramount. Most successful of all the Independents was Laemmle's Independent Motion Picture Company (known as Imp).

The Trust's solid barriers sprung other leaks. Unable to buy film stock from Eastman, the Independents bought stock from English and French factories. In addition, legitimate licensed film companies and film exchanges ran unlicensed, independent companies and exchanges on the side. When the smoke of this second film war had cleared, by about 1917, not only had the Motion Picture Patents Company been busted in court as an illegal trust but also the individual companies who formed the Trust were either dying or dead. The independent companies, for reasons that we will see, propelled the movies into their next era. Many of the original independent companies survive today. The last of the original Trust companies, Vitagraph, died in 1925.

The Film D'Art

An important film influence was to make itself felt toward the end of the new century's first decade. In 1907, a French film company announced the intention of creating a serious, artistic cinema, of bringing together on film the most important playwrights, directors, actors, composers, and painters of the period. The company, which rather pretentiously called itself the Film d'Art, produced its first film in 1908—*The Assassination of the Duke of Guise*. Featuring actors from the Comédie Française and incidental music by Saint-Saëns, the film was hailed as introducing the nobility and seriousness of the stage to the film. Ironically, the movie was a huge cinematic step backward from the level attained by Porter and Hepworth. The Film d'Art ran the movies headlong back into the theatre: theatrical staging, unedited scenes, theatrical acting, theatrical set painting. The Film d'Art showed no more spatial thinking than Méliès films had, and a lot less imagination. The French Film d'Art was the first in a series of attempts to produce "canned theatre," the most recent of which was the American Film Theater of the mid-1970s with its filmed productions of plays like *The Homecoming, The Iceman Cometh,* and *A Delicate Balance.*

The first of these Films d'Art to be seen in the United States was *Queen Elizabeth* (1912), featuring Sarah Bernhardt and members of the Comédie Française, directed by Louis Mercanton. This bombastic film version of Elizabeth's love for Essex, whom she must eventually send to the block, reveals all the plodding staginess of the Film d'Art technique. Characters enter and exit from right and left; groups of soldiers, ladies in waiting, or courtiers stand immobile in the background, just as they are supposed to do on the stage; the actors, Bernhardt included, indulge in a grotesque series of facial grimaces, finger gesticulations, arm swingings, fist clenchings, breast thumpings (once even raising dust from the costume), and quadruple takes. And yet these were among the most skillful stage actors in the world!

One clear lesson of the Film d'Art was that stage acting and film acting were incompatible. The stage, which puts small performers in a large hall, requires larger, more demonstrative movements. The artificiality of this demonstrativeness does not show in a theatre for two reasons: first, the live performance sustains the gestures with the "vibrations," the vitality of the living performer's presence, which assimilates gesture as only one part of a whole performance; second, the performer's voice adds another living note that makes facial expression and gesticulation also merely parts of a whole. In the Film d'Art of *Queen Elizabeth,* gesture and grimace were not parts but the wholes themselves.

The way to improve film acting was not just to make the actors underplay but to let cinematic technique help the actors act. A camera can move in so close to an actor's face that the blinking of an eye or the flicker of a smile can become a significant and sufficient gesture. Or the camera can cut from the actor to the subject of the actor's thoughts or attention, thereby revealing the emotion without requiring a grotesque, overstated thump on the chest. Film acting before Griffith, not only in the Film d'Art but in Méliès and Porter and Hepworth as well, had been so bad precisely because the camera had not yet learned to help the actors.

In *Queen Elizabeth,* for example, there is a scene in which Elizabeth bids adieu to Essex (he's off for Ireland) and then,

after all the court has left, she sinks down on her throne in abject sorrow; she can be a queen, but not a woman. The entire scene—adieu, exit, sorrow—is filmed in one setup. The single take is ridiculous, unrelated to both the content and the composition of the scene. The first part of the scene is a big one: Essex kneels screen left, Elizabeth sits screen right, the courtiers watch, standing around and behind the principals. But after Essex and the court leave, Elizabeth still stands far screen right—alone. What a natural spot for the camera to pan so that she fills the frame; what a natural spot for a close-up so that we can see her sorrow. No wonder Bernhardt acts her unhappiness in such a big way; we can hardly see her way off on the right edge of the screen.

Although the Film d'Art had nothing to do with film art, it had a lot to do with the direction that film art would take. *Queen Elizabeth,* despite its leaden

technique, was a huge success. Its success launched the career of its American distributor, Adolph Zukor, who decided to form an American Film d'Art called Famous Players in Famous Plays, which would one day become Paramount Pictures. Its success also proved that quality pictures and, more important, long pictures could make money. The Motion Picture Patents Company maintained that the public would not sit through a single picture of over fifteen minutes. It was to their advantage to maintain the theory, for the whole film business they had solidified was dependent on one-reel pictures exclusively. Longer pictures would scramble the whole industry; the General Film Company purposely would not distribute any film longer than two reels. *Queen Elizabeth,* a six-reeler, squashed the Trust myth. And D. W. Griffith's epics were only two years away.

4 Griffith

David Wark Griffith never intended to make movies. The accidental path that eventually led him to films stretched from his rural Kentucky home to selling books, picking hops in California, reporting for a Louisville newspaper, and finally writing and acting for the legitimate stage. The young Griffith had decided he was a playwright. One of his plays, *The Fool and the Girl,* even played two tepid weeks in Washington and Baltimore. Like the movies themselves, Griffith's dramatic apprenticeship was rooted in the world of Belasco. It would be Griffith who would most successfully translate the Belasco effects for the screen—melodrama, suspense, pathos, purity. Although today there is a certain pejorativeness in the term that press agents concocted to describe Griffith—"the Belasco of the screen"—there is an ironic aptness in the label that was not then apparent. Griffith began with the same dramatic structures, the same sentimental characters, and the same moral assumptions of the Belasco stage, and he never deserted them, even when his audiences did.

Griffith's playwriting ultimately brought him to the movies. Like all stage actors, Griffith regarded the moving pictures as an artistic slum. But he had written an adaptation of *Tosca,* which he failed to peddle as a stageplay. He then decided to try to sell it to the films. In 1907, out of work, he took his manuscript up to the new Edison studios in the Bronx. The film companies had deserted city rooftops for more spacious and secretive quarters in the Bronx and Brooklyn. Edwin S. Porter, by then head of production of Edison, thought Griffith's *Tosca,* with its many scenes and lengthy plot, too heady for the movies (this was five years before the Film d'Art's *Queen Elizabeth*). Instead of buying Griffith's script, Porter offered him an acting job at five dollars a day. Griffith, recently married to Linda Arvidson, needed the money and took the job. But he insisted on playing under the assumed name of Lawrence Griffith, thinking he would save his real name for the day when one of his plays opened on Broadway. Things would work out differently.

The opening shot of The Adventures of Dollie

Apprenticeship

In Griffith's first role for Porter he played a lumberjack (a very thin lumberjack!) and father in *Rescued from an Eagle's Nest*. When his wife informed him that baby had been swooped away by a huge black bird, Griffith scaled the bird's mountain lair (shot partly inside a studio and partly outdoors on the Palisades, producing a very obvious mismatching of shots), fought the puppet eagle to the death, and brought baby back home. This melodramatic film was not without significance for Griffith's later career. First, Edwin S. Porter provided Griffith's introduction to film technique—Porter being the American director before Griffith who best understood the power and logic of editing in building a story. Second, the thin melodramatic plot was to find its reincarnations in later Griffith movies throughout his career, both in the early short films and in the long epics.

Whether Griffith acquired the taste for the melodramatic suspense of the last-minute rescue from the Belasco stage or the Porter screen, by the time he started to direct his own films that taste had become his own.

After a short career with Edison, Griffith took a job with the Biograph studio, performing the same kinds of acting chores for the head of production there, Wallace C. ("Old Man") McCutcheon. By 1908, the devouring nickelodeon's demand for films was so great that Biograph needed to step up production to several reels per week. The studio needed another director to produce those reels. Griffith, whose imagination had been spotted by Biograph cameraman Arthur Marvin (brother of co-owner Henry Marvin), was offered the job. Griffith wasn't sure he wanted it. He was content with the daily five-dollar wage; failure as a director might cost him the steady income from acting. Biograph promised him that he could go back to acting if he failed as director. The sincerity of the promise was never tested. Griffith directed his first film, *The Adventures of Dollie*, in June 1908.

The Adventures of Dollie displays Griffith's thorough knowledge of the successful formulas of the past. Dollie's one-reel adventures are terribly familiar. An insulted gypsy takes vengeance on a family by kidnapping baby Dollie and hiding her in a water cask. As the gypsies ride away, the cask falls off the wagon and into a stream, where it moves steadily toward the vicious rapids. Dollie eventually escapes a watery death when her cries attract the attention of a nearby boy who is fishing; the picture ends with the inevitable happy family reunion. Griffith uses two motifs that had become standard in filmed melodrama: the spurned gypsy's revenge and the perilous danger to an innocent child. Its clear ancestors are films like *Rescued by Rover, Rescued from an Eagle's Nest, The Lost Child*, in which a mother thinks her baby has been spirited off by a gypsy and runs off in pursuit, and *Her First Adventure* (1908), Biograph's own version of the *Rover* film, made just three months before Griffith's *Dollie*. Despite its debt to the past, the dangerous rapids would recur in later Griffith films, most notably in *Way Down East*, made twelve years later, in which Lillian Gish floats toward the falls on an ice cake.

Although Griffith's film sticks to extremely conventional narrative material, he handles those conventions with a narrative fluidity and symmetry uncommon in films of the period. Griffith establishes the agent of Dollie's rescue, the boy fisherman, in the film's first shot. He walks along the river bank and away from the camera at the same time that Dollie and her family walk toward the camera. This narrative linking in the film's opening shot makes the action's resolution more probable and logical. The final sequence with the floating cask also flows more continuously and rhythmically (using the consistent direction of motion across the frame and cutting on movement) than is usual for films of 1908. And the film's most interestingly planned shot is a deep-focus long shot that shows a farmer cutting grain as the gypsy runs through the field with Dollie in his grasp. Because the farmer is occupied with his task and submerged in the tall stalks, he cannot and does not see the mischief that passes so near him. The shot gives the convincing feeling that this episode of movie fiction has been plucked out of the random and continuous flow of life itself.

It was this paradox of film narrative—that films look so spontaneously real and natural and yet are so fictional and patterned—that Griffith would develop and master in the five years that followed. His general method would be to push each of these paradoxical qualities to its extreme—to make filmed life look as natural and random as real life and yet to make filmed stories as carefully constructed and patterned as any well constructed narrative fictions. If there had been a tendency of film narratives before Griffith, it was either to depict life as so random that the story and its characters were unclear (far shots often failed to pick the people and events out of the background clearly enough for the audience to understand their significance) or, the more common failing, to isolate the fictional events and characters so clearly from the background (which may have been obviously posed or painted) that the shot did not resemble life at all.

Griffith, shouldering the production demand of directing several one-reel pictures every week, had been given an ideal laboratory for experimentation and development. Between 1908 and 1913, clearly Griffith's apprenticeship period, he directed over 400 films, giving him the opportunity to test a new idea immediately, see how and if it worked, and then return to the technique the next week and develop it further. Griffith did not innovate abstractly; he could test each method day by day in front of the camera, rejecting the tools that failed, refining the ones that worked. Griffith's discoveries were empirical, not theoretical. Those discoveries embraced every component of visual, black-and-white cinematic technique.

Griffith realized that the content of the shot should determine the camera's relationship to it, whereas the accepted shot in the film world of 1908 was what would be called the full shot or far shot today. This shot necessarily included the full figures of all the characters in the scene, plus enough of the scenery to show the audience exactly where the characters were and how carefully the set had been painted. This standard shot enjoyed the official blessing of the Motion Picture Patents Company, whose reasoning seemed sensible: why should the public pay the full price to see half an actor when it can see the whole actor for the same money? Griffith revealed the effectiveness of showing half an actor, or even smaller portions.

In his apprentice years, Griffith developed a full series of different shooting perspectives. Beginning with the standard full shot, he moved the camera closer to the players to produce the medium shot—including, say, two actors from the knees up (a shot later christened the "American shot"). And then the camera was positioned still closer to produce the close-up, including only the face and shoulders of a single actor, or the extreme close-up, revealing only the eyes, nose, and mouth. Griffith also saw that he could move the camera in the other direction, further away from the actors. He produced the long shot—a much more distant view of one or more players—which emphasized more of the scenic environment than the far shot. And then he moved the camera still further from the players, producing the extreme long shot that would emphasize huge vistas and panoramas rather than the human figures.

Griffith, of course, was not the first to use these shots. Many of the Lumière "views" were of vast panoramas. *Fred Ott's Sneeze* and the closing shot of *The Great Train Robbery* both used medium to close shots. G. A. Smith's *A Big Swallow* (1900) uses an extreme close-up of a man's mouth (he was supposedy swallowing the camera), and Porter's *Life of an American Fireman* used a close-up insert of a fire-alarm box. But these earlier films used the nonstandard shot for some special photographic or narrative effect (as even the term *insert* implies). Griffith made all of these shots standard and combined them into sequential wholes; he thereby proved that the very idea of standardness was a cinematic lie. One could cut freely between long and medium, close and medium, close and long to produce a whole scene. Griffith broke the theatrical scene into the cinematic unit of shots.

In a sense, his method really was another kind of analogy with the stage, but a much more subtle one than film directors had earlier perceived. Although a scene on the stage is anchored in immovable space, it really is a series of shifting "beats," of emotional pivots and pirouettes, of thrusts and parries, of comings together and splittings apart. Despite the stasis of the setting and the audience's viewing angle, the theatrical scene is not static; it is constantly shifting, changing, and evolving. Griffith translated these stage "beats" into film terms. When the mood shifted, when the emotions changed, the camera shifted. It caught that intimate moment when a single member of a group made up his or her mind to take a significant emotional leap; it caught the smallness of a solitary soldier in the midst of a huge army on a vast battlefield. Griffith discovered that the narrative content of the scene, not the location of the scene, determined the correct placement of his camera and the correct moment to cut from one perspective to another. This discovery is frequently called the "grammar and rhetoric" of film because Griffith discovered that—as with words—there was a way of combining film shots to produce clarity, power, and meaning.

Griffith discovered, at the same time, the power of two moving-camera shots: the pan shot and the traveling shot. Again, both of these shots had been used before. There were pans in the "school of Brighton" films and in *The Great Train Robbery*. There were traveling shots in early Lumière views (a trip through Venice by gondola in 1897) and in an American film show called Hale's Tours, in which the audience sat in a theatre designed as a railroad car and watched films of moving scenery actually shot from a moving railroad car. But Griffith realized that these special shots were just two more potential units in creating the whole. The pan shot, with its horizontal sweeps from left to right or right to left, is not only functional for following the moving action but also transfers its feeling of sweeping movement to the viewer. The eye is sensitive to such shifts in the field of vision and it telegraphs this sensitivity to the brain, which translates it into a physical sensation. The traveling shot (sometimes called a tracking shot because the camera's dolly is often mounted on a track) produces an even more magnified sensation of physical movement; the perfect tool for communicating the internal excitement of people riding rushing trains and galloping horses and racing wagons. Griffith integrated these two moving shots into his cinematic language, using their special emotional qualities when his narrative needed that effect. Griffith's restraint in using the traveling shot—reserved for brief and occasional moments in the midst of a climactic chase or "race for life"—shows how thoroughly he understood its kinetic power.

Griffith also realized that, just as the camera was not the servant of space, neither was the final editing of a film the servant of space or time. The early films—Méliès's, for example—had followed a focal character slavishly from place to place, unable to leap to other places and other people regardless of the needs of the narrative. Griffith discovered that two places vastly separate in space or time could be brought together in the audience's mind. This editing technique, called the cross-cut (or parallel cut, switch-back, or several other synonyms), which produced closeness out of distance, became a standard Griffith tool, fulfilling two primary functions. The cut could be either a leap in space (from the victims of an attack to their potential rescuers) to increase the audience's suspense or awareness, or a leap controlled by the character's mind (from the face of a sad girl to a shot of her husband lying dead on the battlefield) to reveal the character's motivations or perceptions. Both kinds of cross-cuts were attempts to mirror internal human sensation in a concrete, externalized, visual form—either the fear and frenzy of a rescue from a violent attack or a reflective reverie in a quiet moment of joy or melancholy. A third kind of Griffith cross-cut served a more symbolic and intellectual purpose. In *A Corner in Wheat* (1909), Griffith cross-cut between a lavish and lively banquet for the rich and a frozen portrait of the poor, waiting in line for a meager loaf of bread. The cross-cut clearly and effectively underlined the injustice of these simultaneous social conditions. When the Biograph management wondered if audiences would be able to understand these shifts, Griffith's answer revealed both his insight and his influences: "Doesn't Dickens write that way?"

While Griffith's narratives learned to leap from space to space, they also began to deepen the texture of life within each of those spaces. Not content with the two-dimensional settings that dominated the interior scenes of most American films of the era (so flat that many painted their furniture and props onto the backdrop), Griffith insisted on making his interior scenes appear as three-dimensional as his outdoor ones. He thrust desks and tables into the shooting area, perpendicular to the walls of the set and to the frame line, rather than lining them up parallel to the walls, as they would be on the theatrical stage. He pushed pieces of furniture out at oblique angles to the set, the camera, and each other, and he shoved chairs, tables, and vases extremely close to the camera itself, further increasing the sense of depth in the cramped quarters where all the Biograph films were shot. By 1909 Griffith's sense of the difference between theatrical and cinematic space was so clear that he could shoot a film, *The Drunkard's Reformation*, that used the device of a play-within-a-film and depended on our perceiving the contrast between shallow and deep space.

Griffith's innovations went beyond the camera and the editing table. Almost simultaneous with Griffith's debut in films came the debut of the electric light in the studios. Artificial lighting gradually replaced the sun's harsh and inconstant performances. When film companies left Manhattan rooftops for the Bronx and Brooklyn, they also left behind the sun and muslin sheets that diffused its glare. But the first film directors merely used the new arc lights as though they were the sun—to produce bright, even, untuned light with no regard to the tonal and narrative requirements of the scene. Does the scene take place indoors or out? During night or day? Should it feel harsh or gentle, cool or warm? Griffith realized the importance of such questions and the potential effectiveness of lighting in answering them. Indeed, another reason that indoor scenes in early American films looked so flat was that the flat, even sunlight could not possibly duplicate the

texture and atmosphere of indoor life. And so Griffith lit one early film (*The Drunkard's Reformation*, 1909) with a dim, flickering, low-angle light that convincingly imitated a firelight's glow. The scene was not only one of the first indoor scenes in an American film to look like life; it was also tonally and metaphorically related to the film's plot—the drunkard returning from the theatre to the warmth and comfort of his home and family. In *Pippa Passes* (1911) Griffith indicated the passage of time, from morning to night, with lighting alone. Griffith's complete mastery of tonal lighting would culminate in 1919 with *Broken Blossoms*, which is dependent on lighting effects not only for its atmosphere and tone but also for the metaphoric contrast that underlies the film's moral system.

Griffith was as innovative with people as with machines. Early film acting was laughably bad; Griffith set out to improve it. First, he demanded underacting: no more huge gestures and demonstrative poses. Of course, because he had developed the expressive power of his camera and editing, he had the tools to allow a player to underact and still be understood. Second, he showed a much greater attention to selecting actors to play the roles, realizing that the actor's physical type was a crucial element in conveying emotional and intellectual states. Despite the obvious limitations of type casting, a purely visual medium like the films communicates as much or more with physical presences than with flexible, dynamic acting talents—a principle the films still respect today. The very casualness of Griffith's getting a job with Porter reveals how shoddy the early directors were in selecting either actors or types. Third, Griffith shocked his employers with what they considered an obvious waste of time—rehearsals. The actors rehearsed the scenes before Griffith shot them. In an era when directors could scream their instructions

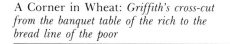

A Corner in Wheat: *Griffith's cross-cut from the banquet table of the rich to the bread line of the poor*

during the shooting, Griffith's method seemed extravagant and unnecessary. Griffith, however, had doubts about creating moods with his actors while he was screaming at them. Finally, Griffith realized the applicability of one of the key artistic principles of the stage: a whole production requires an ensemble, not a collection of individual players. Griffith began building the Biograph stock company as a cohesive group of talented, attuned performers. His success is reflected in the number of important screen actors that Griffith's stock company produced, either for his own films or for the films of others. Mary Pickford, Lionel Barrymore, Lillian and Dorothy Gish, Mae Marsh, Blanche Sweet, Henry B.

Walthall, Robert Harron, and Donald Crisp all had worked for Griffith by 1913.

A close look at three specific Griffith one-reelers reveals his growing mastery of the film form. In *The Lonely Villa* (1909), Griffith's skill in cutting adds excitement to a melodramatic trifle about a wife and children who are attacked by two intruders in her home. Early in the film, Griffith's fluid and rhythmic cutting adds pace to a rather clumsy and unclear exposition that establishes the husband's leaving home while the two assailants hide outside in the bushes. The opening sequence is full of fluid match-cuts—shots from different angles and distances that have been assembled to give the impression of fluid, continuous

The Lonely Villa: *Griffith's cross-cutting. The husband gallops to the rescue . . . of the family under attack at home*

movement—as the husband walks through the house and out the front door. These match-cuts also establish the various domains of the house: the hallways and rooms that will play significant roles in the film's climactic sequence as the wife retreats further and further from the intruders (the steady retreat into the protective depths of the home would become a consistent Griffith motif).

That climactic sequence reveals the power of Griffith's cross-cut. As the intruders begin their assault, Griffith cuts to the husband, many miles distant and ignorant of the danger to his family. The wife retreats to the telephone to inform her husband; Griffith cuts to the husband receiving the call, firmly linking the two distant locations in the narrative flow despite the separation in time and space. Griffith then cuts back and forth between the besieged wife trying to hold out against the attackers and the husband furiously driving home to the rescue. Griffith tightens the screws by cutting each shot shorter and shorter, increasing the tension, excitement, and suspense. When the husband arrives home—just in time—the audience feels as much relief as the besieged wife; we, like her, relax after

the driving finish.

The Lonedale Operator (1911) drives to its climax even more excitingly. The whole film shows a surer and more fluid technique than *Lonely Villa*. The exposition, establishing the relationship of the girl and her beau, establishing that he is a railroad engineer and she a telegraph operator, is much clearer and more detailed than the exposition in the earlier film. The acting is much quieter, much more natural than in *Villa*; the scene in which he proposes to her is humanly credible and warmly touching. Griffith captures the girl's spirit and her joy as she unexpectedly leaps on one of the railroad tracks and walks, tightrope-style, on the track while she talks to her beau. As soon as she and the beau separate, he to his engine and she to her telegraph office, Griffith builds toward the climax with a series of fluid match-cuts showing her entering the office and setting to work. Once the attack begins on her and her office, Griffith begins his relentless and rhythmic cross-cutting, which alternates between three clearly established locales: the attackers on the outside trying to get into the office, the operator inside the office trying to protect herself from the assault, the speeding train (traveling shot) on its way to answer the distress signal that the operator intelligently wired to the next station. Griffith cuts quicker and quicker from outside to inside to train, outside, inside, train, until the beau arrives just in time to find his sweetheart holding the culprits at bay with a wrench she has disguised as a pistol. The girl has brains as well as energy.

Both of these films are pure stories of suspense with very similar devices, although the later one has more human detail, greater realistic texture, and stronger narrative construction. Much more human still is *The New York Hat* (1912), which dispenses with the melodramatic, suspenseful rescue altogether. With a screenplay by Anita Loos (her first, for which she received $15 and an offer to write more), featuring Mary Pickford and Lionel Barrymore, *The New York Hat* is the story of the birth of love. Young Mary longs to escape her drab life and clothing, to attract a gentleman's eye. The young reverend of the parish buys her a stylish hat from New York that she fancies. The town biddies start gossiping, linking Mary and the reverend in sin. He finally silences their talk with a letter from Mary's dying mother asking him to look after the girl. He takes advantage of this opportunity to declare his romantic intentions; she accepts his proposal of marriage.

Griffith puts human flesh on the story's potentially bare bones. To establish Mary's longing for a hat, Griffith breaks down an expositional scene between Mary and her father into two different setups, alternating between a medium two-shot (a shot with two equally important figures) that includes both Mary and her father and a close-up of Mary alone making wistful faces in a mirror. The two alternating setups in the scene establish the crucial emotional premise of the exposition: the gulf between Mary's

little-girl relationship with her moralistic father and Mary's womanly longing to be pretty. And Griffith makes the mirror a key leitmotif of the film, for when Mary finally gets her hat, she returns to the mirror (and the camera to precisely the same setup) to see how charming she looks. Griffith similarly breaks the hat-buying scene into several setups: from Mary's point of view (desiring the hat), from the reverend's point of view (seeing she wants the hat), and then a close two-shot when he makes the purchase, bringing their two heads together, instantly suggesting the direction of their affections.

The film is full of other sensitive human touches. Mary's faces in the mirror are coy and charming; the ugly, snide town gossips are perfect comic caricatures. Griffith would draw fuller portraits of these comic, nasty ladies in *Intolerance* and *Way Down East*. Most personal of all in the film is the disdainful masculine flick of the head that the all-male church elders give, in unison, to the gossipy ladies after their reverend has washed the taint of sin from his relationship with Mary. Griffith is also thumbing his own nose at these morally nearsighted ladies of reform and "uplift."

With a film like *The New York Hat*, Griffith had gone as far and as deeply as he could with the ten-minute picture. Those five years of one-reel films show Griffith laying the foundation not only for his technical achievements but also for the themes and motifs that would dominate his later films. He had made films about periods of American history (such as *1776, or The Hessian Renegades*), films about the contemporary social problems of poverty and vice (such as *The Musketeers of Pig Alley*), films that were stylistically careful adaptations of literary classics (Shakespeare, Poe, Browning, Longfellow) and contemporary novels (Frank Norris, Helen Hunt Jackson). Griffith had also begun making moral-religious allegories—Satan as the

The New York Hat: *the gentlemen thumb their noses at the gossipy matrons*

source of all human error and misery (*The Devil*, 1908); the inevitable choice between the life of sensual pleasure and the life of home and family (*The Two Paths*, 1910); the incompatibility of goodness and the realities of human existence (*The Way of the World*, 1910). Griffith particularly excelled at the close and affectionate study of American rural life—either the gently comic, tender study of rural customs and courtship, as in *A Country Cupid* (1911), or the compassionate view of the difficulty of rural living and survival, as in the hauntingly slow, lyrical, almost mystical shots of the farmer and his horse sowing and planting in *A Corner in Wheat* (1909), establishing the beautiful and natural unity of man, beast, and fields.

Although no member of the audience yet knew Griffith's name (no Patent Company director or actor received screen credit until after 1912), they all knew that Biograph pictures were the best on the market. But by 1913, Griffith wanted to break loose from the one-reel

limit on his thoughts. He had earlier made two-reel films, but the General Film Company insisted on releasing them in two parts, one reel at a time. Now that Griffith had discovered how to say things in the cinematic form, he found he had things he wanted to say.

Griffith made no technical innovations in his longer films that he had not already begun or perfected in the short ones. The longer films used the earlier innovations to assimilate and communicate more complex and more solid material. And that material was simply the Truth, the humanistic gospel according to Saint D. W. He no longer wanted to tell melodramatic stories that culminated in the last-minute rescue, although he never dispensed with either melodrama or the rescue. He wanted the images on the screen to illuminate his personal vision of good and evil. Griffith was not just the cinema's first technician; he was also its first moralist, poet, *auteur*, and master storyteller. A cliché in the criticism of Griffith is that his moral system is

A Corner in Wheat: *the natural unity of man, beast, and field*

essentially that of the Victorian sentimentalist. The positive values are social order, peace, the home and family, womanhood, motherhood, and marital fidelity. The negative values are, correspondingly, social change, war, high life, sexual license, and the broken home. But these specific values are really consequences of Griffith's central vision rather than the vision itself.

The two poles of Griffith's moral world are gentleness and violence. From gentleness come all the virtues of Woman, Peace, and the Home. The figures of gentleness are almost always female; Griffith's women are really girls— luminous, soft, sweet, blonde, frail, child-like, symbols of a delicate ideal rather than living, breathing creatures. Gentleness for Griffith, however, is the ideal, whereas violence is the reality. From violence issue the evils of social upheaval (hence Griffith's hatred of social

reformers), war (hence Griffith's pacifism), and sexual libertinism. The figures of violence are almost always men, for it is man's way to fight and seduce and conquer and reform. Ironically, Griffith's adoration of love and gentleness and simplicity is precisely the same, in its own terms, as that in the later *Easy Rider, Midnight Cowboy,* and *Last Picture Show.*

Griffith's difficulty was integrating his vision into his melodramatic, plotty films. All too often Griffith fell back on two artificial devices that seemed super-imposed on the films rather than an integral part of them. One of them was literally superimposed. He often thrust allegorical meanings on the films by superimposing angels and visions up in the heavens to comment on the earthly action. His allegory also extended to giving characters allegorical names—the Dear One, the Friendless One, the Evil Eye. A second Griffith device was to soup

up the film's meaning with purple, rhetorical titles that told the audience what moral conclusions it should draw from the actions it was about to witness. The titles constantly tell us that war's slaughter is *bitter* and *useless* (italics Griffith's), that women turn to social reform when they can no longer turn a man's fancy, that "looms of fate" weave death that opens up its "opal gates." One of the discoveries about film that Griffith did not make was that the silent film should include as little of its information in titles as possible. One reason that his last-minute rescues were so exciting was that they needed (and used) no titles at all.

Several four-reel films that Griffith shot between the one-reelers of 1912 and the epic films of 1914–15 show both his artistry in transition and his difficulties in wedding moral significance to film action. *Judith of Bethulia* (filmed 1913, released 1914) was the last film Griffith made for Biograph. It is a curious mixture of cinematic strengths and weaknesses. Because Griffith felt self-conscious about his biblical style and subject, his actors were much more stilted and much less carefully observed than in *New York Hat*. Griffith's rendering of the evil of the invader, Holofernes, is also formulaic and hollow. The "orgies" in his tent, metaphoric for the man's evil mind, are represented as a series of clumsy and unevocative semihula dances by the "Maids of the Fishes." Those Fish Maidens revealed a flaw in Griffith's vision that was to persist throughout his film career. Although Griffith knew what purity and goodness were, he never really knew what sin and degeneracy were all about. The abstractness of the lives of sin that people lead in his films inevitably keeps those lives from having any real or credible impact.

Balancing the film's artificiality and the fable-like thinness of the characters is Griffith's skill at cutting and construction. His opening expositional sequence effectively establishes the peacefulness and fertility of life in Bethulia, the importance of the well to its survival, and the thickness of the town walls for its defense. Here is Griffith's civilized ideal of peace and gentleness. Then Griffith introduces the conqueror Holofernes and his attacking army, the forces of violent destruction. The branches in the foreground part, revealing the awesome hordes ready to descend on peaceful Bethulia.

Griffith magnifies the horrifying intensity of the battle scenes with his skillful cutting from side to side, from inside the walls to outside, and back again. These battle scenes clearly show Griffith warming up for the huge sequences in *The Birth of a Nation*, although in *Judith* the battles feel slightly pinched and confined by their being anchored to the walls of the city, a problem he would solve in *Intolerance*. Much freer is Griffith's cutting at the end of the film when the attacking hordes, without their leader, retreat in chaos. Griffith cuts from one shot in which the horses and men run furiously from screen right to screen left to the next in which men and horses stream down a hill at the top of screen left into a valley that is at the bottom of screen right. This collision of contrary movements would not only dominate the battles in *Birth of a Nation* but would also contribute to Eisenstein's theory of the shock value of colliding images.

Also noteworthy in the film are the cross-cuts between the Bethulians starving inside the walls and Judith inside Holofernes' tent preparing to ease their starvation (clearly a variation of the

---

Griffith's framing in The Musketeers of Pig Alley: *the tension of the oversized close-up (Elmer Booth and Harry Carey), the social implication of money that arrives anonymously (to Elmer Booth) at the side of the frame*

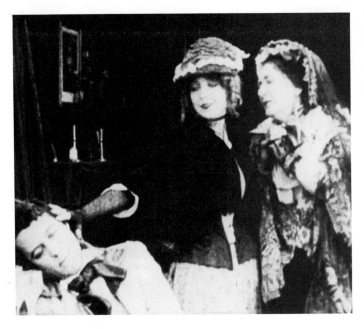

last-minute rescue), and the cross-cuts between Judith's hesitation before killing Holofernes, with whom she has fallen in love, and her vision of her own starving people (the vision that ultimately moves her to commit the murder). Despite Griffith's continuing technical skill and despite the film's vastness, it remains a rather tepid and artificial production.

By 1914, Griffith's innovativeness, the growing lengths and costs of his films, had irked Biograph into kicking him upstairs, making him director of studio production and relieving him of the opportunity to direct films personally. Griffith, however, wanted to make feature films; both his own vision and the new feature-length imports from Italy (*Cabiria, Quo Vadis?*) pointed the way toward longer films. Griffith left Biograph for the independent company, Mutual, signing a contract that gave him the freedom to make one picture of his own each year in addition to making several program pictures of the company's choosing. It was a new beginning for Griffith; it was the end for Biograph. Not only did Griffith leave but so did his

cameraman, G. W. "Billy" Bitzer, and the whole Griffith stock company of actors.

One of Griffith's program pictures for Mutual, *Home Sweet Home* (1914), is another transitional mixture of good and bad; it showed where Griffith had been and indicated where he was to go. Like the later *Intolerance*, *Home Sweet Home* uses four strands of action. Unlike the later film, Griffith does not weave the strands together but keeps them separate, using only the leitmotif of the song, "Home Sweet Home," to unite the four stories, just as the wandering Pippa's song unites the incidents of Griffith's one-reel *Pippa Passes* (1909). In the framing story of *Home Sweet Home,* the composer of the famous song, John Howard Payne, deserts home, mother, and sweetheart for the big city. There he falls to wenching, drinking, degeneracy, and poverty, summoning up just enough of his old home spirit to write his famous song. Payne later dies of unspecified causes in a foreign land, and his hometown sweetheart dies at the same time, presumably from E.S.P.

The second story in the film is the most human and delightful. An Eastern slicer falls in love with the earthy, out-west hashslinger, Apple Pie Mary, played energetically by Mae Marsh. Griffith adds a human, comic touch when Mary first sees the slicer; she immediately starts pulling the curlers out of her hair, revealing her attraction to him. When he later returns to her, she goes through the same curler business again. In this section, the Easterner is about to reject Apple Pie Mary (two different worlds) when he hears a fiddler playing "Home Sweet Home." He rushes back to her—a delightful reunion scene with her crawling under the bed to hide from him—and they marry and live happily ever after. Interestingly, this section, the comic, earthy, rural sequence of the film, is the most entertaining part of it, just as the earthy, comic, down-east sequences of *Way Down East* are the best sections of that film. Griffith repeatedly demonstrates that his best film subjects are those he intimately knew and loved.

The third section of *Home Sweet Home* is a melodramatic Cain-and-Abel story in which brother murders brother. Their mother, about to commit suicide after the dual slaughter, hears another fiddler playing "Home Sweet Home." She gives up her thoughts of suicide and continues living, now resigned to life. The fourth section of the film is a domestic tale of potential marital infidelity. A young wife flirts with a lascivious admirer; as she is about to run off with him to a sinful amour, she hears a fiddler playing "Home Sweet Home." (Those fiddlers are everywhere.) She rejects the lover, returns to her husband, and in the next shot we see the happy married couple, aged and gray, surrounded by a bushel of kids.

The implication of all three stories is clearly that Mr. Payne's song, despite his faulty life, did great good. The film's epilogue picks up this moral nail and drives it home. We return to Payne in some unclear locale; he is either slaving away in Hell or fighting in a foreign war in which he met his death. Payne's home-town sweetheart (played by Lillian Gish) appears to him as a white diaphanous angel, superimposed in the heavens. Her image multiplies until there are many images of her fluttering and floating and beckoning from up there; Payne's image flutters up to join hers. The point Griffith makes is obviously that the results of the man's work cancel out the depravity of the man's life; furthermore, that Payne had the potential for good in him (he could write such a song), but the potential was corrupted by decadent, big-city life.

There is obviously much that is soft-headed in the film. Griffith announces with his opening title that the film is allegorical and not biographical; but the slender, melodramatic stories and the artificial unifying device (that fiddle) cannot support the film's ponderously heavy theme. You can't ask a bon-bon to be a steak. The film's titles are no help either. In the epilogue Griffith tells us:

Master Lust Thoughts
Master Carnality
Master Brutality
Master Worldly
They Pull Hard.

The Bunyanesque personifications seem disproportionate to the slim tales. An earlier title sums up Griffith's sentimentality as Lillian Gish tells her fiancé, "'Til the end of the world and afterward, I shall wait for you." Despite the absurdity of the idea, she makes good on her promise.

The Birth of a Nation and Intolerance

For his own independent project for 1914, Griffith chose a novel by Thomas Dixon, *The Clansman*. The book appealed to Griffith for several reasons. It was a vast story, covering the final years in the graceful life of the old South before the Civil War, the turbulent, violent years of war, and the painful, political years of

Reconstruction. Griffith, a southerner whose father served in the Confederate Army, was also attracted by Dixon's slant. Dixon, also a southerner, saw the Reconstruction era as a period of chaos in which the white South struggled, but survived. It was this film, with dangerous social and political implications, that Griffith set out to make.

No one on the set knew exactly what Griffith's film was all about. Griffith used no shooting script, creating all details of the vast cinema pageant out of his head as he went along. The players only knew that the project was vast: it took six weeks to rehearse and nine weeks to shoot, an incredible amount of time in an era when a director cranked out a film (*Home Sweet Home,* for example) in only a week. It required thousands of men and animals and countless huge and detailed indoor sets. Its cost, $125,000, was the most ever invested in a motion picture. At the film's official premiere in Clune's Auditorium in Los Angeles on February 8, 1915, audiences finally saw how huge Griffith's plan and project were. The film was still called *The Clansman* at that opening. When the author of the novel finally saw the film, however, he told Griffith, in his enthusiasm, that the original title was too tame. Griffith should call his film *The Birth of a Nation.*

The Birth of a Nation is as much a document of American social history as of film history. Though President Wilson described the film as "history written in lightning," its action, which openly praises the Ku Klux Klan, is a very difficult morsel for today's liberal or social activist to swallow. It was just as difficult for the liberals of 1915. The N.A.A.C.P., the president of Harvard University, Jane Addams, and liberal politicians all damned the work for its bigoted, racist portrayal of the Negro. The film was suppressed in some cities for fear of race riots; politicians spoke for or against it according to their dependence on the black vote. At a revival of the film some ten years after its original opening, mobs poured into Chicago to see it as well as to attend a Ku Klux Klan convention. With all of the controversy over the film, it might be wise to look at Griffith's handling of the black man a bit more closely before moving on to the cinematic qualities of the film.

First, a close examination of the film reveals that two of the film's three villains—Lynch (the false reformer) and Sarah (Stoneman's mistress)—are not pure Negroes but mulattoes. Both possess qualities that Griffith had already damned in white men—hypocrisy, selfishness, social reforming, and sexual license. That they were mulattoes indicates that Griffith's main target was not the blacks but miscegenation; the miscegenation theme flows through the movie—in the black legislature, in signs at the black-dominated polling place, in Lynch's attraction to Elsie. The mixing of bloods is the source of evil. Griffith's stance against miscegenation stems from an assumption about blacks and whites that is perhaps more central to the film's offensiveness. For Griffith, whites are whites and blacks blacks; the white race is naturally superior; each race has "its own place." If Griffith's view seems outrageous today, it is certainly a part of his general moral system in which he viewed all social establishments as good because they are established and all attempts to change the Establishment as bad because they are disruptive, violent, and disorderly.

There are good blacks and bad blacks in Griffith's film. The good ones are the "faithful souls" who work in the fields, "know their place," and stay with their white family after the war. If Griffith's separation of good and bad seems an old-fashioned partiality to Uncle Tom, it should be pointed out that *Gone with the Wind,* twenty-five years newer fashioned than *Birth of a Nation* and released every five years to a still adoring public, makes the same distinction between good and bad "darkies." Perhaps Griffith's most

The Birth of a Nation: *Griffith's "historical facsimile" of Ford's Theater*

offensive scene is the one in which the empty state legislature suddenly (with the aid of superimposition and dissolve) springs to life, full of black lawmakers with bare feet on desks, swilling booze, and eating—what else?—fried chicken. But Griffith's treatment of these blacks is not an isolated expression of racial prejudice; it is a part of his whole system of the evil of social change and disruption. And cinematically this legislature scene is a visual marvel!

The brilliance of *The Birth of a Nation* is that it is both strikingly complex and tightly whole. It is a film of brilliant parts carefully tied together by the driving line of the film's narrative. Its hugeness of conception, its acting, its sets, its cinematic devices had not been equalled by any film before it and would not be surpassed by many that followed it. Yet surprisingly, for such an obviously big picture, it is also a highly personal and intimate one.

Its small moments are as impressive as its big ones. Though Griffith summarizes an entire historical era in the evolution of the nation in general and the South in particular, his summary adopts a human focus: two families, one Northern (the Stonemans), one Southern (the Camerons), who, despite the years of death and suffering, survive the war and the reconstruction. The eventual marriage between the two families becomes metaphoric for Griffith's view of the whole nation. Human values—love, sincerity, natural affection—triumph over social movements and social reformers. The close observation of people and their most intimate feelings, the techniques of which Griffith had been developing for five years, propels the film, not its huge battle scenes, its huge dances and political meetings, its detailed "historical facsimiles" of Ford's Theatre and the Appomattox courthouse. The big scenes

serve as the violent social realities with which the gentle, loving people must contend.

Even in the mammoth battle sequences Griffith never deserts his human focus. His rhythmic and energetic editing constantly alternates between distant, extreme long shots of the battles and close concentration on the individual men who are fighting. Griffith takes the time for such touches as his cut from the living, fighting soldiers to a shot of the motionless dead ones who have found "war's peace," his cuts from the valiant human effort on the Union side to shots of a similar effort on the Confederate, including Ben Cameron's heroic charge of the Union lines, ramming the Southern flag down the Union cannon's throat. Griffith increases the power, the violence, the energy of these battle sequences with his sensitivity to cutting on contrary movement across the frame, to cutting in rhythm with the action, and to cutting to different distances and angles that mirror the points of view of the different participants. But in the midst of such violence, Griffith takes time for quiet, tender moments: the moment when the two boys, one Cameron and one Stoneman, die in each other's arms; the moment in which a weeping mother on a hilltop views the destructiveness of the invading army in the valley.

This shot, one of the most celebrated in the film, shows Griffith's control of the masking- or irising-effect, another of the innovations he developed in his apprentice years. The iris-shot masks a certain percentage of the frame, concentrating the viewer's attention completely on a circle or rectangle or some other shape of light within the blackened screen rectangle. The iris, analogous to the theatre spotlight or today's zoom lens, either shrinks the audience's focus from the whole field to a single point or expands our focus from the single point to the whole field. In *Birth of a Nation*'s famous iris-shot, Griffith begins tightly on the weeping mother's face and then irises out to reveal the awesome army below her, the cause of her sorrow. This use of the mask-shot to reveal cause and effect is only one of many in the picture.

Griffith's attention to human dramatic detail dominates the film. He uses animals to define his characters and their emotional states. In the film's opening sequence depicting the gentle, peaceful life of the old South (analogous to the opening sequence of *Judith of Bethulia*), Griffith shows Mister Cameron gently stroking two puppies. Significantly, one of the puppies is black and the other white; it is also significant that a kitten soon begins to play with the pups. The animals become visual metaphors for Griffith's idealized prewar South, a happy mixture of different races and different social classes. Later in the film Griffith cross-cuts between the two lovers, Elsie and Ben, gently playing with a dove while the savage Lynch mistreats a dog. The attitudes of the characters toward animals ultimately reveal their attitudes toward people.

Another of Griffith's artistic devices is his use of the main street in the Piedmont town as a barometer of the film's emotional and social tensions. At the film's opening the street is full of people and carriages: active, sociable, friendly. As the Confederate soldiers first march off to war, the street becomes a carnival: fireworks, cheering townspeople, rhythmic columns of men on horses. Then, when "the little Colonel" (Ben) returns home after the war, the street is desolate, empty, ruined, dusty, dead. And finally, when the town is overrun with carpetbaggers and reconstructionists, drunken gangs of black men rove the street; the street has become a very unfriendly, ungentle place. By capturing human emotion in concrete visual images Griffith successfully renders human feeling rather than a parody of feeling, as in *Queen Elizabeth*.

Birth of a Nation is part mammoth spectacle and part touching human drama. It is also part melodrama and part allegorical vision. Griffith never deserts the constructional principles of his early melodramatic one-reelers as the means to keep his story moving. The suspense and excitement of Griffith's cross-cutting create the dramatic tension of many of the sequences: the attack of a band of

Ben Cameron (Henry B. Walthall) rams the Confederate flag down the throat of the Union cannon

The street as emotional barometer: the total emptiness and loneliness of the "Little Colonel's" return from the war

rejoices as the City of God replaces the Kingdoms of the Earth. There are several remarkable things about this closing vision: its audacity, its irrelevance, and the passionateness and sincerity of Griffith's commitment to it. But, as in *Home Sweet Home*, there is a striking disparity between the film's generalizations and the specific evidence on which they are based, between realistic melodrama and mystical allegory. Exactly how is this City of God to become a reality? Certainly not by the efforts of the Ku Klux Klan alone. It is the evil in the human soul that must be exorcised. And once again Griffith reveals his nearsightedness in probing what he considers evil.

All the evil in the film is instigated by three people. They are evil (1) because they are evil, or (2) because they have mixed blood. They succeed in doing evil because they entice the naturally good but easily tempted Congressman Stoneman. And his temptation stems from his physical deformity and vanity (Griffith brilliantly uses a club foot and a wig to define these traits of Stoneman's), which demand physical proofs of his prowess. According to the film's action, the chaos of the Civil War was the direct result of the nation's Stonemans who became entangled in an evil of which they were totally ignorant or about which they were helpless. Even granting Griffith this preposterous premise (suitable for melodrama but not for history or philosophy), how is one to be sure that the future contains no Stonemans? *Birth of a Nation*'s final vision is an innocent wish rather than the intellectual consequence of what has preceded it. The film remains incredibly solid as human drama and cinematic excitement, incredibly flimsy as abstract intellectualization.

Precisely the same is true of *Intolerance*. This next major film grew directly out of the controversy over *Birth of a Nation*. Griffith's treatment of the blacks provoked public condemnation of the

black renegades (significantly their captain is white) on the defenseless town and the Cameron home (and women); the assassination of Lincoln in Ford's Theatre; the rapacious Gus chasing the littlest Cameron girl through the woods until she falls to her death. The most thrilling sequence of all is, appropriately, the final one in which Griffith gives us not one but two last-minute rescues. Not only does Griffith cross-cut from the victims to the potential agents of their rescue; he cuts between two sets of victims and their common saviors—the Ku Klux Klan—furiously galloping forth to eradicate the forces of rapine and death. Not only is this rescue sequence Griffith's most complex up to this point; it is also his most sensitive to the kinetic excitement of editing rhythms and the moving camera.

But after the dust from the galloping climax has settled, Griffith celebrates the peaceful union of Elsie Stoneman and Ben Cameron with a superimposed allegorical pageant in the heavens. Elsie and Ben see Christ replacing the military general (Alexander the Great?); Christ cuts the Gordian knot and all humanity

man who put such ideas on film. The criticism stung Griffith deeply, especially since he had watered down many of Thomas Dixon's most inflammatory, anti-Negro passages. Griffith began defending himself against the charges of bigotry and hatred; he angrily protested the film's suppression in several cities, writing a pamphlet championing the "Freedom of the Screen." *Intolerance* was to be his cinematic defense, his pamphlet against intellectual censorship in film form. Fortunately for Griffith, *Birth of a Nation* not only stirred a lot of talk; it also made a lot of money. It was the first authentic blockbuster in film history. Griffith would need all that money for *Intolerance*, its cost reputed as high as $2,000,000, its conception so huge that it was to *Birth of a Nation* in scope and complexity as *Birth of a Nation* was to *Judith of Bethulia*.

Ben (Walthall) and Elsie (Lillian Gish) see the City of God replacing the strife of the world

Intolerance was not one story, but four. In Belshazzar's Babylon, the evil high priest conspires against the wise and just king, selling the city to the Persian conqueror, who destroys the nation's happiness and murders its ruler. In Judea, the jealous Pharisees intrigue against Christ and contrive to send the wise and just savior to the cross. In Renaissance France, evil courtiers persuade the Catholic king to slaughter all the Protestant Huguenots. In twentieth-century America, a Boy is falsely convicted of a murder and his wife unjustly robbed of her baby by a group of social reformers; the facts eventually surface to save the Boy from the gallows.

Tying the four stories together are its consistent themes: the machinations of the selfish, the frustrated, and the inferior; the divisiveness of religious and political beliefs; the constant triumph of injustice over justice (except in the modern story); the pervasiveness of violence and viciousness through the centuries. Also tying the stories together is Griffith's brilliant control of editing, which keeps all the parallels in the stories quite clear, and

which creates an even more spectacular climax than in *Birth of a Nation*.

In *Intolerance*, there are four frenzied climaxes; the excitement in each of the narrative lines reinforces the others, all of them driving furiously to their breathtaking conclusions. Griffith's last-minute rescues cross-cut through the centuries. And finally, tying the four stories together, is a symbolic mother-woman, rocking a cradle, bathed in a shaft of light, representing the eternal evolution of humanity, fulfilling the purpose of the creator. This woman, inspired by Whitman's lines, "Endlessly rocks the cradle, Uniter of Here and Hereafter," is a figure of peace, of light (a shaft of light grows steadily brighter on her as the film progresses), of fertility (flowers bloom in her cradle at the end of the film), of the ultimate goodness of man that will eventually triumph.

The film's bigness is obvious: the high walls of Babylon, the hugeness of the palace (and the immense tracking shot that Griffith uses to span it), the battle sequences, the care with each of the film's periods and styles. The costumes, the lighting, the acting styles, the decor are so distinct in each of the four epochs that

The faces of women: The Mountain Girl (Constance Talmadge) and the Little Dear One (Mae Marsh)

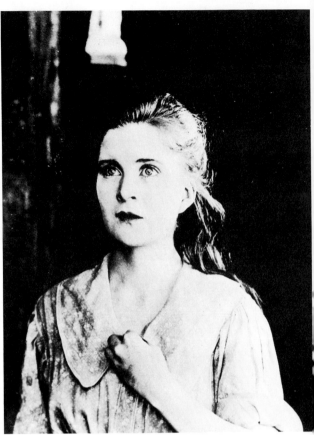

The poignant detail: the Little Dear One grasps her stolen baby's bootie

viewers know exactly whether they are in the squalid, drab poverty of a contemporary slum, the elegant tastefulness of the French court, or the garishness of ancient Babylon. But as with *The Birth of a Nation, Intolerance* is a big film that works because of its little, intimate moments. The film revolves around the faces of women— from the bubbling, jaunty, comically vital face of the Mountain Girl in the Babylon story to the luminous, tear-stained, soulful faces of Brown Eyes in the Huguenot story and the Dear One in the modern story. *Intolerance* makes it perfectly clear that social chaos takes its toll on the women, who are the helpless sufferers of its violence. Significantly, Griffith's mother-symbol of historical continuity is also necessarily a woman. Along with the close-ups of faces, the film is equally attentive to close-ups of hands, particularly in the modern story: the Dear One's wrenched hands as the callous court pronounces judgment on her husband; her hand grasping her imprisoned husband's cap, a tender memory of his warm presence; her hand clutching one of her baby's booties after the social uplifters have carried the infant away.

The film is also rich in the same kind of metaphoric detail found in *Birth of a Nation.* The Dear One shows her humanity and tenderness as she lovingly throws grain to her chickens; when she moves to the oppressive city she keeps a single flower in her flat, a metaphor for all that is beautiful and natural and alive. Significantly, flowers bloom in the symbolic cradle at the end of the film. (Flowers become the same kind of symbol of love and beauty in Griffith's later *Broken Blossoms.*) Yet another touching metaphoric detail is the little toy cart pulled by two white doves in the Babylon sequence—a metaphor for the tender, fragile love between Belshazzar and his queen. After the two and the mountain girl have been slain, Griffith hauntingly

irises out to a shot of the tiny cart and doves, a touching evocation of a beauty that was but is no longer.

Although the film is very deeply felt, Griffith's ideas are once again very shallowly developed. *Intolerance* makes quite clear what kinds of humans and human activities Griffith thoroughly detests: rich meddlers in false charities, unsympathetic judges and courts of law, callous entrepreneurs and businessmen, religious hypocrites, political schemers, white slavers who take advantage of the poverty of the poor, anyone who kills or destroys. Griffith's technique is as effective at conveying hatred as it is at evoking tenderness. His social-reforming ladies are vicious, ugly caricatures of gossiping old women; his intriguing priests and politicians and Pharisees are equally grotesque. One of Griffith's most effective devices of caricature is the cross-cut—particularly the sequence in which he captures the cold, unfeeling inhumanity of the factory owner. Griffith cuts from the shots of the workers being mowed down by police rifles (violent, quick cutting, frenetic) to a shot of the owner of the factory sitting alone in his vast office (a long take, perfectly still, shot from above to emphasize the size of the office and the smallness of the man). The contrast of action and inaction, passion and deadness, in the two shots clearly defines the man's unsympathetic inhumanity to his slaughtered workers. Ten years later Eisenstein would build a whole film, *Strike,* out of such cross-cuts.

Although Griffith's dislikes are clear, the intellectual cement uniting the four stories (and the rocking cradle) is not. The film could as easily have been called "Injustice" or "Intrigue" as *Intolerance.* Griffith was interested in the word intolerance simply because he felt himself the victim of it. But in none of the four stories does intolerance seem so much the cause of evil as pure human nastiness (exactly as in *Birth of a Nation*). And when the film ends with its almost obligatory

The seeds of expressionism: the stark symmetry of the climactic hanging

optimistic vision—more superimposed angels in the heavens; the fields of the prison dissolve into fields of flowers; flowers bloom in the cradle—we once again witness a thematic *non sequitur,* an interpolated wish rather than a consequence of the film's action. Though there may be hope in the Boy's last-minute reprieve, it hardly seems enough to balance a whole film of poverty, destruction, suffering, and injustice.

The audience of 1916 was not so much aware of intellectual inconsistencies in the film as it was of its confusing complexity and its general unpleasantness. The fact that Griffith films can be probed for intellectual and artistic wholeness at all, despite the results of the probe, shows how far Griffith had taken the feature film in only three years (since *Queen Elizabeth*). But unlike *The Birth of a Nation, Intolerance* aroused no social protest; worse, it aroused little audience interest of any kind. Perhaps the film was unpopular because its structural complexity asked too much from its audience. Or perhaps the film was a victim of an historical accident, its obviously pacifistic statement being totally antipathetic to a nation preparing itself emotionally to send its soldiers "Over There." Thomas Ince's pacifist-intellectualistic film, *Civilization,* had made money only six months earlier. Whatever the reason, *Intolerance* was a financial disaster, costing Griffith (its ballooning budget forced him to invest in it personally) all his profits from *Birth of a Nation.* The failure of *Intolerance* began Griffith's financial dependence on other producers and businessmen, from which he would never recover.

1916-1931

The cliché of criticism of Griffith is that with *Intolerance* the director reached a peak from which the only direction was down. The final years of Griffith's career are often dismissed as years of repetition, a retreat into sentimentality, and a lack of attention to audience tastes. There is some truth in the cliché. In the final period of his career, Griffith was no innovator; the cinematic advances of his youth had solidified into a stable, controlled mastery of the film form beyond which he would not or could not go. Some of his major pictures were unsuccessful at the box office and do not seem striking artistic wholes today: *Hearts of the World* (1917), *Orphans of the Storm* (1921), *America* (1924). After the financial fiasco of *Intolerance*, Griffith also had to look to his wallet, a concern that led to many uninspired program pictures to fulfill contracts: *The Idol Dancer* (1920), *One Exciting Night* (1922), *Sally of the Sawdust* (1925), *That Royle Girl* (1926), and perhaps a dozen more.

Despite Griffith's financial problems and lagging artistic imagination, he made two films during his final period that rank just behind his two epics in power and interest. In fact, both of the films—*Broken Blossoms* (1919) and *Way Down East* (1920)—are more entertaining and easier for today's audiences to sit through than either of the huge epics. *Broken Blossoms* is Griffith's most polished, most finished gem. This film, smaller in conception than the two epics, is a tight triangle story of one woman between two men. Out of this triangle come the film's values, rather than from Griffith's subtitles and allegorical visions. If the film is less weighty than the two epics, it is also less pretentious, less intent on intellectualization, and less insistent on its high seriousness. Like so many Griffith films, *Broken Blossoms* is an adaptation of a work of fiction—Thomas Burke's "The Chink and the Child," from his collection *Limehouse Nights*. As with *Birth of a Nation*, Griffith took another man's work and made it his own, as the film's metaphoric title so clearly shows.

The film is Griffith's gentlest, his most explicit and poetic hymn to gentleness. The typical Griffith film shows violence destroying gentleness; the focus of the films is usually on the violent disrupters: war, social upheaval, union protests, political chicanery, sexual debauches. In *Broken Blossoms*, the aura of ideal gentleness dominates the action, punctuated by the violent jabs of the real world. The gentle man in the film comes from the Orient to bring the message of the gentle Buddha to the vicious, violent men of the West. Once he arrives in London's Chinese slum, Limehouse, Cheng Huan runs into the "sordid realities of life"—gambling, whoring, opium smoking—that constitute life in the West.

Then in the film's second section, Griffith switches to the female figure of gentleness, Lucy. Raised by the prize fighter, Battling Burrows, Lucy is an unloved child who spends her time wandering around the Limehouse district, trying to scrape up enough tin foil to buy herself a flower. Flowers, of course, are the visual metaphor for gentleness in the film, as the title clearly indicates. Lucy's gentleness, however, like Cheng Huan's, runs into sordid realities. Her reality is her foster father, Burrows, a brute who uses Lucy as both slavish servant and defenseless punching bag. One of the most poignant touches in the film is Burrow's insistence that Lucy smile for him, regardless of her real feelings. Since she is unable to summon a genuine smile, she uses two fingers to force one.

The next section of the film necessarily brings the two gentle figures together. Cheng Huan is attracted by Lucy's gentle purity, which he instantly perceives. They first meet, appropriately, over the purchase of a flower. She later collapses in his shop after a terrific beating by her foster father. Cheng Huan enthrones her in his room as a Princess of Flowers, and the two celebrate a brief but beautiful union of gentle love. Lucy even smiles without the aid of her fingers for the first time, and Cheng Huan's one weak moment of animal lust (brilliantly communicated by a painfully tight close-up) is soon conquered by his realization of the ideal perfection of his guest and their relationship.

But the realities break in upon the ideal. Burrows finds her at Cheng Huan's, drags her back to their slum room, and begins his inevitable attack.

She retreats to a closet; he smashes it open with an axe, and Griffith creates one of the most accurate renditions of human frenzy in screen history as Lucy frantically starts rushing in a circle inside the closet—trapped, flustered, terrified. The death of all three characters is imminent. Lucy dies from this final beating, Cheng Huan shoots Burrows and then commits *hara-kiri*. Blossoms, despite their loveliness, cannot survive for long in the soil of mortality.

This simple story could descend into either boredom on the one side or sentimental claptrap on the other. Griffith walks a tight-rope between the two abysses. He suffuses the film with the atmosphere of dreams and haze. The two actors who play the gentle figures— Richard Barthelmess and Lillian Gish— have perfectly harmonious faces of inner calm and peace. Their acting is so restrained and so perfectly matched that the two even begin to look alike. The two feel like a single being. Griffith also succeeds in giving the violent villain—played by Donald Crisp—both energy and credibility. Because he is a prize fighter, Burrows comes alive by sustaining the metaphor of boxing; Griffith makes Crisp walk, stand, sway, stagger like an animal in the ring. After Cheng Huan shoots Burrows, Griffith adds one of those observant touches that brilliantly makes the moment come to life. Burrows, reeling under the shot, instinctively puts up his dukes and begins dizzily jabbing at his opponent; after a few weak and faltering feints, Burrows collapses. This realistic detail at the moment of death—for once Griffith gives his villain as much naturalistic attention as his heroes—parallels Lucy's final living gesture in which she uses two fingers to poke her face into a last smile.

Griffith's lighting also sustains the film's mood; *Broken Blossoms* remains one of the most beautifully lit early films in screen history. The lighting of scenes in Cheng Huan's shop and room is an atmospheric blend of beams of light and pools of shadow. Lillian Gish, as the Princess, becomes luminous, surrounded by the gray and black regions of her flowery kingdom. Griffith uses low-key lighting exclusively for these scenes. The lighting is not only atmospheric; it is also a precise visual translation of the film's metaphoric contrast between gentleness and violence. While Lucy is enthroned in Cheng Huan's room, Battling Burrows fights his title match. Griffith cross-cuts between the place of love—the room—and the place of hate—the ring. The boxing ring is harshly lit with bright, even white light; the room is suffused with shafts and shadows. Although *Broken Blossoms'* single mood asks a lot less of its audience than the earlier epics, it keeps its promises.

Way Down East, although more uneven than *Broken Blossoms,* contains sections that are as fine as anything Griffith ever did. The most famous sequence in the film is the climax, the last-minute rescue of Anna Moore (Lillian Gish again), floating steadily toward the deadly falls. Anna Moore's unfortunate sexual error has been discovered by her adopted down-east family; she rushes out of their house into a blinding blizzard, the savagery of the wind and snow becoming visual metaphors for the rage and misery in her own heart. Then Griffith's cross-cutting, his most useful and enduring tool, drives the film's climax by alternating between three separate but related locations: Anna Moore alone in the storm, prostrate on a moving ice cake; her down-east boyfriend (Richard Barthelmess again) searching for her—the agent of her rescue; the ominous falls, toward which the ice cake is moving—the danger from which she must be saved. The falls that Griffith used for these cuts were none other than Niagara Falls; Griffith merely spliced in bits of stock footage. Here was the ultimate proof of the logic of cross-cutting: although the actress was really nowhere near any falls (especially

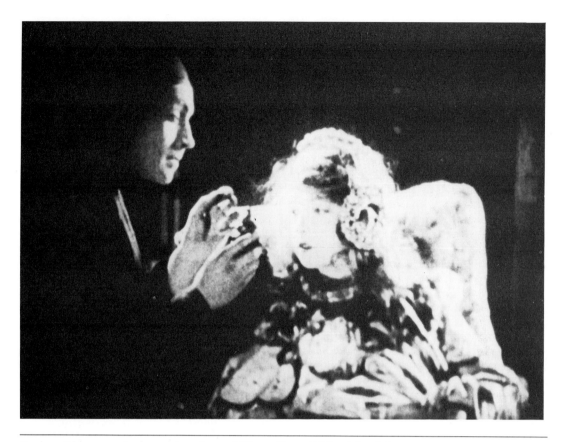

Broken Blossoms: *the harmonious faces of Cheng Huan (Richard Barthelmess) and Lucy (Lillian Gish) in their luminous Kingdom of Peace*

Niagara), the audience felt her nearness because of the narrative links that bound the three locations. Soviet filmmakers would soon seize on this Griffith editing principle, naming it "creative geography."

The uneven, weaker parts of *Way Down East* are the plotty remnants of the original stage melodrama, whose rights Griffith purchased for $175,000 ($50,000 more than the entire budget of *Birth of a Nation* and a sure indication of the film industry's rising costs). Everything in *Way Down East* related to the evil doings of the rich folks reveals the artificial, heavy, and abstract hand of Griffith trying to depict a life-style for which he had neither

sympathy nor understanding. After all, rich people have more things to do with their money than hold fancy-dress balls, act snobbish toward the pure of heart but poor of purse, and seduce innocent virgins with fake marriage vows. Griffith's handling of the rich in the film is a throwback to the Fish Maidens of *Judith of Bethulia*. But the film has two compensating virtues. First, there is the face of Lillian Gish, radiant, luminous, charming, alive. If the problems that the plot gives her seem foolish and artificial, the touching reactions of her eyes and mouth make sense of them. Griffith knew the power of the Gish face; he rivets our gaze on it with close-up after close-up, most of them key-lit to give her hair that shiny, diaphanous glow. The real action of the film takes place not in the film's society but on the Gish face.

The second virtue of the film is Griffith's tender, careful, comic observation of down-east life. He loves the warmth of these rural people, their pettiness, laziness, and short-sightedness as well as their sincerity, simplicity, and compassion. For Griffith, the down-east life, despite its lack of wealth and sophistication, is a model of gentleness, of peacefulness, of poor eyes balanced by rich hearts. In down-east life Griffith saw a mirror for the gentle and fertile life of the South (which he had depicted in the opening section of *Birth of a Nation*) before the violence of military and political wars ripped that life asunder. In his final important film, Griffith again demonstrates that no director could more convincingly and lovingly render the things he knew and loved, and could more laughably and artificially render the things he gathered from books and literary clichés.

There are several theories that attempt to explain Griffith's creative decay in the final fifteen years of his career. Perhaps he ran out of innovative ideas, both technically and intellectually. The solidifying of his cinematic technique may have contributed to the congealing of his ability to make exciting, moving, powerful films. Because his vision was so consistent and yet so thin he may have gone sour on saying the same things without being able to say them in a new way. There might never have been an *Intolerance* to equal or surpass *Birth of a Nation* if the controversy over the first epic hadn't fired Griffith's anger and imagination. A second popular theory is that Griffith's ideas had become outmoded in the twenties. The flapper morality of the jazz age rejected the sentimentality of Griffith's Victorianism. Belasco's melodrama had been supplanted by

urbane, domestic comedy-dramas of sexual innuendo and visual wit. The high life, which Griffith depicted so blackly and so clumsily, was what audiences vicariously wanted to experience. Griffith did not give the public what it wanted. A third theory is that Griffith's own artistic integrity had been corrupted by wealth and success. Renowned as the director-laureate of the world, Griffith substituted dreams of power—ten-hour films, chains of movie theatres and studios all bearing his name, The Griffith—for his artistic seriousness and skill.

The truth probably lies somewhere among the various theories. Griffith certainly seemed to be running out of creative gas. As his pictures became more and more formulaic he was more and more dependent on public acceptance of his formulas—but his formulas, as formulas, were ten to twenty years out of date. The Griffith mastery when he was working at the top of his powers could make Victorian formulas exciting; *Broken Blossoms* and *Way Down East*, both heavily Victorian and sentimental and both released in the early years of the jazz age, were huge box-office successes—as big financial successes as Griffith ever had. If Griffith's later films in the twenties had been as powerful as those two, they might also have pulled in the customers. When the mastery flagged, however, audiences saw the bare bones of sentimentaliy and took themselves to other directors' pictures.

Griffith's *America* (1924) is a sure symptom of his hardening of the creative arteries. Despite its lovely photography, its careful re-creation of American life in 1776, and its brilliantly edited sequence of Paul Revere's ride, the film is an obvious remake of *The Birth of a Nation*, substituting the Revolution for the Civil War. Again there are two families, one Southern, one Northern. Again one of the families is misguided in its political loyalties but not in its moral instincts. Again the villain is an idealization of evil who uses political theory to mask his own selfish drives of sexual, material, and political conquest. And again the film's last-minute rescue resolves its melodramatic problems as well as its political ones, uniting hero and heroine, North and South, Yankee and Tory, common man and aristocrat. The film might just as well have been called *The Birth of a Nation,* that title being at least as appropriate to it as to the film of almost a decade earlier. Griffith was obviously repeating himself.

The final years of Griffith's career were scarred by his disastrous fling with the sound picture. In *Abraham Lincoln* (1930), he returned to American history, but the result was stylistically inept and narratively inert. *The Struggle* (1931) was a sentimental and overstated sociological study of alcoholism. In the true Griffith manner, he depicts alcoholism as a product of the social-reforming ladies who thrust Prohibition on a beer- and wine-drinking nation, converting it to whiskey as a result. It does not seem to occur to him that people might drink because they are unhappy or because they want to or need to. The film was so unsalable that its producers changed Griffith's title to *Ten Nights in a Barroom,* presumably hoping to lure a few alcoholics off the street to see the film. The Hollywood brass was convinced that Griffith was old-fashioned, that his day was done. He spent his final seventeen years living in Los Angeles, barred from an art that he had practically fashioned by himself, his only contribution being several sequences for Hal Roach's *One Million B.C.* in 1941. Public praise for his achievements could not ease the bitterness of his rejection by the business. He died in Hollywood in 1948.

5 The Comics: Mack Sennett and the Chaplin Shorts

In the year that Griffith took his ride on the "El" up to the Edison studios in the Bronx (1907), Mack Sennett took the same ride for the same purpose. Like Griffith, Sennett then wandered from Edison to Biograph to take up a longer residence there. Like Griffith, Sennett later moved from his apprenticeship at Biograph to maturity as an independent producer and director. Sennett even worked for Griffith at Biograph, as director, actor, and writer (he wrote the screenplay for Griffith's *Lonely Villa*). In his years with Griffith, Sennett absorbed many lessons on cutting and shooting and construction. Sennett would later repay his teacher by both adopting his fluid cutting methods and by parodying Griffith's plots and last-minute rescues. Unlike Griffith, however, Sennett always wanted to make comic films. For years he tried to get Biograph to let him make a comic film about cops. He finally got his chance with his own independent company, Keystone, in 1912.

Krazy Keystones

The marriage that Sennett effected between visual, physical, burlesque comedy and the silent film was one of those happy, inevitable unions. The purely visual film medium was perfectly suited to the purely visual comic gags that Sennett concocted. The popularity of Lumières' first comedy, *L'Arroseur arrosée*, foreshadowed the future of the physical gag. Although there were comic films before Sennett—particularly the comic surprises of the trick films and the energy of the chase films—no one before him so forcefully revealed the comic effects of motion, of human bodies and machines and inanimate objects hurtling across the screen and colliding. It may not be coincidence that one of the most famous essays on comedy—Henri Bergson's *Le Rire* (1900)—was contemporary with the early films. Sennett—and later Chaplin, Keaton, Lloyd, Laurel and Hardy, et cetera—would unknowingly apply the

Bergson theories. No theoretical aesthetic ever had the advantage of such concrete and convincing data. The Bergsonian principle that Sennett best demonstrated was that the source of the comic was the conversion of a human being into a machine. We laugh at the mechanical, inelastic motions of a man who fails to alter his responses to suit some change in the environment: the man who slips on a banana peel but continues walking as if no peel were under him until he inevitably falls. Further, we cannot laugh if we have any real fears for the man's safety; we must view him externally as a kind of imperishable machine rather than as a man who can suffer pain and broken bones and bruises.

This conversion of men into machines is at the center of Sennett's comic technique. The characters zip across the screen like mechanical toys, crashing and colliding into bricks, pies, walls, furniture, and one another. Sennett furthers the impression of human machines with his undercranked camera. He discovered that by recording the action at only eight to twelve frames per second and then projecting it at sixteen or twenty, the action became so speeded up that the effect became even more mechanical, more frantic, and hence, more comical. There is never a sense of the Sennett characters as people; reflection and feeling are human activities they never experience. The characters have no real human personalities; their individuation is strictly by physical type—fat, thin, short, tall, dark, fair, and so forth. They are purely externalized creatures, not differing at all, really, from the inanimate objects and moving machines with which they collide. In one of the Sennett films, *The Clever Dummy* (1917), Ben Turpin actually plays a robot—the perfect metaphor for all Sennett's people. The use of people as objects rather than as feeling, thinking beings, makes them perfectly suited to run into trouble with the other objects and machines in their universe. Whatever terrific collisions they suffer, we know that the injury will be no more serious than a dent in an automobile fender. Although many Sennett characters brandish guns that shoot bullets, the audience knows that a bullet is no more lethal than a kick in the pants or a pie in the face. Their automobiles smash into each other at fifty miles an hour, their boats sink, their roller-coaster cars fly off the tracks, they fall down wells, they fall off roofs. Disasters resulting in death in the real world produce only a few dazed moments in the Sennett world. Machines do not feel pain; machines do not die. We can laugh at the Sennett characters because we know they are machines and not people.

Like Griffith, Sennett depended heavily on improvisation. A rough plot outline was the basis for staff meetings each week when Sennett, his cast, and crew would get together to see what wild and zany bits they could inject into the story line. Sennett liked to have an imaginative outside observer, whom he called his "wild card" or "joker," sit in on the staff meetings to toss out the wildest, most farfetched and irrelevant gags he could think up. After a series of gags had been hammered together in the meeting, there was further improvisation and gagging in the course of the shooting. Sennett adhered to only one principle of construction: a gag had to begin, develop, and finish itself off within a hundred seconds. Because Sennett cared so little about whole plots—the individual gag was the beginning and end of his cinematic technique—the films are loosely structured, holding together only by the pace of the movement within them. The stories seldom go anywhere; they end when the series of gags has been played out and the reel of film has been shot. One of the most common Sennett endings is for the clashing characters to end up dazed and exhausted or doused in a pool of water, the ocean, or a well—for example, *Tillie's Punctured Romance, The Surf Girl,* and *The Masquerader.* When the characters are all wet, the action stops.

Sennett films usually conform to one of three structural patterns. In one of the most common, Sennett takes some conventional, almost melodramatic plot—the kind that Griffith used—and then peppers it with gags wherever he can. The plot merely serves as a kind of string to hold the gags together. This kind of structure is a clear sign of the loose script outline that gets gagged up at staff meetings. The plot becomes totally formulaic and passes by unnoticed; only the frenzied movement of the mechanical men and women attracts the eye. The second kind of Sennett structure is even less plotty. This structure could best be described as "riffing"—taking some place or situation and then running through all the gags that might occur there. The third Sennett structure is more whole than the first two. Sennett had a great taste for parodying both the styles and the themes of other famous directors and pictures. In the parody pictures, Sennett not only used individual gags but shaped the whole film in accordance with the model he was burlesquing.

Sennett's first feature film, *Tillie's Punctured Romance* (1914), is a good example of the formula plot that merely serves as a string to tie the gags together. The plot is a completely conventional story of a farm girl who falls prey to the false advances of a city slicker; he wants her only for her money. She leaves the farm for the evil city, inherits money from an uncle who is presumed dead, gets mixed up with rich city folk, has troubles with her fiancé who has another girlfriend, and finally discovers his duplicity. (The film sounds as if it could have been made by Griffith.) But Sennett discards the plot entirely and spends his time sticking in whatever gags he can, gags that are fundamentally irrelevant to the plot.

Tillie, the farm girl, is played by the enormous Marie Dressler; her city-slicker boyfriend is the small and skinny Chaplin (before he adopted the tramp character exclusively). Sennett plays with the disproportion in their sizes, showing Tillie besting her beau in all sorts of contests in which Charlie winds up with a brick or a stone or a boot hitting him in the head or seat of the pants. The "other woman" in the film is played by Mabel Normand, a coy and subtle comedienne who indulges in her own comic shenanigans as a fake waitress at Tillie's grand ball. Sennett includes a hilariously comic dance number with the tiny Charlie and the immense Tillie, he adds a hilarious drunken "elephant" sequence when Tillie overindulges in a café, he draws on the incompetent Keystone cops for the final chase, and he throws all the main characters off the Santa Monica pier and into the Pacific Ocean to end the film. Tillie's enormous bulk is eventually hoisted from the waves by a mechanical winch that predictably slips and throws her back in again several times before fishing her out. The plot of the film is almost nonexistent; the best things in the film are the gratuitous gags, the surprises that Sennett throws in. That which is gratuitous ultimately becomes that which is essential.

Mabel's Dramatic Career (1913) has the same kind of structure. Mabel (Normand), a country gal, and Mack (Sennett), her country swain, are deeply in love. (Sennett acted in his films, too, usually portraying the oafish, sluggish country boy.) Mack's mother objects to the match. The story is further complicated by another woman who arrives from the city and steals Mack's heart away from Mabel. Mack gets his ring back from Mabel, and Mabel slinks sadly off toward the big city. Some unspecified time later, Mack journeys to the city and sees a nickelodeon displaying Mabel's picture. (Many of the early film comedies were about the film business itself.) Mack goes into the theatre to see the show; he sees

Mabel attacked by the villain (Ford Sterling) in a typical film melodrama. Mack, who does not realize he is watching a fiction, fails to keep his aesthetic distance. He pulls out his six-shooter and starts firing at the screen, scaring the shocked customers out of the theatre. Mack also runs out and catches a glimpse of the screen villain at home; naturally, off-screen Ford is a kindly father and husband. But Mack starts shooting again. Someone douses him with a pail of water and the film just stops once the menace has been soaked. The plot of the film is merely a convenience to get Mack to the movie theatre; the film is built around the single gag that Mack cannot separate screen life and real life. The early rural romance is merely expository; it pads the film out so that it fills up a reel; it gives Sennett the chance for a few boy-girl gags.

The Sennett "riffing" films are even more fun; the director does not pay even lip service to any kind of narrative line. These films are structured as a pure series of gags, held together only by pace and by the general locale or situation. Several of the films Chaplin made for Sennett use the "riffing" structure. In *The Masquerader* (1914), Sennett and Chaplin pull as many gags as they can on the premise that a disruptive actor on a movie set can wreak havoc in a studio. Chaplin is the actor; Charlie Murray is the director who boots him out; Charlie sneaks back in as a seductive woman; chaos follows until Charlie winds up soaked in a well and the "riffing" stops. *The Rounders* (1914) "riffs" on the troubles that two drunks (Charlie and Fatty Arbuckle, two obviously contrasting physical types) can get into, and on the reactions of their two shrewish wives. *Getting Acquainted* (1914) "riffs" on the theme of flirtation and mashing in the park.

The Surf Girl (1916) is one of the zaniest of the "riffing" pictures. Wild gag relentlessly follows wild gag for two reels.

The film takes the beach as its starting point and then runs off every gag it can imagine in a beach setting. Sennett uses the ocean, a swimming pool, a roller coaster, a ferris wheel, a beach-front saloon, dressing rooms for changing into bathing suits, showers, beach cabañas, an amusement park, an aviary, motor boats, et cetera. The strong man with the hammer not only rings the gong but sends a fellow surfer flying up the gauge and off into the sea. The swimming pool is a crowded casserole of frantic aquatics—Sennett's undercranked camera makes the pool activities a kind of water ballet turned St. Vitus' dance. An immensely fat man rolls down a slide and into the pool. Everyone in the pool (Sennett uses reverse motion of the camera brilliantly) is vomited out of the water by the impact of the fat man's splash. The two lifeguards, courting a young lady, discover that an ostrich has swallowed her locket. They chase and ride the awkward bird until he finally disgorges the chain. Another lifeguard, swinging on the rings over the pool, loses his pants; the lady who has been pushing him unintentionally flies off with the pants into the pool. An old man suspected of lechery takes shelter in the ball-throwing booth, pretending to be one of the moving mannikins the customers try to hit. Sure enough the customers try to hit him.

This wild mêlée of gags and movement ends with a great anticlimactic joke. The cops hustle all the soaked, brawling surfers into the paddy wagon. As the wagon pulls into the station, the top part strikes the roof of the entrance and separates from the chassis. (Those imcompetent cops can't even build the right-sized garage.) The surfer-felons slowly walk away from the cops, using the top part of the paddy wagon as a shell and cover for their retreat. As the dozen or so legs walk off, looking like a huge beetle, the film comes to a halt. A sure sign of the film's "riffing" premise is that

The Surf Girl: *fun in the pool; the police wagon as beetle*

despite its title no single surf girl plays a role in the picture.

The Sennett parody films are less zany but more whole. Parodying the latest movie hit was a staple of the comic shorts, just as parodying the film hits of the past became a staple of comedy in the 1970s. Chaplin parodied *Carmen* in 1915, the same year that two serious versions of the story were released; there were parodies of stage and filmed melodrama: for example, Vitagraph's delightful *Goodness Gracious;* both Sennett and Hal Roach parodied hits like *The Iron Horse* (*The Iron Nag*) and *The Covered Wagon* (*The Uncovered Wagon, Two Wagons Both Covered*). Some of Sennett's best parodies

were of Griffith, not only of his melodramatic stories but also of his famous last-minute rescues. An early Griffith parody, *Barney Oldfield's Race for a Life* (1913), features a villain (played by Ford Sterling) who ties the young damsel (Mabel Normand) to the railroad tracks and then steals a train (perhaps a parodic glimpse at films like *The Great Train Robbery*) for the express purpose of running over her. Her boyfriend, played by Sennett, is flying to the rescue in an automobile. The cops, also alerted to the danger, furiously pump to the rescue on a handcar. Sennett, in the best Griffith tradition, cuts between four locales: Mabel on the tracks, anxious; Ford in the train, looking forward gleefully to squashing Mabel; Mack and Barney in the auto; the cops on the handcar. Sennett pokes fun at Griffith by drawing out this rescue to an impossible length; the train, which we know is not very far from Mabel's bound body, takes forever to get to it, just long enough for Mack and the cops to get there in time. The film's ending is also intentionally silly. Ford shoots all the cops—who obviously do not die—and then, for some reason, decides to shoot himself. Having no bullets left, he chokes himself, does a pirouette, twirls, and falls, apparently dead of dizziness.

Teddy at the Throttle (1916) is a later, longer, and funnier parody of the same kind. The film not only parodies the Griffith cross-cut but also the Griffith plotting. The story is a triangle. The young man (Bobby Vernon) drops his true girlfriend for the rich society gal; the young man is being manipulated by the villain (Wallace Beery), who thinks he will make money from the society match. The society gal (large) drags the young man (small) out into an unbelievably intense storm—with winds that blow the clothes off the guests at a fancy ball when the door opens, with oceans of rain driving down, with pools of mud several feet deep. She is insistent on getting married pronto. The true girl (Gloria Swanson), who has discovered the deception, pursues them into the storm. The next morning, after a hilarious sequence of rolling around in the water and mud, the villain ties the true girl to the railroad tracks. Her dog, Teddy, carries a message explaining her terrible plight, which she has miraculously managed to write, to her boyfriend. Then comes the Griffith cutting. From Gloria tied to the tracks, to the train chugging toward her, to the agent of her rescue (the dog), who finds the boyfriend and leads him back to

Barney Oldfield's Race for a Life: *Ford Sterling ties Mabel Normand to the tracks in an exaggerated parody of melodramatic gesture and acting*

Mack Sennett himself displays the exaggerated, burlesque acting style of his films with Mabel Normand (Barney Oldfield's Race for a Life)

Gloria. Gloria is, of course, saved just in time, and Teddy continues his canine heroism by treeing the nasty villain.

The Sennett films set a comic standard for zaniness, *non sequitur,* and physical activity that has served as a model ever since—for René Clair, for Richard Lester, for Louis Malle, for Mel Brooks. Not as technical a cinematic innovator as Griffith, Sennett still realized that the tricks the camera could play with motion were highly suited to physical comedy. In a sense, Sennett's method took Méliès's stop-action principle one step further by combining rapid physical activity with the camera's tricks. Sennett also realized that in a world as physically active as his, the camera and editor should do a lot less work than in Griffith's films so as not to detract from the purely physical fun.

Sennett had no need for the close-up, which personalizes and individualizes, which conveys human emotions. The standard Sennett setups are the far shot and long shot, revealing the figures only as types, not as individual people. Whereas Griffith developed his screen "grammar and rhetoric" to transmit human emotion and personality, Sennett purposely needed no such method since his comedy negated both.

In 1916 Sennett scrapped his independent Keystone Company to begin producing comedies for the giants like First National, Paramount, and Pathé. By 1920 Sennett had become a producer and no longer directed films personally. His films had become more expensive and polished, losing much of the improvisatory, slap-dash, slap-happy quality of the Keystones that starred Chaplin, Normand, Sterling, Arbuckle, Chester Conklin, and Mack Swain. But Sennett's parody still created hilarious 1920s films that starred the cross-eyed antiheroic Ben Turpin, the antithesis of movie glamor and romance. Sennett's devotion to frantic movement, irrational surprises, and impossible nonsense created films that starred Billy Bevan, supported by incredibly agile machines like leaping tin lizzies and flipping airplanes, or by menacingly awesome beasts like wild lions and even a viciously snapping oyster. Although Sennett produced sound shorts, his importance died with the silent film, which was his natural medium. The particular qualities of the Sennett style become most obvious when compared with the completely different method and emphasis of his most distinguished disciple.

Charlie

In 1913 Charles Chaplin was touring the American vaudeville stages with an English music-hall act, Fred Karno's English Pantomime Troupe. Either Adam Kessel, the bookmaker-turned-owner of the independent Bison Company, or Sennett himself saw Chaplin's performance as a comic drunk in *A Night in a London Club,* one of the Karno features. They offered Chaplin a job with Sennett's comic branch of Bison, Keystone, thinking Chaplin's comic gymnastic talents perfectly suited to Sennett's style. Chaplin wasn't sure he wanted the job; he shared the prejudice of many stage performers against working for the films. He also was wary of the impermanence and novelty of the movie business. After Chaplin drove Kessel's offer up from $75 to $150 a week, including a one-year guarantee, he decided the risk was worth it. Chaplin joined Keystone late in 1913.

Sennett immediately tried to use Chaplin as one more cog in his factory of human puppets. Sennett capitalized on Chaplin's gymnastic abilities: his ability to fall and stagger and roll and bounce off both people and the floor. Chaplin's smallness was the perfect foil for the fatness of Arbuckle or the hugeness of Dressler. Sennett used Chaplin as mechanical toy. In *The Knockout* (1914), Chaplin makes a brief appearance as referee in a boxing match, ducking, sliding, squirming, and falling between the punching pugilists and the ropes. This was Chaplin as pure physical comic. Sennett used the same gymnastic potential in *The Rounders,* in which Chaplin recreates his drunk act from Karno's troupe.

But tension soon developed between Chaplin and Sennett. Sennett's rapid, pure-motion principle bothered Chaplin, who wanted to add character and individuality to his gymnastics. Chaplin began to evolve the tramp character at Keystone, borrowing the idea of using a cane and hat from the earlier French film comic, Max Linder, borrowing an old pair of Ford Sterling's shoes (much too big for Charlie's feet) and an old pair of Fatty Arbuckle's pants (obviously too big for Charlie). Such individuation was both unwanted and unneeded in Sennett's mechanical world. Sennett neither took the time nor placed the camera close enough to make such characterization count. After one year with Sennett, the gymnastic comic with the hat, cane, and shoes had become so familiar in the nickelodeons that he could negotiate a contract to make his own pictures. In 1915 he left Sennett's Keystone Company for Essanay, which agreed to pay him $1,250 a week and give him the freedom to write and direct his own pictures.

Temperamentally, Chaplin never could see comedy as Sennett saw it. For Sennett, the comic world was a world of silly surfaces; for Chaplin the comic world was a way of getting at the serious world of

Chaplin's first two appearances on film—in Making a Living *(without his tramp's costume but with a characteristically dancing cane) and in* Kid Auto Races at Venice

men and society. For Sennett, comedy was an end; for Chaplin, it was a means. Chaplin's own experience played a tremendous role in shaping his outlook. With his father and mother separated and his mother battling ill health and insanity, Chaplin spent almost two years of his young life in a workhouse for the poor. The boy in the workhouse quickly perceived the power of wealth and social status. The young Chaplin was an outsider, beyond the embrace of social and material comforts. The screen character he created, Charlie (the French call him Charlot), is also an outsider. He is a tramp, a criminal, an immigrant, a worker—someone excluded from the beautiful life. And yet Charlie yearns desperately for that life: he longs for money, for love, for legitimacy, for social station, for etiquette, for superiority, for recognition. Ironically, Charlie as outsider serves to show both the gleaming attractiveness of the beautiful life for those who don't have it and the false emptiness of the beautiful life for those who do. Chaplin was mature enough an artist to show the ambivalence of power and wealth, its attractiveness and its emptiness, an ambivalence that Chaplin the man felt when he became rich and powerful.

The Chaplin comic aesthetic was radically different from Sennett's. The cliché is that Chaplin slowed down Sennett's dizzy pace. He did slow it down; but he did so to put something else in. The structures of the films reveal a key shift. If Sennett's films are merely strings of gags, Chaplin's films are structured as three or four beads on a string. Like Sennett's, Chaplin's film structures break into clear and distinct pieces. But where Sennett's pieces are thirty to ninety seconds long, Chaplin's are five to ten minutes long. He exhausts a situation completely rather than flipping from gag to gag. His Essanay film, *The Tramp* (1915), breaks into four sections: Charlie the tramp protecting the pretty girl from other, meaner tramps; Charlie as farmhand on the girl's farm; Charlie foiling the other tramps' plot to rob the farm; Charlie losing the girl when her wealthy boyfriend arrives. A later film he made for Mutual, *The Adventurer* (1917), also breaks into four sections: Charlie's escape from the police; Charlie rescuing the drowning rich man; Charlie attempting to join the *haut monde* at the rich man's swank party; Charlie's second escape from the police when the rich man betrays him, coupled with his expulsion from the house by the pretty rich girl. This shift in film structure from the gag to the scene demands that each of the sequences be more detailed, fuller; each requires attention to either the situation or the character—rather than the gags alone—to sustain it.

The Chaplin structure not only allows for the examination of character but demands it. The long sequences make a mere string of gags impossible; the gags revolve around the location, the objects, and especially the people in the sequence. The gags actually define the characters. When Charlie twirls his cane at a fancy party (in *The Count*, 1916), and then accidentally stabs the turkey, which he inadvertently swings above his head, he makes us laugh and he also defines his sociable attempts to be suave and his frustrating lack of success at it. Charlie's sly and jaunty crap shooting and card shuffling when surrounded by big, mean opponents (*The Immigrant*, 1917) show he has guts as well as style. Despite the size of his opponents and the social obstacles, Charlie always insists on enjoying the last laugh or the last kick in the pants. His attempts to enjoy the last boot are not only ingenious and funny; they also define Charlie's pluck. Though Charlie is comically incompetent at mastering the social graces of the *haut monde,* he consistently makes up for his lack of etiquette with his wiry toughness and his pragmatic cleverness. Though he eats *pêches melba* very badly (*The Adventurer*), he is very adept at dodging the police. Chaplin's gags alone define Charlie's ironic synthesis of naïve innocence and pragmatic pluck.

Another dimension of the Chaplin tramp is that, despite the toughness and dishonesty that help him survive, he has a kind and generous heart. He never mistreats those who genuinely deserve his sympathy. He demonstrates this trait repeatedly by using a Griffith-like woman who evokes Charlie's milder qualities. The Chaplin woman is invariably blonde, pure, and kind, instantly perceiving the redeeming characteristics in the unworldly tramp. For years Chaplin used the same actress, Edna Purviance, to portray her. For Chaplin, the woman was not just a sentimental character—although she certainly was that; she was also a metaphor for natural human beauty uncorrupted by social definitions and unburied by material possessions. In film after film Charlie shows his affinity with the naturally good and beautiful spirit by allying with her against those who can do him more material good. In *The Tramp* and *Police* (1915), he refuses to ally with fellow robbers and protects Edna instead. In *The Tramp* and *The Immigrant,* he retrieves Edna's stolen money and, without letting her know it, slips it back into her pocket. And yet Chaplin's sense of character and reality is such that after stuffing a whole wad of bills in Edna's pocket, he thinks better of it and takes a few back for himself.

Chaplin's handling of character also comments on the values of the society that produces such people. The villain in the short Chaplin films is invariably Eric Campbell, a huge brute of a man whose superblack, upturned eyebrows look as though they alone contained enough poison to kill a man Charlie's size. Like Sennett, Chaplin uses physical types for comic effect. Unlike Sennett, the physical type also implies moral, social, and psychological values. Eric Campbell, the heavy, is invariably a member of the film's social in-group; he naturally hates Charlie because Charlie is not a member of that group. Eric is the physical giant in *Easy Street* (1917), a very uneasy street that values physical toughness alone; Charlie is the contrasting runt. Eric is the waiter in *The Immigrant* who enjoys pommeling those patrons who are only ten cents short of paying the bill; Charlie is the diner without any money. Eric is the lecherous rich man in *The Rink* (1916); Charlie is the poor waiter (but good skater!). Eric is the believable count in *The Count;* Charlie is merely the clumsy pretender. If the social "ins" are as brutal, as coarse, as empty, as vicious as Eric, then there is some human value in being "out," like Charlie. And how pathetic are Charlie's attempts to get "in" considering he is physically and emotionally incapable of besting Eric for more than a second or two.

Some of the differences between Sennett and Chaplin may be seen most clearly by comparing devices and motifs they both used. Both Sennett and Chaplin used cops. For Sennett, the cops were purely comic characters, whose good will was balanced by their energetic but cross-eyed incompetence. Despite their efforts and frenzy, Sennett's cops can do nothing right. Their cars crash; their boats sink; they fall all over each other as they swarm to answer a call. They are as earnest and as functional as toy soldiers. Chaplin's cops, though not precisely what would be called, in the argot of a later generation, "Pigs," were not very far from it. In *Police,* the cops spend their time leisurely journeying by motor car to answer an emergency call for help; they drink tea and fluff their uniforms and show no concern at all for Edna's distress. The cops in *The Adventurer* are not as satirical, but they do shoot rifles at the escaping Charlie, and their bullets, unlike the bullets in Sennett comedies, look as though they could kill. In one of the films Chaplin himself directed for Sennett, *Getting Acquainted* (1914), the differences between the two comic perspectives are clear; in this film, the cop patrolling the park indiscriminately

Easy Street: *The runt and the giant (Charlie and Eric Campbell)*

clubs anyone on the head who seems to be a masher.

Both Sennett and Chaplin use the chase, but Sennett emphasizes more of the pure motion and frenzy of it whereas Chaplin emphasizes the cleverness and skill of Charlie at avoiding capture. The chase scene at the beginning of *The Adventurer,* the chase up and down the escalator in *The Floorwalker* (1916), the chase on roller skates in *The Rink*—all show Charlie's adeptness at escaping his Establishment pursuers. Chaplin's chases seem more like choreographed ballets whereas Sennett's seem more like flying, colliding bowling pins after the ball has thrown them askew. Chaplin's chases are propelled by character—Charlie's cleverness at avoiding capture, his improvisational ability to dart, spin, zig, and zag—not by the delight in miscellaneous motion. Both Chaplin and Sennett use the motif of the bum who substitutes for the man of wealth and position. But in Sennett (*Comrades,* 1912), the tension is between two bums: one is enjoying the fruits of the masquerade (food, flirtations, a snooze in a real bed) and the other, lacking a costume, is not. In Chaplin's *The Count,* the tension is entirely between the bum and the problems of the situation itself, his unsuccessful attempts to manipulate the social tools that make a count a count (eating, drinking, dancing).

Most of the short Chaplin films contain obvious and pointed social commentary in the action as well as the characters. The comedies treat several controversial themes that we might think the exclusive property of our own generation: drug addiction, poverty, hunger, crime on the streets, homosexuality, religious hypocrisy. In *Police,* Charlie learns that those who want him to go straight only intend to eliminate him as a competitor. He discovers that the preacher who urges him to reform has stolen a man's watch that Charlie considered stealing but didn't because of the preacher's sermon. Charlie's instincts are far more human and unselfish than the platitudes of preachers and reformers. In *The Immigrant,* Charlie juxtaposes the Statue of Liberty with a cattle boat full of immigrants. As soon as a title announces, "The land of liberty," government officials rope all the immigrants together and start checking their identification tags. Men in uniform are inevitably damned in the Chaplin shorts, whether the uniform is a policeman's, a fireman's, a government official's, or a banker's.

East Street is perhaps the most social of the early short films. In the opening sequence, Charlie gets uplifted in the Hope Mission, singing hymns and feasting on Edna's pure face. He is so uplifted that he gives back the collection box he has stolen. Charlie goes off into the world uplifted only to discover that the world is a vicious place, full of hunger, poverty, thieves, drug addicts, bullies, and rapists; Easy Street is not so easy, a jungle world of animals striving to survive. Charlie as

Easy Street: *Charlie gets uplifted in the mission, feasting on the face of Edna Purviance*

cop (still an outcast despite the uniform) subdues all the foes of goodness. In the final sequence, the den of thieves has been miraculously transformed into the New Hope Mission; all the thugs, including the ominous Eric Campbell, have dressed in their Sunday suits and

Sunday smiles, all of them marching meekly and politely into the mission for their own uplifting.

This deliberately contrived, Pollyannaish ending is Chaplin's deliberate way of reducing social optimism to absurdity. The social evils admit of no easy solutions; in fact, they seem to admit of no solutions at all. As Brecht's *Threepenny Opera* put it ten years later with its similarly contrived happy ending, "Victoria's messenger does not come riding often." Chaplin's endings frequently imply this social dimension of false happiness and solution as in *The Vagabond* and *The Immigrant*. In *The Bank* (1915), Charlie wakes up only to discover that the happy ending literally was a dream. The other typical Chaplin ending (*The Tramp, The Adventurer*), less socially oriented but more poignant than the faked happy one, shows Charlie losing in the end, shuffling off down the road again after failing to satisfy his longings.

Though the social and moral implications of the Chaplin shorts are very striking, Chaplin never deserts the objective tool of comedy for making his points. If the endings of the films contain the social and psychological implications, the beginnings of the films are brilliant lessons in the comic way of making an entrance. In film after film Charlie shocks the audience with a daring comic surprise at the beginning from which it never recovers. One of the most brilliant is the beginning of *The Bank*. Charlie strides into the bank, goes directly to the safe, twirls the dials of the huge safe, checking his cuff to make sure that he remembers the combination, finally opens the door of the safe, steps in, and brings out his mop and pail. Not only does Charlie demonstrate the difference between capital and labor; he does it in a stunning surprise of our expectations. At the beginning of *The Immigrant,* people are lying about the boat, obviously seasick. The camera cuts to a heaving Charlie, leaning over the side of the pitching ship.

We expect he is sick like all his fellow passengers. Then he turns around, proudly displaying the fish he has just caught. In *The Tramp,* he enters walking down a dusty road; a car rushes by, spraying him with dust—another contrast of rich and poor. Charlie takes out a brush, whisks himself off, buffs his fingernails, and continues on his way. (There is Charlie's spunk as well as Chaplin's comic technique.) In *A Woman* (1915), Charlie enters by walking through a sprinkler. In *The Floorwalker,* he enters by inquiring about the price of a leg of one of the mannequins in the department store. In *The Adventurer,* he enters by digging himself out of his hiding place, a hole in the sand.

Another of Chaplin's great comic gifts was his ingenuity in using objects. As in Sennett and every other silent comedy, objects were an essential element of Chaplin's comic technique. Unlike Sennett, however, Chaplin did not use objects solely as comic weapons (Sennett's famed pies); the object could be either weapon or tool, could define the character using it, could be used in a surprising and unfamiliar way, could foul Charlie up or help him out. One of the consequences of Chaplin's structure—to exhaust a situation of some length before moving on to the next—was that one of the ways of exhausting a situation was to exhaust all the objects in it. And in exhausting an object, Chaplin frequently transformed it into a completely different thing before our very eyes, not by stopping the camera, as Méliès had, but by simply manipulating it in a surprising and unexpected way. Chaplin, like Méliès, was a kind of magician, but his was a magic without trick.

Chaplin's most famous short film with objects is *One A.M.* (1916). With the exception of a cab driver in the first sequence, Charlie is the only character in the film—except for a roomful of objects. In the film Charlie returns to one of his favorite incarnations, the drunk; the play

One A.M.: *Charlie and the tiger rug*

with objects begins in the first section when the drunken Charlie, returning from a night on the town, gets tangled with the taxi door and then with the taxi meter. Charlie can't find the key to his front door so he climbs in the window, stepping in his goldfish bowl as he does so. Inside the house he finds the key in his vest pocket. Back out the window he goes (foot in goldfish bowl again) so that he can enter properly through the door.

In the film's second section—Charlie in the living room—Chaplin uses every piece of inanimate matter with which he has decorated the set. He feels he is being attacked by the tiger rug on the floor. He tries to walk on a circular table toward a bottle of booze and seltzer; the table spins giddily and Charlie walks a treadmill, unable to reach the booze as he spins faster and faster. He tries to walk up the stairs only to discover himself at the bottom again. Second and third tries to ascend end with him rolled up in the rug covering the stairs. He finally succeeds in

getting upstairs by climbing a coatrack. Upstairs he unsuccessfully tries to dodge the huge pendulum of the clock that swings back and forth in front of his bedroom door.

Then, in the film's third section— Charlie and the bed—the game with objects culminates in a five-minute duel between the drunken tramp and a Murphy bed, which seems to operate according to its own laws. The bed flips down, flips up, reverses itself, loses its frame, bounces, rises, falls as it pleases. Charlie finally beds down in the bathtub. With the bed, Chaplin has succeeded in literally bringing an inanimate object to life. Though he excludes living people to play against in *One A.M.,* Chaplin has not excluded living opponents. These "living" opponents draw their breath of life from the powers of cinema alone. Yet another sign of Chaplin's shrewdness is his refusal to cut or edit in the final bed sequence. The whole episode, except for one cutaway, is a single long take. If we are to

The Pawnshop: *the clock as patient and as jewel (Charlie and Albert Austin)*

believe in the bed's vitality, we must not feel that the director has tricked the bed effects with camera and editing scissors. The lack of cutting rivets our attention on the two combatants. All consciousness of the cinematic medium disappears.

The Pawnshop (1916) is another short masterwork of comic objects. Charlie and a rival worker (he cannot even get along with members of his own class) sling baking dough at each other in the kitchen. When the boss walks in, Charlie nonchalantly starts kneading the dough and then suavely runs it through the wringer of the washing machine. He later tries to dry the dishes by running cups and saucers through the same wringer. When he tries to eat one of Edna's doughnuts it seems a bit heavy to him. He instantly transforms the doughnut into a dumbbell by doing weight-lifting exercises with it and then blithely caps his routine by tossing it in the air to catch on his plate. The dumbbell-doughnut smashes the plate to bits and crashes through to the floor.

Among *The Pawnshop*'s other objects are an immense ladder that Charlie uses as a seesaw, a birdcage that Charlie uses as a hatrack, a piece of string that Charlie transforms into a tightrope, and a fishbowl that Charlie mistakes for a chamber pot. But the film's culminating transformation of an object is Charlie's dismembering a clock that a needy customer has brought in to pawn. Probing the value of the clock, Charlie's deft part-by-part dissection combines the methods of the jeweler (do its parts seem real or fake?), the surgeon (is it sound? are its reflexes good?), and the shopper (do the contents smell fresh?). After the innards of the clock lie in front of him, Charlie winds its shell and its parts begin to dance (in typical Chaplin style, he does not use Méliès's stop-action tricks but a magnet to propel the pieces without camera trickery). Then Charlie adopts the method of the gardener, spraying the jittering "bugs" with oil to exterminate them. Finally, Charlie scrapes the clock's mauled contents into the customer's hat and hands the rubble back to him with a shake of the head: sorry; it won't do.

The most striking and most popular element of the early Chaplin shorts is their pure comic inventiveness. The creation of the tramp character and the objective, concrete depiction of social realities are themselves functions of the comedy. Like Griffith, Chaplin made longer and more famous films after his apprenticeship period. Also like Griffith, Chaplin's later work revealed the increasing self-consciousness and seriousness of the artist. Unlike Griffith, however, Chaplin's expanding self-consciousness demonstrated the richness and complexity of the artist's vision—his thorough understanding of both the character he had created and the world in which that character (and all humans) function. Whereas Griffith's simplistic system pitted idealized goodness against idealized evil, Chaplin's system showed the inherent contradictions within the definitions of good and evil themselves. The comic tramp was himself a walking contradiction, a figure who loathed (and feared) the falsity of the established order and who yearned toward the purity of the ideal but also envied the comforts and rewards of the established society and realized that he had better administer a kick unto others before they kicked unto him. This tension between naïveté and instinctive, tough pragmatism in the Charlie tramp produces the moral ambivalence of the mature Chaplin films: the contrast between societal definitions of paternity and more human ones in *The Kid* (1921), the contrast between societal definitions of morality and more human ones in *The Pilgrim* (1922), the ambivalent contrasts between rich and poor in *City Lights* (1931) and between civilization and nature in *Modern Times* (1936). In his first four years, Chaplin created and developed the character whom he would use to travel across the cultural landscape of American society itself, exploring its inadequacies, inconsistencies, and insufficiencies.

Most unlike Griffith, Chaplin's contribution to the cinema has much more to do with what he does on film than with what he does with film. Whereas Griffith is most important for combining the devices of cinema into a coherent narrative medium, Chaplin is most important for making all consciousness of the cinematic medium disappear so completely that we concentrate solely on the photographic subject rather than the process. This does not mean (as many have claimed) that Chaplin was "uncinematic," that he was ignorant of the means of manipulating the cinematic language. Quite the opposite. One indeed manipulates a language skilfully when all consciousness of manipulation disappears and the language serves solely to communicate the subject matter with complete lucidity. This lucidity allows us to view the hypnotic magic of the Chaplin performance far more intimately and closely than we could if he were on the stage. And Chaplin's insistence on unobtrusive, middle-distance composition and "invisible," restrained editing sustains the spell by producing this hypnotic magic without sleight-of-hand.

Chaplin's early films not only demonstrated the magic of a human performance on film but the magical appeal of the performer on the minds of the public. His millions of new fans rushed to the novelty shops that sold mechanical tramp dolls and plaster tramp statues in his image, much as more recent generations of kiddies have bought Mouseketeer and Beatle and *Star Wars* paraphernalia. In his first five years in the business, 1913–18, Chaplin worked for four different companies; each new job brought him more money, more artistic freedom, and more cultural power. From $150 a week as a Sennett pawn, he progressed to $75,000 for a year with Essanay in 1915–16, to $670,000 for a year with Mutual in 1916–17, to $1,000,000 beginning in 1918 with First National Pictures, a firm which only distributed and exhibited films. This last move left Chaplin as a totally independent producer and owner of his own film studio. With First National the later phases of his career began—with the silent and sound feature film. Although these longer works were more complex and mature contributions to film art, Chaplin never had more cultural impact on the history of film than in his first four years.

6 Movie Czars and Movie Stars

Griffith, Sennett, and Chaplin were the three major artists of the moving picture's second decade, 1905-15. Significantly, all three made their films in America. All three were both the causes and the effects of the rise of the American film in this second decade. After trailing the industries of England and France in the first decade of commercial filmmaking, the American film asserted its dominance in the years just preceding World War I and, with the help of that war, established a commercial supremacy that has never been challenged. The secret of the American rise was both art and industry. The increasing demand of American audiences to see moving pictures, the increasing admissions at the nickelodeon theatres, led, in turn, to greater demands on production and more opportunities to experiment and invent methods that were better than the competition's. The art of a Griffith was partially the result of the audience's demand that the Biograph studio turn out two, three, or more reels a week. The necessity of just making films allowed Griffith's imagination to discover ways of making them better. His discoveries, in turn, produced greater popularity and esteem for the movies, and hence further demands for more films and for better films. The successes of Chaplin and Sennett worked in the same circular way.

World War I came at an opportune time for the American film business. In 1914, just at the time when the European film imagination was beginning to atrophy and the American to swell, the war came along to kill off the European industry. The same chemicals that produced raw film stock were also the essential ingredients of gunpowder. The European governments, given the choice of guns or movies, made the obvious decision. American films, suddenly without any competitors, ruled the screens of America and Europe during the war and just after it, a dominance they have never relinquished despite the efforts of foreign governments to limit their profits and exhibition abroad. When the film industries of France, Germany, Russia, and Scandinavia finally recovered, their roles in world film production were as fertile, imaginative innovators rather than as equal competitors with the dollar doings of Hollywood.

Wealth began pouring into the American film business with the appearance of the nickelodeons in 1905, converting that business into a powerful industry and pushing it to untangle the legal and commercial chaos of its infancy. In 1910, the war against the Trust was raging as the impish Independents valiantly kept fighting and producing pictures. Ten years later all but one of the original Trust companies had folded, and the leaders of the opposition had themselves become more tyrannical and more powerful than their earlier Establishment adversaries. Carl Laemmle, William Fox, Adolph Zukor, Jesse Lasky, Marcus Loew, Samuel Goldfish, Lewis J. Selznick, Louis B. Mayer were all lucky enough to be in the right place at the right time. They were fortunate to be running a studio or buying up theatres at the moment when everyone in America started going to the movies and when everyone abroad went to American movies because there were few others. These men, who became the first movie moguls, had outlasted their Trust competitors simply because they rode the crest of the new wave of film merchandising rather than trying to dam it.

The Trust studios and distributors were unalterably opposed to the feature film. Their business was to market one-hour programs of short films; the new feature film, usually lasting two hours, demanded more personnel and more money than they were ready to invest. For a studio to produce fifty-two feature films a year (the equivalent of one film program per week) would require a huge permanent staff of actors, writers, directors, and technicians, a major investment in equipment, a complex administrative office for scheduling the shooting and selling the films, and so on. Zukor, Goldfish, Laemmle, Fox, and a few others made the investment; the Trust companies did not, certain that the new feature craze was just a passing fancy. The fancy never passed; the Trust companies did.

Although the Trust officially lost the battle in the courts in 1915, it had already lost the war to such opponents as *Queen Elizabeth, Quo Vadis?, Cabiria, The Last Days of Pompeii,* and *The Birth of a Nation.* The public wanted to see feature films.

Stars over Hollywood

The years between 1910 and 1920 determined the direction the American film industry would take. By 1915 the film program consisted of a single feature film supplemented by a short or two, the same practice that survives today (with or without the short). A second current practice was born at the same time—the star system. In the healthy days of the Trust no actor ever received screen credit. Performers were either known by the names of the characters they played—"Little Mary"—or by the studio—the Biograph Girl. There even seems to have been some doubt in the minds of the earliest patrons about whether they were watching a dramatization or real life. The confusion in the mind of the country boy about fiction or reality in *Mabel's Dramatic Career* may have been quite common a few years earlier.

The Trust opposed giving screen credit for the same short-sighted commercial reasons that it opposed the feature film. The Trust reasoned that star actors would cost more than anonymous faces on a screen. Their reasoning was quite correct. But the Independents reasoned that although a star would cost more, a film with a star would earn more. As with the feature film, the Independents had the stronger argument: to make more it was necessary to spend more. The Independents launched their career by stealing the Biograph Girl in 1910 and featuring her in Imp pictures under her real name—Florence Lawrence. They did the same with "Little Mary" Pickford, King Baggott, Arthur Johnson, and many other formerly anonymous players. The power of the star system was such that in 1917—only a few years after its inception—two stars, Chaplin and Mary Pickford, were vying with producers and with each other to become the highest paid performers in the business, both of them signing contracts for over $1,000,000. And every major producer in the industry was trying to sign them and pay them that million.

The movie star, no longer an anonymous character in a film but a human being in his or her own right, instantly seized the imagination of the American public. In 1912, just after audiences started learning their favorites' names, America's first motion picture fan magazine, *Photoplay,* appeared. It and subsequent fan magazines featured pictures, stories, and interviews that made the figure on the screen an even more intimate and personal being for each member of the audience. Producing companies needed publicity departments to sell the stars as well as the pictures to the public. In the middle of the second decade of the century, the exotic and erotic activities of the stars first became items of household gossip. One of the earliest and most impressive of the grand publicity jobs was the packaging of the "lusty, seductive siren," Theda Bara, who made her debut in *A Fool There Was* (1914). Born in Cincinnati as Theodosia Goodman, she was transformed by publicists into an Arabian beauty clad in black who survived less on oxygen and victuals than by wrecking homes and devouring men. She was a mystic semisorceress; her name, they pointed out, bore an anagrammatical relationship to Death (Theda) and Arab (Bara); the blood of the Ptolemies flowed in her veins; and her astrological signs matched Cleopatra's. The character she played—a sexual vampire—was abbreviated to vamp, adding a new noun and verb to the

English language. More significant than all the drivel of the Bara legend was the fact that the public loved the drivel and swallowed it, obviously because it wanted to. Movie publicists had discovered the ease of selling something the public wanted to buy.

The greatest stars of the silent films created their own images and types; the lesser stars merely filled the patterns that the great stars had already sketched. There were imitations of Mary Pickford's spunky, good-hearted, pranksterish little girl with the golden curls. There were sultry sirens in the Theda Bara image, many of them imported from Europe. There were gentle, soulful juveniles— Richard Barthelmess, Charles Ray. There were exotic Latin leading men—Rudolph Valentino, Ramon Novarro. Perhaps even Douglas Fairbanks's conversion from zippy American go-getter to swarthy swashbuckler in the twenties was the result of the influence of this new sexual type. There were lecherous, jaded roués, often from decadent foreign shores—Erich von Stroheim, Owen Moore, Adolphe Menjou. There were stars from the opera, the stage, and even the swimming pool—Geraldine Farrar, Mary Garden, Alla Nazimova, Annette Kellerman. There was the basically pure woman who was inevitably tainted by experience (Lillian Gish); there was the stubborn, sophisticated, and often tragic lady (Gloria Swanson); there was the strong, competent, virile male (Thomas Meighan); there was the serious, tough cowboy with the sad eyes (William S. Hart); there was the fat (John Bunny, Fatty Arbuckle), and the little (Chaplin, Harold Lloyd, Buster Keaton), and so forth. The star and not the play became the thing that caught the consciousness of the public. Hollywood also used the star to catch the public's wallet.

The third major development of the American film's second decade was the move west. As early as 1907, production companies—perhaps evading the law

A gallery of stars. "Little Mary" Pickford in The
Love Light (note how the huge sets and furniture
make her seem truly little), the demure Lillian Gish
with the slickly brilliantined Rod LaRocque, a sultry
Joan Crawford, and a cool Gloria Swanson

or the Patent Company wrecking crews—discovered the felicities of southern California. During the Trust War, the independent companies also took advantage of California's distance from the Trust headquarters in New York and its closeness to the Mexican border, where the company could quickly flee with its negatives and machines. But gradually the more legitimate virtues of California struck the filmmakers. The vast, open plains, the dependability of the sun, the nearby mountains and deserts and ocean, all attracted the eyes of men whose art depended on the power of the visual. D. W. Griffith brought his company west in the winters of 1910 and 1911 and 1912. *The Birth of a Nation* and *Intolerance* were both filmed in California. By 1915 most of the film companies had permanently settled down to business in the Los Angeles suburbs—the most famous of them known as Hollywood. Real estate speculators, who suddenly discovered that miles of apparently useless land were of great use to the movie men, sold it to them by the tens of thousands of acres, and at absurdly reasonable prices. Vast studios, like Thomas Ince's Inceville (which became MGM) and Carl Laemmle's Universal City, with rows of shooting studios, office buildings, storage buildings, back lots (for the outdoor sets), and even vast ranches completely stocked with cattle and horses and other beasts of the field, sprang up near Los Angeles. The founding of the movie capital was the result of three coincidental accidents: weather, topography, and real estate values. Enjoying the harvests of chance, the accidental emperors of the new film world now ruled vast, tangible empires.

The Emperors and Their Rule

The most significant accident in the history of the American film is that this first generation of influential movie producers, those gentlemen who made the concrete decisions about the artistic and moral values worthy of inclusion in films, were themselves deficient in formal education and aesthetic judgment. The first Hollywood producers were not just businessmen; they were a very specific breed of businessmen. Most of them were either Jewish immigrants from Germany or Russia or Poland, or the sons of Jewish immigrants. Most of them came to the movies by accident. They sold herring or furs or gloves or second-hand clothes. They jumped from these businesses into running amusement parks and penny arcades just at the time when Edison's Kinetoscope and the Mutoscope were bringing new life to the novelty business. When movies left the peep-show box for the screen, these arcade owners converted their stores into nickelodeons. They built more and more of these theatres, which became more and more plush. Soon they began producing films for their theatres, what with the pressures of the Trust and its licensing fees. Such was the series of small steps by which a Goldwyn (né Goldfish) or Zukor or Mayer climbed out of the Jewish ghetto and into a multimillion-dollar throne of power over national artistic tastes. It is doubtful that a first generation of producer-aesthetes would have made better movies (look at the likes of *Queen Elizabeth*); but this first generation of film men and film values has left a legacy of sacrificing taste for dollars that Hollywood films have never completely outgrown.

The most powerful film company of the silent era was Paramount Pictures. Paramount was the child of Adolph Zukor, the final stage in the evolution of his Famous Players in Famous Plays. Zukor, who began by distributing *Queen Elizabeth*, jumped aboard the feature-film wagon at the very beginning—and therein lies one of the chief reasons for his success. Zukor's Famous Players company initiated three kinds of pictures: Class A (with stage stars and stage properties, the artsy films), Class B (with established screen players), and Class C (cheap, quick features). Zukor discovered that the Class B films, the ones with Mary Pickford, were far more popular than the high-toned Class A. Zukor dropped the stagey films and made Class B's exclusively. He soon absorbed Jesse Lasky's Feature Play Company, Lewis J. Selznick's Picture Company, Edwin S. Porter's Rex Pictures, Pallas Pictures, and Morosco Pictures; he also absorbed a distributing exchange called Paramount Pictures, which eventually gave its name to the final amalgamation. Zukor bested his competition by buying it out. The huge company then had the power and the money to hire the most popular stars and demand the highest fees from exhibitors who wanted the films of its stars.

A second powerful combine emerged in the mid-twenties: Metro-Goldwyn-Mayer. The monolith was assembled by theatre owner Marcus Loew, who wanted to control the profit from the pictures that he showed in his vast national chain of theatres. In 1924, Loew bought the struggling Metro Picture Company and the struggling Goldwyn Picture Company. Goldwyn had left his own company shortly before the merger, bitter about losing one of those power-financial struggles that dominated the early years of the film business. Loew then put Louis B. Mayer, another theatre owner recently turned producer, in charge of production at Metro-Goldwyn. Mayer brought a young assistant, Irving Thalberg, with him to supervise the shooting of the pictures. With these individual parts, Loew assembled the most solid film factory in America. MGM took over the Goldwyn lot to shoot its films (Goldwyn had earlier taken it over from Ince); the studio then distributed its films to all of the Loew theatres. Loew had finally succeeded in creating the kind of vertically integrated empire that Gaumont and Pathé had established twenty years earlier; he controlled all three branches of the theatrical film business: production, distribution, and exhibition.

Zukor was not slow to follow suit. His company had been working in a similar, octopal manner, snatching up theatres as well as studios and exchanges. One of Zukor's commercial innovations was the system of block booking. The theatre owner had to agree to buy all of Zukor's products to get any of them. If he wanted Mary Pickford or William S. Hart, he had to buy all fifty-two weekly programs from Paramount. But even block booking, tyrannical as it was, was less efficient than owning the theatres. The studio owner not only had to produce films but had to guarantee that each of them would be shown. What better guarantee than to own the theatres to show them?

Understandably, the theatre owner did not enjoy the strong-arm pressures of block booking nor the unavailability of those popular films that had been made by the studios for their own theatres. In 1917, a group of theatre owners joined together specifically as an antidote to Zukor's commercial poison, calling themselves the First National Exhibitors Circuit. First National, managed by W. W. Hodkinson (himself elbowed out of Paramount by Zukor) and J. D. Williams, intended to eliminate the film production company from filmmaking, just as the film production companies were trying to eliminate the independent exhibitor. First National contracted with individual stars (Chaplin, for example, and Harry Langdon) to make pictures for their theatres. The star gained independence and financial backing; the theatre owner gained the lucrative products of popular, established stars. The idea was so felicitous that First National became the third power of the 1920s film world.

Yet another new producing wrinkle was the emergence of the artist as producer. If film producers could turn theatre owners and if theatre owners could turn producers, then artists could also turn

The four United Artists after the signing (from a contemporary newsreel)—
Fairbanks, Griffith, Pickford, and Chaplin

producers and work for themselves. In 1919, D. W. Griffith, Charles Chaplin, Mary Pickford, and Douglas Fairbanks joined together to form the United Artists Corporation. Each would produce his or her own films, which would then be distributed by the common company, United Artists. United Artists owned neither studio nor theatre; it merely released the finished products for distribution. However flimsy such an organization seemed compared with the Goliaths like Paramount, MGM, and First National, the company survived and still does today. In fact, the idea for the company was years ahead of its time,

foreshadowing the commercial practices of the 1960s and '70s. Today, the major "studios" themselves are primarily distributors for pictures that have been filmed by independent producers.

The Hollywood film studios of the 1920s had traveled a long way from Edison's Black Maria. Vast expanses of land and a complex maze of buildings had replaced the single little tar-paper shack that pirouetted with the sun. The Hollywood studio had become an entertainment factory; like any factory it broke the manufacture of its product into a series of parts, and each cell of the whole organism fulfilled its particular function. There was a specific section for writers in the studio—those who conceived the original story ideas, those who wrote the final scenarios, and even those who created the film's subtitles, a separate and highly developed art of its own. There was a specific section for costuming, one for the construction of sets, and another for the care and maintenance of the increasingly complicated equipment, still another for the shooting of the films, and one for publicizing, marketing, and financing the finished product. The arts of the costumer, the cinematographer, the art director, the electrician, and the writer had become as significant as the contributions of the director and actor.

The growth and evolution of the film studio were paralleled by the growth and evolution of the theatre that showed its films. Almost simultaneous with the birth of the feature film came the huge, plush, comfortable movie theatre to show feature films. The two births are interrelated: the same feature phenomenon that turned the studios into rich dinosaurs turned the theatres into rich dinosaurs. The earlier nickelodeons were small and often dirty; the movies migrated from these little stores in the low-rent districts to huge theatres on Broadway. The first of the new palaces was the Strand, constructed on Broadway in 1914, followed immediately by the Vitagraph (now the Criterion). The new theatres could accommodate over two thousand patrons, who trod on carpeted floors and relaxed in plush, padded chairs. The manager of the Strand Theatre, Samuel L. Rothafel (né Rothapfel), soon went on to buy, build, and conceive huge movie palaces of his own. Roxy (his nickname) opened or salvaged a string of mammoth New York houses: the Rialto, Rivoli, Capitol, Roxy, and the Radio City Music Hall, his finale and *chef d'oeuvre*. Roxy brought the same tone of quasi-gentility to the movie theatre that his colleagues, like Zukor and Mayer, brought to the films themselves.

Roxy supplemented the film showing with symphony orchestras, corps de ballets, and live variety acts. Whereas vaudeville had supported the movies in their first years in America, the movies had now begun to support vaudeville. The last survivor of the Roxy era in this country is, of course, Radio City Music Hall, whose live stage show was a major tourist attraction simply because it was a unique anachronism. History, inflation, and labor costs finally caught up with the Music Hall in 1979, however, forcing it to terminate its traditional vaudeville-movie combination in order to preserve the architectural edifice as a functioning relic of America's cultural past.

Roxy decorated the insides of his theatres with the same kinds of flouncing that he used for the film showings. The ushers wore colorful silken uniforms that matched the carpets and walls and were consistent with the theatre's architectural motif. The theatre walls offered ornate carvings in stone, brass, and wood; gargoyles stared from the balconies; plaster copies of Greek statues (attired in fig leaves) gazed down from trellised cupolas, bathed in a red or green floodlight. The Roxy of the West Coast, Sid Grauman, paid as much attention to the outsides of his theatres as Roxy paid to the inside. His Chinese Theatre welcomed the patron with a complex system of pagoda roofs and Oriental carvings; his Egyptian Theatre offered patrons a waterfall and a wishing well as they walked in the door. The pretentiousness, the tacky splendor of these huge movie houses today seems metaphoric of most of the films they showed on their screens.

Morality

The movies have waged a perpetual cold war with the forces of religion and righteousness. In 1897, the moralists denounced the improprieties of the

Rice-Irwin Kiss. Another 1897 film, *Fatima,* which depicted the bumps and grinds of a noted hooch dancer of the day, so offended some members of certain communities that exhibitors superimposed broad white stripes across the screen to cover the areas where Fatima displayed her most lascivious wares. Without question, the censored version of the film is far more offensive and obscene than the original since the two heavily streaked regions of the frame inform the viewer quite precisely about what areas of the body should be considered nasty.

Throughout the nickelodeon era the movies had been criticized as cultivators of iniquity; the theatres had been attacked as unsavory or unsafe. The protests of the moralistic few did not deter the entertainment-minded many from going to the nickelodeons. The parallels between the twentieth-century moralistic controversy over the movies (still continuing today) and the sixteenth-century moralistic controversy over the Elizabethan theatre (also criticized as a breeder of licentiousness and laziness) are striking. The vocal moralists preached; the public continued to go to their favorite public entertainment. The movie cold war suddenly became a very hot one in the early 1920s.

First, the content of films, reflecting the new materialism and moral relativism of the decade, became spicier and more suggestive. The sentimental films of the Griffith era had not disappeared; Griffith's own films, Mary Pickford's, and pictures like Henry King's *Tol'able David* perpetuated the tradition of innocence and purity. But alongside these Victorian films were others suggesting that lust was indeed a human emotion, that married couples indeed indulged in extramarital flirtations (at the least), and that the urbane and wealthy and lustful were not inevitably evil and unhappy. The new materialistic audience (who spent as much as two dollars to get into the plush movie palace) enjoyed films that idolized the material as well as the spiritual. The spiritual sermonizers intensified their letter-writing and speech-making campaigns with concerted public action. Clergymen and laymen united to form panels and committees that would not exactly censor films, but would advise parishioners and the public about which films to see and which to avoid. Behind the censorship drives of some of these organizations lay a thinly veiled antisemitism (an interesting parallel with the similarly antisemitic campaigns against the Hollywood "Reds" of some thirty years later). The moral deficiencies of the movies were yet another strategem of the Jewish infidels, once again poisoning the wells of a Christian nation. Against such attacks, the moral statements and strictures of the industry's own National Board of Review (its name changed from the National Board of Censorship in 1915 and its power undermined by the busting of the Trust that created it) were inadequate and powerless.

The moral ambiguities of the offerings on the motion picture screens were soon accompanied by the scandalous doings of the motion picture people off the screen. In the early twenties, several national scandals rocked the film industry far more severely than had the letters and speeches of the zealots. Hollywood did not just sell pictures to the public; it sold the stars who sold the pictures. Scandal in the life of a star was more serious than any extramarital wink on the screen. In 1920, Mary Pickford, "America's Sweetheart," quietly went to Nevada with her husband, Owen Moore, to get a divorce. Three weeks later "Little Mary" married her male counterpart in innocence and purity, Douglas Fairbanks. The public was not shocked by the divorce alone, since Hollywood divorces had already become old news. But this divorce, followed by the abrupt marriage of these two supposedly healthy, happy, all-American people, was something special. The Pickford-Fairbanks marriage was further complicated by the possibility that the divorce proceeding had been improperly executed ("Little Mary" eventually avoided the stain of bigamy). Though Doug and Mary had done nothing illegal, their illicit premarital romance seemed contradictory to their screen purity. The tremendous public interest in the petty domestic affair clearly revealed the new social importance of the film industry and its vulnerability to attack by newspaper headlines.

In 1921, two consecutive Fatty Arbuckle scandals fed the headlines. In July of that year newspapers reported a mysterious Arbuckle party in Massachusetts that had taken place in 1917. The mysterious detail was that the district attorney of a Massachusetts county had received a $100,000 gift just after the party. The public wondered what the District Attorney had discovered that was worth such a sum to keep quiet. Then in September 1921, Arbuckle threw a second party, this one in San Francisco's St. Francis Hotel. The next morning one of Arbuckle's guests, Virginia Rappe, was found dead in her hotel room. A week later Arbuckle gave himself up to the police, was eventually tried for involuntary manslaughter, and was found not guilty. His innocence in the eyes of the law did not affect his standing in the eyes of the moralists. The Hollywood producers, acceding to the cries of the preachers, barred the evil Fatty from pictures. The great comedian worked in only one more film, James Cruze's bitter satire of Hollywood (*Hollywood,* 1923), although he continued to direct minor films under an assumed name (Will B. Good!). The Hollywood producers threw Arbuckle to the moralists, hoping to still the hissing tongues; the money men preferred a safe surrender to a possibly unsettling and unprofitable confrontation. Some thirty years later the industry made

the same choice when it sacrificed "the Ten" directors and writers to the Red-baiters.

In 1922, "handsome" Wallace Reid died suddenly and mysteriously, generating posthumous scandal when the newspapers discovered he had used drugs. Early in the same year, a minor director, William Desmond Taylor, was found dead in his apartment, another scandal with a vague mixture of sex, murder, and drugs. The Taylor murder hurt the careers of Mabel Normand, the pretty comedienne, and Mary Miles Minter, a little-girl imitation of Mary Pickford, who were both friends of the director. The press, satisfying the hunger of its readers, turned these friendships into something salacious. There was no defense against vague rumor and veiled innuendo. Two more careers were thrown to the yapping dogs to keep them quiet.

Such notoriety brought the film business to the attention of the United States Congress and the edge of federal censorship—the last thing any producer wanted. The industry decided once again to clean its own house, to serve as its own censorship body. Recalling the success of the baseball owners at finding a moralistic commissioner to cleanse the black-sox scandals, the esteemed Judge Landis, the film producers sought their own respected commissioner. In 1922, they found Will H. Hays, President Harding's campaign manager, Postmaster General of the United States, Presbyterian elder, and Republican. Hays became president of the Motion Picture Producers and Distributors of America, an organization supported and financed by all the major film companies in America, known colloquially as the Hays Office, which he headed for twenty-five years. Rather than taking concrete censorship actions, the Hays Office sought to counter bad publicity with good, to keep the press from magnifying its tales of Hollywood debauches, to regularize business

Moguls and Morals—Irving Thalberg, Louis B. Mayer, Will Hays, and Harry Rapf on the Metro-Goldwyn lot

procedures, and to encourage producers to submit their films voluntarily for prerelease examination. The loose, informal advising of the Hays Office in the twenties was another in a series of successful Hollywood attempts to keep films out of the hands of government censors, a strategy that would be duplicated by the enforcement of the Hollywood Production Code of the 1930s and the Motion Picture Rating System of the 1970s.

Films and Filmmakers, 1910–1928

The ever-increasing problem of the American film director was how to make an individualized, special film in a factory system geared toward standardization and mass production. The Griffith era of anarchy and improvisation was rapidly

passing, even as Griffith himself went to work for Zukor. For a director to assemble his own company and begin production without a shooting script and production schedule became unthinkable. Rather than being the artistic creator of his own films, the director was more and more expected to be the mechanic who hammered together the machine that other men, the producer and writer, had earlier designed. Griffith himself noted with dismay the widening gap between producer and director, between the business of making a film and the art of making a film. Each film, rather than being an important work in itself, became only one unit of the studio's yearly output. Though the films had gotten longer and the film business more complex, studio owners considered only the total yearly product, exactly as they did in the Patent Company days of the one-reeler. This industrialization of the film business is most relevant to the career of Thomas Ince, Griffith's contemporary and, after Griffith, the most interesting American director of noncomic films before 1919.

Ince's films are almost the paradigmatic opposites of Griffith's. Whereas Griffth's technique aimed at developing the characters, their emotions, and the metaphoric implications of the action, Ince concentrated ruthlessly on the narrative flow. Ince was as avid a film cutter as Griffith, but whereas Griffith cut to develop rhythm and emotion, Ince cut to keep the story moving. Whereas Griffith consistently used the close-up for intimacy and detail, Ince consistently used the long, far, and extreme far shots, rarely picking the characters' feelings out of the flow of the action. Griffith's interest was primarily on why the characters did something and what that implied symbolically; Ince's focused almost exclusively on what they did. If, on the surface, Ince's method seems thinner and less interesting than

Griffith's, he compensated for it by eliminating Griffith's sticky sentimentality and symbolism. Ince's pretentiously symbolic *Civilization* (1916) is an obvious exception (and an obvious attempt to copy the Griffith formula). However, more typical of Ince is a film like *The Coward* (1915), another Civil War story made the same year as Griffith's, which avoids all the symbolic freight of *Birth of a Nation* to concentrate exclusively on one young man's earning his "red badge of courage." The two titles of the films (the specificity of Ince's, abstractness of Griffith's) are indicative.

Ince was also one of the first directors to discover the power of shooting outdoors. Ince movies could have been made nowhere but in California and the West. The openness and movement that Griffith used for battle scenes and chases were the bases of Ince's films: the stagecoach sweeping down a mountain trail flanked by mountains and plains and sagebrush, the Indians pursuing, the posse galloping across the prairies, the Indians' circle of death as they revolve about the isolated victims, the dust and smoke and powder of the gun battle (a brilliant translation of sound into visual imagery), the dust of the horses' hooves, the silhouettes of the tribe of Apaches on the mesa awaiting the moment to join the attack. One of the most common (and beautiful) Ince images is smoke—the swirling, enveloping movement of gunpowder or dust, shot through refractive beams of light. This smoky haze is an effective contrast with Ince's usual clean, crisp, deep-focus photographic style (yet another marked contrast with Griffith, who depended on soft-focus photography).

Ince movies moved. And they moved because they had the space to move. The outdoor freedom that Porter accidentally discovered for *The Great Train Robbery* became a conscious artistic tool for Ince. It was a tool he would pass on to his successors—John Ford, Howard Hawks, Sam Peckinpah, and many others—who also used the visual contrast of small, moving men in vast western vistas.

Ince, unlike Griffith, quickly tired of directing films. Instead, he became a supervisor of production (a position Griffith found distasteful), in effect a producer, keeping his finger on several different film projects at the same time. Unlike Griffith, Ince insisted on a detailed shooting script, which he eventually approved and stamped "Shoot as is." The Ince director then went about the business of constructing from the producer's blueprint. Ince supplemented the shooting script with a detailed production breakdown and schedule, making sure that all people and animals and equipment went to the right place at the right time for the fewest number of hours. If Griffith was the film's first real director, Ince was its first important producer, instituting the system that uncomfortably divided the artistic responsibility for the film between two people. Ince showed the future studio heads how to run a studio.

Ironically, Ince's career waned in the studio era itself. He was the hardest hit by the failure of the Triangle Film Corporation, which depended on his films and his Culver City studio. In 1915, the president of the Mutual Film Corporation, Harry Aitken, was ousted by his partner, John R. Freuler, in another one of those power struggles for control. Aitken, who personally owned the Mutual contracts of Griffith, Sennett, and Ince, took the three with him to build the Triangle Film Corporation, with the three important directors as the tips of the triangle. But Griffith produced several unimportant program pictures, and Sennett's and Ince's drawing powers were feebler than they had been. The triangle collapsed in 1919. Ince, the movie man of system and efficiency, died mysteriously (another of those strange Hollywood deaths) in 1924, just when the era of system and efficiency had officially arrived with the Mayer-Thalberg rule at MGM, Ince's old lot.

The films of Douglas Fairbanks also reveal the changing values of Hollywood. Fairbanks broke into films with Griffith at Triangle; the young actor was so athletic, so bouncy, so perpetually in motion, that Griffith gave up on him and suggested he go see Mr. Sennett. Triangle eventually let Fairbanks go his own way, pairing him with the scenario writer, Anita Loos, her director-husband, John Emerson, and cameraman, Victor Fleming. Between 1915 and 1920, the group produced a series of breezy, parodic, energetic comedies that combined the star's athleticism, energy, and sincerity with the writer's and director's wit and style. For today's "film generation," which thinks of Fairbanks only as the cavalier who duelled while swinging from a chandelier (Gene Kelly parodied this Doug in *Singin' in the Rain),* his early films are refreshing surprises. They are parodies that make fun of a personality trait (American snobbishness, the fascination with royalty, the hunger for publicity, the ambition to achieve the impossible) or a genre of films (the western, the mystery, the melodrama). Doug is the center of the parody, the magnified version of whatever the film is satirizing. But Doug, because of his naïveté, because of his enthusiasm, because of his obvious love of life and people, always succeeds in engaging our sympathies at the same time that we laugh at him. Loos and Emerson took advantage of the way that Doug overdid everything; they made a virtue of overdoing. And Doug's athleticism, his physical exhilaration, his constant movement, become a delight to watch. Doug can jump around madly, can swing from the beams of the ceiling, can jump from balconies, can ride horses and twirl a rope, can tumble down (or up) a ravine. Doug's acting technique seemed to center

around such questions as: why enter a room through a door when you can jump in through the window? why walk up a flight of stairs when you can leap up them, or swing upstairs on a lighting fixture, or vault through a hole in the downstairs ceiling?

The glorification of the physical in the Fairbanks film led to several key moral principles that the films implicitly, and sometimes explicitly, extolled. One of the key contrasts in the films is between the dull, routine, banal life that Doug must live in conventional society and the imaginative, free, vigorous life he wants to live. Fairbanks was the foe of the dull and regimented; the row upon row of similar desks in the button factory of *Reaching for the Moon* (1917) was an image of everything Fairbanks hated. A consistent metaphor for the routine and businesslike in Fairbanks's films was the accountant's eyeshade; whenever Doug feels the need to drive free and imaginative thoughts out of his head, he clamps on the eyeshade and gets to work. The physical emphasis of Doug's talent also led the star to value the source of the physical, the body. The character Doug played, though guilty of an overly fertile imagination and far-fetched ambitions, was rarely guilty of abusing his body. Doug supplemented his on-screen cleanliness with magazine articles lauding the healthy life and disparaging the unhealthy lures of drink, tobacco, and gluttony.

Yet another Fairbanks moral principle was—despite the joys of the imagination and the tortures of routine—one's imagination should not be too imaginative, and should really bend its efforts to make the conventional, routine life less routine. In *Reaching for the Moon,* Doug tells us that the moon is not worth having because we can't get it. The plot is a sputteringly delightful parody of skullduggery and spying in a small, mythical middle-European kingdom

The Americano gone exotic—Douglas Fairbanks in The Thief of Bagdad

(Vulgaria). But affixed to the plot is the explicit message that one should indeed concentrate and aspire, but only toward that which is worth attaining. Whereas Doug aspires to be a king, his girl only aspires to a husband, house, and children (in New Jersey). In the end she gets her wishes and Doug renounces his "moon shot," returning to the hateful button company, supposedly to use his imagination there; there is a rather uncomfortable vagueness about just how he is going to do so.

The later Fairbanks films of the twenties make quite a contrast with these earlier, breezy ones. Doug is still a great athlete; he still has his smile and energy. But he is no longer a contemporary American trying to strike a blend between his own imaginative impulses and the conventions of society. Doug has been transported to faraway, romantic lands of centuries ago. He is free to perform bizarre and exotic deeds, and although he is usually some kind of thief, he is not, paradoxically, dishonest. In addition to sparking his daring exploits, the faroff themes and places allow Doug to become an explicit sex symbol, gliding through most of the films without his shirt, with limbs clearly defined by a pair of tights or slightly exposed by the scanty cloth that teasingly covers his middle. Although these later Fairbanks films—*The Mark of Zorro* (1920), *Robin Hood* (1922), *The Thief of Bagdad* (1924), *The Black Pirate* (1926)—make for pleasant, visually slick, and charmingly energetic shows, the results seem less important than the incisive wit, the cleverness, and the cultural insight of the earlier Doug films that simultaneously lauded and parodied the excesses of the American Dream.

No two directors more clearly show the problems of the filmmaker in the 1920s than Erich von Stroheim and Cecil B. DeMille. As were Griffith and Ince a few years earlier, the two are almost paradigms for the whole industry. Von Stroheim gave the public what he wanted, DeMille gave it what he thought it wanted. Von Stroheim was a ruthless realist committed to his art and his vision, DeMille was willing to throw any faddish or striking hokum into a film. Von Stroheim's greatest tools were close observation and detail, DeMille's were size and splash. Significantly, DeMille's greatest popularity was in the twenties and fifties, two decades devoted to size and splash. Von Stroheim's films, despite their symbolic excesses and occasionally overstated moralizing, were controlled by the director's taste and intelligence; DeMille's films had everything but taste and intelligence.

Both DeMille and von Stroheim served several apprentice years before emerging as major directors. DeMille shot his first film, *The Squaw Man*, for Jesse Lasky's Feature Play Company in 1913. Later he and his brother William, joined the new production company of Samuel Goldfish and Edgar Selwyn (hence, Gold + wyn, which eventually became Goldwyn). DeMille began keeping track of national trends and tastes. Von Stroheim began as a studio adviser on European military details, then began playing vicious "Huns" (dubbed "the man you love to hate") for Griffith, and finally, in 1919, persuaded Carl Laemmle to let him direct and perform in his own films.

The two films that most clearly reveal the differences in the two men are DeMille's *Male and Female* and von Stroheim's *Blind Husbands*. Both films were released in 1919; both capitalized on the new audience interest in sexual amours and the doings of the rich. Both suggested the importance of sex in human relationships. There the similarities stop. *Male and Female* is a lavish, pretentious, and inconsistent examination of the class question; DeMille's point of view is so vague that he seems to suggest two things at the same time: that masters may marry their servants and that masters may not marry their servants. Although some of the film's confusion stems from J. M. Barrie's play, *The Admirable Crichton*, that DeMille was adapting, the most dazzling stupidities are DeMille's "additions": for example, the film begins with a sequence that does not exist in the original play, a series of shots of oceans and the Grand Canyon, followed by a biblical quote, "God created man in his own image." Both the quotation and this whole Creation sequence—an obvious plea for high seriousness and a theft of Griffithisms— are irrelevant to anything that follows in the film. The stentorian seriousness of the DeMille beginning—the impli- cation that the film one was about to see was Very Significant Art and might even come directly from God—was a consistent DeMille trait that continued into the sound era. Even a modest war- time biography, *The Story of Dr. Wassel* (1944), begins with a "Voice of God" narrator.

DeMille then plunges into the affairs of a contemporary British household, spending most of his time showing the elegance of Gloria Swanson taking a bath (scented with rose water), the water temperature being checked carefully by her maid, Gloria striding carefully and sliding gently into the sunken tub. One of DeMille's titles asks why shouldn't the bathroom express as much elegance as anything else in life, and his even asking such a question is at the heart of what is empty about the film. Meanwhile, DeMille contrasts the high-falutin' ways of Lady Mary (Gloria), who rejects a piece of toast because it is too soft, with the simple ways of Tweeny, her maid. Simple Tweeny is in love with the butler, Crichton (Thomas Meighan). But, alas, he is not simple; he loves Lady Mary; he reads aloud poetry that Tweeny cannot understand but Lady Mary can.

Then the whole family takes a yachting trip and runs aground. A title tells us that they have sailed into "uncharted seas," but we recognize Catalina. Now that the group must survive on a desert isle, DeMille can add yet another locale and style of decor to the film. Having already filmed the Creation and a chic English drawing-room comedy, he can go about filming a kind of Swiss Family Robinson. On the island, it turns out that he who is lower class in one society is upper class in another. Crichton, the butler, becomes the king of the group and they become his servants, simply because he is competent and able to survive, while they all are numbskulls trying to play at being posh in the middle of the wilderness. The only unaltered element is that Crichton still loves Mary (now no longer a Lady); and she discovers that she loves him. One night, fearing for her safety, Crichton follows her to the haunt of the lions where he slays a beast that is about to attack her. The male and female vow their love. And now DeMille throws in the kitchen sink.

There is an instantaneous and unmotivated cross-cut to some Oriental dream kingdom, presumably Babylon (the scene does not exist, of course, in Barrie's play). The only motivation for the shift is the line of poetry that Crichton and Mary have read in the film (Barrie uses the line just once, but DeMille repeats it several times so you don't miss it), "If I were a king of Babylon. . . ." DeMille is not one to leave his ifs iffy. In this Babylon sequence, Crichton is indeed king, and Mary, a title informs us, is a Christian slave. The fact that Babylon had evaporated hundreds of years before Christ does not offend DeMille's sense of history. Despite the irrelevance of the shift, DeMille can trade in the cave man, leopard skin costumes of the island sequence for the lavish, gaudy silks and satins of Hollywood's version of Babylon. Gloria Swanson, slave though she be, appears in flowing gowns and peacock headdress. Because she refuses to share her man with other concubines, the king of Babylon tosses his reluctant mistress to the sacred lions of Ishtar. She is not reluctant at all about these lions as she strides majestically into their lair. All DeMille then shows us is a sacred lion licking his chops and Gloria's empty gown (unbloodied) lying on the floor.

Meanwhile, back on the desert island, Lady Mary and Crichton are in the middle of their marriage ceremony (they luckily happened to have a clergyman in their yachting party) when they spot a ship. Lady Mary says forget the ship; Crichton, however, for some incomprehensible reason, decides that they must go back to society and must not wed. They go back; they don't wed; the picture ends. The tastelessness of the individual episodes is overwhelmed by the tastelessly irrelevant method of stitching them together. The film is clearly one of the bastard progeny of *Intolerance* in its combination of different epochs and locations in a single film. But in *Male and Female*, the diversity is for diversity's sake, merely using the splashiness of set and costume changes. The moral spinelessness of the film, which flirts with unconventionality and then upholds convention for no dramatic or human reason, became a staple of DeMille's fifty-year career. His racy films flirt with naughtiness and sell conventionality; his religious films flirt with righteousness and sell lewdness. In both versions of *The Ten Commandments*, DeMille was more interested in the splashy sinful doings around the golden calf than in the righteous thunder and lightning on the mountain.

Von Stroheim's *Blind Husbands* is a far

less complicated story than *Male and Female*. A doctor and his wife travel to the Alps; he pays her insufficient sexual attention. A German military officer sees the young wife and desires her; she cannot stop herself from desiring him, for she has no other outlet for her desires. The husband's blindness finally clears up; on a climactic hiking trip, the two males confront each other on the pinnacle, and the lecherous rival perishes, more a victim of the mountains and of fate than of the husband. The power of the film lies in von Stroheim's reduction of the quantity of incidents (quantity was DeMille's credo) in order to develop the quality, the feeling, the texture of the incidents he includes. Details develop the film's emotional dynamics: the calm husband's pipe; the wife's provocative ankles and shoes; the German's handling of his monocle and his careful primping with brush, comb, and vaporizer of cologne to make himself sexually attractive; the soulful tune that Margaret (the wife) plays on the piano, joined by von Steuben (the German) on the violin, which shows both her loneliness and her desire (we need no sound to hear the kind of tune the two are playing together).

Von Stroheim's attention to detail inevitably allows him the luxury and subtlety of understatement. Several of the seduction scenes between von Steuben and Margaret take place in rooms, or hallways, or fields where a cross can distantly but clearly be seen in the background; von Stroheim never cuts to a close-up of the cross. The one way to turn subtle symbolism into overstated twaddle would have been to force us to read the crosses symbolically. Von Stroheim, mature artist that he is, knows the power of allusion and understatement.

The director's technique owes its greatest debt to his first master, Griffith. Like Griffith, his two principal tools are the creation of atmosphere and cutting. Von Stroheim's care with sets, lighting,

costumes, and decor is so meticulous in creating his seamy world that you can almost smell it. In *Blind Husbands,* the details of the inn courtyard, of the dining room with its posters and crockery, of the individual bedrooms (so important to the film's plot), of the fog and mist on the pinnacle, all contribute to the tone of the film and the power of each scene.

Von Stroheim's care extended to his editing of the films, using the two Griffith devices of the cross-cut (to show parallel events in different places at the same time) and the subjective cut (to show the mental projection of a character at a particular moment). In *Blind Husbands,* von Stroheim's cross-cutting develops both tension and irony. For example, he shows the doctor delivering a baby at the same time that von Steuben courts his wife, obviously trying to perform the act that produces babies. The most striking subjective cut in *Blind Husbands* comes just after the husband has discovered the Prussian's designs on his wife. Von Stroheim suddenly cuts to a menacing, spot-lit head of the German looming out of the darkness until it eventually fills the frame; it leers grotesquely and points an accusing finger at the doctor.

The grotesque, the ugly, and the repellent are dominant motifs in von Stroheim. André Bazin described von Stroheim's "one simple rule for direction": "Take a close look at the world, keep on doing so, and in the end it will lay bare for you all its cruelty and ugliness." Beneath the elegant surfaces of von Stroheim's characters—their polished manners, white gloves, and spray perfume—there is animal rapaciousness, viciousness, and lust. His films are populated by physical cripples and mental defectives; their physiological ugliness is clearly metaphoric of the moral ugliness of this world. In *Foolish Wives* (1921) the fake Russian Count (von Stroheim again) attempts to rape a helpless, mentally retarded child. At the end of the film, the girl's father kills the "Count" and

Foolish Wives: *Von Stroheim (as the bogus Russian count) defines his murderousness on the pistol range; then he sets his sexual sights on a helpless, mentally retarded child*

dumps his body into the sewer so it can be swept out to sea with the other garbage.

Despite the overwhelming viciousness of the von Stroheim films, these close and careful examinations of bedroom tensions between husbands and wives were very popular with the public. Their less-than-American nastiness and the haughty independence of their non-American director were less popular with the heads of studios and their flunkies. Irving Thalberg, then Carl Laemmle's assistant at Universal, removed von Stroheim from *Merry-Go-Round* (1922) in the middle of shooting, firing him for his "inefficient" (that is, perfectionist and uncompromising) production methods, his wasteful expenditures on "invisible" details (which were actually quite visible in the convincing realism and texture of the overall film), and for his insubordination. Metro Pictures, then in financial trouble, engaged von Stroheim to keep them alive, as he had Universal. (Thalberg would get the opportunity to fire von Stroheim again.)

Von Stroheim's first project at Metro was an adaptation of Frank Norris's brutal novel, *McTeague*. The novel attracted von Stroheim for several reasons. Norris's view of the human dog exactly matched von Stroheim's, whose consistent metaphor was to depict human behavior in animal terms. Like von Stroheim, Norris was a ruthless realist with a taste for the ugly and grotesque. Further, the German family in the novel paralleled von Stroheim's own heritage, and the familiar San Francisco and Oakland settings of the novel appealed to a man who had lived there before he went to Hollywood. The director decided to shoot a precise, literal translation of the novel, scene by scene, page by page. He went on location to San Francisco (in an era of almost exclusive studio shooting) and Death Valley (during the summer!) to obtain absolutely authentic details. As his teacher had done with

Lillian Gish in the snow, von Stroheim's passion for authenticity put one of his players, Jean Hersholt, in the hospital after the gruelling takes in the sand of Death Valley.

The original version of the film ran forty-two reels (*Birth of a Nation,* Griffith's longest film, ran thirteen). Von Stroheim cut it to twenty-four and said he could cut no further. His friend and director-colleague at Metro, Rex Ingram, cut the film to eighteen reels and felt he could cut no more without mutilating it. Irving Thalberg (who had come to Metro with Louis B. Mayer while von Stroheim was at work on *Greed*) turned the film over to the Metro cutting department, where a hack film cutter (Joe W. Farnham) finished the hatchet job. *Greed* was released in ten reels, and the remainder of the negative was deliberately destroyed. Whether a nine-hour, literal translation of a novel is one of the authentic aesthetic possibilities of the cinema will perhaps never be known.

The *Greed* that exists must therefore be judged on the strength of its parts rather than its whole. For one who hasn't read Norris's novel, the film's narrative (certainly its details) is almost incomprehensible. The concrete process of the dissolution of McTeague and Trina's relationship makes no sense in the film at all, for in the novel Norris carefully charts it by moving the couple to shabbier and shabbier living quarters. Each degradation in physical sur-roundings implies emotional and moral degradation. But in *Greed*, although we may notice that the walls of the McTeague household change as the film progresses, we never know exactly when, why, and where the couple has moved. Although in one shot we may notice that Trina's bandaged hand is lacking several fingers, we never learn from the film that she lost them because they became infected as a result of her husband's biting them. The dissolution from happy, human marriage to vicious, selfish animal

The repellent naturalism of Greed: *McTeague (Gibson Gowland) and Trina (ZaSu Pitts) go a-courting in a swamp*

combat—which is the subject of at least half of the Norris novel (and which also must have been of central interest to von Stroheim)—does not exist in the film.

Another reason this sense of dissolution does not exist is that the ten-reel version had to do without two other "love" relationships in the novel that undoubtedly seemed superfluous to a hack film cutter but that are really essential. The relationship between Trina and Mac is bounded, on the one hand, by old Grannis and Miss Baker, an idealized couple of old folks who carry on a pure, genteel, spiritual, "Victorian" love affair, and, on the other, by Zerkow and Maria Macapa, two slovenly human beasts whose "love" is based solely on Zerkow's almost

sexual pleasure in listening to the equally insane Maria's story of her hoard of gold. The only element remaining of this story in *Greed* is the two extremely bizarre, expressionistic shots of long, skinny arms playing with a pile of metallic objects (taken out of the Maria-Zerkow context, these shots in *Greed* seem irrelevantly and pretentiously symbolic). In the novel, we understand the original love of Mac and Trina as a median between the spirituality of the old folks and the crazed passion of the gold lovers. Trina begins as Miss Baker's close friend, somewhat repulsed by Maria's crudeness, and gradually drifts into becoming Maria's confidante. Mac and Trina even move into the squalid hovel where Zerkow and Maria lived (and

which became vacant when Zerkow cut
Maria's throat). Without the two poles of
these other couples, *Greed* has no
barometer to measure the direction and
degree of decay in the central couple.

Despite the incoherence of *Greed* as a
whole, several of the sequences are visual
and dramatic marvels. The wedding
ceremony is a mixture of the comic and
the somber: a delightful parody of
bourgeois wedding customs that is
overshadowed by the sight of a funeral
cortege through an open window (and a
clear premonition of the direction the
marriage will take). The scene in which
Trina realizes that she is alone—with no
one to protect her except the stranger
who is her animal-sensual husband—is a
touching, sensitive examination of internal
feelings and sensations. Von Stroheim
ends the sequence brilliantly as Trina
rushes into the room where Mac sits
patiently alone, throws herself helplessly into his huge arms, kisses him
desperately, and rises instinctively and
involuntarily onto her toes. Von
Stroheim's use of animal symbolism,

particularly his likening the evil Marcus
Schouler to the sneaky cat that constantly
prowls about the cage of McTeague's
bird, is quite effective. And most awesome
visually are the endless wastes of Death
Valley—a seeming infinity of caked sand
and dust under a pitiless, dead sky—the
ultimate stopping place on a journey in
which a dead metal seems the only goal
worth pursuing.

But von Stroheim's point is not so
much a moralistic warning against the
evils of Mammon as it is a minute
examination of what gold does to the
human animal. Gold is the stimulus that
turns men into vultures who viciously
prey on the flesh of their fellows to peck
out a profit. Von Stroheim depicts his
society of animals with a series of the
most realistically detailed scenes in any
American film before the new naturalism
that followed World War II: the
tawdriness of the middle-class American
home; the brutal lust for wealth that
turns husband and wife into murderous
enemies; the human irony that the thirst
for gold, an inanimate object, can

overpower the natural human need for life-sustaining water, chaining a man to a corpse and a cask of gold in the midst of a vast desert where his body can only become food for vultures. It is von Stroheim's view of man, not gold, that dominates the surviving scenes of *Greed*.

That same view of man dominates even the fluffy trifle of a film that Thalberg assigned von Stroheim after *Greed*. *The Merry Widow* (1925) was a safe property, a Viennese operetta that Thalberg was sure von Stroheim could not destroy. Von Stroheim apparently did not destroy it; the film was one of his greatest commercial successes. But von Stroheim, in adapting this operetta fairy tale, devotes a disproportionate amount of attention to the widow's first husband (before she became a widow) rather than her resulting merry widowhood. The husband is a deformed cripple (von Stroheim accentuates the deformity). Worse, he is a cripple with a very obvious sexual fetish; he is attracted to healthy feet—a theme that von Stroheim develops with pointed cutting. Worse still, he is so excited on his wedding night that he collapses and dies on top of his bride, worn out from dragging his gnarled body up to the bed of love. Von Stroheim's handling of this unsavory relationship is not exactly operetta fare. Another brilliant von Stroheim stroke is his depiction of the mental attitudes of the widow's three suitors. All three come to watch her perform at the theatre; all three stare at her through opera glasses. Then von Stroheim cuts to the object of their stares: the cripple watches her feet; the lecherous suitor watches her groin; the young hero watches her face. Such naturalistic touches turn von Stroheim's operetta into a very subtle and salacious parody of an operetta.

Because his production methods seemed extravagant, because he seemed mean and tyrannical, unwholesome and unpleasant, Erich von Stroheim was very easy to fire, even if his films made money. *The Merry Widow* was his last film for MGM. He went to work for Zukor and had as little success with him as with Thalberg. After two projects in 1928, *The Wedding March* and *Queen Kelly*—the latter ending with the cataclysmic introduction of sound that shelved the film—Erich von Stroheim directed only one other film, *Walking Down Broadway* (1932). For over twenty years von Stroheim continued acting in films, most memorably as von Rauffenstein in *Grand Illusion* and Max, the chauffeur, in *Sunset Boulevard*. The irony of this last film was that not only did von Stroheim play a character whose career in films echoed his own, but that he also played the devoted, adoring servant of Gloria Swanson, who was with him at the stormy end of his Hollywood road.

Another interesting and important descendant of Griffith's methods was Henry King's *Tol'able David*. The Soviet director, V. I. Pudovkin, found King's use of cutting to build a scene as instructive and effective as Griffith's. Although *Tol'able David* (1921) is often shrugged off as a piece of American regionalism or a retreat to a bygone era, it is a very powerful film in its own right. King, the student of Griffith and the employee of Ince, combines the very best of both Griffith and Ince in the film. King's world in *Tol'able David* is similar to the Griffith world of *Way Down East*: rural, homey, gently comic, touching, peaceful. Into the peaceful world come the violent figures from outside, three fugitives from justice, who are as vicious, as nasty, as psychotically mean as Battling Burrows. Like Griffith, King defines the characters by their responses to animals (Pudovkin called it the use of the "plastic material"): David lovingly plays with his dog Rocket; the invaders consider stoning a sleeping cat and eventually kill the playful Rocket out of pure meanness.

Like Ince, King avoids the sentimentality of Griffith; the film is sentimental without sentimentality. King shuns

Griffith's symbolism and overstated subtitles. And like Ince, King makes the film's narrative flow, never adding any detail of characterization that does not keep the story moving.

Tol'able David is a David and Goliath story. The three villainous Hatburns, who have cast their shadow (literally) on the sunny rural town, kill David's dog, cause his father to die of a heart attack, and cripple David's older brother, Alan. The villains have destroyed David's home (the source of his comfort and happiness), for the family must leave now that the breadwinners have either died or become disabled. David, who had happy dreams of an adult life in his town, is reduced to a poor clerk. He finally gets the chance to prove his mettle, however, by disposing of all three Goliath Hatburns in brutal and exciting combat; David shows he is a lot more than tol'able.

King shows how to bring a story alive with significant and memorable detail by manipulating the visual, "plastic material." Richard Barthelmess, Griffith's own figure of gentleness and sincerity, plays David; his face and presence contribute greatly to the charm, warmth, and sympathy of the story. King's cutting consistently drives the emotions of the tale; the horror of Alan's injury, its impact on Rose, his wife, comes alive as King repeatedly cuts from the crippled, helpless Alan in bed to a shot of Rose, sitting in a rocking chair, holding their new infant, rocking relentlessly back and forth, back and forth. King's cutting transforms the emotionally neutral act of rocking into a moment of pain, of determination, of savagery, of misery, as the shots of the invalid in bed create the emotional climate for the wife's silent rocking. The rocking is far more successful than the cradle in *Intolerance* because the human focus and the specific causes and effects of the act of rocking are so much more concrete.

Also effective in the film are its details of brutality, which clash, intentionally, with the sweeter strains of the picture. Unlike Griffith and more like Ince, King actually depicted malicious violence on the screen: the death of David's dog, Hatburn's digging his finger into the gunshot wound in David's shoulder, the excruciating, exhausting pain of David's final fight with the last Hatburn. Even in Griffith's *Broken Blossoms*, the beatings of Lucy were more implied than graphically depicted. Also Ince-like is the irreversibility of the disaster that has befallen the characters. Unlike the damage done in *Way Down East*, the pieces of David's life can never be patched together again. His dog and father are dead and his brother is an incurable invalid; there can be no miraculous resuscitations. His home is gone; his innocence will never return.

Several other directors made interesting films in the twenties. Some of them would never make the transition to sound; some of them had only begun a career that would take a clearer shape in the era ahead. James Cruze, whose specialty was satire, made the most celebrated western epic of the decade—*The Covered Wagon* (1923). Rex Ingram, whose most famous film was *The Four Horsemen of the Apocalypse* (1921), was a pictorial master of composition and atmosphere. Josef von Sternberg began his control of physical detail and cinematic atmosphere in *Salvation Hunters* (1925), *Underworld* (1927), and *Docks of New York* (1928). John Ford made his first important western film, *The Iron Horse*, in 1924. King Vidor effectively mixed wartime humor, antiwar propaganda, and a saccharine love story in *The Big Parade* (1925).

Most significant of all the newcomers was the German director, Ernst Lubitsch. Hollywood had begun importing many of the leading directors of Europe: Mauritz Stiller, Victor Sjøstrøm, Fritz Lang, F. W. Murnau, E. A. Dupont. But none found Hollywood so comfortable and so amicable a home as Lubitsch. Mary

Pickford imported him specifically to direct a costume spectacle, *Rosita*, for her. Pickford, like her husband, sought to change her adolescent image: to grow up, cut her curls, and show she was a woman. Lubitsch, who had directed a string of costume pageants in Germany (*Gypsy Blood, Passion, Deception*) which had become popular in America for their comic "humanizing" of history, was Pickford's choice. *Rosita* proved the beginning of the end of Mary Pickford's career, the beginning of Lubitsch's. He immediately turned to polite, witty, understated drawing-room comedies: *The Marriage Circle* (1924), *Lady Windermere's Fan* (1925), *So This is Paris* (1926). His cleverness, his ability to imply much with a trivial detail, his pictorial sense—all would later help him make some of the best early American sound films.

It is striking that, of the thousands of American films made in the twenties and of the hundreds of directors who made them, very few individual filmmakers and works of the decade are memorable (or even remembered). Very few films were asked to be memorable and very few directors were asked to use their own inventiveness and insight to make them so. The director was responsible for finishing the film that had already been designed; and the designers, not knowing what new ideas would work and what new ideas the public would accept, ultimately fell back on the old ideas that had the virtue of being tested. The formula picture, deadening to creativity and the imagination, was a means of making the studio product as standardized and, consequently, as stable as the product of any other factory. From the film's earliest days, competing directors copied each other's successes, but not until the 1920s had high finance made the necessity of copying so binding. If the film conformed to a familiar pattern—western, melodrama, spy story, war story, domestic comedy, spine-tingling serial, biblical epic, historical romance—it could be made.

The most creative directors either invented new formulas or, much more likely, injected their own personal vision into old ones. The films of von Stroheim and Lubitsch were part formula (the general situation and plot outline) and part individual (development of the story, illumination of characters, implications of the action). DeMille's great gift was to whip up any formula so furiously that the audience could not tell that the immense edifice was built of whipped cream.

There were a few directors of the 1920s who worked outside the fences of the Hollywood formulas. One of them was Robert Flaherty, the father of the documentary film, who had been taking his camera and film to Hudson Bay since 1913; the eventual result was *Nanook of the North* (1922). Flaherty discovered that only the documentary filmmaker enjoyed the freedom of the solitary, individual artist, shaping his material with his own methods according to his own perceptions. He enjoyed the freedom of a Griffith or Sennett in the early years when man, camera, and idea were still one, without studio middlemen.

Flaherty's *Nanook* is significant for the beauty of its photography of the white, frozen plains of ice and for its care in revealing the life and life-style of the man who lived there. Flaherty's greatest asset was Nanook's total lack of inhibition before the camera. Although he was clearly conscious of being watched, he did not quite know what a film and camera were (just as he tried to eat a phonograph record in an early sequence of the film). He did not pose for the machine; he did not act. He merely lived his life while Flaherty's camera recorded and, inevitably, commented. One comment, of course, was that Nanook's life was hard, a perpetual battle to survive, a continual struggle for two absolute necessities, food and shelter. But Flaherty's making of the film itself mirrored the hardness of Nanook's life, for Flaherty could only record the

severity of ice and snow if he lived through the blizzards he was recording. The making of the film was a metaphor for the subject of the film, and out of that bitter hardness came a work of art, a product of human accomplishment. So Flaherty necessarily found a virtue in the hardness of Nanook's life, in the struggle itself. For Nanook, life was not hard, it merely was. In Nanook's simplicity, in his strength, his competence, his ability to survive, his ability to forge meaning from nature's savagery, Flaherty depicted a life of fulfillment. Nanook's life was ultimately full and filled. Life, in fact, could be no fuller.

Flaherty's later sound film, *Man of Aran* (1934), also develops the difficulties and the fulfillment of the hard, vital life. By then Flaherty had fled to England. Hollywood, rewarding the dollar success of *Nanook* with more dollars, asked Flaherty to make pictures for commercial release. For Paramount he made *Moana* (1926)—an idyllic study of the life on a South Seas island, a life whose warmth and romanticized easiness were as fulfilling for the natives as Nanook's coldness and hardness were for him. Hollywood, which expected native girls dancing the hula, was disappointed and

teamed Flaherty with other directors, W. S. Van Dyke and F. W. Murnau, for his later films. The fiction directors were expected to add formulaic stories to snatches of Flaherty's documentary photography. The idea was contrary to Flaherty's intentions and inimical to all three directors. To preserve his independence, Flaherty left for England where a whole group of filmmakers applying his principles had begun to produce films.

The Comics

One other group of 1920s films maintained an inventiveness and individuality that remain as fresh today as they were a half-century ago. The silent film, which had already proved itself the ideal medium for physical comedy, continued to nurture its most legitimate children. Several new comic imaginations joined the established Sennett, who still supervised films, and Chaplin, who had begun to make feature films: most significantly, Harold Lloyd, Buster Keaton, Harry Langdon, and Laurel and Hardy. Laurel and Hardy were minor figures in the silents, just beginning their teamwork as sound began seeping into Hollywood. They became popular comics of the sound era, and although sound subtracted nothing from the comic principle they had discovered in the silents, it added little to it either. The Laurel and Hardy team had been patched together by Hal Roach, Sennett's major rival as a producer of comedies, who reasoned that one of his fat players and one of his thin ones might go well together. The premise was entirely Sennett-like and indeed Laurel and Hardy's method was a return to the completely comic, externalized, surface world of Sennett gags.

But Laurel and Hardy films were far more controlled and far more tightly structured than the loose Sennett romps.

Their films inevitably demonstrate the "snowball" principle that Bergson had developed in *Le Rire*. Like the snowball rolling down the mountain, the Laurel and Hardy film gathers greater and greater momentum, greater and greater bulk, as it hurtles toward the valley. Their films demonstrate the classic structure of farce—of Plautus and Feydeau: to begin with a single problem and then multiply that problem to infinity. Compared with the random movement in Sennett or the leisurely tangents of Chaplin, the Laurel and Hardy films are very tightly structured indeed. If an auto gets dented in a traffic jam at the start of the film, every car on the highway gets stripped by the end of it; if a Christmas tree branch gets caught in a door at the start of the film, the tree, the house, the salesmen's car must be totally annihilated by the end of it; if the two partners have trouble with a few nails and tacks when starting to build a house, the film must inevitably end with the house collapsing into a pile of rubble. There is an insane yet perfect logic about the whole process.

As does every great silent-film comedy, the Laurel and Hardy films depend on physical objects; the purely visual, physical medium demands the use of concrete, visible things. But for Laurel and Hardy an object is merely something to be destroyed; their films are built around breaking things. The childishness of this willful destruction demands that the primary emotion of the films be a childish one—spite. The "adults" of this world are all children squashing each other's mud pies. Both Stan Laurel and Oliver Hardy play men who are merely overgrown kiddies. Stan is the weepy, puling, sneaky, and covertly nasty kid, while Oliver is the pompous, bullying, show-off, know-it-all, and inherently incompetent kid. His dignity is as false as Stan's tearfulness; they are both ploys to cover spiteful pettiness. If the premise of the films is much thinner than Chaplin's, or even Sennett's, it is also true that the spiteful

emotion they capture is a genuine, psychologically perceptive one. They mirror our feelings when another car zips in to steal the parking place that we have been patiently waiting for. Their single-keyed emotion and their taut, unidirectional structure did limit their success, however, to the short film. Though Laurel and Hardy made many features in the sound era, the longer films are more interesting in their parts rather than their wholes.

Harold Lloyd, another Hal Roach product, was almost a combination of Chaplin and Fairbanks. Like Charlie, he was a little guy, slightly inept, trying to succeed. Like Fairbanks, he was energetic, athletic, and engagingly charming. Like Doug, his smiles were calculated to snare us as well as the girl. Like Charlie, he had trouble both with objects and the world while trying to achieve his desires. But unlike Charlie—and like Doug—he invariably does achieve those desires, and they are the same material and romantic treasures that Doug always wins. Also like Doug—and unlike Charlie—Lloyd films never imply that the prize he has won was not worth the winning.

Rather than developing character or social commentary, Lloyd generates pure comedy from the situation, from topical satire, from his own limber body, and from the daring stunts he would dream up. In *High and Dizzy* (1921), the first of his high-rise comedies of thrills he demonstrates the variety of his comedy. The film is constructed like the Chaplin shorts, with three rather isolated episodes loosely tied together by the thinnest of narrative threads (but without Chaplin's thematic unity). In the opening sequence, Lloyd plays a young doctor, recently out of medical school, whose practice is so dismal that his phone is gathering cobwebs. When a potential patient appears in his office, the young doctor goes through a series of clever improvisations and disguises to make the woman think the doctor is very busy. In the midst of these frenzied activities, he falls madly in love with the patient who, it turns out, walks in her sleep.

In the film's second section, he strolls down the hall and gets stinking drunk with another young doctor who has distilled some hooch in his medicinal laboratory. Lloyd's topical satire of doctors, admittedly rather gentle, is the same kind that he would use to sketch his comic portrait of the twenties' college generation in *The Freshman* (1924). The comic premise of two drunken doctors also allows Lloyd to demonstrate his ability and agility as pure physical comic, as the two friends, one fat, one thin, dizzily weave down the street and into their hotel. The purely surface, physical comedy instantly suggests Chaplin and Fatty in *The Rounders*. But Lloyd's drunken business is more choreographed, more precisely timed. He and his friend get their feet interlocked; they try to put on the same overcoat; they get hung up (literally) on a lamp post. In the hotel, Lloyd's virtuoso gymnastics (tumbling over the bell desk to get his key; trying to stagger into the elevator) show the kind of physical control and clever responses to a situation that make the clothes-ripping sequence of *The Freshman* so funny.

Lloyd introduces his "comedy of thrills" in the film's third section. It just happens that the sleepwalking patient with whom he is in love lives in the same hotel. She starts sleepwalking out on the hotel ledge, many frightening stories above the hard pavement below. Harold goes out on the ledge to save her and, predictably, gets locked out there when she decides to stroll inside. Lloyd tightropes, trips, stumbles on the ledge, playing on so many different emotions in us at the same time. We feel suspense because he might fall; yet we laugh because we know he won't. We wonder if he was really on the ledge when he shot the sequence (the camera angle and lack of editing trickiness makes us suspect he really performed the stunt). We laugh at the

man's fright and perplexity; we admire his underlying competence and control. It was this same synthesis of cliff-hanging serial and burlesque comedy that created the excitement and success of his feature, *Safety Last* (1923).

Unlike the comedy of Chaplin and Keaton, Lloyd's remains content with emotional and psychological surfaces, never cutting very deeply, never going beyond comic sensations to confront us with ironies and paradoxes. But one interesting source consistently tapped by Lloyd's films is their distilling the urges and values of American society as a whole in the 1920s—the American success ethic of get up and get. Further, the Lloyd comedies reveal an extremely cunning and complex sense of comic construction, setting up a comic problem, developing it clearly and cleverly, and driving it to such dizzying heights (quite literally in the high-rise films) that an audience becomes helplessly hysterical in the presence of Lloyd's comic ingenuity (as opposed to Chaplin's comic genius).

Harry Langdon was Lloyd's opposite: his comic style was constructed almost exclusively of internal sensations and emotional reactions with almost no dependence on external business and physical gags. His career was also the shortest of any of the comic stars of the silents. He broke into films at Mack Sennett's studio in 1924, reached stardom with a series of features directed by Frank Capra in 1926 and 1927, and fell from popularity just as suddenly in 1928 when Langdon went off to direct his own films and when sound invaded Hollywood.

The union of Capra and Langdon was significant for both men, for like Capra's later heroes, Langdon was a figure of innocence trapped in a mean, brutal world where foolish angels should indeed fear to tread. Langdon was a Mr. Deeds or Mr. Smith distilled into their essential and purest naïveté, innocence, and childishness. He was an overgrown baby with a puffy baby body, pudgy baby

High and Dizzy: *Harold Lloyd with a sleepwalking Mildred Davis on a scary ledge*

face, and tiny, slow baby brain. The Langdon-Capra films put this overgrown infant into difficult and dangerous situations from which the child-man could escape only by a miracle (for only a miracle could save an infant in a lion's den).

In *Tramp, Tramp, Tramp* (1926) Harry enters a cross-country walking race to try to win enough money to save his father's business from ruin (a clear Capra motif). Harry's opponents in this athletic contest of strength include not only men who are bigger, tougher, and stronger, but eventually the natural universe itself. Harry miraculously triumphs over an awesome cyclone that levels an entire town but turns around and goes away when Baby Harry hurls a few pebbles at it. In *The Strong Man* (1926) Harry is a weight lifter's assistant who is unexpectedly forced to substitute for his boss. He miraculously manages to subdue a whole gang of bootleggers in the course of his act, ridding a small town of the nasty mobsters who have usurped it

The babyish Harry Langdon flirts with the vamp (Alma Bennett) in Long Pants

(more Capra). Harry's small-town girlfriend in this film, Mary Brown, is blind, a figure as physically helpless and spiritually pure as little Harry himself (and a possible influence on Chaplin, who used a blind girl in *City Lights*). At the end of *The Strong Man* the couple of meeklings inherit the earth. But in *Long Pants* (1927) Harry is unhappy with the purity and innocence of small-town life. He deserts the small-town gal and runs off to the "Big City," in pursuit of an exotic "Bad Woman" who refueled her car in his small town and fueled his romantic dreams. After a series of scrapes with criminals, thieves, and the police, Harry discovers that the apparent Lady of his Dreams is no lady, and he hurries back to his small-town family and sweetheart, a sadder and wiser child.

Although Harry Langdon lacked the comic range and physical gifts of the other silent clowns, his comic style revealed how restrained, how subtle, how slow, how unphysical a silent, physical comedian could be. His films were constructed so that a tiny smile, a blink of the eyes, the wave of a hand, or even, as James Agee observed, a twitch of the muscles at the back of the neck were as significant as a whole sequence of Lloyd's spectacular slips and falls on top of a skyscraper.

Of the new comics, only Buster Keaton could rival Chaplin in his insight into human relationships, into the conflict between the individual man and the immense social machinery that surrounds him; only Keaton could rival Chaplin in making his insight both funny and serious at the same time. On the one hand, the Keaton canon as a whole is thinner, less consistent than the Chaplin canon. The character Keaton fashioned—with his deadpan, blank reaction to the chaos that inevitably and inadvertently blooms around him—lacks the range, the compassionate yearnings, the pitiable disappointments of Chaplin's tramp. On the other hand, Keaton made a single film, *The General* (1926), that is possibly more even, more unified, and more complex in both conception and execution than any individual Chaplin film.

The key difference between Keaton and Chaplin is that Charlie longs to better himself, to accomplish grand things, whereas Keaton merely desires to go about his business. If he fails to reach his modest goal it is not because of his own incompetence or ineptitude but because of the staggeringly huge obstacles the environment throws in his path. Objects inevitably play a role in Keaton films, but unlike the objects in a Chaplin film—which are small and manageable and which Charlie can hold in his hand, or lie in, or sit on—the objects in a Keaton film are immense machines that dwarf the little man. Keaton plays against huge things: an ocean liner he must navigate by himself, a locomotive, a steamboat, a hurricane, a herd of cattle. When he runs into trouble with men, it is never with a single figure (an Eric Campbell); he runs into rivers of antagonists, into armies of opponents: a whole tribe of jungle savages, the entire Union and Confederate armies. Like Charlie, Buster has his troubles with cops, but never with one or just a few cops; in *Cops* (1922), in *Daydreams* (1922), Buster runs into the entire police force. Given the size and complexity of his problems, Buster can take no sensible or meaningful action, despite his most sensible efforts. The perfect metaphor for the Keaton man is in the short film, *Daydreams*, in which Buster, to avoid the police force, takes refuge in the paddle wheel of a ferryboat. The wheel begins turning; Buster begins walking. And walking. And walking. He behaves as sensibly as a man can on a treadmill that he cannot control, but how sensible can life on a treadmill ever be?

Chaplin and Keaton are the two poles of silent comics. Chaplin's great strength is his development of character and the exhausting of a particular comic and social situation; Keaton's strength is the tightness of his narrative structures and his contrast between the numbers one and infinity. Chaplin is sentimental; his gentle smiling women become idols to be revered. Keaton is not sentimental; he stuffs his females into bags and hauls them around like sacks of potatoes; he satirizes their finicky incompetence and even raises his fist to the silly lady in *The General* who feeds their racing locomotive only the teensiest shavings of wood. It was especially appropriate and touching to see the two opposites, Chaplin and Keaton, united in *Limelight* (1952), both playing great clowns who were losing their audiences and their touch. It may be no accident that one of the most significant literary works of our era, *Waiting for Godot,* was produced in the same year as *Limelight* and used the same metaphor of two old vaudeville tramps whose act (in *Godot* their act is their life) had become a bomb. If the Godot of Beckett's title suggests Charlot, it should also be remembered that Beckett wrote a film script especially for Buster Keaton, *Film.* The influence of the pair of comics continues to be felt.

No two films more clearly reveal the contrasting strengths and interests of the two clowns than *The Gold Rush* and *The General,* both of which were made at about the same time (1925-26). Like the short comedies, *The Gold Rush* is an episodic series of highly developed, individual situations. The mortar that keeps these bricks together is a mixture of the film's locale (the white, frozen wastes), the strivings and disappointments of Charlie, and the particular thematic view the film takes of those strivings (the quest for gold and for love, those two familiar goals, in an icy, cannibalistic jungle). All the Chaplin features, including those he made with synchronized sound, would share this common episodic structure. *The Gold Rush* also benefits from the circular pattern of the sequence of episodes: Prologue (the journey to Alaska), the Cabin, the Dance Hall, New Year's Eve, the Dance Hall, the Cabin, Epilogue (the journey home).

The individual sequences of *The Gold Rush* are rich both in Chaplin's comic ingenuity and his ability to render the pathos of the tramp's disappointment, his cruel rejection by the woman he loves. Several of the comic sequences have become justifiably famous. In the first cabin scene, a hungry Charlie cooks his shoe, carves it like a prime rib of beef, salts it to taste, and then eats it like a gourmet, twirling the shoelaces around his fork like spaghetti, sucking the nails in the soles like chicken bones, offering his friend one of the nails as a wishbone. This is the Chaplin who treats one kind of object (a shoe) as if it were another kind of object (a feast), the same minute observation he used in dissecting the clock in *The Pawnshop*. In the dance hall, Charlie hastily ties a rope around his middle to keep his sagging trousers up. He does not know that the other end of the rope is attached to a dog, who then trots around the dance floor following his dancing master. Charlie, however, must follow the leader when the dog takes off after a cat.

But the comic business is matched by the pathos that Charlie can generate, often out of the comic business itself. Charlie's saddest moment is when Georgia, the woman he loves, whose picture and flower he preserves beneath his pillow, callously stands him up on New Year's Eve. When Charlie realizes that it is midnight and she is not coming, he opens his door and listens to the happy townspeople singing "Auld Lang Syne," (an excellent translation of sound—a song—into purely visual terms). The film cuts back and forth between Charlie, the outsider, standing silently and alone in a doorway, and the throng of revelers in the dance hall, clasping hands in a large circle and singing exuberantly together (excellent use of Griffith cross-cutting here). But this pathetic moment would have been impossible without the previous comic one in which Charlie falls asleep and dreams he is entertaining Georgia with his "Oceana Roll." Charlie's joy, his naïve sincerity, his charm, his gentleness, all show on his face as he coyly makes the two rolls kick, step, and twirl over the table on the ends of two forks. The happiness of the comic dream sequence creates the pathos of the subsequently painful reality.

If the reality proves painful for Charlie, it is because the lust for gold makes it so. The film's theme is its consistent indictment of what the pursuit of the material does to the human animal; as in *Greed*, it makes one an inhuman animal. Charlie, the least materialistic of men, has come to the most materialistic of places—a place where life is hard, dangerous, brutal, uncomfortable, and unkind. Unlike the life of Nanook (might Chaplin have been influenced by Flaherty?), in which hardness becomes a virtue in itself, the men who have rushed for gold want to endure hardship only long enough to snatch up enough nuggets to go home and live easy. The quest for gold perverts all human relationships in the film. It creates a Black Larsen who casually murders and purposely fails to help his starving fellows. It creates a Jack, Georgia's handsome boyfriend, who treats his fellow men and women like furniture. Just as Charlie's genuine compassion reveals the emptiness of Jack's protestations of love, Chaplin's film technique makes an unsympathetic villain out of the conventional Hollywood leading man.

The rush toward gold perverts both love and friendship. Georgia herself, though Charlie perceives her inner beauty, has become hardened and callous from her strictly cash relationships with people in the isolated dance hall. And

The Gold Rush: *Charlie's forks dance the "Oceana Roll"*

Charlie's friend, Big Jim McKay, is one of those fair-weather friends whose feelings are the functions of expediency. When Big Jim gets hungry, he literally tries to eat Charlie; although Jim's seeing his buddy as a big chicken is comic, the implied cannibalism of the sequence is not. Later, Big Jim needs Charlie to direct him to his claim; once again Charlie becomes a friend because he is needed. But when Jim and Charlie get stuck in the cabin that teeters precariously on the edge of a cliff, the two men turn into dogs again, each trying to scramble out of the cabin by himself, stepping on the other to do so.

Whereas *The Gold Rush* combines a thematic unity with the episodic structure of exhausting the individual situations, the thematic coherency of *The General* is itself the product of the film's tight narrative unity. *The General* is the first, probably the greatest comic epic in film form. Like every comic epic, *The General* is the story of a journey, of the road (albeit a railroad). As in every comic epic, the protagonist suffers a series of hardships and dangerous adventures before achieving the rewards and comforts of returning home. As in every

comic epic, the protagonist's opponents are both men and nature (particularly those two natural enemies, fire and water). As in every comic epic, there is a comic insufficiency in the protagonist and a disparity between his powers and the task he is asked to accomplish; but like every protagonist in the comic epic, Buster triumphs despite his insufficiencies. Everything in the Chaplin film, every gag, every piece of business, every thematic contrast, is subordinate to the delineation of the lonely tramp's character and the qualities that make him both lonely and superior to the men who have betrayed their humanity to keep from being lonely. Everything in *The General*—every gag, every piece of business—is subordinate to the film's driving narrative, its story of Johnny Gray trying to save his three loves: his girl, his country, and, most important of all, his locomotive. *The Gold Rush* is a comedy of character, *The General* a comedy of narrative.

The great question posed by *The General* in the course of its narrative is how to perform heroic action in a universe that is not heroic. Buster, with his typical deadpan expression, merely tries to go about his business while the world around him goes mad. A metaphor for the feeling of the whole film is the shot in which Buster is so busy chopping wood to feed his engine that he fails to notice that the train is racing past row after row of blue uniforms marching in the opposite direction; he has inadvertently propelled himself behind the enemy's lines. Johnny Gray simply wants to run his train; unfortunately, the Union Army wants to steal the train and use it to destroy his fellow Confederates. In the course of merely trying to save the train, Johnny rescues his lady love and accidentally wins a terrific victory for the South.

That heroism occurs as an accident in *The General* is at the center of its moral thrust. It is an accident that the cannon,

The General: *Johnny (Buster Keaton) goes about his business while his train takes him behind the enemy's lines*

aimed squarely at Johnny, does not go off until the train rounds a curve, discharging its huge ball at the enemy instead of at the protagonist. It is an accident that Buster's train comes to a rail switch just in time to detour the pursuing Union train. Just as wealth, material success, is accidental in *The Gold Rush* (and an accident not worth waiting for), heroism and successful military strategy are accidental in *The General*. And just as Charlie's character exposes the folly of the accidents of wealth, Buster's character exposes the folly of the accidents of heroism. For how less heroic, how less aspiring, less grand can a man be than little Buster? Buster merely uses his shrewd common sense against impossible odds, and he is lucky to get away with it.

The denigration of the heroic is as constant an element of *The General's* narrative as the denigration of gold is in the sequences of *The Gold Rush*. The plot is triggered by Johnny Gray's rejection by the Confederate Army. He fears he has been found wanting, but the Confederacy needs him vitally at home, running his locomotive. Nevertheless, his girl and her family ostracize Johnny as an unheroic coward, a shirker, and the rest of the film demonstrates what heroism really is and what it is really worth. Johnny uses the most pragmatic, least heroic of tools for defeating the northern army: boxes of freight, pieces of wood from a fence, the locomotive's kerosene lantern. Hardheadedness, not gallantry, wins the day.

The gallant and romantic are explicitly burlesqued in the film's final sequence, the battle in which victory results from a combination of stupidity and chance. The northern general, certain that the bridge Johnny earlier set afire is still strong enough to support his supply train, orders it across. The general is wrong; the train and bridge topple magnificently into the river below. In the pitch of battle, Johnny sees the Confederate standard about to fall to the ground. He hastily climbs to what he thinks is a hilltop in a gallant gesture to support the falling flag (a parody of Griffith?), only to discover the embarrassment of feeling the hilltop move. The hilltop is really a disgruntled soldier's back. When the northern officer surrenders to the South according to all the articles and procedures of war—the sequence uses all the formal rigamarole of military honor—Johnny Gray accidentally fires his pistol, disrupting the dignified formality of the ceremony.

Even the film's ending burlesques the conventions of heroism, war, and romance: Johnny wraps his arms around his girl for the final clinch; since he is now an officer, all soldiers must salute him and he must salute in return. In the midst of his embrace, the entire battalion troops past him. After interrupting his embrace for a while, he, in his pragmatic manner, devises a better method. He continues saluting perfunctorily and mechanically, never taking his lips or his eyes away from hers.

Such antiheroism is common to all the Keaton films; he is always the sensible little guy who inadvertently runs up against senseless objects that dwarf him. The thing that distinguishes *The General* is that the senseless object, the huge infernal machine of this film, is war. Men themselves have been transformed into a

---

The pragmatist turns obstacles into tools

machine (an army), and the business of this machine is murder and destruction. This antiheroic comic epic must necessarily become an antiwar story, too, for the military heroism consistently debunked by *The General* is the Circe that turns men into murdering and destructive swine. Buster is never hypnotized, and his film makes sure we keep our eyes open, too. There is absolutely nothing sentimental in the world of *The General*. As soon as Johnny Gray gets a bit sad, Keaton immediately slams him with a joke to rip the pathos off him.

The film is as shrewd, as caustic, as hard-edged as Johnny Gray himself. His girl, a typical figure of sentiment and romance (her name is Annabelle Lee!), is degraded into an incompetent and feeble representative of romantic notions; Johnny Gray ultimately must fight her as well as the pursuing army. There is no place in the world of *The General* for sentiment, for the same reason that there is no place for heroism. Romance and heroism are twins, and *The General* wages war on both. Unlike the Chaplin films, there are no flowers, no roses, in *The General*. As soon as you admit a rose, you must also admit a gun to fight for it.

True, the character Buster plays, Johnny Gray, is a southerner, a seemingly romantic choice. But Buster chose to play a rebel because the South lost the war, because the South was romantically blind about fighting the war, and because the South—like Buster—was the little-guy underdog. Though Johnny plays a southerner, the film is impartial; ultimately Johnny must sneak his train (even its name is a military one) past both the Union and the Confederate lines. Despite the film's comic conclusion and inventive gags, *The General*, with its mixture of burlesque and grimness (many men die in this film), is the spiritual ancestor of that more recent mixture of laughs and war horrors, *Doctor Strangelove*.

The ultimate proof of the power of *The Gold Rush* and *The General* is that they need not be referred to as great silent films; they are merely great films. They require no qualification of any kind, unlike even Griffith's greatest work. For both of them, silence was not a limitation but a virtue. It is inconceivable that the two films could have been any better with sound; in fact, by removing our complete concentration on the visual they could only have been worse.

The power of the Chaplin film comes from the expressiveness of his panto-mime. Mime is mute. To reveal the significant gestures and facial flickers, Chaplin, as is his wont, uses the range of shots from full to close. Only expository shots—the opening shots of the men treking north, the establishing shots of the dance hall, et cetera—pull away from the characters. Chaplin's unobtrusive editing consistently allows the pantomime to play itself out without a cut—for example, in the roll dance.

The power of the Keaton film comes from the contrast between his simple efforts and the immense problems surrounding him. Keaton, the character, is as tight-lipped as he is expressionless. His character is essentially mute. His blank stare says everything that can be said about the chaos he sees. To reveal the contrast of man and chaos, Keaton, as is his wont, uses the range of shots between full and extreme long. His camera works further away from the characters than Chaplin's, consistently comparing them with their surroundings. His cutting is slightly quicker than Chaplin's—to increase the pace and to reveal the different perspectives of man and environment—but never so quick or obtrusive as to make the stunts seem faked.

With such control of physical business, of thematic consistency, of appropriate structure, of placement of the camera, and of functional editing, neither *The Gold Rush* nor *The General* requires speech to speak.

7 The German Golden Age

In the final year of World War I, the German government wondered if its preferring bullets to pictures had not been a tactical error. Whatever the results of the battles at the front, the German nation and German character were losing terribly on the screens of the world. In the early years of the war, the American film, mirroring the nation's neutrality, did not take a consistent side in its view of the conflict in Europe. Some American films expressly advocated neutrality; others, like *Civilization* and *Intolerance,* preached pacifism. But as America itself prepared to enter the war, its films began to prepare it to prepare. In 1916, Vitagraph's J. Stuart Blackton made *The Battle Cry of Peace,* the first of a series of films urging "defenseless America" to defend itself. Blackton was continuing his tradition of making patriotic war films some twenty years after *Tearing Down the Spanish Flag.* The American war films predictably painted the enemy as a villainous, vicious Hun; the evil, sinister, outwardly polished and inwardly corrupt Erich von Stroheim was the perfect stereotype of this newest movie bad guy.

There was no screen antidote to this single stereotypic portrait. The German government decided to produce one. In November 1917, the government collected the tiny, chaotic fragments of the German film industry together into a single, large filmmaking unit, Universum Film A.G., known subsequently to the world as U.F.A. Ufa's job was to make movies that would boost the German spirit at home and sell the German character and position abroad. The war ended before Ufa could accomplish either goal; but the huge movie company, with its studios at Neubabelsberg near Berlin, was still standing after the armistice had been signed. The great era of German films was born in those studios.

The German Golden Age of film was a very short one, from the making of *The Cabinet of Doctor Caligari* (1919) to Hitler's absorption of the German film industry in 1933. The great burst of artistic activity that followed the fall of the Kaiser and the founding of the Weimar Republic, the new spirit of intellectual and creative freedom in Germany, made itself felt in all the arts (in the pictorial and plastic arts, the founding of the Bauhaus group by Kandinsky and Klee; in the theatre, the plays of Brecht and the staging of Erwin Piscator), but especially in the cinema. The great German contribution in these years of intellectual freedom and artistic innovation was, as almost all post-Griffith cinematic innovations have been, merely a refinement of one of the potentialities of the medium that Griffith had discovered. If Griffith's two great accomplishments were his realization of the power of atmosphere and texture within a shot and the power of editing to join shots, it was the genius of the German film to refine and develop the former (the Soviet film developed the latter). The German film, in an era of silence, made the aura, the mood, the tone of the shot's visual qualities speak. It made them speak so well that the best German films of the era contain the barest minimum of subtitles, or none at all.

Further, the German filmmakers realized that the emotional tensions and sensations in a film need not be performed solely for a passive, objective camera. The camera—rather than taking the stance of a distant, impartial observer—could itself mirror the subjective feelings of a single character experiencing an event. To use an analogy with the novel, the German filmmaker realized that the camera, like the pen, could narrate a story in the first person as well as the third. Griffith used an occasional flight into subjectivity—his flashbacks to reveal a character's thoughts, the tracking camera galloping with the horses to the rescue—but Griffith's subjective moments were always in brackets. He used specific conventions to inform the audience that it was entering the personal experience of a single character. The subjectivity in the German film is never set off in brackets; the boundary between subjective and objective perceptions becomes as blurry in the films as it is in our own post-Pirandellian lives.

The dependence of the German film on the evocations of its visual elements led to its becoming completely a studio product. The only way to make sure that the lighting, the decor, the architectural shapes, the relationships of blacks, whites, and grays were perfect was to film in a completely controlled environment. Even outdoor scenes were shot inside the four walls and ceiling of a studio. The vastness, the freedom of the outdoors that had become one of the sources of power of both the American and Swedish film was rejected by the Germans. The result was not only a perfect control of style and decor but also a feeling of claustrophobia that enhanced the mood of many of the best films, which were also claustrophobic in their content. The totally studio-produced films emphasized the importance of the designer, whose job was to conceive and decorate enormous indoor cities. These designers came to films from painting and, especially, from architecture, having absorbed the styles of many of the new artistic movements of postwar Europe: expressionism, cubism, constructivism, other forms of abstraction. The German film could never have exerted its influence without its talented painter-architect designers, the most notable of whom were Hermann Warm, Walther Röhrig, Walther Reimann, Robert Herlth, Albin Grau, and Ërno Metzner.

The emphasis on the studio production and the consolidation of talent in a single studio produced a studio system very different from Hollywood's. Unlike the competing factories of Hollywood, the German studio was far more a combination of artists working with each other because they were devoted to their product rather than to receipts. Although there were competitors with Ufa in the twenties, many of them worked so closely with the major producer that merger was inevitable (Decla-Bioscop, for example). Ufa's great producer, Erich Pommer, was a man of artistic judgment and taste who stimulated mediocre directors to do their very best work (E. A. Dupont's *Variety,*

1925, for example) rather than the reverse. Rather than building a star system, the German studio developed a repertory company, emphasizing the play and not the player, the character and not the personality. The German film actor needed variety and range, not a single trait to be milked over and over again. The greatest of the German repertory actors were Emil Jannings, Werner Krauss, Conrad Veidt, Fritz Körtner, Lil Dagover, Asta Nielsen, Lya de Putti, Pola Negri, and Greta Garbo. Hollywood imported most of them and tried to turn them into stars; the attempt was inconsistently successful.

The German studio also gave a great deal of freedom to its cameramen; they were encouraged to develop new and revealing ways of looking at things. The Hollywood cameraman had become more and more tied to the most functional, most familiar way of recording a scene. Two German cameramen in particular, Fritz Arno Wagner and Karl Freund, used their freedom to show how much a camera could really do.

The German films of this great era were of two types: either fantastic and mystical or realistic and psychological. One was steeped in the traditional German romanticism of love and death, the other revealed the new German intellectual currents of Freud and Weber. In the film of fantasy, the action revolves around the occult, the mysterious, the metaphysical. These are films of fantastic monsters in human dress, of the kingdom beyond the grave, of dream kingdoms of the past and of the future. The German architect-painters could use their imaginations to turn these eerie, abstract, intangible regions into concrete, visual domains. In the realistic film, the action revolves around the inner thoughts and feelings of the characters, their needs, their lusts, their frustrations. Of the Americans, only von Stroheim, perhaps showing his Teutonic origins, made such internalized, sensation-centered films.

Unlike the fantasy films, which are inevitably set in some romantic time and place, the psychological films are set in a squalid and seamy middle-class present. The architect-painters could use their imaginations to turn the tawdry, dirty, depressing rooms, streets, and suburbs into complex and detailed studio slums.

Fantasy

The film that signaled the start of the new German era, *The Cabinet of Doctor Caligari,* appropriately combined both the mystical and the psychological. Although Ernst Lubitsch had been making his historical costume films since 1918, those witty, lavish entertainments were more relevant to his own personal career than to the eventual development of the great German films. Perhaps the one significant influence of the Lubitsch films was the respect and attention they commanded for the art of the designer. It was *Caligari* that set the German film mind in motion for the next decade.

Its central plot was a story of horror, of murder, of superhuman powers. An enigmatic and menacing hypnotist (Werner Krauss) opens a stall at a fair in the town of Holstenwall; his act demonstrates his mastery over another human being whom he has hypnotized, Cesare (Conrad Veidt). Mysteriously a rash of murders breaks out in the town. The police have no clues. The film's protagonist, Francis, suspects the hypnotist, shadows him, and eventually discovers that he forces his slave, Cesare, to murder the innocent victims while the hypnotist substitutes a wax image of Cesare in the coffin-like box to fool the police. Francis continues to follow the murderous master who, it turns out, is also the director of the state insane asylum. The keeper of the insane is himself an insane murderer, a monster who has discovered the medieval formula of Caligari for subduing men's minds.

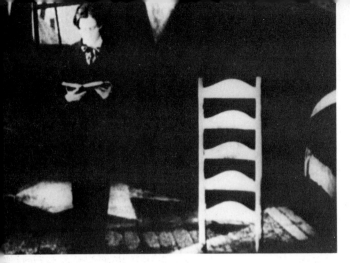

The Cabinet of Doctor Caligari. *A madman's vision of the world: impossibly shaped windows, exaggeratedly high furniture, and geometric shadows*

Francis exposes the monster; the monster goes mad. The orderlies stuff Caligari into a strait jacket and lock the door of his cell. This is as far as the central plot of *Caligari* goes. It is also as far as its writers, Carl Mayer (who would become the most influential of the German scenarists) and Hans Janowitz, wanted it to go.

But *Caligari* goes further. The entire central plot has a frame. The film begins with Francis informing a listener (and us) that he has a most horrifying tale to tell. To set a horrific, supernatural tale within a frame is, of course, a traditional literary device (for example, Henry James's *The Turn of the Screw*), the means to anchor a fantastic story in reality and thereby increase our credulity. The setting of this opening, framing sequence seems like a park—there are trees, vines, a wall, benches. But there is something vaguely disturbing about it: it is too bare, too cold; the girl who walks past seems somnambulistic, ethereal. Only at the end of the film do we discover that the setting for the entire tale is not a park but an insane asylum, that Francis himself is a patient, that many of the characters in his tale are also patients, and that the

so-called Caligari is the director of the asylum. And it is not Caligari who winds up in a cell with a strait jacket but Francis, whose feverish accusations about the director have necessitated his confinement. The surprise at the end of the film is our discovery that the tale we assumed to be one of horror and of superhuman powers is really the product of the imagination of a subhuman brain, a paranoid's fantasy, a madman's hatred of his doctor.

Our discovery of the disease in the narrator's brain suddenly illuminates the principle of the film's decor. Throughout the film the expressionist-cubist world of the horror tale has been striking: the grotesque painted shadows on streets and stairs; the irregular, nonperpendicular chimneys, doors, and windows; the exaggerated heights of the furniture; the two-dimensional, painted rooms; the painted skin and wrinkles of the characters' faces. The grotesque world is not simply a decorative stunt; it is a precise translation of the way Francis, the madman, sees the world. The world of the film is the product of Francis's subjective vision, not of the director's objective one. Robert Wiene, *Caligari*'s director, has intentionally used the decor of the film in a perpetual war against nature.

The striking effect of the film's design (by Warm, Röhrig, and Reimann) is not just the look but the unnatural feel of it. Walls, floors, and ceilings bear a structurally impossible relationship to one another; buildings so constructed could never stand. Skin, that soft and malleable material of nature, becomes caked and frozen with paint. Windows are painted in gnarled and impossible shapes. And most unnatural of all, the world of *Caligari* is a world without sunlight. Shadows of light and dark, shafts where the sun would normally cast its shadow, have been painted on the sets. To use paint to make a shadow where the sun would normally make one emphasizes the fact that no sun

exists. The outdoor scenes feel as if they were shot indoors. And they were. Here was the perfect use of the total studio film. The deliberate unnaturalness of the film is so striking that it is difficult to tell if the acting is intentionally or unintentionally stilted. It is simply appropriate.

The interest in *The Cabinet of Doctor Caligari* is not only in the way the film looks but in the ambiguities that the film-within-a-film generates. Wiene's structure clearly reveals that *Caligari* is no simple horror story. The film is no simple tale told by an idiot either. True, Francis is mad; he has clearly leaped the gulf between control and lack of it. But what pushed him over it? How did he manufacture this particular story and in such detail? Is there no truth at all in his story of the Holstenwall murders? And if the kindly doctor is really not the demented Caligari, why does he look like Caligari when he puts on his glasses? And why does the asylum look no more natural in the frame of the film (supposedly an objective point of view) than it did in Francis's narration? And what is the relevance of the film's clear antagonism to bureaucracy? Wiene ridicules the police and the authorities with their ridiculously high, skinny desks and their red-tape insistence that the hypnotist obtain a permit to perform at the fair—a permit, essentially, to murder. The insane asylum that the doctor heads is yet another bureaucratic enterprise with its procedures, methods, and assistants. Is one bureaucratic institution better than another? Are the assumptions and definitions of one superior to those of the other?

Unfortunately for the critic, *The Cabinet of Doctor Caligari* raises these questions without answering them. Perhaps there are no answers. Perhaps the film's ambiguities stem from the unintentional carelessness of the director with a few details or the conflict between the writers, who conceived one kind of story, and the director, who filmed another. Whatever the underlying reason, the ambiguities of *Caligari* seem to enrich it. How can a world as askew and ajumble as this one give us clear and unambiguous answers?

Perhaps no major work in film history has attracted as many theoretical sticks and stones as *The Cabinet of Caligari*. The major film theorists—André Bazin, Erwin Panofsky, Siegfried Kracauer—are unanimous in believing that the film is a cinematic mistake, that it "prestylizes reality," that it violates the inherent photographic realism of the medium, that it substitutes a world of painted artifice for the rich resources of nature. Despite these later arguments, the film had an immense influence on other filmmakers, not only in Germany but in France, where "Caligarism," though detested by some, inspired many of the early avant-garde experiments in abstract cinema, in film as "painting-in-motion" rather than as realistic narrative of natural events in natural settings. And despite the arguments of the theorists, *The Cabinet of Doctor Caligari* has been capable of intriguing and fascinating audiences, of weaving its mysterious, hypnotic spell, for over sixty years.

Of the mystical children of *Caligari*, Fritz Lang's *Destiny* (1922) is the most interesting. Lang, in collaboration with his author-wife, Thea von Harbou, is more famous for a series of psychological studies of the activities of gamblers, murderers, and spies (*Doctor Mabuse, Spies, M*). But he also made several metaphysical-fantasy films. In *Destiny*, a young girl and her lover enter a new town; on the road they encounter a dark, shadowy, spectral stranger. The stranger has bought a piece of land near the town's cemetery and has enclosed it with an immense stone wall that lacks a door or any other physical means of entering. The girl's lover disappears; when she discovers that he is a prisoner beyond the wall she frenziedly starts to drink a poisonous drug. Lang immediately cuts to the huge wall where she sees the transparent, spectral images of souls entering the region beyond the wall. The means to enter the wall is metaphysical, not physical.

The wall surrounds the kingdom of death; the mysterious stranger is Death himself, and a tired, sad Death he is, superintending the candles of human life that inevitably flicker out. The girl pleads for the life of her lover; Death tiredly offers her a chance to save him, pointing out three candles whose lights have begun to flicker. The girl claims that love can conquer death, and she sets off to save at least one of the three lights. Each of these "lights" is a story in a far-off land: a middle-eastern Moslem city, Renaissance Venice, and a magical China. In all three, the girl and her lover are reincarnated as two young lovers whose monarchs have declared war on their love. In all three reincarnations, the young man dies; the girl's love does not conquer death. After her failure, Death gives the girl one more chance; she can return to life and redeem her lover's being if she can offer another life in trade. She soon runs into a burning hospital to save an infant trapped there. Death meets her inside and asks her for the child as the pawn. She considers and then refuses; she will not kill the infant to save her lover. Instead, the girl herself dies in the fire; her soul and her lover's are thereby reunited as their transparent images climb a hill and stand against the sky. Love, in dying, has, ironically, conquered death.

The power of the film lies in its combination of the pictorial sense of the director and the magnificent visual creations of the designers (Warm, Röhrig, Herlth). The huge, gray wall of Death dwarfs the little, black-clad human figures who stand in front of it; its horizontal and vertical lines run off the frame at top, right, and left—the perfect visual metaphor for the infiniteness and inaccessibility of fate. Death's cave of the candles—a dark, hazy (a special distortion-lens effect), smoky den, punctuated by a numberless collection of thin, white candles with bouncing, waving flames—is an equally perfect visual metaphor for the fragility of human life, the irreversible direction of its progress, and the inexorable control of fate over that progress. Equally memorable is the care taken in creating each of the fantastic kingdoms for the stories of the three lights: the minarets and mosaics of the Arabian city; the canals, the flights of steps, the arched bridges streaming with revelers of the Venice sequence; the flying horse, the flying carpet, the tiny army that emerges from beneath the magician's legs of the China sequence. Lang uses the trick effects of the camera as well as the atmospheric architecture of the designers: superimposition (to depict the souls of the dead), dissolve (to show a dead infant suddenly materializing in Death's arms), vertical masking (to emphasize the height and narrowness of arches and steps), Méliès-style stop-action (to metamorphose a man into a cactus or a pig).

The gimmickiness of the film may make it seem as superficial and banal an exercise as De Mille's *Male and Female* or Fairbanks's *The Thief of Bagdad,* with which it has obvious affinities. Like the DeMille film, *Destiny* uses multiple locales and hence is enhanced by the splash of multiple sets, costumes, and customs. Like the Fairbanks film, it presents the spectator with an entertaining series of surprising cinematic tricks. The Lang film, however, keeps its artistic seriousness because of the unity and consistency of its theme (the war of love and death), because of the clear purpose of its structure (a film descendant of the medieval romance in which the protagonist must face the challenge of a series of tests), and because of the fatalism and melancholy of its tone. If the film resembles DeMille or Fairbanks, it

Destiny. *The Cave of the Candles: thin, fragile white shafts as metaphors for human life (Lil Dagover and Bernhard Götzke)*

also has unmistakable affinities with the work of the later film metaphysician, Ingmar Bergman. The opening scene in the forest in which the coach stops for the stranger feels like the opening sections of both *The Magician* and *The Seventh Seal.* Bergman's coach and forest at the beginning of *The Magician* reveal the same eerie tone as Lang's; the awesome, black-cloaked figures of Death in *Destiny* and *The Seventh Seal* are cousins. And the two directors photograph them the same way: in shadow, as silhouettes against the sky, back-lit so that the faces are only discernible in close-ups. In its mysticism, in its romantic struggle of love and death, which ends in a romantic truce (both triumph), *Destiny* is more than a surface picture of visual splash.

The same cannot be said of a later Lang film of a similar type, *Metropolis* (1926). Although *Metropolis* is a fantasy of the future and technology rather than a fantasy of the past and romance, like

Metropolis: *human beings reduced to disspirited masses of architecture*

Destiny it uses a never-never-land setting to demonstrate an abstract theme. Unfortunately, *Metropolis* is all eyes and no brain, all visual with no convincing vision. The film depicts a world of the future where the rich and intelligent live on the earth's surface with their airplanes and trams and skyscrapers, and the workers—who make the society go—live beneath the surface in dark, imprisoning caverns. Here was Lang's visual translation of the class structure. The banker's son, a young rebel, rejects his father's upper world and goes to live and struggle with the workers of the underworld. There he meets the spirit of the workers—Maria, a proletarian version of the Virgin Mary and Christ all in one—who urges peaceful change and passive progress. Maria is a Christian-Democrat-Humanist (literally Christian since she delivers her political sermons in a white, candle-lit cave full of crosses) who formulates the film's political argument: the heart must mediate between head and hands.

The young hero's banker father will have none of this. He hires the evil scientist, Rotwang, to manufacture a violent, vicious robot who looks exactly like Maria and who will incite the workers to riot; the father's troops can then use the riot to enslave the workers. The workers riot, flood the city, and almost destroy the whole society, until the real Maria appears to tranquilize them with her abstract words of political love. The banker learns his lesson, and his son, appropriately, is designated as the society's official "heart" to mediate between head (his daddy) and hands (he shakes hands with the foreman of the workers).

The film demonstrates the dangers of the purely architectural-pictorial premise of the German studio film. *Metropolis* is a series of stunning pictures with the silliest, wateriest intellectual and dramatic paste holding them together. Lang's primary compositional device was to create

geometrical patterns of men and machines: configurations of row upon row of black-clad workers against the white walls at Maria's political prayer meeting; the geometrical machines and the geometrical patterns of workers who serve them; the circle of workers around the warning gong as the water seeps into the lower city; the fleeing workers in the flooded streets, a river of rushing human bodies that parallels the river of rushing water engulfing their homes. The film resembles nothing so much as a kaleido- scope, a shifting series of interesting visual patterns, from its opening montage of whirring machines to its final triangular configuration of head, heart, and hands.

The emptiness of the film, however, lies in this kaleidoscopic premise. To reduce people to patterns—to units of geometrical architecture—is to convert them from the living into the dead. The whole film is lifeless, inanimate; even the principal players are dead abstractions. The acting in the film is abominable— overstated, inhuman, unconvincing. A further failing of the film is the reduction of complex political con- cepts to romantic drivel. The political opposition—head versus hands—with its facile solution is as theoretically silly as it is blatantly overstated. The political conflict in the film has been drained of vitality as much as the human conflict.

The implications of *Metropolis,* however, did not pass unnoticed in its time. It was one of Hitler's favorite films, and after he had seized control of the government he invited Lang, a leftist and half Jew, to make films for the Nazis. That Lang diminished men into wooden puppets and political problems into romantic abstractions exactly suited Hitler's hypnotic purposes. Perhaps the film's romanticized stupidities and unconscious (or is it conscious?) fascism was more the responsibility of Thea von Harbou, who remained in Germany to join the Nazis after her husband fled. Lang, trained as

The triumph of Metropolis: *human beings become architecture again in the Nazi celebration film,* Triumph of the Will

beneficence of the ruler above. The film sees the benign despot as the only means of shepherding a human race of plodding sheep.

Despite the fascistic implications of the action and *mise-en-scène, Metropolis* is a clever forerunner of many later developments in the American film. Its progeny include, of course, all the science fiction films about the world of the future; several sequences seem to have leaped directly into *Flash Gordon,* particularly the conflict between the blond, Buster-Crabbelike hero (Gustav Fröhlich) and the evil, Emperor-Minglike magician (Rudolf Klein-Rogge). The whirring machines, sparking Jacob's ladders, and bubbling retorts that bring the robot alive in Rotwang's laboratory are the progenitors of all the similar apparatus that transfers the juices of life into the monster in the laboratory of Doctor Frankenstein. As would become typical of future Hollywood films, science is indistinguishable from magic. Rotwang himself leads directly to yet another evil colleague, Doctor Strangelove, who—forty years later—wears Rotwang's black glove to cover permanently the remains of one hand, undoubtedly sizzled or gnarled in the course of one of their hellish experiments. If Lang had stuck to such imaginative details rather than decorating them with intellectual bombast (Lang's decorative version of the *Niebelungen,* 1924, suffers from the same pretentiousness), he might have duplicated the success of his madman, crook, and spy films, which are understandably more popular today.

Of the other films of fantasy and the supernatural, Paul Leni's *Waxworks* (1924) combined the setting of *Caligari* (a fairground "cabinet") with the structure of *Destiny* (three separate stories—of Haroun Al-Raschid, Ivan the Terrible, and Jack the Ripper—in three bizarre and decorative locales). Paul Wegener's and Henrik Galeen's *The Golem* (1920, but previously made by the pair in 1914)—the

an architect, may have decided to tend to the film's pictorial architecture, leaving his scenarist wife to tend to the ideas. What is most fascistic about *Metropolis* is its portrayal of the general lot of human beings as a mass of undistinguished and undistinguishable ciphers, incapable of thought, growth, or development, lacking the mental energy to look after themselves, totally dependent on the

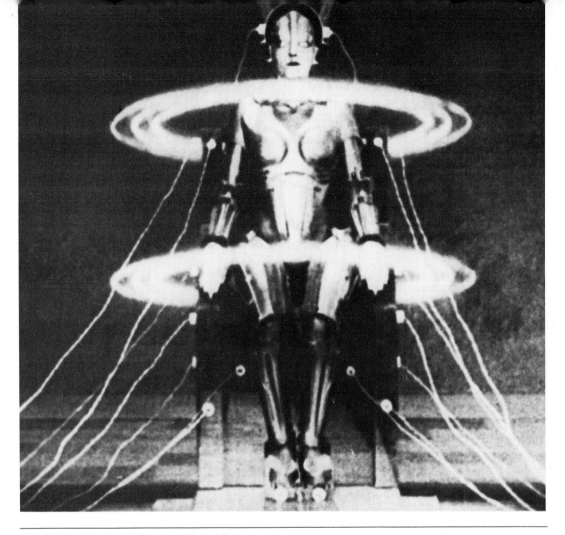

Science as magic: bringing the robot to life

story of a magician-Rabbi who brings a clay statue to life to protect the Jews in the Ghetto—is significant for the twisted architecture of its settings (designed by Hans Poelzig) and the fiery, demonic special effects in the scene when Rabbi Loew brings the man of clay to life (more clear evocations of the later Frankenstein *genre,* including the monster's attraction to an innocent playing child). Their second version of *The Student of Prague* (1926, previously made by Stellan Rye in 1913) is the mythical story of the *Doppelgäinger,* the man who sells his shadow only to effect a divorce between his internal and

external selves. Arthur Robison's *Warning Shadows* (1922) is interesting for its complex and consistent use of the visual effects of shadows: as an element of the film's action; as the profession of one of the main characters, who, like a filmmaker, entertains audiences with shadow plays; as a means of creating a mysterious mood and mystical atmosphere; and as one of the film's key metaphoric motifs.

Perhaps the most noteworthy of the purely horrific descendants of *Caligari* was F. W. Murnau's *Nosferatu* (1922), the first in a long series of movie versions of

Bram Stoker's Dracula story. This film, Murnau's first major success, was distinguished in the aura of horror and gloom with which it surrounded the vampire's neck-piercing activities. Unlike the later incarnations of Dracula—Bela Lugosi, Christopher Lee, and Frank Langella—Murnau's vampire (Max Schreck) was no sexy, suave, debonair figure who stole the lady's heart before he stole her blood. Murnau's vampire was hideously ugly—a shriveled, ashen little man with pointed nose, pointed ears, and pointed head. This ugliness made the sexual implications of the vampire's relationship to humans—particularly the use of a man's bedroom for the primary setting of the nighttime bloodsucking—even more horrifying.

Unlike later Dracula films, in *Nosferatu* the vampire's victim did not die with the first kiss of the count's teeth. The victim remained alive, growing steadily weaker with each successive loss of life-juice to the vampire. The longer relationship of the vampire with each victim gives *Nosferatu* a feeling of mystical parasitism,

of the way that death perpetually feeds off the living. Also memorable are the shots that evoke the deadly emanations of the vampire: the rats scurrying in the streets; the phantom ship sailing by itself with no humans to sail it; the tricky use of negative film and single-frame exposure to depict the gulf between the natural world and the supernatural world of the vampire's castle; the bare, stony walls of the castle itself. Unlike many German films of the period, Murnau deliberately shot these sequences outdoors, in nature, to contrast with the shadowy indoor sequences inside the castle. He rejected the typical studio-sculpted forests and hillocks to reveal the conflict of nature and artifice in the narrative, to emphasize that the existence of this vampire in the world was a subversion of the natural order itself.

Significantly, the underlying theme of *Nosferatu* is the same as *Destiny*'s: the conflict of love and death. The film's heroine consciously seduces the deadly menace, who is attracted to her beauty (more sexual imagery; she can conquer his perverted sexual powers only with the natural sexual powers she possesses). She keeps him out of his coffin until after the sun rises, and he dissolves into the morning air. Just as Cesare could not kill the beautiful Jane in *Caligari*, the vampire cannot kill beauty in *Nosferatu*. Love is the strongest power in the mystical German film.

Realism

F. W. Murnau's *The Last Laugh* (1924) is the most influential of the realistic sons of *Caligari*, and is probably the most even and most satisfying film of the whole German era. *The Last Laugh* teamed the greatest talents of the German film: director, Murnau; producer, Erich Pommer; writer, Carl Mayer; photographer, Karl Freund; designers, Röhrig and Herlth; and central figure, Emil Jannings. The plot is as simple as the plots of the mystical-fantasy films were complex; its emotions are as personal, as human, and as carefully motivated as the concepts of the metaphysical films were abstract.

A porter at a posh hotel (Emil Jannings) bases his self-respect and centers his being on his belief in the importance of his job, which is symbolized by his passionate devotion to his ornate porter's uniform. The uniform both defines his existence and is the only feature that impresses his less fortunate neighbors. Because he is old and feeble the porter is stripped of this uniform and given a new one; he now wears the white linen jacket of the lavatory attendant. The film then details the impact of this loss of dignity on his emotions and on his family and acquaintances. Rather than leaving the porter stooped in abject despair, the film "takes pity on him" and gives him a happy ending: a sudden inheritance of money that turns him into a kindly but gluttonous gobbler of caviar. The effect of this deliberately contrived ending will be discussed in a moment. Worthy of the fullest and most immediate attention in the film is the rendering of the steady degeneration of the porter's soul once he has lost the uniform that covers his body.

One of the film's great virtues is the performance of Jannings, his clear yet subtle portrayal of the two states of the porter's mind. Wearing his uniform Jannings walks quickly and erect; his gestures are smart and precise; his smile and buoyancy make him seem a very

The Last Laugh: *the porter (Emil Jannings) with his uniform and without it*

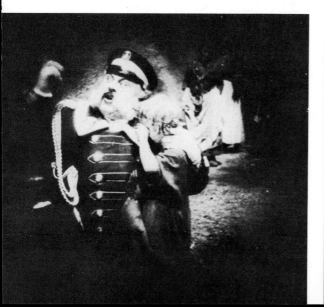

young man. His whole body exudes pride and self-esteem, as well as smugness and vanity. Without the coat he ages fifty years—his body stoops; his gestures are vague and languid; he barely moves at all—he becomes a hunched, old, broken man.

But Jannings does not need to do it alone. The director and cameraman have given him a new and useful ally—the camera itself. Freund's camera tracks and swings and tilts and twirls at key moments in the film. The key principle is not so much that the camera moves for the sake of visual variety, but that it has been freed from its tripod for the sake of illuminating the narrative and psychological content themselves. The camera actually serves as the emotional mirror of the old man's soul; its lens is his own pair of eyes. When the world becomes blurry or confusing or insufferable for him, the camera photographs the way the world feels to him, the way he responds to it. The real action in the film is not between Jannings and other characters (there are no other important characters in the film), but between the warring thoughts and feelings inside the porter's own head. The camera makes this internal warfare clear and becomes, in effect, the other major character with whom Jannings plays his scenes.

The power of the sweeping camera strikes the viewer in the film's first scene: the camera tracks down the elevator and through the bustling lobby of the Atlantic Hotel as if it were one of the guests there, continues through the revolving doors, and stands with the porter in the rain as he hails a cab. The sequence not only imparts excitement with its movement, but also establishes every crucial expository detail the film's action requires: the size and importance of the hotel, the conscientious devotion of the porter to his job, the indifference of the revolving door, which later becomes a metaphor for the circular, inhuman, insensitive relationship of a man to his vocation. The vocation remains; the individual man disappears. Further, the bustling excitement of the moving camera precisely mirrors the porter's own excitement about the significance of the hotel and his high position in it.

When the porter receives his dismissal notice from the manager, the camera shows us the letter and then blurs; the porter can no longer read the piece of paper. When the porter gets frenziedly drunk at his daughter's wedding party, the room starts whirling around madly; the spinning camera mirrors the porter's spinning head. In his drunken reverie, the whole world becomes blurred and distorted; the faces of the musicians look like faces in the distorting mirrors of a fun house; the revolving door of the hotel becomes distorted into an immensely high, narrow space that could crush and dwarf a man. And Murnau even translates sound into subjective visual effects by blurring the shots of the musicians' trumpets, implying that the porter can only hear them as a blur. Whereas the distortion and super-imposition in a film like *Destiny* reveal the supernatural and the immaterial, those same techniques in *The Last Laugh* reveal natural sensations and responses; the effect of a technique is defined by the narrative context of the whole film.

Compared with the externalized, narrative emphasis of Hollywood films, the emphasis on the internalized, emotional state of the character in *The Last Laugh* is striking. With the exception of Chaplin or von Stroheim, the Hollywood filmmakers consistently subordinated character development to telling a story. Even Griffith developed only those feeling states that were functional to the narrative sweep of the entire film. Another radical departure of *The Last Laugh* from the Hollywood films of the twenties was its avoidance of preaching, its depiction of a world of moral grays rather than blacks and whites. On the one hand, the film condemns the inhuman and insensitive social process that values the man's function rather than the man himself. The society (the callous hotel manager serves as its symbol) welcomes the rich in its posh hotels and posh dining rooms, it caters to the rich with a huge staff of personnel, and it sends the functionless members of that staff packing through the revolving door (as one man revolves out, another revolves in). The circle is truly vicious. On the other hand, our particular hotel porter is foppish and vain, egotistical and falsely self-satisfied. For a man to define his essence by a uniform is false and foolish.

On yet another side, the other members of the porter's own lower-middle-class world are themselves callous and petty, unsympathetic and inhumane. They are as vicious as the hotel manager is indifferent. They snigger behind the porter's back when the bent, broken man walks down the street and into his house. Even his own family turn their backs on him. These vicious, gossiping beings are totally unresponsive to the misery of their fellows; they have lost any sense of camaraderie, of compassion for the plight they all share. On still another side, the very social pressures to survive are partially responsible for their petty viciousness. And the porter, to some extent, deserves their unpitying torture, for his earlier attitude toward them, as he smugly paraded down the street in his uniform like a peacock, was as callous as their present one. The complexity of the film's moral system contributes to the feeling that it mirrors life rather than forms some simplistic paradigm for it. In its rendering of character and its relativity of values, *The Last Laugh* was not only a mature contrast with the escapist Hollywood product; it also set a kind of pattern that has, with exceptions of course, continued through the years: the Hollywood film has traditionally been the

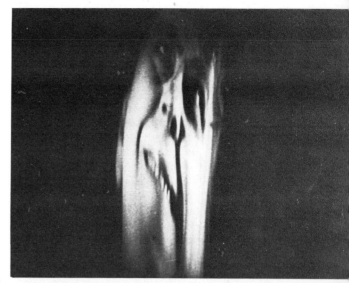

The subjective camera conveys the hung-over porter's view of his neighbor (Emilie Kurz) with the morning coffee

film of action and clear-cut values, the European film of character and moral ambiguities.

The one questionable note in the whole film is its ending: the porter's unexpected discovery of a pot of gold at the end of the rainbow. The contrivance of the legacy is emphasized by the fact that the film's only subtitle wrenches us out of the story and tells us that the rest of the film is chimera. Whereas the film had not previously required a single title to clarify the thoughts or feelings of its characters, it suddenly uses one to show that the filmmaker is sticking something on with narrative paste. The key question about the ending is, is it a deliberate contrivance (a parody of Hollywood's happy ending) or a deliberate attempt to emulate Hollywood and give us a happy ending? Perhaps it is a little of both.

Like the endings of both *Easy Street* and Brecht's *Threepenny Opera,* the artificiality of the film's conclusion is so obvious, the solution so facile, so inconsistent with the social realities that the film itself has defined, that our mind immediately sniffs parody and social comment. However, our hearts are also gladdened by the man's good fortune, particularly because he shares that fortune with the only human being in the film who showed compassion for his suffering—the night watchman. The porter's goodness showers on all those who really need it; he discovers the humanity, the compassion for his fellows that he lacked at the beginning of the film. He has no compassion, however, for those who turned their backs on him. He makes the hotel manager eat crow, and his own family is noticeably absent in his moment of good fortune. The ending satisfies our sense of poetic justice at the same time that it reveals the insufficiency of social justice. Alas for the real porters of the world—and all of us—poetic justice and social justice are incompatible.

If one kind of German realist film was the close examination of a single man's psyche, the other was a sociological examination of a whole political or social milieu. These films, which have since acquired the label, "street films," consistently use the word street in their titles: Karl Grune's *The Street* (1923), Bruno Rahn's *Tragedy of the Street* (1927).

They consistently use the unifying locale of the street as a means of tying together diverse kinds and classes of people and diverse kinds of human activities. In a sense, the street films can be seen as related to the street sections of *The Last Laugh* in which the porter walks between his home and the hotel—the many people he meets on the street, their attitudes, their aspirations, their successes and failures. The street becomes a microcosm of society as a whole.

Perhaps the most interesting of the street films is *The Joyless Street* (1925), the first important film of G. W. Pabst. Pabst's street runs through postwar Vienna, a city of striking contrasts, of rich and poor, of feast and starvation, of family traditions and whoring. The street of Pabst's film is the synthesis of Vienna's two faces: the ugly, starving reality and the courtesan's painted mask. On Pabst's street the poor wait doggedly and frustratedly in line in front of a butcher's shop, hoping that the brutal man will give them a shred of meat. In the same building as the butcher's shop is Mrs. Greifer's night club, a frivolous, gay, orgiastic late-night gathering spot for the rich, which also serves as a brothel. The film examines several lives on that street of contrasts where the women must inevitably choose between the poverty of standing in the slow line for the butcher's meat or the fast line to riches at Mrs. Greifer's (where the butcher is a steady customer). Two women take opposite paths. One (Asta Nielsen) sells her body and eventually commits murder; the other (Greta Garbo) holds out as long as she can and is rescued from selling herself at the last minute. Pabst's street is joyless because it is a dead end of prostitution and early death.

Pabst's realism typically combines a social theme with melodramatic action. Despite the artificiality and contrivance of the film's tubercular whore who murders one of her rivals, the real unity of the film lies in Pabst's consistent condemnation of the society that allows such poverty and such opulence to exist at the same time, that gives no choice to the poor except starvation or capitulation to the perverted values of the opulent. Pabst's innovative technique, befitting the objectivity and moral consciousness of the film, rejects the subjective use of the moving camera. Pabst's camera does move: it tracks down passageways, pans a line of starving faces, walks along a street with its dwellers. But the movement is less intended to mirror the inner feelings than it is to keep the film moving, exciting, vital.

Pabst's cutting, far more important in his films than it is in *Last Laugh* or *Variety,* also aims at cinematic fluidity rather than developing a character's sensations. Pabst's great refinement in cutting was to realize that the director can charge a scene with invisible energy by cutting in the middle of a character's motion. The moving hand or arm or leg, the rising body, the opening door all hide the camera's shift in distance and angle while propelling the eye into the next frame. The consistent cuts on movement in *The Joyless Street* keep the story, for all its overstatement, flowing. In an occasional sequence—for example, Pabst's rendering the frenetic emptiness of the night club with its tapping toes, clapping hands, bouncing knees, bobbing heads—his cutting alone produces energy and rhythm. The later Pabst film, *The Love of Jeanne Ney* (1927), another melodramatic love story played against a political backdrop, develops his principle of cutting on movement still further.

Pabst's cinematic sense and his political vision contributed to his making some of the best early sound films. Pabst brought the traditions of the German studio film into the sound era. His film version of Bertolt Brecht's *The Threepenny Opera* (1931), shows a mastery of the new sound medium. His camera tracks through the studio-built streets of a sleazy beggar's London, descends stairways, marches along with the army of the poor. Bertolt Brecht unsuccessfully sued Pabst for corrupting his play, for changing his antiromantic, anticonventional, deliberately contrived theatre-piece into a romantic, conventionally plotted, realistic movie. Despite Pabst's social views, which paralleled Brecht's, Brecht's condemnation of Pabst's more conventional melo-dramatic treatment—always a Pabst weakness—was quite valid. Pabst converts the story into a conventional boy-girl tale; Mackie meets Polly in the first scene and their lustful amour blooms. Brecht's play avoids showing how or why Mackie and Polly first meet; he has no interest in this kind of exposition and motivation. Pabst makes a twenty-minute scene of the business. Pabst's film milks the antics of the thieves, particularly their comic-clumsy attempts to steal a grandfather clock. It milks the pathos of the march of the poor (pathos is one of those emotions absent from the Brecht canon). It blurs the deliberate contrivance of Brecht's ending by supplying Mackie's release with a motivation: his wife, Polly, and his gang have themselves founded a bank, so Mackie is respectable.

Pabst's emendation is pointedly social. The founding of the bank is a clear jab at the extralegal power of capital and a rather explicit reference to Hitler, the crook who was becoming legitimate. But the Pabst ending blunts the satiric force of the original; Brecht's play is funnier, more bitter, more biting, sharper-edged than Pabst's adaptation. Pabst has weighed Brecht down with unneeded freight: a linear plot and a minutely detailed, atmospheric world of film decor. On the other hand, the cinematic qualities of that world are marvelous. The seamy streets, the smoke-filled, mirrored and paneled café where Mackie first seduces Polly, the cavernous, expressionistic interiors of Peachum's house, the sumptuous, sparkling splendor of the wedding banquet, the tacky gentility of the whorehouse are all exquisite visual

Berlin: The Symphony of a Great City—*the geometry of everyday life*

creations. Unfortunately, Pabst's visuals work contrary to Brecht's vision.

The End of an Era

The key question about the death of the German film is whether it ended with a bang or a whimper—with Hitler's tyranny over the imagination of the individual artist or in the gradual decay that had been afflicting the German film mind for a half-dozen years before Hitler came to power. There is evidence that the claustrophobia of the studio production, the dependence on architecture and paint, which had liberated the visual imagination in 1920, began to inhibit it by 1926. Lang's *Metropolis* was the triumph of the dead, decoration for the sake of pure decorativeness. One year after

Metropolis, 1927, the great writer of studio films, Carl Mayer, and the great photographer of studio films, Karl Freund, broke out of the studio completely to shoot a candid documentary of Berlin life. Edited and constructed by the abstract artist and architect, Walther Ruttmann, *Berlin: Symphony of a Great City* was the antithesis of the traditional German film. It used no story; it was merely a chronological progression of some twenty hours in the city's life, from the arrival of an early morning train to the late-night activities of the Berliners. The film lacked a human protagonist; its protagonist was the city itself. And, like any great city, the protagonist of this film is both good and bad, kind and cruel, cold and warm. It is a place of great activity—which is of questionable meaning or value. It is a place where people sit in cafés in the warm sun and where litter clogs a storm drain. It is a place where people see Charlie Chaplin on a screen and where a girl commits suicide by jumping off a bridge. The film's ultimate comment is that life in Berlin certainly exists in staggering quantity, but whether that life is good or bad, beneficial or brutal is impossible to say. It has all and none of these moral qualities. It is as neutral as life itself.

The power of *Berlin* lies in its candid photography and its rhythmic cutting. To guarantee the authenticity of revealing the city at work and play, Karl Freund, the careful craftsman of both *The Last Laugh* and *Variety,* hid his camera in a truck and drove about the city, hastily and fleetingly shooting the movement that happened to catch his eye. Though the shooting of the film was mostly accident, Walther Ruttmann's editing of it was not. His two controlled editing principles were form and rhythm (this was, after all, two years after *Potemkin*). As he cut from shot to shot, Ruttmann capitalized on either parallels in form (circles, verticals, heavy masses) or contrasts in form. To combine whole sections of shots he used the principles of musical composition, endowing the sequence with a rhythm and tone appropriate to its content. The opening movement of the film, the train approaching the sleeping city, is *allegro moderato*—rhythmic, pulsating, alive with expectation, but a bit cautious, sleepy, hesitant. The next sequence, of the sleeping city waking, is a *largo*—slow, quiet, peaceful. As the city wakes and goes to work, the tempo changes to *allegro vivace*—vibrant, alive, active. There is an *andante* at the lunch hour when work stops, another *allegro* when it begins again, and another *andante* in the quiet, gear-changing hours of the evening between work and play. The film ends with a *presto finale,* a fast, frenzied sequence of neon lights, night life, dancing, music, movies. With its use of pure visual form, musical rhythms, and

real life, *Berlin* is clearly an attempt to break the bounds of studio production.

Another iconoclastic film is *Kuhle Wampe* (1932), Brecht's attempt to redress his movie injury by writing a script of his own. The work rejects the lighting, the atmosphere, the control of the German studio film completely. The film, like the *Berlin Symphony,* feels more Russian than German; its creators (Brecht and Slatan Dudow, the director) are clearly influenced by both Marx and Eisenstein: the montage of bicycle wheels rolling endlessly through the streets, unsuccessful at taking their riders to a job; the montage of rising prices, of evictions for not paying the rent, of the price tags on every human necessity. The film's total rejection of a plot, its use of actual locations, its subordination of people to political discussion are also signs of its rupture with the German film tradition.

If the limitations of the studio film had begun to cramp the German imagination, it was also possible that the exodus of the best film talent to Hollywood had not left enough imaginations in Germany to get cramped. Murnau had gone to Hollywood where, after making the sensitive, internalized, and highly praised study of a married couple's antagonism and reunion (*Sunrise,* 1927), he died in an automobile crash in 1931. Lubitsch had gone to Hollywood, never to return. Pommer had gone to Hollywood and returned, but he may have caught the dollar influenza after being exposed to it. Even those filmmakers who never went to Hollywood could not avoid its influence. As the German film industry had more and more financial difficulties, it was more and more underwritten by Hollywood production dollars. With dollars came directives. Perhaps the Germanness of the German film was bought out.

On the other hand, it is possible that there was no real decline, that Hitler's victory killed a reviving and thriving film imagination with a swift and terrible suddenness. The early German sound films were as good as anyone's. Or better. *The Blue Angel,* despite its American director (von Sternberg), was a completely German film. Its heritage is evident in its careful studio-controlled atmospheres (the contrast between the smoky chiaroscuro of the night club and the bright, clean, ordered whiteness of the professor's classroom), in its close examination of a Jannings character's soul (Professor Unrat's steady degeneration into a beast), and in its cynical portrayal of the nasty, callous insensitivity of the German populace to human suffering. The film was as careful with sound as with pictures: the contrast of Lola's singing and the traditional tune chimed by the town clock, the contrast between the noisy chaos in Unrat's classroom before he enters and the deadly silence when he does. Von Sternberg never made a better film (or as good a one?). Pabst's use of sound was also developing: the wheeze and crash of exploding shells in his antiwar study of the First World War, *Westfront 1918,* the effective contrast of singing soldiers and dying ones, the use of musical leitmotifs in *Threepenny Opera.* Pabst's *Kameradschaft* (1932), his final pre-Nazi sound film, was an extremely daring and innovative work. In this story of international cooperation on the Franco-German border to rescue the victims of a mine disaster, Pabst shot a fiction film that looked as real, as unstaged as a documentary. In this dialogue film, dialogue itself becomes a metaphor (as it does in Renoir's *Grand Illusion*) since the conflict of languages (German and French) underlies the human and political conflicts of the narrative.

Lang's use of sound was equally astute. In *M* there is the asynchronous handling of sound as a mother calls in vain for the daughter who has been murdered, while the camera reveals the empty spaces where no living being stirs. The murderer himself is identified by the Grieg tune he repeatedly whistles, and Lang effectively depicts the moment when the man gets the urge to kill by the increasing intensity and urgency of his whistling. The blind man, who is totally dependent on sound, later recognizes the murderer from this whistled tune. And throughout the film, Lang juxtaposes visual imagery (shadows, a Wanted poster, the little girl's balloon, the dishes on the table for a meal that will never be eaten, the searches and strategies, maps and machinations of the police going about their business) with ironic or contrapuntal commentary on the sound track.

Rather than dying slowly, the German age may well have been translated abruptly from one of gold into one of iron. Ironically, the great era of German films can be seen as merely developing the means that a Hitler would use to manipulate the minds of the public. The German sense of architecture and composition, the rhythms of cutting and movement, would be reincarnated in the masterful propaganda films of Leni Riefenstahl, who lent her great art to bending the German mind. The heroic architectural configurations of her *Triumph of the Will* (1935) are descendants of *Metropolis* and *Niebelungen;* the stirring integration of musical motifs, the control of camera angle, the incorporation of mythic elements all aim at presenting the Führer as a combination of Pagan god of strength and Christian savior of mildness. In *Olympia* (1936–38), the techniques used to consecrate and glorify the body, the athlete, the purely physical are the descendants of the rhythmic editing of Ruttmann and Pabst. With the exception of providing the world with a series of lessons on the use of film as cultural and political propaganda, the German film failed to make any major contribution to the international cinema for forty years, until the new German cinema emerged in the 1970s.

Sound and image in **M**. *As her mother calls for "Ilse," Lang combines these still lifes of emptiness*

8 Soviet Montage

The Russian film was born with the Russian Revolution. Before 1917 the Russian film industry was a colony of Europe—of Pathé or Lumière or Scandinavia's Nordisk. No film was shot in Russia by a Russian company until some ten years after the invention of the moving picture. The films of the next ten years (1907–1917) were strictly for local consumption (very few of them were exported). Costume films, horror films, and melodramas—the typical formulas of Europe and America—were the staples of the pre-1917 Russian film diet. The revolution changed all that.

Marxist political and economic philosophy, which had evolved in the age of machines, adopted the machine art as its own. Lenin considered the cinema the most influential of all the arts. Movies not only entertained but, in the process, molded and reinforced values. The film was a great teacher; with portable power supplies it could be shown to huge groups of people at the same time in every remote corner of the new Soviet Union. While the flickering images held their audiences captive, the events on the screen emphasized the virtues of the new government and encouraged the Russian people to develop those traits that would best further it. Whereas the American film came into the world as an amusing novelty, the Soviet film was created explicitly as teacher, not as clown. In 1919, after a chaotic year in which the Soviets had let the film industry go its own commercial way, the Russian industry passed under government control. The first harvest, however, was six years in coming.

"The foundation of film art is editing," wrote Pudovkin in the preface to the German edition of his book on film technique. Whereas the German innovators concentrated on the look, the feel, the pictorial values of the individual shot, the Soviet innovators concentrated on the effects of joining the shots together. Like so many of the earlier innovations in film technique, the Soviet discoveries were the products of experience and experiment rather than abstract theorizing. Two significant accidents determined the paths the experimentation would take. The first was the shortage of raw film stock. As in the rest of Europe, film stock was scarce in Russia during and just after the war years. The Russian film famine was even more severe, for the still fighting Red and White armies erected blockades against each other to keep supplies from getting through. Lacking quantities of stock, the Soviet filmmakers had to make the most of what they had.

One of the first to make something was Dziga-Vertov, who traveled about the country shooting newsreel footage with his camera, which he called his "Kino-Eye." Vertov then assembled this absolutely unstaged footage (Vertov insisted on unstaged reality throughout his career) into a newsreel called *Kino-Pravda,* creating powerful emotional effects and educational results from the way he joined this real footage together. Vertov brings the ordinary, laborious tasks of building or rebuilding a nation to life (laying an airstrip, planting crops, finishing a tram line) by examining the progress of the task from many stirring and awesome angles that succeeded in endowing the ordinary with wonder. Vertov succeeds in giving inanimate

machines both stature and vitality, revealing, as many of the later Soviet films would do, the powerful potential, the almost sexual fertility of the union of men and machines. Of course, one of the reasons for Vertov's dynamic editing was that he had to shoot with mere scraps of film stock, and many of those scraps were very short.

The scarcity of film stock also created the film workshop of Lev Kuleshov. Kuleshov, who taught a workshop class at the newly established Moscow Film School, led his students in a series of editing experiments. Pudovkin was to become the most famous of those students, but even those filmmakers who did not study with Kuleshov (for example, Eisenstein) could not escape his influence. Lacking the film stock to make whole films of their own, the Kuleshov workshop experimented in drafting scenarios, in editing and re-editing the pieces of film they already had on hand, and in re-editing sequences of feature films imported from the West. The second of the influential accidents directly affected the Kuleshov group. In 1919, a print of Griffith's *Intolerance* successfully wriggled through the anti-Soviet blockade. *Intolerance* became a Kuleshov primer. His

---

Vertov's "Kino-Eye." The camera lens as an extension of human vision; thrusting the moving-picture camera into everyday life (from The Man with the Movie Camera)

students examined its boldness in cutting—cuts to drive the narrative, to integrate tremendously diverse and disjointed material, to intensify emotion with its rhythms, to mirror internal thought and sensations. The Kuleshov workshop screened *Intolerance* incessantly, even re-editing its sequences to examine the resulting effects on the film's power and to discover the reasons for Griffith's particular choices. With such a thorough mastery of the principles of Griffith's cutting, the Soviet directors would extend those principles to their limits—when they got the money and the film.

Until then they experimented. Each of the experiments furthered their control of the effects of editing and their conviction that editing was the basis of film art. Several of the Kuleshov experiments have become classics. In one, Kuleshov used some stock footage of the prerevolutionary actor, Ivan Mozhukin. Mozhukin had fled to Paris (with the majority of the Czarist film industry), where he became a matinee idol of French films. But, unknowingly, he left his face behind on a piece of film to aid the dreaded Bolsheviks. Kuleshov cut the strip of Mozhukin's face into three pieces. He juxtaposed one of the strips with a shot of a plate of hot soup; he juxtaposed the second with a shot of a dead woman in a coffin; he juxtaposed the third with a shot of a little girl playing with a toy bear. When viewers, who had not been let in on the joke, saw the finished cutting they praised Mozhukin's acting: his hunger when confronted with a bowl of soup, his sorrow for his dead "mother" (their interpretation), his joy when watching his "daughter" (another interpretation) playing. Mozhukin's expression was identical in all three cuts; the actor's emotion never changed. The context of the juxtaposed material evoked the emotion in the audience, which then projected it into the actor. Editing alone had created the emotion—as well as a brilliant acting performance!

In another Kuleshov experiment the audience sees a series of five shots: (1) a man walks from the right to left, (2) a woman walks from left to right; (3) they meet and shake hands, the man points; (4) we see a white building; (5) the two walk up a flight of steps. The audience connects the five pieces into a single sequence. A man and woman meet; they go off toward a building that he sees. In reality, the two individual shots of the man and woman walking were made in two distant and different parts of the city; the building he points to is the White House, snipped out of an American film; the steps they ascend belong to a church in yet a third section of the city. Kuleshov's experiment revealed that the impression of geographical unity in a film was unrelated to geographical unity in space. Kuleshov called the result "creative geography." It was the same method Griffith used when he spliced Niagara Falls into the climax of *Way Down East*. A third Kuleshov experiment might, by analogy, be called "creative anatomy." Kuleshov created the impression of a single actress by splicing together the face of one woman, the torso of another, the hands of another, the legs of yet another.

The Kuleshov student learned that editing served three primary purposes in building a film. First, a cut could serve a *narrative* function. For example, a man walks toward the camera; suddenly, something to his right catches his attention and he turns his head. The audience's natural question is: what does he see? The director then cuts to an old tramp who pulls a pistol on the man. The audience's next question is: how will the man react to this attack? The director cuts back to the man to show his fear. And so forth. The narrative cut allows the director to analyze an action into its most interesting elements and then to resynthesize these elements of the event into a powerful sequential action. Another kind of narrative cut is the flash back or forward—a cut that furthers the action by

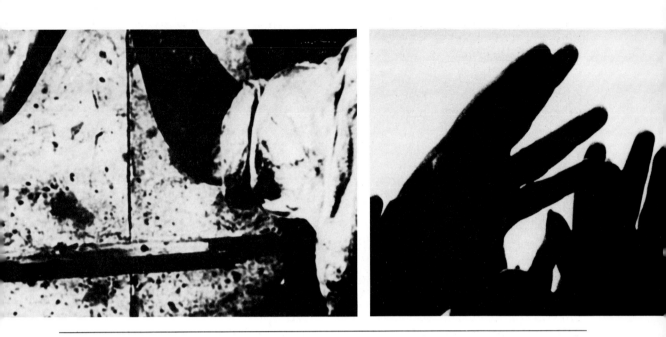

From the final montage sequence of Strike: *the butcher's hand thrusts downward to smash the animal's skull, the people's hands thrust upward in an appeal for mercy*

revealing a character's thoughts at a particular moment. A woman stares dreamily into space; the director cuts to her husband in a faraway prison; the director then cuts back to the woman's face. Yet a third kind of narrative cut is the cross-cut. While the tramp attacks the man with a pistol, the police, aware of the attack, charge to the rescue. These lessons of cutting had all been learned from Griffith.

But the Soviet film students realized that a cut could do more than narrate. They also found that a cut could generate an *intellectual* response. One kind of intellectual cut was the metaphorical-cut or associational-cut. From a group of workers being mowed down by the rifles of soldiers, the director could cut to the slaughter of an ox in a stockyards (as Eisenstein did in *Strike*). The image of the slaughtered ox comments on the action of the slaughtered workers. The director can cut from a streaming procession of striking workers to a shot of a river thawing in the spring, a mass of ice flowing steadily toward the sea (as Pudovkin did in *Mother*). The naturalness, the inevitability of the progress of the streaming ice comments on the force of the streaming workers. A second intellectual effect could be produced by the contrast-cut. The director cuts from the dinner table of a poor man, who eats only a few pieces of bread, to the table of a rich man laden with meats, candles, and wine. The contrast of the two tables comments on the injustice of the fact that two such tables can exist at the same time. Such cuts can also be traced back to Griffith, of course, who executed precisely this intellectual contrast between the table of the rich and the bread line of the poor in *A Corner in Wheat* of 1909. The parallel-cut produces a third kind of intellectual response. From the condemned man sentenced to die at five o'clock, the director cuts to a thief who murders a victim at precisely five o'clock. The parallel acts of violence at the same time reinforce each other. Significantly, the intellectual cut—metaphoric, contrast, or parallel—also has an emotional dimension. The director not only uses the slaughter of the ox but also the sickening, horrifying violence and bloodiness of the murder to make his point. He not only comments on the injustice of the rich man's dinner but makes us hate the rich man for his gluttony and pity the poor man for his need.

The third kind of cut that the Kuleshov students discovered is a purely *emotional* one: the very method of joining the strips of celluloid together, rather than their content, produces an almost subliminal kinetic response in an audience that the director can unobtrusively control. First, the director can cut a sequence rhythmically. He can use shorter and shorter pieces of film, increasing the tempo and tension of the action. Or he can cut a sequence with long pieces of film, producing a feeling of slowness and languidness. By stitching together a series of strips of equal length the director can produce the feeling of a regular, measured beat. The tonal-cut is the director's second method of manipulating an audience's emotions without its conscious awareness of manipulation. He can cut a sequence with steadily darker pictures, producing the impression of oncoming night and growing despair, or with steadily lighter pictures, producing the impression of dawn and rising hope. A third kind of emotional editing is the form-cut, cutting on a similarity or difference in the form of the object in the frame. The director can cut from a spinning roulette wheel to a turning wagon wheel, from a plodding ox to an efficient tractor, from a jabbing pencil to a thrusting sword. A fourth kind of kinetic editing is the directional-cut, in which the director uses the direction of movement across the frame either to keep the action flowing or to produce a

dynamic collision. The director can cut from a group of workers streaming from right to left, to a group of foot soldiers streaming from right to left, to a group of Cossacks on horseback streaming from right to left. Or he can cut from a group of workers streaming from right to left to a group of Cossacks streaming from left to right. Whereas the first series of directional cuts would produce the feeling of speed, continuousness, and flow, the second would produce the sensation of two huge masses smashing into one another. Significantly, a cut that is intended to have an intellectual effect —from pencil to sword—may also serve as a form-cut, as part of a tonal sequence, as part of the film's increasing rhythm, and as a shift in the film's narrative structure all at the same time. A single cut can function on all three levels—narrative, intellectual, emotional—at once. In fact, the Soviet directors discovered that most cuts *must* function on all three levels at once.

To this discovery they gave the name "montage." In French, the word simply means editing; for the Soviet director, the word signified the particular way editing could control the film's structure, meaning, and effect. By 1924, the Kuleshov students had acquired the film, the equipment, and the budgets to turn their lessons into films. They went out to develop their personal notions of montage. The surprise was that, despite the similarities in theory, the individual filmmakers produced strikingly individual and personal films.

Sergei M. Eisenstein

Eisenstein was the greatest filmmaker to apply the principles of Kuleshov, the greatest master of montage. It was Eisenstein's sense of cutting that transformed his didactic lessons on the virtues of brotherhood and Marx into dynamic, moving works of art—even for the non-Marxist. The Eisenstein films break all the rules of narrative construction. They lack a protagonist and focal characters; they lack a linear plot of the rising or falling fortunes of a single man. Although the Eisenstein films lack a conventional plot, they lack neither compelling action nor a unified structure. Although they lack individualized and rounded studies of human personality, they lack neither character nor human compassion.

The Eisenstein film holds together by means of its theme rather than its story: the experience of the workers who learn what it means to strike and to take collective action against a wicked state, the ability of a single revolutionary action on a battleship to unite a whole people, the replacement of a false revolutionary government by a true one, the superiority of the new agricultural and social methods to the old ones. The theme gets its flesh from Eisenstein's depiction of the people who embody it. Although the central character of the Eisenstein film is the mass, the people as a whole, he never forgets that the mass is a combination of individuals. Although the Eisenstein film is full of magnificent shots of streaming rivers of people, he invariably shows the viewer the impassioned faces of the men and women in that river. Like Lang, Eisenstein has the visual ability to convert huge groups of people into complex and striking geometric shapes. Unlike Lang, Eisenstein constantly reminds you that his subject is the dynamic human being, not the kaleidoscopic visual pattern. Also unlike Lang, Eisenstein's geometric compositions, as careful and as visually attractive as they are, are never static. The individual shots are full of dynamic movement; they are not static, metaphoric, or quasi-ballet as in *Metropolis*. That was one of Eisenstein's advantages in shooting outdoors; he had the freedom to move. And Eisenstein's montage increases the sense of movement

and tension as the individual shots collide, crash, explode into each other.

Eisenstein defined his principle of montage as one of collision, of conflict, of contrast. He does not simply build shots into a whole but sees each frame as a unit with a dynamic charge of a particular kind. His goal is to bring the dynamic charge of one frame into conflict with the charge of the next. For example, the shots can conflict directionally—a group of men running from right to left, followed by a shot of soldiers marching from left to right. The shots can conflict in rhythm—a group of people running quickly and chaotically, followed by a group of soldiers marching steadily, slowly, and inexorably. The shots can conflict in bulk—from a mass of workers to a shot of a single worker's face. The shots can conflict in emphasis—from a shot of four silent workers' faces to a shot of a single worker's fist clenched at his side. The shots can conflict in camera angle—from an extreme downward angle on a large crowd to a noble upward angle shot of a member of the crowd. The shots can conflict in the intensity of light—from a dark, dim shot to a blazing, bright one. The shots can conflict in the intensity of emotion—from a shot of fighting, struggling workers to a shot of a single worker's lifeless body, dangling quietly outside the struggle. The shots can conflict in their vitality—from a shot of a living man to a shot of a stone statue. And so forth. Eisenstein's great films are the products of the combinations of his many and diverse gifts—his visual sense of composition, his feeling for rhythm and tempo, his ability to understand and manipulate human emotion, and his perceptive intellect, which could create meaning by joining two seemingly unrelated images.

Eisenstein formally studied engineering and architecture. During the Civil War of 1917, he organized an impromptu theatre troupe in the Red Army. Attracted to the

Potemkin: *from the mass to individual detail, from geometry to people*

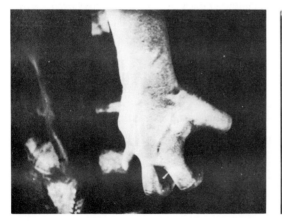

theatre, he started directing plays in Moscow after the war, where he was heavily influenced by the innovative, antinaturalist director, Vsevlod Meyerhold. In one of Eisenstein's stage productions, *The Wise Man* (1922), he used a short film sequence, a pastiche of Vertov's *Kino-Pravda,* within the context of the play. He staged his last play, *Gas Works* (1923), in the Moscow Gas Works. Eisenstein could go no further with stage reality; the leap into films was inevitable. His first film, *Strike* (1924), revealed the bold, broad strokes of a new film master. From the film's opening montage sequence—of whirring machines, spinning gears, factory whistles, of traveling shots along the length of the factory complex, of dynamic, dizzying movement—the film proclaimed that a brilliant cinematic imagination was at work.

The film contains many of the traits that make an Eisenstein film pure Eisenstein. There is the director's control and alternation of moods: from the peaceful, idyllic sequences of the striking workers at rest and play to the violent, vicious slaughter of the workers in their tenements. There is the satirical treatment of the rich and the informers for the rich: the company finks are depicted as sneaky animals (a Griffith touch here); the rich factory owners sip cocktails while the workers starve and die (Griffith cross-cutting, of course). There is the director's sense of visual composition: the geometrical patterns and shapes of the factory and of the workers' tenements where the Cossacks attack. There is Eisenstein's use of metaphor to comment on the action: the sickening slaughter of the dumb and defenseless ox, which comments on the slaughter of the workers. And uniting the film is the Eisenstein vision—the capitalistic, Czarist system is fundamentally inhuman and inhumane, an obstacle not only to physical survival but also to human fellowship, family, and brotherhood.

Potemkin (1925) was Eisenstein's next film. The work was originally intended to depict the entire workers' revolt of 1905. Instead, Eisenstein pared down his conception to a single event in the revolt—the rebellion on the battleship Potemkin and the resulting reprisals from the Czarist army—to serve as a microcosm for the whole year's events. (Ultimately, of course, it foreshadowed the workers' eruption of 1917.) The film's five parts, mirroring the five-act structure of classical drama, form a taut structural whole: from the unity the sailors build on the ship, to the unity between ship and shore, to the unity of the entire fleet. In the first part, subtitled "Men and Maggots," Eisenstein builds the dramatic reasons for the sailors' discontent. The food is infested with maggots; the Czarist doctor looks at the meat closely through his spectacles and declares the meat wholesome, although his glasses magnify the presence of the worms. The officers beat the men and treat them like cattle. Eisenstein brilliantly shows a worker's pain by merely photographing the twitching muscles of his back as he sobs.

In the film's second section, "Drama on the Quarterdeck," the men have had enough. They refuse to agree that their food is edible; when the captain orders all dissenters to be shot, the sailors rebel. By the end of this violent sequence, the ship belongs to the workers. The film's third section, "An Appeal from the Dead," is a quiet, elegiac requiem, a pause between the violent capture of the ship and the violence to follow on the Odessa Steps. One of the sailors has been killed in the battle; his body lies in state on the shore. The workers of Odessa file past it, united in spirit by the sailor's sacrifice. The dead man's action touches and unites the people of Odessa.

The fourth section of the film, "The Odessa Steps," begins gaily enough. The workers of Odessa race out to the Potemkin in their boats, carrying food

  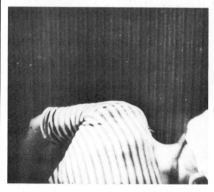

 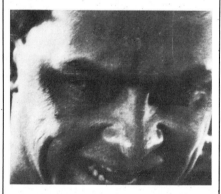 

The plate-smashing sequence in
Potemkin: *a brief action broken into a*
dramatic and dialectic process

and joy to their fellow workers on the ship. There is a union of ship and shore, of sailors and citizens. Other Odessans watch and wave from the shore. Suddenly, Czarist troops march down the steps, butchering every person in their path. The citizens scurry for protection. The soldiers' guns mercilessly fire, slaughtering young and old, men and women, children and mothers. The fifth section of the film, "Meeting the Squadron," is another emotional contrast. From the violence and chaos of the previous section, the mood becomes subdued, tense, expectant. The single battleship races toward the fleet; the ship prepares for battle. Eisenstein builds the suspense with shots of whirring gears, pumping pistons, rising guns. Will the fleet fire? The fleet does not. The comrades of all the fleet cheer one another. The Potemkin has united them all.

The techniques that are uniquely Eisenstein's bring the film to life. The power of his cutting is unmistakable. At the end of section one, Eisenstein wants to emphasize that the men have had it, that the last straw has been laid on the camel's back. A sailor washing the dishes sees a plate inscribed, "Give us this day our daily bread." The biblical platitude infuriates him since they have no decent daily bread. He smashes the plate. To emphasize this act of smashing, Eisenstein divides this physical action, which takes only two or three seconds, into eleven different shots: (1) a close-up of the man's face reflecting his decision to smash the plate; (2) a medium shot as he pulls his arm back with the plate in his right hand; (3) a medium shot of the withdrawing arm; (4) a close shot of his right arm and shoulder pulling back; (5) a medium shot of his right arm starting forward; (6) a medium shot of his determined motion; (7) a close shot of his face showing his determination; (8) a medium-close shot of his face and arm in action; (9) a medium shot of the table

about to receive the blow; (10) a close shot of his relaxed shoulder; (11) a medium shot of the table where the dish has been smashed. Dividing an action into such a process makes the event more violent, more purposeful, and more memorable as a pivotal point in the film. The edited version of the action takes longer than the physical act itself.

Other sequences use a different but equally effective editing plan. No better example of tonal montage exists than in the opening passage of the film's third section, "An Appeal from the Dead." The entire sequence is saturated in the lyric calm of the sailor's death. Eisenstein cuts slowly from shot to shot, each of them growing lighter, revealing the rising of the sun through the fog. In the languid cuts, the sea is calm as glass, ships glide through the mist, their masts silhouetted in the fog, gulls quietly hover in the air. The quiet editing creates a lyrical moment of slow-moving, dark shapes sliding through a gray mist. The editing of the mourning Odessans in the final section of this "Appeal from the Dead" adds a note of strength and human determination to the moody silence. Eisenstein cuts from far shots of the immense mass of people to medium shots of three or four faces, to close-ups of single faces, clenched fists, and outstretched arms. When an antisemite screams, "Down with the Jews," Eisenstein shows the fierceness of the people's unity in a rhythmic editing sequence that shows heads turning, wheeling, in angry response to this voice of narrow inhumanity.

And the most dazzling editorial sequence of all in the film is the slaughter of the innocent Odessans on the Steps. Eisenstein weaves this magic with a series of different kinds of shots: far shots from the bottom of the steps showing the workers running chaotically; traveling shots along the side of the steps that reinforce the movement of the running workers; shots from the top of the steps showing the relentless, metric pace of the marching soldiers, only their boots, their bayonets, and their awesome shadows in the frame; close-ups of the individual workers, their faces expressing horror, fear, sorrow, anger. Eisenstein weaves this tapestry by intercutting the different shots, alternating them according to different principles of his montage of collisions, each of them sustained on the screen for the rhythmically correct number of seconds (or fractions of seconds). And as in the plate-smashing scene, the film time for the sequence on the Odessa Steps is longer than the actual time it would take a group of people to run down a flight of steps. Subjective time, the way it felt to be there, replaces natural time.

But *Potemkin* is more than montage, more than a series of dazzling editing techniques. For a film with a mass protagonist, the faces of individual people are strikingly memorable. Out of the brilliant geometric organization of sailors' hammocks emerge the individual faces of the young sailor who gets beaten and Vakulinchuk, the sailor who leads his comrades in revolt. The sharp-featured, beady-eyed faces of the sneaky ship's doctor, the cunning ship's mate, and the egomaniacal captain convey Eisenstein's condemnation of the vicious ruling class. The most maniacal and vicious face of all is that of the priest, his hair streaming in close-ups framed with light and smoke, his huge iron cross more a dangerous weapon (it sticks in the ship's deck like a dagger) than a symbol of love and mildness. To enhance the lyrical quietness of the "Appeal from the Dead," Eisenstein evokes our sympathies with loving shots of the sorrowing faces of old and young, of men and women. And the most memorable faces of all are those in the most active and violent sequence of all—the Odessa Steps. Eisenstein creates the horror of the slaughter not just with mass murder and chaotic movement but with the individual reactions and sensations of the people who experience

the slaughter: the elderly lady with the pince-nez, the mother with her young son, the student with the glasses, the legless man scurrying at the feet of the crowd, the dark-haired, dark-clad mother with the baby carriage, from whose womb issues not fertile life but blood from the soldiers' bullets and whose carriage hurtles chaotically down the steps, a metaphor for a society with no future. As the soldiers attack, Eisenstein follows the fortunes and reactions of each of these individual faces, using their emotional responses to evoke ours.

If *Potemkin* seems to be Eisenstein's most unified, most satisfying, and most *emotionally* effective film, it is perhaps because so many of its devices are felt rather than noticed. For example, the famous montage of the stone lions (three sequential shots of three statues—a lion sleeping, waking, and rising—so edited as to produce the impression of a single, natural, connected action) has drawn extensive critical and theoretical attention. Clearly the sequence is a rather explicit metaphor (condemned by André Bazin and others for its explicitness) for the rising of the people in power and anger, enraged at the slaughter on the Odessa Steps. But a much more subtle and less explicit metaphor in the film (drawing no commentary at all, although the metaphor runs throughout the film) is Eisenstein's handling of the battleship's guns. At the beginning of the film the guns are lifeless, inert. In the middle of the film the guns come alive to send the ship's defiance to the shore in answer to the slaughter on the Odessa Steps. By the end of the film, the guns are alive with power: rising, turning, and twisting toward the enemy. The guns have come to life because they have now acquired a soul, working as the tools and servants of the true spirit of the people.

But Eisenstein's use of the guns may be even more subtle, for he may be giving the general metaphor of the new soul within the machine a specifically sexual

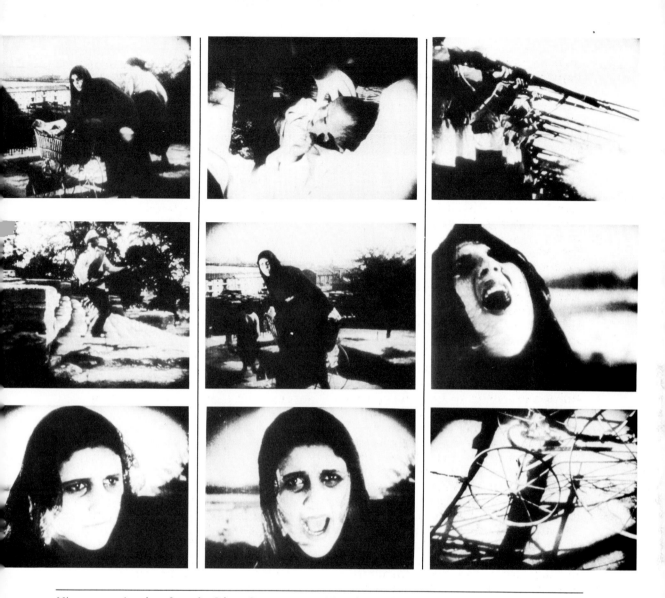

Nine consecutive shots from the Odessa Steps sequence. Note the graphic conflicts between long and close shots, symmetrical and asymmetrical compositions, a human face and the inexorable march of an inhuman armed machine

connotation. Early in the film the guns play a passive, androgynous, asexual role. When a sailor inserts a swab into one of the huge guns, the potential instrument of power serves as a mere receptacle, secreting a gooey oil. Later—in response to the slaughter on the Steps—the guns rise for the first time in the film (and the low angle increases the sexual implications of this rising), and then shoot their answer into a Czarist edifice, knocking it flat. (Only then do the stone lions arise, being born, in a sense, from the semen of the guns.) In the film's final sequence, the guns continue to stand erect and alert, becoming a mechanical extension of the new potency of the men who control them.

Another element of the film that is felt rather than noticed is the sheer musicality of Eisenstein's montage. Although Eisenstein (and most historians and critics) have devoted their time exclusively to discussing the intellectual and argumentative effects of montage, the editing of the strips of film in *Potemkin* also functions on a purely sensual level. Because Eisenstein's major period of theoretical writing followed the making of *Potemkin* by almost a decade, one can argue that he might well have lost touch with a quality of his work that he had manipulated instinctively and spontaneously in his youth. (Such a view would explain the drier, more academic, less exciting sound films that he made after his years of theorizing.)

So much of the viewer's experience of *Potemkin* proceeds not from the eyes to the brain (the film's ideological statements) but from the eyes to the nerves. Like music, one *feels* the film as rhythm, mood, tone, and texture in addition to perceiving its concrete images. Eisenstein's "music" may be generally described as tensely violent, as a nervous, surging, discordant dissonance—qualities that parallel those of the modern music then being composed by his countrymen and contemporaries, Dimitri Shostakovich and Sergei Prokofiev. Interestingly, both composers later wrote music for the Soviet sound film, and the effective collaboration of Eisenstein and Prokofiev on *Alexander Nevsky* and *Ivan the Terrible* revealed how kindred were the spirits of these two "musicians."

Eisenstein's next film, originally titled *October* (1927) but released in the United States as *Ten Days That Shook the World*, is not nearly as careful, consistent, or effective in its manipulation of the sensual effects of visual "music" as *Potemkin*. The film, a loose historical survey of the months between the February Revolution of 1917 and the Bolshevik Revolution of October, is more intellectual, more satirical, and more specifically political than *Potemkin*. Its historical structure also makes it less unified dramatically, less consistent thematically, and less effective emotionally. Unlike *Potemkin*, its parts are far more striking than its whole.

The film's montage still drives its rhythms. During the scenes of rebellion, Eisenstein uses extremely quick cuts (two frames long!) that smash the viewer with an impression of violence, shock, and frenzy. The alternation of these two-frame pieces, the one of a machine gun, the other of a man's face, gives the viewer the smashing sense of the clash and crash of gunfire, although no gun is actually firing at all. Eisenstein uses an opposite editing principle to emphasize that St. Petersburg has been cut in half, extending, slowing down the scene of the raising of the bridges, just as he draws out the plate-smashing scene and the Odessa Steps sequence in *Potemkin*. Two halves of a drawbridge pull apart and rise with infinite slowness. On one of the halves lies the body of a girl whose hair streams into the gap between the halves. On the other half lies the body of a horse, still attached to a wagon. The horse falls into the gap; the wagon remains on the bridge; the horse remains suspended in midair, like the woman's hair, as the bridge continues to rise. After an agonizing wait, the two bodies fall into the river. Significantly, immediately after they fall in the river, Eisenstein cuts to a shot of Bolshevik leaflets and banners falling in the river. The real revolution is as dead as the woman and horse. The new provisional government, the result of this February Revolution, is a failure for the real revolutionists.

The striking device of *October* is less in the emotional power of its montage than in the intellectual commentary of Eisenstein's cutting. His consistent method in this film is to use inanimate objects to

October: *a world of satiric objects. Eisenstein deflates material things into the ugly and the dead*

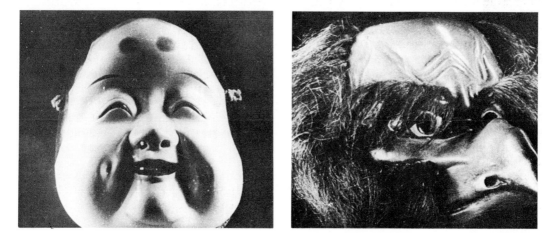

comment on the activities of men. The film's dead things ironically give it its life. Whereas Eisenstein used the method only once in *Potemkin, October* is full of "stone lions" that come to life.

A series of objects comments on the values of Kerensky, leader of the provisional government. As Kerensky poses, Eisenstein cuts to a statuette of Napoleon. Eisenstein further debunks Kerensky by showing all the possessions in his palace: gleaming china plates, goblets of cut glass, chalices of silver, an army of toy soldiers. The burlesque of Kerensky dominates the film. During the Bolshevik Revolution, Kerensky furtively calls the Cossack barracks for help, but the Cossacks have joined the Bolsheviks. The only response to his furtive call is a series of shots of the buttocks of horses, implying both that he is a horse's ass and that even the animals' asses are "voicing" their opinion of the false leader's request. Most damning of Kerensky is the series of shots that shows him fleeing in his Rolls Royce, a little American flag firmly planted on the radiator. Eisenstein repeatedly cuts to the flag to show both Kerensky's flight and his loyalties.

Eisenstein uses other objects satirically. To burlesque the glories of war, he shows a collection of gaudy medals; to burlesque the emptiness of religion (a consistent Eisenstein theme) he shows a series of church icons: crosses, statues of Buddha, wooden figures of primitive gods. All of the statues are inanimate and ugly; all of them emphasize the artificiality of turning the abstraction of a deity into a tangible (and expensive) object. To burlesque the futility of the government officials, Eisenstein plays geometric games with the empty coffee glasses on their conference table. The glasses jump into a circle, a line, a curve, a square; though the patterns of the glasses change, the results of the conference do not. To burlesque the idealism of the Mensheviks, a group that advocated peaceful change rather than revolution, Eisenstein cuts from one

of their speakers to a group of harps plucked languidly by graceful, feminine hands.

The dominant mood of *October* is parody and burlesque. Exemplifying the tone of the film is Kerensky's action when he hears that the Bolsheviks are attacking: he buries his head under the cushions of a sofa and flails his arms and legs frantically and childishly in space. The constant use of inanimate objects is a perfect burlesque tool, a way of turning human activity into wood or glass or stone. The parodic tone of the film's spirit holds together its sprawling, semi-historical structure.

Eisenstein's next film, his last silent, returns to the human world of *Potemkin.* In *Old and New* (1929), Eisenstein demonstrates the difficulties and the virtues for the peasant of discarding the old ways of farming and thinking, of adopting the new collective ways and the new machines. The film represents some departures for Eisenstein. In the manner of Pudovkin, he uses natural (rather than inanimate) imagery—fields, soil, animals, and crops—and he also uses a central figure rather than a mass to embody the film's social progress (although unlike Pudovkin, Eisenstein merely observes the peasant woman's behavior rather than probing or developing her thoughts and feelings).

But Eisenstein was beginning to run into trouble with the Soviet line and leaders. Stalin was dissatisfied with the ending of *Old and New,* finding it untrue to the spirit of the new nation and the people. Eisenstein, an iconoclast, a devoted artist, an avid reader of everything from T. S. Eliot to Joyce and Kafka, from Dickens to Haiku poetry, began to feel the pinch of tightening state control. He did not complete another film for ten years.

Several factors contributed to his silence. Sound had suddenly overtaken the world's film industries and Eisenstein needed time to study the new medium.

He spent several years in America studying, trying to get Paramount to accept one of the scripts that they had contracted him to direct *(Arms and the Man, The War of the Worlds, An American Tragedy)*. Paramount rejected them all. In 1932, Eisenstein and his cameraman, Edouard Tisse, went to Mexico to film an epic of the Mexican people, *Que Viva Mexico!,* financed by Upton Sinclair. Eisenstein fought with Sinclair and the film was cancelled. Eisenstein never got the chance to edit the finished footage, much of which he never saw. A bowdlerized version of the film, assembled by Sol Lesser, was released in 1933 as *Thunder over Mexico.* Returning to the Soviet Union, Eisenstein submitted several film projects that were rejected by the state film committee. Eisenstein was accused of formalism—the great sin of Soviet art. He paid too much attention to the beauty of the work and not enough to the utility of it. His methods were wasteful and time-consuming. His perfectionism was demanding and inconsiderate of budgets and schedules. Then in 1938 he was able to complete his first film in almost a decade, *Alexander Nevsky.*

Eisenstein's theory of the sound film was that the "talkie" was a fundamental error in the use of the medium. There was no artistic purpose in showing a man's lips move while the audience hears the words pour out. For Eisenstein, sound was to be used asynchronously, to do something that the picture did not do. And the picture should continue to do what sound could not do. Sound was to become one more element of a film's montage. The visuals and sound should play against one another, not sing in unison. Although Eisenstein's theory of the sound film was contrary to the practice of his contemporaries, years of experience with the sound film have since proved the solidity of his theory.

Eisenstein, whose use of images had always been musical, was especially interested in the precise synchronization of visual images with musical passages and motifs. One of Eisenstein's best demonstrations of his musical theory is in "The Battle on the Ice" sequence in *Alexander Nevsky* as the invading Teutonic hordes encounter the valiant Russian people who have gathered to defend themselves. Aided by the power and complexity of Prokofiev's score, Eisenstein turns "The Battle on the Ice" into a cinematic symphony. The successive tones and rhythms of the Prokofiev music— slowly expectant, playfully fast, steadily victorious—play both with and against the content of Eisenstein's images of battle and the rhythms and shapes that control the cutting of the images.

Eisenstein's only other completed works before his death in 1948 were two of the three intended parts of *Ivan the Terrible.* In Part II, he experimented with color in two sequences. As with sound, Eisenstein believed that color should not be exploited for its novelty, its colorfulness, but that color should play a functional role in controlling the film's tone and effects. Again, the years would prove his sensitivity to one potential of a cinematic device. The interrelation of color, cutting, movement, and music during the dance sequences of *Saturday Night Fever* (1977), for example, can be traced directly back to Eisenstein's theories of using sound and color in film. But the most striking fact of Eisenstein's twenty-five–year career in films is that he made four pictures in his first five years and three in his next twenty. Eisenstein became a teacher and theoretician; he taught at the State Film School; he wrote lengthily and convincingly on the powers and effects of montage. But his greatest achievements in filmmaking had been accomplished before the end of the silent era. Indeed, his sound films display a self-consciousness in the handling of montage that was deadening to the vitality and the exuberance of the method he applied instinctively in his youth.

To some extent his career mirrors the artistic vitality of the Soviet film as a whole. The Russian film made the transition into the sound era with the greatest difficulty, partially because the Soviet cinematic method was so visual, partially because the great Soviet directors became politically suspect, partially because the Soviet industry had great difficulty acquiring reliable machines to shoot and project sound pictures.

Vsevlod I. Pudovkin

Pudovkin and Eisenstein were friendly opponents. Whereas Eisenstein's theory of montage was one of collision, Pudovkin's was one of linkage. For Pudovkin, the shots of the film combine to build the whole work rather than conflict with one another in dynamic suspension. Although the linkage-collision argument may seem a war of words, of similar but different-sounding abstractions, the differences between the two directors become clear by comparing their films. Whereas the tone and pace of the Eisenstein film is generally nervous and tense, the tone and pace of the Pudovkin film is more languid and relaxed. He reserves the shocking, violent montage effects for occasional sequences of fighting and rebellion. Whereas Eisenstein's usual human focus is the mass, Pudovkin's is the individual, a single human's revolutionary decision rather than the revolutionary action of a whole group. Whereas Eisenstein's montage is rich in intellectual commentary, Pudovkin's usually develops the emotional tone and human feelings within the scene.

Pudovkin, unlike Eisenstein, depended heavily on the performances of individual players; like Griffith, Pudovkin realized that the context of the scene, the immobile face of an actor in close-up, a flickering in the eyes, could communicate more than overt gestures. Pudovkin took Kuleshov's experiment with Mozhukin's face seriously—far more seriously than Kuleshov himself took it (as the overacting in Kuleshov's own film, *By the Law,* shows). Pudovkin believed that the "plastic material"—concrete physical objects—could communicate emotions and ideas more effectively than an actor's grimaces.

Whereas the imagery in Eisenstein's films is primarily inanimate, the imagery in Pudovkin's films is primarily natural: trees, rivers, the sky, the wind. When Eisenstein does use a natural image, for example the sea in *Potemkin,* his choice is a huge, violent natural image rather than a calm, peaceful one. The Eisenstein film is a more exciting, jostling emotional experience; the Pudovkin film is a warmer one.

Like Eisenstein, Pudovkin came to the arts not as artist but as scientist. After studying physics and chemistry, Pudovkin decided to work in films (originally intending to act rather than direct). His admiration for Griffith's *Intolerance* strongly influenced his decision. In 1920, Pudovkin began his studies at the State Film School, entering Kuleshov's workshop two years later. His scientific training ably suited him for his first major film project, *Mechanics of the Brain* (1926), a cinematic investigation of Pavlovian research on conditioned reflexes in animals and children. He took time off from the Pavlov picture to shoot his first fiction film, *Chess Fever* (1925), an ingenious and charming short comedy that paid homage to his teacher, Kuleshov.

Unlike the American comedies, *Chess Fever* is a comedy of editing. Pudovkin surprises us with gags that are solely the results of montage. In the opening sequence, we watch a chess game from underneath the table, seeing only the feet and arms of each of the players making his move. Only later does Pudovkin pull back to show us a single chess player playing the game by himself—he is that infected with the chess fever. Pudovkin's editing fooled us into believing that there were two players, the usual and expected number. The whole film is built out of such Kuleshovian tricks. During the filming of *Chess Fever*, an international chess tournament actually took place in Moscow. Pudovkin sent his camera crew—masquerading as newsreel photographers—to film the tournament and the champion players. Pudovkin then spliced the "newsreel" footage into the plot of the comedy, making the film's action seem to revolve around the tournament. For example, a girl is so upset by her boyfriend's fanatic devotion to chess that she throws one of his chess pieces away. Pudovkin then cuts to a shot of the chess champion, Capablanca, standing and holding a chess piece. It looks as though he caught the piece that

the girl just threw. Purely an editing trick! Pudovkin took Kuleshov's notion of "creative geography" and produced "creative continuity."

Pudovkin's unique style emerged in his later fiction films. In *Mother* (1926), he reveals his ability to combine sensitive treatment of a human story, fluid narrative editing that uses the shock effects of montage for isolated, showcase effects and natural images that comment on the action and reinforce the film's values. *Mother* is an adaptation of a Gorky story (later adapted by Brecht into a play): a tale of a woman who learns that radical action is ultimately the only protection against a wicked state. Her husband is lured into helping a group of strikebreakers; he is shot and killed in a scuffle. The mother then betrays her own

Mother: Pudovkin's use of the "plastic material". Defining a bureaucratic policeman by his gloved hands

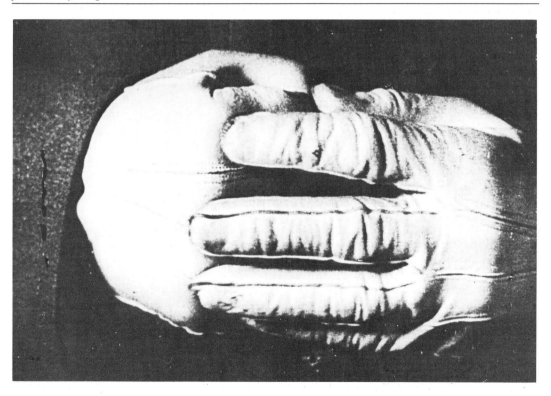

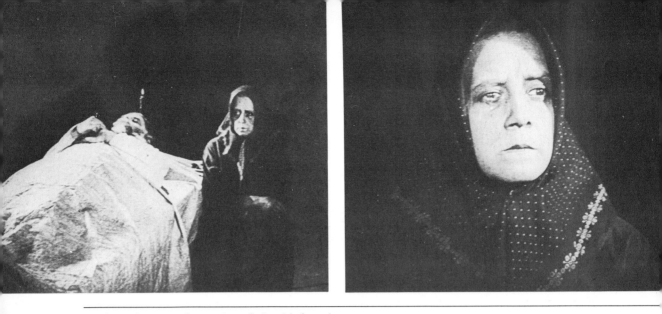

Mother: *the scene of mourning—built with four shots*

son, Pavel, revealing that the boy was in collusion with the workers. At her son's trial, she sees the corruption of justice. The judges are more interested in dozing or breeding race horses than in administering justice; the unsympathetic gallery has come to the trial for a good sadistic show. The unjust social process turns the old lady into a radical herself. She helps her son escape from prison and together they march in the forefront of a workers' demonstration. Although both she and Pavel die, cut down by the bullets and bayonets of the Cossacks, the story of her education serves as a model for all the workers of Russia and a metaphor for the results of their education that would eventually surface in 1917.

Pudovkin's handling of his actors and shaping of the scenes is exceptional. His principle of acting—that actors do not really act in films, that the film's context, its decor, its business, its use of objects, create an acting performance—is demonstrated throughout the film. A most effective example is the scene of mourning in which the mother sits by the corpse of her dead husband. Pudovkin

alternates between several shots: a far shot of the mother sitting beside the bier, the walls gray and bare behind her; a close shot of water dripping in a bucket (the scene's "plastic material"); a close shot of the mother's face, motionless. The mother's face needs no motion. The bareness of the room, the steadily dripping water, our knowledge of the husband's death create all the emotion the scene needs. Her still, quiet face mirrors all the sorrow that has been built around her.

A similar principle creates the viciousness of the strikebreakers, the Black Hundreds. As they make plans in a saloon, Pudovkin uses three kinds of shots: shots of the musicians playing a jolly tune, shots of a man's hands dismembering a fish (the "plastic material"), and shots of the strikebreakers' faces. These men need not grimace and glower to reveal their nastiness; by juxtaposing their discussion with happy, frenetic music and the brutal gutting of a fish, Pudovkin creates all the viciousness he needs.

Significant also is the camera angle

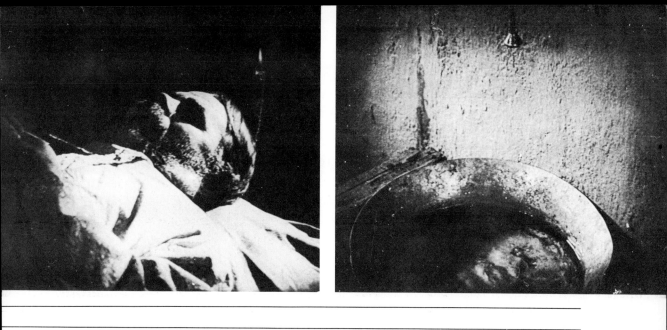

Pudovkin uses to shoot a scene. The far shot of the mourning mother beside the corpse is a down-shot from a high camera position. Pudovkin discovered that the downward angle emphasizes the characters' smallness, their feeling of being alone, their insignificance. Conversely, the extreme upward angle can magnify the self-importance of characters, their smugness and petty self-esteem. Pudovkin uses extreme upward angles for his satiric shots of the factory owners, of the corrupt judges, of the egotisical, self-important policeman (played by Pudovkin himself) who comes to search the mother's house for the strikers' guns. A slight upward angle produces not satire but ennoblement of the figure, making the character grand without delusions of grandeur. Pudovkin's final shots of the mother marching nobly at the head of the demonstration are slight upward shots. In fact, Pudovkin mirrors the state of the mother's mind and the progress of her education with his choice of camera positions. He shoots her from above before her conversion, he shoots her from below to ennoble her

after it. With such control of setting and camera angle, Pudovkin allows his actress, Vera Baranovskaia, to give a brilliant performance. Her performance, of course, is partially the result of his cutting and camera placement.

Pudovkin relies primarily on the narrative cut, on the lessons he had learned from Griffith. Like Griffith, he works for fluidity in building a scene, a fluidity that hides the cut from the viewer so that we synthesize the complete emotional experience. Most reminiscent of Griffith is the flashback in which the mother remembers her son hiding the guns; Pudovkin even uses a Griffith-like iris-in and -out to mark the flashback. Such fluid, narrative cutting was infrequent in Eisenstein. But like Eisenstein, Pudovkin could also use tricky montage effects when he needed the power of a physical assault. To reveal the joy in Pavel's heart when he discovers that his comrades will soon free him from prison, Pudovkin splices together a series of images to evoke the sensation of joy. The director's sensitivity to the actor's needs told him that merely to show a

The beginning of the slaughter in Mother

smile on Pavel's face would be fakey and punchless. Instead, Pudovkin cuts from Pavel's face to a series of beautiful natural images: a flowing river, tree-lined fields, a happy child playing. Pudovkin uses the identical method to reveal the other prisoners' thoughts of home when they hear of the intended escape: he uses cuts of fields, of horses, of plowing, of hands feeling the soil. Like Eisenstein's cuts, the shots are related thematically, not narratively; unlike Eisenstein, the images are natural rather than artificial, warm and human rather than satirical. Pudovkin's famous ice shots, with which the film ends, also echo Eisenstein's metaphorical cuts. Pudovkin cuts repeatedly from the shots of marching workers, steadily growing in mass, rhythm, and purpose, to shots of ice flowing on the river, steadily growing in mass, rhythm, and direction. Although the image of the ice cake echoes Griffith's *Way Down East,* the intellectual function of it does not.

Yet another use of montage for a nonnarrative effect is Pudovkin's cutting of violent sequences; like Eisenstein, Pudovkin knew how to analyze a quick action into its component movements to add emphasis, shock, and drama to the event. For example, in the final demonstration sequence, Pudovkin emphasizes the brutality of the slaughter by breaking the moment of the soldiers' initial attack into thirteen shots: (1) a gloved hand of the commanding officer is raised, close-up; (2) the soldiers raise their rifles, full shot; (3) the workers see the rifles and start to scurry, far shot; (4) the mother and Pavel embrace, medium; (5) the commanding officer's gloved hand drops, close-up; (6) the rifles fire, full shot; (7) a fallen worker's body crashes in a pool of muddy water, close shot, very quick; (8) another worker plunges face first into the water, close, very quick; (9) another body falling (Pavel's), close-up on midsection, quick; (10) the red flag starts to fall, silhouetted against the sky,

close; (11) the falling flag and its bearer reflected in the water as they both fall into the mud; (12) the mother and Pavel continue to embrace, medium close; (13) Pavel falls, still locked in the embrace. Out of the violence and chaos of this moment the mother gains courage, picks up the fallen flag and starts walking slowly toward the advancing troops (excellent series of cuts with contrasting directions and rhythms). Though the mother dies, she dies a new woman and a new metaphorical mother of the nation that is born with her death.

Like *Mother, The End of St. Petersburg* (1927) is a story of political education, of a character who betrays the revolutionists early in the film only to join them before the end of it. A young peasant boy from the country must leave for the city to survive; there is neither enough land nor enough food on the farm to support him. Pudovkin draws a visual contrast between city and country with the opening shots of animals, fields, rivers, and trees (precisely the same images as in *Mother*) contrasted with later shots of factories and city buildings and statues. The boy feels dwarfed in the city of St. Petersburg. Pudovkin shoots from high angles down at the boy, making him seem small and worthless in comparison with the huge statues, high buildings, and vast public squares.

The boy, ignorant of political realities, becomes a strikebreaker and betrays the leaders of the strike, one of whom is his own cousin. The boy feels guilty for his betrayal. He returns to the man's home to give the man's wife the piece of silver he received for his information. Pudovkin's skill in narrative cutting and manipulating detail creates a memorable scene. The boy enters the room. He and the wife look at each other, faces motionless, saying nothing. He slowly walks toward her. In a close-up of his right hand we see him slowly and fumblingly pull the piece of silver from his pocket and put it on the table, the same table where the whole

The End of St. Petersburg. *The deflation of war: soldiers without heads, flying flags, a fancy-speaking orator (note the upward angle to burlesque him), as men die in the smoke and carnage on the battlefield*

family had eaten together earlier in the film. The wife says nothing; she just looks at his face and his coin. The boy says nothing. He slowly turns and walks out the door. The woman's grim silence, a small, seemingly trivial action, teaches him the meaning of his betrayal of another human being.

The second half of the film is a sharp structural shift. Pudovkin abandons the narrative focus on the boy to treat the political events of 1915–17 that converted St. Petersburg to Leningrad: World War I, the February Revolution, Kerensky's Provisional Government, and the October Revolution. Like Eisenstein's *October, The End of St. Petersburg* was intended to commemorate the tenth anniversary of the revolution. Although the film's second half lacks narrative unity (the thin unifying thread is the boy's development into a Bolshevik soldier), it contains some powerful thematic contrasts that Pudovkin draws with his control of montage.

The film makes a brilliant visual contrast between the idealistic glories and the horrifying realities of war. When war is declared Pudovkin shows a procession of marching soldiers, smartly filing into formation. Pudovkin's shot reveals only their bodies from the neck down—their sabres, their uniforms, their medals, their gold braid, their boots. Not their heads. They obviously have no heads. As the parade of soldiers marches off to war, Pudovkin cuts the sequence rhythmically to look and feel like a gaudy carnival: trumpets blare, flags wave, drums rattle, arms wave, girls throw flower petals, an orator speaks (extreme upward angle to burlesque his grandiloquence). From the rhythmic shots of celebration, Pudovkin cuts to a quiet shot of the sky; suddenly a shell explodes, splattering the earth in the foreground. The glory of war has been replaced by the reality. Pudovkin continues with horrifying shots of trenches, fire throwers, smoke, bodies. Not content to let the contrast rest there, Pudovkin cuts back and forth between the violent war at the front and violent men haggling at the stock exchange. While men die in the military war, other men get rich in the financial war. While men die on the battlefield, other men barter at the stock exchange.

Pudovkin's next film, *Storm Over Asia* (1928), is yet another story of revolutionary education, of potential betrayal converted into political camaraderie. A young Mongol hunter learns that the value of his pelts is fixed by the greed of the capitalists, who buy them as cheaply as they can. When the Mongol is captured by his people's enemies (he has since joined the Partisan guerrilla army in their struggle against the imperialists), the young man produces papers that seem to prove him the heir of the great Genghis Khan, papers that he has acquired accidentally and that make him the hero's heir only in the sense that all Mongols rightfully share that heritage. The imperialist rulers (the British Army in the original version, the White Army in the American one), however, try to use the lad to keep his own people in bondage. The young Mongol perceives their viciousness, rejects the rich and soft life they offer him, breaks free from his captors, and leads his people in an uprising that sweeps the usurpers off the land.

The film contains several extraordinary sequences that reveal the director's mastery of his art. The most striking is a montage sequence that deflates both the sanctity of religion (probably influenced by *October*) and the pretentions to gentility of the imperialists. Pudovkin cuts back and forth between the religious icons, which are being scrubbed and brushed and polished for a religious festival, to shots of the rich imperialists, who are also being scrubbed and powdered and dressed to attend the festival. These parallel and intercut activities turn the religious objects into pampered dolls and turn the pampered imperialists into dead wood.

Another brilliant yet much subtler and simpler device is Pudovkin's use of a puddle of muddy water, an exemplary use of his notion of "plastic material." A puddle blocks the town's main road. When a soldier leads the young Mongol to be shot, the Mongol walks directly through the puddle; the soldier carefully walks around it, taking care not to soil his boots. The puddle instantly delineates the class conflict (reminiscent of Chaplin), the difference between the rulers and the people. Interestingly, when the soldier is later commanded to save the Mongol, he runs directly through the puddle in his frenzy and haste.

Satiric cross-cuts in Storm Over Asia: *from powdering and pampering a rich dignitary to polishing up a religious icon*

The film's third remarkable device is the metaphor with which it ends, a howling, furious wind that strips the branches off the trees and the imperalist soldiers off the land. The wind, like the flowing ice in *Mother,* is a natural image; it symbolizes the spirit of the people, rising irresistibly to blow the foreign element from their soil.

Like Eisenstein, Pudovkin believed that the value of the sound film would be its asynchronous, tonal use of sound rather than a synchronized dialogue and picture. In discussing how he would have used sound in the silent *Mother,* Pudovkin said he would have evoked the sorrow of the mourning scene not with the synchronized sound of the mother's weeping but with the steady, hollow sound of the water dripping into the bucket. Like Eisenstein, Pudovkin had difficulty putting his theories into practice. *The Story of a Simple Case* (1932) was originally intended as a sound picture; it was finally released silent. It is uncertain whether the film's difficulties with sound stemmed from the clumsiness of the director with sound or the clumsiness of the Soviet sound machines and technicians. His next sound film, *Deserter* (1933), is his most respected; it is the story of a young German worker who, like the protagonists of Pudovkin's silent films, receives an education in political radicalism. It was originally intended as a German-Soviet coproduction, but the emergence of Hitler forced Pudovkin to finish shooting in Russia. Pudovkin continued directing and acting in films for the next twenty years, until his death in 1953; during those twenty years he directed only about a half-dozen major films. Like Eisenstein, he was castigated for his formalism and his fictional manipulating of official Soviet history; like Eisenstein, he spent much of his later life teaching and writing. But Pudovkin's few sound films lack the stature of his silent films; his purely visual method

never successfully wedded sound to his control of the "plastic material."

Dovzhenko and Others

Alexander Dovzhenko was the third of the great Soviet directors. Though he shared both the political philosophy of Marx and the montage methods of Kuleshov with Eisenstein and Pudovkin, Dovzhenko's style was completely original. Unlike Eisenstein and Pudovkin, Dovzhenko came from the provinces, not the capital, from the Ukraine, not Moscow or St. Petersburg. Dovzhenko's films are saturated in local Ukrainian life and customs as well as in the folk-legend spirit and poetry of the province. Dovzhenko's films desert realism and linear construction even more completely than Eisenstein's or Pudovkin's. His is a world where horses talk, where paintings of heroes in picture frames roll their eyes at the bastardization of their principles, where animals sniff the revolutionary spirit in the air. The Dovzhenko film is structured not as story or even as mass political action but purely as visual metaphor that develops a theme and allows the filmmaker immense elliptical jumps in time, space, and continuity.

Typical of Dovzhenko's films is *Arsenal* (1929), the first of his mature film poems. Made after three years of apprentice directing in which he converted himself from painter of static scenes on canvas to director of moving ones on a screen, *Arsenal's* subject is, roughly, the birth and growth of the revolutionary spirit in the Ukraine. Whereas Eisenstein would develop such a theme by showing the action of a human mass in relation to a single historical event and Pudovkin would develop it by showing a single Ukrainian's revolutionary decision, Dovzhenko seems to spread all the events of the revolutionary years before him on a table and then select those images and those vignettes that appeal to him. The film darts from place to place, from social class to social class, from political meeting to war to church procession to factory to a train chugging through the snow.

Somewhat like the second half of Pudovkin's *St. Petersburg,* Dovzhenko uses a central figure, a soldier who deserts the czar to serve the revolution, as a loose peg on which to hang the film's action. Scenes with the soldier flow through the film's many vignettes. In the final sequence, the White Army captures the soldier, leads him in front of a firing squad, and shoots him. The Ukrainian soldier does not die; the bullets do not strike him. He stands there defiantly. Although the forces of tyranny can capture a single arsenal, although they can shoot a single rebel, they cannot murder the spirit of rebellion and freedom in the hearts of the people. The Ukrainian becomes a metaphor for that spirit. His presence throughout the film has been as metaphor, not as traditional protagonist. Dovzhenko's films are not narratives of events but metaphors for the feeling and the significance of the events.

Individual images and vignettes of a film like *Arsenal* stand out from the whole. Whereas Eisenstein's geometric compositions show him building with the eye of an architect, Dovzhenko's striking compositions in light and space reveal the eye of a painter. Vast shots of sky and clouds, framed at the left by a tall tree and with the thinnest strip of land at the bottom with a group of tiny men trooping across it, are among Dovzhenko's favorite views. A similar principle of composition controls his snow sequences—vast expanses of white, a peasant wife huddled in black beside a grave in the lower-right corner of the frame, a team of horses bearing the husband's body to the grave in the center rearground. Dovzhenko's painter's eye sees the power and tension of shooting with the tilted camera, on an angle to rather than parallel with the world he is filming.

But Dovzhenko's compositions are as impressive for their content as for their look. His shots of war, which dwarf men as tiny dots on the horizon or turn them into motionless statues in silhouette against the sky, also evoke the horrors of useless human slaughter. If Pudovkin deflates war by comparing it with theoretical glories on the one hand and financial realities on the other, Dovzhenko deflates it with haunting images of sheer horror. Dovzhenko cuts repeatedly to the frenzied laughter of a German officer who has been gassed, to a frozen smile on the face of a corpse (a smile of death), to a frozen hand sticking out of a pile of dirt (a single reminder that a whole man once breathed the air).

Dovzhenko's style is also dependent on extended metaphors; whole sequences, not just an occasional montage (Eisenstein's slaughtered ox, Pudovkin's ice), are pure metaphor. In *Arsenal,* Dovzhenko shows the journey of a train, loaded with soldiers of the czar. The train has no brakes; it hurtles faster and faster down the track until its inevitable and disastrous crash, murdering the men who are still aboard. The train becomes a metaphor for the unquestioning servants of political tyranny, blindly accepting the murderous orders of their government. Dovzhenko brings the metaphor alive with his control of montage: tracking shots of the speeding train, of some soldiers frenziedly leaping from it just before the collision, of other soldiers contentedly listening to accordion music in ignorance of their impending doom, and swirling cuts when the train crashes into the station. Dovzhenko dramatizes the death of the soldiers by following the career of the accordion, the former instrument of pleasure. Tossed from the train in the collision, the accordion lies on the ground full of air; suddenly it collapses as all the air goes out of it. The "death" of the accordion is a metaphor for the death of all the soldiers on the metaphoric train.

Dovzhenko's films are of metaphors

Arsenal: *the horrors of war. Frozen statues of death in silhouette . . . a mad laugh . . . a frozen smile . . . a hand*

within metaphors within metaphors, of isolated vignettes, of scenes and characters manifesting themselves without preparation or introduction, playing themselves out on the screen and then disappearing, often never returning to the film at all. The film's general theme and the unity of the director-poet's imagination keep the apparently random scenes together. Dovzhenko's second great silent film-poem, *Earth* (1930), is another series of images and vignettes, this one revolving around the earth, the harvests,

the relationships of people, machines, and the cycles of life. His sound films, *Ivan* (1932), *Aerograd* (1935), and *Schors* (1939), were equally daring, equally episodic, equally imagistic. Not surprisingly, Dovzhenko ran into stiff Soviet criticism; he was the most elliptical director of them all. How could his films be socially useful if the audiences could not follow them? Dovzhenko made only two films in his last fifteen years; he died in 1956. The Pudovkin-Eisenstein pattern had asserted itself again—the great innovative mind stifled by the state's ever-narrowing definitions of artistic utility.

Dziga-Vertov, one of the Soviet Union's pioneers in combining documentary footage with political commitment, experimental cinema with ideological statement, suffered similar artistic strangulation. His *The Man with the Movie Camera* (1929) remains one of the most distinctive and adventurous films of any era. Like Ruttmann's *Berlin,* the film is organized as an examination of a cross-section of life in a major city—its work and play, at night and during the day. Unlike its German predecessor, however, Vertov depicts the ways that the cinema itself has become an intrinsic part of modern life and a marvelous aid to seeing and understanding that life. The film begins with shots of an empty movie theatre. When the patrons arrive, the seats of the theatre fold down by themselves to greet them. The film they see is the film we see—for *The Man with the Movie Camera* is a film-within-a-film about filmmaking. In that film-within-a-film Vertov parallels the lens of the movie camera and its operations to the human eye and its operations—converting the cinema into an extension of human vision. He demonstrates the processes of editing (the winding of film strips into spools on an editing machine) and the relationship of still cinema frames to moving cinema imagery, drawing parallels between the processes of cinema and other societal occupations that depend on machines that spin circularly—the winding of threads, the packing of cigarette boxes, various other whirring wheels and gears for grinding, winding, spinning, and propelling. If Vertov takes the "magic" out of cinema by exposing how it does its tricks, he also endows it with another form of magic—the magic of all processes of modern mechanical life doing their work in the service of human beings.

Like everyone else in the society, the man with the movie camera has a job to do—his special work being to record and reveal the work of everyone else. And like everyone else in the society, the man with the movie camera likes to play. The final section of the film allows the playful camera to dazzle us with its cinematic juggling—slow motion, accelerated motion, split screens, superimpositions, pixillation—sharing this visual magic with the movie audience that has come to the movie theatre to see it play in this very way. For Vertov, the cinema becomes life and life becomes cinema; the two are inseparable. But despite this impressive synthesis of radical form and radical ideology, Vertov made few major films after 1930, the most important being *Three Songs of Lenin* (1934), which combined documentary footage with lyrical passages in honor of the founding father. He died in 1954 after twenty years of reduced influence and enforced idleness.

Lesser film minds enjoyed healthier and longer careers. Abram Room—whose great silent film, *Bed and Sofa* (1926), combined a sensitive, human study of a love triangle with the social problems of abortion and inadequate housing—continued to make competent films in the sound era. Room's realistic human focus and more conventional narrative plotting were more consistent with the new official aesthetic of "socialist realism" than were the methods of the more adventurous silent masters. Esther Shub used montage effects to bring old newsreel footage to life, providing a striking, imaginative, and officially sanctioned view of what it was like to live in *The Russia of Nikolai II and Lev Tolstoy* (1928) and other eras.

In the early years of sound, the more realistic and less elliptical directors triumphed. Perhaps their methods were more compatible with the theoretical demands of the new sound filming. But behind the struggle between realism and abstraction in the films lay a more general battle that was being waged between two conflicting forces in all the Soviet arts: the struggle between socialist realism and constructivist abstraction for control of the "true path" of the People's Revolutionary Art. The central arena for the struggle was the theatre, where the principles of Stanislavski's Moscow Art Theatre (detailed, realistic characters; lucid stories of human interaction in a clear social setting) triumphed over those of Vsevlod Meyerhold's "constructivism" (more abstract and symbolic settings; epic stories of vast social forces and movements). The official canonization of the Stanislavski method (despite the Moscow Art Theatre's czarist and elitist origins) led to the vilification and ostracizing of Meyerhold. (Bertolt Brecht, who first fled Hitler's Germany for the Soviet Union, found a very cool reception there in 1933, for Brecht and Meyerhold held similar theories of the stage.) This conflict of values in the theatre necessarily spilled over into the cinema, where several film directors (Eisenstein, for example) had been extremely influenced by Meyerhold.

Nikolai Ekk, whose *The Road to Life* (1931) was the first great success of the Soviet sound film, found the new socialist-realist assumptions very congenial. His film is both a close, warm study of human feelings and exertion as well as a social lesson on how the "wild boys" of Russia—the homeless juvenile delinquents roaming the streets—found a purpose in life through collective labor. The Vasiliev Brothers' *Chapayev* (1934) became the model for the study of Revolutionary heroes, the human portrayal of a military leader whose great strengths are his energy, his passion, his humor, and his love for the people, and who overcomes his great weaknesses—excessive individuality, a stubborn refusal to study the new ways—to unite his heroic band of guerrillas with the spirit of the entire Red Army. The difference between the Vasilievs' Chapayev and Eisenstein's Nevsky is the difference between the leader as a man of the people and the leader as totem pole or as opera singer in buskins.

Yakov Protazanov was another of the successful realist directors of the first decade of sound, one of the few film directors of the czarist era to return to Soviet Russia. Grigori Kozintsev and Leonid Trauberg founded the actor-oriented "FEX" group (Society for Eccentric Actors) in the silent period in answer to the montage-oriented Kuleshov group. They continued to make films into the 1960s, including the respected color version of Pasternak's translation of *Hamlet* (1964). Mark Donskoi made the careful, literate biographical trilogy of Maxim Gorky's growth from youth to maturity (*Childhood of Maxim Gorky,* 1938; *Out in the World,* 1939; *My Universities,* 1940).

But for almost twenty-five years the imagination and creativity of the Soviet film was tightly reined by a government policy and aesthetic that found it exceedingly difficult to force innovative minds into the prescribed channels of film expression. During the most critical years of film history, from 1929 to 1937—the transitional years between silence and sound—the Russian film industry was controlled by Boris Shumyatsky, a business-minded bureaucrat who viewed his job as bringing the eccentric, "formalistic" artists in line. Shumyatsky's "bringing the artists in line" was as responsible for the silence of Eisenstein in those ten key years as the triumph of socialist realism. Stalin dismissed Shumyatsky in 1937 for failing to produce enough films and enough significant films; the Soviet filmmakers then enjoyed three years of freedom. But the war against Germany in 1940 imposed restrictions on Soviet directors again; certain kinds of films were needed to boost morale at the front and at home. After the war, Stalin clamped down on the directors again. Only since his death in 1953 have Soviet films regained prestige on international screens with such powerful and personal films as Mikhail Kalatozov's *The Cranes are Flying* (1957) and Grigori Chukhrai's *Ballad of a Soldier* (1959). Although the Soviet Union continues to produce a significant number of films each year for its own screens and those of its Eastern Bloc allies, almost none of those films are ever shown or make any impact in Western Europe and the United States. Even the citizens of Czechoslovakia and other Warsaw Pact nations prefer the few Hollywood movies their theatres are allowed to show to the many Soviet films their theatres must show.

The five greatest years of Soviet filmmaking, 1924-29, demonstrated how powerful and important are the effects of simply joining the pieces of celluloid together. In Hollywood, the Eisenstein methods were so admired in the late 1920s that producers began installing metronomes on sets and in cutting rooms to control the rhythms of the movement and cutting. (The metronomic parade and battle sequences in King Vidor's *The Big Parade* would never have been made without Eisenstein and, especially, Pudovkin.)

In the early years of sound, Hollywood did an about-face and began discrediting the jangling, discordant effects of montage. In the 1960s and 70s, however, the quick cutting of television commercials, the tense, violent cutting of action films like *Bullitt, The French Connection,* and the James Bond series, the subjective flashes into the past of *Joanna* and *Z,* the satiric cross-cutting in *Medium Cool,* the symbolic montage sequences in experimental films like Kenneth Anger's *Scorpio Rising,* all proved that montage was once again very much "in."

9 Sound

According to legend, sound unexpectedly descended on the film industry from the skies, like an ancient god out of a machine, when *The Jazz Singer* opened on Broadway on October 5, 1927. Although the success of *The Jazz Singer* ripped apart the film industry of 1927 with incredible speed, preparation for the entrance of sound had been building for over thirty years. The idea for the sound film was born with the film itself. W. K. L. Dickson even claimed to have produced a rough synchronization of word and picture with his Kinetophonograph of 1889.

For the first twenty years of film history inventors worked to wed sight and sound. Many of the same inventors who had developed the first cinema cameras and projectors turned to sound synchronization after the film artists had taken their toys and put them to use. In France, between 1896 and 1900, Auguste Baron, Henri Joly, and Georges Demeny patented various processes of synchronizing moving pictures with sounds recorded on a disc. Between 1900 and 1910, Léon Gaumont demonstrated

various synchronized-sound pictures, both at the World Exposition of 1900 and in his own Paris theatres. In 1910, the German film pioneer, Oscar Messter, produced a film with synchronized sound, *The Green Forest.* And in America, the Edison Company had produced a fifteen-minute, vaguely synchronized musical version of *Mother Goose Tales* (shot in one continuous take!) as early as 1912. Like the pioneers of an earlier film era, the first sound pioneers decorated their inventions with fancy-sounding Greco-Latin names that almost required a special apparatus to pronounce: Phonorama, Graphonocone, Chronophone.

The first practical, dependable synthesis of picture and sound came just after World War I. There were two primary problems that confronted the inventor of a sound-film process. The first, obviously, was synchronization. How were the film and the sound to be kept permanently and constantly "in synch?" The method of coupling a projected film with a recorded disc was dangerous; with two separate machines it was terribly easy for the two to slip "out of synch." The film could break; the stylus could skip. The film musical, *Singin' in the Rain* (1952), a marvelous parody of the transitional era from silent to sound films, revealed the unintentionally comic results when the cavalier's voice issued from the damsel's moving lips. Although the first commercially successful American sound-film process, the Vitaphone, synchronized a recorded disc with the film projector, a more stable method had been developed as early as 1919. Three German inventors had discovered the means of recording the sound track directly on the film itself. Using the principle of the oscilloscope, which converts sound into light beams, the Germans converted the sound into light beams, recorded the beams on the side of the strip of film next to the image, and then built a reader on the projector that could retranslate the light beams into sound. This German discovery, known as the "Tri-Ergon Process," became the ruling sound-film patent of Europe ten years later. In America, a similar sound-on-film process had been developed by Lee de Forest in the early 1920s.

An earlier de Forest invention solved the second problem of the sound film—amplification. The sound not only had to be synchronized. It had to be audible. A film had to make enough noise to reach the ears of the thousands of patrons who filled the huge movie palaces. The earliest phonographs and radios, lacking the means of amplification, could entertain only one listener, who stuck the listening tube in his ears (similar to the stereo systems on today's jet airplanes). In 1906, de Forest patented the audion tube, the little vacuum tube that magnified the sounds it received and drove them into a speaker. De Forest's tube gave birth to many children— radio, the public address system—and grandchildren—television, the high-fidelity music system. It also gave birth to the

sound film. Whatever the system of synchronization, the audion tube magnified the sound so that an entire audience could hear it.

By 1923 de Forest was making and showing little synchronized-sound films of variety acts, singers, politicians, and famous comedians, analogous to the first film strips that Edison made in his Black Maria. De Forest also gave a filmed lecture-demonstration of his sound-on-film process, which he called the Phonofilm. *Singin' in the Rain,* historically relevant as well as brilliantly funny, satirizes the good professor de Forest with its film clip of a horse-faced, nasal-voiced scientist, his nose and forehead grotesquely distorted by a wide-angle lens, stupidly and tautologically telling the audience that it is watching a talking picture. Despite de Forest's success with his sound-on-film process, the Bell Telephone Company's research laboratory, Western Electric, developed and marketed the less dependable sound-on-disc process, christened the Vitaphone, in 1925.

Western Electric offered the Vitaphone to the biggest producer in Hollywood, Adolph Zukor. Paramount did not want it. Neither did any other major company. Their reasons for rejecting sound were obvious; it was an untried and expensive innovation that could only disrupt a business that had become increasingly stable and increasingly profitable. Sound recording was ticklish and expensive; it would only slow down production schedules. Sound equipment was expensive to buy, especially for the theatre owners whose houses would have to be converted before any sound film could be shown. Nor did the competing sound-film processes make the decision easier. On which should the wise theatre owner place a commercial bet? The confusion was like that surrounding competing color television formats of the early 1960s and the competing home video-tape formats of the late 1970s. The wise theatre owner did nothing.

Rejected by the most powerful producers, Western Electric offered Vitaphone in 1926 to Warner Brothers, a family of four producing brothers, whose small company had recently embarked on a costly program of major expansion. Having bought the remains of the Vitagraph Company (the last of the original Trust companies) in 1925, Warners wished to expand their small network of theatres, to achieve full vertical integration, and to take on the big boys—Loew, Zukor, First National— who controlled enough theatre and distribution chains to choke the market for Warners' films. The Warner Brothers bought the Vitaphone. Within three years they had swallowed First National and digested most of the theatres in that chain.

The Warner sound films started cautiously enough. On August 5, 1926, Warners presented a program of short sound films; the first was an address by Will Hays praising the possibilities of the sound film, followed by the New York Philharmonic Orchestra and by leading artists of the opera, the concert, and the music hall. The Vitaphone shorts were no different from de Forest's earlier Phono-film novelties. In addition, Warners presented a feature film on the same program, *Don Juan,* with a synchronized musical score. A canned orchestra had merely replaced the live one in the pit. For over a year the Warners presented a series of similar film programs: short, musical sound films and a feature with synchronized score.

Like the Warners, another lesser producer, William Fox, was a film businessman who gazed enviously at the Zukors and Loews on the heights; he decided to use sound the same way as the Warners did. Early in 1927 Fox began presenting mechanically scored films to match the Warners'. Like the Warners,

Shaw Talks for Movietone: *the playwright scowls his "Mussolini look"*

Fox also presented a series of short novelty films—performances by famous variety artists and conversations with famous people. In addition, Fox inaugurated the first newsreel film with synchronized narration, the Fox-Movietone News. Unlike Vitaphone, the Fox system, called Movietone, was a sound-on-film process, exactly like de Forest's Phonofilm. One of de Forest's assistants, Theodore Case, had apparently pirated the inventor's system, made some slight modifications, and then sold it to Fox.

Fox exploited the novelty of coupling the sound of the human voice with the picture of moving lips. In the Movietone short, *Shaw Talks for Movietone* (1927), the audience is amused solely by seeing the image of the crusty playwright, by hearing his voice, by enjoying his garrulous, improvised pleasantries, and by recognizing the mechanical reproduction of other natural sounds like birds chirping and gravel crackling on the garden path. Visually the film is static and uninteresting. It uses only two setups: a brief far shot as Shaw walks down the

path; a medium shot of Shaw's head and torso that lasts for the duration of the film (at least five minutes without a cut). Perhaps the only reason the film splurged with the second setup was that the honk of an automobile horn (clearly audible on the sound track) "spoiled" the first take a few minutes after the camera started rolling. The moving pictures had become a simple recording device once again. The camera had stopped speaking, speech had replaced pictures. Although it is both delightful and instructive to see a famous figure "canned" for eternity, such a historical recording had nothing to do with film art.

The tendency of the Movietone shorts to use picture as merely an accompaniment for human speech dominated the first sound films that tried to integrate human speech and fictional action. *The Jazz Singer* was neither the first sound film nor the first film to synchronize picture with human speech and song. It was, however, the first film to use synchronized sound as a means of telling a story. Most of the film was shot silent and the musical score later

synchronized with the finished picture. In this respect Warners' *Jazz Singer* went no further than their earlier *Don Juan*. But four sequences used synchronized speech.

In one, the jazz singer returns to his orthodox Jewish home to visit his parents. His mother both enjoys seeing him and listening to his "jazzy" singing. His father, a cantor, does not and orders an end to all profane jazz in his sacred house. The father's command to stop the music is the cue for the film to revert to silence again. In another of the synchronized sequences, Jolson sings his "Mammy" number to an audience in a theatre. The number is exactly like the vaudeville shorts recorded earlier on the Phonofilm, the Vitaphone, and the Movietone—with two differences. In addition to singing his song, Jolson performed for two specific people who were watching him: his girl (backstage) and his mother (in the audience). Jolson not only sang but his song played a functional role in the action of the film: the cantor's son had synthesized the sacred and profane functions of music by becoming a successful entertainer.

The schizophrenia of this first sound

feature—part silent, part sound—revealed both the disadvantages and the advantages of the new medium. Whereas the silent sections of the film used rather flowing camera work and terse narrative cutting, the synchronized sections were, like the 1912 *Mother Goose Tales,* visually static and inert. For Jolson's first song, "Blue Skies," the camera was restricted to two shots: a medium shot of him sitting at the piano; a close shot of his mother responding (used sparingly). Most inert visually of all is the dialogue sequence: a rambling, improvised series of Jewish jokes between choruses of the song—a full shot of Jolson and mama, one long take. The two actors obviously squeeze and huddle together so that their voices can be picked up by the microphone that had been hidden somewhere between them. When the film starts making synchronized noises, the camera stops doing everything but exposing film.

On the other hand, this informal, improvised moment at the piano, though visually dreadful, is the most magical, exciting, and vital sequence of the entire film. Jolson is a poor mime, with hammy, overstated gestures and expressions (and Eugenie Besserer, who plays his mother, may be even worse). But when Jolson acquires a voice, the warmth, the excitement, the vibrations of it, the way its rambling spontaneity lays bare the imagination of the mind that is making up the sounds, convert the overgesturing hands and the overactive eyes into a performance that seems effortlessly natural. The addition of a Vitaphone voice revealed the particular qualities of Al Jolson that made him a star. Not only the eyes are a window of the soul.

Problems

The Jazz Singer was a huge hit; it put new zip in a film business that had begun to sag in 1927. The movie czars who resisted sound because it would disrupt their stable business now had to convert to sound to stay in business. Although studio executives predicted that the sound and silent films would continue to coexist, the admission dollars of the public punctured the theory. Americans no longer wanted to see silent films; they quickly deserted the old mistress for a more attractive new one. Silent films had taught them to see; the new invention of radio had taught them to hear. They would not leave their homes and spend their money if they could not both see and hear at the same time. By 1929 the silent film was dead in America; Hollywood produced a few silent versions of sound films for foreign theatres and for rural American houses that were not yet equipped for sound. In 1926 a few silent films used synchronized music and sound effects as a commercial novelty; in 1929 a few synchronized sound pictures were released silent as a commercial necessity.

Although Hollywood leaped quickly into sound production, it did not leap without stumbling. The new sound film caused filmmakers and film critics three primary problems: artistic, technical, and commercial. The camera, which had spent the last thirty years learning to take an active part in filmed fiction, suddenly became motionless and mute. The camera stood still while the players mouthed their lines. Cuts were rare; visual images became functional rather than expressive. Although the post-Griffith silent film had declared its independence from the stage, the early sound film became the vassal of the theatre once again. Canned theatre could now duplicate the dialogue of the stage hit in an identical film version. The moving picture stopped moving and stopped using pictures. Critics and directors sang a requiem for the film art and said amen.

Typical of the aesthetic blunders of the early sound films was the very first Warner Brothers "all-talking" film, *The*

Lights of New York (1928). The camera stood still to record scenes of seemingly endless dialogue. The director cut sparingly if at all. The decor no longer served any tonal, metaphoric, or narrative function; it was merely a backdrop for speaking bodies. Space was no longer charged with beauty or meaning; it was merely something to talk in. And the talking bodies huddled together so they could all be heard by the single microphone. In a scene in a barbershop, a character began a speech at one end of the room, walked across the room, and started talking only when he had come to a complete rest at the other end. He could not speak until he had parked himself under the mike. In a later scene, two thugs talk to their mobster boss in his office; the crooks sit on the edge of the sofa leaning toward the boss; the boss sits in his desk chair leaning toward his boys. All three actors strain to make sure that their voices can be heard by the single microphone, obviously buried in a canister on a ludicrous table that has no other function in the scene except to hide the microphone.

Worse, the film not only strains to record the dialogue, but the dialogue, once recorded, is not worth hearing. The film's speech is crammed with mixed metaphors ("You think you can take any chicken you want and throw me back in the deck?"), with clichés ("You needed me to stick by you through all the tough times")—with the blatantly obvious and unnecessary. Especially ludicrous are the actors' attempts to render their versions of gangster slang with the most precise, theatrical diction. Although the films had learned to talk, they had not learned to talk well. Compared with the fluidity of a gangster film like von Sternberg's *Underworld* (1927), with its completely effective moments of tough violence and subtle humor, *The Lights of New York* was an abominable regression. The outcry of theorists and critics was understandable.

Many of the aesthetic shortcomings of the early sound films were less the result of theoretical problems than of the practical and technical problems of mastering the new machines. Just as the first generation of film directors had to learn to paint with lens and film, the new generation of directors had to learn both to paint and score at the same time. The stasis, the inertia of the early sound films resulted partially from the difficulty of silencing the whirring camera and partially from the difficulty of recording with a single, fixed microphone. To baffle the camera's clatter, the machine and its operator were imprisoned in a sound-proof glass booth. The camera could neither tilt nor travel. The most it could manage was a slight pan. In the era before sound mixing and the microphone boom, a single microphone had to be buried in a pivotal, stationary spot on the set. Of necessity, the microphone nailed the action to a tiny circle. The comic attempts to hide the mike in *Singin' in the Rain*—in a bush, in the star's bosom—are exaggerated but accurate. Movies could not move if they wanted to be heard.

Yet another problem of the new sound equipment was its tremendous cost. Studios invested huge sums in the new machines to record the voice and new soundproof stages to house them. The theatre owner also faced big expenses, being forced to buy new sound projectors, new speakers, and new wiring to link the two. Both studios and theatres borrowed from the banks to convert to sound. The movies, big business though they were, became subsidiaries of the banks. The two major sound processes in 1930, Western Electric's and R.C.A.'s, were themselves subdivisions of the Morgan and Rockefeller holdings. Studios borrowed from these very banks to buy the equipment that bank money had developed. This interrelationship of movies and high finance has continued for the past fifty years.

The new invention caused commercial problems with people as well as with paper. Studios suddenly discovered that the popular stars and directors of the silent films were now liabilities in the era of speech. The incoming tide of foreign talent—the Negris and Jannings and Stillers and de Puttis—suddenly reversed and started flowing back to native shores. The actor or director with faulty English had no place in the Hollywood world of dialogue film. Lubitsch, Murnau, Garbo stayed, but most returned home. Native American stars also had troubles with dialogue; their voices had to harmonize with the visual images they had projected in the silent era. The beautiful actress with a nasal rasp, the handsome Latin with a squeaky twang might as well have been unable to speak English at all. Diction coaches suddenly opened offices in the studios to polish the pronunciation of those voices that did not irreparably offend the microphone. Along with the diction coaches came dialogue writers, many of them novelists or playwrights, whom the studios also needed. Old stars and old jobs died; new ones were born.

Eisenstein predicted that the sound film would try to solve its problems by taking the path of least resistance: by drifting into dialogue films, by synchronizing picture and sound, by merely exploiting the audience's interest in seeing a picture and hearing a sound at the same time. Hollywood did just that, grandly advertising its films as "all-talking" and even as "100% all-talking, all-singing, and all-dancing." Gunshots, twittering birds, ringing telephones, banging doors became mandatory sound-film effects. Musical numbers became obligatory. Hollywood imported Broadway directors, Broadway players, and Broadway plays. At least the talk in a play had already been proven and its actors had demonstrated their ability to speak it. As in their earliest years, moving pictures became the hand-servants of the theatre, seemingly oblivious of the twenty-five years of development that had created a unique narrative art.

Solutions

While film aesthetes sang the blues, a few creative film artists worked to turn talkies into moving pictures with sound. Two of the greatest directors, René Clair and Eisenstein, refused to throw their handfuls of dirt on the film's grave, certain that the movies could absorb sound rather than the other way round. Hollywood quickly began to solve some of the technical problems. Although the noisy camera had to be encased, it could be released from its glass prison for a few sequences that did not require synchronized dialogue. In *Hallelujah* (1929), King Vidor let his camera roam silently over the fields and then dubbed in the singing of the Negro spirituals. Music in *Hallelujah*, its rhythms precisely synchronized with the visual action and emotional "beats," became one of the powerful sources of the film's meaning and effect—either the exuberant joy of jazz or the soul-heavy sorrow of the spiritual. In *The Love Parade* (1929), Ernst Lubitsch shot ladies sitting in Parisian windows or soldiers marching gallantly in formation with a silent, tracking camera and then dubbed in the song that Maurice Chevalier or Jeanette MacDonald sang. In *All Quiet on the Western Front* (1930), Lewis Milestone shot battle scenes with silent, sweeping tracking shots of the lines of attacking armies and dubbed in the sounds of machine guns and grenades later.

Soon even the dialogue scenes gained mobility with the invention of the camera blimp, a device that slipped over the camera to baffle its clatter without banishing it to a glass island. By 1929 Victor Fleming (in *The Virginian*) could shoot dialogue sequences outdoors,

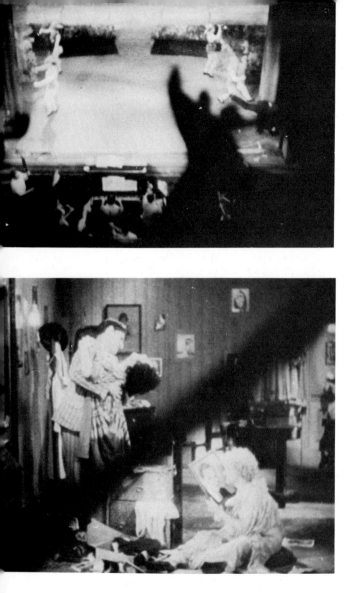

including tracking shots in which men on horseback spoke to passengers on a moving train. And by 1930 Ernst Lubitsch (in *Monte Carlo*) could shoot a long tracking shot on a gravel path in which camera movement, dialogue, and editing worked together with complete fluidity (and cleverness).

Hollywood solved the microphone problem, too. Rouben Mamoulian, one of the directors imported from New York, showed filmic imagination when he suggested using two microphones to shoot a single scene, balancing and regulating the relative volumes of the two with a sound mixer. In Mamoulian's *Applause* (1929), two characters could speak to each other from opposite ends of the room without trotting together to speak into the same flowerpot. Mamoulian added zip to his film by recording indoor scenes with a moving camera, ceaselessly (sometimes too ceaselessly) tracking toward and away from the speakers. He shot other scenes on location, taking advantage of actual and interesting New York sights like the Brooklyn Bridge, the Chrysler Building, and the subway, dubbing in the dialogue later.

An even more flexible method of capturing the voice was the invention of the "boom," a machine that kept the microphone hovering directly above the speaker's head, just out of the camera's frame. Whenever the actor moved, the microphone could silently and faithfully follow. Although the invention of the principle has been credited to either sound technician Eddie Mannix (at MGM) or actor-director Lionel Barrymore, the idea for the machine was probably born

Applause: *adding visual energy to the early talkies. Bizarre camera angles and silhouettes; a tricky split-screen: while Helen Morgan serenades her lover's picture, he caresses the chorus girl down the hall; the girl and her suitor on a Manhattan skyscraper*

when some director (perhaps Barrymore) improvised by tying the mike to a long stick rather than burying it in a bush or canister or telephone receiver.

Just as technicians began to conquer the mechanical problems of sound filming, film directors began to discover the means of using sound artistically in a primarily visual medium. Even a deadly talkie like *The Lights of New York* contained a few imaginative combinations of sound and picture: the Broadway sequence of the film evokes the excitement of the city with a montage of city sights and city sounds; the sequence in which the gangsters shoot a cop is staged in enlarged shadows on a wall coupled with the sounds of a shout, a policeman's whistle, a shot, and the racing motor of the getaway car. René Clair was particularly impressed with some of the effects of a mediocre all-talking, all-singing picture, *Broadway Melody* (1929): while Bessie Love watches the departure of her lover, the director (Harry Beaumont) keeps the camera riveted on her tearful face, dramatizing the departure with sound alone—the door slams, the lover's car drives off. Then just as Bessie is about to break into tears, Beaumont fades out the picture, a single Love sob punctuating the blank, black screen.

Ernst Lubitsch's first two sound films, *The Love Parade* (1929) and *Monte Carlo* (1930), show a creative film mind wrestling with the problems of integrating sound and picture. Although *The Love Parade* has dull, static passages (the long, posed takes of Jeanette MacDonald's songs), this first Lubitsch sound film shows him beginning to weave his tapestry of witty dialogue, of clever and surprising uses of sound, and of deft images that imply much more than they show. The film contains many subtle effects that would have been impossible without synchronized sound: the coordination of the valet's physical business with the precise rhythms of his opening song, an adieu to Paris sung by a dog, Chevalier's flippant and charming asides to the camera, the parody of American tourists who do not look up from their newspapers until they hear how much the castle cost to build, the sexual implications of Chevalier's saying "Yes" in answer to the queen's question at the same time that his head is shaking "No," the parody of the wedding ceremony in which the minister emphasizes the reversal of the sexual roles by pronouncing the couple wife and man, the booming sound of cannon (a typical Lubitsch use of a comic Freudian symbol, combining both picture and sound), which both implies and interrupts the couple's wedding night amours.

Several of Lubitsch's juxtapositions of sound and film are dazzling indications of the comic ingenuity that would later develop into a sound-film masterpiece like *Trouble in Paradise*. As Chevalier starts to tell the queen's chamberlain a sexual anecdote (how Madame Curie cured him of a cold but gave him a French accent), Lubitsch cuts to a camera position outside the window. The remainder of the scene is silent; we cannot hear the joke at all. We don't need to. The slyness of silence is funnier than the joke itself. Similarly, as Chevalier and the queen dine tête-à-tête in her boudoir, Lubitsch, rather than showing us the scene inside the room, shows us the queen's ladies-in-waiting, ministers, and servants narrating the scene they can see from outside her window. Sound allowed Lubitsch to develop one of his favorite comic devices: a scene inside a room can be much more interesting and much more fun if the camera stays outside the room.

In *Monte Carlo,* another Jeanette MacDonald musical, Lubitsch's most famous device was his use of the song, "Beyond the Blue Horizon," as a duet between the singer and a speeding train. As Miss MacDonald sings the song, the sounds of the train (chugging wheels,

Monte Carlo: *this rhythmic montage of eight shots of a speeding train serves as the introduction to "Beyond the Blue Horizon"—joining the Soviet adoration of machines with the exuberance of American song*

tooting whistle, puffing smoke) become her percussion accompaniment, underscored by the equally percussive rhythms of Lubitsch's cutting. Unfortunately, the Lubitsch innovation soon became a Hollywood cliché: those outrageous combinations of speeding trains, a rhythmic song on the sound track, a superimposed calendar with the dates flying off it to mark the passage of time, or a superimposed series of newspapers whose names reveal the train's progress across the country. Lubitsch's original idea had been an innovative and ingenious combination of picture, sound, and cutting—a synthesis of Soviet montage (particularly the fascination with the energy of machines) and American musical comedy (particularly the fascination with the energy of human singing and dancing).

The most innovative early sound films, however, were the animated cartoons of Walt Disney. Disney began as a commercial artist and cartoonist in Kansas City; he made his debut in films with animated ads and satiric, short cartoon films—Fred Newman's Laugh-O-Grams. He migrated to Hollywood in 1923 and produced a series of short films that integrated cartoons and a living girl (called Alice in Cartoonland). By the end of the silent era, he and his animator, Ub Iwerks, had mastered the methods and

art of animation. The "Alice" films, except for the irrelevant, living Alice herself (Disney would again mix people and cartoons two decades later in *Song of the South*), were rich in the mature Disney imagination, particularly in his transposition of physical reality into almost surreal impossibility. For example, as a mouse (Mickey's progenitor) serenades his mousette (Minnie's) in *Alice Plays Cupid* (1925), a barrage of notes flies out of his guitar and streams into her face as she stands on her balcony. The mouse then uses these notes as a ladder, climbing them up to her chamber; that accomplished, he gathers them together with his tail, transposing the ladder of notes into a bouquet of flowers for his Juliet.

But it was sound that turned Disney into one of the most influential producers and respected artists in the film industry. Disney's animated cartoons, which were not compelled to photograph the real world, escaped the tyrannies of sound recording that enslaved the directors of theatrical features. The cartoon—which is pure fantasy, is free from all natural laws, from all human and spatial realities—also granted its creator complete freedom in playing with sound. Just as the pictures could depict impossibilities—animals that act like people, physical stresses that a living organism could never endure—the

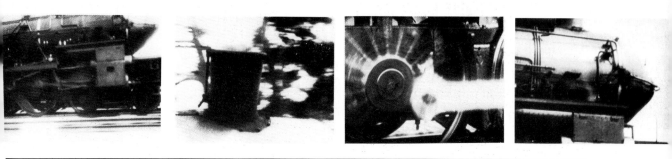

sound track could be equally free and fanciful. Fantastic, unreal pictures could combine in fantastic and imaginative ways with unreal and clever sounds. Or the animated film could develop a counterpoint between its fanciful, unreal sights and the concrete reality of familiar sounds. The imaginative Disney sound cartoon united three of the great traditions of silent filmmaking and carried them into the sound era: the wacky, speedy physical comedy of Mack Sennett; the fantasy and unreality of the world of Méliès and Emile Cohl in which what cannot happen happens; and the Chaplin genius for transforming one kind of object into a totally different one.

Disney's first sound film, *Steamboat Willie* (1928), shows complete mastery of the possible counterpoint of picture and sound. The most imaginative sequence is the "Turkey in the Straw" number. A billy goat has eaten a guitar and a copy of the tune, "Turkey in the Straw." Mickey Mouse starts twisting the goat's tail; the notes again become visible, pouring out of the animal's mouth; the music on the sound track accompanies the visual notes. Then Mickey runs all over the boat using whatever he can find as an accompanying percussive instrument. He rattles on a garbage pail and on a series of different-sized pots; he scratches a washboard; he twists a cat's tail to produce syncopated shrieks; he squeezes a duck's throat to produce rhythmic quacks; he pulls the tails of nursing piglets to produce percussive squeaks; he bangs on a cow's teeth to produce the tones of a xylophone. Whereas the method of the silent film was to create meaning by juxtaposing two dissimilar images, Disney perceived the similarity of apparently dissimilar sounds and images. An Eisenstein simile that the workers (visual) are like oxen (visual) contrasts with Disney's that a cow's teeth (visual) are like a xylophone (sound).

The Skeleton Dance (1929), the first of the Silly Symphonies, is an even more skillful weaving of visual motion, music, and rhythm. The film's opening sequence —an atmospheric painting of the mood of midnight and goblins—combines the eerie, tense whine of violins with percussive effects produced by an owl hooting, bats' wings flapping, wind whistling, and cats screeching. Then the skeletons creep out of their graves. The surprising activities of the bones are carefully coordinated with the percussive beats of the score's rhythm. Disney is not only sensitive to the possibilities of the kinds of sound that a visual image might generate, but also to the punch of coordinating animated movement with the rhythmic effects of the score. This sensitivity to musical tones and rhythms

Disney's clever wedding of sound and visual. Two xylophones: a cow's teeth in Steamboat Willie, *a human skeleton in* The Skeleton Dance

became the outstanding feature of all the Silly Symphonies, eventually culminating in the cinematic tone-poem, *Fantasia* (1941), and in the wildly surreal evaporations of one object into another of the "Pink Elephants" dance in *Dumbo* (1941). Disney's synthesis of image, music, and rhythm had begun with his first sound films. The means of turning sound into a resource for film rather than a liability were being found.

10 France Between the Wars

The French film in the first decade of sound may have been the most imaginative, the most stimulating of its generation: a subtle blend of effective, often poetic, dialogue, evocative visual imagery, perceptive social analysis, complex fictional structures, rich philosophical implication, wit and charm. The maturity of the French film mind in the decade between 1930 and 1940 was partially the result of the growth of the French film mind in the previous decade between 1920 and 1930. The final ten years of the silent film laid the foundations for the great sound structures that would follow in the next ten. René Clair, Jean Renoir, Jacques Feyder, Julien Duvivier, and Jean Epstein all conquered purely visual expression before they began combining picture and word. The sharp chasm that divided the two Hollywood film worlds before and after 1928 was less apparent in the Paris film world. The innovative, experimental minds of the French twenties energetically accepted the artistic challenge of the new talking machine. Although many French plays and playwrights found a welcome on the new French sound stages, just as American plays and playwrights had in America, the French sound film never turned its back on visual expression. The French filmmakers of the silent twenties had learned some very powerful and convincing visual lessons.

Paris of the 1920s was the avant-garde capital of the world in art, music, and the drama. It was the city of Picasso and Dali, of Stravinsky, Milhaud, Poulenc, and Satie, of Cocteau and Stein. The urge to experiment, to invent new forms, to challenge the established artistic norms in music, painting, poetry, and drama also dominated the new machine art of the motion picture. Paris was the city of many modern isms—surrealism, cubism, dadaism. Painters exulted in manipulating the pure shapes and textures and colors of paint on a canvas. The painting did not need to mirror life's external reality; it could mirror its moods, its feelings, its tones, its dreams. The world was irrational; art could mirror that irrationality. Plays did not tell logical stories of rationally motivated actions; playwrights exulted in the irrational, the *non sequitur*. Jean Cocteau wrote a drama about an absurd wedding party at the top of the Eiffel Tower; Gertrude Stein and Tristan Tzara wrote plays whose value was in the sounds of the words rather than in their meaning. Colonies of artists would gather at parties to show each other little works they had sculpted, or painted, or written—works devoted to form and sensation rather than to logic and meaning. At these parties some of the artists would show little movies, created on the same formal principles, to their gathered friends. They discovered that of all the arts, the moving picture was capable of the most bizarre tricks with form: a series of purely visual images, of shapes, of lights, of double exposures, of dissolves, a series of worlds out of focus, moving too fast or too slow, upside down or inside out. The lens and crank could be even more devoted to pure irrational form than chisel or brush.

Ironically, the great experimental leap forward of the French film in the 1920s was also a step backward into the past. In 1919, at the dawn of this avant-garde decade, Louis Delluc and Ricciotto Canudo, two zealous film buffs, founded the first of many subsequent French societies for the presentation and preservation of great films of the past. Delluc and Canudo canonized the movies as the Seventh Art and urged attention to the directors of an earlier era: to Méliès, Zecca, Cohl, Max Linder, Jean Durand, Louis Feuillade. The "Seventh-Art adventists" leaped back into the film past about ten years, ignoring the theatrical, stagey, Comédie-Françaiseish, Film d'Arty pictures of the decade of the war. This first generation of *cinéastes* urged a return to the irrational fantasy of Méliès, to the action-filled chases of Zecca and Sennett, to the tricks with camera speed and motion of Jean Durand's *Onésime Horloger* (1910), in which a magical clock makes the world dizzily speed up or lethargically slow down. Like the French *cinéastes* of the sixties—Godard, Truffaut, Malle—the Paris filmmaker of the twenties not only used film history to pack movies with

historical echoes but also to embellish earlier film ideas with the filmmaker's own distinct and personal extensions of them. The Parisian avant-garde filmmaker of the 1920s used one hand to rip up accepted film conventions and assumptions and the other to pull the traditions of the film past into the movies of the present.

The experimental French films of the twenties were of three approximate types: (1) films of pure visual form; (2) surrealistic film fantasies in which tricks with visual form create the surrealistic-symbolic-irrational film universe; (3) naturalistic studies of human passion and sensation in which symbols and surreal touches help to render elusive human feelings. The three types were far from distinct. A film could begin as an essay in pure form and then change into a surreal dream-fantasy (René Clair's *Entr'acte,* 1924). Sometimes the film would begin as a surreal journey and change into a study of form (Man Ray's *Mysteries of the Chateau Dé,* 1929). Or the film could begin as an impressionistic study of human emotions and relationships only to end as a dream (Jean Renoir's *Little Match Girl,* 1928). Dadaism, surrealism and poetic naturalism flowed into one another to create new and surprising compounds in the movies.

The films of Man Ray are the purest examples of movie dada—of a collage of visual shapes and patterns with no meaning other than the interesting forms themselves. Ray's films began quite literally as collages: he randomly scattered paint, nails, glue, scraps of paper over strips of film, and then exposed the littered film to light, leaving shadows of the objects imprinted on the celluloid. Ray gradually abandoned such accidental methods for more controlled essays in form: *Return to Reason* (1923), a highly ironic title since the film consciously rejects reason, and *Emak Bakia* (1927). In these films a pair of spinning dice become a pair of spinning lights which become a pair of spinning sticks which become a pair of dancing legs. And so forth. Visual similarities and differences of form control Ray's choice of images. Fernand Léger's rhythmic *Ballet Mécanique* (1924) and Marcel Duchamp's comic jest of spinning spirals and nonsense words (closely resembling Ionesco's puns and plays with sound), *Anaemic Cinema* (1926), also begin with the premise of using a succession of visual images related in form, shape, and rhythm rather than in meaning.

The most famous of the surreal films is the Salvador Dali–Luis Buñuel fantasy, *Un Chien andalou* (1929). Like the title, the film is a series of *non sequiturs*, scenes that seem to be related logically and yet are not related. The film teasingly suggests thematic unities and some kind of structural logic. Its action consistently pairs the same man and woman; sexual desires and tensions clearly dominate their confrontations. Dali-Buñuel seem to contrast sexual desire and social convention: the stigmata and ants in the man's hand suggesting Christian sin and human mortality, the man fondling the woman's breasts, the two puritans laboriously being dragged along with the equally heavy burdens of pianos and burros, the doorbell in the shape of a cocktail shaker, the asocial bawdiness of the man in his jester's costume. Despite the whiffs of consistent meaning, *Un Chien andalou* is pure dream, irrational, a series of daring and imaginative vignettes with no rational paste between them. From the opening sequence in which Buñuel slits a lady's eyeball with a razor (in intentionally gruesome closeup) to the final one in which the man and woman wander inexplicably on a rocky beach "in the springtime," the film's goal is to excite, to shock, to tickle, to surprise, to make us "see" differently rather than to preach or explain.

On the other hand, Jean Epstein's *The Fall of the House of Usher* (1928) uses surreal dream effects to create the

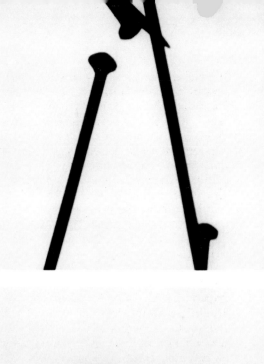

Man Ray's Return to Reason: *exposing the celluloid to nails and thumbtacks, then printing the results in negative*

atmosphere for his lucid Poe plot. Epstein uses the tools of cinematic surrealism— slow-motion effects, out-of-focus lenses, multiple exposure, contrasts of light and shadow, distortion, cavernous, dream-world sets—as a means of rendering Poe's eerie tale. Dada and surrealism become a means for Epstein, not an end—the means of turning the House of Usher into a house of mirrors.

Even the naturalistic psychological studies of human interaction try to probe beneath familiar surfaces to reveal the irrational, chaotic passions, often using the devices of the surrealists to illuminate this subjective world. Alberto Calvalcanti's *Rien que les heures* (1926), on the surface a documentary study of twenty-four hours of Paris life, relies on cinematic tricks to paint the city's moody picture: on freeze frames, double exposures, split-screen effects, obtrusive wipes. Louis Delluc's *Fièvre* (1921), a tense story of desire and death in a seamy waterfront saloon, weaves images of gliding ships and a symbolic rose into its tapestry of naturalistic human conflict in the café. Dimitri Kirsanov's *Menilmontant* (1926) uses quick cutting and the sordid atmosphere of Paris slums to tell its story of two girls from the country who drift into prostitution in the city. The films of Germaine Dulac (*The Smiling Madame Beudet*, 1923) and Marcel L'Herbier (*The Late Matthia Pascal*, 1924) use the tricks of slow motion, distortion, and soft focus subjectively to illuminate thought and emotion.

Even the most important commercial film director of the decade, Abel Gance, applied the surrealist's concern with visual forms, tricks, and devices to the narrative feature film. His *J'Accuse* (1919) and *La Roue* (1923) mix an attack on varying forms of social injustice with an intimate Zolaesque study of human passion and sensuality. His biggest film, *Napoléon* (1927), attempted to make a French epic to rival Griffith's *The Birth of a Nation*, using the heroic leader (rather than Griffith's ordinary citizens) to explore the history of the entire nation in a particular period. (The shift from folksy family to idolized superhuman leader indicates Gance's shift in both dramatic and political emphasis.) For *Napoléon* Gance experimented with several ancestors of future visual processes. His Polyvision, a three-screen process that could either be used as an immense single panoramic view or a triptych of three different views, foreshadowed both Cinerama and other multiscreen experiments. He shot other sequences in color and in what later would be christened 3-D.

The French director of the 1920s delighted in the games that could be played with the camera, in its visual surprises, in its ability to make the familiar world look bizarre. The isms of twentieth-century French painting also captured its cinema.

The culmination of this decade of film painting was a feature that seemed to synthesize and incorporate the history of painting, from Renaissance religious iconography to the modern abstract concern with texture and line: Carl-Theodore Dreyer's *The Passion of Joan of Arc* (1928). Despite its Danish director and German designer (Hermann Warm, the designer of *Caligari*), the film's aesthetics and effects are pure French. Narratively, the film chronicles Joan's long trial and eventual execution at the stake; but the film's narrative structure is merely a skeleton. The picture has no real plot; it is pure passion. The details of Joan's trial are very blurry; the enormity of her suffering, her sorrow, her spiritual fire, her warmth are very clear. The film examines Joan the immense emotional being rather than Joan the historical figure, Joan the militant, or even Joan the religious iconoclast. The sainthood of Dreyer's Joan (played by Falconetti) is not in her words or deeds; it exists within her; it is in her intense ability to feel and suffer and glow. Dreyer's Joan contrasts strikingly with Shaw's, although the film uses some of the same dialogue as Shaw's play. But in Shaw's play Joan's comments are witty and intelligent and shrewd; in Dreyer's film her words seem totally inconsistent with her passion and suffering. Dreyer's Joan, with her glowing face and shiny, tear-filled eyes seems incapable of verbal expression. Words are

The Passion of Joan of Arc. *A film of faces: Joan's (Falconetti), smooth and passionate, with her one compassionate accuser (Antonin Artaud, bareheaded); and the wrinkled imperfections of the faces of her accusers*

irrelevant to her passion. Shaw's Joan is pure intellect, Dreyer's pure passion.

Dreyer's film is more a musical Mass in film form than a dramatic story; it is a St. Joan's Passion in the same way that Bach composed a St. Matthew's Passion. Like Eisenstein, Dreyer's sense of cinematic form is more musical than logical. Unlike Eisenstein, whose "music" was the rhythmic, violent dissonance of the twentieth-century symphony, Dreyer's music is the spiritual passionate calm of the organ fugue or church chorale.

To create a feature film of almost musical sensations rather than story, Dreyer fills the frame with faces rather than events. His camera travels ceaselessly over the faces of the judges and the face of the girl. Huge asymmetrical compositions of human faces fill the screen. The bare white walls of the set make the richly textured human features and human skin leap out at the viewer. The bareness and whiteness of Warm's decor give the film the flavor of medieval starkness and the texture of abstract painting with its sharp clean lines.

To contrast the passionate saint with her fallible accusers, Dreyer uses two different photographic methods. He shoots the accusers in motion. The judges and priests twist, pivot, and lunge with their bodies and faces; Dreyer keeps his camera moving when photographing them to sustain an even greater impression of movement. The accusers are constantly in motion; Joan is always still. Dreyer shoots her motionless with a motionless camera. The maid's passionate calm contrasts with her accusers' nervous activity, her passivity with their action. Dreyer's camera also contrasts the potential ugliness, the deformities, the faults in the faces of the accusers with the smooth, glowing perfection in the face of the maid. The camera prowls over the faces of judges, settling on a wart, a wrinkle, a mis-shapen nose or chin, a roll of facial fat. The shots of Joan, glowingly lit from behind rather than ruthlessly

from the front, turn her skin into a milky silk to contrast with the crust and crevices of the skin of her accusers.

For many critics, *The Passion of Joan of Arc* was the ultimate silent film, the ultimate example of the power of purely visual expression. In comparison with its pictorial beauty and expressiveness, its artistic wholeness, its intellectual and emotional maturity, the silly, static talking pictures that were already playing at competing theatres were ludicrous. Critics and aesthetes justifiably watched with horror as the *kitsch* of a *Jazz Singer* swallowed the art of a *Joan*.

But even the *Joan of Arc*, as moving as its pictures were, contained its own limitations. Although sound and talking were obviously bothersome gimmicks, printed titles—the necessary evil of the silent film—became uncomfortably intrusive in Dreyer's *Joan*. Just as there is something anomalous in his Joan's uttering any words at all, there is something anomalous in interrupting the passionate conflict of human faces to flash printed words on the screen. The titles disrupt the pictorial unity of *Joan of Arc* just as obviously as sound disrupted the pictorial imagination of early talkies. To sustain an unbroken flow of visual images, the film needed sound rather than printed words to perform its vital narrative functions. *Joan of Arc* needed a nondisruptive means of showing us what those compelling faces were thinking, what those mouths were saying. A purely visual cinema, perfectly suited to short, abstract, surreal films, had its own limitations in the full-length narrative film.

René Clair

Like so many French filmmakers of the era, René Clair mastered the purely visual cinema, the painting-in-motion of the twenties, before he began to assault both eye and ear in the thirties. Clair began as cinematic trickster, a choreographer of irrational film ballets; later he used his cinema tricks to turn the realistic and rational world into a place of fantasy and song. Clair looked back admiringly at the zany, frenetic worlds of Sennett, Zecca, and Durand, and that looking backward allowed his own kind of zany frenzy to move forward. Despite Clair's historical influences, despite his maturing as an artist, despite the new adjustments that the talking machines forced him to make, a René Clair movie—silent or sound—is unmistakably Clair. The clearest Clair traits are his delight in physical movement and his comic fancy (falling somewhere between wit and whimsy), which converts two things that are obviously different into things that are surprisingly the same: a funeral becomes a wedding party, a prison is a factory and a factory is a prison, a tussle for a jacket becomes a football game, a provincial French café becomes an Arabian harem. Clair's constant dissolving of differences into similarities is fanciful as well as satirical, designed as much for wildly fantastic imaginative fun as for social commentary. However, Clair's best silent film, *The Italian Straw Hat* (1927), and his best sound films, *Le Million* (1930) and *À Nous la liberté* (1931), are those in which his flights of visual fancy drop the most explosive intellectual bombs on the director's two favorite targets—social convention and money.

Clair's first two films, both silent, contained the seeds of everything that would grow afterward. *Paris qui dort* (*The Crazy Ray*, 1923) is the story of a crazed scientist, appropriately named Dr. Craze, whose mechanical ray has put the populace of the world to sleep, paralyzed in the midst of their activities. Only a handful of Parisians avoid the professor's paralyzing power, those who were above the beams of his machine on the top of the Eiffel Tower or in an airplane. Most Clairish in the film is not its story— although the director would always

feel comfortable with fantasy—but the clever translation of its premise into visual and physical terms.

Clair has great fun with the frozen human statues that dot the streets of Paris, interrupted unsuspectingly in their daily pursuits: the pickpocket paralyzed in flight with the wallet of a frozen victim, the unfaithful wife frozen in the arms of her lover, frozen diners in a café, the paralyzed waiter holding the anticipated bottle of champagne. The witty plights of Clair's frozen people are matched by his comments on social values. One of the first plans of the nonparalyzed survivors is to rob the sleeping banks of all their cash; unfortunately they discover that their hordes of wealth have no value in a sleeping society in which there is nothing to buy. Equally pointed is the way the characters resume their old social roles as soon as Doctor Craze reverses his ray and gets society going again. While the city sleeps, crook and cop, socialite and socialist live and play together; when the city reawakens, the familiar social distinctions also reawaken.

Clair's second film, *Entr'acte,* is less satirical and less logical than his first, but it is more fun. Made specifically as the intermission piece, the entr'acte, for a performance of the Ballets Suedois in Paris, the film is pure movement, pure romp, the whimsical, choreographic Clair rather than the social satirist. The film begins with a series of dadaist *non sequiturs*: two men playing checkers on a high building, two others hunting birds on skyscrapers, a ball dancing on jets of water, a ballerina (shot from underneath) whose billowing skirt spreads and shuts like the petal of a flower. Clair masquerades as pure irrationalist, pure film dadaist. But he quickly reveals the sly comical logic in his cinema madness. The two checker players surprisedly see the Place de la Concorde materialize on their checker board; the dancing ball dangles inexplicably in midair, defying gravity, after the spurting water jets have been turned off; the ballerina turns out to be a bearded man. Clair's irrational images are anomalous, nonsensical surprises rather than a "serious" collage of pure form.

The delightful silliness continues in the second half of the film, which develops a superficially more coherent structure. One of the bird hunters has been accidentally killed; society gathers for his funeral. But the mourners surprisingly dress in white; they gleefully throw rice at the departing hearse; a Sennettesque jet of air blows the ladies' skirts up. The hearse itself is inexplicably drawn by a camel; the mourners break pieces of the funeral wreaths off the hearse and eat them like pretzels. Suddenly, the hearse starts running away by itself; the mourners rush off after it. A Zecca-Sennett chase begins. Clair uses fast motion, slow motion, traveling shots, interpolated cuts of racing cars and roller coasters to add energy and interest to the chase. Eventually the coffin falls off the hearse, the corpse miraculously rises from the box and blithely makes everyone disappear (Méliès stop-action). The film apparently ends as the word "*Fin*" flashes on the screen. But Clair has one more joke up his sleeve: the "corpse" suddenly comes bounding through the word on the screen, like a dog bounding through a paper hoop in the circus. He cavorts in slow motion and then bounds back (reverse motion) through the hoop. Clair's bizarre, nonsensical romp finally comes to its final "*Fin.*"

Clair's silent feature, *The Italian Straw Hat,* which takes its visual style from the era of the pre-Griffith French "prim-itives," from the decor of the Zecca and Linder films, uses that distant visual world to combine the director's romping spirit with his sarcastic sniggers at the pettiness of middle-class conventions. A young bridegroom's horse eats a young lady's straw hat as the groom drives to meet his bride. Since the young lady lost her hat while enjoying an extramarital afternoon with a beau, she must replace

the rare hat to allay her husband's suspicions. The young groom, who looks suspiciously like Max Linder, must juggle his wedding party with his comically frantic attempts to replace the mangled hat. He leads the wedding party out of the church and through the city in an energetic chase that eventually culminates in the town jail. Throughout the chase Clair supplements the physical fun with satiric jabs at the tawdry wedding festivities, the pettiness of the silly, middle-class guests, and the inane social conventions that have created both the tacky wedding and the chase for an Italian straw hat.

The addition of sound gave Clair even more opportunities for comic inventiveness. In his first sound film, *Sous les toits de Paris* (1930), Clair—always the choreographer—discovered the effectiveness of using music as one of the film's leitmotifs and as a means of creating the film's fantasy-like breezy spirit. Clair's films became musical films; music became the perfect unrealistic accompaniment for the ballet-like Clair fantasy world.

Clair's next film, *Le Million* (1931), is an even more fanciful mixture of movement, sound, and music. Its subject is imaginative fancy itself, the way that the line between the "real" and the "fanciful" can be erased by the power of the human imagination. The film revolves about two favorite Clair motifs—money and the chase. A poor French artist discovers that he has won a million francs in the state lottery; unfortunately, the lottery ticket is in the pocket of a coat that has been stolen by a fleeing thief. The film becomes a furious chase for the elusive jacket, carrying the artist through the streets of Paris, into a den of brainy thieves, and finally onto the stage of the Paris Opera. The ballet-like film appropriately ends in a joyous dance as all members of the eventually successful chase join hands in a singing, dancing circle of celebration.

On their way to this final rejoicing, Clair engages his characters in a series of wild adventures that reveal a startlingly imaginative combination of sound and visual images. When the young man finds his coat at the Opera, he grabs it, only to find that the vain, fat tenor insists on using the old coat as part of his atmospheric pauper's costume. The young man, the tenor, and the police engage in a mock-heroic struggle for the jacket. Clair comments on these mock-heroics by adding crowd noises, officials' whistles, and cheering to the sound track while the men play keep-away in the Opera's corridor. The coat has become a football, the struggle has become a game.

Clair's most dazzling sequence uses the sounds of the operatic performance on stage simultaneously to emphasize the difference between real love and operatic clichés of love and to erase those differences. As the film's two lovers sit behind the set on stage pledging their love, the fat tenor and fat soprano, who detest each other, pledge their troth in grandiose song. Clair juxtaposes the saccharine lyrics of the fakey aria with the sincere feelings of the genuine lovers. Clair then caps his contrast of apparently fake and real love with a dazzling visual joke. The stagehands in the flies let loose a horde of artificial autumnal leaves, designed to flutter down on the two operatic lovers on stage. The wonder is that the fakey theatricality of the device underscores the artificiality of operatic love while, at the same time, it converts the equally fictional love of the movie lovers into a tender, lyrical, even magical moment of human interaction. Clair's point is not that movie love is more real than operatic love (what could be less "real" than this—or any—movie's lovers?), nor that movie sets are more real than opera sets (even if Clair's camera makes sure we can see the fake backsides of all the opera's scenery). His point is that our conviction of the "realness" in any work of art has nothing to do with the realness

of the fiction and everything to do with our imagination's response to the fiction. It is on this same basis that the audience in the opera house accepts operatic love as a kind of "real" story. Movies both are and are not more "real" than operas. Movies, like operas, achieve their legitimate ends only by speaking to the human fancy.

Clair's next film, *Á Nous la liberté*, was to be his last masterpiece. Clair again combines his comic inventiveness with the thematic wholeness and seriousness that make a great film. Two convicts escape from prison. One of them, using stolen money, builds a huge factory to manufacture phonograph records and machines; the other, his friend in prison, eventually becomes a worker in that factory. The business tycoon eventually discovers that the life of a "respectable" factory owner, with its rules, its social obligations, its emotional infidelities, its devotion to money and machines, is no different from the life of a prisoner. Neither businessman nor prisoner is truly free. The film ends as the businessman and the worker turn their backs on the factory and on money to stroll off down the road, two tramps, finally free of restraint and convention.

Uniting the film is its consistent examination of the term *liberty* in its title. For Clair, society and freedom are incompatible. Everyone attached to the factory—Clair's microcosm for society as a whole—is a prisoner of his or her role in the system: owner, member of the board, worker, foreman, secretary, all are prisoners of their particular functions. The film's brilliance lies in the director's translation of this Marxist-humanist cliché into imaginative film images. The two central characters, one tall and fat, the other short and skinny, are two spirits from the world of silent comedy, reminiscent of Fatty and Charlie, of Laurel and Hardy. Their ultimate choice of vocation—tramp—also echoes the asocial yet human choice that Charlie

À Nous la Liberté.
*Clair's visual parallels:
the prison as assembly
line, the assembly line as
prison*

makes over and over again. If Clair's
tramps seem indebted to Charlot, Chaplin
later collected the debt by borrowing one
of *Liberté*'s assembly-line scenes for
Modern Times. Clair's little prisoner, the
Chaplinesque dreamer, sits in his place on
the monotonous assembly line. As the
unfinished machines roll past him on the
conveyor belt, he, dreaming of his blonde
lady love (another Chaplin echo), fails to
put his particular screw into the destined
hole. He scampers down the line
following the machine, trying to remedy
his error. The assembly line quickly
becomes chaos, a heap of unfinished
machines and brawling workers. Clair's
assembly-line chaos is not only
Chaplinesque but a perfect way of
showing man's inhuman enslavement to
the machines that man has built.

Clair's consistent technique for illuminating the lack of liberty is visual parallel. The film opens with shots of men in prison, manufacturing little toy horses as they sit in rows on the prison's assembly line; they eat their meals as they sit in rows in the prison's dining room. Later, Clair shows the factory workers sitting in the same rows as the men in prison, eating in the same formations as the men in the prison mess hall. Factory and prison are visually identical. Prison uniforms have become factory uniforms; prison guards have become factory foremen; prison numbers have become workers' numbers.

Clair's decor emphasizes these visual parallels. The vertical bars of the prison are echoed by other verticals throughout the film: vertical rows of flowers (like flowered bars) in front of the young girl's window, vertical wood paneling in the factory owner's office, vertical bars on the windows of the factory. The factory's bare courtyard looks exactly like the prison yard. The film's music also emphasizes parallels. Its title song, a bouncy march about "liberty," recurs throughout the film; it often has little to do with liberty. As in *Le Million*, Clair juxtaposes the words of a song with contrasting events. The prisoners sing the "Liberty Song" as the film opens; they sing it lifelessly and dully as they work dispiritedly on the prison assembly line. The chorus line of convicts singing about liberty is not only ironic but also introduces the typical Clair spirit of unreality and fantasy at the beginning of the film. Later, a pretty young miss sings the "Liberty Song" at her bowered window (the one with the flowery bars). Suddenly her song slows down and stops. She was only mouthing the words to a record: another Clair device that is surprising, funny, ironic, and a clever comment on the lack of liberty. Of course, Clair's choice of a phonograph factory is just as much a part of the film's metaphorical wholeness as his use of the prison and the ironic

"Liberty Song." The factory turns music into an artifact; that which should be spontaneous and free becomes a machine. Even music lacks liberty in this society.

The film hits its visual and thematic climax in the wild scene in which the social elite gather to honor the great factory owner (former crook) who has created this phonographic empire. The ceremony begins with perfect formality: the guests wearing top hats and tails (symbols of social convention), the orators sitting stiffly on the rostrum, the workers standing in formation listening to the boring, droning speeches. Suddenly a wind sweeps (both visual and sound effect) through the factory courtyard. It drowns out the silly speech of the old rhetorician; it blows the top hats all over the courtyard; it scatters the factory's profits—bills of money—all over the ground. The liberating wind turns the factory into a swarming mass of chaotic free activity. In the most Sennettesque manner, the dignitaries abandon their dignity to chase their blowing top hats and the blowing bills all over the courtyard in frenzied, choreographed patterns.

After this climax, the film's final section—a quiet, peaceful coda—shows the effect of this whistling wind of freedom. The two prisoners become tramps; all of the factory's workers sit by the river dreamily fishing; the now totally automated factory continues producing phonographs without any workers at all. In Clair's idyll, the people are free to be human, leaving the machines to tend the machines. It is work itself, and the society that requires its citizens to work to survive, that ultimately deprives a person of liberty. Work and freedom are antithetical. If Clair's idealistic solution of this dilemma seems too idyllic, too fanciful in the film's final scene, perhaps the director had the same kind of point in mind as Chaplin had in *Easy Street* or *The Gold Rush*. The obviously facile solution magnifies the problem.

With *Le Million* and *À Nous la liberté* René Clair hit an obvious peak of both style and vision. After two less important films in France, Clair made his first English-language film, *The Ghost Goes West* (1936), a fantasy about a social-climbing American who buys a Scottish castle and transports it, block by block, complete with ghost, back to Florida. The film has some very Clairish satire of the American *nouveau riche* (played by Eugene Pallette), but otherwise it is a rather sticky creampuff. During the war years, Clair understandably stayed in Hollywood where he made more fantasies (*I Married a Witch*, 1944), and the most ingenious comedy-mystery by a director other than Hitchcock, *And Then There Were None* (1945). When Clair returned to France after the war, his wit was gentler, the whimsy thicker, the decor more lush. Later Clair films never matched the combination of exuberance, style, cinematic control, structural parallel, and thematic consistency of *Le Million* and *À Nous la liberté*.

Jean Renoir

Like René Clair, Jean Renoir started making films in the twenties and reached the peak of his powers in the thirties. Like Clair, Renoir was a social satirist. But there the similarities between the two directors very clearly stop. Renoir's satire was bitter and melancholy whereas Clair's was ebullient and whimsical. Clair's satire condemned institutions and praised the spirit of man; Renoir's satire declared hollow institutions to be the inevitable products of erroneous men. Like Clair, Renoir saw that the claims of nature and civilization were antithetical; unlike Clair, Renoir never resolves the dilemma by simplistically espousing one of the two alternatives. For Renoir realized both the attractiveness of nature that seems so innocent and the need of human beings for civilization that seems so complicated.

Indeed, civilization and not fields and woods *is* nature for twentieth-century human beings.

Clair's roots were firmly planted in ballet and in song, Renoir's in painting, in the sensitivity to light and shadow, form and texture that he inherited from his father. Clair's physical comedy instantly made itself at home in exciting silent films; Renoir's method matured slowly, requiring dialogue and the structural complexities of the dialogue film before his pictures could paint his personal view of the human condition. If Clair's visual cleverness quickly hit its peak, it just as quickly fell from it. Renoir's canon was fuller, richer, with significant films stretching into the color and wide-screen eras of the 1950s. Clair was the more ingenious, Renoir the deeper, more perceptive artist.

The Renoir silent films are darker, slower, more brooding than Clair's. In *The Little Match Girl* (1928), Renoir adapts Andersen's fairly tale of the little match seller who dreams of happiness in toyland and perishes in the snow of reality. The film is suffused with the heavy atmosphere of death. The opening sections, Renoir's depiction of reality in the cold, snowy city, reveal the director's impressionistic eye. He paints the world with exaggerated harshness, with extreme blacks and whites: glaring lamps (obvious spot lighting), black silhouettes, grotesque shadows. Renoir's impressionism makes the real world surreal; the visual contrasts of dark and light are that intense.

In the second sequence, the little girl's dream, Renoir is free to play with all the devices of the French cinematic tricksters: double exposures, irrational sequences of images, blurred focus, superimposition. But again the results are strikingly different from Clair's effusive use of the same tricks. Even in the toy shop window the atmosphere is heavy and dark. The shapes of this toy world are jagged and sharp; the lighting creates harsh tones of over-darkness and extra-whiteness.

Whereas Clair's lighting is appropriately even and bright, Renoir's is consistently tonal and moody. Even the toys threaten the little girl—soldiers in formation, an aggressive ball, the ominous jack-in-the-box who becomes the pursuing figure of death.

In the final section of the film, the girl and her soldier-protector futilely flee from their black pursuer. Their flight through the clouds becomes a horrifying, nightmare chase, not a joyfully Clairish one; it ends in the girl's dream-death in an impressionistic cemetery. The petals of flowers descend onto her dying body; the petals of the dream dissolve into the snowflakes of reality. The little match girl lies frozen, buried under a mountain of snow. Only a few scattered boxes of matches reveal that she once existed.

Although later Renoir films became less fantastic, the effects of tonal lighting, the overhanging mood of death, the bitterness underlying the superficial gaiety were all constants. Even the utopianly comic *Crime of Monsieur Lange* (1936) ends with a murder and the probable disintegration of a happy human society. A publishing house becomes a joyous communistic utopia for the production of western movies, chronicling the adventures of the cowboy hero, Arizona Jim. Renoir shows his particular debt to the film past with his satiric handling of a movie cowboy, clearly based on William S. Hart, known in France as Rio Jim. Arizona Jim's creator, M. Lange, who has never been to Arizona, becomes founder and father of the happy commune; all workers benefit equally from the films that they jointly produce and in which they all joyfully perform. In this particular film's conflict of art and nature, it is artifice that is truly benign.

But the old capitalistic owner returns to seize possession of his now successful publishing house. To preserve the house's freedom, Lange shoots the boss and becomes a fugitive from justice. The continued success of the Arizona Jim

commune is highly doubtful. Despite the brief era of social perfection and happiness, reality returns to awaken its vassals from the dream world. The disintegration of the social idyll in *Monsieur Lange* seems to speak directly to Clair's creation of such an idyll in *À Nous la liberté*.

Throughout the 1930s Renoir's films threw a cold, hard light on the crumbling social and political structures of Europe. Renoir juxtaposed the tinkle of ironic laughter with the overwhelming sense of dissolution and decay; an effete aristocracy was gradually sinking under the weight of its own artificial and lifeless conventions, and the new rising classes were barrenly following in the empty steps of their former masters. The thirties, in France as well as in America, had become the age of the scenarist, and Renoir's scenarios (which he wrote himself in collaboration with one or two other writers) novelistically emphasized parallel events, parallel structures, parallel characters, parallel reactions, parallel details. The attention to visual and intellectual parallels gave the Renoir film the richness and complexity of the novel. But the literary structures of the films were supported by Renoir's sensitivity to the visual: shots of nature, of faces, of social groupings visually generate the film's meaning and control its tone. *Boudu Saved from Drowning* (1932), an exuberantly comic clash between a tramp, a pure man of nature, and the stifling conventions of polite, bourgeois society; *Toni* (1934), a sensitively tragic clash between the passions of love and the societal conventions—law, marriage—that unsuccessfully attempt to harness those passions; and an adaptation of Gorky's *The Lower Depths* (1936), which attracted Renoir with its bitter microcosmic study of human beings in society—all show the director warming up for his greatest films at the end of the decade.

Grand Illusion (1937) is also a microcosmic study. Its superficial action is the story of two French soldiers who eventually escape from a German prisoner-of-war camp during World War I. Its real action is metaphor: the death of the old ruling class of the European aristocracy and the growth of the new ruling classes of the workers and bourgeoisie. The prisoner-of-war camp is Renoir's microcosm for European society. The prison contains French and Russian and English, professors and actors and mechanics and bankers, nobility and capital and labor.

At the top of the social hierarchy is the German commander, Rauffenstein (played by Erich von Stroheim), and the French captain, Boeldieu (played by Pierre Fresnay). Though the two men fight on opposite sides, they are identical: they both use a monocle; they both wear white gloves; they both share the same prejudices and snobberies, the same tastes in wines, foods, and horses. The supreme irony of the film is that the German commander must kill this man to whom he feels most closely allied because the rules of the war game demand that the commanding officer of the prison shoot men trying to escape, just as they demand that the prisoner-gentleman attempt to escape. The two men are inflexibly frozen in their codes, their rules, and their duties. Although the French prisoners live better than their German guards, although they sip fine wine and sup on *pâté de foie gras,* their duty is to escape.

The two tougher, hardier prisoners do escape, while Boeldieu, attired in his white gloves, smartly covers for them and gives up his life in gentlemanly sacrifice. Maréchal (played by Jean Gabin), a mechanic, and Rosenthal (played by Marcel Dalio), a Rothschildean Jew whose family owns banks, land, and several chateaux, escape together from the German prison. The animosities, the tensions, the prejudices of the two men surface as the going gets rough, but the two finally make it to Switzerland—and

they make it together. They are the new Europe.

Renoir sustains the film's metaphor with his sense of style, construction, and imagery. The film opens on a gramophone horn; the machine plays "Frou, Frou, Frou," a popular French song; we are in the French camp. A few minutes later, the camera captures a second gramophone horn; the machine plays a Strauss waltz; we are in the German camp. The songs have changed; the camps are the same. Most indicative of the film's tone and statement is the drag-show sequence in which the French prisoners entertain each other dressed as cancan girls in the latest imported Paris frocks. Just before the show, the French prisoners receive word that the German army has captured the French town of Douaumont. Despite their sadness, the show must go on—to show their *esprit.* In the middle of the drag show, the French receive word that the Allies have recaptured Douaumont. Maréchal makes the announcement; the cancan boys stop dancing and rip off their wigs to cheer; they all sing the "Marseillaise." Renoir's shots of these rouged, lipsticked men singing the patriotic hymn—moments before, they had been singing a frivolous tune—equates the two songs and reveals the irony and paradoxes about a notion such as patriotism, simultaneously serious and silly, deadly and tawdry, transcendant and transvestite.

Music is one of the film's leitmotifs. The musical trifle, "Frou, Frou, Frou" recurs several times. When the captured French prisoners first hear a German military band, united by the rhythmic tramping of marching feet and the soaring descant of piping fifes, Boeldieu remarks, "I hate fifes." Another unifying musical motif is "Il était un petit navire," which we hear played for the first time by Boeldieu on a little toy fife as a ruse to help Maréchal and Rosenthal escape; the tune diverts Rauffenstein's attention but leads to the death of the man who hated fifes. Later, on the icy road, when the crippled Rosenthal and the impatient Maréchal quarrel and threaten to separate, Rosenthal starts singing, "Il était un petit navire," in defiance and anger. As Maréchal stalks away from his lame comrade he unconsciously starts to sing the same song. The song ultimately brings Maréchal back to his wounded comrade; he will not desert him again.

Consistent visual imagery is another source of the film's unity. Renoir's camera contrasts things that are hard, cold, and dead with things that are soft, warm, and vital. The final sequences of the film take place during the winter; the consistent pictures of snow and frozen ground throw their cold, damp shadow over the entire film. The two escaped prisoners must struggle across an immense meadow of snow to reach safety in Switzerland. Yet ironically, the Swiss border, the place of refuge, is invisible. It is impossible to distinguish different nations beneath a common blanket of snow. Only the German officer's announcement that the two have made it informs us where the snow of Germany ends and the snow of Switzerland begins. That one can make such nationalistic distinctions between things that are really the same is one of the film's grand illusions, an illusion that freezes the human heart and condition to death.

Equally cold is the bare, stony castle that keeps the prisoners captive. And unforgettable is the piece of iron that replaces Rauffenstein's chin; it supports his face since his real chin has been shot away. Rauffenstein himself is literally held together by metal—in the chin, the back, the knee—the living embodiment of the film's contrast of the vital and the dead. The one warm thing in the prison-castle is Rauffenstein's little geranium, which he carefully guards and nurtures. When Boeldieu dies, Rauffenstein lops off the one blossom himself; he knows that his

Grand Illusion: *The coldness of stone and metal: Von Rauffenstein (Von Stroheim), Boeldieu (Pierre Fresnay), and Maréchal (Jean Gabin) in the German fortress. Maréchal finds warmth on the little farm: a farm not a prison, straw not stone, loose clothing not uniforms*

world is dead. Emphatically warm and vital are the woman and child, Elsa and Lotte, that Maréchal and Rosenthal encounter on their flight. Elsa's warmth touches the soldier Maréchal, as does her little daughter, Lotte, with her sparkling blue eyes. Maréchal vows to return to this warmth after the war is over. But will he? He tells her he will return in French, a language she cannot understand. His promise is never received; will it ever be kept?

It is, of course, another sign of Renoir's brilliance that he has built this dialogue film around the ironies of language—languages that separate people or bind them together as effectively as national boundaries. Indeed, language differences are national differences. So in this film that is full of disastrous political illusions, it is difficult to determine which is the "grand" one. That war can resolve political issues? That national boundaries exist? That national boundaries do not exist? That class distinctions do not exist? That national distinctions are stronger than class distinctions? That class distinctions are stronger than national distinctions? Or perhaps it is simply that the "grandest illusion" is that the First World War was the "war to end all wars," since none of the conflicts for which it was fought—drawing acceptable national boundaries, declaring racial supremacies, bridging linguistic barriers, resolving class differences—had been resolved in the Europe of 1937.

Grand Illusion pointedly condemns the decadent, wasteful artificiality of the ruling class that has caused the very war that will kill it. With the Great War, the aristocracy of Europe committed elegant suicide. To turn life into a cold murderous game with a series of artificial rules is ultimately to turn life into death. But how can a class that has lived according to certain codes and manners for centuries suddenly change to fit the new bourgeois and proletarian times?

Rather than being villains, von Rauffenstein and Boeldieu are stunningly admirable for their taste, their elegance, and their honor. Is it their fault that they have been condemned by history to live in a century that does not need those virtues?

These ironies and paradoxes become the central issues of one of Renoir's subsequent films, perhaps his greatest, *The Rules of the Game* (1939). The film depicts the dead values of a dead society—two dead societies, in fact—the society of wealthy masters and the society of genteel, parasitic servants who ape their masters. Both masters and servants value good form over sincerity and the open expression of human emotion. The inevitable result is death. But as in *Grand Illusion*, the dancers in this dance of death are sincere, elegant, honorable human beings, trying to balance the demands of social form with the demands of human spontaneity. Like the aristocrats of *Grand Illusion*, they find that the conflicting demands are ultimately, and unfortunately, mutually exclusive and unbalanceable.

Renoir's complex structural parallels play off two love stories against each other. In the main plot, a young romantic aviator, André Jurieux, openly confesses his love to a stylish upper-class married lady, Christine de la Chesnaye. Although the rules of the game do not prohibit adultery, they do condemn such frank, open, sincere expressions of it. In the subplot, the adulterous lady's maid begins her own adulterous dabbling with a new servant, Marceau, a poacher, an outsider (like André), not a genteel servant like her own husband, Schumacher. The servants, who ostracize Marceau, are just as snobbish and conventional as their masters who ostracize André because he is romantic and Christine because she is foreign. The two love plots cross paths. The maid's jealous husband, who also has problems observing the rules of the game,

The Rules of the Game. *The perfect orderliness of conventionalized murder:
the aristocrats at the hunt*

mistakenly shoots the aviator, thinking
that André is his wife's new suitor. The
romantic aviator dies but the game goes
on. Marquis de la Chesnaye, Christine's
husband, formally announces to his guests
that André has met with a "regrettable
accident"; the group willingly and
unemotionally agrees to accept the baron's
obvious lie as a gentlemanly display of
good form.

Renoir's sense of style and imagery
again sustain the film. Its most
memorable visual sequence is the rabbit
hunt, a metaphor for the society's
murderous conventionality and
insensitivity. The wealthy masters go off
to shoot rabbits; this hunt, like the lives
of the rich, has its etiquette, its rules, its

gentility. It is a totally destructive yet
conventionalized form of killing. The
servants also serve as accomplices in the
murder, for their job is to beat the trees
and bushes, driving the pheasants and
rabbits out of their cover and into the
open where they can be gunned down.
Servants and masters are partners in this
murderous game. Renoir fills the screen
for five minutes with an agonized ballet
of helpless, dying animals: they run across
the screen accompanied by the bushy
scamper of their little feet on the sound
track, we hear the crack of a rifle, the
furry animal stops, flips, spins, and
stretches out (in slight slow motion) to
die. The sickening, horrifying beauty of
this dance of death is at the heart of the

*The marquis (Marcel Dalio)
with one of his mechanical pets
and Octave, the sponger (played
by Renoir himself)*

film's meaning and tone. The whole film is a dance of death. While the skeletons dance on stage at the marquis's evening party, men shoot real bullets at one another in the audience.

Another of the film's visual metaphors is the marquis's collection of mechanical toys—ornate, clockwork birds and music boxes. The marquis converts the living into the dead, the body into a machine. He collects people—his wife and mistress—the way he collects toys, and he prefers stuffed but predictable machines to breathing, unpredictable people. The marquis's delight in the mechanical mirrors his society's worship of mechanical social rules and its disrespect for people, for whom the rules have theoretically been written. The aviator uses his machine to reach his beloved; the marquis uses his as an alternative to loving. The rules of the game and love are incompatible. The sincere, loving, naïve aviator is gunned down—like a rabbit.

And yet Renoir's method is not so naïve as to condemn artifice and praise the simplicities of spontaneity. For one thing, the Marquis de la Chesnaye—Renoir's representative of civilization—is a compassionate, considerate man who is trying not to hurt anyone, whereas the aviator—Renoir's representative of spontaneity—is a selfish, blundering fool. Although La Chesnaye's music boxes are indeed mechanical, they also represent a degree of orderly and delicate perfection toward which human life might well aspire. La Chesnaye's human problem is that he would like to achieve an impossible ideal—a world in which the demands of love and order are harmonious rather than mutually exclusive. As he tells his gamekeeper, he wants no fences around his property and he also wants no rabbits. It is not La Chesnaye's fault that the perfect grace of the eighteenth century (the century that produced his chateau, his lifestyle, and the Mozart on the sound track), a world in which the demands of spontaneity and convention may have been properly balanced, no longer exists in the twentieth century with its airplanes, motor cars, bourgeoisie, and the Nazis massing on the borders of France. As in *Grand Illusion*, the source of evil in *The Rules of the Game* is extremely complex: it is rooted partly in the human personality, partly in the demands of social convention, partly in nature itself, and partly in history, which has posed dilemmas greater than the powers of people to solve.

Renoir's comedies of manners were dark, bitter, and very uncomical. The death, the decay, the antisemitism, the organized murder that Renoir depicted in his films prophetically surfaced with the Second World War. Renoir, like Clair, made films in the United States during the war: *Swamp Water* (1941), *The Southerner* (1945), *Diary of a Chambermaid* (1946). After the war, he, like Clair, returned to France. But Renoir's talents had been less dulled by the war and the years in Hollywood. His eye, his sense of style, his perception of social structures and human relationships were still keen. Renoir would serve as an historical bridge, uniting the tradition of French literary filmmaking with the emerging cinematic breeziness of the *nouvelle vague*.

Vigo, Carné, and Others

Not all French films were successful at combining literariness with the visual powers of moving pictures. As in America, the early sound years in France produced a curious and inert hybrid, the filmed play. "Canned theatre" became one obvious but clumsy way to solve the dialogue problem in French as well as American films. The success of the French playwright, Marcel Pagnol, as a producer and director of dialogue films was symptomatic. But in translating plays for the camera, Pagnol showed more cinematic sense than did many theatre-inspired Hollywood directors. He often preferred shooting outdoors to shooting on the sound stage, a very untheatrical choice. He also had the vision to ask cinematically-minded directors to work for him, like Jean Renoir *(Toni).*

The young iconoclast, Jean Vigo, however, was totally unfettered by the theatrical and literary biases of the early thirties. Vigo made only four films—two

shorts, one of medium length, one feature—before his death in 1934 at the age of twenty-nine. That Vigo should be free of the deadening conventions of canned theatre was entirely appropriate, for freedom was Vigo's primary theme. Unlike Clair, whose ballet-like romps created a naïve dream-world for the free human spirit, and unlike Renoir, whose films evoke a bitter, sardonic laugh at the human attempts to wriggle free from suffocating social conventions and their own fallibility, Vigo's films show the determined and successful efforts of his characters to create temporary pockets of freedom in the midst of the society that confines them.

Zéro de Conduite (1933) contrasts the energetic, joyous freedom of boyhood with the constrictive restraint of the prison-like school that the children must attend. The boys eventually rebel against their captors, staging a demonstration on alumni day in front of all the wooden guests. They lower the flag of France and raise the skull-and-crossbones. They stand erect against the sky as the film ends. The freedom of Vigo's surprising images reveals the spirit of this film about freedom.

Vigo's primary visual choice is to subvert realistic, three-dimensional, deep-focus space and replace it with an imaginative, metaphoric sense of space that takes its spatial coordinates not from the architecture and scenery of the physical world but from the emotions and sensations of his characters. In the opening sequence of the film, two young boys, in a moment of youthful communion, transform the cramped space of a train compartment into an imaginative realm of play and joy. The shots from varied angles and perspectives in the tiny compartment (brilliantly photographed by Boris Kaufman, whose ability to shoot improvisationally in real locations would later contribute greatly to the American film) turn the tight physical space into an openly magical, mental universe. The spatial magic of the opening sequence is matched by that of the final shot, as the four young boys, apparently climbing to the peak of a tiled roof, seem to ascend into the sky itself, since Vigo has deliberately stripped the shot of all familiar spatial coordinates.

Surprisingly beautiful in the film is the slow-motion pillow fight in the bare, sterile dormitory. The scene—another radical transformation of space, this time achieved by transforming time—is a metaphor for the whole film: in the midst of the confining, regularized room the children leap and bound, swing pillows, spill feathers in ballet-like slow motion, the feathers falling about their bodies and laughing faces like snow. Indicative of the film's tone is Vigo's handling of the teacher-jailers as comic grotesques (perhaps the Eisenstein influence here) with sharp, ugly faces or fat, round bodies. They sneak around corners; they steal the kids' candy. Most grotesque of all is the school's principal—a three-foot dwarf with a pointed beard. The highest authority of the system is the smallest man; his mind is as small as his body. Not surprisingly, this snide, iconoclastic film was banned by the French government in 1933 because it ridiculed authority. The film was not shown in France until after the war in 1945 when all forms of repression and restraint became understandably unpopular.

If *Zéro de Conduite* was the young director's youthful, rebellious, sarcastic swipe at authority and the system, his next film, *L'Atalante* (1934) is a mature investigation of two people discovering what is important within the system. Two young people, recently married, discover each other's love, then drift apart and separate, and then find each other again, now knowing how empty their lives are without each other. Tying the film together is the river barge, L'Atalante, where the newlyweds must live. The young man owns the barge and running the boat is his life. Juliette (the young

bride) longs for life on the shore. The barge becomes the source of the plot's complication, the rival that drives the young man and woman apart. Although Juliette does not know it, the open space of the shore, which seems so attractive, is really more confining, less free than the apparently cramped space on the barge. As in *Zéro de Conduite*, Vigo has set himself the problem of translating emotion into spatial coordinates, and the cramped, cluttered space on the barge is spiritually and emotionally richer than the deep but dead space on shore. The barge, adrift on the river, gliding on the water, in the sunlight, through the fog, becomes, like the community established by the boys in *Zéro de Conduite*, an ideal community—man, wife, old crew member, young apprentice—because it is not contaminated by contact with society at all.

The film's opening sequence begins the contrast of ship and shore. The man and woman are married on shore; the wedding party is stiff, formal, wooden; the marriage ceremony feels more like a funeral; the guests seem dead; their faces are unfeeling; they wear black. Only on the barge do the two young people loosen up and begin to feel what getting married really means: not a deadening social ceremony but a fertile union of two minds and bodies. Vigo's gorgeous traveling shots of the barge on the water, either from extremely high or low angles, consistently evoke the beauty of river life. His sincerity in rendering human emotions, which he accomplishes by means of understatement and implication, is evident in the images that imply much more than they say: Juliette's desire to listen to the radio, her one contact with the shore; the lonely Juliette sitting huddled up alone in the fog; the separated man and woman, each sleeping alone in separate beds (before, they had always slept together). Vigo's sense of the grotesque—another carry-over from *Zéro de Conduite*—adds a unique and symbolic

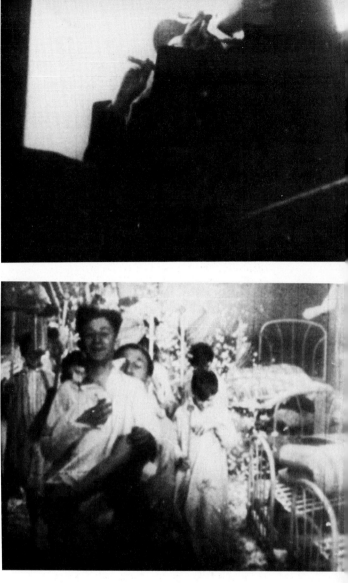

Zéro de Conduite. *The subversion of three-dimensional space: two boys puffing cigars in the train car, the slow-motion procession after the feathers fly, the final ascent toward the sky*

air to the old sailor (Michel Simon), who has made the water his home, and the clownish peddler (reminiscent of the jester in *Chien andalou*), who evokes Juliette's longings for the life on shore. Because the two young people really love each other, and because Vigo has rendered that love so intimately and so sincerely, we feel complete relief and delight when they return to each other and the idyllic life on L'Atalante. The barge casts off and continues its journey up river.

Like the films of Renoir, the films of Jacques Feyder and Marcel Carné took their literariness from the novel rather than the stage. In this age of the scenarist, both directors enlisted talented minds to write their scripts. Charles Spaak (who also wrote *Grand Illusion* for Renoir) wrote for Feyder the scripts of *Le Grand Jeu* (1934), *Carnival in Flanders* (1935), and *Pension Mimosas* (1935). Even more fruitful was the collaboration of the novelist-poet, Jacques Prévert, and Carné. Prévert, whose poetic obsessions with fatalism and death dominated even his light comedies *(Bizarre, Bizarre, 1937)*, wrote Carné a series of scripts in which admirable men die (for no reason other than that men die), in which people are dragged against their wills into complicated webs of human interactions from which there is no escape, in which people lose what they want and achieve what they do not want, in which symbolic figures of death weave pointedly through the realistic action, in which images of fog and gloom and chaos dampen the film's tone and symbolize the world's emptiness.

Like Renoir, Carné-Prévert explore what is clearly the key theme of the 1930s, freedom. But for Carné-Prévert the limit to human freedom is the nature of the race itself: its fallibility, its mortality, its existence in a completely irrational, indifferent universe. Prévert's existential void is the precursor of Camus's or Beckett's; his characters not only wait for Godot (love is clearly their Godot), but

wait for it very incompetently, never attaining the desired love because of some failing within themselves, within the desired lover, or merely within the cosmos. Although the Carné-Prévert films echo the decay, the waste, the death of Renoir's, they lack the surface level of ironic comedy, of polished manners, of genteel laughter. The serio-comic irony of Renoir contrasts with the hollowness, the sadness, the profound despair of Carné.

In *Port of Shadows* (1938), a young soldier, past unknown (we know only that he is running away from something), is steadily dragged into a complicated human net of murderers, thieves, and outcasts, all because of the woman he loves, who loves him in return. One of the film's leitmotifs is a small dog that follows the soldier (Jean Gabin) everywhere, instinctively, irrationally attached to this man who helped save his life at the beginning of the film. In the same way, the soldier is instinctively, irrationally attached to Nelly. He abandons his own attempts to escape, protects Nelly instead, and is suddenly and unexpectedly gunned down at the end of the film, the victim of his love, his self-sacrifice, his commitment to a human being outside of himself.

The film is dominated by the empty, seamy people who surround the soldier and Nelly: the fat owner of the toy shop, Zabel (Michel Simon), who is Nelly's foster father and also her lecherous captor; the slimy, petty mobster who takes the loss of Nelly as a blow to his self-importance; the nihilistic painter (a Prévert surrogate) who paints death in all his pictures and eventually commits suicide so that the fleeing soldier can use his passport and clothes. The film is dominated also by images of shadows and fog—of rain, of dimly lit streets, wet pavements, shadowy figures in silhouette. The gray muteness of the film is the perfect visual accompaniment to the inexorable closing of the jaws of the trap around the soldier and his love. The trap is life itself; his two ways of facing the trap—fight and flight—are equally unsuccessful.

The richest, the most complex of the Carné-Prévert films, one of the greatest literary-novelistic films of all time, is *The Children of Paradise* (1943-45). As with Dostoyevsky, or Tolstoy, or Dickens, the viewer of *Les Enfants du Paradis* lives through a very complicated series of interlocking events with a great many complex and interesting figures over a long period of time. The feeling of complexity, of immensity, and of depth in the film is overwhelming. There are four central characters: two actors, a woman, and a murderous thief. All have difficulty deciding what they really want; each achieves tremendous material success only to discover that the success is meaningless.

Central to the film is the contrast between the two actors: one, Frederick Lemaître (Pierre Brasseur) is the man of words who acts with his mouth; the other, Baptiste Debureau (Jean-Louis Barrault), is the mime who acts with his body. Although both Frederick and Baptiste are historical figures—two famous French actors of the nineteenth century—the film treats them as metaphorical opposites rather than as biographical subjects. Frederick is the man of surfaces, of words, of fine talk and phrases; he becomes a huge success in cheap, hack dramas which he saves with his own imaginative theatrics; he also runs up debts, trifles with the ladies, treats his colleagues with contempt. His life is richly barren. Baptiste is the man of real feeling and the real artist; he is moonstruck; his ability to feel and love makes him the artist that he is. Although Frederick is the matinee idol of Paris, Baptiste's ethereal mime is the delight of artists, thinkers, and the common people.

Between the two actors stands a woman named Garance (Arletty), after the flower, who casually becomes Frederick's mistress although Baptiste is the man who really loves her. The young Garance thought that love was very simple, that bodies were to be tasted and then tossed away when the flavor had departed. Her view of love's simplicity conflicted with the complexity of Baptiste's passion; when she casually offers him her body, he, seeing her as a pure spirit of beauty, declines the offer. Only years later, after she has found wealth and glamor as the mistress of a rich count, does she realize the power of Baptiste's passion, the power that makes him a great mime. And only then does Baptiste realize that he should never have declined Garance's offer. But when she returns, Garance sees that Baptiste is saddled with a wife, whom he does not love, and a child. The two are just as far apart as ever.

The fourth character, Lacenaire (Marcel Herrand), is not a man of the theatre but a thief with a taste for murder, a man who lives his life as though it were the theatre. Lacenaire, like Frederick, is a man of words; in private he writes plays and in public he makes embroidered, fatalistic, lengthy speeches about the futility of life. He is a man of costumes: of overstarched, overwhite shirts, fancy canes, curled hair, finely spun words—a glossy, empty servant of death who treats both life and the living as banal jokes. His one passion is indulging his contempt for others and his vain love for himself.

Carné and Prévert use the theatre as the film's central metaphor. The first and second parts of the film both open on a theatre curtain; the curtain rises to reveal the world of *Les Enfants* behind it. Both the first and second parts of the film end with the curtain coming down. Although the theatre is Carné's metaphor, the film never degenerates into the static talkiness of the canned-theatre films. (Ten years later, both Max Ophuls and Jean Renoir would use the theatre or circus tent as a metaphor without inhibiting the film's cinematic freedom.) Carné sustains his theatre metaphor by paralleling the dramatic, fictional roles of the actors on stage with their actual longings and

Les Enfants du Paradis.
*The theatre as life and life
as the theatre: Frederick
(Pierre Brasseur) as
Harlequin, Garance
(Arletty) as the Moon Lady,
Baptiste (Jean-Louis
Barrault) as Pierrot*

choices as human beings off stage. In the playlets on stage there are bandits, lovers, police, and deaths; in their off-stage lives there are bandits, lovers, police, and deaths. The on-stage character played by Frederick—Harlequin—is, like Frederick, bouncy, playful, spirited, charming, superficially happy. Baptiste's dramatic role as Pierrot is like Baptiste himself: sad, mellow, moonstruck, tender, unfortunate. Just as Pierrot loses the beautiful moon lady (played by Garance) to Harlequin, Baptiste loses Garance to Frederick. The theatre is life and life is the theatre.

The title of the film itself is part of its theatre metaphor. The "Paradise" of the title is not a heavenly, metaphysical one but an earthly one: it is the slang name for the second balcony, the highest, cheapest seats in the theatre, the seats where sit the masses, those who love the theatre and mix intimately in all its passions. The chaotic, seething, energetic masses (the "gods") in "Paradise" parallel the masses just outside the theatre on the teeming, vital, packed Boulevard du Temple, also known as the "Street of Crime." There is no particular order or reason or meaning for all the human activity in "Paradise" or the "Street of Crime." The life merely is; it exists in all its energy, its contradictions, its desires, its disappointments, its feelings. It, ironically, is the only kind of paradise there is. Out of this huge human "audience," Carné and Prévert have merely selected four specific performers to demonstrate their roles. The ending of a drama in life, however, is not always happy, as it sometimes is on the stage (of course, Baptiste's mimes always have unhappy endings). In fact, given Prévert's nihilism, the ending in life is never happy; at the most it is ambiguous.

Weaving through the film is a dirty, vulgar old-clothes man called Jericho, who is Prévert's symbolic reminder of the sordid, mortal realities behind all our dreams of the ideal. Jericho, with his prophetic biblical name of death and dissolution, is also a thief, an informer,

The seething activity in "the gods"

and an eavesdropper. He spies on people's lives, spreading gloom and doubt wherever he goes. Baptiste hates Jericho, for the old tramp reminds him of the etherealness, the unreality of the moonbeams on which he bases both his life and his art. Baptiste hates Jericho so much that he creates a character just like him for one of his mime plays whom Pierrot kills. In an original version of the script, Baptiste was also going to kill Jericho.

Instead, Jericho merely stands at Baptiste's side at the end of the film. Baptiste has just lost Garance once more, perhaps never to see her again. He follows her through the "Street of Crime," vainly calling her name, trying to attract her attention. But Garance cannot hear him; the swirling masses of humanity slow Baptiste's pursuit, effectively choking him off, keeping him from reaching his love. At his side stands Jericho, a metaphor for broken dreams, unfulfilled hopes, irrational fate, human mortality—the true "crimes" of human existence. Surrounded by all this human activity, so alive and yet so senseless, Baptiste is swallowed by the crowd, by his "audience," and the curtain falls.

Les Enfants du Paradis was a kind of intermission in an era which had lasted for some twenty years before the Second World War and would last for another fifteen after it. *Children of Paradise* could not be finished and released until after the Liberation liberated both the creative energy and the necessary francs. For the first fifteen years after the war the best French films—those of Ophuls, Bresson, Tati, and Renoir—very clearly looked backward to the literary-scenario films of the prewar era. Not until 1959 would the French film imagination strike off in a new direction.

11 The American Studio Years: 1930–1945

In the 1930s Americans went to the movies; in the 1980s they go to a movie. The difference is not merely semantic. In 1938 there were some eighty million movie admissions every week, a figure representing 65 percent of the population of the United States. In 1978 there were fewer than twenty million movie admissions every week, less than 10 percent of the population of the United States. Over five hundred feature films were produced in the United States in 1937; fewer than one hundred were produced and distributed in 1978. The film industry of the 1930s thrived on a felicitous circle of economic dependence on attendance, exhibition, and production. The huge number of movie admissions necessitated a huge number of theatres, which necessitated a huge number of films to be shown in the theatres, which necessitated large, busy studios that could produce enough films to keep the theatres filled. Only after the Second World War did the circle of dependence reverse itself and turn vicious.

The need for enormous quantities of films guaranteed the survival of the studio system, which was geared for production in quantity. The huge studios of the 1920s converted to sound by merely adding new departments to their already complex organizations; specialization and division of labor, two pillars of the silent-film factories, became even more essential to the sound-film factory. New departments of music, of sound mixing and dubbing, of sound technicians and machinery joined the older, established departments on the studio lot. The writing department became even more specialized; some writers roughed out general treatments, others broke the treatment into its shot-by-shot elements, and still others added the necessary dialogue.

The film property traveled through the studio, from department to department, from story idea to finished script, until it finally landed in the hands of its director, often on the day before shooting began. After fifteen to thirty shooting days, the director relinquished the negative to the cutting department, which edited the film into its final form, as instructed by the film's producer. Only the most important directors enjoyed the opportunity to shape the script before shooting and to cut the exposed footage afterward. From the cutting department the film went to distribution offices, and from them to the waiting chains of theatres that the company itself owned. The film product rolled down the assembly line from original idea to final showing, all stages controlled by the studio factory. The film industry had evolved its structure for the next fifteen rich years, from 1930 to 1946.

The years of wealth were not without their moments of worry. At first, the Wall Street crash of 1929 exerted curiously little effect on the film business. Although America was officially broke, Americans kept scraping up dimes, quarters, and dollars to see movies. The economic sag first hit the movie industry in 1933; admissions sagged, theatres closed, production dropped. But prudent studio economy measures, the aid of government dollars, and a new moralistic path of righteousness nursed the film business back to health.

In 1930, Martin Quigley, a Roman Catholic layman, and Daniel Lord, S.J., drafted the Hollywood Production Code, another in a series of the motion picture industry's official statements on the proper moral content of films. But the Code might never have been enforced if the Catholic Legion of Decency had not threatened an economic boycott in 1933, the same year that movie revenues first began to feel the Depression. In 1934, Joseph I. Breen, another Roman Catholic layman, went to work for the "Hays Office" as the head of its new Production Code Administration, an agency that would award the industry's seal of approval only to those films that observed the Code's moral restrictions. Any producer or distributor who released a film without the industry's seal would be fined $25,000 (and every major producer

and distributor was a member of the MPPDA and subject, therefore, to its rulings).

The Code declared that movies were to avoid brutality (by gangsters and especially by the police), they were to avoid depicting any kind of sexual promiscuity (unwedded, extramarital, or "unnatural"), and they were to avoid making any illegal or immoral life seem either possible or pleasant (goodbye to the gangsters who lived well until the law gunned them down). The Production Code viewed marriage as more a sacred institution than a sexual one; the bedroom (with obligatory twin beds) of a married couple became more ornate and holy than a cathedral. Even more restrictive were the new Code's specific prohibitions against certain words. Not only were "sex," "God," "hell," and "damn" forbidden, but so were such flavorful and healthy Americanisms as "guts," "nuts," "nerts," and "louse," which were considered deficient in gentility and "tone." Ironically, the Code, which Hollywood adopted for business reasons in 1934, perished some thirty years later for the same reasons. The very words and deeds that crimped sales in the 1930s spurred them in the 1960s.

In addition to soothing its audiences' moral sensitivities, Hollywood pulled itself out of the Depression by appealing to its audiences' greed. Double features—two pictures for the price of one—became standard in all but the poshest of first-run theatres. Hollywood added a third attraction to the two movies; audiences could play exciting games between the films—Keno, Bingo, Screeno—which promised to send them home with cash or a set of dishes as well as with many hours of uplifting entertainment. The studios survived the financial crisis of 1933 and profits shot up in 1935; they survived the crisis of 1938 and profits shot up in 1939. The boom years of the war eliminated all money crises for several more years. The film industry enjoyed its biggest business year in 1946 (despite the blockbuster years of the late 1970s, the film industry's profits have never been proportionately higher than those of 1946).

The studio system produced an obvious tension between film art and film business. Art cannot be mass produced; creativity does not work in departments and on schedules. Although Hollywood produced some seventy-five hundred feature films between 1930 and 1945, only some two dozen directors and two hundred films maintain their original power and entertainment value (as opposed to their "camp" value) today. Despite the tension between commerce and creativity, there are surprising parallels between the Hollywood film of 1930 to 1945 and the rich era of English drama, 1576 to 1642. Like the Renaissance drama, the studio films were tremendously popular with vast audiences of diverse social, economic, and educational backgrounds. The Elizabethan plays and players were products of repertory theatre companies with a permanent staff of writers, actors, technicians, managers, costumers, and designers; the films were products of repertory film studios with similar permanent staffs. Like the Elizabethan theatre company, the film studio spread the acting parts among its regular stable of actors, each of whom played a specific kind of role over and over again—old man, comic, juvenile, leading man or lady, dancer, singer, child. Just as Shakespeare's Will Kemp or Richard Burbage bounced from comic or tragic part to comic or tragic part, Mickey Rooney and Clark Gable bounced for MGM. And like the films of the studio era, the Elizabethan plays were drenched in the theatrical customs, clichés, and conventions of their age: the tragic scenes of Senecan gore, the bawdy use of the comic Vice, the pastoral convention of a magical, fanciful forest. And just as a Shakespeare, a Marlowe, or a Jonson

could turn a convention into a trait of personal style, so too a Lubitsch, a von Sternberg, or a Ford could make a studio convention completely his own. The most striking differences between Elizabethan plays and the studio films are, first, that the studios produced no Shakespeare (but then neither has any other art at any other time) and, second, that thousands of the hack, completely conventional, and clichéd films of the 1930s still survive, but only a few hundred (presumably the best) of the thousands of plays written between 1576 and 1642 have not been lost.

There are two ways of looking at the artistic products of a repertory system for the manufacture of popular dramatic entertainment. The critic can look at the greatest products of the system—its Shakespeares and Jonsons—or at its most typical and conventional products. Any fair assessment of the studio system must do both.

Film Cycles and Cinematic Conventions

The studio system controlled both the subjects of film narrative and the cinematic style in which they were shot. Formulas for fictional construction, characterization, decor, and photography dominated Hollywood's films. A key principle in the selection of story material was simply that an idea that had worked before would probably work again. Films were not special, individual conceptions but tended to bunch together as types, in cycles. The new sound equipment introduced audiences to the hard-bitten, tough argot of mobsters; Hollywood produced a cycle of pictures that made the tough talk of gangsters as familiar as polite conversation around the family dinner table. The first gangster cycle glorified the amoral brutality of the underworld: *Little Caesar, Scarface, Public Enemy.* Later gangster cycles, purified by the antiviolence, antiillegality sections of the Breen Code, merely put the tough-talking guys on the right side of the law—that is, on the other side of the badge—*Public Hero Number I, The Last Gangster.* A cycle of films about prisons, "the big house," spun off from the mobster films; the big house also had its euphonious argot, its underworld morality, its tough characters both behind bars and behind the warden's desk: *The Big House, San Quentin, The Criminal Code.* Yet another close relative of the mobster cycle was the journalism cycle. The newspaper reporters often seemed like gangsters who had accidentally ended up behind a typewriter rather than a tommy gun; they talked and acted as tough as the crooks their assignments forced them to cover: *The Front Page, Big News, The Power of the Press.* It is no accident that Ben Hecht, the greatest screen writer of rapid, bullet-like, flavorful tough talk, wrote gangster pictures, prison pictures, and newspaper pictures. The pictures were all variations on the same brutal, tough-guy cycle. And Hecht, of course, had scores of imitators.

A succession of musical cycles accompanied the cops-and-robbers cycles. Just as synchronized sound brought the pungent, brittle crackle of thug talk to American audiences, synchronization also brought the possibility of complex rhythmic and musical effects. Singing and dancing could be synchronized to the exact beat; picture and sound could be wed in their own kind of sound-visual montage. The earliest talking pictures were inevitably singing pictures. De Forest's earliest Phonofilms and Warners' earliest Vitaphone shorts used singers and vaudeville entertainers. *The Jazz Singer* was more a singy than a talky; even *The Lights of New York*—the first of the gangster talkies—used several long musical numbers in Hawk Miller's night club. Musical sequences were almost obligatory in early talkies (even *The Blue Angel* and *Morocco*).

The first musical films were either filmed versions of Broadway shows with their original stars or suave, continental musical-comic pictures *à la* Lubitsch with Maurice Chevalier, Jeanette MacDonald, Jack Buchanan, or Miriam Hopkins. The second cycle of musicals was a series of "backstage" stories—the struggling young composer (who happens to be a slumming millionaire but wants to make it on his own talents), the young hopeful in the chorus (who is catapulted to stardom when the leading lady falls ill), et cetera —with the musical numbers directed by Busby Berkeley. The Berkeley musicals were highly schizophrenic mixtures of the blandest, thinnest dramatic sections and the most dazzling, kaleidoscopic visual style for the musical sections. The effect of the new Hollywood Code on these backstage musicals was especially obvious—particularly in the difference between the tough, vulgar, sexually frank dialogue of *42nd Street* and the saccharine, virginified dialogue of *Golddiggers of 1933*, only six months later.

Other musical cycles included the smoother, more intimate and integrated comedies-of-romance-with-music with Fred Astaire and Ginger Rogers or the ornately costumed operettas with Nelson Eddy, Jeanette MacDonald, Allan Jones, and Risë Stevens. America's greatest composers for the musical theatre, the Gershwins, Jerome Kern, Rodgers and Hart, Cole Porter, wrote original songs and scores for Hollywood musicals. There were musicals with children (Shirley Temple and Bobby Breen); musicals with the fresh young ingenue, Deanna Durbin; musicals on ice (Sonja Henie); and later, even musicals under water (Esther Williams).

Any successful Hollywood film spawned a dozen imitations. Hollywood's studio years were like the 1960 television years when one successful spy show begot a dozen progeny on all three networks. Like television, the Hollywood of the thirties faced the weekly pressure of entertaining a huge percentage of the national population; as in television, fear

The monochrome musical. Busby Berkeley's kaleidoscopic white pianos on a black floor (Golddiggers of 1935), *Fred Astaire's variations on black and white, circle and line, light and shadow* (Top Hat, Swingtime)

of a dollar disaster was a constant spur to producing safe mediocrities. The parallels with television programming are even more obvious with those successful films that spawned not only imitations but sequels. The film series was the ancestor of the television series: the Andy Hardy pictures, the Maisie series, the Charlie Chan films, Mr. Moto, Philo Vance, Henry Aldrich, and—the closest parallel with television of all—the series of films springing from MGM's *Young Doctor Kildare*. Yet another studio formula was to patch together a film with all the available stars on the lot, using some flimsy narrative thread to unite the stars' fragments: Paramount's *Big Broadcasts* (of 1932, 1936, 1937, and 1938), MGM's *Broadway Melodies* (of 1936, 1938, and 1940). The studios made the same films over and over again, with similar titles or different ones.

Formulas for style were as binding as formulas for plotting. Despite the hundreds of different Hollywood directors in the decade, the Hollywood films, with surprisingly few exceptions, looked strikingly alike. The studio system was as pervasive in erasing stylistic differences as it was in blurring differences of theme and story. The director not only inherited an unalterable, detailed scenario but a completed series of sets and costumes and a studio crew of cameramen, electricians, and soundmen. Any director's impulses toward personal style were suppressed before shooting began by the studio's general policies of lighting, design, cinematography, and cutting.

The key characteristic of film style in the studio era was that sound films were talking films. The talk was better, now that writers of screen dialogue knew how to write screen dialogue. The scenes of talk were smoother, now that the speakers could move from place to place and both camera and microphone could follow them. But talk, rather than images, still propelled the talkies. The reign of talk produced further stylistic consequences. The camera's position and angle illuminated the speaker and the other characters' reactions to the speech rather than obscuring them in the hope of illuminating something else. Extreme high and low angles, extreme close shots, extreme far shots, tilts, and whirls were uncommon in even the most visually imaginative films. Cutting was as functional as the shooting. Quick cutting distracted the audience from the speaker's words. Montage, one of the most expressive tools of silent films, was reserved for occasional and obvious showcase effects: passage of time, summary of a character's activities. Film lighting was also functional rather than tonal—clear, bright, even—so as not to detract from the speakers. Scenes were lit for the stars, not for the dramatic atmosphere. Designers and cameramen used light to make the pretty people even prettier, shaping their heads with light to make those box-office faces stand out from the backgrounds.

Despite their common assumptions and conventions, each of the studios displayed a unique personality in applying them. Perhaps the two giants—MGM and Paramount—were the most distinctive and the most different from one another. MGM was the studio with almost dictatorial central control—exerted by Louis B. Mayer and Irving Thalberg. Paramount, under B. P. Schulberg, was a much looser organization, granting more freedom to individual producers, directors, and writers. MGM was a studio of stars: Greta Garbo, Jean Harlow, Joan Crawford, Norma Shearer, Katharine Hepburn, Clark Gable, Lionel Barrymore, Spencer Tracy. Paramount was a studio of writers and directors: Ernst Lubitsch, Josef von Sternberg, Cecil B. DeMille, Leo McCarey, Preston Sturges, Billy Wilder. In the early 1930s Paramount was the iconoclast's haven: the home of Mae West, W. C. Fields, and the Marx Brothers. The studio permitted the sexual excesses of von Sternberg and the sexual sniggers of Lubitsch. MGM flattened all excesses into a shiny, respectable wholesomeness. When the Marx Brothers left Paramount for MGM they quickly lost their lunacy and their spark. Ironically, in the 1930s the MGM policy seemed the much wiser of the two, for Louis B. Mayer's devotion to family entertainment made MGM the most respected (and successful) film factory in Hollywood, while B. P. Schulberg's chaotic individuality ran Paramount into severe financial difficulties, resulting in the studio's loss of many of its stars (Jeanette MacDonald accompanied the Marx Brothers to MGM) and Schulberg's loss of his job.

None of the other studios were as distinctive as these two at the extremes. Warner Brothers, which invested less money in production values (sets,

The spoils of crime in Scarface: *fancy apartments, pretty women (Paul Muni, Karen Morley)*

costumes, crowds), was more dependent on good talk, and the dialogue in the early Warners' pictures was as sharp, as fast, and as good as anyone's. The studio specialized in gangster films, biographies, and musicals, directed by Howard Hawks (in 1932), William Wellman, Mervyn LeRoy, William Dieterle, Michael Curtiz, and Busby Berkeley, and starring such sharp talkers as James Cagney, Edward G. Robinson, Paul Muni, Humphrey Bogart, Bette Davis, Ida Lupino, Dick Powell,

Ruby Keeler, and Joan Blondell. Twentieth Century–Fox excelled in historical and adventure films directed by John Ford, Henry King, and Henry Hathaway with Tyrone Power and Henry Fonda, in show business musicals with Don Ameche and Alice Faye (and, later, with Betty Grable and Dan Dailey), and in the folksy comedies of Will Rogers and Shirley Temple. R.K.O. is most memorable for the smooth musicals of Fred Astaire and Ginger Rogers, the suave comedies with Cary Grant, and the occasional film by Howard Hawks (*Bringing Up Baby*), Orson Welles (*Citizen Kane, The Magnificent Ambersons*), and John Ford (*The Informer*). Universal excelled in the horror films—Frankenstein, Dracula, and the Wolf Man—directed by James Whale and Tod Browning, in the later comedies of W. C. Fields, and—at the opposite extreme—in the saccharine singing pictures of Deanna Durbin and Gloria Jean. The two "minor" studios, Republic and Monogram, specialized in cheap Westerns and cheap hoodlum pictures respectively. A later generation of French *cinéastes* has subsequently canonized the B-offerings of these cheapie-quickie studios as superior to many of the glossier offerings of the major studios.

The studio film of the thirties took the path of Ince rather than the path of Griffith: the American film became an externalized, narrative medium. What the characters did—and, as a corollary, what they said—became the movies' concern. Questions of why they did or said what they did or how it felt to do or say it became almost irrelevant. Human psychology, the world of sensations and inner feelings, motivation, all became formulaic, the most functional kind of shorthand solely to serve the narrative incidents.

These studio conventions posed the greatest obstacle to the creativity of the individual filmmaker. Not only were the minor directors—the staff hacks, the directors of "B" pictures now needed as the thinner halves of the double features—dominated by studio producers and policies, but even some of Hollywood's most respected directors earned that respect by executing studio commands with the greatest economy, efficiency, and polish. Hollywood's directors were not expected to be poet-painter-thinkers like Renoir, Carné, or Vigo; American directors were more like sergeants than generals, draftsmen than architects. Even when Renoir, Clair, and Lang came to Hollywood to make films, their films—despite obvious touches of personal insight, theme, and composition—acquired Hollywood's slick, impersonal sheen.

The studios forced their best directors to be eclectic. A director jumped from jungle adventure to backstage musical to historical pageant to contemporary comedy to operetta to gangsters. The director's sole qualification for handling so many styles and settings was his ability to get any job done well. He was more director in the stage sense of the word, the man who puts together someone else's idea, rather than a film *auteur*. Discussions of studio directors often dwell on one's fine sense of cutting, or another's clean use of light, or a third's close attention to costume and decor. This is to consider the director as a competent mechanic, the equivalent of equating Shakespeare's art with his control of metrics; it is substituting a means for an end.

Typical of the competent impersonality of the studio era are the careers of Warner Brothers' Mervyn LeRoy and MGM's W. S. Van Dyke. LeRoy, within a three-year period, directed *Little Caesar*, the tough story of a mobster's rise and fall; *I Am a Fugitive from a Chain Gang*, a tough tale of brutality in a southern prison; and the inane "dramatic" sections of the backstage musical, *Golddiggers of 1933*. In those same three years, 1930–1933, LeRoy directed twenty other films, including journalism pictures,

homespun comedies, and show-business musicals. LeRoy's later work was just as eclectic, from the patriotic adventure, *The F.B.I. Story*, to the heavy, sour musical pancake, *Gypsy*. Although a director like LeRoy obviously knew his craft, it seems impossible to say whether he knew or felt anything else. Woody Van Dyke's films are equally schizophrenic; there was adventure (*Trader Horn; Tarzan, the Ape Man*), light comedy (*The Thin Man* series), costume pageant (*Marie Antoinette*), historial romance with music (*San Francisco*), operetta (*Rose Marie, Sweethearts*), as well as contributions to MGM series pictures (*Andy Hardy Gets Spring Fever, Dr. Kildare's Victory*). To find any *auteur*ishness in the work of such directors is highly pedantic fishing.

The studio era produced several of these "smorgasbord" directors who could be depended upon to cook up a slick, palatable, occasionally powerful product regardless of its particular ingredients: Michael Curtiz (*Charge of the Light Brigade, Dodge City, The Private Lives of Elizabeth and Essex, Casablanca, Yankee Doodle Dandy, Mildred Pierce, Night and Day*), William Dieterle (*The Firebird, A Midsummer Night's Dream, The Story of Louis Pasteur, The Life of Emile Zola, Juarez*), Lewis Milestone (*All Quiet on the Western Front, The Front Page, Rain, Anything Goes, Of Mice and Men*), Victor Fleming (*Treasure Island, The Wizard of Oz, Gone with the Wind*, which was begun by Cukor and finished by Fleming).

In addition to asking their directors to select from the smorgasbord, the studios found that some directors did a better job with a single dish. Some directed comedies primarily: Gregory LaCava (*She Married Her Boss, My Man Godfrey*), Sam Wood (*A Day at the Races, A Night at the Opera, Goodbye, Mr. Chips*), Leo McCarey (*Duck Soup, Ruggles of Red Gap, Going My Way*), Edward Sutherland (*Mississippi, Poppy*). Other directors specialized in adventure films or mysteries: Tod Browning (*Dracula, Freaks*), William

Chaplin's women. With the ideally beautiful statue and flower seller (Virginia Cherrill) in City Lights

Wellman (*The Public Enemy, The Ox-Bow Incident, The Story of G.I. Joe, The High and the Mighty*), James Whale (*Frankenstein, The Kiss Before the Mirror, The Man in the Iron Mask*), Henry Hathaway (*Come On Marines, Lives of a Bengal Lancer*). George Cukor and Clarence Brown, because they worked well with actors and dialogue, specialized in adapting stageplays into films; Mark Sandrich and Roy Del Ruth directed musicals primarily. But even the specialists took their turn at the smorgasbord table—the comic director occasionally being served a costume pageant, the adventure director dishing up a musical.

If the conventional studio films displayed any consistent personality it was one that reflected the general moral assumptions and human values of the era as a whole rather than that of any individual director. Almost all the films took the view that the sincere, the sensitive, the human would inevitably triumph over the hypocritical, the callous, the chaos of social machinery. American movie audiences, escaping from the realities of the Depression outside the movie theatre, withdrew inside to see

human grit triumph over suffering and human kindness triumph over financial, political, and moral chicanery. If the optimism of Hollywood films provided the audiences with the tranquilizer it needed, it also strengthened the audience's belief that eventually good people would make bad times better.

The American film offered not only escape but also subtle propaganda. Whereas many Americans lacked the money to buy warm clothing, American movie characters wore fashionable gowns and well-tailored suits. Whereas many Americans lacked the money to pay the rent, American movie characters lived in elegant apartments filled with expensive furniture. The tasteful richness of the studio films, supported by the inexorable workings of poetic justice in their plots, answered a very deep need in a people working hard to achieve the kind of comfort, ease, and plenty that it saw in the films every week. Just as the cynical materialism of the 1920s succeeded the innocence and purity of the Griffith era, the optimism and wholesomeness of the 1930s succeeded the values of the jazz age. Many of the Hollywood studio films

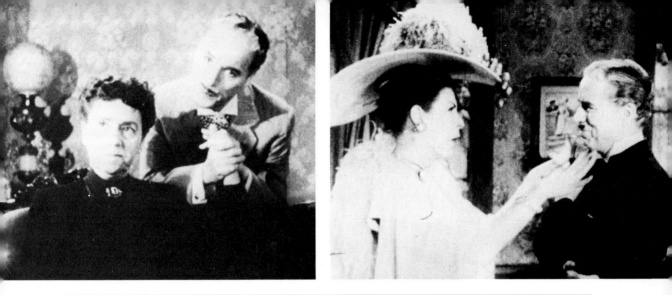

With the ugly and vulgar realities of his wives (Margaret Hoffman, Martha Raye) in Monsieur Verdoux

are more interesting as social documents than as personal, powerful works of art. As in the 1920s, the greatest individual directors were those who could avoid the clichéd convention or those who could inject their own personal insight and energy into the convention.

The Comics

Some of the most distinctive American films of the 1930s, like those of the 1910s and 1920s were comedies. Chaplin survived the transition to sound by making no transition at all. His first two sound films, *City Lights* and *Modern Times*, used a synchronized score and sound effects but almost no synchronized speech (like *Don Juan* and other early Vitaphone features). Chaplin was certain that Charlie, the little tramp, was a man of mime, a character who could not survive in a world of words. In *City Lights* (1931), Charlie's pantomime takes him into the society of the rich, where he makes friends with a suicidal millionaire who is friendly and human when drunk, cold and callous when sober (a possible

influence on Brecht's *Puntila and His Servant Matti,* with the same kind of schizophrenic rich man). Charlie's closeness to the world of the rich allows him to help a poor blind girl who, significant in the Chaplin symbolism, sells flowers to keep herself alive. Charlie scrapes up enough money to pay for the girl's operation; she recovers her eyesight and eventually discovers her benefactor. But Charlie perceives that he and the girl are further apart than ever; she longs for a rich, respectable suitor—not the outsider, the tramp. An agonizingly poignant closeup of Charlie's face ends the film with an unanswered and perhaps unanswerable question. Does the girl accept Charlie for what he is and can the two possibly share a life together? Or are their worlds too far apart and must the tramp take leave of his lady of the flowers, the inevitable loser again?

In *City Lights* Chaplin raises the question of whether the Tramp is capable of achieving sexual-romantic love, of, in effect, finding a sexual partner; in *Modern Times* (1936) Chaplin asks if the Tramp is capable of achieving marriage. But marriages can only exist within the social system that authorizes them. Marriages require homes, and homes require payments, and payments require jobs. So in *Modern Times*, the little Tramp, as always, is at the mercy of the social order, especially of the immense industrial machinery of our increasingly technological society. At the end of *Modern Times*, the Tramp and his "wife" walk away from the camera and from society, for their kind of marriage cannot survive in such a society.

Modern Times would be Chaplin's last stand against the modern dialogue times and the last incarnation of the tramp. Certain that the pantomimic tramp had no place in a realistic dialogue world, Chaplin dropped Charlot for *The Great Dictator* (1940). Chaplin now played two roles: a little Jewish barber, closely akin to his underdog tramp, and the villainous top-dog Führer, whom Chaplin—with his short, toothbrush moustache—resembled. (Or did Hitler, who loathed Chaplin's spontaneous, compassionate, demystifying comedy, really resemble Chaplin?) The comic action of the film pleads eloquently and ironically for the rights of individual human expression against the stifling, murderous power of the tyrant. Unfortunately, Chaplin discovered that the dialogue film could plead with speeches as well as with comic action. The overt didacticism of the film's final speech, a sincere but clichéd appeal for peace and understanding, loses the power of Chaplin's comic objectivity, which scores its points with shrewd human observation and insight rather than with saccharine sentimentality.

The same overt moralizing and sentimentality cloud the brilliance of Chaplin's last two masterpieces, *Monsieur Verdoux* and *Limelight*. *Monsieur Verdoux* (1947), like *The Great Dictator*, begins with a brilliant serio-comic premise: a delightful, witty, urbane gentleman marries a series of rich women specifically to bump them off, using the dead ladies' legacies to support his crippled wife and child on an idyllic country estate. The film necessarily questions the relationship of the means of an action to its end, whether murder is justifiable if its ultimate purpose is virtuous. The film develops its theme with a series of acidly hilarious vignettes in which Chaplin goes about his murderous business in the most fastidious, matter-of-fact way. Most hilarious of all are his frustrating attempts to dispose of the coarse, clumsy, big-mouth wife played in perfect counterpoint to Chaplin's diminutive suaveness by Martha Raye.

But as in *The Great Dictator* Chaplin deserts comic objectivity at the end of *Monsieur Verdoux* to turn the film's implications into rather bald and pedestrian prose: society commits the same crimes and accepts the same assumptions as Monsieur Verdoux, except on a much larger scale. The explicit accusation was unnecessary. The same blend of comic insight and uncomfortable sentimentality pulls *Limelight* (1952) in two directions. The flashback scenes that recreate the music-hall routines of the old vaudevillian are brilliantly funny and touching, the former music-hall clown's ultimate tribute to the world that fostered his mime and art. The scenes in the present—of Calvero trying to control another human destiny now that he has lost control of his own—suffer from overstatement and melodrama.

Chaplin maintained his power and individuality in the studio era because he needed to make no concessions to Hollywood's commercial structure, to the new sound machines, or to the new optimistic temper of the times. Chaplin ran his own studio; the success and popularity of his films guaranteed him theatres in which to exhibit them without having to own them and profits to make more of his own pictures as he wanted to make them without the interference of producer or president of the board. Chaplin's cinematic technique, even in the silent era, was never dependent on montage or intrusive camera work. The unobtrusive cinematic style of the talking films was perfectly suited to Chaplin, whose cinema style had always been unobtrusive, emphasizing what he was shooting rather than the way he was shooting it. Despite his hesitation in adopting dialogue, Chaplin's personal film style was completely consistent with the visual conventions of the dialogue film.

Walt Disney, like Chaplin, made the transition into the studio era by maintaining his commercial and, consequently, artistic independence. Disney, whose fantasies of sight and sound, drawing and music, movement and rhythm had evolved in the first years of sound, found one further ally in the 1930s—color. Whereas the realistic, live-action studio films were trying to tame the effects of color, to blur its garishness, to make its hues mirror nature rather than some color-mad dream world, Disney's animated fantasies could use such color madness as one more fantastic, unreal element. The counterpoint of picture and music in the Disney cartoon acquired a third contrapuntal line. Shifts in color could accompany the shifting tones of the music. When the action and music became ominous and eerie, the screen world could turn icy blue; when the action and music became heated and intense, the screen world could turn a torrid red-orange. Color, like rhythm and music, became kinetic, not naturalistic. The same advantage that Disney enjoyed over realistic films in the free use of sound also gave him the freedom to manipulate color. Disney brought color to his Silly Symphonies, to his animal characters (Mickey, Donald, and Pluto), and eventually to his first feature film, *Snow White and the Seven Dwarfs* (1938).

The Disney fantasies of color and motion were perfectly suited to the audience's craving for happiness, wholesomeness, and optimism in films. His "Who's Afraid of the Big, Bad Wolf?" from *The Three Little Pigs* (1933), not only became a popular song but also a metaphor for the whole country's cheerful defiance of the big, bad social wolf, the Depression. But Disney's happy cleanliness began taking its toll on his visual imagination. *Snow White* was to be a foreshadowing of things to come. Disney gradually deserted the short for the feature, the fantasy-abstract film of color, music, and movement for the sentimental story film that attempted to blend fantasy and realism. Even in 1938 critics noticed a tension in *Snow White* between the fantastic rendering of the animals and dwarfs and the clumsy, sticky attempts at naturalism in rendering the people. The tension resolved itself as Disney moved steadily away from color-sound abstract painting (his *Fantasia* of 1941 was its culmination) toward turning human emotions into romantic, saccharine cartoons of emotion.

A third director of silent comedies found the new conventions of sound liberating rather than constricting. Ernst Lubitsch, whose camera had learned to comment on a character or situation by shooting an apparently insignificant detail that was loaded with implications, discovered that sound, as well as pictures, could make such touches. In his first sound films, the continental musicals, he mastered the new machines and learned to make the sound film as fluid and effortless as the silent one. But his greatest sound films were dialogue pictures, slick comedies of manners, translated by his cinematic imagination from the stage into his unique film terms: *Design for Living* (1933), *Angel* (1936), *Ninotchka* (1939), *To Be or Not to Be* (1942), and, especially, *Trouble in Paradise* (1932). *Trouble in Paradise* is such a subtle, deceptively artless film that its bold, imaginative mixture of picture and sound seems completely consistent with the shiny conventionalities of studio-era films.

Trouble in Paradise is the story of an urbane, elegant crook, whose charm and social graces allow him to work his way

into the hotels and houses and hearts of
the very rich where he performs his
clever, high-stake thievery. Eventually the
master crook, Gaston Monescu (Herbert
Marshall) finds himself caught between
his love for two women, Mariette Colet
(Kay Francis), the rich perfume heiress he
is swindling, and Lily (Miriam Hopkins),
his clever accomplice in crime. Because
he is a thief, because he is merely a
pretender to propriety in the gleaming
world of the rich and proper, because his
past has determined his future, Monescu
eventually leaves Mariette for Lily.

Lubitsch brings this droll carnival of
thieves to life with his dry, witty control
of picture, sound, and speech. The film
opens on a shot of a garbage pail. A man
picks up the pail and tosses its contents
into his "truck." Except that "truck" turns
out to be a gondola, for this is a garbage
man in Venice, city of romance. As the
garbage gondola journeys on its route,
Lubitsch shoots the gleaming water of
the canals and the picturesque *pallazos*

surrounding them; the garbage gondolier
sings plaintively, "O Sole Mio." The
romantic song continues as the garbage
gondola continues off-screen. Not only
has Lubitsch deflated picture-postcard
romance, one of the film's themes, but he
also has underscored, metaphorically, the
film's action, which reveals the "garbage"
beneath the pretty surfaces in the lives of
the film's "beautiful people."

A later blending of music and picture
similarly deflates the world of the rich.
When the characters go to the opera, a
symbol of snobbery and social status,
Lubitsch summarizes the proceedings by
concentrating on the conductor's score.
With the camera riveted on that score,
the soprano torridly sings (off-screen), "I
love you, I love you." Then the pages
begin to riffle, steadily turning by
themselves to some point near the end of
the opera. The soprano just as torridly
sings (still off-screen) with the same notes
"I hate you." The device is a brilliant
means of handling the passing of time, of

ridiculing opera plots and passions, and of burlesquing the values of high society that force people to pursue fashionable amusements that do not amuse them.

Lubitsch handles Monescu's sexual relationships with his two ladies with the greatest wryness and subtlcty. In the first sequence, Lily and Monescu fall in love by discovering each other's crooked cleverness. The two sit in Monescu's elegant hotel suite, eating supper and drinking wine. Like the opening garbage gondola of the film, the scene plays the elegant, polite surfaces off against the genuine corruption beneath: the two are not Baron and Countess enjoying a slyly seductive supper but two crooks trying to fleece one another. As the two trade polished banalities they subtly steal each other's watches, wallets, jewelry. After discovering and sorting out each other's goods, Monescu bends over to kiss Lily as she sits on a sofa. Lubitsch dissolves to an empty sofa. Then he cuts to a male arm, its white sleeve implying a discarded dinner jacket, hanging a "Do Not Disturb" sign on the door of his hotel room. Later, in a dazzlingly clever series of cuts, Lubitsch implies the direction of Madame Colet's and Monescu's intentions by throwing the intertwined shadows of their embracing bodies on the coverlet of her bed. The implications of such juxtapositions are obvious, clearly a sign of the screen's pre-Breen sexual maturity.

Add to Lubitsch's subtle images and clever music his satiric handling of the minor characters, themselves rich fools or covert crooks (Edward Everett Horton, Charles Ruggles, C. Aubrey Smith), and Samson Raphaelson's sparkling, effortless dialogue, which consistently pins a new tail on an old cliché: "A bird in the hand is worth two in jail"; "If you behave like a gentlemen, I'll break your neck"; "I love you as a crook, but don't become one of those useless, good-for-nothing gigolos"; "a member of the *nouveau* poor." The combined ingredients make *Trouble in Paradise* the most polished comedy of manners in the history of American film.

Frank Capra also directed comedies of manners. But instead of the suave manners of a shiny Europe in Lubitsch's films, Capra focused on the ingenuous, homespun manners of the most American America. Although Capra's career in films stems from silent comedy when he was a gag man and staff director at both the Sennett and the Hal Roach studios, Capra

---

Lubitsch's sexual wit in Trouble in Paradise—*from a reflection of the embracing lovers in the mirror to the shadows of their intertwined bodies on the bed*

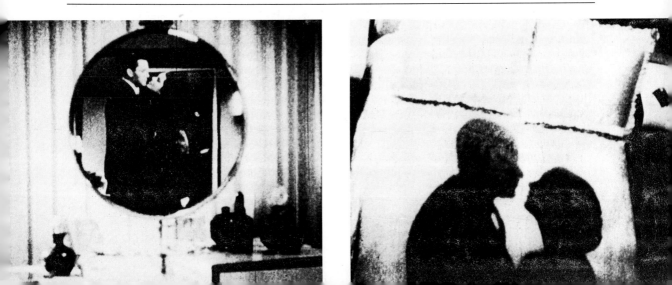

became an important director in the era of the talkies after he had come to the then tiny Columbia studio. There he met Robert Riskin, the man who was to write all his important scripts. The Capra-Riskin film was generally a witty contemporary morality play that pitted a good man—invariably a "little guy" who is naïve, sincere, folksy, unaffected, unintellectual, apolitical—against evil social forces: money, politics, affectation, social status, human insensitivity. The "little guy" converts the social heretics to the human truth, usually by making the film's heroine, who embodies the false societal assumptions, fall in love with him. The "little guy" emerges from the struggle not only victorious but also wiser about the ways of the world.

It Happened One Night (1934) examines the clash of a snooping newspaper reporter (Clark Gable) and a rich society girl (Claudette Colbert) fleeing her wealthy father to marry a worthless boyfriend. The two travel cross-country by bus, discovering the hazards as well as the charms of rural, uncitified America— motels, bad roads, hitchhiking, and, most significantly, people. In *Mr. Deeds Goes to Town* (1936), a young man from the country (Gary Cooper) inherits a pile of money and comes to the city to discover how to spend it. The city folk belittle the country ways of the hero "hick," and leading the laughter is the snobbish lady reporter (Jean Arthur) with whom Deeds has fallen in love. Deeds eventually converts the lady and eventually discovers that he must use his money to help the poor and starving. A whole family of happy, poor, humane eccentrics struggles comically against the forces of money, sophistication, and industrialization in *You Can't Take It with You* (1938). In *Mr. Smith Goes to Washington* (1939), Mr. Deeds has merely changed his name to Smith and his problem has changed from money to politics. Although Capra was no cinematic innovator, and although his vision may

seem corny and populistic today, the consistency of Capra's material, his solid scripts, the perceptive comic characterizations, the informal, under-stated acting in his films all make them sincere and clever statements of the era's conventional optimism and folksy humanism.

Like Frank Capra and unlike Ernst Lubitsch, Preston Sturges wrote and directed witty moral comedies on native American subjects. But like Lubitsch and unlike Capra, Sturges was an ironist and satirist who stood many of the era's wholesome and optimistic clichés and conventions on their ear. *The Great McGinty* (1940), the first film Sturges directed after a distinguished career in the 1930s as a Hollywood screenwriter (he wrote the script for Mitchell Leisen's brilliantly clever *Easy Living*, 1937), ridicules American democratic politics and the naïve notion that the voter really controls the government. *Christmas in July* (1940) ridicules the American dream of getting rich quick without hard work; the hero thinks up snappy advertising slogans. *The Lady Eve* (1941) is a burlesque of American sexual-romantic conventions, particularly the naïve, Puritanical insistence on virginity, purity, and innocence. And *Sullivan's Travels* (1942) is perhaps an explicit nip at Capra, the story of a Hollywood director who is weary of making entertaining fluff and aspires to make films laden with Serious Moral and Social Significance. In the course of his travels, the director discovers both the social utility and human nobility of "merely" making people laugh.

During the war years, Sturges courageously extended his satire to American perceptions of the war, our role in the conflict, our confused sexual standards in wartime (*The Miracle of Morgan's Creek*, 1943), and our superficial definitions of heroism and patriotism (*Hail! the Conquering Hero*, 1944). Sturges could get away with his audacious iconoclasm because of the comic richness and subtlety of his scripts, the spirited wit and charm of his acting ensemble, the ingenuity of his physical slapstick comedy sequences, and ultimately because, very much like Capra, his apparent antithesis, Sturges films suggested that the real disease was merely a slight case of social and moral myopia rather than an inoperable cancer in both the American people and the American way of life.

As with the silent comedies, many of the sound comedies wore the personalities of their comics rather than their directors. Because Langdon and Keaton and other purely pantomimic clowns who were schooled in the silent tradition never successfully combined talk and movement, Hollywood imported clowns from Broadway who had already effected the combination. The Marx Brothers even shot their first films in New York. In 1929 they recreated their current stage hit, *Cocoanuts*, for the screen. The Marx Brothers combined the great traditions of American physical comedy with a verbal humor that perfectly suited their physical types. The Marx Brothers looked funny: Groucho's moustache and eyebrows and baggy pants, Chico's hats and sly beady eyes, Harpo's hair and silly smiles. The Marx Brothers talked funny: Groucho's nasal gravel, Chico's accent, Harpo's beeps. And the Marx Brothers walked funny. Like the Sennett silent comedies, the plots of the Marx Brothers' films were irrelevant: romantic clichés with obligatory musical numbers and sappy doings of the juvenile and ingenue. The zany comics invariably dropped into this conventional world, and while it went about its predictable, Hollywood business, they merely did their own unpredictable things.

Those unpredictable things were either visual or verbal insanities. The great silent comedies have no funnier sequences than many of those in the Marx films: the football sequence in *Horsefeathers* (1932), the mirror scene in *Duck Soup*

(1933), the stateroom packed with human sardines or the split-second timing of the bed-shifting sequence in *A Night at the Opera* (1936), the scene in which the brothers invade the midget's teeny room with the teeny furniture in *At the Circus* (1939), the "more wood" sequence in *Go West* (1940), in which the brothers strip a train to keep the locomotive racing. And for brilliant verbal double talk there is the "Why-a-duck?" sequence in *Cocoanuts* in which Groucho tries to sell Chico a piece of island property with a viaduct (why-a-duck), the "Party of the First Part" sequence in *A Night at the Opera* in which Groucho and Chico burlesque legalistic jargon by tearing apart a contract (literally) clause by sanity clause, and there is the "Tootsie Frootsie Ice Cream" sequence of *A Day at the Races* (1937) in which Chico sells Groucho a coded manual for betting the ponies, and then another manual to decode the first manual, and then yet another manual to decode that manual, and so forth to infinity. The Marx Brothers films revealed the key elements of American sound comedy—comic physical types, suited to their comic personalities, suited to the physical-comic situations, suited to the verbal wit. Comic talkies had to move as well as talk.

Another Broadway import—Mae West—fulfilled the same comic formula. West had her comic personality, a parody of the amoral, sensual female who frankly enjoyed nice clothes, nice food, and a nice tumble in the hay. She physically suited that personality. No petite, lithe, virginal ingenue was Mae, but a buxom, hefty broad who looked like a cross between a curvy stripper and a fullback for Notre Dame. Her rolling eyes, her gyrating hips, her falling, throaty voice consciously tried to unmask an opponent or undress a friend. And her comic lines fit the eyes, the voice, and the body: "Beulah, peel me a grape"; "Are you packin' a rod or are you just glad to see me?" Even her croaking "Oh"

W. C. Fields caught in the trap of respectable American bourgeois life in The Bank Dick

was more a sigh than an exclamation and said much more than oh. Like the Marx Brothers' plots, Mae West's film stories, which she wrote herself, were slender lines on which to hang her own personal business: her gyrations, her groans, her comments, her songs. The films' action inevitably ran Mae up against the wall of respectability and legality. And if she avoided prison and legal censure at the end of the film, it was primarily because her impulses were human and sympathetic even if her activities were somewhat under the table (or under the bed).

Ironically, only one Mae West film, *She Done Him Wrong* (1933), is, because of its pre-Breen date, a real Mae West film. Most suggestive (and most characteristic of Mae's style) in the film are her songs. One of them is her set of dirty lyrics to the familiar tune, "Frankie and Johnny"; after all, Frankie didn't shoot Johnny just because she saw him with another woman in a public bar. The second song was often referred to as "THAT song"; its noneuphemistic title was "I Like a Guy What Takes His Time" and its subject was exactly what the title implies it to be. A third song, "I Wonder Where My Easy

Rider's Gone," was not about horse-back or motorcycle riding.

The effect of the Breen Code was obvious in her next film, which was forced to change its title from *It Ain't No Sin* (with its obvious implications) to *I'm No Angel* (1933), although the plot of the film allowed Mae to defend her personal code of morality against the sanctimonious assumptions of the bluenoses. And in *Belle of the Nineties,* when Mae sings "My Old Flame," although the significance of the flame is clear in the innuendoes of her eyes and voice, it has no explicit life in the song's lyrics. Despite the financial success of *She Done Him Wrong,* Mae West's film career was cut up and cut short by the moralistic scissors of the Breen sanctions against sexuality and the glamorous portrayal of vice. In her later films—*Goin' to Town* (1935), *Klondike Annie* (1936), and even *My Little Chickadee* (1940) with W. C. Fields—Mae West becomes a sterilized, clean-scrubbed caricature of her own sexuality, which was, in its original frankness, a caricature of sexuality in the first place.

W. C. Fields was another great comedian of the sound stage. Like Mae West and the Marx Brothers, Fields's comedy stemmed from himself rather than from the stories in which he found himself. Like Mae West and the Marxes, Fields combined a comic personality, a comic physical type, and a style of verbal wit that fitted both his mind and body. Fields also came to films from the stage, but the former vaudevillian, famous today for his gravelly, whiskey voice, began his film career in silent comedies directed by Edward Sutherland, Gregory LaCava, and—of all people—D. W. Griffith. Although it is impossible to imagine Fields without his voice, his neglected roots in silent films reveal that Fields's funniness, like that of all the great American screen comics, is fundamentally physical. An occasional sequence from one of the sound films reveals his powers as pure physical clown: his clumsy attempts to play croquet in *Poppy* (1936), the battle with bent pool cues in *Six of a Kind* (1934), and his deft juggling in *The Old-Fashioned Way* (1934). Physically funny, too, is the Fields body—the booze-bloated nose, the beer belly—which he tries to dignify with the spiffiest, most fastidiously selected period costumes.

Like his physical appearance, the Fields character is a mixture of external polish and inner nastiness. Fields is the great spinner of words—of melodious euphemisms, euphonious malapropisms, florid rhetoric. His affectation of polite speech is like all his other pretentions to politeness—pure sham. Beneath the fancy waistcoats and purple prose beats the heart of a dirty old man who drinks, smokes, swears, and gambles, who hates women (especially sweet old ones), children (especially cute little ones), animals, and all respectable social institutions (especially marriage, work, honest business dealings, and the law). In films like *Tillie and Gus* (1934), *It's a Gift* (1934), and especially *The Bank Dick* (1940), Fields—like the Marx Brothers and Mae West—was the foe of everything sentimental and nice. In an era of glamorized sentimentality and niceness, their essential vulgarity and comic crudeness were especially refreshing.

von Sternberg, Ford, Hawks, Hitchcock, Welles

Of the noncomic directors whose films were obvious exceptions to the studio rule, the films of Josef von Sternberg have perhaps worn the least well. Visually the von Sternberg films are gleaming gems, rich in atmospheric detail, shimmering pools of light and contrasting shadow, the excitement of a perpetually moving, prowling camera, the luminous face of Marlene Dietrich—in shadow, in blazing light, veiled, feathered, powdered, hazed. The von Sternberg film looks dazzling beside the stiff, static, neon-lit feeling of the typical studio film. But beneath von Sternberg's gleaming surfaces—the exotic locales, the symbolic details, the smoke, the shafts of light, the audacious sexual innuendoes that could only have gotten past the censors who didn't understand them—his films suffer from some of the same ills of formulaic plotting and undeveloped characterization as do their more stylistically conventional brothers.

The Blue Angel (1930), von Sternberg's second sound film, is perhaps his best, for it suffers least from a hollowness in the guts. Ironically, von Sternberg shot the film in Germany for Ufa. In the early sound years, Hollywood suddenly discovered a new problem—breaking the language barrier. The silents simply substituted new titles in new languages as the film leaped from country to country. But with sound, before film distributors discovered dubbing and subtitling, Hollywood's plan was to shoot the same film in Europe with different languages and different casts. Von Sternberg went to Germany to take part in this cinematic internationalism.

The Blue Angel is a Circe story. A bewitching woman, the nightclub singer, Lola Lola (Marlene Dietrich), steadily turns an orderly, almost lifeless school teacher (Emil Jannings) into a beast; he even crows like a cock to show his transformation. Professor Unrat eventually dies from this dramatic change of air, his conversion from school teacher to night-club clown. If the film is von Sternberg's best it is because the director renders every step in Professor Unrat's demise with the greatest intimacy and clarity, and he renders the sexual energy that destroys the man with an equal clarity. Atmosphere and visual images in the film are not independent entities but the means to depict the two conflicting characters and life-styles. Both picture and sound establish the two opposite worlds at the beginning of the film.

The Blue Angel: *the hazy, chaotic clutter of the nightclub, the antiseptic order and clarity of the classroom*

Professor Unrat's classroom is white, clean, bright, desks arranged in geometric regularity; the Blue Angel club where Lola sings is smoky, hazy, chaotic, dim. Professor Unrat's classroom is silent except for the drone of his voice; the Blue Angel is noisy, bustling, full of shouts and song. The antiseptic silence of Unrat's classroom is emphasized by the song of a choir that drifts in through an open window; in the Blue Angel Lola sings songs of a far less spiritual kind.

Like the great silent films of Jannings's past, *The Blue Angel* refuses to draw either romantic or moralistic conclusions. Professor Unrat's ascetic life is sterile, schematic, so crammed with routine that it lacks the breath of life; he, like his caged bird, is dead. Lola's sensual life is totally selfish, amoral, blind to the existence of any other being but herself; she is committed to love, not to love someone—as her famous song, "Falling in Love Again," so clearly indicates. Neither of the two lives is superior to the other. The film's business is not moral comment but merely the human story of what happens to a man from one life who tastes a drop of another. The wine that at first makes him drunk eventually poisons him. Although Lola frees him from his cage and makes him sing, his song, like the man himself, becomes cracked and empty. His final metamorphosis is not into the singing bird but into the kind of pathetic clown that he saw in Lola's dressing room when he first met her. That clown both foreshadows Unrat's fate and implies that Lola's collection of human husks is endless. The shattered professor creeps back to his old classroom to die. The only consistent moral comment in the film is on the professor's callous students who fail to see that as both strict disciplinarian and broken clown Unrat is a human being and deserves human sympathy. The film's young students are vicious, inhuman vultures, like the porter's neighbors in *The Last Laugh,* and rather obviously Nazis-to-be.

The von Sternberg–Dietrich American films are as dazzling visually as *The Blue Angel* (in fact, even more dazzling). They have individual moments of keen psychological insight. But they consistently depend on brilliant surfaces—in particular, the glimmering, shimmering close-ups of Dietrich's face—to imply the sexual and psychological intensity beneath the surface. But how clearly and how fully do these images reveal that underlying material? Take, for example, the final shot in *Morocco* (1930), the first of von Sternberg's Dietrich films made in this country. The hero (Gary Cooper), a member of the Foreign Legion, has marched off over the sands of the desert to fight. Marlene, in a wildly romantic moment, rejects her rich suitor and plunges off to follow Cooper over the sands, just as each peasant Arab woman follows her beloved Legionnaire dragging her goods and her goats behind her. Now Marlene is not the kind of woman to travel with goats. The awkwardness of her crossing the desert is emphasized by her need to remove her high-heeled shoes before setting off over the sand dunes. To make such a wildly romantic gesture believable, the director's responsibility is to structure the whole film so that we believe Marlene really loves the soldier *that* much. But the Dietrich-Cooper relationship has no life in the film's narrative at all. He falls in love with her in public (she is a night-club singer again). They play only one scene together *in camera,* in which little is said and nothing is done. The ending remains an incredible romantic pose. On the other hand, if the final shot is narrative nonsense, it is visually gorgeous: a beautiful composition of waves of blowing white sand, a sliver of dark sky, black specks of human figures dotting the sand at the corners of the frame.

There are other beautiful things in *Morocco.* There is von Sternberg symbolism in the scene in which Marlene must decide between life with the rich suitor (Adolphe Menjou) and life with the man she loves. To emphasize the struggle and decision, Marlene hears the military trumpet call (fine use of sound as symbol) announcing the Legion's departure from the town; at the same time, she nervously fingers a string of pearls her suitor has given her (a metaphor for the rewards of the wealthy life). As Marlene makes up

her mind she unconsciously tugs so hard at the necklace that the string breaks and the pearls scatter all over the floor. The meaning of her decision is clear. The film's finest, most stunning psychological moment is Marlene's first appearance in the Moroccan night club. She is dressed as a man in tails; she sings, Evelike, about selling apples, which she offers as she sings. A lesbian is obviously attracted to the male-clad performer. Marlene, knowing the woman's intentions, toys with her while singing and then matter-of-factly walks up to her and kisses her on the mouth. Nothing that happens later in the film has the same psychological intensity or interest.

The von Sternberg films are consistently packed with beautiful pictures and unexplored psychological details. *Shanghai Express* (1932), the fourth von Sternberg–Dietrich feature, is a story of the reawakening and reaffirmation of love between Marlene (now the shady Shanghai Lily) and Captain Harvey (Clive Brook), a proper officer in the British Army—played against a backdrop of robbers and revolutionaries in exotic China. As in *Morocco,* von Sternberg captures the texture and look of an exotic locale with a brilliant opening sequence, relying on Lee Garmes's constantly tracking, moving, prowling camera to capture the bustling activity and scurrying people of the eastern railway station. As in *Morocco,* the pictures of Marlene Dietrich are luminous, her face radiant in a streak of light against a darkened backdrop; they look striking even in the stills.

But as in *Morocco* much of the overt psychological narrative has been suppressed, von Sternberg relying instead on the sexual energy implied by the Dietrich close-ups and the film's calm and cool rhythm, reinforced by agonizingly long dissolves. The past relationship between Lily and Harvey fell apart when he refused to trust her, believing he had been sexually betrayed. The plot of

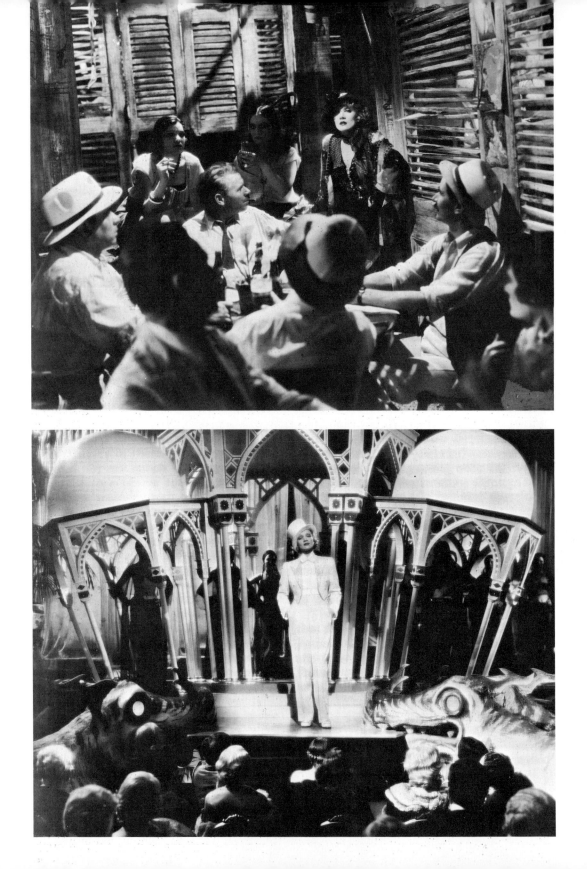

Shanghai Express gives him a second chance to put his faith in her, and he eventually passes this test. Clearly, Lily, like the oriental prostitute who shares her compartment (Anna May Wong), has her own powerful and personal system of morality, as opposed to the superficial and self-righteous moralism of the European passengers on the train. When Lily offers her body to the Chinese bandit in exchange for Captain Harvey's eyesight, the officer, unaware of her sacrifice, condemns her a second time for her apparent sexual licentiousness according to the same standards as the other proper passengers on the train. Because he never receives any concrete information to the contrary, he is forced to accept Lily's fidelity to him on trust alone—"purely a question of faith." It is on the basis of this faith alone—whatever the sexual surfaces and moral appearances—that love between human beings becomes possible. But we audiences must also accept much of the film's psychological material—primarily that there is anything worth loving about the cold, priggish Harvey in the first place—solely on our faith in von Sternberg's visual imagery rather than because of his film's narrative connections.

The final three von Sternberg–Dietrich films became progressively more bizarre, as if the Austrian director were (like von Stroheim) daring the race of Puritans to stop him and, at the same time, were (like Lubitsch) laughing at the sexual childishness of the race of Puritans for accepting his mythic, Circean hogwash as the genuine sexual article. *The Blonde Venus* (1932)—which contains enough plot for four films—features Marlene as loving wife, tempted adulteress, devoted mother, cheap whore in a Southwestern border town, and international sensation of the music hall. Despite the film's wandering and globe-circling plot, it is redeemed by its moments of sensual intensity and sexual audacity: the sensuous, tactile liquidity of the opening scene as

Dietrich swims in a shimmering, limpid stream (and as Herbert Marshall, impersonating a Boy Scout—at the age of 42!—voyeuristically watches this hypnotic Lorelei); the dusty, smoky chiaroscuro of the cheap dive in the Tex-Mex border town; the astonishing visual contrasts of the "Hot Voodoo" number, in which the Blonde Venus, complete with platinum fright wig, pokes her head out of the gruesome black body of a gorilla's costume; Miss Dietrich in white top hat and tails (the lesbian motif again), the very masculine guise that attracts the applause and adoration of her masculine admirers. More than anything else, von Sternberg seems to wonder how many grotesque and outlandish hoops he can make his Blonde Venus jump through without his audience's catching on to the sardonic and satirically contemptuous game.

The coming of the Code and the Hays Office in no way inhibited the director's sexual fantasies but seemed to spur them to new heights. *The Scarlet Empress* (1934) begins with the dreams of the sweet blonde seven-year-old child who later becomes Catherine the Great of Russia. The child's nighttime visions are sado-masochistic fantasies, including the agonizing screams of tortured men on the rack and, in what may be the most deSade-like image ever presented in a "respectable" studio-era film, the hanging of male bodies inside huge bells, so that their swinging legs and heels can bang against the bells and send their reverberating peels out over the town and countryside.

Later, the grown-up author of these dreams marries the madman who is the heir to the Russian throne, an idiot whose sexual activities are confined to drilling holes in people's walls so he can watch them and whose favorite playthings are inert toy soldiers (clearly von Sternberg implies something about the Prince's own inert toy soldier). The frustrated bride conceives a son by casually offering

---

Von Sternberg putting his Blonde Venus through hoops. Dietrich as sleazy whore and international star

herself to one of the palace guards, and with the eventual support of the entire army (which obviously supports her because of the way she has been "supporting" it) she leads the Revolution and seizes the throne (riding a milk white stallion and wearing a white hussar's costume—the white/black and male/female tensions again). The bells of all Russia (and those bells have been a consistent visual and aural motif of the film since the film's opening dream sequence) peel out with something resembling joy.

What is equally striking about *The Scarlet Empress* is that it is essentially a silent film. Von Sternberg reveals his roots in the visual richness of the silents by shooting whole scenes with only musical accompaniment: the spectacular wedding ceremony that alternates long shots of the immense cathedral, its columns and candles, with agonizingly immense close-ups of Miss Dietrich's face shot through her lace veil; the Bacchanalian wedding feast with its sensational traveling shot spanning an immense table covered with steaming broths, littered plates, and the sugared carcasses of beasts. Most of all like the silent film, *The Scarlet Empress* does not attempt to tell its story with dialogue (or even with pictures). The film probably devotes more screen time to printed titles than any film made since 1930. But as in his other films, this is a sure sign that von Sternberg either could not or would not manage a narrative skilfully.

Von Sternberg broke away from Dietrich to direct films without her after 1935: specifically, the unfinished *I, Claudius* (1937), with Charles Laughton, Emlyn Williams, and Merle Oberon; *The Shanghai Gesture* (1941) and *Macao* (1951), with their exotic, von Sternbergian Far-East locales; *The Saga of Anatahan* (1953), a film he directed for the Japanese film industry. But von Sternberg's most influential and prolific period as a director ended when he and Dietrich separated.

John Ford is the spiritual descendant of D. W. Griffith. Like Griffith, Ford's values are traditional and sentimental: the pure woman, the home, the family, law, decency, democracy. Like Griffith—and like the two other important Roman Catholic directors of the studio era, Frank Capra and Leo McCarey—Ford was a populist who praised the little people and the institutions that protected the little people while he damned those who selfishly twisted the system to grab money and power. Like Griffith, but unlike Capra or McCarey, Ford's method emphasized visual images rather than talk and violent dramatic action rather than wry comedy or pathos. Ford also tended to use the myth of the settling of the West as his central metaphor for the human spirit and the spirit of America, bringing civilization and fruitfulness to the savage wilderness.

The Ford films are as striking visually as von Sternberg's. Like von Sternberg, Ford's technique paints with extremes of dark and light. But von Sternberg used darkness to emphasize the luminescence of his shafts of light; Ford used shafts of light to emphasize the darkness. The Ford world is one of night, fog, rain, and shadow. The dark form in silhouette replaces von Sternberg's light-saturated faces surrounded by darkness. The dominant photographic method of von Sternberg is his Germanically moving camera; Ford's camera, often managed by Joseph August or Gregg Toland, composes in space, in width and depth. Dominating Ford's films are the vast vistas of the plains, mountains, and sky, the shots-in-depth of a group of human faces or figures, tensely composed, shot slightly from below. But Ford never substituted picture taking for picture making. Although the films became allegories of good and evil—the misty lighting, the weather, the characterizations all supporting the allegory—Ford's best films never forgot the studio prescription that a film must tell a good story.

The Scarlet Empress: *the spectacular wedding sequence*

The Informer: *Ford's feeling for people is reflected in the strength and uniqueness of their faces*

Ford's film career began early in the years of the silents, but he did not become a major influence until 1935 with *The Informer*. Ford, like Capra, never achieved real distinction until he found the proper scenarist-collaborator—Dudley Nichols. *The Informer* is a story of the Irish Revolution, with which Ford, an Irishman, was naturally in sympathy. Gypo, a former member of the I.R.A., betrays his closest friend and former comrades to the hated British. Gypo has been expelled from the party specifically because they fear his weakness. The film is the story of Gypo's succumbing to that weakness and eventually paying, both physically and mentally, for his mistake. The film's power is its achievement in making Gypo's tortured mind manifest, in showing the man's hurts, hopes, fears, and conflicts.

Ford accomplishes his psychological translation by the consistently subjective use of Joseph August's camera, which mirrors Gypo's mind with dissolves, blurred focuses, and physical projections of the man's frightened mind. Ford bathes the film in fog. The fog is not only the perfect visual climate for the dim, damp story; it is also a metaphor for the era's moral fog and for the psychological fog inside Gypo's head. Like the storm scene in *King Lear* (and in Griffith's *Way Down East*), the physical universe in Ford films takes its tone from the insides of men's heads. Memorable in *The Informer* is not only the metaphorical fog but the metaphorical blind man— dressed in black, silhouetted in the mist, tapping steadily with his cane—who seems to follow Gypo everywhere. The blind man is both an internal and external symbol: of Gypo's internal sense of guilt, which he cannot escape, and of the pursuit of the revolutionaries, whose justice he also cannot escape. Ford's symbols consistently work because they have a life on several literal and symbolic levels at the same time. Assigning them a specific single meaning inevitably shrinks them into something smaller than Ford intended.

The Informer has other strengths. It has a series of fine performances in the smaller roles in which Ford depicts how other Irishmen casually betray the cause and their fellows every day for money or booze. It has a series of brilliant scenes in which Ford depicts Gypo's growing irrationality and torment: his awkwardness in the house of mourning, his frenzy in spending the pieces of Judas money to buy drinks for the people he has betrayed, his final asking for forgiveness from his victim's mother as he lies dying in the church. As with Ford's visual symbols, his religious allusions in the film live on the dramatic level as well as on an intellectual one. Today the film's most glaring weaknesses seem to be an overstated performance from its star (Victor McLaglen) and a hackneyed musical score (by Max Steiner) that instructs the audience how to react with glaring exclamation points on the sound track. Ford, despite his talent, could not quite pull free from studio conventionality, and the score of *The Informer* is a reminder of the commercial bondage that lasted throughout his career. Ford himself estimates that he made only about six films—out of over one hundred!—that he wanted to make and in the way he wanted to make them.

Ford's greatest weakness (other than studio policy, which he could not control), like Griffith's, was his rather limited and traditional personal vision, which he made uncomfortably specific. Discussions of political and moral questions invariably become simplistic and banal in Ford films. One of the most outstanding examples is James Stewart's classroom lecture on liberty and freedom in *The Man Who Shot Liberty Valance* (1962). The entire film, including the irony that the vicious villain

bears the name of "Liberty," is an allegorical study of the bringing of democracy and civilization to the Old West, an allegory of liberty as opposed to license. When the film makes its point with story, characterization, or images (for example, the opening shot of the civilizing train slicing through the barren prairies), it is effective; when the film stops for a discussion of political or emotional issues, it is not. Action, character, and image fuse together in the best Ford films; among the best of them, because it is so active, so human, and so richly visual, is *Stagecoach* (1939).

For a film that masquerades as an action-packed western, *Stagecoach* is an intimate film of human interaction rather than exciting events. Although there is a thrilling Indians-versus-stagecoach chase in the final ten minutes of the film, followed by an obligatory (and very underplayed) gunfight just after the chase, *Stagecoach* for ninety minutes of its length is a film of faces and personalities. The coach itself becomes Ford's metaphor for civilized society. Like the train in *The Iron Horse* and *Liberty Valance* and the truck in *The Grapes of Wrath*, the stagecoach is a machine built by civilized hands that sets out to tame the vast uncivilized western wastes. Although Ford's films examine what civilization does *to* men as well as *for* men (particularly in *The Searchers*, 1956, and *Cheyenne Autumn*, 1964), in *Stagecoach* the key dramatic conflict is between the humanness of the coach society and the savagery of the Apaches.

Inside Ford's stagecoach is a whole society of people, of different social classes and mental habits: banker, sheriff, outlaw, salesman, doctor, prim wife, dance-hall "singer," gambler, stage driver. Ford and Dudley Nichols carefully distinguish between the human traits of each: the gambler's chivalry and polish, the outlaw's sense of fairness, the doctor's drunken kindness, the delicate lady's shedding of her prejudices, the sheriff's

Bringing civilization to the wilderness: Ford's stagecoach slices through the barren beauty of Monument Valley; inside a rustic shack, a microcosm of society breaks bread

the good-hearted outlaw get away with his woman, the singer (a euphemism for prostitute), at the end of the film; the singer, despite her toughness, gently helps the doctor bring a baby into the world; the outlaw loves the girl despite the societally defined shadiness of her past.

The single unredeemed character in the film is the rich banker who has stolen $50,000 from his own bank and is now running away with it. Despite his selfish violation of the law, the banker is the most outspoken on the immorality of the doctor, singer, and outlaw, and the most dogmatic in pontificating on the government's duty to protect his own self-important person. The banker, who views the law as written for his personal convenience, is pure Griffith. Ford's preference for the good-hearted, simple people—good-hearted despite their human fallibilities—over the evil-hearted rich is another Griffith dichotomy. And the prim, proper, moralistic, uplifting society of old hens, who viciously toss the doctor and singer out of town at the beginning of the film, seems to have leaped directly out of *Intolerance* or *Way Down East*. Despite the brilliantly exciting staging and cutting of the stagecoach's climactic battle with the Apaches, *Stagecoach* is a film about warm people and the important human values. So is *The Grapes of Wrath* (1940), *My Darling Clementine* (1946), and the other great Ford films.

If John Ford was the sound film's Griffith, Howard Hawks was its Ince. Compared with Ford, Hawks's films are more brutal and less sentimental, more active and less moralistic. Like Ince's, Hawks's movies are striking in their driving narratives rather than their examinations of psychology or emotional interaction. The psychological insight in a Hawks film functionally serves the narrative line. If Ince used his "soul fights" to move his narratives, the Hawks pictures contain similar conflicts between a man's outer actions and his inner urges.

human concern for the outlaw's safety, the salesman's citified, dude-like cowardice. Beneath their superficial tensions and differences, all these people (with one exception) eventually reveal an underlying warmth, kindness, and camaraderie that makes them equally decent human beings. The doctor sobers up to deliver the lady's baby; the whiskey salesman overcomes some of his anti-western squeamishness; the sheriff lets

Howard Hawks is the most deceptively artless of the great Hollywood "studio" directors: his visual style lacks the stunning, tricky idiosyncracies of a von Sternberg or a Lubitsch; his narrative style lacks the political and moral allegories of a Ford or a Capra. Hawks films merely seem to be well paced, well told, functionally shot genre pictures—gangster films, westerns, screwball comedies, and the like. But the ultimate testimony to Hawks's powers and abilities may well be that he created at least one film that might serve as the very best representative example of almost every American genre: the best gangster film (*Scarface*, 1932), prison picture (*The Criminal Code*, 1930), western (*Red River*, 1948; *Rio Bravo*, 1957), backstage comedy (*Twentieth Century*, 1934), newspaper picture (*His Girl Friday*, 1940), whodunit (*The Big Sleep*, 1946), and screwball comedy (*Bringing Up Baby*, 1938). When a director succeeds so deeply and so broadly with these genre films, it is necessary to look more closely at the unique spirit and talent that created them.

That these films are at least arguably the very best examples of their genres is perhaps due to two facts. First, Howard Hawks was not really a studio director, a staff member employed by a single studio (as Ford and von Sternberg were). He was an independent producer for much of his career and his films were released by various studios (Warner Brothers, R.K.O., and Columbia among them). He was not assigned genre pictures; he made the films he wanted to make in the way he wanted to make them. Second, Hawks was one of the greatest narrative craftsmen—perhaps the greatest—of the entire studio era (he is von Sternberg's opposite in this strength). He wrote or coauthored every script he shot, and his ability to shape the scenes he wanted to shoot and eliminate those he did not was so extraordinary that he was frequently called in to help other directors solve particular narrative problems with whole films or single scenes. Hawks's special skill was an ability to convert plays and novels into cinematic narratives that were invariably richer, tighter, more complex, and more perceptive than the originals.

The aesthetic of omission, of implying what is not explicitly and overtly stated, is an essential feature of Hawks's narrative mastery. Beneath the generic surfaces of his narratives lie complex tensions between the characters' verbal façades and their unverbalized feelings. In both the comedies and the adventure films, Hawks characters tend not to talk about their feelings overtly—first, because words can be easily and hollowly manipulated; second, because Hawks characters attempt to protect themselves, either through silences or torrents of chatter, not wanting to make the costly emotional mistake of investing their trust in someone unworthy of it. Most of the great Hawks films are stories of the evolution of trust, of growing faith in another human being, and the goal of the entire narrative is to reveal to the central pair (either two men or a man and a woman) that they have good reason to invest their faith in one another. The Hawks films, then, are primarily subtextual and psychological studies of the ego and of intellect, a counterpoint between mind and feeling (in contrast to many other Hollywood directors, like Ford, Capra, or von Sternberg, for whom the center of interest is the naked heart). The intellect controls the character's surface; the genuine feelings lie beneath; and the resolution of the Hawks narrative almost always brings the characters to a synthesis of the perceptions of the brain and the affections of the heart.

On the surface, *Twentieth Century* is a battle of wills, a study of two egomaniacal theatre people (played by Carole Lombard and John Barrymore) who fight to the egoistic death. Beneath the battle there is love (for they would not fight if they did not love), respect for each other's abilities, each other's strength, each other's egos. In the same way, although Hildy (Rosalind Russell) in *His Girl Friday* thinks she wants a sweet, normal married life with an insurance salesman (Ralph Bellamy), the fact is that she belongs with Walter Burns (Cary Grant) because, beneath their arguments and banter and battles, they complete each other. They are both newspaper "men." Hildy's life can be full only if she *does* what she does well, not if she tries to feel what she feels she ought to feel (this tenet is as central to the Hawks philosophy as any). And in the same way, the scientist David (Grant) in *Bringing Up Baby* can free himself from his emotional and psychological cage only by experiencing the spontaneity and unpredictability of a Susan (Katharine Hepburn) rather than by being emotionally devoured by his more proper fiancée, aptly named Miss Swallow. Although the plot of *Bringing Up Baby* seems to be a loony chase after dinosaur bones and escaped leopards, it really is an adventure in emotional education (like Antonioni's *L'Avventura*) in which David learns how to be a complete human being. The journalistic adventures of *His Girl Friday* and the theatrical adventures of *Twentieth Century* teach their characters the same lesson.

Hawks's alterations of Raymond Chandler's *The Big Sleep* clearly reveal both his psychological interests and his thematic commitments. Hawks builds the surface of the film as a maze of murders and bewilderingly proliferating names (Sean Regan, Eddie Mars, Joe Brody, A. G. Geiger, Carol Lundgren, Harry Jones) designed to lead the central pair, Marlowe (Humphrey Bogart) and Mrs. Rutledge (Lauren Bacall), to the knowledge that they can trust each other, if only because they work well together. It would be both foolish and dangerous for Marlowe to trust her if she is not really "wonderful" (as he ironically describes

her); many of the film's murdered men go to their "big sleeps" because they invest their affections in worthless women. The twists and turns of Hawks's narrative allow Vivian (a lesser character in the Chandler novel) to demonstrate her loyalty and sincerity, not by telling Marlowe about them but by demonstrating them as she helps him escape his big sleep.

Despite its apparently different cowboy surface, *Red River* is a very similar narrative. The prologue of the film (which does not exist in the Borden Chase story on which Hawks's film is based) carefully and cleverly establishes every narrative detail the film will require for its conclusion. Thomas Dunson (John Wayne) builds an immense cattle spread from the mating of his bull with the calf of a young boy, Matthew Garth (Montgomery Clift). After the Civil War, it becomes necessary to drive the now huge herd a thousand miles to market, from Texas to Kansas City. During the drive, Dunson's inflexibility—his refusal to change his mind or alter a decision, his strict sense of vengeful justice—threatens the success of the entire venture. Matthew usurps Dunson's authority and proves more flexible and more popular with the men he leads. The younger, "softer" man succeeds by altering the ultimate destination, bringing the herd to the new railroad line in Abilene and establishing the Chisholm Trail.

Beneath the surfaces of this familiar American western lie several deliberate epic and biblical parallels. The founding of the herd itself, with its suggestion of mythic animal coupling, echoes any number of similar copulations in Greek mythology. As in the Old Testament's "Exodus" and Homer's *Odyssey*, the group must make a long and arduous journey, beset with many kinds of enemies— natural and human, geographical and psychological, external attackers (Indians, rustlers) and internal conflicts stemming from human insufficiency and unreliability. As in Homer's *Iliad* and *Odyssey,* there is a wise old choric Nestor or Mentor (the cook, Nadine Groot, played by Walter Brennan), who serves as the work's moral commentator and barometer (Groot is a minor figure who plays no such role in Chase's story). As in "Exodus" the group must cross a body of water named "The Red" at the beginning of their journey. And as in "Exodus" Moses's hubris, his tendency to judge the weaknesses of mortals too harshly, leads to a change in leaders; Joshua, not Moses, takes the Children of Israel to the Promised Land, and Matthew, not Dunson, takes the herd to Abilene. The herd, like the Children of Israel, is both the progeny and the responsibility of its father-leaders, Dunson (always called by his last name) and Matthew (always called by his first).

In transferring the materials of older epics to these new American surroundings, Hawks sought to accomplish several ends. First, he argues that the history of America—part fact and part legend, part truth and part fiction —is exactly the kind of material out of which those earlier epics were made. *Red River,* part story and part history, is, as a work of art, exactly parallel to an *Iliad, Odyssey,* or "Exodus" in both content and spirit. Second, Hawks uses the epic context to examine his essential notion of human completeness and complementariness. Dunson is so purely hard and male ("the man with a bull" and without a woman) that his virtue is an extremely solitary one; he can build a civilization out of the wilderness but he cannot keep the civilization together once he has built it. Matthew ("the boy with a calf") has the milder gifts of fertility and civilizing; he can bind men and societies together. The historical process examined by Hawks in the film is, in effect, the passing of America's need from the one kind of leader to the other. But only with both

can one produce a whole civilization; one needs both the builder and the binder, the hard and the soft, the male and the female, the bull and the calf.

The climax of the film, an apparent showdown gunfight between the two leaders, reveals the usual and ultimate Hawks synthesis of love and trust demonstrated by action. Although some find the ending of *Red River* an optimistic, arbitrary avoiding of the gunfight toward which westerns invariably build, this opinion reflects a lack of understanding of both Hawks in general and the particular narrative he has carefully built. Dunson has come gunning for Matthew because he views the boy's taking the herd from him as a disloyal act, a usurpation, a denial of their love and work together that built the immense herd in the first place. (Hawks fills the frame with thousands of cows at the start of the promised duel, the very tangible, visible proof of the fertility of the Dunson-Matthew union.) Matthew, on the other hand, has taken the herd from Dunson as an extension of his love and loyalty, knowing that only his leadership can bring their invested labors to fruition. Matthew knows (from that very prologue added by Hawks) that Dunson will not shoot a man who does not intend to shoot him; he also knows (again established in the prologue) that Dunson reads a man's eyes to determine if and when he intends to shoot. As Dunson strides toward Matthew, the younger man's eyes (carefully scrutinized by Hawks's camera) reveal that he will never shoot. One does not shoot the people one loves. Dunson must observe that love in action, and Matthew accordingly demonstrates in action (as every major Hawks character must do) exactly what he feels beneath the surface. The film ends with an affirmation of love, friendship, fraternity, paternity, and "marriage," as almost every Hawks film does. Despite their screwball or adventurous surfaces,

these essential human feelings—and their definition by concrete human action—are the real subjects of Howard Hawks's films.

Although Alfred Hitchcock was a product of the British rather than American studio system, his work is very much a part of the American studio tradition. The British film industry has maintained a symbiotic relationship with Hollywood since the end of World War I, a relationship intensified by their common language after the conversion to sound. Hitchcock's affinity with the American system is clear in the popularity of his British films in America and in his smooth, effortless emigration from the British studio to Hollywood in 1939. The assumptions of the British and American studio systems were essentially the same.

Although Alfred Hitchcock directed his first film as early as 1925 (*The Pleasure Garden*), he, like John Ford, did not become a major influence until 1935 with *The Man Who Knew Too Much* and *The 39 Steps*. *The 39 Steps* is a prototype Hitchcock film. The plot is a mad chase from London to Scotland and back again. The chase throws the crime-tracking runners into the most wildly diverse and incongruous settings: a Scottish farmhouse, a plush manor house, a vaudeville theatre. The action is a mad attempt to solve the film's great riddle, what Hitchcock called the "MacGuffin," the meaning of "the 39 steps." That riddle is buried inside the head of the vaudeville performer, Mr. Memory, who, when publicly confronted with the question in front of an audience, is torn by his commitment to his art (he prides himself in knowing all) and his commitment to his fellow conspirators.

As in so many of his films, Hitchcock delights in showing the most horrible crimes taking place in the most public places: amusement parks, concert halls, theatres, buses, trains. And like so many Hitchcock films, *The 39 Steps* is a completely apolitical story of political intrigue. Except for the war-time films (*Saboteur, Foreign Correspondent, Notorious,* and *Lifeboat*), which are explicitly anti-Nazi, and *North by Northwest,* which is fuzzily anti-Communist, the two political sides in Hitchcock films are us and them. He deliberately refuses to cloud a good story with ideology. For the same reason, Hitchcock films inevitably take place in the world of the rich; they are totally divorced from such social-realist problems as poverty, hunger, and injustice. The Hitchcock actors are smooth, slick males like Cary Grant, Ray Milland, and James Stewart and cold, sleek ladies (usually blonde with strong, almost sterile features) like Joan Fontaine, Ingrid Bergman, Grace Kelly, and Eva Marie Saint. *The 39 Steps* uses the slick Robert Donat and the cool Madeleine Carroll.

The Hitchcock films are a unique blend of story, style, and a deceptively complex technique. Hitchcock mixes the macabre and the funny, mystery and whimsy, suspense and sardonic laughter. While the film's gripping story drives relentlessly forward, Hitchcock takes time out to focus on a subtle physical detail or bit of human irony. The plots revolve about the wildest improbabilities in the most bizarre locales: vast, international conspiracies; little old ladies who are really spies; psychotic killers who impersonate their dead mothers; secret codes memorized by vaudeville entertainers; chases that culminate on carousels, in concert halls, in theatres, on the Statue of Liberty or Mount Rushmore. Beneath almost every Hitchcock film is the structure of the Sennett chase, the breathtaking, accelerating rush toward a climactic

solution. But Hitchcock personalizes the wildly improbable chase by making each of the racers surprisingly human, comically vulnerable, fallibly credible. Murderers, psychotics, and spies become as human as the little old lady next door. The most insane, exotic tales hang on the tiniest, most trivial details—a rare brand of herb tea, a glass of milk, a bird cage, a glove, a native folk song, a cigarette lighter, an inquisitive cocker spaniel. Frenzied suspense and wry understatement are the ultimate Hitchcock ingredients, bizarre psychological states beneath the most banal surfaces the essential Hitchcock theme.

If there is a single Hitchcock theme that personalizes his vision and makes him more than the supreme technician and trickster, it is the fuzzy and indistinguishable line between normal and abnormal human behavior. The ordinary fears of normal human beings—of heights, of meeting a stranger on a train where no escape is possible, of being alone in a sleazy motel room—are subtly transformed into bizarrely abnormal occurrences. Perhaps the best early Hitchcock example of this transformation is in *The Man Who Knew Too Much* (1934) in which everyone's fear of a trip to the dentist is transformed by the fact that this particularly menacing dentist is a member of an international conspiracy of murderers. Hitchcock would blur the line between normal and ordinary, sane and psychotic, even more in his films of the 1950s, in which the most ordinary human pursuits shade gradually into the most forbidden sexual-social taboos.

Hitchcock's two greatest technical tools are his command of cutting and his control of what Pudovkin called the "plastic material." Hitchcock's films are so rich in tiny yet revealing "plastic" details that if they had been made by Lubitsch the devices would have been called "Lubitsch touches." In *Suspicion* (1941), Hitchcock ingeniously reveals that Joan Fontaine is falling in love with Cary

Grant. There is a close-up of a fashionable magazine; the pages flip until the book remains open on the picture of the handsome socialite (Grant). Then a lady's hand enters the frame and sets a pair of glasses down on the picture in the magazine. Because we know that Joan Fontaine wears glasses in the film, the scene instantly reveals that Miss Fontaine is looking at a picture of Grant and, further, that she has specifically removed the glasses in his photographic presence. The un-Hollywoodish, unglamorous use of glasses for women also functions in *Strangers on a Train* when the killer goes berserk upon staring into the face of a young girl with glittering glasses (the woman he murdered also wore glasses). Hitchcock's awareness of the power of concrete detail is such that when the detail is not exactly right in its natural state he fixes it up to emphasize it. In *Suspicion,* to hypnotize us with a glass of milk that Joan Fontaine thinks is poisoned, Hitchcock puts a tiny light inside the glass to make the milk truly glow in the darkness. In *Spellbound* (1945), he makes a revolver truly dominate the foreground by photographing an immense, six-times-larger-than-life model.

In an era of functional narrative cutting, Hitchcock's editing alone tightened the screws of suspense. As Sylvia Sidney slices roast beef at the dinner table in *Sabotage* (1936), Hitchcock's cutting shows her passion building until she drives the knife into her villainous husband. The same quick cutting creates the suspense of the final fight in *Saboteur* (1942) as the Nazi spy slips off the Statue of Liberty to his death, the frenzy of the spinning carousel at the end of *Strangers on a Train* (1951), the brutality of Janet Leigh's death in *Psycho* (1960) as Hitchcock cuts from shots of the victim's face, to shots of the slashing knife, to shots of the bloodstreaked water swirling down the drain of the shower.

Hitchcock films provide perfect

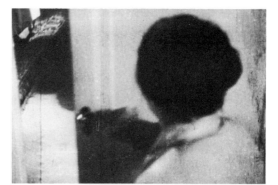

The 39 Steps. *The sound-and-picture montage: from cleaning lady's discovery to train's scream*

textbook examples of how to cut picture and sound together. In *The 39 Steps* (1935), the landlady walks into a room where she sees the shadow of a corpse; her eyes widen and her mouth begins to erupt into a scream. Hitchcock immediately cuts to the shriek of a train whistle and a shot of the train racing toward Scotland. The screaming train replaces the human scream and startles us with its unnatural shrillness. Indeed, Hitchcock used the same device—a mechanical scream replacing a human one when a landlady discovers a corpse—in his very first sound film, *Blackmail* (1929).

In *Strangers on a Train,* Hitchcock weds sound and cutting perfectly in the tennis sequence. The hero (Farley Granger) must play a tennis match knowing that the murderer (Robert Walker) is, at that very moment, trying to plant a false clue that will establish his guilt. To avoid suspicion, Granger must finish off the tennis match before he finishes off the killer. Hitchcock makes the suspenseful delay unbearable with languid, rhythmic cutting from one player to the other to the crowd, player to player to crowd, underscoring the plodding sequence with no sound other than the steady plop, plop, plop of racquet hitting ball.

The 39 Steps is a mystery-with-psychology Hitchcock film (the other kind he makes being the psychology-with-mystery). In the course of running madly toward solving the film's cloak-and-dagger mystery, Hitchcock invests his film time in making the individual psychological moments of the picture come alive. The major alteration in Hitchcock's adapting John Buchan's World War I spy story for film was his deliberately and slyly building every scene around a sexual confrontation, none of which existed in the original. In the opening scene between Robert Donat and the female spy who is subsequently killed, Hitchcock enjoys the sexual matter-of-factness of the woman's inviting herself to a stranger's flat, where she calmly sits eating cheese and telling her outlandish story. In the scene in the Scottish farmer's house, Hitchcock deftly sketches with a few subtle strokes a whole lifetime's relationship between the moralistic farmer and his sympathetic

wife. Most ironic of all the sequences is the one in which the fleeing Donat escapes his pursuers by spending the night in a hotel room with Madeleine Carroll, handcuffed in bed to a woman who detests him, since he earlier escaped the police on the train to Scotland by barging into her compartment and kissing her on the mouth.

The flair of Hitchcock's breathless construction and subtly ironic sequences is matched by his complete control of his craft. To depict the death of the spy, a necessary but potentially dangerous starting point for the story, Hitchcock underplays the sequence by making the woman rush into Donat's room obviously upset and flustered, run toward the camera quickly, and then suddenly collapse on his bed, a knife sticking out of her back in the foreground of the frame. Then the phone rings (brilliant juxtaposition of visual and sound). To underscore Mr. Memory's confusion about telling the audience the truth about the 39 steps, Hitchcock shoots the man's face in tight close-up from below and on a tilt; the composition of the shot dramatizes the tension in his mind. Hitchcock's tilted camera constantly plays such dramatic functions in his films. Of course, Hitchcock subtly points the road back to Mr. Memory all along because Robert Donat unconsciously whistles the theme song of the man's act throughout the film. But Donat, no Mr. Memory, cannot remember where he heard the tune that keeps running through his head. Hitchcock repeatedly uses the sound medium by building entire films around musical leitmotifs.

The film's final scene is a brilliant synthesis of its action, irony, comedy, and psychology. Mr. Memory lies dying on the floor in the wings of the theatre. Though he is dying, he insists on telling the police the complicated formula he has memorized—his pride in his work is that great. Meanwhile, a line of chorines dances on stage (in the rearground of the frame). Meanwhile, Robert Donat puts his arm around Madeleine Carroll (in the foreground), and suddenly we discover the same dangling handcuff on his wrist that has been there for the last hour of the film. This final ironic detail undercuts completely the romance of the ending, a perfect indication of the Hitchcock style and tone.

Unlike Hitchcock, Lubitsch, Chaplin, Hawks, or Ford, whose reputations rest on a great number of impressive films, critical respect for Orson Welles rests primarily on one film, *Citizen Kane*. The film's greatness can be discussed on several different levels: its technical innovation, its structural complexity, its complicated handling of narrative point-of-view, its controversy as a biography of a famous American, its philosophical search for meaningful human values, its sociological study of the "American Dream," its acting, its literacy, its individuality. Orson Welles, the young sensation of both the stage and radio, had been invited to bring his Mercury Theatre group to Hollywood in 1941 to make any film he chose. Welles was twenty-six. The film, *Citizen Kane,* was both his first and the last he would ever be so free to make. Like an earlier *enfant terrible* of Hollywood, Erich von Stroheim, Welles insisted on supervising everything himself: acting, directing, writing, editing, designing sets, even sewing costumes. And like von Stroheim, Welles soon saw the Hollywood lords giving his negative to other hands for slicing and later found the gates of the lords' studios locked against him.

From its opening sequence, *Citizen Kane* is no ordinary film. It begins in quiet and darkness: a wire fence with a "No Trespassing" sign; a series of tracking shots and dissolves past a weird menagerie that bring us closer to the old, creepy house and eventually into the room of the dying man; his expressionistic death, with the echoing, rasping sound of the word "Rosebud" on

Citizen Kane: *The expressionism of Kane's death*

his lips; the glass ball floating through space in slow motion before shattering; the nurse entering the room to attend to the dead man, seen in a distorted, extreme wide-angle shot. As if this beginning were not elliptical enough, Welles shatters the dark mood of death with the blaring music and glaring, overexposed images of the newsreel documentary. From moody expressionism, the film jumps to a brilliant parody of "The March of Time": the march-time music on the sound track, the booming "voice-of-God" narration, the overly descriptive printed titles, the purple prose, the little diagrams and maps, the clumsy newsreel photography, the flat interviews with reporters. The newsreel ends as abruptly as it began and is followed by a scene in the projection room in which the reporters discuss the newsreel's defects, a scene played entirely in shadow, drenched in smoke, backlit by shafts of light from the projection booth. The scene is as garishly shadowed as the preceding newsreel was flat and overexposed. Three sequences, three completely different film styles.

The film's technical brilliance continues throughout. Even today it seems striking in its extreme up-angle shots (how many Hollywood sets before *Citizen Kane* had ceilings?), its consistently extreme contrasts of dark and light (much of the film was lit from behind), its vast shots in depth revealing interaction between foreground and rearground. Welles was lucky to have the cinematic eye of Gregg Toland behind his camera. He was also lucky to have the new fast film and the new bright lights.

But Welles also shows genuine cinematic inventiveness in editing several of the sequences. The most striking sequence reveals the widening emotional

The deliberate overexposure of the newsreel's peeping camera trying to catch a glimpse of Mr. Kane and the shafts and shadows of the projection sequence, lit almost totally from behind

gulf between Kane and his first wife. As the two eat breakfast together at their dining table, Welles executes a montage series of vignettes, each of which shows the two moving further apart physically. At the end of the sequence, the two, who had begun sitting next to each other, talking cheerily, sit at opposite ends of the long table, not talking at all; she is reading a competing newspaper—the supreme insult to a newspaper publisher.

Welles's control of sound is as careful as his manipulation of image. The years in radio made him aware of sound's dramatic power, an advantage he enjoyed over those directors who graduated to sound from the silents. The overloud narration of the newsreel sequence, the echoing emptiness of Mr. Thatcher's mausoleum-library, the contrast between the amplified and unamplified human voice at Kane's political rally, the shrieking tones of the opera singer trying to master her craft, the flat smallness of the voices in the immense rooms of Kane's huge chateau, all are examples of an ear trained in the power of the microphone and the loudspeaker.

Citizen Kane is also one of the most complexly structured pieces of film narrative in cinema history. Resembling nothing so much as Faulkner's *Absalom, Absalom!*, *Citizen Kane* is, like the Faulkner novel, an immense jigsaw puzzle (like the puzzles Susan assembles in Kane's castle). The director and screenwriter (Herman J. Mankiewicz) lead the audience through a seemingly chaotic collection of events and human fragments until all the pieces of the puzzle are fitted together. Although both Welles and Faulkner seem to wander confusingly over an immense expanse of time and space, both artists carefully follow a well-charted if intricate map to the ultimate revelation. Although Welles and Mankiewicz may not have been directly influenced by Faulkner, they were also working at the time on a screen adaptation of Joseph Conrad's *Heart of Darkness*, whose complex story-within-a-story, imagery, theme, and central character (Kurtz—even the name is similar) bear obvious affinities to *Kane*.

The cinematic structure of *Citizen Kane*'s first sequence is a microcosm of the whole film. Just as Welles's camera begins outside the fence of Charles Foster Kane's house and then steadily moves closer until it comes to rest on the man himself, so the whole film begins on the outside of Kane and steadily moves inward until it eventually exposes the emptiness at the man's core. The first section, the newsreel, is the most externalized report of all, a sweeping summary of the facts and dates of Kane's life with no attempt at understanding his motivation. The newsreel is useful for the film, not only because it gives us a completely surface report but also because it gives us a series of road signs, concrete incidents and dates, to which Welles will return later in the film and which keep the film's sprawling structure moving in a clear, coherent direction.

The film's second section is narrated by Mr. Thatcher, the banker who first brought young Charles to the city. Or rather it is narrated by Mr. Thatcher's memoirs, since the man is now dead. Thatcher's section primarily covers Kane's boyhood and youth, from the time he left his parents in Colorado to the time he founded the newspaper in New York. Since Thatcher never cared for Kane and since his written rather than spoken words tell his story, his report remains very much on the outside of Kane. It is, however, part of the narrative game of *Citizen Kane* that many of the events narrated by "Thatcher" (and the others) could not possibly have been perceived in the way we witness them (the closeness of mother and boy captured in the excruciatingly tight close-ups of their faces; the boy's sled, Rosebud, lying alone in the snow, as the howl of a train whistle on the sound track implies that Thatcher and the boy have already departed). Despite the human narrative voices in the

The shot in depth. Jed Leland (Joseph Cotten) and Bernstein (Everett Sloane) speak in the foreground while Charlie Kane (Orson Welles) dances with chorus girls in the rearground

Welles's "dissolve-montage." As Leland tells his story in the foreground, the events dissolve into the frame in the rearground—a technique borrowed from the stage

The erosion of time. The youthful Leland, Kane, and Bernstein (Cotten, Welles, Sloane) and the aged Thatcher, Kane, and Bernstein (George Coulouris, Welles, Sloane). In his youth, Kane signs a "Declaration of Principles"; broken by both age and the Depression, he signs away his holdings

film, the real narrative is told by Welles's camera, which sees more clearly and deeply than any human observer. That counterpoint—between human vision and an artist's vision—is also an element of the film's complexity.

The film's third section, ostensibly narrated by Mr. Bernstein, Kane's business associate, begins to turn inward. Bernstein begins where Thatcher left off—from the founding of the newspaper through the marriage with the first Mrs. Kane. But because Bernstein idolized Kane and because Bernstein never deserted him, the section concentrates solely on the young, energetic, iconoclastic Charlie Kane, the man with spirit and vision. Bernstein never explores the hollow depths beneath the flashy shallows.

The fourth section, Jed Leland's, begins the depth sounding. Jed is Kane's former best friend, now his cynical enemy. Kane fired Jed when Jed refused to desert his principles to suit his boss; Jed's very presence reminded Kane of the principles he had left behind. Jed's section picks up where Bernstein's leaves off: from the marriage with the first Mrs. Kane to the Chicago opera debut of Susan Alexander, who has become the second Mrs. Kane. Bernstein's section takes Kane to the peak of his happiness and success; Jed's shows the beginning of Kane's bitter descent.

The film's fifth section, Susan Alexander's, continues the descent. Now a booze-soaked singer in sleazy cafés, Susan begins her section with her operatic career under Kane and continues it through their horrifying life in the huge castle, Xanadu, that Kane supposedly had built for her; she ends with the time she finally walks out on him, despite his money, his screaming, and his threats. Kane, attractively youthful and rebellious in the film's early sections, is now a broken, empty, ugly old tyrant.

The film's examination is complete except for the epilogue, which mirrors the film's opening prologue. Like the prologue, the epilogue focuses on Xanadu, the house, as well as Kane, the man. In the epilogue, the reporter, whose presence has tied together all the film's sections, tries once more to find the meaning of the clue that has propelled his search, the meaning of Kane's last word, "Rosebud." The reporter, who has remained faceless throughout the film, gives up. (Welles consistently shot the reporter from behind, not wanting to blur the focus on Kane by adding the psychological complexity of his searcher.) The reporter will never find Rosebud. After he resigns the search, Welles shows some workmen throwing piles of junk that Kane had collected during his lifetime into a furnace. One of the pieces of junk is Kane's childhood sleigh; its name is Rosebud. The wood goes up in flames; the object becomes a column of smoke, swallowed up by the invisible air. The camera pulls steadily away from the Kane house, dissolving steadily until it stands once more outside the fence with the "No Trespassing" sign. The film's final sequence is a mirror image, an identical reversal of its opening one. The circle has been completed.

The film's key moral question is what happened to Charles Foster Kane. What did he do wrong? What destroyed his youthful hopes and excitement? The answer is a dark, sickly spot at the heart of Kane's values and, by implication, at the heart of the values of American life. The three abstract themes that constantly flow through *Citizen Kane* are wealth, power, and love. The questions that the film raises are whether the first two exclude the third, and whether a life that excludes the third is worth living at all. Kane obviously has wealth; his wealth bought him newspapers and his newspapers brought him power. But Kane thinks that money and power can buy him the affection of human beings. Kane is a man of quantities. He collects things in quantity: newspapers, *objets d'art,* junk. When he runs for governor, he attempts to collect the people's hearts in the same way that he collects statues and paintings. The word "love" echoes through his whole political campaign. But hearts cannot be bought and stored like statues.

Failing to earn the people's love, Kane decides to demonstrate his power by making them love his creation, the opera singer, Susan Alexander. But Kane is no Svengali; his Trilby is a dud. Despite Kane's mortal power he is not God; he cannot reshape nature; he cannot alter Susan's stringy tonsils. Kane fails to collect the people's hearts with his creation just as he failed with his political lovemaking. And so instead of collecting the hearts of the people *en masse,* Kane decides to collect a single human heart—Susan's. He becomes her absolute tyrant; he builds her a huge house, a private universe, where he is sole master of a single human destiny. The house becomes Susan's prison. It is full of dead statues and dead souls. Susan is merely one more piece of stuff that Kane has collected, the only living object in a house full of crates and crates of junk. Susan rebels; she leaves. Kane has not succeeded in collecting a single human heart. The most appropriate epitaph at his death is the silent cellar full of crated marble and stone, the dead objects he has ravished with his checkbook from the museums, cathedrals, and chateaux of Europe.

Rosebud, the sleigh, is also an object. But it is an object of Kane's youth, not his maturity, an object of wood rather than of stone. It is an object that he did not buy. He kept Rosebud because, like his mother's old wood stove, the object had sentimental value. He was also sentimentally attached to snow and snowscapes: Kane's glass ball with the snow scene deliberately recalls the snowy images of Mr. Thatcher's visit to young Charles in Colorado. Young Kane was ripped away from his snowy childhood, his family, and life with Rosebud, by the discovery of the Colorado silver lode on the land that the Kane family fortuitously owned. And so Rosebud, in Kane's mind anyway, represented the opposite of everything his life had become, youth rather than corrupt maturity, life with living nature rather than dead objects, genuine human emotion (with his mother particularly) rather than cash substitutes.

The final views of Kane—as a tiny dark figure, dwarfed by grotesque arches, his reflection multiplied to infinity

Rosebud was, in Frost's words, the road not taken. Even Kane himself told Thatcher that he could have been a really great man if he had not been rich. But what man, what American, would not have taken Kane's road? That question makes Kane's story both tragic and philosophically disturbing. Kane's barren,

lifeless journey is so inevitable. One only misses the Rosebuds in life as a sentimental afterthought. For this reason, the Rosebud symbol is both poignant and silly, nostalgic and sentimentalized, important and totally unimportant to the reality of Charles Foster Kane's life.

Significantly, no human observer at all discovers the meaning of "Rosebud." Welles's naked camera alone discovers the answer to the film's opening riddle, completing the work's artistic pattern. Works of art are much more knowable, more discoverable and recoverable, than living human beings—especially great and complicated ones. The pattern completed by the discovery of Rosebud is, arguably, the only classical tragedy—in spirit and shape—that Hollywood ever produced out of native American materials. Like the hero of classical tragedy, Kane is an immense human being with immense social power. Like Marlowe's Faustus or Shakespeare's Macbeth (a favorite Welles role), Kane is an overreacher, a man who dares the cosmos by seeking to accomplish more than a mortal can. The very virtues of such a figure—his energy, will, ambition—lead directly to his tragic flaw, as virtues inevitably do in classical tragedy. Finally, as in the classical tragedy, there is something inevitable about Kane's tragic journey; elements inherent in the man's character and in the cosmos itself conspire to produce the tragic result. Kane would not be Kane, the most powerful and interesting being in the film (after all, Thatcher can only sign pieces of paper, while Leland can only rip up pieces of paper), if he were not the overreacher he is. Being that overreacher, he is necessarily doomed to his particular tragic failure.

Citizen Kane was shocking to its audiences in 1941. Instead of Hollywood's flat gloss, the film was sombre and grotesque. Instead of a tight, well-made story, the action sprawled over more than sixty years, requiring its performers to make tremendous transitions in acting and appearance. Orson Welles (as Kane) evolved from a dashing, Gablesque youth to a bald-headed ogre; Joseph Cotten (as Leland) evolved from a smooth Ivy Leaguer to a doddering, senile old man. Audiences found *Citizen Kane* distinctly unpleasant and brooding. There were no last-minute changes of heart, no romantic reconciliations. *Citizen Kane* followed its tragic premises to their logical, gloomy end. Even more disturbing for Hollywood was the enmity the film produced in the press, particularly in the Hearst chain. William Randolph Hearst saw obvious and infuriating parallels between himself and Charles Foster Kane, between Susan Alexander and his own artistic protégée, Marion Davies, between Kane's Florida castle, Xanadu, and his own California castle, San Simeon. The pressures of the press, and the film's unspectacular showing at the box office, led Welles's boss, R.K.O., to tie the reins around the director's head.

Welles's next film, *The Magnificent Ambersons* (1942), is certainly his next-best work. Like *Citizen Kane*, the film examines an egomaniacal, selfish mind that sees other human beings as his pawns. Like *Citizen Kane,* the film contains some striking compositions in depth and shadow, some brilliant montage sequences (particularly the opening section showing the passage of time—Joseph Cotten trying on each year's new fashions while facing a mirror), and some highly effective film acting. But Welles tacks a formulaic happy ending on the film as the vain,

callous young Amberson (Tim Holt) undergoes a miraculous change of heart and sees the egotistical folly of his ways. Despite the Hollywood ending, the film did no better at the box office. R.K.O. relieved Welles of his duties on his next film, *Journey Into Fear,* before he had the chance to edit it. Later Welles films, *The Lady from Shanghai* (1947), *Macbeth* (1950), *Touch of Evil* (1958), *Mr. Arkadin* (1962), are, like *Citizen Kane,* obsessed with the themes of the corrupting influence of power and money, with the manipulation of human beings as mere pawns in a vicious game, with a human's choice between a selfish commitment to himself and a responsible commitment to others. But the later films, despite their striking moments, become, like Welles's acting itself, mannered caricatures of his greatest work. The Welles pose and the Welles cult have outlived the Welles genius.

Although Hollywood had won the battle with *Citizen Kane,* it would lose the war. The film, despite Hollywood's attempts to hide it and silence its creator, would become the most influential film in American film history after *Birth of a Nation.* Personal and individual rather than factory made, iconoclastic rather than conventional, daring rather than safe, innovative rather than formulaic, bitter rather than sickly sweet, thoughtful rather than escapist, *Citizen Kane* would point the way to the film things to come. In 1941 those things were not very far away.

12 Hollywood in Transition: 1946–1965

In 1946 the American film business grossed $1,700,000,000, the peak box-office year in the fifty-year history of the American film industry. Twelve years later, in 1958, box-office receipts fell below a billion dollars; by 1962 receipts had fallen to $900,000,000, slightly more than half the 1946 gross. While box-office income steadily fell, production costs—labor, equipment, materials—steadily rose along with the nation's soaring, inflated economy. The two vectors of rising costs and falling revenues seemed to point directly toward the cemetery for both Hollywood and the commercial American film. Yet in 1968, theatre box offices collected $1,300,000,000 (box office receipts having risen every year since 1963). In 1974 theatres grossed almost two billion dollars. And by 1979 domestic box-office grosses neared 2.5 billion dollars. The figures indicate that the American film industry emerged from a difficult transitional period and solidified itself commercially by redefining its product and its audience. Between 1948 and 1963 lay fifteen years of groping.

Even before World War II, the two forces that would crush the old Hollywood had begun their assault. First, United States courts had begun to rule that the film industry's methods of distributing motion pictures represented an illegal restraint of open trade. Block booking was unfair to the individual competitive exhibitors, requiring them to book many pictures they did not want in order to get the few they did. Over the course of the 1920s and 1930s, the general tendency of American judicial and legislative pressure was to reduce the number of films the exhibitor could be forced to buy as a block. In addition, the studio-owned chains of theatres gave even greater monopolistic control of the market to the "Majors," the biggest Hollywood production companies who could use their commercial and artistic power to control the industry's profits and practices. The industry knew that the day would come when the line that tied theatre to studio would have to be cut. The war postponed that day.

Second, by the mid-1930s a new electronic toy that combined picture and sound—television—had been demonstrated by its scientist creators. At first Hollywood laughed at the silly toy;

by the late 1940s, Hollywood had begun to fight; less than ten years later Hollywood had surrendered.

The war helped postpone the battle. A fighting America needed movies to take its mind off the war; both soldiers overseas and their families at home needed to escape to the movies. America also needed films for education: to train the soldiers to do their jobs, to teach them "why we fight," to give both information and encouragement to the folks at home who wondered how the fight was going and if the fight was worth it. Hollywood sent many of its best directors—Frank Capra, William Wyler, Fred Zinnemann, John Huston, John Ford, Garson Kanin—to make documentary films for the government and the armed forces. While Hollywood did its part, its profits conveniently rose. The government added special war taxes to theatre tickets; Americans who went to the movies not only enjoyed themselves but patriotically contributed to the war effort.

After the war, the Supreme Court's 1948 decision in *U.S.* v. *Paramount Pictures, Inc.* was the ultimate in a lengthy series of court rulings that the studios must sell their theatres. The guaranteed outlet for the studio's product—good, bad, or mediocre—was closed. Each film would have to be good enough to sell itself. Meanwhile, more and more Americans bought television sets. Events like the 1948 Rose Bowl game and parade, the 1948 political conventions, and the weekly "Uncle Miltie" kept Americans looking at the box in their living rooms or, more likely at first, in the living rooms of their neighbors. The movies declared war on the box. No Hollywood film could be shown on television; no film star could appear on a television program. So Americans stayed home to watch British movies on the box and the new stars that television itself developed.

These specific legal and commercial woes were accompanied by a general shift of American mood in the years following the war that also contributed to the ills of a troubled industry. The Cold War years of suspicion—dislike of foreign entanglements in general and the increasing fear of the "Red Menace" in particular—also produced a distrust of certain institutions within the United States. Because the film industry was so active in the war effort against the Nazis, because so many Hollywood producers and screenwriters were Jewish, because so many Jewish intellectuals seemed sympathetic to liberal political positions, and because the most extreme right-wing American opinion saw the entire war as a sacrifice of native American lives to save the Jews in German concentration camps, it was not surprising that these rivers of reaction coalesced into a social attack on the motion picture industry as a whole. Whereas for four decades American suspicion had concentrated on Hollywood's sexual and moral excesses, in the decade following the war distrust shifted to Hollywood's political and social positions.

The first set of hearings of the House Un-American Activities Committee in 1947, investigating Communist infiltration of the motion picture industry, produced the highly publicized national scandal of the "Hollywood Ten." Ten screenwriters, directors, and producers, who had been accused of Communist leanings, attacked the congressional committee itself as an unconstitutional violation of America's first-amendment guarantees of freedom of speech. The Ten were sentenced to a year in prison for contempt of Congress, and the motion picture industry reacted fearfully by instituting a blacklist—no known or suspected Communist or Communist sympathizer would be permitted to work in any capacity on a Hollywood film. The second set of Congressional hearings of 1951–1952 gave witnesses two choices. If they admitted a previous membership in the Communist

Party, they were obligated to name everyone else with whom they had been associated at that time or suffer a contempt of Congress sentence as had the Hollywood Ten. The other choice was to avoid answering any questions whatever on the basis of the Constitution's fifth amendment guarantee against self-incrimination. Although "taking the Fifth" kept the witness out of prison, it also kept the witness out of work—thanks to the industry's blacklist. The result of these hearings—and the controversial blacklist, the damaging publicity in the press, the threats of boycott against Hollywood films by the American Legion, the lists of suspected Communists or Communist sympathizers in publications such as *Red Channels*—was an even greater weakening of the industry's crumbling commercial and social strength.

The biggest, richest studios were hit the hardest. Two former assets suddenly became liabilities: property and people. In 1949, MGM declared wage cutbacks and immense layoffs. The giant studio's rows of sound stages and acres of outdoor sets became increasingly empty; the huge film factories now owned vast expanses of expensive and barren land. Even more costly than land were the contracts with people—technicians, featured players, and stars—that required the studio to pay their salaries although it had no pictures for them to make. MGM allowed the contracts of its greatest stars, formerly the studio's richest commercial resource, to lapse. Every big studio extricated itself from the tangle of its obligations with financially disastrous slowness. A small studio, like Columbia, with very few stars under contract, a small lot, and no theatres, stayed healthier in those years of thinner profits. Columbia also showed foresight by being the first film studio to establish a television-producing division, Screen Gems, in 1951, when television was still an infant. The big movie houses suffered with the big studios. On a week

night, only a few hundred patrons scattered themselves about a house built for three thousand. One by one the ornate palaces came down, to be replaced by supermarkets, shopping centers, and high-rise apartment buildings.

By 1952 Hollywood knew that television could not be throttled. If films and television were to coexist, the movies would have to give the public what TV did not. The most obvious difference between movies and TV was the size of the screen. Television's visual thinking was necessarily in inches whereas movies could compose in feet and yards. Films also enjoyed the advantage of over fifty years of technological research in color, properties of lenses, and special laboratory effects; the infant television art had not yet developed color or video tape. Hollywood's two primary weapons against television were to be size and technical gimmickry.

One of the industry's first sallies was 3-D, a three-dimensional, stereoscopic effect produced by shooting the action with two lenses simultaneously at a specified distance apart. Two interlocked projections then threw the two perspectives on a single screen simultaneously, the audience using plastic polaroid glasses to meld the two images into a single three-dimensional one. The idea was not new; even before the twentieth century, a viewer could see a three-dimensional version of a still photograph by looking at two related photos through a stereoscope. A popular American commercial toy, the Viewmaster, uses the same principle of fusing two pictures to present a single three-dimensional scenic view. Despite the familiarity of the stereoscopic principle, to see it in a full-length, active, feature film was a great novelty. Hollywood rushed into 3-D production in 1952 with *Bwana Devil, House of Wax, Creature from the Black Lagoon, The French Line, Kiss Me Kate, Murders in the Rue Morgue,* and *Fort Ti.*

Color tinting of black-and-white silent films.

Top left, Edison's Annabella Dances: *swirls of color and motion.*

Top right, Méliès's Paris to Monte Carlo: *the automobile is always red.*

Center and bottom, Intolerance: *worshiping Ishtar and Belshazzar's feast.*

The Technicolor musical: Gentlemen Prefer Blondes.
Above, two "little" girls from Little Rock (Jane Russell and Marilyn Monroe).
Below, "Diamonds Are a Girl's Best Friend" (Monroe).

The Technicolor musical: Singin' in the Rain.
Top, "Gotta Dance" (Cyd Charisse and Gene Kelly); center, the hoofer among his memories (Kelly); bottom, "You were Meant for Me": stylized unreality (Kelly and Debbie Reynolds as abstract shapes of magenta light).

The color system of
Red Desert.
Giulia (Monica Vitti) in the drab, imprisoning environment of contemporary reality; Giulia and Corrado (Richard Harris) in the sexual atmosphere of the red-walled shack; rocks like flesh in the brilliant sunshine; the hotel room gone pink after sexual consummation.

Color and composition in Jacques Tati's Playtime.
*Above, Hulot's first entrance in the rearground while the tourists watch in the
foreground—monochrome drabness, harsh rectangularity; below, a traffic jam as
carousel—pastel colors, flowers, and rectangles that have melted into circles.*

Abstract animation. Above, Oskar Fischinger's
Allegretto, *Jordan Belson's* Allures, *John*
Whitney's computerized Matrix. *Top right, a real*
fern in Stan Brakhage's Mothlight. *Right, three*
consecutive frames of Robert Breer's Blazes.

Color and composition in Rosemary's Baby.
Top, in Rosemary's kitchen, bright light, crisp white
and yellow (Ruth Gordon and Mia Farrow on
opposite sides of the CinemaScope frame); center, the
apartment of her devilish neighbor (Sidney
Blackmer), dominated by dark brown, amber, and
deep red; bottom, Rosemary's hallucinatory
copulation with the devil synthesizes the white and
the red as she floats on an oceanic mattress.

Left, altering the same space in Michael Snow's Wavelength.

Right, Scorpio Rising: *the motorcycle man surrounded by the iconography of his universe . . . the sensuous dream of what he would both like to become and possess.*

Audiences eagerly left their television sets to experience the gimmick that attacked them with knives, arrows, stampedes of animals, avalanches, and Jane Russell's bust; the thrill of 3-D was that the formerly confined, flat, projected picture convincingly threatened to leap out of its frame at the audience.

Although there were long lines of eager patrons at the box office of *House of Wax,* the novelty, once experienced, did not bring many of them back again. Some blame the death of 3-D on the clumsy glasses that it required, but the obvious cause of death was that any pure novelty, like the earliest filmstrips, becomes boring when it is no longer novel. 3-D was pure novelty; the thrill of being run over by a train is identical to that of being run over by a herd of cattle. Further, because 3-D required the theatre owner to make costly additions and renovations to the equipment, the exhibitors declared a war of neglect against the process and hastened its demise. Business at 3-D films fell off so quickly that Alfred Hitchcock, who had shot *Dial M for Murder* (1953) in the new process, released it in the conventional two dimensions. The only later attempts to revive 3-D have been in a few "sexploitation" films (for example, *Kiss My Analyst* or *The Stewardesses*) that promised especially titillating sequences for those who visited the "skin houses." Andy Warhol's decision to make his *Frankenstein* (1974) in 3-D undoubtedly reflected an awareness that the process could produce only three effects: the horrific, the pornographic, and the "camp."

A second movie novelty, released almost simultaneously with 3-D, also promised thrills. Cinerama, unlike 3-D, dazzled its patrons by bringing the audience into the picture, rather than the picture into the audience. Cinerama originally used three interlocked cameras and four interlocked projectors (one for sound). The final prints were not projected on top of one another (as in 3-D) but side by side. The result was a screen that was really three screens. The wide, deeply curved screen and the relative positions of the three cameras worked on the eye's peripheral vision to make the mind believe that the body was actually in motion. The difference between a ride in an automobile and a conventionally filmed ride is that in an automobile the world also moves past on the sides, not just straight ahead. Cinerama's huge triple screen duplicated this impression of peripheral movement.

Like 3-D, the idea was not new. As early as the Paris World's Exposition of 1900, the energetic inventor-cinematographers had begun displaying wrap-around, multiscreen film processes. (Multiscreen experiments have long been popular at world fairs, for example, the New York fair of 1963–1964 and Expo '67 in Montreal.) As early as the mid-twenties, Abel Gance incorporated triple-screen effects into his fictional feature film *Napoléon.* In 1938, Fred Waller, Cinerama's inventor, began research on the process. But when *This Is Cinerama* opened in 1952, audiences choked—quite literally—with a film novelty that sent them racing down a roller coaster track and soaring over the Rocky Mountains. A magnificent seven-track stereophonic sound system accompanied the galloping pictures; sounds could travel from left to right across the screen or jump from behind the screen to behind the audience's heads.

If Cinerama survived much longer than its gimmicky sibling, 3-D, it was not because Cinerama was less gimmicky. Lacking (at first) any fictional interest, Cinerama was even more dependent than 3-D on the surface grandeur of picture and sound. But Cinerama was more carefully marketed than 3-D. Because of the complex projection machinery, only a few theatres in major cities were equipped for the process. Seeing Cinerama became a special, exciting event; the film was sold as a "road-show" attraction with reserved seats, noncontinuous performances, high prices. Customers returned to Cinerama because they could see a Cinerama film so infrequently. And although Cinerama repeatedly offered its predictable postcard scenery and its obligatory rides and chases, the films were stunning travelogues and not embarrassing dramatic drivel like 3-D.

Cinerama faced new troubles when it too tried to combine its gimmick with narrative: *The Wonderful World of the Brothers Grimm* (1962), *It's a Mad, Mad, Mad, Mad World* (1963), *How the West Was Won* (1963). As with 3-D, what Aristotle called "Spectacle" (he found it the least important dramatic element) overwhelmed the more essential dramatic ingredients of plot, character, and ideas. In 1968, Stanley Kubrick's *2001* subordinated Cinerama's tricks to the film's sociological and metaphysical journey, letting the big screen and racing camera work for the story rather than letting the story work for the effects. Despite the artistic and commercial success of the Kubrick film, Cinerama now seems as dead as 3-D. Only one film has been released in Cinerama since *2001* (*Ice Station Zebra*, 1969), and the 1973 rerelease of *This is Cinerama*, made twenty-one years earlier, parallels the retreat into the past with the rerelease of *House of Wax* in 1972. If the process has no future, it is partially because the mid-1970s combination of 70mm film, Panavision lenses, and Dolby Stereo soundtracks on magnetic tape comes close to reproducing the immense sights and sounds of Cinerama without the clumsy multimachine methods of the earlier process. In 1952 the gimmick successfully pulled Americans away from the small screen at home, but not enough of them at once to offer the film industry any real commercial salvation.

A third movie gimmick of the early 1950s also took advantage of the size of the movie screen. The novelty, christened CinemaScope, was the most durable and functional of them all, requiring neither special projectors, special film, nor special optical glasses (this lack of special equipment especially pleased the theatre owners). The action was recorded by a single, conventional movie camera on conventional 35mm film. A special anamorphic lens squeezed the images horizontally to fit the width of the standard film. When projected with a corresponding anamorphic lens on the projector, the distortions disappear and a huge, wide image stretches across the theatre screen. Once again the "novelty" was not new. As early as 1928, a French scientist named Henri Chrétien had invented an anamorphic lens for the motion picture camera; in 1952, the executives of Twentieth Century–Fox visited Professor Chrétien, then retired to a Riviera villa, and bought the rights to his anamorphic process. The first CinemaScope feature, *The Robe* (1953), convinced both Fox and the industry that the process was a sound one. The screen had been made wide with a minimum of trouble and expense. A parade of screen-widening "scopes" and "visions" followed Fox's CinemaScope, some of them using an anamorphic lens, some of them achieving screen width by widening the film to 50mm, 55mm, 65mm, or 70mm: Todd-AO, Metroscope, VistaVision, Panavision, Super Panavision, and Ultra Panavision.

Ultimately it was size and grandeur that triumphed, not depth-perception or motion effects. As early as 1930, Eisenstein advocated a flexible screen size, a principle he called the "dynamic square." He reasoned that the conventional screen, with its four-to-three ratio of width to height, was too inflexible. The screen, he reasoned, should be capable of becoming very wide for certain sequences, very narrow and long for others, a perfect square for balanced compositions. But Eisenstein's principles were much closer to Griffith's use of masking or irising than to the wide screen's equally inflexible commitment to width. George Stevens complained that CinemaScope made photographing a python more appropriate than a person. How could a horizontal picture frame, with a five-to-two ratio of width to height, enclose a vertical subject? Like sound in the early years, the new technological invention was a mixed blessing, adding some new film possibilities and destroying many of the old compositional virtues. What many critics of the wide screen did not perceive at the time was that just as deep focus permitted contrapuntal relationships between near and far within the frame (as in Renoir's films or *Citizen Kane*), the wide screen permitted contrapuntal relationships between left, center, and right. The wide screen, like sound, became an inescapable fact of film life and the artists eventually came to terms with it. By the mid-1960s the wide-screen revolution was as complete as the sound revolution of the 1930s, and the wide screen, like sound, would become the basis of a new generation's film aesthetics.

The battle with television was partially responsible for another technical revolution in the 1950s—the almost total conversion to color. From the earliest days of moving pictures, inventors and filmmakers sought to combine color with recorded movement. The early Méliès films were hand-tinted frame by frame, but such meticulous painting was no substitute for color photography. Most silent films (Griffith's and Gance's most notably) were bathed in color tints, adding a cast of pale blue for night sequences, a cast of red-orange for passionate, heated sequences, a yellow cast for certain effects, a green cast for others. Such coloring effects were obviously tonal, like the accompanying music, rather than an intrinsic part of the film's photographic conception. As early as 1908, Charles Urban patented a color photographic process, which he called Kinemacolor. But business opposition from the then-powerful Film Trust kept Kinemacolor off American screens.

In 1917, the Technicolor Corporation was founded in the United States. Supported by all the major studios, Technicolor enjoyed monopolistic control over all color experimentation and shooting in this country. Douglas Fairbanks's *The Black Pirate* (1926) and the musical *Rio Rita* (1929) used the early Technicolor process, which added a garish grandeur to the costumes and scenery but sickly, unstable pinks or oranges to human flesh. In the 1920s Technicolor was, like Urban's Kinemacolor, a two-color process: two strips of film exposed by two separate lenses, one strip photographically sensitive to the blue-green colors of the spectrum, the other sensitive to the red-orange colors, then bonded together in the final processing. But by 1933 Technicolor had perfected a more accurate three-color process: three strips of film, one sensitive to blue, the second to red, the third to yellow, originally requiring a bulky three-lens camera for the three rolls of film. *La Cucaracha* (1935) was the first Technicolor three-color short, Disney's *Trees and Flowers* (1932) the first Technicolor cartoon, and Rouben Mamoulian's *Becky Sharp* (1935) the first three-color Technicolor feature. Hollywood could have converted to color almost at the same time it converted to sound. But expenses and priorities dictated that most talkies use black-and-white film, which was, itself, becoming faster, subtler, more responsive to minimal light, easier to use under any conditions. Color was reserved for special novelty effects—for Disney cartoons, for lavish spectacles that needed the decoration of color and could afford the slowness and expense of color shooting (for example, Michael Curtiz's *The Adventures of Robin Hood,* 1938; Victor Fleming's *Gone with the Wind* and *The Wizard of Oz,* both 1939).

Before World War II, color was both a monopoly and a sacred mystery. Color negatives were processed and printed behind closed doors; special Technicolor consultants and cameramen were almost as important on the set of a color film as the director and producer. Natalie Kalmus, the wife of Herbert Kalmus who invented the process, became Technicolor's artistic director and constructed an official aesthetic code for the use of color (she preferred the quiet, muted effects of pastels), a code as binding on a film's color values as was the Hays Code on its moral values. Every film that used Technicolor was required to hire Mrs. Kalmus as "Technicolor Consultant."

The war, which demanded that the film industry keep up production while tightening its belt, generally excluded the luxury of color filming (with the notable English exception of Laurence Olivier's *Henry V,* 1944, in which the splendid color intensified the film's propagandistic appeal to the Englishman's traditional sense of courage). Most wartime American color films also had propaganda value—Minnelli's *Meet Me in St. Louis* (1944), which depicted the homespun life and traditions that the boys were fighting to save; DeMille's *The Story of Dr. Wassel* (1944), a hymn to an American war hero.

After the war, Hollywood needed color to fight television, which—at least until the 1960s—could offer audiences only black-and-white. Technicolor, formerly without competitors, had kept costs up and production down. Hollywood began encouraging a new competing color process, Eastmancolor. The new process was one of the spoils of war, a pirated copy of the German Agfacolor monopack. The monopack color film bonded the three strips of color-sensitive film together in a single roll. A color film could be shot with an ordinary one-lens camera. Color emulsions became progressively faster, more sensitive, more flexible. A series of new color processes—DeLuxe, Metrocolor, Warnercolor—were all variations of Eastmancolor. During the 1950s black-and-white gradually became the exception, and color, even for serious dramas, little comedies, and low-budget westerns, became the rule. As the technology of color cinematography improved, film artists learned, as they did with sound, that a new technique was not only a gimmick but also a way to fulfill essential dramatic functions. Color movies ceased to be merely colorful and began using color to tell the film's story and control the film's tone.

Although the movies fought TV by offering audiences visual treats that television lacked, Hollywood finally capitulated to television by deciding to work with it rather than against it. If television would not die, then it would need old movies and filmed installments of a series to sustain its diet. Columbia Pictures, Walt Disney *(Disneyland)*, Warner Brothers, Twentieth Century–Fox, MGM, and Universal all began making 30- and 60-minute weekly shows—as well as commercials—for TV, while several new companies bought old film studios expressly to make television films: Revue bought the old Republic studio and Desilu the R.K.O. studio. Hollywood also lifted its ban against films and film stars appearing on television. In 1956, Hollywood first sold its films to television, the sole provision being that the film had to have been produced before 1948. Since 1956, however, Hollywood has sold more and more recent films to the networks; many of last year's movies appear on this year's television. In a sense, TV has replaced the old fourth- and fifth-run neighborhood movie houses, all of which have disappeared. By 1956, the war with television was over and, although the armistice had clearly defined the movies' future relationship with its living-room audiences, the future with its audiences in theatres was still uncertain.

Films in the Transitional Period

With the collapse of the studio structure, the dictatorial head of production, and the quantitative demands of a large yearly output, producing films became similar to producing stageplays. Like the theatre producer, the new film producer concentrated on shaping and selling a single project at a time rather than a whole year's output of more than a dozen films. Like United Artists, David Selznick, and Samuel Goldwyn of earlier years, Hollywood feature-film production, even within the studios, had "gone independent." The more independent producer selected the property, the stars, and the director, raised the money, and supervised the selling of the finished film. Perhaps the production company rented space on a studio lot; perhaps it used the studio's distribution offices to help sell the film. But the producer, not the studio, made the picture. With no lot, no long-term contracts with stars, no staffs of writers and technicians, the producer assembled a production company for a particular film, disbanded it when the film was finished, and assembled another for the next film.

The individual producers, forced to make each film pay for itself, searched for stable, predictable production values. One of the axioms they discovered was that the most dependable films were either very expensive or very cheap. A very expensive film could make back its investment with huge publicity campaigns and high ticket prices at road-show engagements. The theory translated itself into practice with big films like *The Greatest Show on Earth, The Ten Commandments, The Robe, The Bridge on the River Kwai, Ben Hur,* and *Spartacus.* But the 1950s were also the years of *I Was a Teenage Werewolf, I Was a Teenage Frankenstein, Hercules, Hannibal, Joy Ride,* and *Riot in Juvenile Prison.* American-International Pictures, the only new producing company to be founded in a decade of studio collapse, built itself entirely on low-budget films with topical themes—horror, science fiction, rock and roll, juvenile delinquency, and beach parties—that could be shot in less than two weeks and budgeted at under $250,000. Joseph E. Levine built himself a commercial empire on films with Steve Reeves and a cast of Italians which were produced for under $150,000 in Italy and then dubbed into English. Roger Corman built his empire by teaming Vincent Price with Edgar Allen Poe. The very inexpensive film could make back its investment in two weeks of saturation booking at neighborhood theatres and drive-ins—yet another gimmick to pull Americans out of the living room. In an era of unstable business values the movies had become a lure for daring speculators, just as they had been before 1917.

For major productions, the studio and independent producer became dependent on popular novels and popular plays, properties that had excited the public in other forms and would conceivably excite it again. American movies had been using the commercial power of a popular novel or play for forty years, ever since Kalem adapted *Ben Hur* in 1907 and later paid $25,000 in damages for failing to obtain legal rights to the book. In 1920, D. W. Griffith paid $175,000 for the rights to the old stage melodrama, *Way Down East,* and although no one had ever previously paid so much for a property, Griffith's financial investment was still a wise one. Throughout the studio years, both silent and talking, Hollywood adapted successful books, from *The Four Horsemen of the Apocalypse* to *Gone with the Wind.* But the percentage of adaptations that attempted to reproduce a book faithfully in return for trading on the book's popularity was rather low. Studios employed dozens of

On The Waterfront: *New York "method" naturalism. Marlon Brando with Eva Marie Saint and Rod Steiger*

young writers either to invent totally original screenplays or to fashion almost original scripts loosely based on little-known stories and plays. If the studio years preceding World War II have been called the Age of the Scenarist, the years following the war must be called the Age of the Adaptation. Lacking large, permanent staffs of screen writers, both studio and independent producers bought established, already-written properties that merely needed translating into film form: *The Caine Mutiny, Marjorie Morningstar, Exodus, From Here to Eternity, Not as a Stranger, Tea and Sympathy, My Fair Lady, Sweet Bird of Youth,* and so forth, for several hundred titles. It was easier for a producer to raise money for a film that was considered "presold"; it was easier to sell one of these familiar properties back to the public after the film had been finished.

Because both fiction and the stage have traditionally remained freer of sexual and moral restrictions than films—there have never been any official codes for books or plays—it was inevitable that fresh breezes would blow from the original works into the screen adaptations of them. Because television applied even stricter moral regulations to its programs than the 1934 Breen Code did to films, film producers could lure audiences to the theatre with promises of franker, racier, "more adult" entertainment. The content of films adapted from novels like *Peyton Place, From Here to Eternity, Compulsion, Advise and Consent, Suddenly Last Summer,* and *Butterfield 8* could not possibly avoid references to adultery, fornication, or homosexuality, topics that were perfectly suited to Hollywood's audience war with television.

The war against the Code began officially in 1953 with Otto Preminger's deliberate decision to release *The Moon Is Blue* without the Code's seal of approval. Not only was Preminger's the first major American movie not to bear a seal in the almost twenty years of awarding them; it also demonstrated the commercial and publicity value of not receiving a seal of moral approval. The war declared by Preminger would end fifteen years later with the elimination of the 1930 Code and the adoption of the more flexible system of rating the "maturity" of a film's content. During the fifteen years between 1953 and 1968, the strict moral principles of the Code repeatedly slid and bent, for

The Pawnbroker: *Rod Steiger trapped in the cage of his pawnshop and (with Geraldine Fitzgerald) in the cage of New York's modern architecture*

in the search to find a lure that television lacked, the film industry seized upon sexual relationships and social criticism.

But the sexual-social films of the transitional years were very different from 1970's "liberated" films. The sharp producer of the 1950s had merely found a clever way of injecting sexual tidbits and social questions into the old 1934 formulas for morality, motivation, and plotting. Otto Preminger and Stanley Kramer were particularly good at turning "explosive," "controversial" material into films that could offend no one. Preminger's *cause celebre, The Moon Is Blue,* merely added a few "naughty" words (for example, *virgin* and *mistress*!), a few leering eyebrows, and a few bedroom situations to a completely conventional, and stale, comedy of manners. The difference in the sexual maturity of this leering, juvenile treatment of sex and the treatment in a film like Lubitsch's *Trouble in Paradise* is the difference between mud pies and Sacher Torte. Equally puerile is Preminger's *Advise and Consent* (1962), which turns homosexuality into a melodramatic plot complication and which, in the best Joe McCarthy style, turns the crusading leftist into an

unscrupulous villain and the bigoted, filibustering southern crook into a nice old guy. Preminger's two most enjoyable postwar films, *The Man with the Golden Arm* (1955) and *Anatomy of a Murder* (1959), use very quiet understated acting and very effective jazz scores (by Elmer Bernstein and Duke Ellington respectively) to make the stories more absorbing and the heavy-handed social commentary less obvious.

Stanley Kramer became the era's sentimental liberal. In *The Defiant Ones* (1958), he examined race relations by showing a black man and a white man escaping from a southern prison. Chained together, they are forced to come to terms with one another. The terms, the problems, and their solutions are completely predictable from the moment the men flee. In *On the Beach* (1959), the entire human race is about to perish from atomic fallout. Kramer's film depicts this staggering human catastrophe as a nuisance that is about to interfere with several pretty love affairs. Kramer portrays the sentimental consequences of universal death, but none of its human or social causes. Perhaps the soul of Stanley Kramer is best presented by the judge in

Judgment at Nuremberg (1961). Played by Spencer Tracy (who, along with Henry Fonda, was everyone's favorite movie liberal), the head judge at the Nuremberg trials defines himself as a Maine Republican who thought F.D.R. was a great man. Such a definition is specially designed to offend no one's principles. Amazingly, the film's *scène à faire,* in which the judge explains the legal principles on which he is going to find the German defendants guilty, never takes place. Kramer cuts from the judge asking for dissenting opinions, a clear forum for possible debate, to the judge pronouncing sentence on the guilty. The precise standard of guilt remains unclear. The film remains a vehicle for a predictable, melodramatic display of war horrors and the broken, psychotic, deformed humans who emerge from the war to parade to the witness stand and do their twitchy things for Kramer's perpetually zooming lens.

The tension between social consciousness and Hollywood cliché is very strong in the films of the transitional era. The tension accounts for some of the pretentiousness and some of the staleness of those films today. William Wyler's *The Best Years of Our Lives* (1946) maintains its freshness because its social theme—the problem of the returning serviceman adjusting to civilian life—has been completely absorbed by a compelling story, a credible study of more general problems of human relationships, and because of Gregg Toland's subtly effective camera work. But Elia Kazan's *Gentleman's Agreement* (1947), a study of suburban antisemitism, and *Pinky* (1949), a study of a black girl who passes for white, seem both worn and thin because a rather obvious statement of a social problem has been substituted for both plot and people. Kazan, a cold-war liberal in the era of Hollywood blacklisting, had the problem of making social-problem films that would neither offend an audience nor cost him his job. He solved the problem in his best

films by turning social statements into human statements—*A Streetcar Named Desire* (1951), *Viva Zapata!* (1952), *On the Waterfront* (1954), *East of Eden* (1955), *A Face in the Crowd* (1957)—all of which sustain their social issues with dynamic acting performances by Marlon Brando (the prototypic Kazan actor), Vivien Leigh, James Dean, Jo van Fleet, Rod Steiger, Andy Griffith, and others. In these films Kazan brought the earthy, realist acting style of New York's Group Theater to Hollywood.

Several other American filmmakers of the era also attempted to use New York styles to escape the studio clichés of Hollywood—in particular, the use of real New York locations and established New York actors (*Marty*, 1955; *Twelve Angry Men*, 1957; *A View from the Bridge*, 1962; *The Pawnbroker*, 1965). Many of these "New York films" owed their texture and impact not so much to their director (usually Sidney Lumet) but to the apparent spontaneity of location shooting and lighting, which could be attributed to a single cinematographer, Boris Kaufman, who had demonstrated the same ability in his collaboration with Jean Vigo two decades earlier.

John Huston also faced the tension between cinema style and significant statement. His generally fine *Treasure of the Sierra Madre* (1948) is marred by heavy-handed symbolism (a money bag on a cactus) that is more in the spirit of MGM's *Greed* than von Stroheim's. If Kazan's films, with their credibly earthy acting, revealed his background in the theatre, Huston's revealed his background as a scriptwriter with their taut and subtle scripts in which individual human weaknesses usually destroy the best laid plans of mice and men: *The Maltese Falcon* (1941), *The Asphalt Jungle* (1950), *The African Queen* (1951), and *Beat the Devil* (1954). Huston, however, caught the pretentiousness bug, and his later films seemed to demand more than he could muster stylistically (*Moulin Rouge*, 1953;

Moby Dick, 1956) or intellectually (*Freud,* 1963; *Night of the Iguana,* 1964).

The best films of the transition era were neither pretentious in size, spectacle, and grandeur, nor pretentious in their attempts at intellectual statement. The best American films of the fifteen years following the war were the same kinds of films that seemed best before the war: driving, engaging stories; credible, if not psychologically complex, characters; functional camera work and editing; appropriate and economical dialogue. The American film was still a narrative medium, not a thematic or psychological one.

Several of the directors who made the best films before the war also made the best films after it. Alfred Hitchcock, despite his new opportunity to revel in the aberrant personality, never forgot to keep his stories driving toward a breathless climax. Hitchcock, always the technical innovator, accepted the challenge of the new technical devices (3-D, color, CinemaScope) of the transitional era with glee. His *Rope* (1948) was an audacious technical experiment in which Hitchcock decided to shoot his tale of murder and homosexuality in extremely long, ten-minute takes, using almost no editing devices at all (and this from a master of editing!). The decade from 1950 to 1960 was an extremely fertile one for Hitchcock, ranking with the English years of 1935 to 1940 as one of his two most significant periods.

In *Strangers on a Train* (1951) Hitchcock juxtaposes murder and a bizarrely perverted sexuality with the conventional social assumptions about success and normality—exactly as he did with *Psycho* (1960), the film that closes the decade. In *Rear Window* (1954), *To Catch a Thief* (1955), and *Vertigo* (1958), Hitchcock examines the thin line between fantasy and reality, perversion and normality, vice and virtue. Since the 1950s have come to be seen as a decade committed to the "straight" and normal, Hitchcock's sly

examinations of the sexual aberrations beneath the ordinary placid surfaces of American life were especially appropriate. *Rear Window* is perhaps Hitchcock's most explicit examination of the moviegoer's forbidden fantasies, a film in which photography itself becomes a metaphor for voyeurism, and the audience in the theatre, like the photographer in the film, gets its kicks from spying on the lives, particularly the intimate sexual-emotional lives, of people in the frame.

The Man Who Knew Too Much (1956) and *North by Northwest* (1959) return to the English films of the 1930s (quite literally with *The Man Who Knew Too Much*) in which slick, innocent, and endangered men run for their lives and run toward the vaguely political menace that has entangled them. As in his earliest films, Hitchcock remained the master of the "plastic material": the sparkling jewels in *To Catch a Thief,* the crop-dusting plane over the flat midwestern plains in *North by Northwest,* the stuffed birds in *Psycho,* the photographer's flashbulb and camera in *Rear Window* (indeed, an immense telephoto lens, which James Stewart holds on his lap, becomes one of slyest comic phalluses in the history of film).

John Ford continued his mythification of the civilizing of the Old West: *My Darling Clementine* (1946), Ford's legend of Wyatt Earp; *Fort Apache* (1948), *She Wore a Yellow Ribbon* (1949), and *Wagonmaster* (1950), Ford's trilogy examining the role of the cavalry in the civilization process; and the allegorical *The Man Who Shot Liberty Valance* (1962). Ford also displayed his Irish background and commitment in the touchingly warm *The Quiet Man* (1952) as well as his commitment to America and Irish Americans in *The Long Gray Line* (1954) and *The Last Hurrah* (1959). Howard Hawks made the late Westerns, *Rio Bravo* (1957) and *El Dorado* (1967). Unlike Hitchcock, however, both Hawks and Ford seemed stylistically uncomfortable with color and the wide screen. For Ford, color seemed irrelevant, and the wide screen tended to weigh his films down with a heavy, slow, and static non-rhythm. Hawks was so clumsy with the big screen (*Land of the Pharaohs*, 1955) that his most lively later films deliberately used as small a screen as possible.

The western film remained one of the most exciting and entertaining of the transitional era: George Stevens's *Shane* (1953), Fred Zinnemann's *High Noon* (1952), Nicholas Ray's *Johnny Guitar* (1954), as well as several of the films of Budd Boetticher, Jacques Tourneur, Anthony Mann, and Samuel Fuller. But in the transitional era the conventions of this long-lived Hollywood genre began to stretch in several different directions. Some western films—most notably Anthony Mann's (*Winchester 73*, 1950; *Bend of the River*, 1951) and Budd Boetticher's (*Decision at Sundown*, 1957; *The Tall T*, 1957; *Buchanan Rides Alone*, 1958)—maintained the conventional attitudes of the genre toward violence and killing. Violence was a legitimate means of establishing law and civilization or a legitimate assertion of a man's self and self-respect against elemental enemies. These "classic" westerns, like Ford's *Stagecoach* and Hawks's *Red River* were attempts to reveal and mythify American history by examining the essential human and social qualities that produced the American nation (and its ideals) in the first place.

But other westerns of the fifties began taking the conventions of the genre toward their next evolutionary stage of the sixties and seventies. On the one hand, a director could use the mythic background of the Old West to discuss contemporary American values (disguise was an especially useful ploy in an era of blacklisting). *High Noon*, in its attack on the timidity of the respectable majority and its contempt for the think-alike, act-alike mentality, is clearly about the American social climate of 1952. The John Sturges westerns (*Bad Day at Black Rock*, 1954; *Gunfight at the OK Corral*, 1957) similarly mix contemporary moralizing with the western's setting and action. On the other hand, a director could take the violence of westerns as symptomatic of deranged and psychotic human behavior; the forging of this "ideal" American nation was corrupt from its very beginning. The "good" gunman who guns down the bad one becomes himself a brutal and brutalized semipsychotic (most notably in *Shane* and in Samuel Fuller's orgies of violence, *I Shot Jesse James*, 1949; *Run of the Arrow*, 1957). *Johnny Guitar* may be one of the most bizarrely deranged westerns ever made, its tense hysteria magnified by the screeching gaudiness of its Trucolor, a two-color process as false as its name, favored by the quickie Republic studio because of its cheapness.

Another familiar Hollywood genre found its conventions stretching and pulling in the decade after the war. The gangster film began turning very dark, concentrating on the inevitability of crime in urban America, on crime as a symptom of the society's disease, on criminals who are not simply selfish and tough (like Rico or Scarface) but deranged, on policemen who are as diseased as the men they track down, on peripheral characters who are frequently physical or mental cripples, and on visual images that are consistently shadowy, dark, and dim. The French critics coined a name, the *film noir*, for this subgenre of films about gangsters who are not tough but sick and about gangsterism that is incurably rooted in society itself. Edward Dmytryk's *Crossfire* (1947) is a black mixture of murder, antisemitism, and homosexuality. Robert Rossen's *Body and Soul* (1947) and Abraham Polonsky's *Force of Evil* (1949) both use John Garfield as a child of the

---

Rebel Without a Cause: *the rebel (James Dean) pulls his domesticated and effeminized father (Jim Backus) off the floor*

slums facing the inevitable decision between an unprofitable honesty and lucrative crookedness. Garfield was perhaps the prototypic *film noir* hero and the "bad girl"—Gloria Grahame, Jean Hagen, Shelley Winters, the early Marilyn Monroe—its prototypically used and abused woman. The title of Huston's *The Asphalt Jungle* could serve as a metaphor for the whole genre. In Robert Siodmak's *Cry of the City* (1948), the cop becomes possessed with the task of tracking down the criminal, who happens to be his boyhood pal as well as a man that the cop secretly envies. Henry Hathaway's *Call Northside 777* (1948) uses real locations rather than studio interiors, which give it a sense of reality, immediacy, and urgency. James Cagney stars in Raoul Walsh's *White Heat* (1949), in which the old-style breezy Cagney gangster has become psychotic. Jules Dassin depicts the brutality of prison life (*Brute Force*, 1947), the brutality of urban life (*Naked City*, 1948), and the commercial brutality of the San Francisco vegetable market (*Thieves' Highway*, 1949). In Fritz Lang's *The Big Heat* (1953) women become mere pawns (and the victims of gruesome crimes) in the war between cops and criminals.

An outgrowth of the *film noir* was a new genre that also showed marked affinities with the western. The "rebellious youth" films of the 1950s—particularly Laslo Benedek's *The Wild One* (1953) and Nicholas Ray's *Rebel Without a Cause* (1955)—were also a violent reaction against a decaying and diseased society. But whereas the gangster chose violence as a defense against the brutal hardness of city life, the youths rebel against the sterility, monotony, and conformity of adult life. Despite Ray's ironic title, these rebels most certainly do have a cause. Just as the western hero has his horse, his means to freedom, and the gangster his automobile, his means of destruction, the youths have their motorcycles and automobiles, which are both instruments of freedom and destruction. The

machines take the youths away from the confined mediocrity of adult life and give them the exhilaration of movement in open spaces (like the cowboy's horse); but the machines also destroy property, people, and even their masters themselves. The youth films developed new folk heroes, Marlon Brando and James Dean, who were to contemporary society what John Wayne, Gary Cooper, and Randolph Scott had been to the Old West.

American comic films after the war were particularly uninventive, especially considering the richness of the preceding thirty-five years. The newest comic performers were Bud Abbott and Lou Costello, who seemed to be built on the old physical premises of Laurel and Hardy or the Marx Brothers—one fat, one thin; one smart, one dumb; one clumsy, one suave. But despite their physical humor, Abbott and Costello were primarily verbal comics (Who's on first?); the only way to use them in a film was to plunge the bungling, cowardly, klutzy Lou into dangerous or horrifying situations. And so Abbott and Costello met murderers, the Invisible Man, Frankenstein, Dracula, and the Wolf Man in an attempt to squeeze laughs from spine-tingling contrasts of humor and horror.

Succeeding Abbott and Costello in 1950 were Martin and Lewis, another team combining a wacky, zany clown and a cloyingly slick "straight" man. (Interestingly, none of the classic comedy-film teams—Laurel and Hardy, the Marx Brothers, the Sennett repertory clowns—had any use for a human being who was "straight.") Martin and Lewis contrasted not so much physically as mentally: the one brash, noisy, nasal, the other oily, loose, controlled. But the weakness of their films is that their wacky personalities were drowned in predictable, overplotted situation comedies (many of the American classic comedians were notoriously independent of plotting).

The same problem plagues the films that Jerry Lewis made alone after 1956. Although the French intellectual critics rate Jerry Lewis alongside Chaplin and Keaton, no American over fourteen can sit through a Jerry Lewis film. Lewis's problem seems to be a conflict between character and plot, a zany conception forced to march through a completely formulaic story. The first reel or two of a Lewis film is brilliantly funny as Lewis reveals the particular comic nuttiness of the main character. But then, the exposition at an end, the nutty professor, shopkeeper, errand boy, or whatever, must trudge through more than an hour of, Will he get the girl? or, Will he keep his job? Lewis runs out of comic ideas for a character or situation after about twenty minutes. Unlike any of the great American film clowns, Lewis's funniness stems entirely from technique rather than a unique personality and vision of experience.

The director-crafted comedy of manners also declined after the war. Frank Capra (*It's a Wonderful Life*, 1946; *State of the Union*, 1948; *Riding High*, 1950; *A Hole in the Head*, 1959) made films that were feeble shadows of his greatest work. Preston Sturges also made mellower and thinner comedies after the war (*Mad Wednesday*, 1947; *Unfaithfully Yours*, 1948; *The Beautiful Blonde from Bashful Bend*, 1949). The best postwar comedies of manners were Billy Wilder's, who with his coauthor, I. A. L. Diamond, preserved the tradition of comic collaboration between director and scenarist.

Wilder's comedy juxtaposed verbal wit with a sinister, morally disturbing environment: comedy and the corruption of a post-war Berlin in rubble (*A Foreign Affair*, 1948), comedy and a psychotic has-been of the silent screen (*Sunset Boulevard*, 1950); and a concentration camp (*Stalag 17*, 1953); and the gangster underworld (*Some Like It Hot*, 1959); and the corruption of Madison Avenue (*The*

Apartment, 1961); and the cold war in the now rebuilt and industrialized Berlin (*One, Two, Three*, 1962). The films vary in their balance of comedy and moral seriousness. *Sunset Boulevard* is most interested in the perversion of human values that turns Norma Desmond (Gloria Swanson) into a fanatic worshipper of her dead past and Joe (William Holden) into a male prostitute willing to sell head, heart, and body for the hope of an equally dead future. Wilder's film examines the human dreams and emotions a person must sell to purchase success. *Some Like It Hot*, the opposite extreme, tries to get as many gags as it can out of Jack Lemmon and Tony Curtis in drag with an all-girl orchestra.

Musicals in the postwar years were also undergoing a transition, one that may have produced Hollywood's greatest musical films. Before the war, Hollywood musicals were slight concoctions (invariably focusing on the doings of show folk). Musical numbers wove through a scanty plot about love among entertainers as Ruby Keeler, Dick Powell, Fred Astaire, Ginger Rogers, Eleanor Powell or Rita Hayworth sang and danced in the show-business world of theatres and night clubs. The films had no pretensions to psychological realism or serious human relationships; the plots were almost invisible trifles to hold the musical numbers together. In the 1960s, however, filmed musicals, following the pattern of Broadway shows (which, of course, they were adapting), became realistic and psychological. World War II and Nazis and street gangs and death had become subjects for Broadway musical comedy. The unserious fluff of Rodgers and Hart had been replaced by the romantic seriousness of Rodgers and Hammerstein.

In the "integrated" musical, as the Rodgers-Hammerstein type and its successors came to be known, one did not assume that singing and psychological interaction were mutually exclusive (as they were in earlier Broadway shows and Hollywood musical films). The "integrated" show tried to imagine under what conditions a human being might sing in reality. Although it was difficult to convince a Broadway audience that a group of juvenile delinquents would sing to each other before cutting each other's throats, the task was even more difficult for the films. The stage, at least, enjoys the unreality of cardboard and plaster and paint and spotlight. But how to make a film audience believe that a group of juvenile delinquents would pirouette down a real New York street with real graffiti on the walls and real garbage in the gutter? How to make an audience believe that a woman would sing a song standing on a real tugboat in the middle of New York harbor?

The director of early musical films did not have such problems. Musical films were obviously unreal, unserious spoofs that never tried to be believable. A director like Busby Berkeley could twirl his camera, his dancers, their pianos, fiddles, and fountains, in grandiose and grotesquely imaginative patterns precisely because his musical numbers owed no allegiance to either logic or reality. Although it is almost taken for granted that color is the musical's natural medium, it is worth mentioning that without black-and-white there would have been no Busby Berkeley or Fred Astaire —or not the same ones. Berkeley's kaleidoscopic visual conceptions depended on the contrast of white and black (say, white dresses gleaming off a polished black floor), and Fred Astaire, in top hat and tails, literally *was* black and white. Significantly, every Astaire color movie of the 1940s and 1950s conceived at least one musical number in which contemporary color was translated into the visual monochrome values of his 1930s musicals (for example, the title song in *Funny Face,* performed exclusively in the red-oranges of a photographic darkroom).

Musical films just after the war, while they did become lavish, ornate, Technicolor spectaculars (as so many films did), maintained their stylized unreality. The MGM musicals produced by Arthur Freed in particular combined surrealistically imaginative musical numbers, pleasant scores, an exciting use of color, and funny, spoofing plots that often still revolved around showfolk: Vincente Minnelli's *The Pirate* (1948), *An American in Paris* (1952), *The Bandwagon* (1953); Charles Walters's *Easter Parade* (1948), *Summer Stock* (1950); Stanley Donen and Gene Kelly's *On the Town* (1949) and *Singin' in the Rain* (1952); Donen's *Seven Brides for Seven Brothers* (1954) and *Funny Face* (1957).

The best of the musicals were those with musical numbers conceived and choreographed by Gene Kelly, particularly *An American in Paris* and *Singin' in the Rain.* In *Paris,* Kelly's ballet, combining George Gershwin's tone poem with French impressionistic painting, received the most critical attention. Although the lengthy ballet borders on the pretentious and fits very clumsily into the film's plot, the dream-ballet by itself is a brilliant demonstration of the powers of a purely abstract cinema. Its integration of music, color, dance, decor, costumes, editing, and camera movement is as sensually and formally "pure" cinema as any abstract filmmaker has ever attempted. Equally exuberant and imaginative was the staging of "By Strauss" in a Paris bistro, the staging of "I'll Build a Stairway to Paradise" on a Paris music-hall stage, and Kelly's casual singing, hoofing, and whistling of "I've Got Rhythm" for a group of Paris kids.

Singin' in the Rain boasts perhaps the funniest screenplay of any musical film, the best of Betty Comden and Adolph Green's many Hollywood spoofs, both in films and on the stage. Every musical number in *Singin' in the Rain* combines both music and fun, pleasant movement and wry spoof: the opening musical montage in which Kelly rises from sleazy hoofer to movie star, the staging of the title song in which Kelly tap dances in rain puddles (!), the surrealistic ballet, "Gotta Dance," in which Kelly romanticizes a young entertainer's rise to the top.

Indicative of the shifting styles in film musicals is the difference between the love song, "You Were Meant for Me," of *Singin' in the Rain,* and the love song, "One Hand, One Heart," of *West Side Story* (1961). In the earlier film, Kelly leads his lady onto a sound stage, turns on atmospheric colored lights, turns on an artificial wind machine, and then sings, surrounded by stylized unreality. In *West Side Story,* girl and boy pledge their troth in her bedroom, shortly after climbing out of bed, the sheets of which are noticeably rumpled. Whichever style you prefer, the difference between the two is obvious. The shifting styles must partially account for the conversion of Gene Kelly's imaginativeness of *Singin' in the Rain* and *Les Girls* to the predictable dullness of *Hello Dolly!* (1969).

By the mid-1950s, MGM had already begun deserting original musical ideas, assigning Vincente Minnelli to adapt stage shows like *Brigadoon* and *Kismet.* The original screen musical died with the original screenplay. It also died with the studio system that produced a certain number of musical films each year and kept a stable of musical talent stocked expressly for that purpose. With the death of the studios that developed such musical talent, the world was condemned to a future with no new Gene Kellys, Judy Garlands, and Fred Astaires, who no longer had a school for study nor a showcase for displaying their wares. The repertory musical performer needs a repertory system.

Finding the Audience

Despite the gimmicks, despite the wide screen, despite the sexual innuendos, despite the industry's claim that movies

The grime and unglamor of the Italian neorealist world—stripping the bed of its sheets in The Bicycle Thief

were better than ever, movie income and movie admissions continued to fall. In an effort to give the public what television could not, Hollywood discovered that it could not give much of it anything for very long. The public yawned respectfully through a big spectacle and returned to the television set; it bought a ticket for one supposedly racy film, discovered it was not very racy, and returned to the television set. In order to please its public, Hollywood had to discover who its public was. It could not assume, as Mayer and Zukor and Cohn did in the thirties, that its public was all of the people all of the time.

The signs that would eventually point the way had begun to appear just after the war. A series of foreign films—with DeSica's *The Bicycle Thief* (1948) being, perhaps, the first important import —proved that a particular kind of film, inexpensively produced, more obviously sociological and less escapist than the Hollywood film, could attract interested audiences to small theatres while slick Hollywood films played to empty houses in large ones. More and more little neighborhood theatres that could no longer do business as fourth-run houses for Hollywood films found a second life as "art houses" showing foreign pictures like *La Strada* (1954), *Les Diaboliques* (1955), and *Nights of Cabiria* (1957). The foreign film was certainly unlike anything that the networks could present on television: introspective, with dialogue requiring the audience to read printed words, sensitive to intellectual and social questions, sexually mature, with refreshing and un-Americanized insights into other cultures, other values, and other peoples. And these foreign imports were never required to submit themselves to the moral approval of the Hays Office Code. There had been a call for "art houses" and an "art movement" in the 1930s, which had been answered in a few major cities by a few theatres. But the small art house of under 500 seats, with its elitist fare, ran contrary to the old financial tides of 1940 when the big movie palaces of several thousand seats filled up every night with customers eager to see Cary Grant or Greer Garson. With television, however, the commercial tides had turned.

Hollywood discovered that movies had indeed become an elitist, not a popular, art. Just as the legitimate theatre had been the art for *some* in the thirties when movies were the art for *everyone,* so movies had become the art for some when television became the art for all. Whereas movies had been the casual everyday form of entertainment before the war, television supplied that kind of entertainment after it. Movies, then, had to be aimed at the minority audience that wanted the kind of show that television could not or would not provide. The elitism of the 1970 movie audience becomes clear when comparing the average cost of a ticket in 1946 and 1970. Although films grossed almost the same amount of money in both years, in 1946 the average movie seat cost a bit over forty cents; in 1970 the average seat cost a bit under two dollars. By the end of the decade the average cost had doubled again to almost $3.50.

There is no clearer sign of the generation gap than in the difference between the television and movie audience in this country. The majority of filmgoers in the 1980s are under thirty, educated, and live in or near the cities. Hollywood aims its films at their values, their interests, their styles, using their themes, their music, their moral codes. If movies now are directed at the young and urban, television, like films in the thirties, is aimed at rural and suburban families. The important rating systems that determine a show's popularity are very attentive to figures from the Midwest and South as well as from New York City. But for a new film to be successful, it needs favorable reviews from the big-city critics. Television programs are aimed at the kind of audience who went to the movies in the thirties and forties; in fact much of its audience is composed of those very people. Television formulas—family comedies, mysteries, westerns, hospital dramas, courtroom dramas—are the old movie formulas. They have not changed because the audience has not changed. Films and film audiences have changed.

The movies have learned to coexist with television. They have scrapped their huge movie palaces and replaced them with 500-seat theatres that are easier to fill despite their four dollar ticket prices. They have chopped big theatres into two or even three smaller theatres on the same property, a much more economical use of land and space in cities like New York and London where rent is very high: New York's Baronet/Coronet, Cinema I and II, Loew's State 1 and 2; London's Cinecenta 1, 2, 3, and 4, Paramount 1 and 2. Television, which threatened to swallow the film studios, has itself been swallowed. Over 75 percent of the film footage shot in Hollywood is for television production.

The old studios survived the years of drift and struggle solely on the steady income from TV filming. The same relationship that existed between "A" and "B" pictures in the studio era exists between feature and television production in the 1980s. Movies are Hollywood's proudest product; television shows and commercials are Hollywood's steady staples.

The fifteen years following World War II may have been the least exciting, least imaginative, least innovative years in the *art* of the American film since Griffith founded that art in 1908. The bustling production in quantity of the studio years had died; the imaginative production in quality of the last fifteen years had not yet been born. Although some four thousand films were made in those years—many of them good ones—the American film lacked the unifying spirit, direction, and purpose that distinguished it in its two previous major eras (1915–1929, 1930–1946). Hollywood slowly stumbled through the maze of conflicting production values, eventually emerging from what seems like a time warp.

Note that in the last sentence "Hollywood" has been personified. That personification is especially appropriate today when Hollywood, former world capital of film production, is now only a metaphor, a phrase that symbolizes the American film business, American film values, the movies. In 1968, for example, there were almost as many feature films shot in New York City as in Hollywood. "Hollywood" films have included MGM's release of *2001: A Space Odyssey* (made in Britain with an American director, an American technological process, and British crew), Paramount's release of *Romeo and Juliet* (an Italian film with an English cast) and *If . . .* (thoroughly English), and Twentieth Century–Fox's release of Richard Lester's totally English *The Three Musketeers*.

In 1973 the MGM and Twentieth Century–Fox back lots were both sold to make room for apartment houses, office buildings, and shopping malls. Although Leo the Lion still roars before several films each year, MGM is more in the hotel business these days (the MGM Grand Hotels in Las Vegas and Reno) than the film business, financing and distributing a few films each year but no longer making them. The Warner Brothers studio is now the Burbank Studio, shared by Warners, Columbia, and several other production companies. One of the only major Hollywood studios to remain intact, Universal, has done so by supporting itself almost completely with television production (both series filming and made-for-TV "movies"), with a large hotel on its grounds, and by advertising its tours as a major attraction for visitors to Southern California.

Although today the American film business—yearly gross, weekly admissions, audience vitality and interest—is thriving, the theoretical capital of that business, Hollywood, is a movie ghost town, dead as a production center of feature films. With so many companies filming in New York City, San Francisco, Europe, the Great West, and all over the many regions of America (many states have established film boards specifically to lure film production companies), Hollywood itself is suffering the worst feature film production crisis in its history. The new movie audiences have rejected both the old Hollywood moral values and the visual production values of the studios that produced them.

13 Neorealisms and New Waves

After the Second World War, European directors did exactly what they did after the First World War. They climbed out from under five years of wartime rubble and disrupted production, somehow scraped together enough money and film stock to assemble a motion picture, and began making films that showed extraordinary sincerity, perceptivity and artistic control. While American films searched for a new identity, the best films came from Europe. The films were best not because they often revealed portions of naked bodies together in a bathtub or on a sofa, not because the actors spoke a chic but incomprehensible tongue, not because the films were bathed in obscure, symbolic, pretentious meanings, and not because American audiences had become cultural snobs—as so many chauvinistic American film critics and film executives claimed. The films were best because they raised the same questions in cinematic form that had been raised in the best novels, plays, poems, and philosophical essays of the twentieth century. And the Americans who had become the new movie audience, those who found it easy to leave their television sets, were precisely those who were reading the books.

To call the new European films more existential than the American would perhaps seem pretentious; it would also seem to agree with those American critics who found the European films both dreary and depressing. But in the tradition of Mann, Proust, Pirandello, and Sartre (and, by the way, of Renoir, Carné, Murnau, and Pabst), the new European film searched for meaningful, life-giving human values in a world in which absolute values had obviously crumbled. This kind of film would almost always produce what Hollywood would call (and has called) an unhappy—or at least highly ambiguous—ending. What are happy endings? Hollywood has traditionally, in thousands of films, used one of two—or both. In fact, there are only two happy endings: (1) Good triumphs over Evil; (2) John gets Jane. Historically these endings have always been appropriate to comedy—Plautus, Shakespeare, Molière—and melodrama. But they are inappropriate to tragedy, if we define tragedy as action pertaining to Man (whereas comedy pertains to men) that examines the human condition (whereas comedy examines the social condition). And the tragic human condition, as expressed by tragic dramatists from Aeschylus to Beckett, can be summarized by a single line from Albert Camus's play, *Caligula:* "Men die; and they are not happy."

The two Hollywood endings, and all comic endings, are incompatible with Caligula's cry. Previously, neither American producers nor American movie audiences had wanted such an idea to sneak into the local movie house. The only directors of American films who consistently suggested such a disturbing idea were Erich von Stroheim, Charles Chaplin, and Orson Welles. All three of them were banned from Hollywood; all three of them became extremely popular with the same audiences who enjoy foreign films. The American films before 1960 that do not end with either of the two familiar happy formulas make up a small and select group—among them, *Broken Blossoms, Greed, City Lights, The Grapes of Wrath, Citizen Kane, The Treasure of the Sierra Madre,* and *Sunset Boulevard.* (Not a bad group of American films!) Hollywood's victory of good over evil presented a severe problem in a world in which both terms were difficult to define. When Hollywood's John got Jane, they lived happily ever after; when reality's John got Jane, the problems of communication, compatibility, and day-to-day "unromance" began. Many European films began with a marriage rather than ended with one. A serious examination of tragic human problems could not be squeezed into the old Hollywood formulas—hence the tension between intellectual probing and melodramatic formula in the Kramer-Preminger films and other American films of the years that followed the war.

The great films of postwar Europe, despite the individuality of the particular directors, share several traits that contrast with the American films. First, very few of them were faithful adaptations of familiar books and plays. The films were often original conceptions, carefully shaped by the director and scenarist working in unison (in fact, the director was usually credited as coauthor). This collaboration of director and scenarist revealed a continuity in the European film tradition (before the war, its great films had been produced with collaborations like Murnau-Mayer and Carné-Prévert).

Second, the postwar European films continued the prewar tradition of structuring themselves around a theme or psychological problem rather than around a story. Like *Grand Illusion, The Children of Paradise, Potemkin,* or *The Last Laugh,* the films of Vittorio DeSica, Federico Fellini, Ingmar Bergman, and Michelangelo Antonioni were not so much linear narratives as they were comparisons of human conduct, human emotional states, and conflicts between the social whole and the human unit.

Third, the focus on psychology and theme brought these films into the mainstream of twentieth-century thought and literature. The thematic and psychological questions in these films could only be the same as those in Camus, Mann, Kafka, Beckett, and Ionesco.

Fourth, European directors knew that they were free to manipulate film style, that certain kinds of thematic inquiries or psychological states required a totally different handling of the camera and sound track. The directors of *Caligari, The Fall of the House of Usher,* and *À Nous la liberté* had earlier realized the same principle.

In effect, the postwar European cinema brought the movies into the mainstream of "modernism," the key twentieth-century movement that produced nonrepresentational painting, atonal music, absurd drama, and the stream-of-consciousness novel, and whose two tenets were the self-conscious

Open City: *from the death of a single valiant priest, the boys walk back to the city, arm in arm*

dressed-as-the-sick-soul-of-Europe" pictures, the years after 1945 were remarkable in that so many European directors had something to say and knew how to say it.

Italian Neorealism

Not since 1913 had Italy been an important international film power. The huge silent spectacles of 1912 and 1913 were swiftly replaced by the Griffith films, which were not only big but active. Early Italian sound films traveled between the two poles of pro-Mussolini propaganda and escapist comedies and musical romances, so-called "White Telephone" pictures (because of the inevitable white telephone in the fancily decorated apartments that served as sets for these films). Italian films under Mussolini were remarkably similar to German films under Hitler. Despite the financial aid Mussolini extended to the film industry, despite his founding of a huge film studio (Cinecittá) and film school (Centro Sperimentale), the Italian film remained frozen by its commitment to either dogma or drivel. After the overthrow of Mussolini and the expulsion of the Nazis, the Italian filmmakers, well trained at their craft and highly experienced in film production, used the new freedom to combine their skill in making pictures with the subjects about which they wanted to make pictures. Just as the freedom following World War I unlocked the minds of the German and Soviet directors, the freedom following World War II released the Italian imagination.

Even as the Nazis were evacuating Rome, Roberto Rossellini began shooting *Open City (Roma, Cittá Aperta,* 1945). Rossellini made the film under the most difficult conditions, closely resembling the early production problems of the Soviet filmmakers: raw film stock was scarce, money for constructing sets was even scarcer, actors were difficult to find,

questioning of all social and moral values and the self-conscious manipulation of the conventions of the art itself. Like the great European directors before 1940, postwar European filmmakers were both thinkers and poets. And the postwar film audience, especially in America, was receptive to their films, allowing them to make more and more of them. Although several American critics shuddered at the thought of "Antoniennui" or "come-

slickness and polish were impossible without the controlled lighting of studio filming. Rossellini turned defects into virtues. He willingly sacrificed polish for reality, actors for people, settings for real locations, written scenes for improvisation, fiction for life. Rossellini often preferred laborers and peasants to actors (another striking parallel with Eisenstein and Pudovkin). He carried his camera all over the city and fleetingly shot the real city on the run.

Open City contrasted the humane, committed, unified struggle of the Italian people for freedom—the unity of priests, workers, intellectuals, adults, children—with the brutality of the Nazi invaders who used the most loathsome methods (torture, bribery, manipulation of the dependence on drugs or sexual gratification) to enslave the weaker Italians or to force them to betray their fellows. The two styles of the film—the natural, open, realistic, crisply lit texture of the scenes with the Resistance figures; the cramped, stilted, artificial, shadowy texture of the scenes with the Nazis—supported the film's thematic contrast.

At the end of the film a single member of the Resistance, a committed priest, is executed by the Nazi oppressors for his service to the people. But as he dies, Rossellini's camera captures the activities of the children of Rome and a far shot of the city itself, for from the death of this one person will come the freedom of the future generation of this about-to-be opened city. *Open City* became the unofficial cornerstone of a new movement in Italian cinema—neorealism.

Cesare Zavattini, scenarist for so many of the neorealist Italian films, defined the principles of the genre: to show things as they are, not as they seem; to use facts rather than fictions; to depict common people rather than silken heroes; to reveal the everyday rather than the exceptional; to show people's relationship to their real society rather than to their romantic dreams. The neorealist film

developed the influence of the social environment on basic human needs: the need for food, shelter, vocation, love, familial comforts, sexual gratification. In the tradition of Marxist thought (yet another parallel with the classic Soviet films), the neorealist films repeatedly show that unjust and perverted social structures threaten to warp and pervert the essential and internal human values.

Vittorio DeSica's *The Bicycle Thief* (1948) is one of the best and most representative embodiments of the neorealist theories. DeSica, a popular stage and film actor in the 1930s and director of escapist fluff films in the early 1940s, directed the neorealist *Shoeshine* in 1946 (script by Zavattini), a poignant study of the perversion and destruction of a pair of Roman children by both the gangsters and police who are using them. *The Bicycle Thief* (Zavattini script again) is another study of degradation and perversion. Its original title, *Bicycle Thieves,* is far more appropriate than the amended translation, simply because there are two bicycle thieves in the film: the man who steals the protagonist's bike and the protagonist himself, who eventually becomes a bicycle thief out of necessity.

From the film's opening shots DeSica begins his development of the kind of social environment that turns men into bicycle thieves: there are many men without work; there are very few jobs; the men have wives and children to support; the man with a bicycle is one of the lucky working few. To get his bicycle out of the pawn shop, Antonio's wife takes her wedding sheets to pawn in exchange for the bike. The poignancy of her sacrifice is underscored by DeSica's panning shot of row upon row upon row of pawned bridal sheets—other wives and families have been forced to make the same sacrifice of sentimental mementos for practical necessity. DeSica's camera constantly emphasizes the quantities of people and of things that are embraced by his story rather than implying that his

The Bicycle Thief: *father and son search desperately in a downpour for the irreplaceable bicycle*

tale is of the exceptional few. The film is filled with panning or tracking shots of rows and rows of men, of houses, of bicycles, of bicycle parts.

The film's narrative is Antonio's desperate search for his stolen bicycle. Without the bicycle he has no job; without a job his family starves. The man and his young son, Bruno, roam the streets, catching an occasional glimpse of the stolen bike or the shadow of the figure who stole it. Throughout the film the boy's relationship with his father serves as barometer of the effects of the agonizing search on the man's soul. Father and son drift further apart; the man even strikes the boy. When Antonio finally corners the thief, he discovers that the young man is as poor as he is. Even

more pathetic, the thief is epileptic. The thief's mother and neighbors protect the young man against Antonio; the man who has been robbed discovers that he, in turn, has become the culprit in his attempts to get his bicycle back from a man who needs it as desperately as he does. The young bicycle thief is no thief but simply a starving, sick, desperate man like himself.

Realizing the impossibility of ever getting his own bicycle back, Antonio is tempted by the sight of the many unattended bicycles around him. The man cannot resist the temptation. He steals a bicycle himself, is swiftly caught, and then beaten and abused by the angry citizens who ignorantly denounce him as a villainous thief. The man's degradation is complete. Bruno both sees and hears his father's ultimate degradation. The father sits alone—empty, hurt, beaten. His son sits alongside him, silently. The boy slowly and gently slips his hand inside his father's. Despite the terrible social humiliation, the humanity and affection of father and son have been restored.

DeSica claims that an American producer offered him millions to make *Bicycle Thieves* with Cary Grant as Antonio. DeSica rejected both the money and the star. Instead, he cast a young metal worker, a nonactor, as the desperate father. DeSica's preference reveals many of the principles of neorealism. Reality rather than romance, earthiness rather than sparkle, the common man rather than the idol. Instead of Hollywood's bright sets and stylish clothes, the Italian directors showed primitive kitchens, squalid living rooms, peeling walls, baggy, torn clothing, streets that almost stank of urine and garbage (no telephones here, much less white ones!). Instead of the Hollywood love goddess, the neorealist lady incarnate was Anna Magnani: coarse, fiery, indefatigable, too plump, too strong, too sweaty. Zavattini claimed that the neorealist film was as attached to the present as sweat was to skin. Both the idea and the imagery are significant.

The essential theme of the neorealist film was the conflict between the contemporary common man and the immense sociological forces that were completely external to himself and yet completely determined his existence: first the war, after it the means of making a living and the struggle to keep a home and family together. In the three or four years following the war, many Italian directors developed their own variations on this essential theme: Rossellini's *Paisán* (1946) and *Germany Year Zero* (1947), in which Rossellini examined the rubble, hunger, and unemployment of postwar Berlin as sensitively as DeSica had with

postwar Rome; Allessandro Blasetti's *Un Giorno nella vita* (1946); Luigi Zampa's *Vivere in pace* (1946), *L'Onorevole Angelina* (1947), *Anni Difficili* (1947); Alberto Lattuada's *The Crime of Giovanni Episcopo* (1947) and *Senza Pieta* (1948); Giuseppi de Santis's *Caccia Tragica* (1947) and *Bitter Rice* (1949). In many of these films, despite the social squalor and economic misery surrounding them, the central figures succeed in asserting the human and the humanity within themselves. The films are about misery without surrendering to misery.

But by 1950 neorealism had begun to change its course. Either the new stability of postwar Europe or the new prosperity of the Italian film industry shifted the Italian film's focus away from the sociological struggle with squalor. The films become increasingly psychological and less sociological. Although critics tried to elucidate the continuity of the movement by coining terms like poetic neorealism, romantic neorealism, or historical neorealism, such terms were not quite compatible with the original neorealist premise. The Italian film, while still valuing the realist actor and the realist milieu, had begun to use more polished scripts, more carefully constructed sets, more conventional fictional structures and themes, and highly professional actors. Even the original neorealist directors wandered away from earlier styles and themes. Rossellini became an international director, making carefully crafted and produced pictures all over the world, most of them starring his new wife, Ingrid Bergman. DeSica made a utopian folk fantasy, *Miracle in Milan* (1951), and a highly personal study of old age, *Umberto D* (1952), that seemed far more interested in Umberto's mind and feelings than in old-age benefits. DeSica, however, probably strayed least from the original Zavattini principles, as his later *The Roof* (1956) and *Two Women* (1961) show.

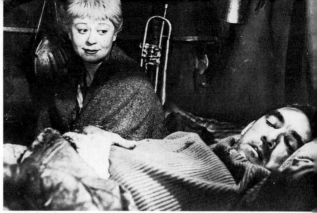

Sophia Loren won an Academy Award for her ability to play an unglamorous, Anna-Magnaniesque woman in *Two Women*, valiantly fighting the *Ur*-problems of neorealism: the war, hunger, and the assault on her family. In *The Garden of the Finzi-Continis* (1971) DeSica again depicts the struggle of individual people and whole families against the viciousness of social systems and the brutalities of war. But this late film—with its nostalgic look backward at the world of the rich; its softer, more sentimentalized human beings; its dependence on lengthy discussions; and its lush color pictorialism —seemed antithetical to the style and spirit of the earlier DeSica.

The potential direction of Italian realism was predicted by the earliest of the films later hailed by critics as neorealist: Luchino Visconti's *Ossessione* (1942). Visconti's film, an unauthorized adaptation of James M. Cain's novel of sexual sordidness and passion, *The Postman Always Rings Twice*, uses squalid settings and realistic rather than romantic human types as background for its personal, psychological action. Social realism becomes the film's milieu, its soil, rather than its subject. Visconti's films consistently depart from the Zavattini definitions, using the social reality to define the personal problems of the characters rather than to be the focus of the films themselves. For this reason, Visconti felt equally comfortable in the social reality of contemporary squalor:

Ossessione, La Terra Trema (1948), *Rocco and His Brothers* (1960)—or historical sumptuousness: *Senso* (1954), *The Leopard* (1960), *The Damned* (1969), *Death in Venice* (1971).

That Visconti's interest was more in the interrelationship of human passion and stylistic decor than in societal forces can be clearly seen in the difference between his films in color and those in black and white. For Visconti (as, perhaps, for DeSica) black and white was the medium for depicting poverty, deprivation, and the raw, baser human passions; color was the medium for depicting the rich, the elegant, and the more complex and contradictory thoughts and feelings. In *The Damned* the characters and their social system were both literally equated with the decor, for their corrupt and decadent passions were mirrored by the opulently decadent decor, which was itself the mirror of the vicious political system these people had created and nurtured.

Visconti's late films put many of the commonly accepted views about film to their severest test: particularly that human beings are the focal interest of narrative films, and that film might be defined as a moving image. In his late color films, people seem to be reduced to mere puppets, mere elements of decor, and the image not only does not move but, in *Death in Venice* especially, seems subservient to the musical track. In his discussion of *La Terra Trema*, André Bazin referred to the extreme length—three to

La Strada: *Gelsomina (Giulietta Masina) and Zampano (Anthony Quinn). Love despite the obstacles*

four minutes—of all of Visconti's shots as they tracked and panned endlessly, observing the characters' actions. In *Death in Venice* the shots are equally lengthy and the camera tracks and pans as much, assisted by a new ally—the zoom lens—which seems to slide through three or four maneuvers in every shot.

But unlike *La Terra Trema*, the dominant photographic subject of *Death in Venice* seems to be the characters' non-actions, as if they are posing for stills. They sit motionless—almost a Panavision postcard—allowing the eye to soak up the magnificent details of the decor: its elegance, its accurate re-creation of an historical era, its visual taste and beauty. And as the eye absorbs this static scene, the only thing other than the camera that moves is the music of Mahler on the sound track, rising to heights of ecstasy. Whether the music successfully re-creates and transmits the passion in the main character's soul (clearly its intention) is a matter for debate, but the result (despite the film's pictorial and musical beauties) seems less complex and less compelling than the original novella by Thomas Mann.

Fellini, Antonioni, and Others

Although Federico Fellini's apprentice-ship was in the most neorealistic of neorealisms—he assisted Rossellini and Sergio Amidei on the scenarios for both

Open City and *Paisán*—the mature Fellini is a pure romantic. Fellini prefers the exotic places of romance—the circus, the variety theatre, the night club—to the squalid slums of reality. His characters search for happiness, for love, for meaning, not for social security. If Anna Magnani is the soul of neorealism, Giulietta Masina is the soul of Fellini, his wife offscreen and the central figure of many of his films, including *La Strada* and *Nights of Cabiria,* two of his greatest. Giulietta Masina, with the glowing eyes, the smirking mouth, the deep dimples, wildly joyful, wildly sad, is to Anna Magnani as a sunbeam is to a packhorse. In both *La Strada* (1954) and *Nights of Cabiria* (1957) Masina plays a pure spirit of love, a being of the heart not of the mind.

In the earlier film, she is Gelsomina, the clownish fool, apprenticed to the strong man, Zampano (Anthony Quinn), who uses her as servant, performer, cook, and concubine—a piece of human chattel. Despite her rough treatment from the boorish animal-man, Gelsomina comes to love this human with whom she shares her life. But he—afraid of human commitment, afraid of emotional strings—betrays her, leaves her alone to die in the snow. He kills her in the same careless and callous way that he killed that other clownish soul, the acrobat (Richard Basehart), who had felt the rays of Gelsomina's hypnotic passion. Only after Gelsomina is dead, when the strong man hears the haunting, sweet-sad song that she once played on her trumpet, does the supposedly strong man learn how weak and alone he is as he sobs helplessly in a vast cold empty universe of sand, sea, and sky.

As Cabiria, Giulietta Masina plays once again the spirit of pure love trampled by the realities of human selfishness. Cabiria is the purehearted whore, forced to sell her love since no one will take it for nothing. The film opens with a boyfriend stealing her purse and throwing her in the river. Every sequence duplicates the disillusionment of this opening one. A film star casually picks her up and takes her to a fancy night club, using her as a weapon against his mistress, whom he is trying to infuriate. The mistress ends up in the actor's bed; Cabiria spends the night in his bathroom, her only companion a tiny puppy. Cabiria goes to a music hall. A hypnotist entrances her into enacting all her romantic, childlike fantasies, symbolized by the appearance of her ideal lover, named "Oscar." Cabiria's tender dreams become merely sport for the hooting, crass members of the audience. Worse, a gentleman who has watched the performance, claiming that his name really is Oscar, introduces himself to Cabiria and begins her most serious romantic hope in the film. But after she sells her house and her furniture, gladly leaving her old life behind for the love of a man she knows almost nothing about, she discovers that he too only wants her purse.

Though he takes her money he cannot throw her into the sea. He cannot kill her as he had planned. Cabiria's final disillusionment is the ultimate magnification of the opening scene, the ultimate disappointment, the comedy of the opening scene turned tragic and horrifying by the compelling events between the two scenes. But Cabiria does not die. In one of the most truly ironic and metaphorical endings in film history, closely paralleling the ending of *The Children of Paradise*, the weeping, sobbing Cabiria encounters a group of festive, singing youngsters as she walks on the road back to town (and, metaphorically, to life). They sing as she sobs; they do not notice her tears; their singing does not stop her tears; but she continues walking with them, participating

vicariously in their song. The laughter and tears of Cabiria's life, of Everyman's life, have been brilliantly juxtaposed.

Fellini's greatest works are inevitably works of laughter and tears. His sheer romanticism is underscored by his composer, Nino Rota, whose scores mix melodiousness and mysteriousness, exoticism and sweetness. Fellini gets into trouble when he deserts feeling for thought. *La Dolce Vita* (1959) is a sterile thematic exercise, an overstated contrast of Sensuality versus Spirituality. In the film's first sequence, a helicopter pilot, towing a wooden statue of Christ, looks down and waves at three girls in bikinis, sunning themselves on a Roman roof. The film, intellectually, is over. Christ has been petrified into wood; he is the tool of modern machinery (the helicopter); people are more interested in bosoms and bikinis than in Christ. Although the film has nothing more to say, Fellini continues for two hours, contrasting sensual things—night clubs, orgiastic parties, chic gatherings—with the corruption of spiritual things—a verbose intellectual commits suicide, a group of crazy children pretend to see a miraculous vision.

Weakest of all in the film is Fellini's symbolic summation of the dichotomy. A blonde adolescent child, dressed all in white, beckons to the central character (Marcello Mastroianni), but he, alas, cannot hear her. Her call is drowned by the sound of wind, waves, and human revellers. Although it is obvious that the girl symbolizes the abstractions of Purity, Innocence, Goodness, and Peace, it is not at all clear exactly what concrete, human life choices she symbolizes. *Juliet of the Spirits* (1966), another examination of the same duality—Sensuality versus Spirituality, which must be considered Fellini's primary theme—suffers from a similar over-schematization. Its one striking virtue is a dazzling use of color that Fellini manipulates to underscore the thematic opposition (pale cool green and lavender versus brilliant white, orange, and yellow). Indeed, whereas black-and-white was to be Fellini's medium for analysis and conflict, color in the 1970s was to become his medium for synthesis and accord. *Satyricon* (1969) synthesized the Sensual and the Spiritual by pushing the purity of sensual expression to its limit, so that this elevation of the sensual became an apotheosis of spirit as well (*Casanova*, 1976, attempted the same synthesis). Fellini never interrupts the flow of his visual-sensual circus in *Satyricon* for symbolic dichotomies and abstract generalizations. The result is a hypnotic journey through a surrealistic dream world that, like Fellini's other circuses, has no function other than to be savored and experienced for the way it looks and feels.

What substitutes for thought in Fellini is a romantic rebelliousness and an ambivalent reaction to the grotesque. A consistent Fellini target is the Roman Catholic Church. For Fellini, the Church is a hypocritical and empty show that bilks its public by playing on its insecurities and fears. The Church is the archsensualist masquerading as spiritualist. In *La Strada*, Fellini photographs a solemn Church procession with a neon sign reading "Bar" prominently in the foreground; he further debases the religious spectacle by showing the tacky cardboard backing on the glowing pictures of the saints. In *La Dolce Vita*, the Church supports the lies of hysterical children because the lies will produce a profit in *lire* and souls. One of Fellini's most devastating blows at the Church is in *Nights of Cabiria*. A society of human unfortunates takes a desperate outing to a religious festival, where they are greeted by canned prayers on loudspeakers (prominently in the foreground of Fellini's frame) and greedy vendors hawking sacred candles and secular candies. Fellini transforms a spiritual event into a commercial carnival. Even more grotesque, this delegation of

prostitutes is led by a crippled pimp and dope pusher who has come to the festival specifically to be made to walk again. Perhaps he needs healthy legs to collect even more profits from the sales of body and needle. A much later Fellini swipe at the Church, that rivals *Cabiria* in its venom and cynicism, is in *Fellini—Roma* (1972) with its monstrously funny fashion show of clerical clothing and priestly paraphernalia. As in all his earlier films, Fellini's attack reduces the spiritual claims of the Church to the absurd by depicting its total preoccupation with the material and mundane.

Whereas Fellini treats organized religion with grotesque bitterness and comical contempt, he treats the glamorous world of the rich with a stylish grotesqueness that reveals both its emptiness and its fascination. Fellini films are jammed with the grotesque faces and costumes of the *haut monde*, ladies in long silken gowns and geometrically shaped lorgnettes, their teased hair climbing to the ceiling and their aquiline noses dragging toward the floor, effete gentlemen with fleeting eyes and fluttering hands. The lesbian ladies in the posh night club of *Nights of Cabiria*, the society party in *La Dolce Vita*, the patrons of the health spa in *8½*, the Roman revellers at feasts and orgies in *Fellini Satyricon*, are all examples of the grotesquely ugly—in costume, makeup, gestures, features, shapes, sizes—that Fellini finds hauntingly attractive. In *Juliet of the Spirits*, Fellini uses flashing, blinding color to make the wealthy sensualists even more beautiful-ugly. Fellini's social criticism of the fashionably idle pulls him one way; his hypnotized attraction to their visually stunning exteriors and their uncompromising sensuality pulls him another.

Fellini's greatest film, his most impressive synthesis of dramatic power, personal vision, and cinematic control, is probably *8½* (1963). Perhaps the quintessential modernist feature film, the

subject of *8½* is simply itself. It is not merely about filmmaking (like Truffaut's *Day for Night*); it is about the making of this very film, a film which the director finds impossible to make but which has been made nonetheless. The protagonist of the film (Marcello Mastroianni again) is a film director himself. Because of his nervousness and tension, he is relaxing, preparing for his next film, at a fashionable health spa. Preparing for the project, the director is flooded with images out of his film and memories out of his life, which get thoroughly and inextricably confused. He puts his living relationships into fictional structures; he draws his fictional ideas from his personal experiences of the past and present (just as Fellini does with more tenderness and less agony a decade later in *Amarcord*, 1974, another color film of synthesis and reconciliation). The director's emotional problem in the film—and undoubtedly Marcello represents Fellini here—is wondering whether he is successful at either life or art, wondering whether he

hasn't prostituted his life for his art and his art for his life, whether he has the right or the ability to make films.

Although *8½* tempts critics to treat it as an abstract Pirandellian disquisition on life and art, reality and illusion, its major strength, like Fellini's, is as human drama. Fellini successfully roots the drama in Marcello's thoughts and sensations. The film begins with Marcello's nightmare: he feels trapped inside a hot, smoky automobile during a mammoth traffic jam. He longs to escape from the car, to fly high above the earth. The remainder of the film works on the man's anxiety and longing, his desire to break free of the bonds of his life, his desire to soar in life and art. He searches throughout the film for an actress to portray a pure lady in white. Is she the illusory panacea that will make sense of both his personal relationships and his artistic purpose? Is she a reference to the girl in white in *La Dolce Vita* whom Fellini now sees as a facile and naïve solution to a complex artistic and human problem? By the end of the film, Marcello seems to renounce the search. He attends a gala party for his film. The party becomes a gigantic circus composed of all the characters of his memories and of his film. Fellini's camera swirls in an excited circle as the parade of Marcello's creatures dances about a circus ring, that familiar Fellini setting. Marcello stares at the dancing creatures; he then steps into their circle and joins the dance. His life is what it is; his art is what it is. There is nothing for him to do but live it and create it. The artist's tension has been resolved; he cannot be separated from the dancing ring of his thoughts, his loves, his creations, his memories. The film that could not be made has been made because whatever Marcello's (and Fellini's) deficiencies as a human being, he is a maker of films. That is his dance.

Like Fellini, Michelangelo Antonioni's roots are in neorealism. While Rossellini and DeSica were making their documentary-style features, Antonioni was making documentary shorts about the lives of peasants and farmers. But Antonioni soon deserted the documentary for the highly polished and stylized drama of personal sensations. He quickly evolved a principle of art that was quite the antithesis of Zavattini's neorealism. Whereas neorealism uses the external social environment to define a human being, Antonioni uses the emotions of a human being to define the external physical environment. For Antonioni, the world takes its color from the character, rather than the character taking color from the world. In fact, when Antonioni finally adopted color photography in *The Red Desert* in 1964, the above metaphor for Antonioni's method became a cinematic reality. Whereas Fellini deserted neorealism in favor of a romantic flair that exposed the director's hand guiding every flamboyant filmic detail, Antonioni deserted neorealism by blurring objective reality and burying the action within the subjective perceptions of the central

8½: the artist (Marcello Mastroianni) among his memories; the circle and circus of the film director's life

characters. After apprentice work on *I Vinti* (1952), *Le Amiche* (1955), and *Il Grido* (1957), Antonioni achieved complete mastery over his method with *L'Avventura* (1960).

Rather than using the camera merely to record dialogue, movement, and facial reaction, Antonioni's method concentrates as much on the scenic environment as on the people in the environment. The environment reflects the people in it. And not just socially. The emotional resonances of the environment convey the internal states of the people within it. Among Antonioni's favorite photographic subjects are the slick, hard-surfaced materials of modern architecture: glass, aluminum, terrazzo. The cold, alien surfaces are metaphors for the hollowness a character feels at that dramatic moment. The angular furniture, the stony objects, and the glossy floor of the apartment at the beginning of *L'Eclisse* (1961) brilliantly evoke the coldness, the emptiness, the deadness in a former human relationship as Vittoria (Monica Vitti) breaks off with her lover. Significantly, Antonioni underscores the scene's shiny, hard look with silence—no music, almost no words, a few scraping sounds of hard objects on stone-like floors and furniture. *La Notte* (1960) begins with a similar feeling of hollowness and death, created by the slick, shiny glass windows and the bare white corridors of the hospital where the author and his wife (Marcello Mastroianni and Jeanne Moreau) visit a dying friend. The beginning of *Blow Up* (1966) surrounds a group of carnivalesque merrymakers with wet, shiny terrazzo courtyards and hard, cold aluminum-and-glass apartment buildings. The beginnings of Antonioni films consistently use the scenic environment to define both the film's social milieu and emotional climate.

Other Antonioni environments come to mind: the rocky barren island where the empty barren holidaymakers search for Anna in *L'Avventura;* the steel flagpoles with the ropes hollowly clanging against them in *L'Eclisse,* the gray-brown ugliness of the factory belching smoke in *The Red Desert,* the endless desert of *Zabriskie Point* (1970). Perhaps Antonioni's favorite object for emotional definition is the white wall: Sandro's flat in *L'Avventura,* the hospital corridors in *La Notte,* the hotel corridor in *Red Desert,* the photographer's studio in *Blow Up.* In *Red Desert,* Giulia (Monica Vitta again) searches for some color to make the hard white wall of her shop feel more comfortable. The Antonioni character's feeling of affinity with the hard white wall is constantly emphasized by a piece of business that recurs through all the films—the character stands against the wall and then circles around the room, back and palms pressing against the plaster. The Antonioni characters are wall-bound.

A tendency of criticism of Antonioni is to push his films into one of two clichéd and comfortable categories. The first tendency is to turn the artistic principle of the films upside down by taking the subordinate social and material environment as the real stuff of the film. According to such critics, *L'Avventura* is about the evils of wealth, *L'Eclisse* condemns the stock exchange, *Red Desert* denounces industrialization, *Blow Up* contrasts illusion and reality. However, Antonioni accepts the fact that people today live with the stock exchange, with factories, with ambiguities. What else can he do with a fact? What he is interested in is how do they live with them, how does it feel to do so, what are the problems in doing so. Modern life is the inescapable fact out of which all the Antonioni films grow; that fact is the foundation of his films, not the focus. Why focus on the obvious? The great Antonioni films are not about modern society itself but about the emotional tension between the sensitive central character (Monica Vitti, Jeanne Moreau, David Hemmings) and the society surrounding him or, more often, her.

The white wall in
L'Avventura: *Sandro
and Anna (Gabriele
Ferzetti and Lea
Massari); Sandro and
Claudia (Ferzetti and
Monica Vitti)*

The second cliché of Antonioni criticism is that all his characters live lives that are boring and empty, meaningless and sterile, and that his subject is sterility and meaninglessness in the abstract. Ironically, most of the Antonioni characters manage to survive (Jack Nicholson in *The Passenger*, 1975, is an obvious exception); they do not commit suicide, which would be the logical conclusion of a premise of total emptiness. Most of the central Antonioni figures find some value that helps them live, and most of the Antonioni films end with some cautiously positive implication. Sandro and Claudia in *L'Avventura* come together in a moment of mutual sympathy—beautifully and sensitively depicted by her placing her white hand on his black hair—without saying a word.

NEOREALISMS AND NEW WAVES   293

The ending of *L'Eclisse* implies, with a long series of visual images, again without dialogue, that human relationships continue to provide temporary if not ultimate relief from loneliness. The photographer at the end of *Blow Up* realizes that his life has a meaning to him, if to no one else, that, like the carnival clowns with their invisible tennis ball, he can play his own life's game with the same energy and conviction, even if that game has no ultimate meaning or absolute meaningfulness to anyone else. The ending of *Red Desert* is so explicitly positive that it is uncomfortably inconsistent with the usual Antonioni reliance on visual imagery. Giulia walks by the factory exactly as she did in the film's opening sequence; the smoke stack still belches its poisonous smoke. Giulia's young son asks her if the smoke will kill the little birds that might fly through it. Giulia answers that the birds have long since learned not to fly through the smoke. The parallel of the birds to Giulia, and the smoke to the industrial world surrounding her, implies that Giulia too has learned something.

The real subject of the Antonioni films is education. So many of the films are circular; they seem to end where they began: *L'Eclisse, Red Desert, Blow Up.* Although the characters walk around in a physical circle, they do not walk around in an emotional one. In the course of their journeys, they learn the pervasiveness of emptiness and the possible if temporary ways of combating it. For such a theme, Antonioni's visual images are the only means of rendering each emotional stage of the journey clearly, convincingly, and sensitively. The images become Antonioni's "objective correlatives"; he is as dependent on visual images for these correlatives as was the director of *Broken Blossoms, The Cabinet of Caligari, The Last Laugh,* and *Greed.* No other director of sound films is as dependent on pictures and as free of words as Antonioni.

He rejects words for two reasons. First, words are not a very effective tool for communicating internal states of feeling. Vague, imprecise feelings of loneliness, uneasiness, *angst* do not lend themselves to the terse summary required of movie dialogue. The more lucidly and lengthily a person talks about his or her own internal feelings (either in life or in art), the more we distrust the sincerity of the feelings and the depth of the self-awareness. Second, Antonioni does not trust words as a genuine means of human communication. If his characters succeed in discovering anything meaningful at all, they invariably do so by physical contact, by moments of laughter or calm, by a union of temporarily harmonizing vibrations rather than by discussion and conversation. Antonioni summarizes his opinion of words in *Red Desert* with the self-satisfied engineer (Richard Harris), whose commitment to his vocation and his selfish pleasures has put blinders on his ability to feel and to question. While making a play for the groping, longing Giulia, he sums up his philosophy of experience in a tidy, coherent speech of clichéd banalities. Giulia's perceptive reply deflates the man's smug complacency: "That's a fine bunch of words." At its emotional climax, the same film contains Antonioni's ultimate metaphor for the worthlessness of words when Giulia addresses her lengthiest and most explicit revelation of her innermost feelings to a Scandinavian sailor who cannot understand a word of the Italian she is speaking. Words are antipathetic to Antonioni because both his artistic premise and his philosophical vision deny their value and utility.

L'Avventura is probably Antonioni's most whole, most careful, most completely realized film. Despite the impression that the film wanders, it travels steadily toward its final moment of human reconciliation and compassion in which Claudia can feel sympathy for the weakness of Sandro and in which Sandro can feel the terrible pathos of his need to betray Claudia. The film is a series of betrayals. Anna betrays her friend, Claudia, by making her wait downstairs while she viciously devours Sandro in an afternoon of casual lovemaking. The middle-aged couple (Giulia and Corrado) survives daily on little betrayals—stinging, hateful words that hurt. Giulia betrays Corrado with the adolescent boy who paints nothing but nudes. Sandro has betrayed his talent as an architect by selling out to the pressures of finance. Antonioni brilliantly captures Sandro's bitterness as the former architect deliberately spills ink on a young architectural student's careful line drawing of the town's cathedral. Sandro's betrayals are also sexual. He betrays Anna by lusting after Claudia before Anna disappears. And even after the touching, fulfilling moments with Claudia, he callously flirts with the tasteless American publicity seeker in the very hotel where Claudia waits in bed for his return.

But if Sandro's education is to discover the human weakness that makes betrayal so inevitable, Claudia's education is to discover that betrayal is a fact of human life and to ignore that fact is to cut herself off completely from the human. Though Antonioni invests most of the film in exposing human weaknesses, he does so only because no genuine human relationship is possible without an understanding of the nature of the beast. The terms human and betrayal are unfortunately synonymous; any meaningful human relationship must start from that definition. *L'Avventura* is a journey and adventure that bring Sandro and Claudia to that starting point.

If *L'Avventura* is the fullest and most sensitive statement of Antonioni's vision, *The Red Desert* is the most revealing of his technique. *Red Desert*, Antonioni's first color film, is a film about colors, as its title indicates. Giulia's troubles with reality are mirrored by her troubles with colors. Color in the film is not Fellini's flamboyant visual show but Antonioni's

Clutching at love. Monica Vitti and Gabriele Ferzetti in L'Avventura

use of the visual to mirror the character's internal states and, ultimately, to communicate the film's subject. *Red Desert* often uses a long lens that blurs the background into a mass of indistinguishable colors; that effect mirrors the way Giulia herself sees color: frightening, aggressive, uncontrollable, indistinguishable. She is so uncomfortable with colors that she cannot pick one to cover the walls of her shop. Giulia's discomfort with colors is a metaphor for her discomfort with the reality that surrounds her—all of its sights, sounds, smells, uncertainties. In a later sequence in the engineer's hotel room, the walls change color from their original hard gray to warm pink. The walls are now pink because Giulia feels them pink, with her body next to a warm, strong man. He, ironically, neither cares how she feels nor how she feels the walls.

Though Antonioni's method disparages words, he does not forget sounds. Sound is a crucial element in *Red Desert* and in all Antonioni films (even his deliberate silences reveal a knowledge of the power of sound). In *The Red Desert* sound and color operate similarly. Giulia sees her everyday life as a grayish poisonous choking existence, punctuated by the frightening grotesque colors of the factory pipes (hence the gray-brownishness of the shots of the factory, the mud, the fog, and the striking blues and oranges of the pipe lines). Accompanying the shots of the oppressive factory are the incessant thumping, beating, chugging noises of the factory machines on the sound track.

Later in the film, Giulia tells her child a beautiful fairy tale of an ideally serene life on a far-off paradisiacal isle. Suddenly the screen changes from its sordid browns and grays to shots of brilliant blue waters and sparkling pink sand—the same pink as in the hotel room scene, and carefully dyed pink by the director to look that way. With the appearance of beautiful clear inviting images, the irritating noises on the sound track melt away to be replaced by the sound of gentle waves lapping on the beach and the serene singing of an angelic soprano. The rocks of the island seem as soft, as sinuous, as inviting as human flesh. Indeed, the entire island sequence—with its brilliant colors, sensuous terrain, and hypnotic music—is a temptation to escape, to the very suicide Giulia has already attempted, not to a place of beauty and harmony but into the comfort of nothingness, the ease of nonexistence. For this reason, Corrado's hotel room turns the same pink as the island's rocks; Giulia has discovered a temporary island of sensuous nonbeing —which she discovers to be as false and lifeless as the fairy tale she tells her son.

By his careful control of image, color, and sound, Antonioni tells the story of this woman's mental journey. Despite the oppressive factory, despite her inattentive husband, despite her suicide attempt, despite her callous lover, despite her scare about her son's legs, she, like the little birds, has learned how to avoid the poisonous smoke of reality by acknowledging its existence.

Pietro Germi was Italy's greatest film satirist of the postwar period. Germi made several imitative neorealist films just after the war, the most interesting being *In the Name of the Law* (1949), a contrast between social hypocrisies and the underlying moral realities in a Mafia-dominated Sicily. This contrast of the appearance and the reality, the external show and the internal emotion, later became Germi's dominant theme in his great satirical comedies, *Divorce—Italian Style* (1962), *Seduced and Abandoned* (1964), *The Birds, the Bees, and the Italians* (1966), and *Alfredo, Alfredo* (1972). In the first of these films, murder seems a practical social tool, there being no easier legal way to break a stifling marriage contract. In *Seduced and Abandoned*, a Sicilian family insists on maintaining its honor to the death. And death is precisely the result of the worship of the dead word, honor, despite the hilariously comic machinations to get the deflowered daughter engaged, disengaged, and eventually married. The concept of honor becomes an empty word that the characters frenziedly uphold with the most ludicrous, hypocritical, and silly seriousness. Reflecting the attitude of the film's director toward the archaic and artificial social code is the police inspector, a Roman, who is trying to bring civilized northern law to the chaotic southern island. The inspector, baffled by the empty words, the frenzied familial threats, the moral contradictions, the comic attempts at rape and murder, stares at the map of Italy. He puts his hand over the island of Sicily, covering it up. As he gazes at the amended Italy, he quips, "Better, much better."

Although it received less critical attention than the two earlier films, *The Birds, the Bees, and the Italians* is equal to Germi's greatest work; it is another powerful mixture of Germi's stinging social commentary and his hilarious farcical social comedy. The film leaves Sicily for a northern Italian city, Germi implying that hypocrisy and sterile social values are not indigenous to any particular region. In a town of grotesque lechers, drunkards, and gossips, a society whose every thought (if not deed) is lewd, two unmarried people dare to live together openly. Their love is the purest, tenderest human feeling in the film. The town lechers, hypocritically supporting the official moral code, refuse to let the two people live together warmly and sincerely while their own emotional lives remain blunted and covert. Using the moral clichés, the townspeople drive the couple apart, forcing her to leave town and him to jump off a roof.

Despite the obvious seriousness of the film's stand against hypocrisy, Germi carries the story off with almost the flavor of farce. Every lecher is comically and grotesquely individuated. Richly comic are their social gatherings when they all get together, gossiping viciously out of one side of the mouth and excitedly arranging a liaison out of the other. Richly comic is the seduction scene of the young girl from the country who comes to town and succeeds in shopping at each of the stores without spending any money. Equally comic and telling is the scene in which the businessmen's wives visit the now pregnant farm girl and arrange all the details of buying her off. And richly comic is the scene in a sleazy night club, supposedly a lurid strip joint, where the tawdry bourgeois townspeople go for a night of "fun." The night club seems a deliberate bourgeois parody of the posh night clubs of Fellini and Antonioni. Neither chic nor exotic, the tacky café wakes up and puts on its *dolce vita* only when the soused and senseless customers enter. The most lurid entertainment comes not from one of the hired strippers but from a nymphomaniac wife who suffers from the constant desire to take off her clothes. The Germi world in this film is the Fellini world gone bourgeois —with warts. By mixing farcical grotesques with the enormous suffering that the comic hypocrites inflict on less callous, more sincere beings, Germi achieves his particular serio-comic blend.

The grotesquely satirical political comedy of Lina Wertmüller: Mimi (Gian-Carlo Giannini) and family in disguise in The Seduction of Mimi

The descendants of neorealism took several other directions. Mario Monicelli's *The Organizer* (1964) applied neorealistic principles to a historical study, the fight for fair wages and working conditions by a group of early-twentieth-century strikers. Vittorio de Seta, a documentary filmmaker, combined documentary and fiction for his feature, *The Bandits of Orgosolo* (1961), one of the precursors of "*cinéma vérité.*" Marco Bellochio satirically examined the clumsy attempts of the bored rich to carve a meaning out of their lives by dabbling in romance and Marxist politics in *China Is Near* (1967). And Lina Wertmüller, the most recent descendant of the Italian neorealist tradition (a quite literal descendant since she served her apprenticeship with Fellini) seems to combine Germi's human satire with DeSica's political analysis. Her major films (*The Seduction of Mimi*, 1972; *Love and Anarchy,* 1973; *All Screwed Up,* 1974; *Swept Away . . . ,* 1974; *Seven Beauties,* 1976) reveal both a Marxist analysis of contemporary social problems and an exuberant comic sensitivity to human sexual, psychological, and moral dilemmas.

Most neorealistic of the second-generation postwar directors is Ermanno Olmi. In *Il Posto* (*The Sound of Trumpets*, 1961), Olmi studies a young adolescent boy's absorption into the machinery of bureaucratic industrialized society. The boy leaves home, takes a civil service examination, gets a job as messenger, and finally earns a clerk's desk in the bureaucratic office. The film ends with a brilliant sound effect, not the glorious sound of trumpets but the cranking of a mimeograph machine. The boy has been "duplicated," cranked through the industrial process to emerge as one more identical sheet of paper on which his future for the next fifty years has been printed.

Although Olmi clearly condemns the dehumanizing mechanistic pattern that turns a boy into a faceless man, he handles his subject from two perspectives: from his own view, which judges and condemns, and from the boy's, who sees the whole process as something very exciting and adult. The job frees him from his home; it gives him some sense of financial security; it brings him into contact with girls. Whereas Olmi's view condemns the prison-like regimented process of taking a civil service examination, the boy excitedly, earnestly tries to pass it. Whereas Olmi's view exposes the hollow tawdry sterility of the company's New Year's Eve party, a sad evening of manufactured fun that is no fun at all, the young boy fights his initial fright, drinks a bit of wine, dances, and actually enjoys himself. Perhaps Olmi's point is that "the piece of paper" is ignorant about being ground through a machine and hence can enjoy it. The two contrasting views of the same social process add both a touching humanness and artistic richness to the film.

The two most interesting and influential Italian *auteurs* to emerge in the 1960s were Pier Paolo Pasolini and Bernardo Bertolucci. Both were Marxists who sought to combine a passion for politics with a passion for cinema. Pasolini's career began neorealistically enough with *Accattone* (1961), a study of a brash, poor young man in a Roman slum, trying to earn enough money to survive and, at the same time, preserve enough of his spiritual identity so that his survival is worth it. Pasolini later drifted from neorealism to elliptical poetic allegories of moral and political degradation. Bertolucci's first major success, *Before the Revolution* (1964), set the pattern for his more famous films to follow—a study of the interrelationship between political structures and sexual or emotional fulfillment. While Pasolini's films are more abstract, more elliptical, and more ferociously aggressive moral-political investigations, enlivened and propelled by striking and dazzling bursts of visual imagery, Bertolucci's conform to a more familiar narrative pattern, which combines political events in a particular society with richly rendered human characters, lushly luxuriant color settings (often of the recent past), and carefully structured strings of narrative action. Bertolucci might be thought of as combining the leftist social conscience of a DeSica with the more personal, psychological, and sexual perceptions of a Visconti or Antonioni. Pasolini was more the Eisenstein or Vertov of Italian political cinema (like the two Soviet masters, Pasolini wrote rich and complex theoretical essays on film "language" as a form of visual-intellectual poetry) while Bertolucci is more its Pudovkin.

In Pasolini's *Teorema* (*Theorem*, 1968), its very title informing us that it is a logical exercise, a beautiful young man succeeds in blasting apart the apparently solid foundations of an apparently solid bourgeois family simply by making every member of it fall in love with him—the maid, daughter, artist son (whose notions of truth and beauty are so devastated by the confrontation that his "action painting" becomes a process of urinating on canvas), mother, and high-finance,

Salo: *sexual slavery as a metaphor for moral and political bondage*

businessman father. At the end of the
film, the businessman has been so
overwhelmed by his passion, his
commitment to a forbidden, antibourgeois
love, that he wanders about the town's
railroad station, seeking to pick up
hustlers or make quick sexual contacts of
the most degraded sort. The final image
of the film shows him wandering in a
wasteland, naked, the rocks and sand of
the hilly desert seething with volcanic
steam. The grand bourgeois has been
absolutely stripped of all the moral, social,
and political apparatus by which he lived
his life—no clothes, no sense of direction,
no civilization, no concrete location, no
purpose, a total moral and social leper.
The theorem that underlies this stripping
process is, quite simply, that sexual
passion knows no moral or social
boundaries and those who least know this
truth—the grandest, *hautest* bourgeoisie—

are most easily and completely overwhelmed by the discovery of the flimsy
assumptions on which their entire lives
are based.

Salo (1977), the last film Pasolini made
before he was murdered in a sexual
incident that might well have taken place
in one of his films, is an even more
extreme, more aggressive, and more
repellent allegorical theorem. In this piece
of cinema cruelty (in Antonin Artaud's
sense of the term), the audience is
subjected to a horrifying vision of political
totalitarianism disguised as sado-
masochistic sexuality. In 1943, four
pillars of Italian Fascistic society—a duke,
a priest, a judge, and a general (indeed,
precisely the same four pillars of society
that recur in the plays of Jean Genet)
—gather a specially selected group
of extremely beautiful young boys and
girls in a large palatial house and then

proceed to make them perform every imaginable sexual atrocity for their own pleasure. The beautiful young people are permitted to indulge in any sexual wish, so long as it is not a normal, natural, or tender one. Pasolini fills the screen for two hours with orgies of sexual torture and oppression—buggery, voyeurism, casual murder, pornographic songs and stories (since the "singers" resemble Marlene Dietrich, Pasolini may well be commenting on the pornographic underpinnings of the most accepted bourgeois cinema), mutilation, branding, scalping, the consumption of human feces. Pasolini's point in this *reductio ad absurdum* of sexual decorum is to show that these sexual perversions, the very opposite of bourgeois society's standards and beliefs, is, like Fascism itself, a product of bourgeois society—of its ruling nobility, clergy, laws, and armies. Pasolini's other films alternate between this shattering allegorical mode (*Pigpen*, 1969) and more distanced visual style pieces with political underpinnings (*The Gospel According to St. Matthew*, 1963; *Medea*, 1971).

The political films of Bernardo Bertolucci are much easier to take and, as a result, are understandably much more popular. In *Before the Revolution, The Conformist* (1971), and *Last Tango in Paris* (1973), Bertolucci examines the interrelationship between political issues and sexual drives not, as Pasolini does, by revealing the radical anarchic power of sexual passion but, instead, by showing that political and sexual commitments weave together in complex and mysterious ways. The rich, bored dilettantes are no more committed to Marxist ideology than they are to their own lusts and seductions in *Before the Revolution*. They play around with both and succeed in fulfilling neither. In *The Conformist* the central figure's ideological emptiness is intimately connected with his lack of sexual identity, his need to assert his masculine *machismo* while covering up

his intrinsic homosexuality. He can betray ideals, his friends, his professor, his lover, his wife, his principles because he is a zero—both ideologically and sexually.

1900 (1976), a mammoth, epic, four-hour-plus history of Italy in the twentieth century, might be considered a sort of Italian *Gone with the Wind*, as if shot in color by Pudovkin (as in *Gone with the Wind* and *The Birth of a Nation*, the intermission comes with the return from a war, and Part 2 examines a political reconstruction). Bertolucci shifts his personal focus from sexual lust to friendship—a study of the limits on and the possibilities for friendship of two men, born on the same day on the same estate in 1900 (on the day that Verdi died, signifying the death of nineteenth century romanticism) but in the two opposite classes of landowner and peasant. Bertolucci examines the closeness of the two boys (their comradely discoveries of nature, sex, and death together; the genuine emotional ties that bind them) and the barriers to that friendship (their different financial, educational, and moral backgrounds; their different sexual and sensual tastes; their different attitudes toward the phenomena of the century—two wars; the labor, union, and workers' movements—and toward private property itself). Ultimately, Bertolucci's synthesis (and, in contrast to Pasolini, there is a synthesis, not an insistently irreversible analysis) is that the two men are and are not close, can and cannot be friends, can and cannot overcome the facts of social history that both bind and separate them. Even as cantankerous old men, the two "friends" can only agree to differ.

For thirty-five years the Italian film has started with the surface of reality as its initial premise. But the Italian filmmaker has been free to manipulate the realistic surfaces of rich or poor, of past or present, and to probe beneath those surfaces with sociological commentary, psychological insight, sexual allegory,

1900: Time passes but nothing changes. Landowner (Robert deNiro) and worker (Gerard Depardieu) as friends/enemies/friends/enemies . . .

farce comedy, philosophical ennui, bizarre romance. Though they are both committed to realism, though they are both Italian and contemporaries, no two film directors are as dissimilar as Federico Fellini and Michelangelo Antonioni. The postwar Italian film has been so rich and diverse because the filmmakers have been encouraged to use their imaginations and because, ironically, the Italian film industry has been supported by American dollars to stimulate that encouragement.

Yet a further irony concerning the Hollywood dollar is that it not only stimulated the Italian art films but the cheap trash films as well. A series of quasi-Roman, quasi-Biblical "spectacle" films starring the American muscleman, Steve Reeves, could be shot for under $250,000 in Italy and then dubbed into English for mass release in American neighborhood theatres and drive-ins. A series of Italian "Spaghetti Westerns," many of them starring Clint Eastwood and directed by Sergio Leone, not only made money but attracted a cult, a coterie of intellectual admirers: many of them French, many of them the same fans who admired the raw garish violence of the Roger Corman horror films of the same era. Leone's success with the cheap violent western was so great that he was given the chance to shoot a major high-budget western, *Once Upon a Time in the West* (1969), which perhaps serves as an example of the slowest-paced, most naturalistically detailed, most ponderously heavy, and most visually dazzling collection of western clichés ever made.

In its early years the postwar Italian cinema showed the American industry how to combine ideas, social comment, realistic human observation, and poetic visual techniques with the motion picture form; in its later years it seemed to pander more and more to the very movie conventions and practices it previously had tried to subvert. In the late 1970s, with its greatest directors either dead (DeSica, Visconti, Pasolini, Germi) or working all over Europe on international coproductions or on multi-million-dollar visual extravaganzas (Bertolucci, Fellini, Antonioni), and with Lina Wertmüller the only imaginative filmmaker to have emerged in fifteen years, the Italian cinema no longer enjoys the artistic influence and international importance of a decade ago.

France—Postwar Classicism

The postwar Italian film sprang from the reality that the director sought to capture with camera and film; the postwar French film sprang from the director's stylistic concern with the way a camera can capture reality. Although both François Truffaut and Jean-Luc Godard attacked the formalism, the stylization, the artificiality in the films of their predecessors, their own works are as stylized, as preoccupied with cinematic form and perception as the works they sought to supplant. That the postwar French cinema should be formalistic is not surprising; the prewar French cinema was formalistic, beginning with the abstract films of the twenties through the musical romps of Clair and the literariness of Renoir and Carné. To approach reality through the manipulation of artistic form has been an aesthetic premise of the French creative mind from Racine to Proust to Ionesco. The postwar French cinema is very much in the same tradition.

The sameness is emphasized by the fact that the great prewar directors—Clair, Renoir, Carné, Cocteau—also made films after the war. René Clair returned to France to combine fantasy, song, and social satire once again in films that were frothy mixtures of physical movement, stylized decor, and music—among them, *Le Silence est d'or* (1947), a nostalgic tribute to the Zecca-Méliès years of the French film; *Beauty and the Devil* (1949), an ironic treatment of the Faust legend; and

Beauties of the Night (1952), the romantic reveries of a daydreaming musician.

Whereas Clair returned to France to make films that were softer, sweeter, and weaker than his earlier work, Renoir returned to make at least three films that are arguably as great as or greater than his masterpieces of the 1930s. The three films—*The River* (1951), *The Golden Coach* (1953), and *French Cancan* (1954)—might be considered a kind of trilogy. All three are in color and use color not only beautifully but also as a metaphoric and thematic element in their human investigations. All three are set in periods or places far distant from postwar France: India's Bengal region (*The River*), South America of the 1800s (*The Golden Coach*), and Montmartre of the 1890s (*French Cancan*). And all three examine the conflicting human choices of contempt and consent, commitment and alienation, vocation and love. The primary duality of all three films is the usual Renoir conflict between art and nature (or life), but in these late films the conflict becomes a communion as the very artfulness of the films themselves—their visual beauty as well as their structural complexity—reveals how one can indeed make life into art and thereby synthesize the opposites of art and nature.

The River, shot in India by a French director with a Bengali crew, featuring a cast of both Indians and westerners, is about this clash of cultures and values. Using the vibrant colors of the Indian landscape, the pulsing music of the sitar, the myths of the Hindu religion, and the contemplative philosophy of the Indian people, Renoir's film shows a group of "crippled" westerners—crippled either physically or spiritually by the war, by political chaos, and by personal disappointment—healing their minds and feelings by seeking to achieve a harmony with the eternal cycles of nature: birth, life, and death. *The Golden Coach* continues the examination of clashing cultures. A group of Spanish aristocrats

try to impose their decadent tastes and values on the unformed freedom of the New World. Ironically, another group of Europeans, the members of an acting troupe (led by Anna Magnani), are far more successful at communicating with their New World audience. Art is a more powerful force than politics, and the director, through his leading actress, argues for the validity of art as a human vocation. And *French Cancan* addresses the same issue. Renoir depicts a theatrical producer (played by the aging Jean Gabin who, like Renoir himself, is twenty years older than he was when he made *The Lower Depths* or *Grand Illusion*) who, also like Renoir, defines art as his life.

Marcel Carné, deprived of Jacques Prévert's scripts, never regained the power of his *Les Enfants du Paradis* although he made almost a dozen films examining human failure, lost love, and inexorable death. Jean Cocteau made several films in strikingly different though equally formalistic film styles: the claustrophobic naturalism of *Les Parents Terribles* (1948), a complicated tangle of sexuality, incest, parental rivalry, and jealousy; the poetic symbolism of *Orphée* (1950), an expressionistic study of the artist's ambivalent relationship with love and death; and *Beauty and the Beast* (1946), which mixed Cocteau's realism and symbolism quite effectively in the story of Belle's growing love for the physically ugly yet humanly loving beast. The impression of these stylistically eclectic Cocteau films is that they are the works of a cinematic amateur (in the original sense of the word). The artist, having given birth to his personal and symbolic world on the stage, on the page, and on canvas, also decided to people the screen with his personal fantasies, images, motifs, and symbols. Like Renoir, Cocteau's primary theme was that only the work of art was capable of effecting a synthesis of the conflicting demands of art and nature, of form and freedom. Cocteau's commitment to art is even more

fervent than Renoir's, for Cocteau sees the artist alone as capable of achieving immortality through the created work, which cannot wither into ugliness and die like the body of the mortal artist itself. As befits his deification of art, Cocteau's films are generally more fanciful, more symbolic, more claustrophobically stylized, more otherworldly than Renoir's who, even in his late period, holds the demands of art and reality in balance.

Of the new French directors in the fifteen years following the war, the three greatest were Max Ophuls, Robert Bresson, and Jacques Tati. All three of them made films very much in the Clair-Carné-Renoir tradition; all three of them had, in fact, made films before 1945. Whereas the end of the war signaled a shift in an entirely new direction for the Italian film, the end of

the war in France extended an earlier one. The break with French tradition came in 1959, and, as we shall see, it was not a complete break at all.

Max Ophuls made films in Italy, Holland, and the United States after fleeing his German homeland and Hitler in 1933. Ophuls's reputation today rests almost entirely on three films he made in France between 1950 and his death in 1955; *La Ronde* (1950), *Madame de . . .* (1953), and *Lola Montès* (1955). Ophuls is clearly an international rather than a French director. And yet he found a home in France at a particularly apt time for his particular talents—a time when French film values favored the literate, almost theatrical script and the ornate, carefully styled studio production. Ophuls's greatest artistic resemblance is to two other internationalized Germans,

Ernst Lubitsch and Erich von Stroheim, whose contrasting qualities he seems to synthesize. Ophuls's films combine Lubitsch's light, mocking, sexually wise touch with von Stroheim's perception of human desire and social corruption.

The Ophuls films all revolve around sexual intrigue in conflict with the social regulations against such intrigue. The Ophuls characters continue to carry on their intrigues while either hypocritically ignoring the social tensions (as the liars do in *La Ronde* and *Madame de . . .*) or openly defying social convention (as Lola does). In developing a consistent theme, Ophuls also prefers consistent stylistic conventions. The plots are not linear stories but a string of vignettes, held together either by the setting (the Vienna of *La Ronde,* the circus tent of *Lola Montès*) or an object (the earrings of *Madame de . . .*). By deemphasizing the story, Ophuls illuminates key structural balances, comparisons and contrasts of similar actions in different circumstances or different actions in similar ones. Such balancing takes the viewer directly to the center of Ophuls's moral statement on love, feelings, and social custom, just as structural balancing fulfilled precisely the same function in *Grand Illusion* or *Rules of the Game.* Also similar to Renoir— particularly the postwar Renoir— is Ophuls's deliberate choice of an artificial, theatrical setting (the sound stage in *La Ronde,* the circus tent in *Lola Montès*), which provides not only a nonrealistically appropriate setting for Ophuls's comedies of sociosexual manners but also raises intentional questions about the shams of real human activity and the realness of acting and impersonation.

La Ronde is one of the finest translations of a stage work into film. The film is completely theatrical and completely cinematic. Ophuls effected the translation much as Olivier did with his *Henry V* several years earlier—by coming to terms with the aesthetic fact that the stage is verbal and stylized and that the film is visual and intensely real-seeming. Ophuls neither erases the stage artificiality (as so many American adaptations of stage plays try to do) nor the film's visual realism (as a few American adaptations—*Top Banana, Li'l Abner, South Pacific*—tried to do). The setting in *La Ronde* is both an undisguised sound stage and the city of Vienna around 1900. Ophuls's camera wanders about the sound stage at will between the two poles of obvious stage set and realistic bedroom, between a metaphorical carousel, symbolic of the film's everturning dance of sexual relationships, and a real boudoir. "To wander" is an especially appropriate verb, for Ophuls keeps his camera perpetually on the move, spinning, gliding, flowing, traveling around the sound stage. Ophuls's German heritage is especially clear in his moving camera. The gliding photography adds not only visual energy but also continuity between the potentially disparate vignettes. And Ophuls's wandering camera has an ally: the director has invented a narrator, a character who does not exist in the original play, who speaks directly for the filmmaker to the audience. The urbane, perceptive, witty narrator (Anton Walbrook) wanders, as the camera wanders, as he speaks for Ophuls. Director, camera, and narrator are one.

The single view they present is of sexual desire and the lies people tell to others and to themselves to obtain the objects of their desires. Ophuls's view of human relationships is the same as Arthur Schnitzler's, author of the original play (both Lubitsch and von Stroheim also liked Schnitzler). Schnitzler's play is a series of ten wryly comic seductions, all of which, except the last, denote the sexual climax with a line of asterisks in the text. The play's unique structure gives its author several interesting perspectives, which Ophuls pointedly borrows. Because

the scenes do not depict sexual activity but the events leading up to and away from the activity, the obvious focus of each scene is on the emotional reactions before (usually sexual excitement, clichéd lies, mental fencing) and after (usually disillusionment, callousness, and guilt) the asterisks. The play's aim (and Ophuls's aim, too) is decidedly psychological, not sexual—hence the ridiculousness of Roger Vadim's later, explicitly sexy version of the play (*Circle of Love,* 1964). Furthermore, Schnitzler's play uses each character in two successive seduction scenes, leading to obvious comparisons of each character's actions, words, poses, and emotions in each sexual situation. And third, the Schnitzler play is constructed with an increasing complexity; the lies that each of the characters tells get fancier and fancier with each subsequent scene; the sexual confrontations steadily climb the social and intellectual ladder beginning with whore and ending with count. All classes, all people, play the same games, each in his or her own way.

Ophuls preserves filmically the

intentions of Schnitzler's witty play: the stylized settings, the graceful camera, the understated acting, the charming waltz that plays as the characters change beds, the elegant and careful details of each setting, the urbane and confidential patter of the narrator. Especially clever is Ophuls's discovery of cinematic equivalents for Schnitzler's asterisks, usually handled on the stage by dimming and then brightening the lights. To denote the sexual climax, Ophuls's camera often gracefully tracks away from the lovers, riveting itself on an object, and then later (perhaps after a dissolve) tracks back to them. His cleverest device is the sequence in which the film abruptly stops and jump-cuts to the narrator holding up a strip of film and a pair of editing scissors, shaking his head in concern over the lewdness of the scene he is about to censor. The narrator snips the sensual strip from the reel and the film jumps back to the two sated lovers. Perhaps the weakest section of the film is the last few sequences; the director shies away from Schnitzler's increasing verbal complexities in the later scenes. As a result, the concluding scenes are not different enough from the early ones and the film's repetitive structure becomes an obligatory burden (the film simply *must* complete the circle) rather than the clever means to ever more revealing psychological insights and moral paradoxes.

The moral view of Ophuls's *La Ronde* is not simply that sex is frothy and fun. The film poses a moral tension between natural human responses and unnatural social restrictions. The result is that the only time the characters cannot lie to each other is when they are lying with each other, during the "asterisks" of each scene. There is an underlying sad antithesis of human feeling and human callousness; the human brain's subjection to social rules and theories of proper human responses devastatingly turns both men and women into masses of contradictions of which they are totally ignorant.

This same antithesis between experience and convention propels *Lola Montès*, but Lola (Martine Carol) resolves the contradiction by remaining unflinchingly true to her feelings, regardless of the risk, regardless of the consequences. The story of Lola is the fictional biography of a real human being, a famous (or infamous) courtesan of the nineteenth century, who took a series of brilliant lovers—a famous composer (Liszt), a ruling Bavarian prince. But Lola falls on evil fortune; she becomes a circus performer, forced to parade her life's story before a crass and ogling audience, selling gossip and kisses for a quarter. Lola has, on the surface, fallen from great lover to circus freak and two-bit whore. Her new lover is the fat and slimy ringmaster (Peter Ustinov) who, though he loves her, salaciously revels in Lola's past, his present mastery over her, and the money he makes from her life. Lola's conquerors are those common mortal ones, circumstance and time, as her sick and aging body requires more and more whiskey to keep it going.

Despite the change in Lola's fortunes, despite the public tawdriness of her new life and lover, Lola is still Lola. She refuses to bow to convention, to play safe. Even her deliberate public display of her past is an unconventional act of defiance. If the past is all that remains of her life, then she will live in that past, even in front of a circus audience that gets a vicarious thrill from it. Though her doctor advises her that she is too weak, too ill to make her high platform leap that climactically ends her act, she insists on making the leap. And contrary to all circus-film clichés, Lola does not leap to her death at the end of *Lola Montès* (although she will, of course, leap to it one day). Lola cannot live her life in any way other than a series of dangerous leaps. What is important is not whether the leap is successful but that she always makes the leap.

But *Lola Montès* is more than an examination of a romantic life-style. It is one of the most dazzling of visual shows—in both color and CinemaScope. The circus within the film is matched by Ophuls's visual circus of mammoth action, swirling colors, and brilliant decor. Each of the sequences has its own unique color and tone: the warm browns, oranges, and ambers of the rustic affair with the composer; the cold whites, silvers, and pale blues of the affair with the prince; the dazzling reds and golds of the circus, glowing in the blackness of the circus tent. The film's composition is as effective as its color. Ophuls was one of the first directors to compose not *in* the wide screen but *for* the wide screen. The big shots—in the circus tent, in the palace—truly fill the frame. Ophuls's constantly moving camera, his panoramic staging, and his careful decor decrease the impression of the screen's great width by adding fullness and balance to the frame. Ophuls constantly splits the wide screen with contrapuntal verticals, breaking the horizontal expanse with lamps, chandeliers, ropes, drapes, pillars.

Lola Montès. *Composition for the wide screen: filling the frame, contrapuntal verticals (Martine Carol and Anton Walbrook)*

For his intimate close-ups, Ophuls rejects the conventional single face in the center of the frame, a composition that clashes with the wide screen; he either frames two faces that tensely balance one another on opposite sides of the screen or frames a single face that is balanced asymmetrically by an object or rearground action on the opposite side of the frame. Ophuls's favorite camera maneuver in the film is the circular track that moves round and round the action, keeping the figures contrapuntally balanced around an invisible pole in the center of the wide frame. The circular motion is not only active and interesting pictorially; it is the perfect cinematic parallel for the film's metaphorical circus tent, which becomes a microcosm for all earthly places and all human experience. Ophuls's turning camera, his metaphorical setting, and the very structure of *Lola Montès*, turn all human experience into a vivid circus and all spectators in the film theatre into spectators in the circus tent.

Robert Bresson, though equally careful

with narrative structure, details of decor and pictorial composition, is a completely different kind of filmmaker. Subdued rather than flamboyant, quiet rather than gaudy, introspective rather than extrovertedly spectacular, Bresson's and Ophuls's films are as far apart as Brittany and Vienna. Bresson has made less than a dozen films in a career of thirty-five years, the most important of them being *The Ladies of the Bois de Boulogne* (1944-45), *Diary of a Country Priest* (1951), *A Man Escaped* (1956), *Pickpocket* (1959),

and *Lancelot du lac* (1974). Bresson takes two, three, even five years to make a single film. His slowness and care as a craftsman seem to mirror the quietness, the slow pace, the internalized probing of his films. Whereas the Ophuls films are dizzying visual shows, the Bresson films feel more like novels. Bresson's favorite transitional device is the slow fade out and fade in, strikingly parallel to the novelistic end of one chapter and beginning of the next. Like the novelist, Bresson can either tell his story through

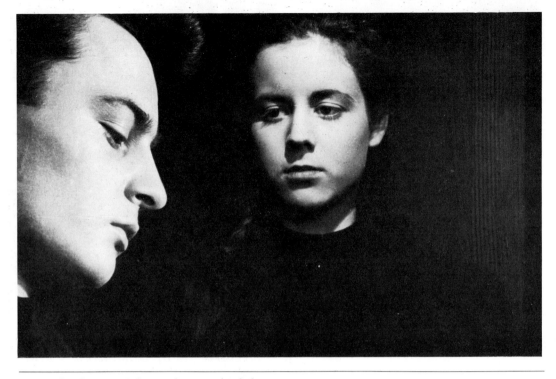

Diary of a Country Priest: *soft eyes and soft faces*

an omniscient third person *(The Ladies of the Bois de Boulogne)* or a confessional first person *(Diary of a Country Priest)*. The *Diary* even uses the narrator's voice as the priest makes entries in his journal.

Bresson's primary theme is the battle of spiritual innocence with the corruption of the world. Bresson, a devout Roman Catholic, searches for spiritual meaning and salvation in a world that has obviously lost them. In *Diary of a Country Priest,* a young, innocent curé faces the worldly evils about him: a cynical, nihilistic doctor commits suicide; a wealthy count substitutes money and influence for morality and faith; the faith of the count's wife wavers at the loss of her son; the count's neurotic daughter viciously implicates the priest in the countess's death; the peasants of the countryside remain indifferent and

hostile. As a priest, the man fails. He succeeds only in bringing a moment of faith and peace to the countess. The other members of his parish remain tied to their selfish cares and physical concerns. But as a man, the priest succeeds completely. He dies of cancer, unshaken in his faith to the end, certain that "all is grace." His spirit wins the battle with his body. The Bresson cinematic technique—unselfconscious, unspectacular, effortlessly transparent— never diverts our attention from the man's internal struggle and the thematic basis of that struggle, spiritual and physical health. The film's structure consistently contrasts the priest's spiritual stability with the weakness and fears of those around him. Bresson's camera lingers on faces, on eyes, on the priest's hands, purposely taking the time not just to slow the pace but to allow the human details to register in our minds and feelings.

Jacques Tati is the great comic of the French film, probably the greatest film mime and visual comic since Chaplin and Keaton. Like Bresson, Tati works slowly, controlling every detail of the film himself from script to cutting; like Bresson, Tati refuses to compromise with either technicians or producers. As a result, though Tati's first film appearance was as early as 1932, he has made only five feature films: *Jour de Fête* (1949), *Mr. Hulot's Holiday* (1953), *My Uncle* (1958), *Playtime* (1968), and *Traffic* (1972). Like Chaplin and Keaton, Tati came to films from the music hall. Before taking to the stage, Tati took to sport—tennis, boxing, soccer. Tati's comedy—for example, his famous tennis pantomime—often combines the athletic field and the music hall. But Tati is sensitive not only to the comic possibilities of his body but also to the visually comic possibilities of the film: a paint can that mysteriously floats on the water and drifts over to the painter at exactly the moment he needs it in *Mr. Hulot's Holiday*; a house that appears to roll its eyes as two people walk inside its windows in *My Uncle*; travel posters exotically beckoning the tourist with a picture of the same modern Hiltonesque hotel in the center of every exotic locale in *Playtime*.

Like Chaplin and Keaton, Tati plays the same character in each film, and the character he plays is inevitably a loner, an outsider, a charming fool whose human incompetence is preferable to the inhuman competence of the life around him. Tati's Mr. Hulot (even the name Hulot recalls Charlot) merely goes about his business, totally unaware that the world around him has gone mad and that his naïve attention to his own business turns its orderly madness into comic chaos. In *Jour de Fête*, Tati plays a clumsy rural postman who discovers the apparent efficiency and speed of the American postal system. Tati's zany attempts to convert himself into a speedy efficient machine produce great visual gags as well as chaos in the little town. As always with Tati, that which seems efficient and modern is ultimately inefficient and wasteful.

For *Mr. Hulot's Holiday*, Tati creates Monsieur Hulot, an apparently conventional pipe-smoking easygoing middle-class gentleman who comes to spend a conventional week at a completely conventional middle-class resort. Monsieur Hulot, again like Chaplin and Keaton, unfortunately runs afoul of objects. His troubles with a canoe, with his car, with a donkey, with a warehouse full of fireworks, reduce the conventional, routinized tourist resort to unconventional hysteria. Tati's comic attack exposes the resort—supposedly a place devoted to leisure and fun—as the domain of the dull, the monotonous, the dead. M. Hulot is the force who converts the dead place of play into a genuine funhouse by bombarding it (quite literally at its climax) with uncanny objects, sounds, and movements. We in the theatre, like those few vacationers who take the time to notice Hulot's spontaneous, disruptive activities, also discover what genuine, active fun really is.

My Uncle features Monsieur Hulot again—this time as an old-fashioned, simple, mild uncle of a family of upper-middle-class suburbanites. Hulot's simple, unaffected ways contrast with the complicated machinery of his suburban relatives' lives: their fancy gadgets that open the garage doors and kitchen shelves (inconsistently); their bizarrely shaped furniture that is designed for everything but comfort and function; their gravel-lined flagstone-paved "garden" that is suitable for everything but growing things and enjoying the sun. In this struggle of man versus the artifact, the gadgets win the battle (they always do

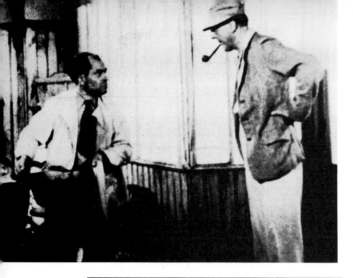

M. Hulot's first entrance (Jacques Tati) in Mr. Hulot's Holiday (compare this entrance with that in the color film, Playtime, in the color section)

in physical comedy), but M. Hulot wins the satirical war.

Playtime brings a group of American tourists to Paris. Hulot, more a passive observer than the central figure of the film, accompanies a group on their tour of a modern industrial exposition and a fancy nightclub that has just been glued together for fashionable Parisians and American tourists. The film's joke, as well as its serious point, is that Paris—the Paris of the travel folders and romance—does not exist. The old Paris has been replaced by aluminum-and-glass skyscrapers and neon-lit prefabricated restaurants. Paris is no different from New York—hence the irony of the American tourists. The film is a clear extension of *My Uncle,* the ultimate blow at "modernity."

But the blow wears a hilariously comic glove. Tati ridicules the slick surfaces of modern life with hysterical visual gags: the tiles of the dance floor have been pasted down so recently that they stick to the dancers' high-stepping shoes; a plate-glass door is so invisible that the customers cannot tell whether the doorman actually opens the door or merely mimes it. Tati also uses sound

hilariously in the film. Unlike Chaplin or Keaton, Tati is a child of the sound era; his physical comedy never ignores its possibilities. Athough *Playtime* has so little dialogue that it requires no subtitles, Tati develops aural gags like a plastic-and-foam-rubber sofa that makes grotesque breathing and sucking noises when Hulot sits on it and a miraculous modern door that makes absolutely no noise even when slammed with the most violent force.

Like *Mr. Hulot's Holiday,* the underlying theme of *Playtime* is the creative use of leisure and the genuine fun that can result from active perception rather than the passive acceptance of planned and canned routines. The American tourists of *Playtime* parallel the vacationers in *Holiday,* and in *Playtime* they eventually do have fun, despite their overly packaged tour, simply by observing the oddities of Hulot and, even more important, the surprising oddities of the world itself. Like *Mr. Hulot's Holiday, Playtime* is very much about itself, about our having fun by watching a film closely and by finding its comic inventions for ourselves rather than being fed them by a prepackaging film director. There is not a single close-up in the film; our eye must pick out visual and comic significance for itself. In their blend of social satire, wry human charm, imaginative physical gags, and the creative use of the visual and aural devices of the cinema itself, the films of Jacques Tati have not been surpassed by those of any other postwar film comic, French or otherwise.

Two other major French directors of the years just following the war were Henri-Georges Clouzot and René Clément. Clouzot is a cinematically conventional director of suspenseful melodramas. Both *The Wages of Fear* (1953) and *Les Diaboliques* (1955) mix chills, horror, sexual intrigue, and taut suspense. *Diabolique* is the more celebrated of the two, a story of a supposedly dead man who keeps reappearing to terrify his living wife—and a shrieking audience. But *The Wages of Fear* is a purer representative of the Clouzot method: an agonizingly tense, long journey of two trucks transporting nitroglycerin through the jungles of South America (portentously and pretentiously remade by William Friedkin as *Sorcerer* in 1977). Most illustrative of Clouzot's bitter, sordid premise is the film's final sequence. One truck has finally made it; the dangerous cargo has been unloaded; the young protagonist sits at the wheel, driving the now harmless truck back home. He is on his way to see his mistress again. He turns on the radio and listens joyfully to a pleasant version of the "Blue Danube Waltz." He turns the wheel in rhythm with the music; he sways back and forth over the mountain road. He misses a curve and the truck plunges down a ravine, taking the man to his waltz-time death.

Clément's most important film is *Forbidden Games* (1952), a war-time story of two children who are both affected and infected by the murderous world of their elders. A young girl's parents and puppy are machine gunned by a strafing German airplane. The girl, too horrified by the death of her parents, fixes her fascination on the dead puppy, refusing to believe it is dead; she tries to keep it and play with it. She is adopted by a family of Pyrenees farmers who, through their young son, teach her that dead things must be buried. The girl buries the puppy. She becomes so fascinated with burying things that she and the young boy go about the countryside killing living beings—flies, spiders, toads—specifically so they can bury them.

Attached to all the burials is that symbol of the cemetery, the cross. Clément equates Christianity and the forces of death. In their quest to bury bigger and bigger things the two children attack bigger animals and steal crosses out of the town cemetery for them. Eventually their private cemetery is discovered; they are punished for their activity, which ironically merely mimics that of their elders. The little girl is sent back to Paris as an orphan, separated from the boy and the family she has come to love.

But Clément's later films fail to duplicate the thematic seriousness and artistic integrity of *Forbidden Games*. Clément has been responsible for *Gervaise* (1956), a heavy and stilted translation of Zola, with Maria Schell; for *Purple Noon* (1959), a psychological, picture-postcard mystery that uses Alain Delon's body in the same way that Roger Vadim used Brigitte Bardot's and Jane Fonda's; for *Is Paris Burning?* (1966), an epic, Franco-American coproduction shot in France but rooted in Hollywood; and for *Rider on the Rain* (1971), a horrific suspense story with sexual overtones (like *Purple Noon*) in which Clément attempted to show the New Wave directors that he too could evoke Hitchcock.

1959 and After

In the years following the war a new generation of Frenchmen became addicted to the movies. These *cinéastes* first became film critics rather than filmmakers, simply because in France, as in America, the studio establishment had solidified enough to keep new minds out. These cinephiles did not like the film establishment's ornately-staged, heavily-plotted, over-scripted, unspontaneous, leaden films. In *Cahiers du Cinéma*, the journal founded by film theorist André Bazin, the young critics François Truffaut, Jean-Luc Godard, and Claude Chabrol ripped apart the films of Clément, Clouzot, Aurenche and Bost (*Symphonie Pastorale*, 1946; *The Red and the Black*, 1948), and others of the same literary, talky, studio-crafted, theatrical

type. These *Cahiers* critics retreated a generation, to the 1930s of Clair, Renoir, and Vigo, where they found the zest and spontaneity of what they considered the authentic French tradition. Just as the French directors of the 1920s leaped backward to the primitive exuberance of Cohl, Zecca, and Sennett, the French directors of the 1960s leaped backward to the films of the 1920s and 1930s. Just as the French films of the 1920s combined echoes of the past with bizarre innovations for the future, the films of Truffaut and Godard were to be full of echoes of Vigo, Bogart, Hitchcock, Hawks, Renoir, combined with inge- niously elliptical, irrational techniques. The year 1959 was the year that the critics persuaded adventurous financial backers to give them the opportunity to make films. It was the year of Truffaut's *The 400 Blows* (its very title an echo of Méliès's *The Four Hundred Blows of the Devil*) and Godard's *Breathless*.

The young François Truffaut, like the young Vigo and the young Renoir, built his early films on the central artistic idea of freedom, both in human relationships and in film technique. Truffaut's early protagonists were rebels, loners, or misfits who felt stifled by the conventional social definitions. Antoine, the thirteen-year-old protagonist of *The 400 Blows*, must endure a prison-like school and a school-like prison, sentenced to both by hypocritical, unsympathetic, unperceptive adults. Charlie Kohler of Truffaut's *Shoot*

the Piano Player (1960) has deliberately cut himself free of the ropes of fame and fortune as a concert pianist, preferring his job in a small smoky bar— uncommitted, unburdened, untied. Catherine of *Jules and Jim* (1961) feels so uncomfortable with all definitions—wife, mistress, mother, friend, woman—that she commits suicide. Truffaut's early cinematic style was as anxious to rip the cords as his characters were. The early films are dazzlingly elliptical, omitting huge transitional sections of time and emotional development. His construction emphasizes the key moments of interaction and conflict rather than the motivational gaps between the moments. This elliptical leaping gave the Truffaut films an intensity, a spontaneity, a lightness that more rationally plotted films lacked.

Truffaut also delighted in mixing cinematic styles. *The 400 Blows* ranges from sentimental traveling shots of Antoine's tear-stained face, underscored by Jean Constantin's lush music, to improvised, candid comic scenes in the schoolroom, echoing Vigo's candid work with school children; from a *cinéma vérité* interview between Antoine and a prying social worker, to agonizingly long, subjective traveling shots as Antoine escapes the reform school and races toward the sea. The film then ends with a deliberately startling surprise, a freeze-frame of the boy staring ahead, presumably implying the ambiguity of the future that lies ahead of him. *Shoot the Piano Player* contains a most audacious, irrelevant interruption. A character swears that he is telling the truth. "May my mother drop dead," he says. Truffaut then cuts to a shot of an old lady by a stove who suddenly clutches her heart and collapses on the floor. Truffaut then returns to the story without further comment. In *Jules and Jim,* Truffaut undercranks the camera for Sennettesque effects; he uses a subjective traveling shot as the three characters race across a bridge; he uses newsreel footage of World War I that is horribly distorted by his contemporary anamorphic lens; he uses a brief freeze-frame to capture a moment of Catherine's beauty; he uses slow motion as Catherine drives her car off a pier to her death, prolonging the suicide, making the moment sad and slow. The trick and the surprise were intrinsic to Truffaut's method. They perfectly accompanied the stories and people he had chosen to film. They gave the film's action the Truffaut spirit.

Charlie Kohler finds it impossible to divorce himself from human commitment and human emotion in *Shoot the Piano Player.* Charlie, as a flashback reveals, was once the famous concert pianist, Edouard Saroyan. Edouard's wife, the woman he loved, felt her husband's career steadily tearing him away from her. She resolves the tension by jumping out a window to her death. Saroyan resolves his guilt by becoming Charlie Kohler, honky-tonk pianist, determined to avoid any further human involvement, human conflict, love. He sits at his piano expressionless, grimly banging out his honky-tonk tunes.

But life catches up with Charlie, forcing him to make a human response—just as it catches up with Bogart in *Casablanca* and Jean Gabin in *Port of Shadows,* both of whom are specifically evoked by the film. Charlie cannot stop himself from helping Léna, from defending her against the bullying owner of the bar (whom he accidentally kills), from falling in love

with her despite his decision not to love. And like his first love, Léna dies, accidentally caught in the middle of a gunfight between Charlie's brothers and two gangsters. Accidents in the film are ironic and horrifying, senseless yet pervasive. Truffaut captures the pathos of Léna's death in her poignant, agonizing slide down a hill of white snow; it is deliberately drawn out in slow motion, like Catherine's suicide in *Jules and Jim,* to prolong its sadness. Charlie has lost his love again. In the film's final shot, he has returned to his piano once again, banging out the same haunting tune—grim, expressionless, determined. The film paradoxically maintains that it is the nature of love to be lost but that to protect oneself from the pain of loss by not loving is not to live at all.

Jules and Jim is another study of the relationship of love and life. Catherine refuses to live any longer than she can love, feel, respond freely, act impulsively. She travels with a bottle of vitriol as a potential means of escape from a life that

Antoine at the sea: the final freeze-frame of The 400 Blows

Jules and Jim: *Supremely sunny moments (Jeanne Moreau)*

might one day hang too heavily about her neck. She is a creature of whim, of impulse, of change. She can dress up like a Jackie-Cooganesque kid; she can race across a bridge; she can dive into the Seine to shake up her complacent companions. The same impulsiveness later drives both her and Jim off a pier to their deaths. Truffaut establishes Catherine as a pure spirit, an incarnation of the goddess of love. Her face and smile identically match the statue of the love goddess that Jules and Jim discover on an archaeological trip. But the pure spirit of love has difficulties surviving in the real world of geographical boundaries, marriage laws, child bearing, and political wars. Though Catherine enjoys supremely sunny moments with Jim, with Jules, with the two of them together, the moments lose their sunlight when they become months and years. She cannot remain happy with anyone for very long. And so she cuts the rope that binds her both to life and to Jules and Jim by driving her car off a pier, taking Jim with her, while Jules, like us in the

audience, can only watch. Once again permanent love and human reality are mutually exclusive.

The Truffaut filmography splits rather neatly into two halves—a group of early films in black and white (which earned him his initial respect and reputation) and a decade of films in color (which, despite their craft and subtlety, have never achieved the critical recognition of his first three films). Like Renoir, who also shifted from black and white, Truffaut's color films reject the pessimism of his monochrome films and seek to establish syntheses—between the human being and the social whole, between private emotion and artistic vocation. The two recurrent themes of Truffaut's later films are education and art, both of which grow out of his earliest work (*The 400 Blows* most explicitly—and apprehensively— concerns itself with education, while both Charlie Kohler of *Piano Player* and Catherine of *Jules and Jim* have converted themselves into characters, into works of art). After several transitional pieces in a variety of styles—the melodramatic love triangle of *The Soft Skin* (1964), a repressive world of the future in *Fahrenheit 451* (1966), and a Hitchcock dissertation in *The Bride Wore Black* (1968)—the second half of Truffaut's career begins with the return to Antoine Doinel in *Stolen Kisses* (1969).

Antoine Doinel is Truffaut's alter ego; his adventures on film parallel Truffaut's own personal experiences as a child and young man; the maturing of the actor who plays Doinel, Jean-Pierre Léaud, precisely parallels the maturing of the film director behind the camera who discovered the young boy and nurtured his early career. Léaud is Truffaut's spiritual son, much as Truffaut claims that André Bazin was his own spiritual father. But the maturing experienced together by Truffaut and Léaud (like the relationship between Truffaut and Bazin) comes about solely because of the cinema, because of sharing the experience of that art. And so the Doinel films allow Truffaut to unite both of his primary themes—education and art—simply because the mutual experiencing of art produces their shared education.

In *Stolen Kisses* (1969), young Doinel blunders at both love and work, clumsily groping toward self-fulfillment in both. In *Bed and Board* (1970), Antoine is married, with a child of his own (the educational cycle has begun again) as well as a mistress who fulfills his fantasies. (Antoine is still a half-committed blunderer, the consistent trait of his adult life.) And in *Love on the Run* (1979) Antoine gets divorced (still the blunderer), but his novel has finally been published (his own creation of a work of art)—a novel that is really an exploration of his own autobiographical experiences with women, transmuted into art (like the novel in *The Man Who Loved Women*, 1977, and the Doinel cycle as a whole).

Despite his creation of this work, Antoine continues to run after the same women in his life/novel (running is the essential Doinel metaphor, established in the magnificent running sequence that closes *The 400 Blows*). So the transforming of life into art in no way erases or resolves the aches and tensions of life (it does not resolve them for Charlie Kohler or the man who loved women either); the work of art merely exists alongside the life it depicts—a separate but closely related chronicle. *Love on the Run* reinforces this conclusion with a cinematic metaphor—its compilation of film clips from all the previous Doinel movies (including the brief "Antoine et Collette" from *Love at Twenty*, 1962)—for the film is not only the story of an adult Doinel looking back on his life but of the adult Truffaut looking back on the entire cycle of Doinel films. And this cycle of films (like Doinel's novel) is not only Truffaut's art but his life as well.

The Wild Child (1970), on its surface an almost documentary-style study (Truffaut's only black-and-white film between 1965 and 1979), is also devoted to education. A late eighteenth-century scientist succeeds in taming a wild boy—a child who had spent his entire early life as a beast in the forest—and introduces him to the luxuries of civilization: speech, clothes, shelter, and, most important, love. That the film is much closer to the Doinel cycle than it might seem from its case-history surface can be seen in Truffaut's dedication of the film to Jean-Pierre Léaud, that Truffaut himself played the scientist who taught the boy (just as Jean Renoir played roles in many of his own films), and that the Truffaut-Léaud relationship is unmistakably significant to *The Wild Child*. Just as both the boy and the scientist grow into fuller human beings as the result of the educational process in *The Wild Child*, both Truffaut and Léaud, who were themselves outlaws and outcasts, grew into mature and full human beings under the tutorship of the director and in the process of creating works of art, the ultimate product of civilization.

The central Truffaut theme had

Day for Night: *Life as art as life as art.*
Jean-Pierre Léaud (with Valentina Cortese) as a
love-sick actor, playing a love-sick character, in a
Truffaut movie, featuring Truffaut in the role of a
film director

evolved into one that was quite close to Renoir's: the relationship of art to nature and the ability of art to contain nature and to become its own nature. *The Wild Child* looks less sympathetically at the claims of nature than *The 400 Blows* or *Jules and Jim.* In contrast to the exuberant natural spontaneity of the earlier rebels is the savagery of the wild child who is both unfettered and inhuman. Although wild children certainly live freely, they do not live well with other human beings and they do not create works of art. The stylish artistry of the film itself is a testimony to the value of art and supports its fable. Truffaut demonstrates the powerful claims of art in his careful cinematic re-creation of the life of an earlier century (one of the cinema's unique gifts), in its sensitive human study of man and boy, and in its cinematic devices that consciously evoke the visual values of an earlier cinematic era, particularly D. W. Griffith's. Truffaut's use of irising, of scenes of silence, of black-and-white whose silvery monochrome looks more like the older orthochromatic film than the newer panchromatic stock, all reveal the director retreating into the cinematic past for his study of the historical past.

Precisely the same tension between art and nature propels *Day for Night* (1973), a film that Truffaut was seemingly destined to make, since its subject is the process of filmmaking itself. As with *The Wild Child,* Truffaut plays a role in his own film—a similar role—the patient, paternal teacher-master who is responsible for the success of a complex project. As with *The Wild Child,* the film develops the conflict and resultant synthesis of art and nature, for the filmmaking process is none other than that of converting the totally artificial into the seemingly natural. A film produces candle effects with electric lights, rain and fire with valves and hoses, snow with suds of foam, an artfully "artless" ironic touch (a kitten eating the remains of an amorous breakfast) with a specially selected (and unnaturally uncooperative) cat, and deadly accidents with the leaps of a nimble stuntman. The term that gives the film its title, *day-for-night* (in French, *La Nuit Americaine*—"American Night"), is itself a synthesis of art and nature, the term that Hollywood coined in the era when the movies invariably produced the effect of nighttime by shooting during the day with a blue filter.

But the synthesis of art and nature in *Day for Night* goes even deeper. Those in the film business ultimately turn their lives into the service of art. Their own personal difficulties—the loss of a lover, separation from a husband, even the grief from the death of a leading player—are subordinate to the end of making the picture. Whatever happens in their lives, they make the picture—for ultimately their art is their life. As in the late Renoir films, the dedication to art indeed becomes natural for people who define themselves as being artists.

That Truffaut's film is close to Fellini's *8½* is obvious not only in its subject but in the recurring dream sequence which deliberately echoes the anguished fantasies of Fellini's film as well as Bergman's ominous dream sequences in

Wild Strawberries. But the difference between Fellini's tortured view of the tension between life and art and Truffaut's more playful view becomes clear in *Day for Night*'s turning this potential dream of *angst* into a joke, a parody. Whereas the Truffaut dream begins frighteningly, each successive repetition reveals more and more glee as Truffaut's little boy unashamedly seizes possession of his great prize—the stills for *Citizen Kane* (just as the child Antoine Doinel steals film stills in *The 400 Blows*). Whereas Fellini's director dreams of frustration and Bergman's doctor dreams of death, Truffaut's director dreams of how the commitment to art turns the fears of death into a celebration of life.

The two major Truffaut films of the late 1970s—*The Story of Adele H* (1975) and *Small Change* (1976)—respectively develop the compulsive surrender to a mania that leads to madness and death and the commitment to education that leads to a celebration of life. Adele is Truffaut's return to the compulsiveness of Catherine in *Jules and Jim*, a woman whose passion is so intense that her commitment to a work of art outside herself (her intimate, personal memoirs—which parallel Antoine's novel) is insufficient to purge the violence of her emotions. Adele H (like Ophuls's Madame de . . . , another woman with an incomplete name but a completely consuming passion), follows her passion wherever it leads her—Nova Scotia, Barbados—converting her life itself into such a deeply perfect work of art (like Catherine) that it seals itself off completely from the influence or even awareness of social reality.

In *Small Change* Truffaut returns to the classroom of *The 400 Blows* of two decades earlier (and to that of Vigo's *Zéro de Conduite*, two decades before that, a parallel reinforced by the film's beginning at the end of the summer vacation). As opposed to the black-and-white psychological repression and emotional torture of the earlier films, *Small Change* is a thoroughly sunny color film that (like *The Wild Child*) neither denies the imaginative freedom of childhood nor the civilizing rationality of adulthood. The old, dark wooden desks of both the Vigo and the earlier Truffaut schoolrooms have been replaced by bright, light, modern ones; the old repressive, vicious teachers have been replaced by a genuinely concerned and kind one (he exactly parallels the patient father-teacher figures played by Truffaut himself in *The Wild Child* and *Day for Night*). In this synthesis of child and adult, life and cinema, teaching and living, social utility and personal expression, education is art is feeling is life.

Jean-Luc Godard took the idea for his first feature film, *Breathless*, from Truffaut. Michel Poiccard, the gangster-lover-hero of the film, is very much a Truffaut figure, a synthesis of Charlie, Catherine, and Antoine Doinel. But *Breathless* and Michel Poiccard were as close as Godard's films ever came to Truffaut's. Whereas Truffaut's films are consistent in both theme and technique, the Godard films are consistent in their inconsistency, their eclecticism, their mixing of many different kinds of ideas and cinematic principles.

Godard, paradoxically, supports several contradictory ideas and filmic methods at the same time. On the one hand, he finds human experience irrational and inexplicable: the sudden accidental deaths at the end of *Vivre sa vie* (1962) and *Masculine/Feminine* (1966), the chance murder of the policeman in *Breathless*. On the other hand, Godard flirts with Brechtian devices and politics, and Brecht's premise was that both art and human problems must be viewed as strictly rational and hence solvable. The parable of turning a man into a soldier in *Les Carabiniers* (1963) echoes that parable in Brecht's *A Man's a Man* (written in 1924); the explicitly numbered scenes of *Vivre sa vie* and *Masculine/Feminine* and the

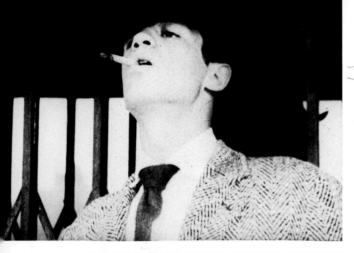

The first shot of Breathless: *Jean-Paul Belmondo playing Michel Poicard playing Humphrey Bogart*

concrete references to B. B. in *La Chinoise* (1968) are unmistakable. On the one hand, Godard is fond of allegorical, metaphorical parables: *Les Carabiniers*, *Alphaville* (1965), *Weekend* (1969). On the other, he is fond of recitations of concrete facts and figures: the prostitution figures in *Vivre sa vie*, the Maoist students' speeches in *La Chinoise*, the truck drivers' debate in *Weekend*, the discussions of imagemaking in *Le Gai Savoir* (1968) and of both radical politics and democracy (a tape recorded interview with a character named Eve Democracy) in *Sympathy for the Devil* (1969).

Godard depicts both irrational moments of fleeting sensation and long-winded speeches of abstract rational argument, both moments of violent action and hours of inactive discussion, outrageous intrusions of the director's favorite film titles and sequences and long unedited sequences in which the director attempts to efface himself completely. Like Truffaut's, Godard's film career breaks into two parts—the decade preceding and following 1968. But Godard's films never evolve toward Truffaut's synthesis of life and art; instead, Godard's films progressively reflect a fear that the familiar solutions of art are precisely antithetical to the necessary solutions for life—particularly political life. And so Godard's films become not progressively whole and controlled but progressively fractured and fragmented. Rather than resolving his contradictions, Godard's evolving work seeks to explore and emphasize those very contradictions.

Breathless, his very first feature, remains the most realistic, most whole, and strongest narrative of the Godard films. Godard examines the life of Michel Poiccard (Jean-Paul Belmondo), alias Laszlo Kovacs (the same name as the American cinematographer who began by filming B-pictures for American-International and who later shot *Easy Rider* and *Five Easy Pieces*). Poiccard is indeed a petty crook in the Monogram, B-picture tradition, a casual car thief who kills a policeman by chance, gets emotionally entangled with his girl (Jean Seberg), and is gunned down eventually by the police after the girl tips them off. The remarkable thing about the film is not its simple story but its Bogartesque character: brazen, charming, free, refusing to warp human emotions into words or human conduct into laws. Remarkable also are the emotional moments of the film: the startlingly real interaction between Michel and Patricia in her room and bed, Michel's buoyant good humor as he drives the car just before he sees the cop, the sentimental but touching ending (a deliberate echo of Lucy's dying gesture in *Broken Blossoms*) as the dying Michel bids a funny-sad farewell to the woman who betrayed him because she was afraid to love him.

To like Godard for *Breathless* is perhaps to like Godard for being Truffaut. But even in *Breathless* the unique Godard devices—the assault against logic, the sudden and abrupt event, the detachment of the viewer from the illusion of the film—control the work. As Michel drives the stolen car, his lengthy monologue on life and the countryside is addressed

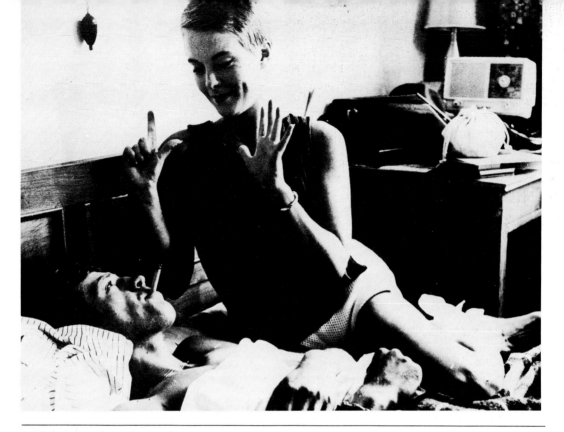

Michel (Belmondo) and Patricia (Jean Seberg) in the bedroom

directly to us, an artifice that Godard emphasizes with his jump-cutting, which destroys the visual continuity of time and space. Michel's shooting of the policeman becomes a distant puppet show because of Godard's nonfluid, jumbled cutting of the sequence and his games with camera speed. As Michel walks on the Champs Elysées, an automobile suddenly strikes and kills an unsuspecting pedestrian. Again Godard's jump-cutting and Raoul Coutard's hand-held camera give the event the convincing feeling of accident, chance, the unexpected. Michel takes a casual look at the dead pedestrian, shrugs, and keeps walking. The fragments of human passion, the juggled editing and jiggled camera, are pure Godard, not Truffaut.

The primary strength of Godard films of the next half decade is the director's continuing ability to catch flashing, elusive moments of passion, joy, or pain with the most surprising and unconventional narrative techniques. *Vivre sa vie,* a supposedly cold, detached, rational study of a girl who drifts into prostitution and is accidentally killed, contains perceptive and revealing moments of human interaction. In the film's first scene, the girl and her husband separate; Godard catches the emptiness, the hollowness of the relationship by shooting the film in a café, full of the sounds of tinkling cups and passing traffic, behind the two speakers' backs. The faces of the man and woman never appear in the scene, except in a brief reflection in the mirror opposite the counter at which they are sitting. Also effective in the film is the girl going about the business of being a prostitute—with the very old, the very

young, the ugly, and the handsome—in the most matter-of-fact way while Godard's sound track gives us, in counterpoint, a dry recitation of facts and figures on prostitution. The girl's teasing of a young man in a pool room, her sentimental weeping at a screening of Dreyer's *Joan of Arc*, and her lengthy but touching discussion of the meaning of life with an old philosopher in a café also contribute to the roundness of her portrait.

Masculine/Feminine also succeeds because of its charming or touching moments. Godard seeks to capture the world, the feelings, the vitality of the young, the generation of "Marx and Coca Cola." Godard relies on improvisational interviews with his young central figures, whose charm, spontaneity, and honesty in front of the camera are infectious. The suddenness of the boy's chance death (Jean-Pierre Léaud again) at the end of the film parallels the irrational abruptness

Vivre sa vie: *going about the business of prostitution; irrational and accidental death*

of the deaths in *Breathless* and *Vivre sa vie*. Godard again handles death anticlimactically. We only discover that the boy has fallen off a building to his death when his girlfriends report the accident to the police. The clicking clatter of the bureaucratic typewriter recording the account in the coldest, most mechanical manner contrasts poignantly with the breathing, vital energy of the living boy. Life and death, energy and deadness are that close and that far apart in the world of Godard.

Les Carabiniers and *Weekend* get their energy from the power of Godard's fable rather than the charm of his characters. *Les Carabiniers* is a wryly comic, Brechtian parable of two country bumpkins—ironically named Michelangelo and Ulysses, a synthesis of classical, Renaissance, and modern civilization—who leave the farm to go to war. The recruiting officer promises them the world; instead, the yokels merely bring back picture postcards of the world. Except, ironically, those postcards *are* the world, just as Ulysses and Michelangelo are Western civilization. When the two clowns return to a combat whose issues, strategies, and warring sides are intentionally unclear and undeveloped, they inadvertently get tangled up in some kind of political and military intrigue. The result of this entanglement is their death—they are incomprehensibly and unexpectedly gunned down by their officer. Throughout the film the two soldiers have described their travels and exploits to their women at home on wry little postcards that make no separation between the pleasant places they visit and the numbers of people they butcher. This naïvely bitter, comic, Brechtian device points directly to the film's statement: those who butcher get butchered in return.

The dominant mood of *Weekend*, another film about butchery, is not wryness but animalistic brutality. The film begins realistically enough; Godard takes realistic man's animal-like possessiveness toward his automobile as the film's starting point. As the central couple travel on a highway to a weekend with their in-laws, Godard transports them from the land of the living to parable land. Using an agonizingly long, stifling traffic jam on the highway—intentionally made agonizing by the director's repetitious and unending traveling shot of the jam—Godard leads us gradually from reality into metaphor: from traffic jam to a land of wrecked automobiles and mutilated crash victims, to a land of open human hostility and warfare, to a land of cannibalistic savages slaughtering pigs and people with equal appetite. Cannibalism is the ultimate metaphor for modern society.

But on his way to this ultimate reduction, Godard cannot restrain himself from adding capricious, playful touches: a journey through literature land where the characters meet figures out of books (perhaps a parody of Truffaut's *Fahrenheit 451*); a political discussion of colonialism by two truck drivers, one white, one black, as they both devour meaty sandwiches; a secret code employed by the cannibalistic bands based entirely on film titles and characters—Potemkin, Gosta Berling, Arizona Jules. The latter is one of the innest of in-group jokes, apparently a combination of Arizona Jim (the parody of Rio Jim in Renoir's *Crime of Monsieur Lange*) and *Jules and Jim*. Godard is wry when serious and serious when wry.

If Godard's overall career reveals a consistent pattern, it is that he began by using bizarre devices of cinematic perception as a means to tell rather conventional narratives—the means to bring his characters to life—and he became progressively more concerned with cinematic perception—irrational nonnarrative; bizarre manipulation of space and time—as an end in itself. The one subject Godard's films consistently explore is the cultural process of making and receiving images—on film, television, radio news, printed advertisements, billboards, book jackets, popular songs. The first shot in Godard's first feature captures Jean-Paul Belmondo gazing upon a sexy pin-up in a tabloid newspaper. While this shot in *Breathless* served to define the interests, the cultural level, and the sexual commitments of the character, successive Godard films became increasingly interested in precisely what people were seeing and reading in those magazines and other media of cultural dissemination rather than in who these people were—or, rather, Godard became convinced that people unwillingly and unconsciously become the products of those very drawings and advertisements.

Three of Godard's pre-1968 films most committed to a study of imagemaking are *Contempt* (1963), a film explicitly about the making of film images (with Fritz Lang in the role of a director and Brigitte Bardot as a sex-object star), *The Married Woman* (1964), an analysis of the commoditization of women, marriage, "beauty," and "romance" in modern society, and *Two or Three Things I Know About Her* (1966), a return to the milieu of prostitution of *Vivre sa vie* but with the emphasis on the milieu (cafés, cars, city streets, architecture) rather than on the business of prostitution. As his films move toward 1968, Godard becomes increasingly convinced that one cannot make movies—or any other kind of art work—about anything without first understanding how one is making them and why.

The Paris riots of May–June 1968 intensified Godard's political commitments, leading him to organize a political cell (he called it the Dziga-Vertov Group, after the Soviet innovator of the *Kino-Pravda*) for making films, in opposition to the Appollonian, bourgeois model of the individual artist-creator. The character played by Yves Montand in *Tout va bien* (1972) is, like Godard, a film director who explains that he could no longer continue making adventurously artistic feature films after the events of 1968 (Montand obviously speaks for Godard here). But Montand's choice becomes a cynical one; he decides to shoot the most vapid and exploitative television commercials exclusively. Unlike this character, Godard has decided to become the analyst rather than the manipulator of modern cultural packaging.

Another important influence on Godard's work must have been the revolutionary political films from embattled Third World countries (like the mammoth *Hour of the Furnaces* from Argentina), which were first shown frequently in Europe the same year as the Paris riots. The political discussions in Godard's films, beginning with *La Chinoise* (especially the colonialism debate in *Weekend* and black radical rhetoric in *Sympathy for the Devil*), seem to have been inspired by similar discussions in Third World films. Godard was unfortunate, however, in being a highly educated European; whereas these Third World films advocate stirring political actions and passionately address a unified working-class audience, Godard's discussions are highly abstract, distant, and dry analyses of semiotic theory addressed to the most educated and elitist members of the culture. Having reached an apparent end point with these films of communication theory (*Pravda* and *Vent d'est*, both 1969; *Letter to Jane*, 1972; *Numero deux*, 1975), Godard has gone to work for Francis Ford Coppola (*Every Man for Himself*, 1980). Perhaps there will be a third period of his career.

The tension between formal experimentation and political commitment is also central to the work of Alain Resnais. Although Resnais has been consistently linked with both Truffaut and Godard, he is a completely different kind of filmmaker. Ten years older than Truffaut and Godard, Resnais's career in films began not as *cinéaste* and critic but as film editor and documentary filmmaker. His most important early films studied the works of artists (Van Gogh, Gauguin, Picasso's "Guernica") or examined the horrors of the Nazi concentration camps (*Night and Fog,* 1955), two types which set the pattern for his two interests: art (the purity of form) and ideas. But as with Truffaut and Godard, 1959 was the year of Resnais's first feature, *Hiroshima Mon Amour,* and critics assumed his work was part of the same "wave," despite the differences in his films.

Resnais begins with a far more literary premise than Truffaut or Godard. His films are neither improvised nor spontaneous. Like Bresson and Renoir, Resnais begins with detailed, literate, highly polished scripts. Although Resnais does not adapt novels into films—he believes a work must be written specifically for the film—he asks novelists to write his original scripts: Marguerite Duras, Alain Robbe-Grillet, Jean Cayrol. Resnais respects literateness, complex construction, and poetic speech. His films are thoughtful, slow, tightly controlled, and perhaps cold and heavy in comparison with the breezy, erratic, makeshift feeling of the early Truffaut and Godard films. If Resnais and the younger men are constantly compared, it is probably because all three share one thematic premise and one formal principle. First, Resnais films examine the possibility of love, of sincere emotional interaction, in the world as it is, with its politics, its wars, its social inequities, its "rules of the game." Second, because one of the key Resnais themes is the effect of time, the interrelation of past, present, and future, his narratives are frequently elliptical, jump-cutting in time and space even more freely than Truffaut's or Godard's.

There the similarities end. The early Truffaut and Godard films were obviously works of much younger, much more optimistic, much more zestful men. There is something very sad, very cold, very dead about the life and the people in the Resnais films. In *Hiroshima Mon Amour,* a French woman and a Japanese man try to build something more between them than a single night in bed. She is an actress who has come to Hiroshima to make a peace film; he is an architect trying to build the ruined city up from its ashes. But they are separated by more than cultural distance. Between them is the past. For him, there is Hiroshima, the burned-out home of his youth. For her, Nevers, the little French town where she loved a German soldier in the occupation army whom the villagers murdered when the Nazis evacuated. Both have burned-out pasts.

To show the intrusion of these pasts into the present, Resnais, the sensitive editor, continually cuts shots of Nevers and the Hiroshima carnage into the shots of the present. At the film's opening, the two embracing lovers' arms seem to be covered with radioactive dust. As they make love, Resnais's camera tracks through the Hiroshima war museum, showing the burnt buildings and mutilated bodies. When the man accuses the woman of not knowing what it was like, Resnais cuts in flashes of her experience in Nevers. The result of this assault of the past on the present is an emotional gulf between them that can never be bridged. The final sequence of the film, lasting almost an hour, is a sterile, silent walk by the couple through the city: to a restaurant, a railroad station, an empty, desolate public square. The scenes of silence, of cold stone, of harsh neon lights, of antiseptic modern buildings rising from the rubble, all underscore the emptiness and the futility of their relationship.

Last Year at Marienbad (1961) is another dazzling film of the living dead. Resnais captures the ornate details of an elegant and elaborate chateau: its mirrors and chandeliers, its carved walls and ceilings,

Framing and space in Last Year at Marienbad: *watching a couple in a framed mirror; playing almost-checkers against a painted checkerboard; the woman (Delphine Seyrig) posed in front of a formal garden that may either be real or* trompe l'oeil

its formal gardens. His editing adds to the visual excitement, jumping about the castle so freely that he erases time and space completely. The film's problem, however, is translating the hypnotic visual show into some kind of coherent human experience. Time and space have been so thoroughly obliterated that every character and event in the film is totally ambiguous. A man may or may not meet a woman at what may or may not be a health resort; he may or may not have met her there one year before. He may or may not ask her to leave the resort with him, to flee the man who may or may not be her husband. At the end of the film, they may or may not leave the chateau together.

In this maze of time and faces, several dominant themes are quite clear. One of them is the contrast between sincere emotional interaction and stifling artificial conventions, as evoked by the cold, sterile ornateness of the castle itself and the woman's sinister "husband," who is both murderous (he enjoys the pistol range) and is infallible (he cannot be defeated at the matchstick game). A second clear theme is time itself. The man claims to have met the woman last year, but what exactly is a year? She has photographs in her room, clear mementos of the past, but the pictures seem to be of her in the present. At one point in the film a man bumps into a woman and spills her drink. Some forty-five minutes of film time continue from this point. Then Resnais returns to the spilled-drink sequence, with the characters in exactly the same positions as when the drink was spilled. Has Resnais equated forty-five minutes of screen time with an instantaneous flash of thought and feeling in a particular character's mind? And if it is a subjective flash, whose is it? Although the film's structure strikingly resembles the stream-of-consciousness narration of modern fiction, it is difficult to determine whose consciousness is streaming in the film—the man's, the woman's, the director-*auteur's*, or some combination of all of them? Perhaps the film is not to be interpreted at all but to be savored for its cold images and sensitive moments, much like *Chien andalou* or *Ballet Mécanique*. But these abstract-surrealist films were only two reels long.

La Guerre est finie (1966), a much less heralded Resnais film, is a much warmer, much more human film than either of his first two features. The film is also more lucid and comprehensible, reserving Resnais's jump-cutting into the past for special, isolated moments of the film that specifically evoke the past. Like the earlier films, *La Guerre est finie* asks how a man lives in the present given the fact of his past and, further, how he makes personal sense of his life if it makes no absolute sense.

Thirty years after the Spanish Civil War, a man (Yves Montand) continues to work for the Spanish underground, making regular trips into Spain from France to bring the Spanish workers revolutionary literature and strategy. Though the war is indeed over, it is not over for the man who has defined his life by fighting it and whose relationships with other people—friends, lover, mistress—are defined by his vocation. The climactic moment of the film comes when his vocation is challenged by a group of young leftists who find his methods and his crusade archaic, worthless, ineffective; they advocate not intellectual conversion and organization of the workers but violent revolution and dynamiting the society. The man rejects their callous challenge and continues to make his trips to Spain, fighting the finished war in his own way. And they, so Resnais implies, will continue to fight their war in their way long after it too is over. The important thing about the war for a participant is not the winning of it—for the film doubts that a just war can ever be won—but the fighting of it.

Like Truffaut's film career, Resnais's work divides roughly into a decade of agonized, existential (and somewhat political) black-and-white films and a later decade of more contented and more formal color style pieces (success seems to take its toll on anger and agony—except for Godard, who rebelled against his own success). *La Guerre est finie* was Resnais's last political film, and his next, *Je T'aime, Je T'aime* (1968), rather cynically used a science-fiction format to experiment with the tenses of film narrative—suggesting that *Marienbad*'s dizzying spatio-temporal leaps would make perfectly ordinary sense if we knew that the subjective consciousness of the central character was being manipulated by a time machine. For Resnais, the true time machine is cinema itself. *Providence* (1977) similarly uses his athletic, subjective editing to examine the narrative process rather than political commitment; Resnais studies a novelist's consciousness, wandering back and forth between the novel he is writing and the life he is living. Resnais's complete embracing of these purely formal (and formalistic) questions—whatever the psychological beauties of the films—has led to an obvious diminution of his critical reputation.

Several other French filmmakers—though not of the stature of Godard, Truffaut, and Resnais—also contributed to the reputation of the French film in the 1960s. Claude Chabrol was the first of the *Cahiers* critics to make a film. In films like *Les Cousins* (1959), *Les Bonnes Femmes* (1959), *Landru* (1962), *Les Biches* (1968), *Le Boucher* (1969), and *Violette* (1978), Chabrol reveals an interesting contrapuntal tension between the sexual passions of his characters and the carefully detailed, stiflingly bourgeois social environment. Chabrol specializes in case studies of bizarre psychological types and personal relationships that inevitably culminate in a grotesque murder.

Roger Vadim's first film, *And God Created Woman* (1956), also preceded the 1959 wave. Vadim began with a rough,

honest sexuality that made Brigitte Bardot a star, but his subsequent films became ponderously ornate, tasteless style pieces that leer as coyly at sex as Cecil B. DeMille ever did: *Les Liaisons Dangereuses* (1959), *Circle of Love* (1964), *Barbarella* (1968).

If Vadim was France's DeMille, Jacques Demy was its Busby Berkeley. In *The Umbrellas of Cherbourg* (1964), Demy took the tritest of melodramatic plots (boy loves girl; he goes into the army; she marries a rich suitor; he returns; their love can never be again) and decorated it with the richest frosting he could find. The film is 100 percent all-singing; even the most banal ideas—needing a penicillin shot, asking for a liter of gas—get the benefit of Michel Legrand's lush score. And the film's art director, Bernard Evein, adopted the aesthetics of the department-store window: if the wallpaper is orange with lavender flowers then the women must wear lavender dresses with orange flowers. When people match the wall paper, more subtle and psychological principles of fictional construction get overlooked.

Demy's wife, Agnes Varda, is a totally different kind of filmmaker: probing, thoughtful, intellectually sensitive to the problems of the artist and the difficulty of making life both happy and full. In *Cleo from Five to Seven* (1962), *Le Bonheur* (1965), and *Lion's Love* (1969), her central characters are all either women or artists and their problem is to come to terms with the undeniable fact of both physical and psychic pain. Similarly introspective are Eric Rohmer's gentle "Moral Tales" of love and longing—*My Night at Maud's* (1968), *Claire's Knee* (1971), and *Chloe in the Afternoon* (1972). Rohmer, like Truffaut, Godard, and Chabrol, graduated to the making of cinema from the *Cahiers du Cinéma*, which he edited after Bazin's death. A fifth of the *Cahiers* critics to make films, Jacques Rivette, explores the magic, the mystery of

Z: the synthesis of spy thriller and revolutionary political document

making and responding to stories in the
first place—in *Paris nous appartiennent*
(1961), *L'Amour fou* (1968), and especially
in the exuberant and improvisational
Celine and Julie Go Boating (1974).

Louis Malle is one of the most eclectic
directors of the first French Wave. In *The
Lovers* (1958), he shapes a graceful literary
study of the manners and world of the
very rich, culminating in the woman
throwing over both industrialist husband
and polo-playing lover to leave with the
young student with whom she spends the
night. *Zazie dans le Métro* (1960) is a
delightfully breezy, illogical, spirited film
that uses cinematic tricks to recreate the
literary and linguistic gags of Raymond
Queneau's novel. The film is one of
surprise and freedom, the director's hymn
to the spontaneous and unfettered. The
zany illogic of the film's story, editing,
and staging mirrors the illogic that little
Zazie embodies by being a petite
eight-year-old who knows how to talk

dirty. *Murmur of the Heart* (1971) seems a
synthesis of these earlier styles with its
child's-eye view of the restraints of adult
life and a wealthy, attractive mother's
attempts to manage both her family and
her love life. Malle's American film, *Pretty
Baby* (1977), similarly explores the
imaginativeness of children, the vibrancy
of American jazz, the richness of period
decor, and the moral constraints and
confusions of adult sexuality.

French filmmakers of the second Wave,
those to emerge in the late 1960s and
1970s, fit the paradigm suggested by the
opposite evolutions of Truffaut and
Godard. One group of younger
filmmakers concentrates entirely on
personal, experiential studies of human
sensation and interaction while the other
makes explicitly activist political films.
The most popular films of the latter
group have been Costa-Gavras's violent
and violently political films (*Z*, 1968; *The
Confession*, 1970; and *State of Siege*, 1973),

which, like the films of Godard and Resnais, mix their political radicalism with deliberately erratic and radical film styles: mixtures of driving suspense and social comment, human spontaneity and political commitment, elliptical jumps into the past and future, freeze-frames and slow motion, satirical comedy and passionate sincerity. Costa-Gavras's New Wave ancestry is especially apparent in the refreshing camera work of Raoul Coutard—prowling over faces, running through a crowd—whose work added similar insight and energy to *Breathless*, *Les Carabiniers*, and *Jules and Jim*. Gillo Pontecorvo (*The Battle of Algiers*, 1966; *Burn!*, 1970) is another radical in both style and ideology who uses the apparent surfaces of documentary, *cinéma-vérité* realism to give both life and immediacy to studies of commitment and liberation. Of course the discovery and development of the *cinéma vérité* documentary style was also a French contribution (as its name implies) of the New Wave era, the most influential films in that style probably being Jean Rouch's *Chronique d'un été* (1961) and Chris Marker's *Le Joli Mai* (1962).

Foremost of the personal, domestic group are the films of Alain Tanner, who applies a Marxist political analysis to the personal lives of middle-class citizens. Though Tanner is Swiss, his films are very French in look, language, and psychological theme. *The Salamander* (1972), *The Middle of the World* (1974), and *Jonah, Who Will Be 25 in the Year 2000* (1976) examine the tangled interconnections of erotic sensitivity, familial responsibility, vocational fulfillment, and political sensibility. The Tanner characters, who tend to be just slightly off beat, mildly extraordinary people living extremely ordinary, middle-class lives, attempt to balance these conflicting commitments—which threaten to rip apart the fabric of contemporary domestic life—without betraying themselves or any one of them. Among

the other newer New Wave directors to watch are Charles Tachella (*Cousin, Cousine*, 1975); Tanner's assistant, Claude Goretta (*The Wonderful Crook*, 1975; *The Lacemaker*, 1977); Truffaut's assistant, Bertrand Blier (*Going Places*, 1974; *Get Out Your Handkerchiefs*, 1978); Jean Eustache (*The Mother and the Whore*, 1973); Nelly Kaplan (*Charles et Lucie*, 1979); and Claude Miller (*The Better Way*, 1976). Among the New Wave characteristics these films share are their careful rendering of the textures of internal human sensations and experiences (particularly their sensitivity to women and to antimachismo states of male consciousness) and their elliptical narrative structures that emphasize internal psychological development rather than a linear, chronological presentation of events.

The French (and Italian) Revolution

Perhaps the most important contribution of the French and Italian postwar cinemas was not the addition of at least a dozen masters of the film art and several dozen masterpieces of film art to the body of world cinema. Even more significant— from the vantage point of over three decades of hindsight—is the way that these two national movements revolutionized the values and aesthetics of the motion picture, affecting and influencing the entire world's cinema in the sound era as much as Griffith, Murnau, or Eisenstein did in the silents. The stylistic revolution that began in Italy and culminated in France spread worldwide, eventually capturing the cinema of America, Europe, and even the Third World. The Italian movement was more concerned with content than style—the close, careful observation of ordinary human beings in their social contexts—and hence its great impact on national cinemas, like those of Czechoslovakia or Third World nations, which produced films that juxtaposed sympathetic, close studies of working- and lower-class people with a discussion of political issues. But the French movement essentially created a new content through style—and hence its great impact in America. That new style came at a propitious moment to fill an aesthetic void—at a time when the American cinema had become bankrupt in both content and style. Hollywood films attempted to apply the old stylistic values to the new wide-screen color film; the two European cinemas discovered what to do with the wide screen and, later, color.

As in the past, in both the Griffith and the Lubitsch-Clair eras, a technological discovery produced a new style that determined a new content. Whereas the old narrow-screen black-and-white film was a more distant, objective, rational experience (perfectly suited to lengthy scenes of dialogue, a rational narrative continuity, and images that essentially supported a film's story and issues), the new wide-screen color film was a more immediate, subjective, and kinetic experience (in which the physical sensations produced by the images and sounds were often the primary bases for understanding a film's story and issues). Composition in the "Golden Frame" (as the narrow screen was called) was indeed composition *in* the frame, deriving from classical conceptions of space, balance, proportion, and perspective. Although the best Hollywood directors noted how poorly suited was the stretched-out wide-screen's shape to such compositional values, they merely tried to apply them as best they could. But effective wide-screen composition was to become composition *out* of the frame, in the sense that the screen no longer produced compositions of images to be viewed but instead used its images to strike, assault, and prod the viewer into experiencing sensations that mirrored those of the characters. The sheer size and grandeur of the wide screen aided and necessitated its physical

assault. And so all the cinematic tricks—the freeze-frames, the jiggling hand-held camera, the zoom lens, the elliptical jumps in the plot, the jump- and shock-cutting—all became ways of conveying subjective sensations to an audience.

This new stylistic assumption determined the content of the two kinds of film that primarily used it. The subject of the films either became experiential itself—the feelings, sensations, and experiences of people living through an ultimate or exquisite moment of their lives, often ending with a Joycean "epiphany" of discovery (Truffaut, early Godard, Antonioni, Fellini, Rohmer). Or the subject of the films became political, using radical stylistic devices to produce a fuller perception of political and social realities, obviously and even admittedly influenced by Brecht (such as the later Godard, Costa-Gavras, and Pontecorvo films). Or the subject of the films became some mysterious and personal combination of politics and experiential sensations (Resnais, Bertolucci, Pasolini, Tanner). Ultimately, the films were about perception—either of emotional or social, inner or outer, realities. And they used all the cinema's devices of perception to make the audience perceive.

It is interesting (and perhaps ironic) that these discoveries were made by the disciples of André Bazin, for Bazin's view was that cinema was the ultimate transcriber of reality, the ultimate discovery of the means of getting nature into our power by reproducing it. For Bazin, the filmmaker's role was to disappear completely, making the film reveal the reality in front of the lens rather than to mirror the personal perceptions of the filmmaker. Bazin's favorite filmmakers—von Stroheim, Welles, Renoir, Flaherty, Chaplin, Rossellini—were those who "put their faith in reality" rather than in the image, as did Eisenstein (who constructed his own reality by means of montage). Bazin's

New Wave disciples are much more in the modernist tradition of defining reality as only that which each person can subjectively perceive. (There is no reality; there are only our own realities.) As a result, the cinematic tricks of these French directors were far more intrusive and self-conscious in their manipulations of "reality"—of spatial, temporal, and causal continuity—than Bazin's theory encouraged.

But then Bazin, who died in 1958, did not live to see the total conversion to the wide screen and color. In all fairness to Bazin, he did envision the possibility of a future period when the stylistic demands of the cinema would change. He noted that the cinema had attained a stability of style and technique that had remained constant for over two decades (as indeed they had since the introduction of synchronized sound), and he predicted that the introduction of a radically different technology might well produce a radically different cinema style and content. Then came the technological revolution, and the postwar cinemas of Italy and France (Bazin's disciples among them) brought the rest of the world into its next cinematic era.

14 Emerging National Traditions

The decades of the 1950s, 60s, and 70s saw the emergence of other distinctive and important national movements, the products of many of the same causes that produced the postwar French and Italian successes. First, the postwar period encouraged personality and individuality in the cinema—new things to "say" and new ways to "say" them—because the old formulae and stylistic assumptions were breaking down. Second, and closely related, the audience, the technology, and the world were all changing. Times of instability and change tend to encourage originality rather than formula. Third— and also closely related—the American film industry was in severe trouble artistically and commercially. Prizes at international film festivals (a new sign of the times) not only brought honor to previously unknown film artists and industries but, perhaps more important, bookings. American films were no longer powerful or attractive enough to keep foreign films off the screen, either abroad or in America itself. Ironically, by the mid-1970s the wheel came full circle. By adopting the styles and assumptions of the foreign film movements, the American cinema not only became strong enough again to keep most foreign competition off American screens but began winning the prizes at the international film festivals as well.

Sweden

The name of Ingmar Bergman is as synonymous with the new cinematic directions of the last twenty-five years as Fellini's, Antonioni's, or Godard's. Bergman, like Truffaut and Godard, is the product of a rich national film tradition. The Swedish film industry, though never producing a great number of films, enjoys a long and distinguished history. Bergman, an actor, playwright, and stage director, learned his film craft from Alf Sjöberg, Sweden's most important director in the first two decades of sound production. And Sjöberg learned his craft in the silent era of Victor Sjöström and Mauritz Stiller.

Both Stiller and Sjöström combined the visual and poetic power of the northern landscapes with stories of realistic passions and mystical influences—exactly as

The Seventh Seal: *Death as confessor. The equation of black, death, darkness, and the Church*

Bergman would do forty years later. The three consistent traits of the Swedish silents were, first, their use of natural imagery to evoke and convey human passions as in Sjöström's use of the sea in *A Man There Was* (1916), and of the mountains and fjords in *The Outlaw and His Wife* (1917), and Stiller's use of the lake of ice in *Sir Arne's Treasure* (1919), and of the snow and mountains in *The Atonement of Gosta Berling* (1923); second, their satirical and critical condemnation of social hypocrisies and injustices, as in Sjöström's *The Outlaw and His Wife,* and Stiller's *Erotikon* (1920); and third, the influence of cosmic, metaphysical forces in human affairs. The eerie, ghostly carriage that comes for the tramp who dies at precisely midnight on New Year's Eve in Sjöström's *The Phantom Carriage* (1920) is clearly the ancestor of the hearse that comes for Isak Borg in Bergman's *Wild Strawberries*, and Sjöström's figure of death with his scythe is an equally clear ancestor of Death in Bergman's *The Seventh Seal*. The films of Sjöström and Stiller were so influential that both men came to Hollywood to work for Zukor or Mayer. Even the title of Sjöström's most important American film, *The Wind* (1927), implies the story's interpenetration of nature and human responses. The metaphorical unity in the Swedish film tradition is striking, for Victor Sjöström —Sweden's first film master—played the role of the old doctor in Bergman's *Wild Strawberries*.

Bergman directed his first film, *Crisis,*

in 1945. For ten years Bergman and his first photographer, Gunnar Fischer, felt their way together within the film form, discovering how to synthesize the drama (Bergman's first love) with the visual image, building a stock company of actors sensitive to each other and to the director: Max von Sydow, Gunnar Bjørnstrand, Eva Dahlbeck, Ingrid Thulin, Harriet Andersson, Bibi Andersson. *Smiles of a Summer Night* (1955) was probably Bergman's first fully mature work, although critics in retrospect now point to signs of the Bergman mastery in *Thirst* (1949), *Monika* (1952), and *The Naked Night* (1953). But it was *The Seventh Seal* (1956) that first conquered audiences throughout the world, and within two years Bergman had produced two more films, *Wild Strawberries* (1957) and *The Magician* (1958), to cement his reputation. These three films—*The Seventh Seal, Wild Strawberries,* and *The Magician*—make up a central unit in the Bergman canon, a complementary trilogy of films despite their differences in tone, style, and historical milieu. The films represent the best of Bergman's early period; they are also a pool of ideas and images from which all his later work seems to be drawn.

The key question about *The Seventh Seal* is whether it is a metaphysical allegory told in earthly terms, or whether it is an earthly allegory told in metaphysical terms. Its story is of a medieval knight, Antoninus Blok, who returns home from the crusades only to encounter Death waiting for him on a desolate, rocky beach. Blok challenges Death to a game of chess, knowing the inevitable result but obviously playing for time. Blok wants the time for one reason: to discover the value of living. Everywhere around him he sees death: from the crusades, from the plague, from flagellation and superstition. Is there life?

At the end of the film, Blok loses the chess game and Death overtakes him and his party. But, as Blok himself says, the delay has been most significant, for the knight has accomplished one important vital action. He has helped a young family of simple innocent folk escape the clutches of Death. This happy family of father (significantly named Joseph), mother (named Mary), and infant becomes the film's trinity of life. At the end of the film, they stand by the sea in the sunlight, watching Death lead the knight and his party across a hilltop in shadow.

The film's central contrast is the opposition of the ways of life and the forces of death. The Church—organized, dogmatic religion—becomes emblematic of everything in the film connected with death. The Church instigated the deadly crusades. The Church decorates its walls with pictures of death. The Church inspires men to frenzies of prayer and mourning and mortification. The Church burns human scapegoats to keep the congregation in terror. The men of the Church wear black, the color of death. In fact, Antoninus mistakes the figure of Death for a priest when he makes confession. Bergman underscores the minions of death with darkness, shadows, and the religious smoke of the censer or the stake. This "holy" smoke dominates the religious sequences, befouling the clarity of the scene with a substance that seems like both fog and poison.

Opposed to the film's dark moments are its moment of life, clarity, and light. The scenes between Joseph and Mary—the two strolling players—are slightly overexposed, brilliantly bathed in light. The scene in which Blok partakes of their happiness, when the group sits in the sunshine to eat wild strawberries, is another scene of peace and light. Nature is not always dark and dead; it is also bright and sweet. The real religion, the real humanity in the film stems from the sincere, unselfish feelings the characters have for one another—husband for wife; parent for child; the cynical squire for his

The Seventh Seal. *Mary (Bibi Andersson) and Joseph (Nils Poppe): two actors in the sunlight*

master the knight, for the tormented farm girl, and the tortured actor Joseph. In the course of the film, Antoninus Blok discovers the value of those feelings and feels them himself.

In Bergman's allegory we all play chess with Death. Life and death are inseparably close. One of the film's most haunting and, at the same time, most comic sequences is the one in which Death chops down the tree in which Skat, an actor, is hiding. Skat plummets to his death while Bergman's camera remains riveted to the sawed-off trunk of the tree. Immediately after the sound of the crashing tree, a cute little squirrel jumps on the tree stump and twitches its nose. Life and death are that close. And so are comedy and tragedy, for Bergman uses

comedy as sardonic earthy comment on a serious film's weighty and philosophical themes. Like the gravedigger in *Hamlet*, the squire in *The Seventh Seal* (and Granny in the later *Magician*) treats death as a bitter and hopeless joke. Since we all play chess with death and since we all must suffer through that hopeless joke, the only question about the game is how long it will last and how well we will play it. To play it well, to live, is to love and not to hate the body and the mortal as the Church urges in Bergman's metaphor. In this sense Antoninus Blok wins the game with Death; it is the only way that game can be won.

Wild Strawberries puts the same theme in modern dress. The film begins with a vision of death, the old man's dream in which he sees a hearse roll down a desolate street, in which he sees himself inside the hearse's coffin, in which the vision of himself in the coffin grabs hold of the dreamer and tries to pull him into it, in which he sees that time has stopped, that the clocks have no hands. Bergman increases the dream's impression of whiteness, of desolation, of unreality by overexposing the whole vision, giving the dream world the pale texture of a ghostly shroud. Then the old doctor wakes up. Since he perceives the closeness of death he is haunted by questions about the value of the life he has lived. Ironically, this doctor, Isak Borg (played by Sjøstrøm), aged 78, is about to be honored by society for the value of his life's work; a university is to award him an honorary degree. Despite the university's assessment of his life's worth, the doctor is not so certain about it. The rest of the film shows him groping for an answer. Like *The Seventh Seal*, the film is structured as a journey. As Borg travels along the road toward the university, three kinds of encounters influence his thought: encounters with his present relationships (son, housekeeper, daughter-in-law, mother), encounters with people on the road (three young, robust hikers and a bickering, middle-aged married couple), encounters with visions of his past that keep crowding into his brain.

When Borg examines his present relationships he sees nothing but emptiness and sterility. He has tyrannized his old housekeeper of some forty years, taking her completely for granted, never realizing that she has served him as faithfully and as lovingly as any wife ever could. His mother is a shell of a human being, living totally in the past, measuring her life by the little scrapbook mementos and childhood trinkets that she has dutifully preserved. But even worse is Borg's relationship with his son and daughter-in-law. He has tyrannized them, too, refusing to give his son the financial

means to be independent. Borg's great legacy to his son is transferring his bitterness, his nihilism, his contempt for life. So successfully has Borg passed on this dowry that the son and daughter-in-law are in danger of separating. The son hates life so bitterly that he refuses to bring children into it.

The two groups that Borg encounters on the road are diametric opposites. The youths are shining, vital, energetic; they devour life with a callous yet honest robustness (Ibsen called it the Viking Spirit), unfettered by social convention, disillusionment, and failure. The middle-aged couple are slaves of a now empty passion, tied to one another by habit, by argument, and by the need to share futility. Both encounters trigger Borg's visions. The pair with blasted lives produces Borg's bitterest moment in which he attends a hell-like school (the scene echoes the school scene in Strindberg's *A Dream Play*) and receives pedantic, empty lectures from the husband. The doctor's life has been as empty and pedantic as that schoolroom.

But the young trio, particularly the girl, stimulates Borg to dream of his childhood, his dazzling summers at the family summer house, where he felt both bitter disappointment (in romance) and the blinding happiness of youth. Bergman

---

Wild Strawberries. *Official societal definitions of a meaningful life—the Doctor (Victor Sjøstrøm) honored by the university*

Wild Strawberries. *Summer, sunlight, whiteness, and the memories of youth*

shoots these summer scenes with a clarity, a brilliance, and a whiteness that echo the scenes between Mary and Joseph in *The Seventh Seal*. Summer and sunshine, in fact, are consistent Bergman metaphors for moments of human happiness in *Smiles of a Summer Night, Monika, Summer Interlude* (1950), *The Virgin Spring* (1959), and *Persona*. As in *The Seventh Seal*, there are wild strawberries, tart and sweet, alive, fresh. Borg's final vision of his summer youth is of a brilliant sunshiny day, the whole family outdoors in the clear bright air, the girls and boys in white, his mother and father, despite their emotional difficulties, alone together in a boat on the lake.

Like Antoninus Blok, Isak Borg translates his vision into human action. At the end of his journey, he realizes the irrelevancy of the university's social pageant. Instead, he shows his human responsiveness by proposing marriage to his housekeeper, by offering to ease his pressure on his son, and by, in effect, reconciling son and daughter-in-law to one another. Borg has taken a journey toward life, and the film's implication is that he has helped his son do the same, preparing him to procreate new life. Borg contentedly falls asleep, no longer haunted by clocks without hands.

In *The Magician*, Bergman turns from the relationship of death to life to examine the relationship of art to life. *The Magician* is also a story of the road. A nineteenth-century magic lanternist and his assistants travel by coach to a town where they are stopped by the local authorities. These bureaucratic devotees of pure reason are anxious to see the lanternist display his wares, to see if his illusion is powerful enough to unsettle their rational reality. The magician's art is indeed powerful enough to drive one spectator to hang himself and another to the point of madness. And yet the bureaucrats judge the man's performance a failure. In the midst of his dejection, word comes to the lanternist that his presence is desired at court. He will be honored by both the coin and prestige of the throne. In an unexpected mood of joy and triumph and (of course) sunshine, the magician's coach sets out for the court.

The great power of *The Magician* is that the film operates on two levels simultaneously. There are, in fact, two magicians; one of them is Vogler, the lanternist; the other is Bergman, the filmmaker. Both Vogler and Bergman work on the principle that the trick, the fake, the illusion can seize the mind more powerfully than the expected reality. Vogler's life is a tissue of lies and tricks. He is not mute as he pretends to be; his hair is dyed; his assistant is not a boy but his wife. Everything about the man is false—a game of mirrors and deceptive appearances like his lantern show. But the same is true of the film director's art. Bergman plays tricks on *his* audience as ruthlessly as Vogler plays them on his.

The film's opening scene is a forest during a thunderstorm; it is a dark and ominous one: murky, shadowy, back-lit in a gothic manner that consciously evokes John Ford. In this first sequence, Bergman introduces us to a dark, shadowy figure who seems to be an apparition of death (a conscious parody of his own Death figure in *The Seventh Seal*?) and who appears to die in the coach before the magician arrives at the town. But later in the film we discover that the figure is not dead at all. The director has deliberately tricked us into believing him dead. He also tricks us with the magician's apparent muteness and his assistant's sex. But his ultimate trick on us is also the magician's ultimate trick on the bureaucrat: Vogler mysteriously lures the official to an attic, locks him in, and then reduces him to absolute terror with thumping sounds, invisible attacks, and the vision of a detached eyeball swimming in an ink well. Bergman reduces us to terror, too; the sequence is so inexplicable, so evocative of the powers of the unknown, so tensely controlled in its rhythm of sounds and cutting.

As though Bergman hasn't demonstrated the magician-director's powers convincingly enough, he ends the film with a grand artistic caprice. The film director has the instant power to change failure to victory, gloom to triumph: he can introduce a messenger with a letter from the king; he can add the music of trumpets and triumph to the sound track; he can shoot the scene in bright sunshine rather than murky shadow. The artistic principle behind all this conscious trickery is simply to show that reason, that the forces of society, have an undeniable power; society can put people in jail or decree their failure. But the irrational, the weapon of the artist, also has an undeniable power; its appearances can capture not the reason but the feelings of man. And feeling, as both *The Seventh Seal* and *Wild Strawberries* assert, is an essential human function.

The later Bergman films return again and again to the same ground as these central three. The films that Bergman himself designated as his trilogy—*Through a Glass Darkly* (1961), *Winter Light* (1962), and *The Silence* (1962)—all seek meaningful personal values—love—in a world in which human life has no

absolute purpose other than to be. *Cries and Whispers* (1973) returns to the issue of *Wild Strawberries*: the way that the awareness of an impending death defines the values of living. And *Persona* (1967) combines the self-concious cinematic tricks of *The Magician* with a psychoanalytic study of a mind that, like Isak Borg and Antoninus Blok, views the experience of living as a bleak and lifeless lie. That *Persona* parallels *The Magician*'s concern with art and illusion is especially clear in the surname of the actress, Vogler, which is the same as the magician's.

But despite the similarities of these to the earlier films, the Bergman cinematic style had altered radically. Whereas the earlier films generated their philosophical meanings through lucid dialogue, supported by appropriate images and well-plotted literary structures (revealing Bergman's origins in the theatre), the later films incorporated the elliptical and irrational cinematic devices of the French masters, their disruption of spatial, temporal, and causal continuity. Bergman's stylistic shift may be partly the result of his observation of these French manipulations of cinematic perception, partly the result of his realization that the probing of human perception and internal psychology required a more elusive technique, and partly the result of his switching to a more experimental cinematographer, Sven Nykvist, who replaced Gunnar Fischer in the 1960s. The late Bergman films are increasingly concerned with internal psychology—the fears, anguish, and even diseases of individual human brains—as though devoting themselves entirely to the anguished dream world of Isak Borg or the irrational illusionistic world of magician Vogler's attic.

Persona is Bergman's late masterpiece, his most complex film, his most difficult, and his most dazzling display of technical virtuosity. On its surface, the film is a psychological case study of Elizabeth Vogler, a famous and successful actress who went blank on stage during a performance of *Electra* and has refused to speak since. Her refusal to communicate is symptomatic of her feeling that human existence is merely a collection of meaningless lies, that there is nothing to achieve, that success is an illusion and happiness is the biggest lie of them all. For Elizabeth, to speak is to lie. She is treated in a mental hospital by the young, energetic, and dedicated nurse, Alma, and the cure then takes both of them out of the hospital to the seaside home of the hospital's head psychiatrist. At that seaside retreat, where the nurse does all the talking, the two women share both moments of tender intimacy and of intense hatred. The end of this process is the actress's apparent return to communication, to her life on the stage and with her family, and Nurse Alma's return to her job, somewhat shaken by the experience but continuing on her way.

What complicates the case study is Bergman's elliptical and nonlinear way of telling this story, which gives rise to several motifs that extend far beyond a simple examination of an aberrant human mind. First, Bergman presents his film not as a mirror of human events but quite frankly as a film about human events. The process of making and watching the film plays a role in the film. *Persona* begins with the illumination of a projection bulb, with the spooling of a reel of film on the projector, with the familiar projection leader that counts down the numbers—11, 10, 9 . . .—on a screen before a film begins, and with several miscellaneous clips of other films interspersed (a slapstick comedy, an animated cartoon). It ends with a loop of film slipping out of the projection gate, with sprocket holes, with the white glare of a blank screen and the extinguishing of the projection bulb with which the film began. Between these two self-referential devices the film refers to itself by, at one point, showing the camera filming a scene

(it is the scene of the actress onstage in *Electra* and gives rise to the question of whether she is acting on the stage or on a sound-stage), and, at another, by the film's appearing to stop, rip, and burn in the projection gate.

Bergman calls attention to the film as a film because he wants to emphasize that what follows is a fiction, an illusion—a sequence of light and shadow on a flat screen. The audience has entered the world of art and chimera, not of nature and reality. But Bergman's film then gives this clear dichotomy another twist, for is the world of nature any more solid, any more real than the one of artistic illusion? That is the question that propels the rest of the film after its projectionist prologue. For example, at one point in the film Alma believes she hears Elizabeth Vogler speak to her—and we believe we hear her too. But Elizabeth denies speaking, and indeed the words were so soft and so misty that we begin to doubt what we thought we heard and wonder if she really did speak or if Alma merely imagined it. At another point in the film, Alma believes she hears a noise in the house and discovers Elizabeth's husband, who mistakes the nurse for his own wife and begins making love to Alma as Elizabeth watches. And yet he cannot possibly be there in that house; he must be the product of Alma's imagination. And yet there he stands, concretely before us and before the nurse. These are only two of the film's sequences that intentionally cast doubt on the reliability of the senses. Is the concrete world any more tangible, any more "real" than the "intangible" world of the imagination? Are the two so easily separated as the words *tangible* and *intangible* imply? And if the illusion can be as tangible as the reality, is this film (which has proclaimed itself as illusory from its start) any less real than any other phenomenon in nature?

This phenomenological collapse of the familiar distinction between illusion and reality leads Bergman to collapse another familiar kind of distinction. Nothing is usually so unique and consistent, in art or in the psychoanalyst's definitions, as individual human personality. Bergman has titled his film *Persona*, a term which can refer either to a role in the drama (as in *dramatis personae*) or to a psychological type in reality (as in Jungian terminology or split persona-lity). One of the assumptions of such terminology is that individual and distinct *personae* exist. The film apparently presents us with two opposite, antithetical *personae*—nurse and patient (can an opposition be clearer?). Each has her own part to play and even her own "costume" (patient's gown, nurse's uniform).

The patient is "ill" because she has discovered the futility, the instability, the lies of all life's definitions: success, marriage, family, wealth. The head psychiatrist explains this illness as Elizabeth's escape from the lies of life by silence, as merely a role (like her roles on the stage) created out of apathy and of which she will become bored. That the psychiatrist is right is irrelevant, for the doctor fails to perceive that the very truths, terms, and definitions of her science are indeed the very lies that Elizabeth (and Bergman) has discovered and cannot accept.

Nurse Alma would appear to be Elizabeth's opposite: contented with her job, with her fiancé (whom she admittedly does not love), with her optimistic and unquestioning acceptance of reality's ambiguities as solid verities. And then Bergman collapses these two opposites—nurse and patient—into one. For the nurse does all the talking; she ironically is the one actually undergoing the psychoanalytic treatment while Elizabeth plays the psychiatrist and merely listens. (A further irony is that Alma describes herself as a good listener. And perhaps she is, for she starts listening to herself.) The film is Alma's psychodrama, not Elizabeth's. It is Alma who confesses

her doubts and insecurities; it is Alma who is driven to acts of violence, inconsistency, jealousy, frenzy, and paranoia. One suspects that Elizabeth is playing her psychiatrist's role rather deliberately, if only to prove that she is capable of reaching another human being, no matter how vicious that reaching becomes.

Bergman's film constantly emphasizes that the two women are one and the one is two. First, the two women (played by Liv Ullman and Bibi Andersson) look strikingly alike. Second, there is the magnificent ghostly scene before the mirror (which may or may not be a dream since it looks as if it were shot through a fog or gray gauze), in which the two women embrace, their two heads seemingly emerging from a single body. Finally, there is the lengthy scene at the kitchen table that Bergman shoots in its entirety twice. First, he shoots Alma's entire story from her point of view, camera riveted on Elizabeth—who is wearing a black sweater and black headband—moving the camera steadily toward Elizabeth's face with a series of lap dissolves (a series of shots that overlap and seem to melt into one another). Then Bergman shoots the story over again from Elizabeth's point of view, camera riveted on Alma (a conventional film would shoot the sequence twice but cut back and forth between the two points of view in the final editing)—who is wearing an identical "costume" of black sweater and black headband—the camera again moving steadily closer to the subject's face with another series of identical lap dissolves (at exactly the same points of the speech as in Elizabeth's previous sequence). The faces begin to mirror each other. Finally, Bergman literally blends the two faces into one (thesis-antithesis-synthesis), using half of each woman's face to make the entire composite portrait (and it is impossible to tell whose face forms the left side and whose the right; it is impossible to tell at whom exactly one is

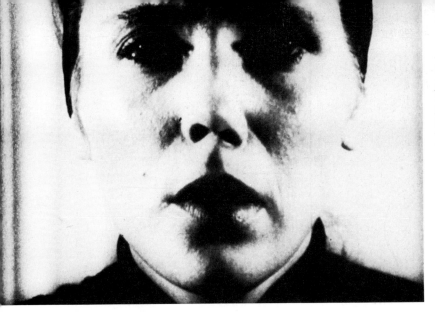

looking). The two opposite *personae* are literally, tangibly one—a concrete illusion that Bergman has produced by means of the filmmaker's art.

The ultimate impression of *Persona* is of an elusive coherency, a unified but hauntingly evasive treatment of the issues of illusion and reality, art and nature, tangibility and insubstantiality, subjectivity and objectivity, definitions and definability. The result of this meeting of the two *personae* is that Elizabeth succeeds in shaking Alma, in giving her an "existential shudder" (the same shudder that produced the actress's silence initially). And Bergman's film is intended to haunt his audience with the same kind of shudder as he pulls the rug of our comfortable and functional definitions of reality and psychology out from under our feet. Bergman could accomplish this shudder only by eschewing the conventional linear narrative, by boldly proclaiming the discontinuity of time and space, by interjecting reminders that the cinema, grand illusion though it is, is no grander an illusion than the reality that we accept as tangible and real. Only Bergman's elusive, elliptical, antirational style could convey a vision of life as elusive, indefinable, and irrational without betraying it. Though the film begins by

proclaiming that it is art and not life, what Bergman paradoxically means is that the film is life indeed.

Although Ingmar Bergman is the unquestioned directorial star of the postwar Swedish industry, several later and lesser lights have appeared in the last decade: the lush, pictorial, fatalistic romanticism of Bo Widerberg's *Elvira Madigan* (1967); the close, affectionate observation of Swedish immigrants in Jan Troell's *The Emigrants* (1972); the frank sexuality and the probing of the relationship between mind and body in Vilgot Sjøman's *I Am Curious* (Yellow and Blue, 1969) or the elegant depiction of incest in Sjøman's *My Sister, My Love* (1969). These last works were very close to a Swedish "subgenre" that became familiar to many American audiences who may never even have heard of Ingmar Bergman. Using its reputation as one of the world's most sexually liberated nations, Sweden unleashed a series of sexploitation films on the world market—*Inga, Helga, 491, I a Woman* (Parts 1, 2, and 3!)—that played extended runs on New York's 42nd Street and in the seamier neighborhoods of many other cities. Like the Italian cinema, the Swedish industry discovered it could make money from its trash as well as its art.

The Man in the White Suit: *the realistic texture of the British documentary tradition flavoring the comedy of Alec Guinness, surrounded by the tubes and wires of his scientific apparatus*

The English Social Realists

The British film has never quite recovered the experimental and artistic uniqueness of the era of Hepworth, Urban, Smith, Williamson, and Collings, which disappeared just before the First World War. The common language made England such a Hollywood colony that the British government passed special quota laws to protect the native cinema in the era of the talkies. A British theatre owner, to stay in business, was obliged to show a certain quota of British-made films. These quotas protected no one and produced a flood of artless, craftless cheapies that served as second features (sometimes screened at 10 A.M.) for the American films that everyone came to see. If a British film did score an international success—such as Alexander Korda's *The Private Life of Henry the Eighth* (1933) or Hitchcock's *The 39 Steps*—its director or star almost immediately departed for Hollywood. Charles Laughton and Leslie Howard were as much a part of the Hollywood of the past

as Richard Burton, Julie Christie, Peter Sellers, Glenda Jackson, Michael York, and Peter O'Toole are of the "Hollywood" of today. Alfred Hitchcock's conversion to Hollywood budgets and procedures has been duplicated by the similar conversion of David Lean—from his stylish Dickens adaptations like *Great Expectations* (1946) and *Oliver Twist* (1947), to *The Bridge on the River Kwai* (1957), *Lawrence of Arabia* (1962), *Doctor Zhivago* (1965), and *Ryan's Daughter* (1970). Carol Reed has also gone the same route from taut Hitchcockesque thrillers like *Odd Man Out* (1947) and *The Third Man* (1949) to *Oliver!* (1968).

For fifteen years after the Second World War, the British film seemed synonymous with four cinematically conventional, although carefully crafted, genres. First, there were the highly polished, fluently acted adaptations of the literary classics: Lean's films of Dickens, Olivier's later adaptations of Shakespeare (*Hamlet*, 1948; *Richard III*, 1955), and Anthony Asquith's adaptations of Rattigan and Wilde (*The Winslow Boy*, 1949; *The Browning Version*, 1951; and *The Importance of Being Earnest*, 1952). Second, there were the suspenseful mystery thrillers— tightly edited, subtly acted—of wartime military assignments or postwar political cabals. Third, there were the understated satirical "little" comedies made at the Ealing Studios by Robert Hamer (*Kind Hearts and Coronets*, 1949; *Father Brown*, 1954), Alexander Mackendrick (*Tight Little Island*, 1948; *The Man in the White Suit*, 1951; *The Ladykillers*, 1955), Charles Crichton (*The Lavender Hill Mob*, 1951), and Anthony Kimmins (*The Captain's Paradise*, 1953). Most of these films starred Alec Guinness. And fourth, there were the lavish ballet spectacles of Michael Powell and Emeric Pressburger (*The Red Shoes*, 1948; *The Tales of Hoffman*, 1950). The general traits of all four of these British genres were a subtle understatement, expert acting, carefully realistic decor, and a firm control of taut narrative construction.

Among the most distinctive and significant work in the British film between the era of Charles Urban and 1959 was the documentary film movement of the 1930s and 1940s. Sponsored by the government and directed by filmmakers like John Grierson, Paul Rotha, Basil Wright, Harry Watt, Edgar Anstey, and Humphrey Jennings, the British documentaries developed the craft of capturing the surfaces of reality to illuminate the essences beneath them. The realist texture that seemed to distinguish British fictional films from Hollywood's was especially obvious in the purely realist documentary films. To some extent, the new British film of 1959 began with a similar premise. This new British film was the product of several influences: of the British documentary tradition; of the new class-conscious British novels and plays by authors like John Osborne, John Braine, Arnold Wesker, Alan Sillitoe, and Alun Owen; of the Italian neorealist films; of the new spirit of free cinema that was emerging in France at the same time. The result of these many influences was a series of films that was radically different from the polished, elegant, escapist films of Lean, Asquith, and Reed.

The new British films, like the Italian neorealist ones, emphasized the poverty of the worker, the squalor of working-class life, the difficulty of keeping a home and keeping one's self-respect at the same time, the social assumptions that sentence a person with no education and a working-class dialect to a lifetime of bare survival. To emphasize the dreary mediocrity of the working-class life, the British directors turned their cameras on the oppressive smoke of factories, the dull and drizzly weather at their stifling seaside resorts, the dingy and smoky feel of the pubs where they try to escape, the bare and faded austerity of the rooms they can afford to rent. In the midst of this intentionally barren and gray world, the directors focus on a common man reacting to his surroundings—bitter, brutal, angry, tough. These heroes of the films, traditionally labeled "angry young men," react in one of two ways to the working-class prisons of their lives: they try to grab some of the swag of the upper-class life for themselves, or, failing that, they break things. Their tragedy is usually that their only talent is loving and society does not reward that kind of talent.

Jack Clayton's *Room at the Top* (1959) was the first of the working-class British films to earn an international reputation and to make money. Clayton did not come to the films as a young rebel but as a tireless perfectionist-craftsman who had worked his way up in the British film industry. Clayton's care and craftsmanship were as responsible for the film's success as was its sociological content. Joe Lampton (Laurence Harvey), an ambitious young man with a provincial accent and a provincial education, takes a job at Brown's factory in a northern industrial city. Joe quickly learns the economic facts of life. He becomes enamored of a posh residential area of the city known as "the top," a hill that dominates the town. Most attractive of all the houses on "the top" is that of Mr. Brown, the owner of the factory and commercial lord of the town. Brown himself had worked his way out of the working class, only to don class snobbery and to join the Conservative Club once he had gotten to "the top."

Joe sets his sights on Susan, Brown's daughter, a rich, pretty, but emotionally shallow girl who responds to human affection with the same intensity as to a brisk set of tennis. On his way to capturing Susan, Joe meets an older, warmer woman (Simone Signoret) who reveals to him what two people are capable of feeling for one another. She,

Two angry young men surrounded by the shabby respectability of their working-class lives: Laurence Harvey, Hermione Baddely, and Simone Signoret in Room at the Top; *Richard Burton and Mary Ure in* Look Back in Anger.

automobile accident. And so Joe marries Susan. He gets his room at the top. Only now he does not want it. He sits in a taxi on the day of his gala socialite wedding. It should be the great moment of his life, the realization of his driving ambition. But Susan sits next to him chattering about how "super" their life will be together. And Joe's eyes fill with tears. Their life together will be anything but super, top or no top.

Clayton's handling of the film shows his experience and craft. He gets the best English-language performance of her career from Simone Signoret and the most virile, least mannered performance of his career from Laurence Harvey. Compositionally, Clayton has not only exerted great care in bathing the film in wet, dreary, smoky grays but also in surrounding the characters with the importance of Brown's name and power in the industrial town. On billboards, outside railway windows, reflected in the puddles on the street, hanging on one of his smokestacks, is the name of Brown, an ever-present reminder of the temptation of money and power, the temptation to which Joe easily yields, unwittingly damning himself.

That Clayton's commitment is more to his craft than to his class-conscious subject matter becomes clearer in his subsequent films—*The Innocents* (1961), *The Pumpkin Eater* (1963), and *The Great Gatsby* (1974). *The Innocents* leaves the gray dirty world of the present for the costumed grace of a country manor house of the nineties. Clayton adapts Henry James's *The Turn of the Screw*, a novella with one of the most debated critical questions in literary history. Has James written a story of real ghosts or a story of phantoms created by the neurotic brain of a sexually starved woman? Clayton decides, as have many literary critics, that the ambiguity in the story is intentional, that James deliberately refuses to show whether the ghosts are real or imaginary. His problem is to translate this ambiguity into cinema, for

escaping her callous, brutal husband, falls in love with Joe, and he falls in love with both the strength of her mind and the warmth of her body. But fate grabs hold of Joe. Just when Joe has decided that the relationship with Susan Brown is valueless, Susan becomes pregnant and her father compels Joe to marry her. When Joe tells his mistress that he is going to marry Susan, she becomes so upset that she kills herself in an

the camera can be quite convincing in its demonstration that a being either is or is not there. By letting the governess's point of view control every shot of the ghosts—we never see them except from her vantage point—the director ingeniously sustains the doubt about their existence apart from her. The result of this careful manipulation of point of view is a combination of a chilling story of terror and evil with a psychological mystery about the potential fallibility of the human brain. Does the evil in the universe torture the children to death or does the evil in the human mind kill them? With the passing of the mid-sixties, however, Clayton's influence and power have also passed.

Tony Richardson was the first and most fortunate of the British directors to take advantage of the success of *Room at the Top*. In 1959, Richardson directed the film version of John Osborne's *Look Back in Anger*, three years after he had directed the sharp, tongue-lashing stageplay at London's Royal Court Theatre. Within three years Richardson had directed three similar films: two adaptations of realist, class-conscious plays (*The Entertainer*, 1960; *A Taste of Honey*, 1962); and an adaptation of Alan Sillitoe's anti-establishment, class-conscious novel, *The Loneliness of the Long-Distance Runner* (1962). These four early Richardson films are similar in their strengths and weaknesses. All depend heavily on the literateness of the original works. All are brilliantly acted, both in the major roles and in the tiny character parts. Richardson's experience as a stage director no doubt aided his actors, but actors like Richard Burton, Claire Bloom, Mary Ure, Laurence Olivier, Brenda DaBanzie, Rita Tushingham, Murray Melvin, and Tom Courtenay made his task somewhat easier. Cinematically, the Richardson films feel like stageplays, punctuated by shots of grimy slums, run-down rooms, unamusing amusement parks, and dirty children. *Loneliness of the Long-Distance Runner* is the most adventurous of the films cinematically, allowing the freeness of the novel and the new cinematic winds blowing from across the channel to help him escape the tyrannies of stage dialogue and stage setting, of stage time and stage place.

Later Richardson films—*Tom Jones* (1963), *The Loved One* (1965), *The Charge of the Light Brigade* (1968)—leave the grime of working-class England and the bitterness of social-outcast laborers far behind. The angry naturalistic sincerity of the four early films is replaced by higher budgets, bigger casts, and colorful settings, thousands of miles and hundreds of years distant from industrial Britain. *Tom Jones*, a consistently delightful film, succeeds because of two Richardson strengths—its debt to the original Fielding fable and its fine performances. But there is something impersonal about the film's inconsistent weaving of cinematic styles: part romance, part Feydeau bedroom farce, part Sennett romp, part gratuitous naturalism with its shots of horsemen's spurs drawing real blood from their abused mounts. Richardson's stylistic bankruptcy is especially clear in *The Loved One*, a desperate and outrageous attempt to copy the mixture of humor and horror of Kubrick's *Dr. Strangelove*. Its satire of American burial festivities—and the culture that created them—consistently falls off the stylistic tightrope between farce and social polemic that *Strangelove* so carefully walks. Richardson's later films have moved even further from the shrill, engaging energy of his commitment to the social rebels of his early films. For Richardson, as for his friend Osborne, success has not been altogether kind.

For five years English directors made film variations on the Clayton-Richardson themes: the young, uneducated, often unintelligent working man or woman sentenced by industrial society to an inescapable yet unendurable life of drabness and mediocrity. Quite significantly, not one of these social-realist

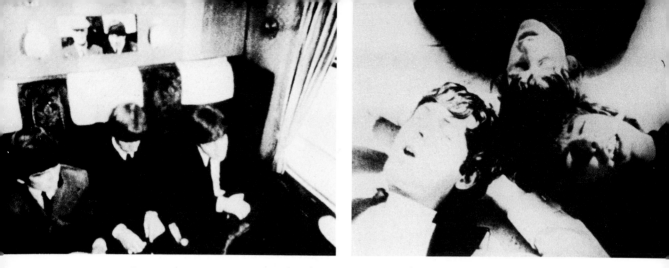

A Hard Day's Night—*cinematic fun and games with the Beatles*

films was shot in color. Color was as antithetical to the smoke and fog of working-class Britain as it was to the poverty of neorealist Italy. Karel Reisz's *Saturday Night and Sunday Morning* (1961) and *Morgan!* (1966) and Sidney J. Furie's *The Leather Boys* (1963) mix stories of rebellious young have-nots with a carefully realistic depiction of the social milieu that condemns them to the prison of their economic class. Other British films of the same era, with widely different themes and characters, share the same texture and smell of cinematic naturalism—from the factory tensions of Guy Green's *The Angry Silence* (1959), to the realistically brutal world of success in Lindsay Anderson's *This Sporting Life* (1963), to the neurotic occultism of Bryan Forbes's *Seance on a Wet Afternoon* (1964), to the realism of a Midlands mining town in Jack Cardiff's *Sons and Lovers* (1960), to the fashionable social world of John Schlesinger's *Darling* (1965), to the study of pathetic senility in Forbes's *The Whisperers* (1967).

The one obvious exception to this school of social realism was the work of Richard Lester, an American expatriate who united the Beatles with the cinematic ellipticality of Truffaut and Godard. The results—*A Hard Day's Night* (1964) and *Help!* (1965)—were buoyant, seemingly effortless romps through the streets and fields of illogic. But later Lester films reveal that the quality of his pictures varies inversely with the strength of his original material. There is a tension between the realistic material in *The Knack* (1965) and *How I Won the War* (1967) and Lester's formalistic games at the editing table. This tension produces not the lightness of the Beatle films but the self-conscious heavy-handedness of a director strangling his material with his own cleverness. Lester's success with *The Three Musketeers* (1974) and its successors is another indication that the real content of his films is his playful manipulation of lightweight material that has no intrinsic content. Perhaps Lester's strongest mixture of ebullient romp, intriguing narrative, and insightful human psychology is *Petulia* (1968), a film that looks even better now than when it was made.

Since 1963 the line dividing London and Hollywood has blurred again. Tony Richardson's desertion of native themes for Hollywood production values was a paradigm for the British industry as a whole. Karel Reisz deserted the slums for the Technicolor internationalism of *Isadora* (1968); Lindsay Anderson's surface realism continued in *If . . .* (1968), augmented by the new Hollywood conventions of youthful romanticism, lush Technicolor pictorialism, and Pirandellian games with the inseparability of reality and illusion; Bryan Forbes directed the Technicolor all-star disaster, *The Madwoman of Chaillot* (1969); John Schlesinger was almost as comfortable with the American social fringes in *Midnight Cowboy* (1969) as he was with the British ones in *Darling*. British and American styles were so indistinguishable that there was no essential stylistic difference between two parallel film adaptations of historical stageplays, Fred Zinnemann's *A Man for All Seasons* (1966) and Anthony Harvey's *The Lion in Winter* (1968), except for Zinnemann's superior ability to translate a talky drama into a moving picture.

By the mid-1970s a new group of British directors had solidified their positions as the most interesting to watch in the future. Ken Russell was the most audacious and gaudy British stylist, a director with a brilliant visual sense of decor and a strong yearning to say things of Significance—the significance of which was frequently buried beneath the scenery and wallpaper. Russell, whose training came in filming biographies (mostly of composers) for television, directed his first highly acclaimed film in 1969, *Women in Love*. The solidity of the D. H. Lawrence characters and the effectiveness of the novel's symbolism helped anchor Russell's visual flights of fancy in solid fictional ground. His film of *The Boy Friend* (1972) avoided the tension between style and ideas by having none of the latter; it (like his later *Tommy*, 1975) was as pure a style piece as has ever been made, a self-contained history of the musical film. But Russell's "psychological" studies of Tchaikovsky (*The Music Lovers*, 1970) and medieval religious fanaticism (*The Devils*, 1971) seemed to have more to do with

stereotypic romantic and sexual poses than psychological subtlety and revelation, and both seemed to lose their intended intellectual and psychological complexity beneath the striking but simple surfaces of the decor.

John Schlesinger is a completely different kind of stylist, the most literate, verbal, and psychological of the new British directors. Schlesinger's primary concern is to reveal the normal, ordinary sense behind the lives of people whom society would define as most abnormal, freaky, and bizarre. For Schlesinger, "abnormal," "aberrant" people live lives that seem completely normal and make perfect sense from their point of view, and the Schlesinger films develop precisely this subjective point of view. The young man's erratic and erotic fantasies in *Billy Liar* (1963), the bizarre sexual and career values of the world of high fashion in *Darling*, the down-and-out lives of hustlers and bums in *Midnight Cowboy*, the bisexual triangles in *Sunday, Bloody Sunday* (1971) are not examples of human freaks but examples of the way even the most bizarre-seeming human types are not so bizzare, but merely people trying to satisfy the most common human needs: security and love. With *Day of the Locust* (1975), however, Schlesinger seems to have lost the human sense and solidity beneath the freaky facade. And *Yanks* (1979) looks as if it might have been made by any British director thirty years before. Schlesinger's promise of the 1960s and early 70s has not been fulfilled later in the decade.

Nor has Lindsay Anderson's, who remains the British director most devoted to rebellion against a stagnant and repressive bourgeois society and bourgeois mentality. Anderson's rebellion is embodied by his violent central characters who usually want to break (or machine gun) the elements in society that repress them: Richard Harris in *This Sporting Life* and Malcolm McDowell (who was to the early 1970s what James Dean was to the

1950s) in *If . . .* and *O, Lucky Man!* (1973). Anderson's rebellion also determines his cinematic style; he avoids the literate coherency of a Schlesinger or the lush pictorialness of a Russell by making violent attacks on the continuity of space, time, and action. Whereas structure, character, and dialogue are Schlesinger's strengths (the dramatic values) and spatial composition is Russell's (the pictorial values), Anderson's primary strength is his battle with continuity at the editing table. Anderson is the British director most obviously influenced by the French, particularly by Godard (and Godard's interpretation of Brechtian theory). Like the French New Wave directors, Anderson was a film critic (and editor of the film journal, *Sequence*) who turned filmmaker. The key question about his future is whether his rebellious leftist anger can remain free of cliché and his self-conscious film trickery remain fresh and functional (rather than derivative and gratuitous).

As in its earlier periods, the British film is at least as notable for its actors as it is for its directors. With performers such as Tom Courtenay, Albert Finney, Rita Tushingham, Vanessa and Lynn Redgrave, Alan Bates, Richard Attenborough, Richard Harris, Julie Christie, Dirk Bogarde, Maggie Smith, Malcolm McDowell, Michael York, Glenda Jackson, and Oliver Reed, the British industry continues to demonstrate that British actors are among the most interesting, most talented, and best trained in the world.

The Czech Renaissance

No cinema better demonstrates the interrelationship of film art and political freedom than the cinema of little Czechoslovakia, a country that has probably been invaded, occupied, and liberated more times in this century than any other. The Czech Golden Age of cinema (or "Czech film miracle" or "Czech New Wave" as it has also been called) was an extremely short one, a bit longer than five years (roughly, 1963 to 1969), during which time over a dozen Czech films won major awards at the important international film festivals, including two nearly successive Academy Awards for Best Foreign Language Film of 1965 (*The Shop on Main Street*) and 1967 (*Closely Watched Trains*). The years of Czechoslovakian film mastery coincided with the only years since the Munich Agreement of 1938 that the Czech people and Czech artists enjoyed a measure of intellectual and creative freedom. Before this brief eruption, the Czech cinema was one of startings and stoppings, of promising beginnings cut short by political repression and artistic censorship. Although the American filmmaker suffered the commercial repression of a Louis B. Mayer and the moral suppression of the Hays Code, the history of the Czech cinema reveals that the censorship of bureaucratic political committees can be even more devastating to the individual artist.

In the late silent and early sound periods, the Czech cinema had begun to develop an integrity and individuality (as in the films of Gustav Machatý, Otakar Vávra, and Martin Frič) that was destroyed by the Nazi occupation of 1939. After the war the Czech cinema made another new beginning. Led by a group of young filmmakers who had organized their intentions in the final year of the Nazi occupation, the cinema was the first of the industries that was nationalized after the liberation. But this promise was cut short by the Soviet occupation and Stalinization of 1948 and there followed over a decade of repressive rule: the purges, the tightening of the Iron Curtain, the cultural isolation of the Cold War. The fears and repressive climate of the McCarthy years in the United States were marked and mirrored by parallel (and much more severe) activities on the other side of the Iron Curtain (as can be seen in Costa-Gavras's *The Confession*, as well as in Jaromil Jireš's Czech film, *The Joke*, 1968). Signs of a political thaw began to appear in 1961, and the Czech Golden Age of cinema sprang up through the cracks until the Soviet tanks rolled into Prague in August 1968.

During the decades of occupation and repression, two significant institutions were founded that would later contribute to the greatness of the Czech film in its years of freedom. Just as the Fascists founded a film school and built an efficient studio in Mussolini's Italy that would later be put to use by significant artists in a period of artistic freedom, the noted Czech film school, the F.A.M.U., was founded in 1947, and the Barrandov Studios were built into one of the best-equipped production facilities in Europe during the Nazi occupation. The great Czech films and filmmakers would come from this film school (five intensive years of training at state expense) and film studio as soon as the filmmakers were free to combine their artistic imaginations with their technical capabilities.

The Czech masterpieces were of four general types, including two that had undergone a transformation in the previous years of Soviet suppression. One of these was the story of Resistance to the Nazi Occupation, a safe subject in the Stalinist era since opinion of the Nazis was quite unanimous. But under the Soviets, the Resistance film mirrored the values of socialist-realism, primarily by presenting a positive, heroic, almost super-human figure as the embodiment of political resistance—like Schors and Chapayev in those Soviet sound films. In the mature Czech films of the 1960s, however, the central figure of Resistance was frequently weak, lazy, slovenly, and comic—nonheroic, all-too-human figures who eventually choose or are forced to take a political stand. This study of the comic antihero confronted by the demands of war is a long-standing Czech literary tradition, perhaps most memorable in Hašek's famous novel, *The Good Soldier Schweik*.

Such are the "heroes" of Jiří Weiss's *The Coward* (1961), the study of a cowardly rural schoolteacher who eventually decides to sacrifice himself rather than to select ten of his fellow townspeople to be slaughtered by the Nazis; of Jan Kadár's and Elmar Klos's *Death is Called Engelchen* (1963), the study of a wounded Czech partisan who wonders if his sacrifice has been worth the struggle; of Zbyněk Brynych's *The Fifth Horseman is Fear* (1964), the story of an aged and cowardly Jewish doctor who must choose between protecting himself and helping another human being who has dedicated himself to helping the doctor's people; as well as of both of the Academy-Award-winning Czech films. Significantly, the anti-Nazi genre continues in the post-1968 era of Soviet occupation—it is still not controversial to hate Nazis. Jaromil Jireš's *And My Love to the Swallows* (1971) is another story of the Resistance, but this film's protagonist—a beautiful young girl—is a saint, a perfect and perfectly contented martyr, obviously cut from the idealized cloth of socialist-realism.

A second genre, the historical costume drama, also popular during the years of suppression, was less popular in the 1960s. As in Hitler's Germany and Mussolini's Italy, a film could avoid delicate political issues by avoiding contemporary life altogether. In the sixties this escapist tendency continued, but of special note are František Vláčil's *Marketa Lazarova* (1968), a mammoth and carefully detailed historical spectacle, and Jiří Weiss's *The Golden Fern* (1963), a beautiful cinematic adaptation of a Czech fairytale. In the forest on midsummer eve, a shepherd discovers and steals the mystical golden fern, a magical token that allows him to fulfill all his wishes as long as he keeps possession of it. Of special interest and beauty in the film are its

Loves of a Blonde: *comic stabs at adolescent love and tenderness (Vladimir Brecholt and Nana Brechkova)*

attention to the styles of decor and costume (there are three—peasant village life, Hapsburg nobility, and High Turk) and its ability to translate such fanciful and mystical material into the concrete reality of cinema (in particular, Weiss's use of natural imagery, lighting, and camera movement to develop the conflict of man and Nature for possession of the fern). Both *Marketa Lazarova* and *The Golden Fern* were shot by the same talented cinematographer, Bedrich Batka.

The third of the Czech genres of the 1960s—the film of contemporary life, of contemporary human and social problems—had a very different analogue in the era of Soviet suppression. Under the Soviets, the Czech cinema eulogized the noble worker, limned the praises of the collective society, depicted the beauty of the factory, and dedicated itself to the idealistic proposition that with hard work and collective cooperation Life Would Be Beautiful. The mature Czech films of the 1960s doubted the values of collectivization, suggested that work did not equal happiness and implied that the essential human problems were internal, psychological, and personal rather than external and social.

These films of contemporary life tend in two opposite directions. Many of them set their studies of human personality against a clear social and political background. Věra Chytilová, perhaps the most important and accomplished woman director of postwar Europe, made careful studies of feminist problems (*The Ceiling*, 1962; *Daisies*, 1966; *Fruits of Paradise*, 1969). Jan Němec's *The Report on the Party and the Guests* (1966), a satire on conformity, was banned for over a year, even in the liberalized Czechoslovakia. Jaromil Jireš's *The Joke* is an explicitly anti-Stalinist and anti-Soviet film, the story of a man who seeks revenge for his earlier imprisonment and injustice in the 1950s era of the purges. Evald Schorm's *Courage for Everyday* (1964) and Jiří Weiss's *Ninety in the Shade* (1964) both use suicide as a means of exposing the potential alienation and sterility of living in such a constrained, highly regulated society. Indeed, the number of these Czech films that use the motif of suicide (either attempted or successful) is striking.

The other tendency of the contemporary films is to avoid political problems altogether and to turn themselves into pure studies of human sensations and experiences. These "experiential" films represent one of the truly unique (and most influential) accomplishments of the Czech cinema: personal, subtle, internal, touching, probing. Many have no plots; there are few incidents or events; almost nothing happens. But in the course of this nothing the audience discovers how it feels to be these people, how they feel life and how they feel about life. The purest expressions of these "experiential" films are the sympathetic satires of Miloš Forman (*Black Peter*, 1963; *Loves of a Blonde*, 1965; *The Firemen's Ball*, 1967) and the delicately sensitive film of Ivan Passer, *Intimate Lighting* (1965), who began as Forman's scenarist. But upon closer inspection, the truly unique and attractive quality of the Czech cinema—whether Second World War Resistance, costume drama, or study of a contemporary social problem—is this experiential quality. Regardless of their settings, the primary focus of the great Czech films of the 1960s is the internal quality and texture of human experience.

Precisely the same is true of the fourth genre of Czech films of the period, the surreal or futuristic allegory. Jan Schmidt is the master of this genre and his short film, *Josef Kilian* (1963), codirected by Pavel Juráček, has been frequently compared with the work of another Czech master, Franz Kafka. Josef K's world becomes a frightening, hysterical nightmare, and the experiential quality that Schmidt and Juráček develop is that of wandering in a labyrinth of terrifying dreams. Schmidt's later science-fiction film, *The End of August at the Ozone Hotel* (1968), script by Juráček, is a brutal and frightening odyssey of survivors from atomic holocaust, all of them women, roaming about the countryside, murdering other living beings—a snake, a dog, a cow—for the sport of it. They are desperately searching for a man to renew the species, and when they find him—a gentle, civilized old man—they murder him too. Schmidt's point seems to be that such a race is better off perishing.

Perhaps the most anarchic and surreal director of the era is Juraj Jakubisko, a Slovak. The Slovak and Czech production centers are separate (the Czech studio, Barrandov, is in Prague, the Slovak in Bratislava), the cultures and traditions are separate, the religions were originally separate (the Czechs Protestant, the Slovaks Catholic). Jakubisko seems to have the same relationship to the Czech cinema as Dovzhenko, a Ukrainian, had to the Moscow-based Soviet cinema. Like Dovzhenko, Jakubisko's films (*The Deserters and the Nomads*, 1968; *Birds, Orphans, and Fools*, 1969) seem anarchically poetic and erratically disconnected: a series of striking images that mix a blunt sexuality, politics, religion, audacious visual stunts, and experiential frenzy, cohering neither in plot nor in temporal continuity. As in many of the Czechoslovakian films there is an undercurrent of fatalism and nihilism in Jakubisko. The protagonist of *Birds, Orphans, and Fools*, who has lived his life like a gleeful child (a bird, an orphan, and a fool), manages to commit one of the most super-suicides—an orgy of self-annihilation—ever seen on the screen by simultaneously hanging, drowning, and incinerating himself. It is no wonder that Juráček and Jakubisko, two of the most daring and pessimistic of the period's directors, have not been permitted to make films by the new authorities.

The Czech cinematic style reveals the pervasiveness and influence of both the French and Italian movements and might be described as a perfect synthesis of Italian neorealism—particularly the compassionate, more internal human studies of *Umberto D* or *Nights of Cabiria*—and the compositional and editing spontaneity of the French New Wave—its elliptical cutting, its jumbling of film time, its hand-held camera and *cinéma vérité* authenticity. No surer sign of French influence exists than the half-dozen major Czech films—Forman's *Black Peter* and Passer's *Intimate Lighting* among them—that end with a Truffaut freeze-frame.

But to these foreign influences the Czechs added two uniquely Czechoslovakian traits. The first was an undiluted and unswerving commitment to illuminating internal human passions and sensations. Although the Czech films usually preferred shooting in real locations, the dominant imagery of this cinema is not natural (though nature often plays a memorable role as a film's supporting and secondary imagery). The dominant imagery of the Czech cinema was the human face, and in capturing that image the Czech directors avoided the standard "American shot" by keeping the camera much closer to the faces (many of which belong to nonprofessional actors). The Czech films also avoided the glossy facial lighting of the Hollywood

Closely Watched Trains. *The human texture of Czech realism. Miloš (Václav Neckár) whispers his sexual secret to the pro-Nazi train inspector (Vlastimil Brodsky)*

studios, preferring much more natural and tonal lighting in much more realistic environments. These Czech devices reduced the apparent artfulness of the cinema's handling of human beings, substituting a feeling of naturalness, spontaneity, and absolute authenticity. This feeling of spontaneity was essential to the films' stories as well as their styles, for the films were frequently about the ability of people to act spontaneously.

A second Czech trait was the intermingling of comedy and seriousness, producing films that were quite remarkable in their range of emotions from hilarious laughter to touching pathos to sudden horror. And this range of effects was also one of the ideas and subjects of the films, for the Czech films implied that life was indeed a mixture of lightness and seriousness, of living through a time fraught with dangers and demanding the most difficult choices (this often subjugated people knows about difficult choices). A most difficult existence still remains rich in smiles and jokes, though death waits (and not even unexpectedly) around the next corner. In their serio-comic blend the Czechs distilled the tragic modern history of their tyrannized little nation into a positive vision of life that saw humor in even the darkest moments and that (with a few exceptions) refused to surrender its faith in human exertion, commitment, and integrity.

Jiří Menzel's *Closely Watched Trains* is as good an example of this Czech spirit as any. The film's story (scripted by Bohumil Hrabak, from his short story) is of a comical young man, Miloš Hrma, who has taken a job as an apprentice at a train station during the Nazi Occupation—primarily to avoid any serious or difficult labor. Despite its wartime setting, the film seems to be a sex comedy, concentrating on the sexual inadequacies, failures, and fears of the inexperienced boy, who is a clumsy apprentice at love as well as at work. Menzel spends most of his time developing the boy's comic qualities: his ridiculously skinny and gawky body (its pathetically ostrich-like shape emphasized by his initial and repetitive appearance in only his shirt, his bird-skinny legs sticking out underneath); his naïve adoration of his train controller's uniform (symbolized by his comical worship of his cap, which he wears even in bed); his comical ancestors (the grandfather, a magician who attempted to conjure the Nazi tanks out of Czechoslovakia; the father, a former train employee who retired at the age of 48 to spend the rest of his life in bed); his naïve, bird-like, eyes-closed attempts to peck a kiss at his girlfriend, Maša, usually without success (in contrast to his coworker, Hubicka, for whom sexual intimacy is as natural as breathing). Comic sexual symbols dominate the film: the official, bureaucratic train stamps that are held up to the mouth and blown upon (in close-up); the long neck of a goose that the station master's wife rubs continually up and down, up and down, to force the food down its neck; the perpetual rip in the station master's

leather sofa, a hole opened by the athletic sexual activity on the sofa.

But beneath the sexual comedy are darker elements, even while Menzel refuses to desert his comic spirit and pratfalls. Menzel reminds us that Czechoslovakia is at war and occupied by the Nazis by depicting an air raid, yet depicting it in a strangely comic way. During the raid, the boy sleeps in a photographer's studio where he has just failed to make love to Maša. In that same studio a giggling group of sexy girls had been photographed earlier, their bodies protruding above a cartoon drawing of an airplane. During the air raid, Menzel keeps his camera on that comic, cartoon plane while real planes drop their potentially deadly bombs. And the air raid ends comically when the photographer awakens in his bed only to discover that he is sleeping outdoors, the walls of his studio having been blown away. His reaction is uncontrolled and exuberant laughter.

The boy's reaction to this night of lost and clumsily unfulfilled love is not comic, however. Menzel continues his subtle development of the film's serious undercurrents when the boy tries to ease his sexual failure and frustration with another act of impotency: he tries to commit suicide by slashing his wrists as he sits in a hot and steamy bathtub. But even the suicide has a comic balance, for the boy's final act of bidding the world goodbye is to remove his precious cap (he doesn't want to dishonor it), and Miloš is only saved from death when a comically clumsy workman punches a hole in the bathroom wall and sees the scrawny, limp form in the tub.

The ultimate surfacing of seriousness is the film's climax, when the boy performs the mission of blowing up a Nazi ammunition train and is suddenly and unexpectedly machine-gunned by a Nazi guard. The term *climax* is especially relevant to this final act, for Miloš's body lies sprawled on the top of a train car in a sexual position, and this implied coitus in which he implants his explosive charge into the passive train is as successful as his sexual intercourse of the night before with Viktoria Freie (the woman who brought him the explosive charge to blow up the train as well as provided her body for Miloš to exercise his first successful sexual charge). The result of the boy's ultimate and final "coitus" is the mammoth orgasm of the exploding train. As if the ironic juxtaposition of sex and war were not clear enough in the boy's mission and death, Menzel adds another (and comic) level by cross-cutting back and forth between the boy's mission and a ridiculous punitive inquiry taking place in the train station itself (an ironic variation on the Griffith cross-cut!), which also has a sexual basis and which serves as a diversionary tactic to allow the successful act of war. Inside the train station, the Chief Train Inspector, himself a ridiculous combination of comic and serious elements (his speeches turn Hitler's rhetoric into hilariously funny bombastic clichés), grills Hubicka about the sexual encounter with Miss Svata, in which he decorated her buttocks with the official train inspector's stamps. While the Chief Inspector is aggrieved by this "insult to the Third Reich" and the other inspectors busily study the photographs of Miss Svata's decorated *derrière,* Miloš insults the Third Reich by blowing up one of its trains.

The reaction to the train explosion and the boy's death (though Hubicka and the others do not yet know Miloš has been killed) is joy: the same exuberant laughter with which the photographer greeted the disappearance of his studio (they were, after all, American bombs—bombs of liberation). The station's clock chimes happily, just as it has chimed after each of the previous sexual encounters on the station master's sofa. Menzel's point is clearly that a clumsy boy has become a man—both sexually and politically—

that his previous impotency has been succeeded by an act of fertility. But our intellectual understanding of that positive point is balanced and complicated by our emotional awareness that he will never exercise his manhood again and that in gaining his manhood he has lost his life. Maša's sad realization parallels the audience's, for she knows that Miloš is dead when the wind of the explosion blows his cap (which he would never willingly remove) to her feet. Details count for Menzel, and he transforms the comic symbol of the cap into a touching monument to the boy's memory. In this strange variation on the familiar *Buildungsroman,* the long comic apprenticeship produces a period of maturity that is strikingly and tragically brief.

The Shop on Main Street, produced and directed by Jan Kadár and Elmar Klos, also mixes the comic and the serious, although not so exuberantly or contrapuntally as *Closely Watched Trains.* According to Kadár, in his collaboration with Klos he took responsibility for the shooting and the handling of the actors while Klos served as producer and supervised the cutting. If so, *The Shop on Main Street* owes its greatest debt to Kadár's work with actors and their earlier *Death is Called Engelchen,* with its brilliant leaps backward and forward in time and space, was more dependent on the cutting of Klos. The central figure of *The Shop on Main Street* is another comical figure, Tono, a lazy, poor provider who would rather spend time strolling with his dog than working at a job, and who prefers the company of the loyal and affectionate animal to that of his shrewish and grasping wife. Tono attempts to remain apolitical in a political era, in sharp contrast to his brother-in-law who has devoted himself to serving the Nazi regime so he can parade around as one of the little town's most influential (and richest) citizens. Tono is obviously a Chaplinesque figure (he even notes the resemblance to Chaplin when he wears a new derby) who wants to have as little to do with work, respectability, and the Establishment as possible. (In particular, he has nothing to do with the huge and ugly "Tower of Babel" being built by the town as a symbol of its submission and capitulation to the Fascists.)

The film's central situation is that Tono's brother-in-law uses his influence to give Tono a "present," one of the spoils of Fascism. He makes Tono the "Aryan Controller" of a Jewish widow's supposedly prosperous shop. Every Jewish business must have its "Aryan Controller," who then reaps a handsome share of the profits. Several ironies proceed from this gift. First, the old widow Lautmann (played brilliantly by the Polish-Jewish actress, Ida Kaminska) is both a bit deaf and completely unaware of the new political regime in the little Slovak town. She not only cannot hear the words when Tono tells her he is her "Aryan Controller"; she cannot even comprehend what the words mean and imply. And the comic and sympathetic Tono has neither the heart nor the patience to make her understand. So he offers to work for her as her assistant (a concept she can understand), and he spends his time in assisting her in the shop and in mending her old furniture (he is a carpenter by trade) in her apartment. She believes, ironically, that he is merely helping her out of kindness and charity, while he, the "Controller," is, ironically, merely a clerk and apprentice.

Another irony is that the shop is almost bankrupt and cannot make anyone, even an "Aryan Controller," rich. The shop's only commodity is buttons. Mrs. Lautmann survives not from the shop's sales but from charity; the town's other Jewish merchants all contribute to her support. Faced with having to support Mrs. Lautmann's shop and her Aryan Controller as well, the Jewish merchants agree to pay Tono handsomely to serve as her assistant. And thus history and politics create one of the strangest commercial arrangements—the Jews in effect hire Tono to serve as an Aryan Controller of a Jewish business.

The comedy, and the stability, of this commercial arrangement crumble when the Fascists decide that all the town's Jews must be shipped out (obviously to concentration camps). Tono now faces a crisis of decision, one of those terrible dilemmas that confront the protagonists of Czech films (and must have confronted the Czechs during the years of Occupation). Does Tono protect the fragile old woman—hide her from the police to spare her the pain of leaving and of comprehension that would obviously kill her? Or does he protect himself—send the old woman packing? On the one hand, Kadár has carefully and sensitively developed Tono's affection for the pathetic, kind, and uncomprehending old lady who treats Tono as her own son. On the other, Kadár has just as clearly developed what happened to Tono's friend, Kuchar, who aided the town's Jews; he was branded a "White Jew" and brutally murdered as a result. Tono vacillates, making one decision and then the other. His crisis of indecision ultimately leads to his unintentionally murdering the old woman and then hanging himself when he feels the horror of his inhuman brutality.

Again affectionate and ironic comedy have turned to horror. The film's point perhaps is that a human being *must* choose and that apolitical stances are impossible in political times (and what times are not?). Or possibly the film's point is that in political eras of inhumanity and illegality, life presents human beings with choices that cannot be made and that cannot possibly turn out well. The film's recurring dream sequence—of Tono's waltzing with Mrs. Lautmann in slow motion, in the bright (and overexposed) sunlight—might well imply that life must make sense before human choices can make sense. On the other hand (and here is that magnificent Czech balance and complexity again), Tono's dream is a dream.

Of the pure comedies, Miloš Forman is the master. An affectionate satirist who pokes fun at human folly, he also realizes that folly is what makes people human. Forman's satire is gentle and compassionate rather than corrosive and vicious (like Kubrick's). Two of Forman's three Czech films (*Black Peter, Loves of a Blonde*) and two of his American films (*Taking Off*, 1971; *Hair*, 1979) are youth films that examine the generation gap, while his other major films, *The Firemen's Ball* and *One Flew Over the Cuckoo's Nest* (1975), examine the follies and insanities of bourgeois adulthood, a secondary theme of the youth films. Forman's primary satirical subjects are youthful clumsiness (in this sense Forman's work is related to Menzel's film) and adult boredom. The folly of youth for Forman is that it is so earnest and so clumsy. Sexual pursuit is the primary activity, but the pursuit is awkward, callous, and mechanical. Sexual success is the only emblem of human importance, and Forman's youths devote their lives to feeding their egos and vanities with this kind of food. Forman's adults, meanwhile, spend their lives in their apartments, conversing about nothing but the evils of their children, bored with the books they read, the television they watch, and especially bored with one another. If it were not for the follies of youth, the adults would seemingly have nothing to occupy their lives at all. In *Taking Off,* however (and here Forman senses the difference between American and Czech parents), the adults also occupy themselves by imitating the follies of youth, which is a double folly.

Forman's three favorite domains are the dance hall, the kitchen, and the bedroom—three distinct and essential social centers. Dances are society's and youth's institutionalized means of sexual pursuit, and Forman delights in examining the clumsy and self-conscious games that people play in the dance hall. Using a *cinéma vérité* method of photographing actual dance halls and mixing his players with the real "revellers" (like Mack Sennett in *Tango Tangles!*), Forman continually reveals how difficult it is for young people to act naturally and effectively in such a situation, how the major business of a dance is not dancing but finding a dance partner, and how most of the people at a dance spend most of their time defending themselves against the very thing they have come to the dance to get. The kitchen is the inevitable social center of the individual family, the place where the boring, painful, yet inevitable discussions of the worthlessness of youth take place. The clumsiness that Forman captures in this social center is that no one listens to what the others are saying (or cares), no one (father, mother, child) agrees on the issues of the discussion, and no one in the kitchen cares about the results of the discussion, since there will obviously be none, something that everyone in the kitchen already knows but feels compelled to continue anyway. The bedroom is the personal and private social center where the results of the sexual pursuit culminate. The clumsiness that Forman brilliantly captures in these scenes (in particular the seduction scenes between Mila and Andula in *Loves of a Blonde*) reveals how such monumentally important matters of human experience culminate in such awkward, pedestrian, and limited physical acts.

One of the most beautiful, least publicized, and most emblematic of the spirit of the Czech film is Ivan Passer's *Intimate Lighting*. The film is one of those "experiential" studies in which nothing happens; instead the film examines a collection of people—their feelings, hopes, frustrations, and contentment. The occasion for the film is the visit of a cellist from the city to play a concert at a music school in the provinces. This

Intimate Lighting. *The union of nature, man, and music*

occasion unites a series of human oppositions: the city musician with his former chum who now runs the provincial music school; the cellist's sexy and sophisticated mistress with the wife and children of the country musician; the two musicians of a middle generation with the country musician's father (also a musician) and mother of an earlier generation; the values of city life with those of country life; the values of the educated and cultured with those of the peasant farmers; the values of the modern age with the eternal values of the countryside. The film devotes itself to the commonplace, to the banal, to the frustrations of the two musician-friends (roads not taken and successes not achieved). The best that the city musician can do is play solo performances in the provinces, and the best that the country musician can do is devote himself to a provincial music school.

But even in these modest and mediocre attainments Passer develops the

satisfaction, the contentment, the comfort that life can bring. At the center of the film's style, study, and subject is music. *Intimate Lighting* may be the best film about music and with (instrumental) music ever made. Its sound track—from the opening titles in which a conductor leads the school's orchestra through a rehearsal for the concert, to its final freeze-frame—is saturated with music. There is music "to bring tears" at a funeral. There is nature's music in the waving of wheat in the fields. There is exuberant beer-barrel music and song at the wake after the funeral. The men play chamber music to relax (and bicker) after dinner. The two friends cannot talk to one another without music on the phonograph. Their friendship exists through music, in music, and with music. There is even music in the rhythmic snores of the old man at night. *Intimate Lighting* depicts the way the rhythms of music mirror the rhythms of life and the way that music can unite and synthesize all social strata and human differences. Though life has its banalities and disappointments and frustrations, it also has its music, which is beautiful and vibrant and sweet.

One further contribution of the Czech cinema that cannot be overlooked is its accomplishments in animation and in puppet cinema, most notably the work of Jiří Trnka (*The Devil on Springs,* 1946; *The Emperor's Nightingale,* 1949; *Song of the Prairie,* 1949; *The Hand,* 1964). Trnka's work is significant, not only for its new and imaginative standards in puppet films but also for its founding an entire school and studio for animation and puppetry, of which Karel Zeman (*Baron Münchhausen,* 1962) is probably the most distinguished disciple.

The other cinemas of Eastern and Central Europe endured the same Stalinist and anti-Stalinist twists and turns as the Czech cinema, producing similar periods of fertility and barrenness. After the Czech cinema, the Polish cinema is the most interesting. The most fertile period of the Polish cinema preceded the Czech era by almost a decade (1955-1964), produced primarily by the founding of another major film school (the Lodz Film School in 1948) and the splitting of the Polish industry into individual artistic production units in 1955. These smaller production units granted the Polish directors a new freedom and allowed the exercise of more individuality; the two most talented directors, Andrej Wajda (of the KADR unit) and Roman Polanski (of the KAMERA unit), took advantage of this new opportunity.

As in Czechoslovakia, the Nazi Occupation and the Resistance to it were favored subjects of the Polish cinema, and no one made more powerful films on the Occupation era than Andrej Wajda. As opposed to the serio-comic, neorealist, intimately personal style of the Czech war films, Wajda's style is more active, more violent, more baroque, and less internalized. The Wajda films (*Kanal,* 1957; *Ashes and Diamonds,* 1958) consistently use a grotesque visual imagery (for example, the claustrophobic Warsaw sewers in *Kanal*), and the recurrent Wajda image seems to be of rubble, ashes, and garbage. His is a barren, ruined world, and the ruined landscapes are metaphoric of the ruined spirits and minds of those who must live there. *Ashes and Diamonds* is a spectacularly visual film (far more consciously spectacular than the Czech war films), with grotesque and bizarre lighting effects (its extreme backlighting and low-angle camera work reminiscent of *Citizen Kane*), with two brilliantly climactic murder scenes that juxtapose the deaths with striking visual images (the startling eruption of fireworks at the moment of death, the dark stains of blood oozing into a white sheet drying in the sun), and with the compelling performance of one of the most interesting (and least known) stars in the history of cinema, Zbigniew Cybulski.

Roman Polanski's style is also more grotesque and externalized than the Czechs', but Polanski's primary theme is not the rubble of war but the ominousness of the universe itself. Polanski's Polish films use an extremely simple situation built around a single object and very few characters (two men carry a wardrobe out of the sea in *Two Men and a Wardrobe,* 1958; three people sail a boat out to sea in *Knife in the Water,* 1962). But Polanski endows these simple events with allegorical significance, primarily by charging the entire universe with a menacing, hostile spirit that turns the most simple and commonplace human events into terrifying combats of great magnitude. In *Knife in the Water* he endows the simple meeting of the three with menace by his use of lenses (primarily wide-angle lenses that magnify and distort distances), by his camera placement (using grotesque angles so that characters or objects dominate others or even blot them out entirely), and by the muted tension and jousting beneath the spare dialogue, props (that hypnotic knife), and movement.

In *Rosemary's Baby* (1968), his first successful American film (after leaving Poland in 1964 when the nation's film policies shifted), Polanski added color as another way for the universe to manifest its terrifying presence (the comparison between the sharp, clean colors of the married couple's apartment and the baroque, warm, sickeningly rich colors of the devilish neighbors' apartment). And *Chinatown* (1974) transfers its study of cosmic malevolence to the American socio-political scene. On its surface a detective "caper" set in Los Angeles of the mid-1930s—like the Raymond Chandler and Dashiell Hammett novels, as well as films like John Huston's *The Maltese Falcon* and Howard Hawks's *The Big Sleep*—*Chinatown* is a tortuous journey through a maze of murders and clues that exposes the interlinked sexual and political corruption at the center of a most paranoid vision of American life. Polanski cleverly weds the nation's "Watergate mood"—the suspicion of inextricable strands of corruption linking everyone in high places—and a gleaming Technicolor world of beautiful images (intensifying the metaphor of ugliness beneath the beautiful surfaces) with his general view that if the universe has any detectable order at all, it is surely a malevolent one (as in his *Macbeth*, 1971).

There were other Polish directors who made effective films in its greatest decade: Aleksander Ford, who had been making films since 1929 (*The Young Chopin*, 1952; *Five Boys from Barska Street*, 1953), and Jerzy Skolimowski, a novelist who began as a script writer for both Wajda and Polanski (scripted *Knife in the Water;* directed *Walkover*, 1965, and *Barrier*, 1966, in Poland; directed *Le Départ*, 1967, in Belgium), were the most significant.

The early Hungarian cinema is probably most notable for the talents it exported to the rest of the world after their Hungarian apprenticeships: Béla Lugosi; Hollywood directors Michael Curtiz, Andre de Toth, and Paul Fejos; the noted British producer and director, Alexander Korda; and the international film theorists, László Moholy-Nagy and Béla Balázs. The best-known international representative of the new Hungarian cinema of the 1960s and 70s is Miklós Jancsó (*Cantata*, 1962; *The Red and the White*, 1967; *The Confrontation*, 1968).

The primary contribution of the Yugoslavian cinema is its famed Zagreb animation studio, the most innovative, imaginative, and influential source of animation films in the world since 1957. In live-action films, the Yugoslavian cinema is one of the youngest in Europe, with no native production until after the Second World War. Its most influential "new wave" director is the brilliantly clever political and social satirist, Dušan Makavejev (*A Man Is Not a Bird*, 1965; *The Switchboard Operator*, 1967; *Innocence Unprotected*, 1968; *WR—Mysteries of the Organism*, 1971).

Das neue Kino

Almost simultaneously with the spiritual and political death of the Eastern European cinemas came the rebirth of the West German cinema. While it would be an exaggeration to say that for thirty-five years, from 1932 to 1967, the film industry of Germany did not produce a single film of international significance (with the exception of Leni Riefenstahl's controversial documentaries of the 1930s), the exaggeration would be a slight one. Among the scattered postwar German films to be seen in America were Rolf Thiele's *Rosemary* (1959), a neorealist study of the life and death of a Berlin prostitute; the delightful impersonations of Horst Bücholz in Kurt Hoffman's adaptation of Thomas Mann's comic novel *The Confessions of Felix Krull* (1958); and the poignant ironies of Bernhard Wicki's *The Bridge* (1960), the chronicle of a group of helpless German schoolchildren slaughtered while defending a worthless bridge against the invading American army in the final days of the war. Volker Schlöndorff's *Young Törless* (1966), which parallels sado-masochistic torture in a boy's school with the moral and psychological conditions for Nazism in Hitler's Germany, was either the last of these occasional German films to achieve international recognition or the first representative of the new and genuine German film movement. In the late 1960s and early 70s, the first feature films of three young German filmmakers appeared within four years of one another—Werner Herzog (*Signs of Life*, 1967), Rainer Werner Fassbinder (*Love Is Colder Than Death*, 1969), and Wim Wenders (*The Goalie's Anxiety at the Penalty Kick*, 1971). All three men were born within three years of each other (Herzog in 1942, Fassbinder and Wenders in 1945); all were about twenty-five when their first features appeared. These three young directors, who have steadily achieved greater international recognition, form the nucleus of the most interesting, promising, and productive new national film movement of the last decade.

In truth, the new German films have not made the same impact on American audiences as did the French and Italian films of two decades ago. No single German film has enjoyed the commercial success and artistic recognition of *Bicycle Thief, La Strada, Jules and Jim, Breathless*, or *Shop on Main Street*. There are both cultural and commercial reasons for the slighter American reception of these recent films. First, there are fewer small "art cinemas" in America devoted to showing foreign films than there were two decades ago. The reduced number of theatres means a much smaller audience for such films than in the period when significant numbers of American filmgoers first turned hungrily to the

European imports to escape from the predictable Hollywood pap. Today's younger audiences seem contented with the new Hollywood's offerings (and unwilling to read subtitles), while the older audiences who continue to patronize foreign films prefer the same older kinds of French, Swedish, and Italian styles and subjects that attracted them two decades ago (many of them made, of course, by the same directors). Second, the new German films are not more difficult than the previous generations of European films, but they are difficult in a different way—colder, harder-edged, more stylized, more austere, more ironic, less romantic, less warm, and less charming than Fellini, Truffaut, Tanner, Bertolucci, or Forman. There is consequently not much money to be made from these films, which not only diminishes their American theatrical distribution but also the attention they receive in the American press. Most of these German films are shown primarily on college campuses in America by film societies in 16mm versions or in an occasional retrospective by a big city art house or museum of modern art. But the recent movement of international financing into English-language productions by Wenders (*The American Friend*, 1977), Fassbinder (*Despair*, 1978) and Herzog (*Nosferatu*, 1979), the major American publicity campaign for this last film as well as the surprising commercial success of Fassbinder's *The Marriage of Maria Braun* (1979), all indicate that these filmmakers may yet attract the attention and audiences they deserve in the United States.

That the new German cinema has made little impact in America is ironic, for one of its traits is a conscious debt to the American cinema. Wenders's *Kings of the Road* (1977) is both a western (two buddies riding in open spaces) and an *Easy Rider* (they ride in a modern machine, a truck, rather than on horseback, accompanied by American rock music). His *American Friend* is a *film noir* that evokes many American movies: Hitchcock's *Strangers on a Train* (one stranger proposes the murder of another stranger, based on a novel by Patricia Highsmith, who also wrote *Strangers on a Train*), Bette Davis's *Dark Victory* (a man is going blind as a result of a mysterious terminal disease), *The French Connection* (an international Mafia-style conspiracy, shot in various cities all over the globe), American westerns (the American wears a cowboy hat and describes himself as "a cowboy in Hamburg"), and that cowboy is played by American actor Dennis Hopper (a frequent performer in American westerns as a "bad guy" and whose last memorable appearance was in *Easy Rider*). There are also appearances by American directors Nicholas Ray (who directed Hopper in *Rebel Without a Cause*) and Samuel Fuller (who, like Ray, specialized in violent stories of masculine self-assertion).

Fassbinder's films are packed with conscious homages to those two Hollywood directors from Germany, Douglas Sirk and Max Ophuls. One Fassbinder film, *Ali: Fear Eats the Soul* (1974) is a specific remake of Sirk's *All that Heaven Allows* (1956), and another, *The Bitter Tears of Petra von Kant* (1972), dissects the same female conflicts between love, success, and power as Sirk's *Imitation of Life* (1959). Fassbinder's repetitive use of glass reflections on windows, mirrors, and table tops deliberately recalls Sirk's use of the same glass materials; the graceful, lengthy tracking shots in many of the Fassbinder films recall the camera style of Max Ophuls. And one of the more interesting lines of movie genealogy can be traced with the appearance of Eddie Constantine in *Beware of a Holy Whore* (1970), who comes to Fassbinder via Godard's *Alphaville,* and came to Godard via a series of low-budget French crime films based on American Monogram mysteries. Fassbinder also acknowledges Godard as a way-station between American movies and the New German Cinema by using Anna Karina, Godard's first wife and leading lady, as the French mistress in *Chinese Roulette* (1976). Although Werner Herzog's conscious debt to American culture and American movies may be smaller than Wenders's or Fassbinder's, *Stroszek* (1977) contains a brilliant satire of the plastic surfaces of American life (mobile homes, fast-food restaurants, formica furniture) as well as a brilliant satire of American bank-robbing westerns.

If one characteristic of the New German films is their debt to foreign movies, another is their debt to a native German film tradition—the Expressionistic style pieces of the 1920s. The Fassbinder films unmistakably evoke the stylized, symmetrical, highly patterned visual world of Fritz Lang: the visual emphasis on extremely slow choreographic human movements and statuesquely frozen human poses, sharply defined by the bare, hard white walls behind them, linked by the traveling of a typically German moving camera. The opening shots of *Fox and His Friends* at a circus sideshow clearly link Fox, who performs as "the talking head," with Cesare of *The Cabinet of Dr. Caligari*. If Fassbinder's films recall the visual stylization of Lang's, Herzog's recall the spiritual, mystical trances of such films as *Caligari, Destiny, Warning Shadows,* and *Nosferatu*—quite literally, of course, since Herzog remade *Nosferatu* as an homage to Murnau's. The slow rhythms of the Herzog films, their reliance on extended, lengthy shots of frozen human figures in hypnotically entrancing landscapes, evoke the dreamlike rhythm of the Expressionist world rather than Fassbinder's evocation of its look. Like the characters of many Expressionist films, Herzog's central figures are possessed by manias and demons that drag them inexorably into the realms of their desires and their imaginations. One of Herzog's most Expressionist experiments was *Heart of Glass* (1976), in which he hypnotized the entire cast during shooting, to achieve the impression that the entire world of the film had been plunged into a deep trance. Although Wenders is the most apparently realist of the three directors, his work can be compared with that of Murnau, the most realist German director of the 1920s—in particular Wenders's use of physical settings as a mirror of subjective human sensations (as in Murnau's *The Last Laugh* and *Sunrise*), and his contrast of cramped indoor architectural spaces with open, vast, freer outdoor spaces (as in Murnau's *Nosferatu*).

If two of the new German characteristics can be traced to the traditions of film, the third can be traced to their attitude toward the traditions of narrative. The new German films are all "new narratives." Rather than forging stories that are credible chains of chronological events, the German films push narrative construction in its two opposite directions—either the distanced political parable in the manner of Bertolt Brecht or the extremely internalized sensation-centered rendering of human emotion and experience. Fassbinder's work is the most consciously Brechtian—the title of one of his films, *Mother Küsters Goes to Heaven* (1975), is a deliberate echo of Brecht's famous *Mother Courage*. The Fassbinder narratives, like those of Brecht, develop a detached irony that allows the audience to perceive the broad political, psychological, or moral outlines of the tale rather than to become intimately attached to the feelings and fortunes of its central character or characters. Such parables always tend toward the allegorical and always take the form of complex and explicit elaborations of a simple moral-political lesson: that personal catastrophe gives one great economic power in contemporary society (*Mother Küsters*), that certain forms of sexual-romantic love require the antagonism of bourgeois society to exist (*Ali*), that even social outcasts like homosexuals are more loyal to their

economic class than to their sexual comrades (*Fox*), that the myth of the bourgeois artist—tyrannically reducing everyone in life to slaves for the sake of Art—is also the myth of Fascism (*Satan's Brew,* 1976), that the political and economic recovery of postwar Germany was achieved by acts of moral prostitution (*Maria Braun*). On the other hand, Herzog and Wenders make extremely internalized experiential narratives that are far less political, far less detached, far more tactile, and far more engrossing than Fassbinder's. Herzog depends almost exclusively on the shadings, textures, and rhythms of his visual imagery to transfer the internal sensations of his characters directly to the conscious and unconscious perceptions of the viewer. Wenders's narratives, much closer to the movie norm, still depend on a highly elliptical and subtle interplay of external narrative event and sensuously evocative and internalized visual imagery.

Rainer Werner Fassbinder is the most prolific of the new German directors—he has made over two dozen feature films in ten years, in addition to writing several plays and staging several theatrical productions in the same period. Fassbinder's roots, like Ingmar Bergman's, are in the theatre and his films have never deserted the theatre's elegant, economical stylization. Like Bergman and D. W. Griffith, Fassbinder prefers the theatrical method of working with an acting ensemble rather than with individual types and stars, and over the last decade the faces of the Fassbinder players have become almost as familiar as the Griffith or Bergman stock companies—Irm Hermann, Margit Carstensen, Hanna Schygulla, Brigitte Mira, Kurt Raab, Volker Spengler, Marquard Böhm, Harry Baer. Despite the speed of his production and shooting, Fassbinder's style and control have evolved slowly and steadily. His frenetic productivity of eleven films in 1969–1970 has slowed greatly to permit greater investment of his time, care, and control. The stylistic experiments of these early films, which tended in any number of contradictory directions—the mannered *film noir* of *The American Soldier* (1970), the maniacal mixture of movie making and love making in *Beware of a Holy Whore,* a chaotic movie about movie chaos, and the undramatic, almost *cinéma vérité* study of dull, drab middle-class life of *Why Does Herr R Run Amok?* (1969)—have fused into a consistent Fassbinder look, style, and tone.

There are three primary Fassbinder visual and social settings: the very drab, very stifling, very tawdry world of the working- and middle-class—their apartments, bars, offices, and shops (*The Merchant of the Four Seasons,* 1972; *Mother Küsters; Ali*); the cold, hard, shiny elegance of the world of the rich and famous (*Petra von Kant; Fox; Chinese Roulette; Satan's Brew*); and the distant, detached, frigid elegance of the world of the near or distant past (*Effi Briest,* 1974; *Despair*). The visual characteristic that links these three social realms is their unrelenting hardness and coldness, their lack of comfort, softness, or human charm. Both private human homes and places of public habitation become inhuman and uninhabitable in the Fassbinder world; they are mausoleums or, like Fox's apartment, museums. Whether cutely cluttered or chicly bare, Fassbinder films are set in the Land of the Dead. For this reason, Fassbinder films are almost exclusively indoor films, claustrophobically enclosed by the rooms his characters are forced to inhabit (another clear parallel to the German Expressionist films and the American Sirk and Ophuls films, which depicted similarly claustrophobic, indoor worlds).

Fassbinder's favorite images in these settings are gleamingly bright, reflectively repellent surfaces—walls and furniture that do not embrace with their softness but repel with their glossy, glassy shine. Among the most memorable of these

Effi Briest: *Effi (Hanna Schygulla) engulfed by the curtains, carvings, mirrors, and paintings of her world*

surfaces are the gleaming white tiles of the public toilet in *Satan's Brew,* the gleaming white marble where Fox lies dead in *Fox and His Friends,* or the gleaming white walls and transparent glass shelves of *Chinese Roulette.* Even the early *Beware of a Holy Whore* is dominated by the pervasively bright white walls of a Spanish hotel. Given his visual preoccupation with the hard and shiny, it is not surprising that Fassbinder's favorite visual material is glass—windows (either broken into many panes or whole in huge transparent sheets), mirrors (either small or large, ornately carved or simply framed, uniquely shaped or purely rectangular), and glass-panelled doors. In *Chinese Roulette*, even the tables and shelving are made of glass. Although the fascination with glass also comes to Fassbinder via Ophuls and, especially, Sirk, the material serves several explicit symbolic and metaphoric purposes in the Fassbinder world.

Glass is both a means and a barrier to communication. It both permits one to see through it and confines one's vision to its surface. It is both transparent and solid, invisible and visible, revealing and blinding. In *Petra von Kant,* Marlene (Irm Hermann), Petra's loving secretary, observes Petra's tender scenes of affection with other women from the other side of a glass window—she is both screened off from the scene she is witnessing and a visual participant in that scene, both distant from it and close to it. Effi Briest is perpetually surrounded by the windows, mirrors, and doorways of her upper-class life. She is capable of seeing herself and seeing the life around her, but she is also screened from the outdoors and limited to observing only her surface characteristics in a mirror. The glass of *Effi Briest* becomes a metaphor both for Effi's being ineffably stuck in her world of glass and, at the same time, incapable of seeing it or penetrating it at all. In *Chinese Roulette,* the constant reflections of the characters' faces off the glass furniture of their lives implies that their elegant, genteel personalities are themselves pure surfaces that disguise the jealousy, pettiness, selfishness, and viciousness beneath. Like the crippled little girl in the film (Fassbinder uses physical and mental cripples—like the idiot brother Ernst in *Satan's Brew*—as symbols of the true personalities beneath the elegant surfaces), the characters are moral cripples, and their moral weaknesses finally surface during the psychological game of Chinese roulette, which the crippled girl proposes, organizes, and conducts.

Although both Ophuls and Sirk used glass for social and psychological commentary, Fassbinder's glass imagery is more insistent and more deliberately Brechtian. For Sirk, glass was an ironic visual leitmotif that never evolved into an explicit and systematic critique of social assumptions and personal definitions (his films were produced, after all, by Ross Hunter at Universal in the 1950s). Ophuls's use of glass was more pointed but also more charming and affectionate. That characters could see neither themselves or their worlds because of the blinding reflections was simply, for Ophuls, an inevitable and understandable flaw in human social and emotional vision, a flaw rooted in the general human condition rather than in a specific political condition. But for Fassbinder, glass serves as a deliberate Brechtian distancing device—Brecht's famous *Verfremsdungeffekt* or "Alienation Effect," designed to remove the spectator from the illusion of reality in the spectacle and the temptation to sympathize with its players. Not only does the glass in *Effi Briest* separate Effi from her world without her knowing it; it separates us from Effi, reducing her to a social marionette rather than building her into an attractive and rounded psychological being. The glass reflections in Fassbinder films deliberately push us, too, behind glass windows (quite literally, since we see films through frames constructed by lenses of glass). This distancing coldness allows the Fassbinder films to achieve their goal as parable-like allegories of the bourgeois social condition—accompanied by a savage comic irony that, in Brecht as well as Fassbinder, almost inevitably accompanies this kind of narrative.

The central theme of Fassbinder's work, as consistent as his panes of glass, is power—social power, economic power, psychological power, erotic power, often translated into specific scenes of sado-masochistic dominance and subservience. The characters in Fassbinder films exercise terrible power over others, just as the filmmaker himself exercises a terrible power over his audience. *Satan's Brew* begins and ends with a quotation from Antonin Artaud, and the union of Artaud and Brecht, the theatre of cruelty with the theatre of ideas, mental punishment with political discussion, is as important to Fassbinder as it was to Pasolini and Polanski. The director, Jeff, of *Beware of a Holy Whore*, Petra von Kant, and the crippled Angela of *Chinese Roulette* are all maniacal figures who exercise enormous power over everyone whose lives touch theirs. The irony, however, is that their enormous power is only temporary; although some figures are completely mesmerized by the master—most often indicated by characters who are absolutely and obediently mute like Marlene in *Petra von Kant* and Traunitz in *Chinese Roulette*—others break away to enslave the master. Other central Fassbinder figures are completely mistaken in the power they think they possess—the sexual power of Effi Briest and Fox is much lighter than the social and economic power that engulfs them, and the mercantile power of the merchant of the four seasons is equally illusory and inadequate. As in the plays of Jean Gênet, the characters in Fassbinder films both love to dominate and to be dominated, and many of the films chronicle the revolutions of this sado-masochistic circle. Fassbinder's ultimate sado-masochistic power study is of the writer, Walter Kranz, in *Satan's Brew*, who converts society as a whole into his slave—all for the sake of his "art."

These power studies lead Fassbinder to the occasional but very striking use of low camera angles in every film. His camera unexpectedly drops to the floor, emphasizing the legs, and, often, the boots of a character in the foreground of the frame, translating the emotional dynamics of the relationship into the visual perspective of the shooting angle. Significantly, when the dominating character loses his or her power—the lonely Petra at the end of *Bitter Tears*, the dead body of the forsaken Fox— Fassbinder's camera returns to the extremely low angle to reveal the reversal of dominant and subservient roles. Fassbinder's method also leads him to use concrete physical objects as metaphors for internal states of consciousness—the dolls and fashion mannequins of *Petra von Kant*, the ripe fruit and vegetables of *The Merchant of the Four Seasons*, the dead flies in *Satan's Brew*, the chocolates of *Despair*. A recurrent Fassbinder metaphor is the breaking of cups or glasses, symptomatic of the crumbling of a human personality, usually as a result of getting drunk (particularly of drinking too much cognac too early in the morning).

Ali: Fear Eats the Soul is one of Fassbinder's most popular and accessible works, the strange love story of a middle-aged widow and a young, almost-Black Moroccan who meet, marry, and confront the societal rejection and isolation that would expectedly greet such a marriage. The film is an obvious remake of Douglas Sirk's *All That Heaven Allows*, but the differences between the Sirk film and the Fassbinder show a degree of psychological perceptivity and artistic courage in the German work that the American one either did not or could not achieve. Sirk's middle-aged widow was an upper-class, graceful, and attractive woman (played by Jane Wyman, who, though approaching middle–age, was still a pretty Hollywood movie star); Fassbinder's widow, Emmy, is an old, wrinkled, frumpy, working-class cleaning lady (played by Brigitte Mira, who plays most of Fassbinder's matrons). Sirk's young sexual male was impersonated by Rock Hudson, who played a gardener (which put him in a different social class

Ali: Fear Eats the Soul. *Emmy (Brigitte Mira) and Ali (El Hedi Ben Salem): Fassbinder's radically odd couple*

from those whose trees he pruned, but also gave him a "natural" dignity—a quality that the film emphasized by frequent references to Thoreau's *Walden*). Although Sirk's film made it fairly clear (or as clear as a 1956 Hollywood film could) that the gardener was an attractive sexual object, his embodiment by the very pretty, very perfect-looking, and not very virile Hudson converted the sexual male into a pretty mannequin. Fassbinder's Ali, on the other hand, is a total social outcast (a Black, unlettered stranger in a strange land) but a very powerful graceful male presence, seething with an animal energy and sexuality (as well as an underlying spiritual wholeness and tenderness). While the philosophical positions of the Hudson character in the Sirk film had to be inferred from his forestrial vocation and the Thoreau quotations, Ali's thoughtful world view comes to us in his short, not fully grammatical, existential utterings: "Work much, think little" or "Fear eats the soul."

The ultimate difference between the Sirk and Fassbinder films is that whereas the central narrative question in Sirk was "Can she marry this man?"—a marriage of course opposed by all her friends,

family, and social set—Fassbinder goes beyond to a much more ironic and challenging problem. Of course the same groups oppose the widow's marriage at first (her family, her neighbors, her grocer, the people with whom she works); but the two actually marry at the conclusion of the film's first third (the marriage was merely implied by the final scene in Sirk's film), leaving Fassbinder's final narrative sections for several ironic twists. The animosity of the social milieu that surrounds the married couple softens—particularly when people find there is something to be gained (usually financial) by befriending the strange couple. And only when the animosity of the society softens does the central couple suffer an emotional crisis. Their love has been nurtured and intensified by the antagonism that separates them from everyone else. How can they maintain their affection without those outside enemies? Without living in a world of their own? That question for Fassbinder is the most interesting one about such a relationship—not Can they marry? but Can they stay married? Must social acceptance and the tensions of everyday living necessarily corrupt the lonely need and exotic passion that were the bases for their relationship in the first place? That kind of question seemed beyond Sirk and any other Hollywood film of the era that so influenced Fassbinder.

Fox and His Friends, despite its homosexual milieu, is a similarly ironic parable of the conflict between personal erotic relationships and the surrounding bourgeois economic and moral landscape. Fox, a working-class boy-man (played by Fassbinder himself) who survives by working in carnivals and as a hustler, wins 500,000 marks in the lottery. The money gives him an entry into the world of "finer things," and he manages to acquire a very pretty new lover, a very "smart set" of new friends, a fancy apartment stocked with paintings and antique furniture, a very expensive sports car, fashionable clothes, and other cultural benefits such as pretentious meals in French restaurants, pretentiously chic dinner and cocktail parties, and exotic vacations in far-off Marrakech. He lends immense amounts of money to Eugen, his lover, which help prop up the boy's tottering family business, and he carelessly signs legal contracts that will defraud him of both his money and his property.

Fassbinder carefully details the conspiracy of the entire surrounding society to fleece Fox, particularly showing that everyone with whom he does business is, like Fox himself, a homosexual—the antique dealer, the clothes salesman, the lawyer, Eugen himself. Although they all share this apparently antisocial, antibourgeois sexual preference, all of these homosexuals are perfectly acceptable in the proper bourgeois world (represented by Eugen's father and mother or the travel agent) because they accept all the bourgeois assumptions about money, property, and possessions. Their economic loyalties are much stronger (and much more socially significant) than their sexual ones. Fox, who has blindly, romantically, willingly done everything for the love of Eugen—he, like Emmy and Ali, is the pure and true romantic in the film—ends completely stripped of everything—no lover, no friends, no car, no apartment, no money, and no life. In a truly ironic final image, Fox lies dead of an overdose of valium on the cold white shiny tiles and stones of a public building—appropriately enough, one of those new underground shopping emporia—while two teenage boys rob the corpse of both its remaining Deutschmarks and the denim jacket that has been Fox's trademark, accompanied by the bitterly cold gaiety of carnival music.

Satan's Brew may be Fassbinder's most amusing synthesis of political allegory, visual style, and human hysteria. The tyrannical political poet, Walter Kranz, becomes Fassbinder's embodiment of the Myth of the Artist in bourgeois society. For Fassbinder, the Myth of the Artist is identical to the Myth of Fascism, and the perfect Artist is also the perfect Fascist—and vice versa. Kranz tyrannizes everyone in his life—his wife, who seems permanently married to the kitchen and who perpetually demands money, money, money; several mistresses, one of whom he visits with the permission of her husband and another of whom he apparently murders in one of the funniest sado-masochistic sexual scenes ever filmed (she reaches her climax by writing a check); a totally adoring nitwit from the country (complete with ridiculously thick comic glasses) whom he swindles and converts into a piece of slavish furniture; his idiot brother (who collects dead flies); even his own parents (whom he robs of

Fox and His Friends: *Fox (Fassbinder himself) with his lover, Eugen (Peter Chatel), in the overstuffed, overdecorated, bourgeois "museum" that is their home*

their funeral money). All of these people (and several others) become Kranz's willing slaves because, after all, he is an Artist, and Artists are divine, and They never have enough money, and, therefore, anything They do for their Art or for money is justified and justifiable. The patience and ministrations of Kranz's adoring slaves is apparently rewarded, for the man, who had written nothing for two years, finally produces a new work—a sort of journal, novel, tract—titled, appropriately enough, "No Ceremony for the Führer's Dead Dog." Having apparently murdered one person, contributed to the terminal illness of his wife, blackmailed another person, and robbed several others, the Artist has finally produced a Work. But when Kranz reports his idiot brother Ernst to the police as the murderer of the mistress he himself killed, Ernst shoots Kranz in the back, an assassination that apparently ends the dictator's rule.

But Fassbinder has another trick and twist up his allegorical sleeve. Ernst only apparently shoots Kranz, just as the mistress is only apparently dead, for in the film's final scene, the supposedly dead mistress visits Kranz's apartment and a bucket of cold water revives the supposedly dead Kranz. After demonstrating that the pistol merely fired blanks, complete with the red dye that makes a very real and deadly looking wound, the characters giggle with glee in an almost satanic celebration of a comic witches' Sabbath. The audience realizes that the entire narrative has been a fake, a sham, a joke; there has been no real story and no real characters. All the film's personages, in their stereotypically comic one-dimensionality, have all been creatures out of Kranz's imagination— indeed, they are the characters in his novel, his Work of Art. But there is no Walter Kranz; Fassbinder himself is the true Walter Kranz, for he has swindled, and teased, and prodded, and hypnotized us as mercilessly as Kranz

did any of his victims. The art of Fascism is that it tyrannically reduces us to its hypnotic slaves, which we willingly become, and the fascism of Art is that it works in precisely the same way and for the same reasons.

Werner Herzog makes both documentaries and fictional feature films, but the differences between them are not nearly so great as such terms imply. Even Herzog's documentaries are far less concerned with the objective recording of events, processes, or conditions than with the internal, emotional, and experiential sensations of undergoing a particular event, process, or condition. *Land of Silence and Darkness* (1971) attempts to recreate the sensation of experiencing the world as a blind and deaf human being (quite a task for film, whose two tools are visual imagery and recorded sounds). *The Great Ecstasy of the Sculptor Steiner* (1974) attempts to transfer the ski jumper's sensation of flying from the film's subject to its audience. And *La Soufrière* (1977), a documentary about an anticipated volcanic catastrophe on the island of Guadaloupe that does not take place, is more interested in transferring the mysterious emptiness, desolation, and loneliness of the evacuated city of Basse Terre than in chronicling a scientific or seismic event. Whether in his documentaries or in his fictional films, Herzog depends entirely on the poetic sensations and evocations of his visual imagery, invariably distinguished by its intense silence, its haunting stillness, its mysterious impenetrability, its hypnotic slowness. One of the most memorable and essential of these images is the shot of ten thousand windmills in Herzog's first feature—*Signs of Life*. Herzog's camera slowly and silently pans across the valley of a Greek island filled with all those windmills, each of them turning silently, hypnotically, mysteriously, continuously from the silent force of an unseen wind.

Among Herzog's favorite images are natural settings that are barren, rough, uncivilized, untamed, and, essentially, untameable. The arid rocky island of Cos in *Signs of Life,* the lushly dense, green Amazonian jungle of *Aguirre, the Wrath of God* (1972), or the flat dusty brown Wisconsin plains of *Stroszek* (1977) are the typical visual environments to which Herzog's German characters have been transported. These people are very much away from "home," and the forbidding, desolate landscapes emphasize their separation and isolation. These visual jungles and deserts are the only "homes" these driven people will or can know. Herzog's soundtracks are as careful as his visual imagery; he gives particular attention to musical themes and the musical scoring of both speech and noises—the repetitive use of intense and mysterious silences; the calls, cries, and hoots of birds in *Aguirre;* the musical passages by Pochelbel and Mozart that open *Kaspar Hauser* (1974); the clash of languages (German and English) and the ironic clash of musical styles (German glockenspiel music as opposed to American pop-rock) in *Stroszek,* or the breathlessly rapid, almost incomprehensible chant of the auctioneer in the same film, a chant that is both a jumble of language and a complex musical passage.

At the center of the Herzog narrative is a single character who follows his single-minded determination to an inevitable and irreversible end. The Herzog characters are driven by compulsions from within that can neither be softened nor averted. Aguirre, the Spanish conquistador, is driven to seek the mythical city of El Dorado in the depths of the South American jungle. He tyrannically and unswervingly pushes his pathetic little band of steadily dwindling Europeans into the heart of the immense and unknown continent, refusing to alter his determination despite the murderous natives, the devastating heat, the crippling diseases, the dense forest, and the angry uncharted waters. Aguirre becomes a

Aguirre, the Wrath of God. *Aguirre (Klaus Kinski) demonically enclosed in his universe of one*

determined and wrathful god who ignores the evidence and arguments of both men and nature. The result is complete catastrophe—the death of everyone on the pathetically small raft that Aguirre has forged to tame the continent. The final shot of the film is both a dazzling cinematic device and Herzog's brilliant visual metaphor for Aguirre's mind and world. As the leader stands firmly atop his raft, littered with the bodies of his followers and the frenetic scrambling of what seem like ten thousand monkeys, moving inexorably toward his own certain death, Herzog's camera hovers above Aguirre in the air (undoubtedly from a helicopter, but used so fluidly and unobtrusively that we never feel its vibrations nor see its shadow). The hovering airborne camera then traces a full, 360 degree circle around the raft, ringing the man and his kingdom off from the rest of the world, revealing that Aguirre's physical and mental universes are essentially a non-human world of one.

He is their sole human occupant, just as the single desire to reach El Dorado is the sole occupant of his brain. He has succeeded in translating his intangible imagination into a concrete physical world. Unfortunately, it is a very small world—the size of a wooden raft—and he is the only person who can live there (and even he cannot live there for long).

Other Herzog figures similarly attempt to mold the physical world according to the shapes of their imagination, and they predictably run into trouble when it fails to respond so malleably. Like Aguirre, the residents of a small German town in *Heart of Glass* become obsessed with a mythical quest that leads to death and destruction —not the discovery of El Dorado but the rediscovery of a secret formula for making the perfect ruby-red glass for which the town is famous. Like Aguirre, the innocent child-man Kaspar Hauser sees the universe with a singleness of personal vision that clashes with the assumptions of all those citizens who teach him to see it differently by teaching him to speak. And the central characters of *Signs of Life* and *Stroszek,* both of them named Stroszek, eventually follow their own instincts and visions by rebelling against a dull and deadening social order that they have come to find stifling and enslaving.

In *Signs of Life*, Stroszek is a Nazi soldier, wounded in action against the Partisans on Crete at the beginning of the film and assigned to duty for the duration of the war on the apparently peaceful and placid Greek island of Cos, where he is to recover from his injuries. The island's sunny placidity becomes a prison of lethargy, reducing the German soldiers to lazy, plodding performers of petty, meaningless routines. To some extent, Herzog's political point about the Nazi army as an occupational force is that its power was not a result of its efficiency or brutality but of its banality; it produced discipline and order by numbing its servants with boredom.

Herzog makes the stagnant lifelessness of this daily routine almost tactile with shots of the glaring white walls of Greek houses shining in the bright sunlight, with contrasting textures such as thin stalks of waving weeds against the heavy, stiff, still marble slabs of that earlier civilization, and with immense far shots of the town and the terrain that emphasize their stillness, emptiness, and deadness. Dominating the film are metaphoric images of imprisonment—a soldier devises a trap to catch cockroaches and another to catch fish; the eyes and ears of a tiny wooden owl are moved by a living fly trapped inside it; a soldier can hypnotize a chicken by pushing its beak to the ground and chalking a straight line in front of it. Stroszek refuses to be a trapped fly or hypnotized chicken, rebelling against this cage of dull normality. His moment of epiphany comes at the sight of those hypnotically turning windmills, trapped like himself in perpetual circles of repetitive motion, responding passively to a force unseen and uncontrollable. But Stroszek's rebellion is a comic one; he seizes the fort and arsenal he has been assigned to defend and bombards the town and its occupying army with the fireworks he has constructed there (like M. Hulot on holiday).

The later Stroszek's rebellion in *Stroszek* is less comic and less exuberant. As in *Signs of Life,* the central issues of the film are freedom, spontaneity, and enslavement. Its first shot is of a narrow prison corridor as Stroszek is about to gain his freedom (he has been imprisoned for some unspecified disorderly conduct produced by his drinking), and the shot immediately raises the central question of whether this man will ever be free. Stroszek, an inarticulate unshaven drunken bum, is, like Kaspar Hauser, an innocent and "natural man" who has no alternative but to live in human society (he is played by Herzog's discovery, Bruno S., who also played Kaspar).

Stroszek. *Stroszek (Bruno S.) and Herr Scheidt (Clemens Scheitz) in a parodic robbery of an American barbershop*

Stroszek's best "friends" are his musical instruments (an accordion, a glockenspiel, a bugle, a grand piano), with whom he spontaneously "converses," and his parrot, who knows only a few repetitive scraps of speech. After protecting Eva, a prostitute, from the repeated beating of two thugs, Stroszek, Eva, and his neighbor, old Herr Scheidt, seek a new life of freedom in the "Land of the Free"—by moving to Wisconsin. But here Stroszek discovers a more subtle form of social enslavement, no longer the brutal torture of Berlin thugs but the polite and smiling imprisonment of bankers and financial obligations—one's job (he works as an automobile mechanic, Eva as a waitress in a Howard Johnson–style truck stop), one's debts (both their television set and their mobile home have been bought on payments), and, especially, the shiny falsity of modern America's plastic landscape (even Stroszek's mattress is wrapped in plastic). This Stroszek is as trapped in the thin shiny surfaces of modern America as the Stroszek in *Signs of Life* was trapped in the sun, weeds, and stones of arid Greece.

Eva is also trapped—by her inability to live life in any other way but as a prostitute. Her departure with two truck drivers triggers Stroszek's ultimate collapse—he sinks into drunken inactivity, loses the mobile home and television set to the bank, attempts to become a bank robber in revenge (he and the tiny old Herr Scheidt, who speak nothing but German, become a marvelous parody of Butch Cassidy and the Sundance Kid), but has to settle for a barber shop. He eventually commits suicide as he travels in the vicious circle of a mountain chair lift. As in *Signs of Life,* Herzog uses images of perpetual circularity as metaphors for human enslavement. The chair lift on which Stroszek takes his final ride is an unending circular journey; before climbing aboard, Stroszek sets his truck in gear and turns the steering wheel so that the truck continues to travel around the parking lot in perpetual circles by itself after Stroszek has walked away from it. As the image of the constantly turning truck indicates, the close connection between human life and mechanical processes is another of the consistent metaphors of this highly metaphoric film. Trucks, which might produce the freedom of travel and linear movement, become consistent images of enclosure and containment. Significantly, Stroszek's mobile home is pulled behind a truck, like a semitrailer, and the "home" itself merely becomes a visual variation of the long, confining body of a truck. Other "life" machines in this film (which could also have been titled "Signs of Life") include an incubator, where a premature baby lies under glass, unaware of the cage of life that awaits it; a voltage meter that Herr Scheidt uses to measure the "animal magnetism" of living beings; and a metal detector that a Wisconsin auto mechanic uses to search the plains for traces of a suspected corpse.

In *Stroszek's* metaphoric definition of the human condition, man occupies a position midway between the machine and the animal. For this reason, the most striking images in *Stroszek* are, like the final shot in *Aguirre,* those with which this highly imagistic film ends; and, as in *Signs of Life,* they are images of encaged animals. In *Stroszek,* like the child in the incubator, these animals are "under glass." Just before his suicidal ride in the chair lift, Stroszek visits an amusement arcade where several diversions have been devised to entertain passing tourists. In one glass cage is the "Fire Chief Rabbit"—a living rabbit forced to ride a toy fire engine when a customer drops a coin in the slot (Herzog cross-cuts between the Fire Chief Rabbit and Stroszek's truck, which has caught on fire and which real firemen rush to extinguish). In another glass cage is the "Dancing Chicken"—a chicken strutting about on a circular turntable that resembles a record disc, another enslaving circle (Stroszek himself, in his love of music, has also been a sort of dancing chicken). And in the final glass cage is the "Piano-Playing Chicken"—who pecks out a tune on a toy piano with its beak (the animal most of all like Stroszek, who has also pecked out tunes on his piano and glockenspiel). Unlike the Stroszek of *Signs of Life,* who discovered and demonstrated his own vital signs by rebelling against the stifling Nazi regimen, this later Stroszek finds his only possible source of freedom in death, for the enslaving trap in *Stroszek* is life itself, which incomprehensibly has suspended human beings in the abyss between organic animal vitality and the perpetual motion of soulless machines.

Wim Wenders's films are most like American movies in both their style and their content. They are also about American movies—and the pervasive force of American culture in general. Characters in Wenders films drink Jack Daniels whiskey, listen to American rock music on American juke boxes, discuss American novels, drive American cars, delight in American names, and, in effect, attempt to recreate the lifestyles and values of characters—particularly male characters—in American films. The goalie in *The Goalie's Anxiety at the Penalty Kick* (1971) attends a showing of Howard Hawks's *Red Line 7000* and a newspaper in *Alice in the Cities* (1974) announces the death of John Ford. If Wenders films glorify American culture and American movies, they also glorify the art of cinema itself. French directors Jean Eustache and Gerard Blain play roles in *The American Friend,* as do American directors Ray and Fuller, and the two buddies of *Kings of the Road,* in explicating a passage from Faulkner's *The Wild Palms,* are also paying their respects to Godard's *Breathless,* in which Patricia explicates a passage from the same novel.

The vocation of one of the two major characters in *Kings of the Road* is to service motion picture projectors, maintaining the machines that allow the art of cinema to exist. The shadow-show that the two friends mime behind a movie screen, their three-dimensional flesh-and-blood bodies converted into two-dimensional silhouettes by the work light behind them, is a tribute both to the magic of silent comedy (their routine is a very Chaplinesque or Laurel and Hardyish one) and to the hypnotic magic of cinema in general (their antics entrance a group of noisy children, impatient for the equipment to be repaired and the film to begin, into mute and adoring silence). This "live" shadow-show becomes itself a piece of cinema—two-dimensional, moving, silent silhouettes on a white screen, created by the powers of light. The crimes against life in *Kings of the Road* are crimes against cinema— projectionists who do not care whether the image is properly framed or focussed, whether their equipment is clean and well-oiled; filmmakers who debase the art of cinema by turning love into pornography and violence.

The central narrative issue and interest of *Kings of the Road* is this intersection of life and cinema. As its title indicates, the film is a story of people on the road—like Chaplin's Tramp, like Huck Finn, like Jack Kerouac's wanderers, like cowboys in American westerns. The road is a place of total freedom from social entanglements; the two men in the truck, like the cowboys on their mounts, belong everywhere and nowhere. One of the men, Robert, the projector repairman, would be analogous to, say, the piano tuner who rode from frontier town to town to service that essential piece of dance-hall entertainment equipment (did anyone ever make a western about a piano tuner?). Rather than being the roaming gunslinger, the figure of death, Robert is a figure of entertainment, joy, amusement, life. His decision to disentangle himself from the world, to live on the road, to keep his life moving by keeping himself in perpetual motion, is a long-standing one. His new traveling companion and passenger, Bruno, a child psychologist who has just broken with his wife, is still emotionally entangled and confined by his life—his unfulfilling relationship with his father, his wife, and with children themselves (an irony—given his vocation). In riding along together, the two "kings of the road," who begin as opposites, achieve a synthesis; the tangled Bruno discovers the openness, the cleanness, the simplicity, the wholeness of the road, of being at one, and at home, with himself.

The American Friend is also about achieving a synthesis of opposites and a wholeness with oneself. At the center of the film is another contrast of two men—Tom Ripley (Dennis Hopper), an American wheeler-dealer engaged in various shady business transactions (the "cowboy in Hamburg"), and Jonathan Zimmerman (Bruno Ganz), a Swiss framemaker and art restorer who lives in Hamburg with his wife and child. The two men come together when Zimmerman makes the frame for one of the paintings Ripley sells, a picture by a noted American painter presumed dead. On the surface, the two men appear to be as opposite as Switzerland and the American West—the one a quiet, careful, devoted craftsman and family man, the other a rootless, valueless, slippery, shuffling wanderer, attached to nothing and no one. But the two are not so different as they seem. There is an emptiness at the center of each man's life. The framemaker's life is all frame and no picture; it has shape but no image to shape. Wenders emphasizes this condition with images of empty frames that Zimmerman carefully scrutinizes, despite their emptiness. Ripley's life is also all surface, all style, and no accomplishment. He may look like a cowboy, talk like a cowboy, walk like a cowboy, but all he does is serve as middleman for a mildly unethical scheme to drive up the prices of a painter's works. Both are foreigners in Hamburg. Both are spiritually homeless.

Closely related to the contrast of these two different men who are not entirely different at all is a contrast of vision and action. The film is built around metaphors for human vision: the framemaker suffers from a terminal disease that attacks the eyes; Wenders packs the film with a little history of objects and devices that have extended the powers of human vision—painted canvases, a Stereopticon, a Zoetrope, peep-hole viewers, an illuminated electrified painting (significantly, it is of a train named "The General"), a Polaroid Land camera, and television. The references to movies are the most central of these visual metaphors (just as they are in *Kings of the Road*) yet among the most subtle. The framemaker, Zimmerman, is a surrogate for a filmmaker, whose business is also making frames. And the cowboy, Ripley, is the typical subject of movies— quirky, active, aggressive, violent, intriguingly unpredictable. In order to achieve a whole movie, one needs both

Alice in the Cities. *Rudiger Vogler, Wenders's alterego in his black-and-white films, surveys the bleak American landscape with his Polaroid*

frame and subject, shape and content. In the same way, for Ripley to become whole he needs a frame, a shape for his actions; and for Zimmerman to become whole, he needs an action, a content, for his frames.

The film unites the two men by plunging them into just such an action that unites them. One of the Mafia-style men with whom Ripley associates needs to assassinate a member of a rival organization. Zimmerman seems a perfect choice for the job: he is dying and has nothing to lose; he can make a lot of money to provide for his wife and child after his death; and he has no motive for the murder and no connection with either of the rival organizations. Zimmerman's eventual agreement to perform the one simple anonymous murder, however, inexorably drags both Ripley and Zimmerman into a proliferating series of additional murders, violent confrontations, and breathless escapes. There is, of course, a sense in which the accelerating and expanding violence into which the two men are drawn is a terrible trap—a sense that Wenders emphasizes by images of confinement, entanglement, and enclosure (tunnels, narrow escalators, confined passageways of trains, labyrinthine corridors). But there is also a sense in which the violence becomes an

assertive, existential act of human defiance against emptiness, inactivity, and meaninglessness—a sense that Wenders emphasizes with the extremely open, vast images (parallel to the open images of *Kings of the Road*) that dominate the final scene of the film.

As acts of human existential assertion that achieve their meaning solely from being violent, dangerous, and deadly, the activities of the two men in *The American Friend* become precisely parallel to such assertive existential actions in the masculine films of Nicholas Ray and Samuel Fuller—two of the directors whom Wenders has (deliberately and pointedly) cast in the film. Unlike Ray and Fuller, whose films embrace such actions with fewer doubts and suspicions, Wenders balances the exhilaration of such accomplishment with the ironic awareness that engaging in such a process also plunges the performers into a trap of inevitability; there is no turning back or returning to the beginning of the game. Zimmerman's growing estrangement from his wife indicates his steady and irreversible attachment to Ripley as a new "wife" and way of life. The sequence of violent events must be played out to its end. But since Zimmerman was fated from the beginning to die at the end anyway (and who is not?), Wenders ironically reveals the meaningfulness of Zimmerman's choice and his steady acceptance of the consequences of that choice, even while destroying the solid frame of his previous peaceful existence. The explicit development of these emotional ironies and existential paradoxes seems (like Fassbinder's manipulation of Sirk) far beyond the scope, interests, and perceptions of Wenders's American friends, Ray and Fuller.

The American Friend is perhaps the most interesting and intriguing combination of old American movie action and new German film style, of narrative complexity, emotional sensitivity, and

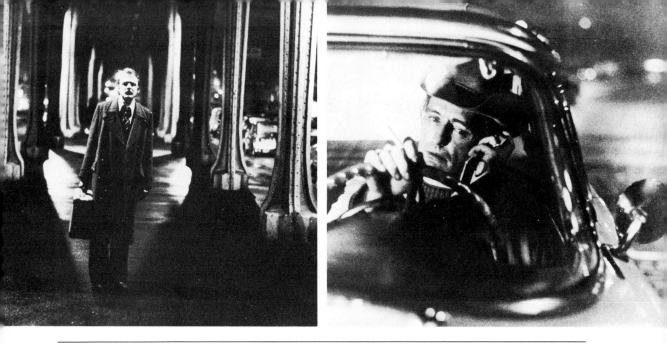

The American Friend: *The framemaker (Bruno Ganz) framed by the oppressive confines of modern architecture, the cowboy in Hamburg (Dennis Hopper) framed by the CinemaScope windshield of his 1950s car*

philosophical inquiry, that the new German cinema has produced in its first decade. But the German cinema movement—like Fassbinder, Herzog, and Wenders themselves—is still very young. In addition to these three major figures, Jean-Marie Straub, Volker Schlöndorff, Werner Schroeter, Hans Giessendorffer, Reinhard Hauff, and Wolfgang Staudte have also contributed in the last decade to the growing significance of the new German cinema. As the movement achieves greater stature, greater maturity, and greater recognition, there will undoubtedly be others.

Cinemas East

The Japanese cinema first conquered the West when Akira Kurosawa's *Rashomon* won the Grand Prize at the Venice Film Festival of 1951. In the wake of *Rashomon* followed a series of imaginative and impressive films from Japan, directed by Kurosawa and by other masters of a cinema that had previously been unknown to Western audiences: Kenji Mizoguchi, Yasujiro Ozu, Teinosuke Kinugasa, Kon Ichikawa, Hiroshi Inagaki, and many others. The decade of the 1950s proved to be Japan's richest cinematic era—both commercially and artistically—as a result of many of the same forces that stimulated the new Western film industries in the same period: the receptivity to new forms of film expression; the new market for non-American films; and the new period of political and intellectual freedom. Like many of the European nations, the Japanese cinema emerged from over a decade of political constraints caused both by the Second World War and its aftermath of normalization. What was equally surprising for both Western audiences and critics was not simply the maturity of Japanese films in this decade but the richness and depth of the Japanese film tradition; Mizoguchi, Ozu, and Kinugasa had been directing films since the 1920s.

The Japanese cinema developed under conditions that kept it approximately ten years behind the cinemas of the West, a lag that worked in its favor in the 1950s, for the Japanese film industry felt the crippling effects of television almost a decade later than the industries of America and Europe. So too, the early period of primitivism lasted a decade longer in Japan, at least into the mid-1920s. Although there were commercial reasons for this retardation—a lag in organizing the industry, problems with machines and film—the primary reasons were aesthetic. First, women did not appear in Japanese films until the mid-1920s, women's roles being played by female impersonators, called *oyama* (Kinugasa's career began as an *oyama*). This sacrifice of naturalness and authenticity tended to keep the Japanese cinema tied to its theatrical roots (where men also played the female roles) and kept it from asserting the kind of naturalness and spontaneity that gradually evolved in the films of the West between 1905 and 1915. Second, the Japanese cinema used a narrator to explain the film to the audience. Called the *benshi*, this narrator's presence not only eliminated the need for printed titles but also for a "grammar and rhetoric" of the cinema itself. With a human being to do the speaking, the cinema itself did not need to "speak" in its own unique and powerful terms. All the early Western masters of the cinema—Griffith, Eisenstein, Murnau, et al.—were specifically those who discovered ways to make a purely visual "language" communicative.

These backward Japanese cinematic traditions died slowly and unwillingly. The *oyama* disrupted film production in 1922 by calling a strike when they saw they were to be replaced by women. The

benshi, who had made themselves into one of the primary attractions of the Japanese cinema (often an audience attended a film merely to enjoy the commentary of a clever and popular *benshi*), fought extinction even more vigorously. In 1932 the *benshi* and the theatre musicians called a strike against the entire film industry; some *benshi* turned off the sound track of the early sound films so they could do their act; on at least one occasion the *benshi* union hired thugs to assault an official of one of the studios that was converting to sound.

When sound finally came to the Japanese cinema it too came almost a decade later than to the film industries of the West. The first successful sound film was not shot in Japan until 1931—*The Neighbor's Wife and Mine*, directed by Heinosuke Gosho. In 1932 only 45 of some 400 Japanese films used synchronized sound. Ozu did not shoot his first sound film until 1936, and silent production did not die completely until 1937.

The coming of sound to Japan was quickly followed by the coming of war, and the Japanese government demanded that the film industry support the war effort with films reflecting national militaristic policies. An equally repressive policy restricted the Japanese film industry after the war when the American Occupation Forces created a cultural "reorientation" committee, which banned certain subjects (for example, all Japanese period dramas because they were feudalistic and militaristic) and demanded others (for example, the values of peaceful living and democratic institutions). Which brings us again to 1950 and *Rashomon*.

On the other hand, the Japanese film industry had developed a number of practices and traditions that would work for rather than against it when a period of commercial, technical, and political equality would enable it to compete on the world's screens. First, the Japanese film industry was the only other film industry in the world organized like the American one—around the studio system. Whereas studios in other countries were either buildings where individual production companies rented space (like the American studios in the 1970s) or a single monolithic production company owned by the state, the Japanese system was composed of several competing commercial companies, with their own writers, directors, actors, and technicians working under contract, which were in the business of conceiving, making, and selling films. The four Japanese studios that became most familiar to Western audiences were Nikkatsu (the oldest, founded in 1912—Ichikawa's studio); Shochiku (founded in 1920 and for three decades the commercial leader—Ozu's studio); Toho (founded in the 1930s by the amalgamation of several smaller companies—Kurosawa's primary studio; exploiter of Japanese monster pictures, like *Godzilla;* developer of Japan's own wide-screen, anamorphic process, Tohoscope); and Daiei (founded during the war—producer of *Rashomon, Gate of Hell,* and Mizoguchi's later films).

One of the obvious implications of such a studio system is production in quantity, and the Japanese industry regularly produced over four hundred feature films each year, second only to Hollywood in its most golden Studio Era and leader in quantitative output when American production fell in the 1950s. As in the United States, this production in quantity guaranteed a very large number of very bad to passably mediocre films every year. But as in the U.S., it also guaranteed a significant number of films every year that would rank among the art's finest achievements.

The Japanese studio system avoided many of the evils of the American system, but it produced others. A primary advantage was that the system was built around the director rather than the producer or star. The Japanese "producer" is comparable to the First Assistant Director in Hollywood, a person who, despite the title, is really the assistant to the producer and who manages production details but makes no decisions. The Japanese director is a more powerful audience attraction than a film's star, and it is the director's name—not the star's—that frequently appears above the title in Japanese films. As a result, Japanese stars earn far less money than their counterparts in the West and consequently enjoy far less power. The Japanese director is the paternalistic head of his own production "family"—the Japanese film industry being modeled to some extent as a mirror of Japanese society. The disadvantages of such a system—more comfortable and less competitive than Hollywood's—are, first, that genuinely talented directors must serve long apprenticeships in order to work themselves up the familial ladder. Japan does not import instant talents from outside its studio system—no Rouben Mamoulians or Mike Nichols who come from the theatre; no François Truffauts, Jean-Luc Godards, Lindsay Andersons, and Peter Bogdanovichs who come from film journals. A second disadvantage is that the paternalistic system tends to perpetuate mediocrity and incompetence, for no member of any family is thrown out of it for mediocrity.

In its film subjects the Japanese cinema also bears a striking resemblance to American movies; Japanese films tend to bunch themselves in clear-cut genres and cycles. In fact, Japanese genres are even more specifically defined and definable than their American counterparts. The basic division is between the *jidai-geki,* a period or costume film set in Japan's past, and *gendai-geki,* a film of modern life. But within these two basic genres there are many subgenres. The *jidai-geki* can be further subdivided into the particular period of Japanese history it depicts— Tokugawa period, Meishi period, and so on. The *gendai-geki* has such subgenres as the *shomin-geki* (middle-class comedy), the "mother picture" (a mother's relationship to her children), the "wife picture" (the difficulties of marriage for women), the "nonsense picture" (farcical comedies), and the "youth picture" (the wild doings of youth, parallel to Hollywood's "beach-blanket" genre of the 1950s and 1960s). As in Hollywood films, the least able directors freeze these genres into collections of their most banal and predictable conventions, whereas the most talented ones breathe life into the film either by developing those conventions with great personal intensity and sensitivity or by reversing the conventional expectations altogether.

Given the quantity and diversity of Japanese production, it is more difficult to find consistent traits of style than in the more unified movements of Italy, France, or Czechoslovakia. Again, the parallel with the American Studio Era is the illustrative one—an era in which Lubitsch, Ford, Hawks, Capra, von Sternberg, Sturges, Cukor, and W. C. Fields all made films at the same time. Two consistent structural traits seem to dominate the best Japanese films, however, and both of these traits are descendants of the Japanese theatrical traditions of the Kabuki and the Noh.

First, the best films are ruthlessly economical in their concentration on the central theme. Rather than fill up the script with flavorful and atmospheric touches to "flesh out" a film—in a sense diverting an audience from the central issue and giving the film a feeling of life's randomness—the great Japanese films seem to rivet every incident of the plot, every character, every visual image, and every line of dialogue to the film's single thematic question (and there is usually only one). A second, and related, structural trait is the Japanese concern for symmetry. Many of the best Japanese films are not close studies of individual people or pairs but of a fairly large group of people who make different choices, take different paths in life, and thereby come to different ends. This structural feeling for symmetry keeps these multipath "journeys" moving along side by side in the audience's mind, all of the paths united, of course, by the single thematic issue that has produced the "journey" in the first place.

Unlike the French or Czech cinemas, there is no single consistent trait of visual style that dominates the Japanese cinema. Those three directors who, at least from a Western perspective, appear to be Japan's greatest film artists—Akira Kurosawa, Kenji Mizoguchi, and Yasujiro Ozu—have three completely different visual senses and use three completely different cinematographic principles. These very visual differences are what make them such unique and individual stylists.

Akira Kurosawa is the Japanese director most popular in the West—perhaps more popular in the West than in Japan—but he also seems the Japanese director with the greatest power, the greatest range, and the greatest stylistic imagination and inventiveness. Kurosawa is the only one of the three Japanese directors with effective films in both the *jidai-* and *gendai-geki*. He is also the only one of the Japanese masters who is obviously influenced by films of the West. Kurosawa's *samurai* films are closely related to American westerns (and have been remade as westerns); his films move with the swift, violent pace of American films rather than the more leisurely pace of Japanese films; and he is clearly influenced by Western cinematic styles, especially the use of the subjective traveling camera, the use of extreme deep-focus photography, and, consequently, the use of very fast film stock. Kurosawa also seems to share an artistic trait with such Western directors as Hitchcock and Truffaut—the urge to tackle very difficult stylistic problems that require him to push himself beyond the artistic frontiers he has already charted and conquered.

Rashomon (1950) clearly demonstrates

Kurosawa's thematic concerns and stylistic maturity (he had been directing films since 1943). The film is famous as the essential cinematic demonstration of the relativity and subjectivity of truth—and that it is. But of greater interest in the film is, first, Kurosawa's stylistic control that conveys and convinces us of that subjectivity and, second, what he says human beings should do with their lives given the relativity and subjectivity of truth.

The film uses what might be described as six different cinematic styles, six separate camera strategies, each corresponding to one of the levels of the film's realities. Two of the six sections are "frames," not the central incident itself but ways of telling or finding out about the incident. One of these two frames is primary: two men telling a third about the incident as they sit beneath the ruins of the Rashomon Gate during a rainstorm; the other is, in effect, a frame-within-a-frame: the testimony of the three participants in the incident to a "judge" who is attempting to discover exactly what happened and why. The remaining four sections are four different versions of what happened and why, each of them mirroring the attitudes, perceptions, and personality of the witness. The single concrete fact is that a man lies dead in the forest. But human beings need to assign a cause, to see a reason for a catastrophic fact, and the film becomes a search for this reason.

The film's primary frame introduces this search as two men, a Woodcutter and a Priest (representatives of the secular and sacred orders), feel compelled to tell their story to a stranger, perhaps to aid their search, perhaps to ease their suspicion that the search has no end. Kurosawa sets this frame during a furious and violent rainstorm, from which the only refuge is a pitiful shelter of architectural ruins. Although rainstorms are almost a cliché of the Japanese cinema, Kurosawa clearly uses this storm

as a concrete external image of both the internal mental agony of the unfulfilled search and the chaotic social instability of the era: a period of lawlessness, bandits, plagues, famine, war, and, like the Rashomon Gate itself, ruins. Kurosawa is a master at using concrete natural imagery to evoke abstract and internal human sensations, a technique he brings to perfection in his later *Throne of Blood* (1957). What is intriguing about the Woodcutter's introduction is that he tells the Listener that this incident is especially terrible, worse even than the social chaos of the present. The Listener, whose curiosity is understandably aroused—he serves as the viewer's surrogate in this respect—agrees to listen to the tale in the course of waiting out the storm.

For these scenes at the Gate, Kurosawa uses a conventionally objective cutting and photographic method. He cuts freely—from various distances and angles—to make the viewer a privileged observer, leading us from place to place, always giving us the most interesting and revealing point of view. The dominant motif is the driving sound and image of the incessant rain. But for his frame-within-a-frame—the testimony before the "judge"—Kurosawa uses a totally different visual principle. Kurosawa keeps his camera in a single spot, at about the eye level of a seated observer, while the speakers stare directly at the camera to tell their story. The implication is obvious; the camera is the "judge" and has become the new viewer-surrogate; the camera-judge takes the evidence, attempting to provide the viewer-judge with the means to draw a conclusion. Kurosawa returns to this courtyard (it is not a court*room*, since the camera-judge, as well as the witnesses, are obviously sitting on the ground outdoors) after each of the versions of the tale, just as he returns to the Rashomon Gate after each of the testimonies in the court. So the viewer has the continual feeling of going from the version of the incident to the

Rashomon: *The bride fighting the bandit like a tiger cat (Toshiro Mifune and Machiko Kyo)*

the woman, he describes her in sensual terms—as a cool breeze—and Kurosawa's camera watches a gust of wind ripple through the leaves and across the characters' clothes, accompanied by the rippling tinkle of a celeste. Kurosawa's primary subjective device in the sequence, however, is the violent, furious pace of his tracking and panning shots, the camera's incessant energetic movement, translating Tojamaro's predatory stalking into visual terms. It is also Kurosawa's way of translating the way Tojamaro sees himself: aggressive, restless, dominant, assertive.

According to Tojamaro, his conquest of the woman was exactly that: an assertive masculine act in which he subdues the woman first by his strength and then by his passion. They struggle violently for a dagger—a struggle which he exuberantly enjoys—until he kisses her and she feels the earth reel. Except Kurosawa's subjective camera is quite ironic at this point, for it does not mirror the way the woman feels Tojamaro's kiss (the usual implication of "dizzy" camera movements, as in *The Last Laugh),* but the way Tojamaro feels she feels his kiss. The bandit then bests the husband in fair, violent, valiant combat ("He fought marvellously"), again the virile male displaying the theoretical characteristics of masculinity. Kurosawa's camera catches the flashy *samurai* swordsmanship and the final kill as Tojamaro perceives it: with violent movement of the participants, violent camera movement, and violent cutting. Violence, pace, and movement are the three stylistic keys of the section: in action, in emotion, in camera movement, and in editing (a perfect synthesis of form and content).

The woman (Machiko Kyo) tells a completely different version in style, tone, emphasis, and action. According to the way she sees both herself and the event, she is a "poor helpless woman" (she depicts herself as just as stereotypically "feminine" as Tojamaro is self-

court, to the Gate, and returning again in the opposite direction. Kurosawa's clearly established visual perspectives and the symmetry of his structure keep the location in both space and time completely clear in the viewer's mind.

The first three versions of the incident are those of each of the three principal participants. Each is completely different in human motivation, in the sequence of events, in its emotional tone, and in its visual style. The first version is that of the bandit, Tojamaro, played as a sensual, virile, exuberant male animal by Toshiro Mifune. Tojamaro's version emphasizes the physical sensations of the confrontation—the heat of the day, the glare of the sun, the sting of the gnats that he repeatedly swats—which Kurosawa depicts subjectively, from Tojamaro's point of view. When Tojamaro first sees

stereotypedly "masculine"). Although her version begins after the sexual consummation, her obvious implication is that she had no choice but to submit meekly to the rape of a strong and determined animal (as opposed to the bandit's description of her struggling like a tigercat). It serves both her self-image and her credibility for her to avoid any references to the sexual act itself. So too, the bandit plays a very small role in her version of the incident, and the few glimpses she provides are of a whooping, subrational, subhuman savage, a grotesque caricature of the bandit's masculinity in his own version. The bandit scarcely exists for her because the real object of her concern is her husband, the only one whose reactions to the rape matter. And his reaction is a cold, pitiless, piercing stare. She retrieves her dagger, still stuck in the trunk of a tree (a point

Rashomon: *Husband and bandit (Masayuki Mori and Mifune); husband, bride, and the lethally connecting dagger (Mori and Kyo)*

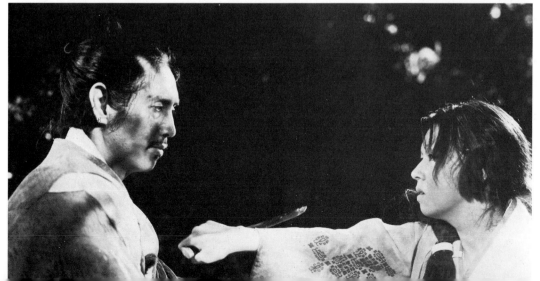

of agreement with Tojamaro's version) and he continues to stare. She starts moving toward him, the dagger erect, and his hypnotic stare continues. For this sequence, Kurosawa's aim is to increase the tension and suspense, and rather than using traveling shots he uses the classic suspense device of the cinema, the cross-cut. As Kurosawa cuts back and forth between the brutally still husband and the seemingly mesmerized wife, hypnotically moving steadily toward him with the knife, the music on the sound track (which sounds unfortunately close to Ravel's "Bolero") pulses and swells, mirroring the tension of the moment for the wife who has been caught in a kind of trance. The result, however, is that she faints, and upon awaking she finds the dagger in her husband's chest (different murder weapon than in Tojamaro's story). Interestingly, Kurosawa does not depict her discovery of the knife visually but merely lets her tell that part of the story to the camera-audience-judge.

The woman's dead husband tells the third version of the story, a feat that Kurosawa accomplishes mystically by using a female medium to summon the man's spirit from the other world and to serve as the vessel of the husband's perceptions. As "he" tells "his" story, Kurosawa uses uniquely cinematic devices to convert this intangible and metaphysical presence into a concrete, tangible, and credible reality. (The Japanese were masters at turning metaphysical spirits into concrete visual realities without making them seem ludicrous, as in Kurosawa's later *Throne of Blood* and Mizoguchi's *Ugetsu*.) A man's voice issues from the woman-medium's lips, and that voice is not only foreign to the apparent sex of the speaker but also strange in its pitch, tone, and timbre—echoing, breathy, hollow, sounding like a phonograph record played at too slow a speed in an underground cavern. Kurosawa supports the bizarre sound with a striking visual image: the medium's

white veils float and flap violently in the wind that has suddenly entered the courtyard, clashing with its previous stillness. The wind is a blast from the supernatural and accompanies, perhaps even carries, the voice of the spirit from that other world.

In contrast to the writhing agony of the medium is the stillness and quiet of the husband's version of the incident itself, toward which his attitude is one of sad resignation. For the husband (played with majestic silence by Masayuki Mori), the woman hardly exists. For him, the essential relationship is between himself and the bandit, two honorable men both caught in the trap of a worthless woman. Whereas the versions of both bandit and wife proceed from stereotypic sexual definitions, the husband's proceeds from the stereotype of honor. The husband sees his action as completely self-determined, completely a matter of his own conscience and his own decision. The mood of that decision is quiet stillness, and Kurosawa shoots the scene of decision from a high angle with the fixed camera and very long takes—as opposed to the predatory traveling shots and the tense cross-cutting of the earlier versions. According to the husband, he does not die by being bested in combat (Tojamaro's version) nor as a result of a hypnotic trance that impels his wife toward him with the dagger (as in hers) but as a result of his own decision—to commit *hara-kiri* according to the *samurai*'s precepts of honor.

But the Woodcutter, who we know (from an earlier traveling shot) discovered the body and who we now find out actually witnessed the entire incident, sees all three versions as concoctions of lies—even the dead man's: "There was no knife." One cannot even depend on supernatural beings for the truth. The Woodcutter then tells his version of the incident, an "objective account" of an outside observer. Interestingly, the Woodcutter is played by

Takashi Shimura, a regular member of the Kurosawa acting family and a figure whom Kurosawa uses consistently as the objective, rational, balanced center of an intense human action (Shimura plays the leader of the *Seven Samurai* who survives to bury his fallen comrades; he plays the equivalent of the Macduff role in *Throne of Blood*).

In the Woodcutter's "objective" account, all three characters are weaker, smaller, and sillier than in their own. The bandit sentimentally begs for forgiveness and blubberingly offers to marry the woman he defiled; the husband is a jittery coward; the wife is a selfish and cackling shrew who simply wants the two men to fight over her. Because both men are so cowardly and so comical in this version, they have a good deal of trouble working up a fight. They both shake with fright, their hands trembling so convulsively they can barely hold their swords, much less make contact with the other's. Their whoops are not masculine assertions of strength (as in the bandit's version) but nervous squeals of sheer terror. Each offers a very tentative poke of a sword-thrust only to scurry away furtively for cover.

For this sequence, Kurosawa uses the generally fixed camera, shooting at some distance from the participants, reducing their stature and the impression of violence, reducing their sloppy swordsmanship to a comic parody of their fight in the bandit's version. One of the most comic of Kurosawa's images is his shot of the tips of the two swords, each shakily and tentatively entering the frame from its opposite sides, trying (but not very hard) to cross in the middle of the frame, only to lose heart, pull back, and evacuate the frame altogether. (Kurosawa uses a similar comic image of weapons entering opposite sides of the frame in *Yojimbo*.) Accompanying these distant comic images is Kurosawa's sound track: no violent whoops (as in the bandit's version), no pulsating music (as in the

wife's), no stillness (as in the husband's), but the sniveling sounds of male whimpers, sobs, and whines, punctuated by the hysterically vulgar cackles of the wife that serve as their goad to combat (and occasionally scare them apart just when they are beginning to get close enough to tangle). Eventually the fight blunders to its climax as the husband loses his weapon and backs away (a long, slow tracking shot rather than a rapid, violent one), trips, and is killed. Even as he whines for mercy, the bandit sobbingly and quiveringly pushes his sword home.

Several questions arise, however, from this "objective" report. First, can an outside observer actually feel the personal and internal resonances of such an intense event? Does his comical, low, and essentially deflating view of human passion and action accurately present the participants' feelings? The Woodcutter's consistent tendency in the film has been to see all forms of human exertion as essentially low and vile. Is he any more to be trusted than the others? Second, if he is to be trusted (however warily), what does his version imply about human behavior, given the conflicting but consistent attempts of the other versions to ennoble human passions and enrich the reasons for human responses? Clearly, the participants do not see their own actions as petty and silly, or they do not say so. But there is the difficulty. Are the participants "lying"—as the Woodcutter believes—or are they telling the "truth" as they perceive it? Lying implies the intention to deceive about what they know to be true. Is that what the characters are doing? Or are they simply telling what they "know" to be true—even if each of them, including the Woodcutter, "knows" something different to be true?

This is the ambiguity that the film poses. But *Rashomon*'s final sequence, which returns us to the ruins of the Rashomon Gate, provides Kurosawa's synthesis of the conflicting versions and resolution of the ambiguity through human action. As the Woodcutter's story finishes, the three men hear the cries of an infant, obviously abandoned to the storm and the ruins by its parents. The Listener's reaction is to steal the baby's clothes and blanket: "We can't live unless we act selfishly these days." The Woodcutter prevents him and protects the helpless infant by drawing a dagger— obviously the mysteriously missing knife that belonged to the wife in all versions of the story except the Woodcutter's. The sudden appearance of this concrete object serves two ironic purposes. First, it shows that the Woodcutter, too, is capable of acting selfishly, of stealing from the victims of misfortune. Second, it undermines the objectivity of his report because it proves that he is really a participant in the incident itself. He has something to hide, and so it is to his advantage to make people believe there was no dagger (as he has said all along) and that the husband died on Tojamaro's sword. The Listener backs away from the Woodcutter's stolen dagger, laughs (for he perceives these ironies that make the Woodcutter no better a man than he), and walks off into the cascades of rain.

The Woodcutter then reaches for the infant, and the Priest's assumption is that now this other thief wants to steal what little protection against life's harshness the infant still has. The Priest's faith in human beings has been so shaken that he now assumes people act from the most selfish and lowest of motives. Instead, the Woodcutter tells the Priest that he will adopt the infant, that he already has six children and a seventh will not make much difference. The two men apologize to one another—the Woodcutter for his callousness and selfishness, the Priest for his lack of faith—and the two men bow. The rain has suddenly stopped, the Woodcutter walks away from the Gate with his new child in his arms, and Kurosawa's tracking camera walks with him as he leaves the ruins of the

Rashomon Gate behind him. The sun finally shines.

Kurosawa's point is that ambiguity, vanity, subjectivity, and self-interest are unavoidable facts of human existence, and that certainty, selflessness, and objectivity are unattainable. All that people can do is their best, or what they feel is their best. They must assert themselves in action as best they can, realizing that it is both impossible to know if that action is really best and to know anything about human experience except what they "know" in their own subjective perceptions.

Kurosawa might be considered the most existential of the Japanese directors: a person is what he or she does simply because it is impossible to discover what anything is in any other way. What a person feels, thinks, or intends is unknowable, even by that person. All four versions of the incident were attempts, in effect, to explain away a brutal, selfish human act that should never have occurred in the first place. Once the inhumane deed has been done, the reasons for it become irrelevant. This same view dominates the other Kurosawa masterpieces of the decade. Kurosawa's two most interesting *samurai* films—*Seven Samurai* (1954) and *Yojimbo* (1961)—work the theme into two opposite situations, both borrowed from the American western. *Seven Samurai* is a variation on the ranchers-against-the-farmers western (like *Shane*), except in Kurosawa's film they are the farmers against the bandits. *Yojimbo* is the story of the paid gun (sword) for hire who rides (stalks) into a small town that is split between two warring but equally crooked rival factions and succeeds in cleaning up both sides. *Seven Samurai* develops the theme of human assertion and action through cooperation—regardless of differences in temperament, background, social class, and personal style. *Yojimbo* develops the theme of self-assertion and individual integrity, the man who can sell his sword but not his values. Kurosawa paid his debt to the American western when both *Rashomon* and *Seven Samurai* were remade by Hollywood as westerns (*The Outrage*, 1964, and *The Magnificent Seven*, 1960, respectively). But the western's debt to Kurosawa may be even greater, for one of his startling and original stylistic devices in *Seven Samurai*—using the lyricism of slow motion to heighten the climactic moment of death in a duel—became a cliché of the "new" western.

Kurosawa's most important *gendai-geki* is *Ikiru* (*Living*, 1952), another extension of his belief in the assertion of human dignity through action, regardless of the reasons for or the consequences of the action. Takashi Shimura plays the major role in a Kurosawa film for once (Kurosawa tends to use Shimura in a supporting role and the more active, assertive Mifune in the major role). *Ikiru* is the story of a petty bureaucrat who has wasted most of his life and who discovers that he is dying of cancer. He decides to dedicate his final days to accomplishing one important thing before his death. The film is as sensitive, as personal, as close in its human observation as the *samurai* stories are active and violent.

But perhaps no two films reveal Kurosawa's stylistic range so well as his two films of 1957, both of them film adaptations of Western classics of the drama: Shakespeare's *Macbeth (Throne of Blood)* and Maxim Gorky's *The Lower Depths*. The two literary texts pose opposite cinematic problems: Shakespeare's magnificent language and sprawling structure; Gorky's claustrophobic, discursive, and philosophic study of a social mass rather than a single protagonist. Kurosawa solved these opposite stylistic problems in opposite ways. He dispensed altogether with Shakespeare's text and translated the spirit of the play's theme and poetry into concrete visual symbols; he kept the text of the Gorky play almost verbatim (it is a far more literal translation of the play than Renoir's 1936 version) and shot the entire film in confined and cramped settings. The results of these opposite approaches of the same year unquestionably rank among the ten finest cinematic adaptations of dramatic works in film history.

In *Throne of Blood* Kurosawa translated Shakespeare's poetry (the references to blood, to the chaos in nature), theme (the valiant man tempted and destroyed by both the evil in himself and in the cosmos —which are identical), and characters (the strong warrior, the grasping wife) into purely visual terms. In a film that is as visually magnificent as any Kurosawa (or anyone else) ever made, it is worth noting his consistent choices: the dominant method is to depict the interrelationship and interpenetration of natural, supernatural, and psychological forces. At the beginning of the film, nature is "out of joint"—there is a violent wind and furious rain storm (as in *Rashomon*). Lord Washizu (the Macbeth figure, played by Mifune) and his friend, Miki (Banquo), attempt to ride through a forest, which attacks them on every side with lightning, tortuous branches, and diverting bypaths (Kurosawa's tracking shots again increase the impression of violence and fury). The tangled, "breathing" forest is both metaphoric of the internal maze in Washizu's mind as well as the ensnaring temptations of the supernatural order, which is about to angle for his soul. This imprisoning forest in the film's early sequence is mirrored by the liberating forest in the late sequence when a moving, man-made forest (the forest's new "soul" is human not superhuman) restores the balance of nature and purges the results of the initial human experience with a forest.

Another of Kurosawa's images linking man, nature, and supernature is fog: the misty white smoke of steamy clouds seemingly rising from beneath the earth. The fog is metaphoric of the universe's poisonous temptations as well as the moral fog in Washizu's mind. When

Consistent imagery in Throne of Blood. *The witch sits blanketed by the mist of the forest; the usurper collapses into the mist at the feet of the moving, human forest*

Washizu first sees the Witch, she is sitting on the earth, seemingly rising out of the fog which blankets her legs and feet. And her skin is the same chalk white as that pestilential mist. And then Kurosawa makes a dazzling leap from the metaphysical to the psychological plane, for Lady Washizu (Lady Macbeth) has the same chalk-white skin, and she continually sits motionless—while she "argues" with her husband, while he performs the murder—in a position identical to that of the Witch. The Witch and Lady Washizu and the fog are white and are earthbound. While Washizu argues with his wife about their course of action, he continually stands up and paces about (the camera pacing with him) as he defends the selfless, humane position; but when he relents and accepts her arguments, he too sits down— earthbound, motionless. At the end of the film, when the wood comes to the castle to reclaim the initial debt of the forest, Washizu's own men shoot him full of arrows (he becomes a sort of monstrous tree himself), and he eventually collapses to the earth in a cloud of mist. He is now permanently bound to the earth and the fog.

The Lower Depths avoids such stunning natural images and uses, instead, the imagery of the human face and the social grouping. Rather than make a dazzling pictorial film, which Kurosawa obviously could have done, he emphasizes the cramped little dwelling that serves as the physical boundary and the shelter of a social microcosm. He also uses another potential of the modern screen—its greater capability of rendering depth-of-field—to turn the film's primary visual principle into a contrasting series of planes of depth, usually by basing all his compositions on some variation of the receding triangle. (There are very few shots in which there is only a single being in the frame. Even in a character's most isolated moments there is a face or a body or two in the rearground.) *The*

Lower Depths is a study of a social whole, and these triangulations in depth continually emphasize that the whole is inescapable and omnipresent.

In addition to this deliberate stylistic confinement, the film mirrors Kurosawa's vision of life as clearly as any. At its conclusion a group of characters erupt into an exuberant, rhythmic, vital dance—an absolutely compelling mixture of rhythmic sounds, physical movement, and film cutting. At the same time, another character commits suicide. That juxtaposition is the Kurosawa statement, a point he greatly emphasizes, in comparison to the Gorky play, by inventing this dance. There is life and death, dance and suicide, elation and annihilation, but life and the dance go on.

Kenji Mizoguchi was a director of an earlier generation whose career came to its artistic culmination as Kurosawa's began to expand. Compared with Kurosawa, Mizoguchi employs a more consistent and single visual style, a more consistent theme and setting, and a much narrower range of emotion and tone. Mizoguchi specializes in period dramas, and his milieu is not simply the past but the past as seen in folk legends, fairy tales, and paintings. Whereas Kurosawa saturates the past with modern realism and intellectual issues, Mizoguchi develops the distant mildness, softness, and stateliness of that past. His primary attraction to the past is its apparent synthesis of art and nature—the way the natural life of the past has been frozen (and enshrined) by the art of the legend and the drawing. Many of Mizoguchi's central figures are themselves artists: the actress Taki no Shiraito in the 1933 silent film of the same name; the troupe of players in *The Story of the Last Chrysanthemums* (1939); the artist Utamaro in *Utamaro and His Five Women* (1946); the potter in *Ugetsu* (1953). For Mizoguchi, the business of the artist is the conversion of life into the perfection and precision of art, and the business of the cinema is both the conversion of life into art and the reverse conversion of art (a folk tale, for example) into the "living" vitality of cinema. No clearer blending of the domains of art and nature exists than in the opening of *Ugetsu* which begins with paintings of nature (under the titles) and dissolves into shots of nature.

In his photographic style Mizoguchi mirrors this art-as-nature-as-art synthesis. Where Kurosawa uses a traveling camera and deep focus, Mizoguchi uses a generally fixed camera (when it travels, it does so slowly and gracefully) and soft focus. Mizoguchi's shots of Japanese settings—fields, mountains, lakes—are much softer and flatter than Kurosawa's shots of nature, deliberately turning these natural settings into evocations of Japanese prints and paintings. Mizoguchi tends to use back- and side-lighting for these outdoor shots, not only softening them and reducing the depth-of-field but also giving them a hazy, limpid glow. Even in the moments of human agitation (for example, the sister's suicide in *Sansho the Bailiff*, 1954), nature remains soft, still, and quiet. The girl drowns herself in a placid pool of glassy water, framed by statuesque, motionless, and gauzy trees that watch but do not react (as opposed to Kurosawa's nature whose tumult mirrors human agitation).

In his structure, Mizoguchi is also more classical and more literary than Kurosawa; Mizoguchi's major films are perfect examples of the Japanese sense of symmetry. Whereas Kurosawa's symmetry (in *Rashomon, Seven Samurai, Throne of Blood*) is often blurred by the violence and energy of his action, Mizoguchi's stately pace emphasizes his structural purity (and symmetry is another of the ways that art improves on nature). Mizoguchi's primary structural device is the separation of the leading characters, each of them traveling different paths—quite literally since the journey is essential to many Mizoguchi films. *Taki no Shiraito* traces the separate paths of the actress and the young law

student until fate draws the paths together; *Utamaro* follows the artist's "journey" as well as that of each of his women; *Sansho* is a series of separations—father from wife and children, mother from children, son from daughter—and eventual reunions with both the living and dead. The symmetry of *Sansho* is so perfect that there are two fathers in the film (Sansho and Zushio's father), two sons (Taro and Zushio), two separations (the mother from Zushio and Anju; Zushio from Anju), two children (Zushio and Anju), two reunions with the living (Zushio with Taro and Zushio with his mother), and two reunions with the dead at their shrines (Zushio at his father's tomb and at the lake where Anju drowned).

Ugetsu is a perfect Mizoguchi film in structure, theme, visual style, and tone. There are four central characters—a potter and his wife, the potter's brother and his wife—each of whom travels a separate path and comes to a different end. The men, pursuing the false goals of money, fame, and lust, both discover the worthlessness of these goals, primarily because the wives trod a road that led to their rape (one is murdered by soldiers, the other becomes a prostitute). Mizoguchi brings the film to life by the elegance of this symmetry and the magnificence of his visual technique which dissolves nature into the mystical and concretizes the mystical into nature.

As the characters travel by boat on a misty lake to bring their goods to market (the potter is driven by his desire for riches), Mizoguchi converts the lake into a misty, ethereal Acheron; the thick fog converts the natural lake into an apparently supernatural netherworld. As opposed to Kurosawa's fog, which seethes, breathes, and floats, Mizoguchi's fog seems to sit and stifle. Out of this fog, the characters see a boat floating toward them, a mystical and eerie boat, seemingly floating on the fog itself. Inside the boat lies a chalk white, corpselike figure who

Ugetsu: *Mizoguchi's elegantly balanced composition as the potter enjoys a picnic with a ghost; the physical concreteness of ghostly confrontation—Lady Wakasa (Machiko Kyo) and the potter (Masayuki Mori)*

looks like a ghost and is even taken for a ghost by the characters. No, he says, he is not a ghost but a man who has been beaten and robbed by pirates. He warns the characters against going further— especially because of the danger to the women. But the potter presses onward.

Not heeding this warning from a man who looks like a ghost, the potter comes face-to-face with ghosts who look like people. First, the potter falls under the spell of Lady Wakasa (Machiko Kyo again, who specialized in beautiful sirens), who tempts him by flattering his artistry and gains possession of his body by satisfying his sensuality. Their moments of sensual union are echoed by the diaphanous, shiny glow of nature in Mizoguchi's typically luminous photography. But Mizoguchi keeps his comment on the action clear by continually cross-cutting between the other characters on their "paths." While the potter falls under the dreamily sensual spell of Lady Wakasa, his wife is murdered by a group of soldiers on the road, his brother cheats his way into fulfilling his dreams of becoming a *samurai*, and his brother's wife is raped on the road by bandits (a brutal sexual

encounter that comments on the potter's).

The potter's diaphanous dream world collapses when he awakes one morning to discover that Lady Wakasa has been dead for years and that her house is a mere pile of ruins (Mizoguchi shoots this "morning after" discovery in a much harsher and brighter light than is usual for him). The potter, penniless and broken, returns home to join his wife (the usual Mizoguchi reunion after separation). Although the wife who greets him appears to be a corporeal being, he discovers the next morning from his neighbors that she has been killed and that he has spent the night with yet another ghost (a second "morning after" discovery—and a clear example of the Mizoguchi symmetry). He decides to devote his life to honoring his wife's grave (just as the son honors the graves of his sister and father in *Sansho),* and the spirit of his wife returns to him again —this time as an incorporeal voice. She tells him that her spirit will remain perpetually beside him (a beneficent supernatural presence, in contrast to the deleterious Lady Wakasa) and that he should return to his pottery. Both the potter and the brother renounce their false ambitions and return to the normal cycles of their lives.

Mizoguchi's moral system is more sentimental and more conventional than Kurosawa's. He advocates the usual humanistic virtues of love, fidelity, and selflessness as opposed to the selfish drives of lust, power, and money, but he mixes these values with the traditional Japanese virtues of patience, submission, humility, and resignation. Mizoguchi, however, brings this traditional morality to life in *Ugetsu* by making his reality look so shimmeringly unreal and his unreality look so very real, by the mysticizing of nature and the naturalizing of mysticism.

Yasujiro Ozu, Mizoguchi's contemporary, is the master of the *shomin-geki* —the modern-day, middle-class comedy. Ozu's primary subjects are the surfaces, forms, rituals, and processes of middle-class (or upper-middle-class) life itself. His films are dominated by scenes of eating, both at home and in restaurants, scenes at the office, scenes of men drinking together in bars. They are films about the central social processes: work, marriage, family life, friendship. And they are films that mirror the modernization of Japanese life: television sets, neon lights, modern architecture, furniture, and offices. The women gossip, the men play golf, and the children both go to school and watch television.

As a stylist Ozu is a real oddity, in many ways challenging most of the West's cinema theory. It is probably not unfair to say that of all the world's highly respected directors in the entire history of film, there is none more visually spare than Ozu. Perhaps the unkindest possible description of Ozu's style would be that he makes "women's pictures" of endless dialogue in the made-for-TV Hollywood fashion of taking pictures of faces and mouths. And all his pictures are alike, so that it is impossible to tell one from the other. In truth, the titles of many of the Ozu films are so similar that they sound like the same film (*Late Spring*, 1949;

Early Spring, 1956; *Late Autumn*, 1960; *End of Summer*, 1961; *Autumn Afternoon*, 1962). In truth, the subjects of them are invariably similar—parents and children; if, when, and who to marry—and the actors recur from one film to another. In truth, all of them have a similar tone—a subtly understated pathos and comedy that play against one another in delicate counterpoint.

Most striking of all, the films are consistently devoid of scenes and moments that are purely visual. There is perhaps a higher percentage of talk in an Ozu film than in anybody else's ever; the only scenes without talk tend to be either conventional "establishing shots"—the building or location where the dialogue is about to take place—or a brief (and often very effective) reaction shot after a dialogue scene. Such visual images usually last less than ten seconds. Ozu's editing is invisible (intentionally, so as not to divert attention from the talk or the people); the color is unspectacular, indeed unnoticeable or even downright ugly; the camera seems confined to eye level as if it were sitting on the floor of one of those Japanese houses (clearly to increase the sense of intimacy). And from these films it would appear that there is nothing colder, uglier, and more sterile than contemporary Japanese houses, offices, office corridors, quick-lunch restaurants, and bars, all of which have walls so hard and bare, floors so highly polished, that they appear unfit for human life. But the counterpoint of warm vital human life in a cold sterile environment is at the center of Ozu's vision: all of his films are indeed variations on the single theme that people *do* manage to live—and not badly either—in the midst of spectacularly glossy ugliness simply by remaining human and trusting in the human (rather than the inanimate) institutions.

Ozu's strengths are structural and psychological rather than visual. Like Kurosawa and Mizoguchi, Ozu inevitably uses the multiple human focus, examining

parallel actions, reactions, and choices in
the lives of different people. Unlike
Kurosawa and Mizoguchi, Ozu tends
toward parallelism, the similarity of
responses that play against one another
contrapuntally, rather than contrast;
unlike Kurosawa's multiple points of view
in *Rashomon* and Mizoguchi's multiple
paths in *Ugetsu*, Ozu builds his films as
very subtle variations on a single issue—
say, getting married—revealing the
attitudes of old and young, married and
single, parents and children, widowers
and adolescents toward the central issue.
Ozu is the master of counterpoint; in his
purity, delicacy, and deceptive complexity,
he is a kind of J. S. Bach of cinema. An
inevitable Ozu effect is that just at that
point when one wonders if anything is
going to happen and if the film is going
anywhere (some forty-five minutes into
it), the film's structure, idea, warmth,
subtlety, and charm grab hold of the
viewer and refuse to let go until the end
of the study.

Ozu's *Ohayo* (*Good Morning*, 1959),
which is not one of his "seasonal" studies
of marriage, is a good example of his
method and concerns. The film's subject
is etiquette, the formal pleasantries of life
(like saying, "Good Morning") that enable
human beings to live together. The film
reveals the social tensions of life—
women's gossip, the suspicion of a
neighbor's dishonesty, the fear of being
snubbed—and demonstrates that the
social niceties are truly necessities for
easing these tensions. At the center of the
film are two children (Ozu has always
liked the world of children, beginning
with his first silent triumph, *I Was Born
But . . .* , 1932). The two boys want their
father to buy them a television set; when
he refuses they get angry and he tells
them that they talk too much. The oldest
boy says that adults talk too much, too,
that they say useless things like, "Good
Morning." And so the two boys refuse to
talk altogether, throwing the neighbors,
their teachers, their friends, and their

Late Autumn: *the modern domestic world of
Ozu—women in the home, men at the bar*

own family into confusion. Ozu comically
and deftly shows that the "useless"
amenities of life are extremely useful for
keeping society at peace. Ironically, the
boys have their own social ritual—a
marvelous little amenity in which they
have developed the ability to fart

automatically when they are pushed on the forehead. To the boys that is a useful ritual, while to say "Good Morning" is useless. Ozu, without any specific comment and overemphasis, reveals how necessary all our social rituals are— including a father's giving in to his kids and buying them a TV. From such a film one can see that Ozu's true subject is the extraordinary ordinary and the interesting boring.

Of the lesser Japanese directors, Kon Ichikawa is perhaps the most interesting. Ichikawa's primary distinction is in the intensity and savagery of his ideological argument, which usually examines the depravity and degeneration of the human animal. Ichikawa's first noted film, *The Harp of Burma* (1956), is one of his milder studies: the examination of a soldier in Burma in the final days of the Second World War who first disguises himself as a priest in order to survive and who subsequently becomes a true convert to the priestly values, primarily as a result of the war horrors he has seen (and Ichikawa's camera occasionally has shown). But his *Fires on the Plain* (1959), another story of the final days of the war, concentrates on the horrors exclusively, on a man's innate determination to survive (although he is ill with consumption), even if it means murdering and eating other human beings to keep himself alive. Ichikawa's *Odd Obsession* (1959) is set in the Ozu environment of the upper-middle-class family, but this family occupies itself with bizarre sexual games that eventually destroy all the players. Kon Ichikawa also directed the mammoth record of the *Tokyo Olympiad* (1964).

Kinugasa's *Gate of Hell* and Inagaki's *Samurai* (both 1953) were two of Japan's first color films and are visually magnificent in their application of splendid color photography to the *jidai-geki*. Hiroshi Teshigahara's *Woman in the Dunes* (1964) is remarkable for its minute, tactile examination of a bizarre human conversion. A man from a modern city on vacation in the dunes is imprisoned by the people who live there, forced to serve as the husband of a woman who lost her previous one. He begins by resisting this imprisonment, trying to escape, loathing the pervasive and omnipotent sand that seeps into his hair, clothes, food, bed, and soul. Only when he ceases to fight the sand and decides instead to study its laws and work with it (he calculates a way to distill precious, life-giving water from the sand) does his prison suddenly become a home. He discovers that sand is certainly no worse a physical environment than the sterile technological society that he came from.

The Japanese film industry, like the industries of the West, underwent severe commercial changes in the decade following 1950. The Japanese discovered that many of their cheaper and exploitative productions—monster pictures (*Godzilla, Rodan*), invasions from outer space (*The Mysterians*)—could make money abroad. And so Japan was continually invaded by prehistoric monsters or visitors from another planet who devoured or incinerated plastic models of Japan's major cities before they were repulsed by some new weapon or old bacillus. As the Japanese bought (and manufactured) more and more television sets, Japanese film attendance dropped. The Japanese film industry had learned from the West, however, that this was one monster that could not be repulsed. The Japanese studios began production for television from the start—and even began operating television stations themselves. Since the mid-1960s, however, the Japanese industry has been remarkably silent, not so much in its quantitative production, which is still high, but its quality. Kurosawa has done little in over a decade (one magnificent color film, *Dodes' Ka-den*, 1970, and one Soviet production, *Derzu Usala,* 1975), and there have been no new Ozus or Mizoguchis to replace the generation that has died. The most promising young Japanese director is Nagisa Oshima, who mixes radical film technique, radical politics, and a radical sexuality in such films as *In the Realm of the Senses* (1976) and *The Man Who Left His Will on Film* (1970).

The West discovered the Indian cinema much as it did the Japanese. Satyajit Ray's *Pather Panchali* (1955) won a special prize at the 1956 Cannes Film Festival, and his next film, *Aparajito* (1956), won the Grand Prize at Venice the following year. Unlike the Japanese cinema, Indian cinema offered no rich unknown cache of artistry; instead the West discovered that Satyajit Ray *was* the Indian cinema. Not that the Indian film industry was not prolific: India produced some three hundred feature films in 1958, second only to Japan (but ahead of America) in the quantity of feature production. In the 1970s, India became the world leader in the number of feature films produced each year. But several causes—unique both to Indian society and its film industry—keep quantity up and quality down.

First, India is a vast nation of over five hundred million people, and movies remain the only form of popular entertainment accessible to the masses. There are very few television sets in India *per capita,* and the percentage of that *capita* that can afford to buy them is very small. This pressure to provide mass entertainment for a huge and highly uneducated and unsophisticated audience has led to a consistent mediocrity, a devotion to formula and convention, and a fear of experimentation.

Second, and even more difficult for the film industry, India is a nation without a common language. There are over a dozen Indian languages—every one of them a mystery to the speakers of the others—the most common of which are Hindi, Bengali, Telugu, Marathi, and Tamil. This language barrier caused little difficulty in the silent era. The Indian

silent film industry, effectively established in 1913 by the magical, mythological films of Dadasaheb Phalke and developed by pioneers such as Dhiren Ganguly, Debaki Bose, and Chandulal Shah, may well have been more artistically advanced than the silent Japanese cinema. But the coming of sound, which liberated the Japanese cinema from the *benshi,* imprisoned the Indian cinema in the Tower of Babel. Indian film production is necessarily narrow and regional in its outlook, which reduces any inclination to appeal to an international market.

Third, the Indian cinema has been subject to ruthless government intervention and censorship. Under the British, themes of independence were forbidden; under the government of free India, "decadent" Western influences were forbidden. In addition to limiting its artistic freedom, the Indian government taxes the film industry heavily; its huge audiences provide handsome revenues, even with the extremely low ticket prices. Further, the Indian government levied severe import quotas that restricted the supply of raw film stock. Even more ironic, an Indian print that had been shown abroad was subject to duty as "imported" film upon returning home.

Fourth, the Indian film industry itself is a victim of corrupt profiteering practices. Independent producers who want to make a quick killing, rather than established film companies, are the rule. In the 1930s, however, India's studios were more solid organizations; the most famous of them, Bombay Talkies, was a cooperative familial studio—modeled on Germany's UFA where Bombay Talkies' owners, Himansu Rai and Devika Rani, had worked. But the independent speculator, who usually did not have enough money to complete a film once it was started and therefore needed to beg, borrow, deal, and swindle more as the shooting went along, came to dominate the industry in the 1940s.

The speculator could get that money

only because, fifth, the Indian film industry has been totally dominated by the star system since the familial studios collapsed in the 1940s. And it has been a star system with a vengeance, making the power and salaries of the Hollywood luminaries look puny. Because only a producer with a major star could get the money to finish a film, stars became so popular and enjoyed such power that they commanded immense salaries (at least half of it paid under the table in untaxable "black money") and might work on as many as a dozen films at once, dropping in periodically on each of the production units as the star's schedule and inclinations permitted. Music was the supporting "star" of an Indian film (the music director is the second highest paid position in the Indian film industry); for decades, of the hundreds of films shot each year in India, there was *not one* without singing and dancing. The Indian film became so conventional that its foremost historians (Barnouw and Krishnaswamy) described the formula succinctly as "A star, six songs, and three dances."

To such assumptions and conventions Satyajit Ray was, and remains, a stranger. Ray was a student of serious Indian literature and philosophy; his father was a friend of Rabindranath Tagore, India's greatest writer of the twentieth century, and Ray was a personal student of Tagore's. But Ray was also, like many of his Western counterparts, a *cinéaste;* he was the cofounder of the first film society in India, the Calcutta Film Society, in 1947. So one might see Ray as uniting the traditions of serious Indian literature with those of Western cinema (avoiding Indian cinematic traditions altogether). The influence of Western cinema is unmistakable in Ray's films, particularly Italian neorealism and the graceful structure of the French classical cinema of the 1930s. Ray was particularly influenced by observing Jean Renoir make *The River* in Calcutta in 1951, when he spoke frequently with the classical French director. Although Ray is a Bengali, his outlook is an international, humanistic one—an attitude that perhaps makes his work more popular in the rest of the world than it is in Bengal.

In the Indian cinematic tradition, Ray makes "Socials"—the two opposite genres of Indian films being Mythologicals and Socials, corresponding roughly to Japan's *jidai-* and *gendai-geki.* But Indian Socials typically drown modern social issues (say, the caste question or the subjugation of women) in sentimental, saccharine claptrap (there are no social solutions, only tragic endings), while the Mythologicals display their fantastic hokum undiluted by reality. (Ray himself pokes gentle fun at this hokum in the film-within-a-film sequence of *The World of Apu,* 1958, which parodies one of these Mythologicals, yet, at the same time, shows the intense audience devotion to it.) Ray's *Pather Panchali* avoided all these Indian film traditions: no star (Ray, in the manner of the Soviets, Italians, and Czechs, even used some nonprofessional actors); no songs and dances (although there was a brilliant instrumental score by Ravi Shankar); a cinematographer who had never shot a motion picture before (the distinguished still photographer, Subrata Mitra); and shooting on location (Indian films were exclusively studio films, even for outdoor scenes, a choice that aided their flight from reality). Ray's film wanted to have as much to do with reality as possible.

Ray's Apu trilogy (*Pather Panchali, Aparajito,* and *The World of Apu*) is one film that is three and three films that are one. In adapting a mammoth novel by Bibhuti Bannerjee, Ray seems to have perceived (as did von Stroheim before him and Coppola after him) that the best way to make a film of a novel without losing its texture and complexity was to make three films. The Ray trilogy employs a complex and carefully conceived structure that is apparent in the unity of the individual films as well as in the overall conception of the trilogy. The subject of the trilogy is the growth of a young Indian boy from his peasant, rural youth to a mature and educated adulthood in the city, an Indian variation on the *Buildungsroman*. The three films devote themselves to childhood, adolescence, and adulthood respectively. In all three films deaths play a pivotal role in the boy's growth and development: the death of the old aunt and his sister in *Pather Panchali;* the death of his father and mother in *Aparajito;* the death of his wife (the hardest one for him to accept) in *The World of Apu.* In counterpoint to these deaths, all three films end identically: Apu is on the road ("Pather Panchali" means "Song of the Road"), moving from the country to the city, implying the continuity of life and growth.

At the end of *Pather Panchali,* the remains of the family battered by death leave the little peasant village to try to live better in the city. At the end of *Aparajito,* Apu pulls himself together after the death of his mother and takes the path back to the city and the university. At the end of *The World of Apu* (a film which was almost entirely Ray's own invention and which revealed his ability to graft his own material onto that of the original novel without leaving any traces of the stitching), Apu is back on the road, returning to Calcutta again, his young son on his back. For Apu, it is also his most explicit return to life, on which he had turned his back after the death of his wife. A sign of the complexity and precision of Ray's structural conception is that at the end of this final installment Apu's young son is almost exactly the same age as the child Apu in the first one, living a similar life (unfettered but fatherless), now on his way to the city with a newly returned father. The song of the road has come full circle.

Ray's themes and concerns are clear in the trilogy. First, there is his sympathetic

and microscopic examination of the points of view of all the major characters. Although much of *Pather Panchali* gives the child's-eye view of life (and death), the mother's-eye view of that struggle also gets Ray's careful attention. She often seems cross and vicious, but she has the heavy responsibiliy of keeping the family together and alive with her husband not only penniless but absent. That responsibility proves too much for her when she fails to protect her daughter, Durga, from death. The mother is caught between her tenderness, her responsibility, and her shame—and Ray catches those conflicting pressures as well. In *Aparajito* the same (but older) mother is caught between her selfish need to keep her son with her and her selfless desire to see him do well in life; the boy is caught between his attachment to his mother and his ambition to succeed and to study. Ray's films excel in the many-sidedness of these human portraits. Another many-sided portrait of Ray's is the wastrel husband: in *Pather Panchali* the husband is literate, sensitive, and poetic but a poor provider; in *The World of Apu* the same becomes true of Apu, his son. The wastrel husband recurs in many later Ray films—*The Music Room* (1958) and *Mahanagar* (1963) in particular.

Perhaps Ray's essential theme, however, is his ultimate commitment to life, to human exertion, and to the cycles of nature of which man is a small and uncomprehending part. Ray's films are acutely aware that life is often painful, that people can be petty, that sorrow is inescapable and death inevitable. As he shows in the Apu trilogy, life is defined by death. But despite this awareness, Ray reveals that people continue to travel the road of life, that the continuity of that road has been decreed by nature, and that the road has a clear, sweet, and compelling song.

Ray's dominant technique for rendering the human feelings that are so central to his films may be described as the

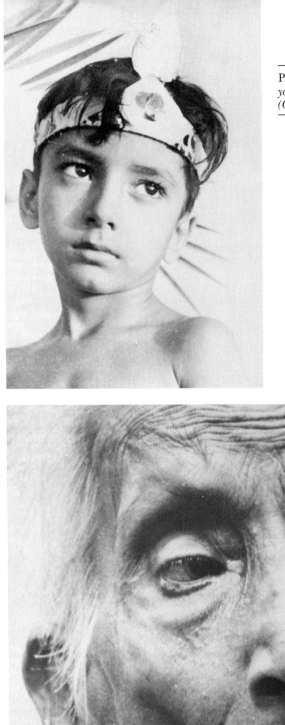

Pather Panchali: *the worlds of youth and age. The young Apu (Subir Banerji) and the old aunt (Chunibala Devi)*

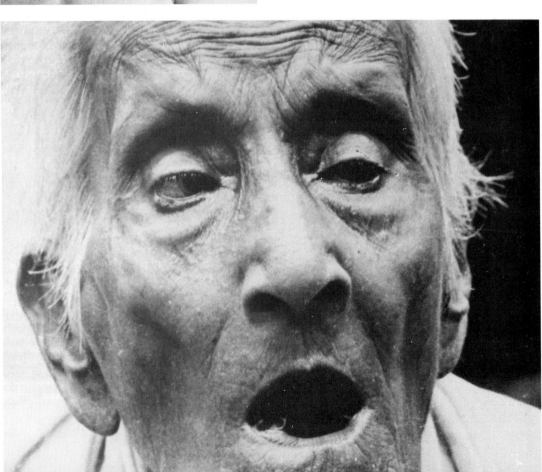

prolonged reaction shot: a device that he uses constantly and that is absolutely unique to his work. Ray's concern is not human action but the essential moment of human reaction to an event of great personal significance; the prolonged moment of reaction serves as the culmination and ultimate definition of that significance. Ray leaves his camera riveted on the person's face, a face that usually remains as motionless as his or her body, and the camera simply continues watching, watching, watching. The stillness, the silence of the facial-physical reaction, coupled with the extreme length of the take, allows that face to serve as a kind of sponge—slowly absorbing all of the events, feelings, and images that have been built around it until both the face and the audience are saturated with that feeling. These reaction shots, so still and yet so long, convert a totally external objectivity into a truly internal experience for both the character and the audience. One of the best (of many possible) examples is the painful moment of parting between mother and son in *Aparajito* as he goes off to the city, to the university, and, in effect, to his own life. Ray's camera holds on her motionless face and body; she stands still in the dusty arch of a doorway that seems to frame and to fix her forever, watching his back recede down the village path. She stands there, and stands, and stands—her feelings of loss flickering beneath the surface of her placid face, locked into the doorway of her own now empty life. It is *the* moment of separation.

Another of Ray's tools is his masterful visual imagery, often charged with symbolic connotations. In *Pather Panchali* there is the magnificent sequence of the mother's nighttime vigil beside the bed of her feverish daughter. Outside the little house a storm rages, rattling the shutters, banging at the door, sending gusts of wind through the cracks, trying to blow out the little candle of light at the bedside. The storm personifies the attack

The child's-eye view of the awesome train, slicing through the fields of grain in Pather Panchali

of nature and death on the little household, and the mother, in trying to save her daughter, is, in effect, trying to bar the raging natural forces from her shaky home. Those forces win, however, as a gust slips through to extinguish the candle. Another haunting and symbolic image of the same film is the magnificent shot of a speeding train, powerfully slicing through the fields of waving grain, leaving behind its awesome trail of floating smoke. With the train, awesomely depicted as the child Apu perceives the magical monster, Ray juxtaposes the old and new worlds (one of his constant themes), the adult, modern world outside the little village and the little world of the child. (Apu's globe of the world in *Aparajito* serves a similar symbolic function, but Apu is then old enough to understand the relationship between region and world.) Trains play an increasingly important role in Apu's life, constantly carrying him from city to village and back to the city again, and so the wondrous image of his boyhood becomes a commonplace method of transportation in his adulthood.

Ray's mastery of imagery, and his

awareness that pace and understatement in recording an image are essential to its effectiveness (rather than just the image itself), is especially clear in the haunting image that follows the death of Apu's father in *Aparajito*. Ray cuts to a shot of birds leaving their roost and flying off into the sky. Now this parallel of flying birds and a departing human soul is an obvious literary cliché; it is doubtful that any verbal simile could redeem its triteness. Ray's visual simile, however, is a moment of great beauty. First, he couples the sudden collapse of the father's head on his pillow (the precise moment of death) with an unexplained crack or snap on the sound track. That snapping sound then serves as the impetus (a "gunshot") that scares the birds, for Ray cuts suddenly and sharply from the father's face to the birds making a sudden departure on precisely that sudden sound. He then follows this technique of sharp suddenness with a very brief (perhaps five seconds) shot of the birds flying, a lyrical, graceful moment of swirling shapes and floating wings that lasts so briefly that the audience acutely feels its graceful ephemerality rather than perceives the precise meaning of the symbolism. By keeping his camera riveted to the human face for long periods of time and by keeping it on his symbolic images only fleetingly and suggestively, Ray achieves his combination of maturity, subtlety, clarity, and compassion.

The Ray films that succeeded the trilogy are equally interesting in their careful views of Indian life and are often quite as effective. In *The Music Room* Ray examines the collapse of the old India— its traditions and its art—and the rise of the new bourgeoisie. *Devi* (*Goddess*, 1960) is also a clash of old and new, a study of the old religious prejudices and fanaticism that can destroy human happiness. *Mahanagar* (*The Big City*) examines family life in the new Calcutta, particularly the new status of women. And *Kanchenjungha* (1962), Ray's first

color film, is a less anguished, more placid, Indian *L'Avventura*, the problems and frustrations of wealthy married couples on vacation in Darjeeling. All of these films are significant for their sensitive development of human reactions, for their social analysis (particularly the contrast of old and new), and for their resonant visual imagery. The only films shot in India other than Ray's and Renoir's *The River* that have been widely seen in the West are those of James Ivory, an American who works in India (*Shakespeare Wallah*, 1965; *Bombay Talkie*, 1970) and has been heavily influenced by Ray.

Third World Cinemas

The term "Third World Film" does not so much describe a national tradition as provide a heading for many spiritually related but geographically scattered national cinemas: those films from the underdeveloped emerging nations of Africa, Asia, and South America that explicitly examine the political, social, and cultural issues of those nations. Although Brazil is one of those countries that has produced Third World films, the popular romantic-erotic fantasy, *Dona Flor and Her Two Husbands* (1978), with its escape from social realities, would probably not be considered one of them. Nor would either the personal, psychological studies of Satyajit Ray or the popular Socials and Mythologicals produced for India's vast popular audience. Nor would the Kung Fus from Hong Kong. On the other hand, some European films (*The Battle of Algiers, State of Siege*) and some American Black films (like Melvin van Peebles's *Sweet Sweetback's Baadasssss Song*) have been considered spiritual products of the Third World even though the films were produced and directed by Americans or Europeans. To keep an already muddy metaphor from becoming any more murky, it would make sense to define a

Third World film by both its national origin and its cultural content.

These countries produce films either to educate their own citizens about the cultural history and contemporary conditions of the nation or to present that nation's problems and positions to the citizens of the rest of the world—or both. The films fulfill both a national and an international function; as such, their clearest historical analogy is to the Soviet silent classics of the 1920s. Like the new Soviet Union, these nations are emerging from decades or even centuries of cultural exploitation—economic domination by foreign interests, political domination by autocratic governments which concentrated power in the hands of the few for the benefit of the few and kept the bulk of the population largely illiterate and very poor. As in the new Soviet Union, films could be used to educate an audience unable to read and ignorant of the goals and methods of a new government. As in the Soviet Union, films could be projected in the most remote regions of these often topographically tortuous countries with the aid of portable power supplies (the Cuban documentary, *For the First Time,* 1967, describes the introduction of motion pictures to a village of Cuban peasants). As in the Soviet Union, films could combine their political lessons with moving stories of human action, often mingling native symbols and folk elements with their didactic tales of social values.

No clearer parallels with the early Soviet movement can be found than in several specific devices of these Third World films. The ending of the Cuban film, *The Last Supper* (1977), parallels those of Pudovkin's films: a montage series of metaphoric cross-cuts links the uprising of an oppressed people with the inevitable and irreversible processes of nature. The ending of the Chilean film, *The Promised Land* (1973), like Pudovkin's *Mother,* shows a failed revolution of the past passing on its spirit to the future and, like Dovzhenko's *Arsenal,* develops the mystically unkillable power of the people. The Argentinean *Hour of the Furnaces* (1968) includes such specific Eisenstein echoes as the use of stone statues in a Buenos Aires cemetery as a metaphor for cultural deadness (paralleling Eisenstein's similar use of statues in *Potemkin* and *October*) and the metaphoric killing of beasts in a slaughterhouse (parallel to the famous montage symbolism of *Strike*—except that the Argentine film ironically juxtaposes its slaughter with the jaunty Bachian counterpoint of the merry Swingle Singers on its soundtrack). True, none of these Third World countries has yet produced works of cinema art and abstract theory to rival the achievements of Eisenstein, Pudovkin, Dovzhenko, and Vertov. But despite the general cultural and economic poverty of the new Soviet Union, its artists were not at all underdeveloped, descending as they did from a cultural tradition that included Turgenev, Tolstoy, Dostoyevsky, Chekhov, Gogol, and Gorky. Indeed, the very tension between artistic complexity and social utility that so plagued Soviet films and filmmakers has been largely avoided by these Third World countries, whose artists culturally come from the people.

The methods and goals of film production in these Third World countries can be divided into three very broad categories. First, one country, Cuba, with an extremely well-developed, sophisticated, and nationalized film industry, can rival the industries of all but a few countries of the world in the quality and quantity of its output. Like Lenin, Castro declared the cinema the most important and socially useful of the arts; as a result, the Cuban government, like the Soviet Union, founded and funded a national film school and film production company (ICAIC—El Instituto Cubano por el Arte e Industria Cinematograficos). Although ICAIC produces mainly documentaries, it also makes several narrative feature films each year, for the Cubans discovered, as did the Soviets, that the populace preferred Hollywood-style stories to didactic documentaries. ICAIC also produces a weekly television program, *24 Frames Per Second,* which contributes to the Cuban audience's sophisticated appreciation of cinema processes as well as the political implications of image making—the semiotic problems that so haunt and consume Godard. During the brief periods of the progressive Torres regime in Bolivia and the Allende regime in Chile, the cinemas of these two South American nations began to move toward a Cuban-style nationalized industry. But the coups d'etat that ended both leftist regimes also ended their developing cinemas.

Second, several Third World countries make a very small number of feature films for both national consumption and international distribution (for example, Senegal, Egypt, Ethiopia—and Brazil). Because the population of many of these countries is small, these films seek international distribution to expand their impact and justify their cost. And because the governments of some of these countries are still politically repressive (for example, Brazil's), the political content of these films is often guarded and metaphoric—more ironic, less radical, less explicitly Marxist, less dominated by revolutionary rhetoric than the films of Cuba or those of the third group.

That third group of films comprises those from South American countries with such repressive totalitarian governments that the films become underground acts of rebellion and sedition in themselves—films from Argentina, Chile, Bolivia, Peru. Because these films are so dangerous to make—*The Hour of the Furnaces* and *The Battle of Chile* (1973) are two outstanding examples—these films could never be shown in the countries that produced them without a revolutionary change in

their governments. These films have been produced almost exclusively for international distribution (the voice-over narration of *The Battle of Chile* is in English) to rally international opinion against the ruling regimes of those countries.

Despite these differences in the methods of their production and distribution, Third World films share several general themes. The first is an attack on the dominating cultural presence of the more affluent nations of Europe and America—the British presence in *Night of Counting the Years* (Egypt, 1969), a film by Shadi Abdelsalam (Satyajit Ray's films approach the spirit of Third World films in their view of the British in India), the French presence in the films of Ousmane Sembene (Senegal), the American presence in the South American films. These films often reveal the power of foreign influences in their conflict between imported products, processes, or customs with strictly native ones—the bottles of Evian water, Coca-Cola, and J & B Scotch whiskey in Sembene's *Xala* (Senegal, 1975) or the conflict of both Christianity and Islam with native African religious rituals in his *Ceddo* (Senegal, 1976); the magazine advertisements for American consumer products in *The Hour of the Furnaces* (directed by Fernando Solanas and Octavio Getino); the juxtaposition of the ritual magic of Black African slaves with the rituals of Christian Easter in Tomas Gutierrez Alea's *The Last Supper;* the presence of the American "Progress Corps" in Jorge Sanjines's *Blood of the Condor* (Bolivia, 1969).

A second major theme is the crushing, unimaginable poverty of vast segments of the peasant population—whether of the Andes Indians of *Blood of the Condor,* the feudal farmers of Haile Gerima's *Harvest: 3000 Years* (Ethiopia, 1975), the migrant workers of Miguel Littin's *The Jackal of Nahueltoro* and *The Promised Land* (Chile, 1969, 1973), or the impoverished family

Clashes of cultures. Black African song and a sleeping white aristocrat (Nelson Villagra) in The Last Supper; *native African costumes and customs with Westernized gifts at the wedding of* Xala

in the barren drought-burned plains of Brazil's Northeast in Nelson Pereira dos Santos's *Vidas Secas* (Brazil, 1963).

A third theme, like the title of Eisenstein's 1928 film, might be called "Old and New," the contrast of the old backward ways of farming, living, thinking with newer, more progressive ones—the conflicts of national and tribal law in *Night of Counting the Years,* of ancient and modern customs in *Xala;* the examinations of the new systems of education and the new social role of women in the Cuban documentaries, *The New School* (1973) and *With the Cuban Women* (1975), and of the general patterns of historical evolution in the Cuban fictional classic, *Lucia* (1969). A final theme that unites many of these films is the implication that these scattered countries, continents, and peoples are indeed united by common cultural problems and common cultural goals— that the exploited peoples of India, Viet Nam, Africa, Cuba, Argentina, Bolivia, Chile share a common need and common enemy.

Like Humberto Solas's *Lucia,* many of these Third World films have become contemporary classics (particularly in Europe where they are shown more widely and greeted with more enthusiasm than in America), and several talented filmmakers from emerging nations have themselves begun to emerge as world class directors. *Lucia* is a film in the tradition that stretches from Griffith's *The Birth of a Nation* to Bertolucci's *1900*—a mammoth cinematic epic that juxtaposes personal human emotions with immense historical events and political processes (indeed, Bertolucci's political epic, which chronicles the same years, seems heavily influenced by it). Solas divides his epic into three periods—1895, 1932, and 196 . . .—each of them reflecting a particular political struggle of the Cuban people (first, the War of Independence from Spain; then, the first Cuban political revolution against the dictator Machado;

finally, the continuing worker's revolution under Castro). Uniting the film is a woman named Lucia—or rather, three different women with the same name (the female focus and the recurrent name parallel similar unifying devices in Griffith's *Intolerance*). In each of the film's eras, there is a conflict between Lucia's romantic love and the political events that surround and threaten that love.

The 1895 Lucia surrenders to her sexual passion for Rafael, although such a passion is forbidden in the proper, highly Europeanized upper-class world of 1895 Cuba. Her Rafael, an undercover Spanish agent, seduces Lucia as a means of capturing an arsenal held by the Cuban guerilla army. The result is that Lucia becomes the unknowing cause of her country's defeat, of her brother's death, and of her own horrifying rape. She becomes so crazed by the brutal betrayal (her experience parallels that of another female character in the film, Fernandina, a nun who is raped by soldiers on the battlefield) that she murders Rafael. The 1932 Lucia is a member of the haute bourgeoisie who falls in love with Aldo, a young radical student, and marries him, supporting his political struggle by, in effect, joining the working class (she goes to work in a factory) and participating in the street demonstrations of the Cuban women. After the succcess of the insurrection against Machado, Aldo discovers that their revolution has become corrupt (this was, after all, an insurrection of the bourgeoisie—and Battista would be its end product). Aldo continues his fight against the new status quo, machine-gunning the mayor of Havana on the steps of the city hall (this assassination is a piece of Cuban history), himself dying in the struggle. Lucia remains alone with both her personal and political future shattered. The 196 . . . Lucia is a member of the working class who has recently married her very energetic and attractive Tomas. Unfortunately, Tomas, in addition to his masculine charm, is also enslaved by the old masculine ways of thinking; he converts his new wife into his domestic prisoner, refusing to allow her to work in the fields, to be seen in public, or to learn to read and write, all because of his sexual jealousy and macho possessiveness. Lucia rebels and deserts him, but the two live very unhappily apart. (The section sets itself the propagandistic problem of supporting marriage while opposing the enslavement of the wife.) In the film's final shot, after their reunion, Lucia continues to insist on her rights to be free and Tomas on his rights to possess her. The film (like *1900*) ends on this unresolved argument—implying that the battle has not been won and the struggle of Cuban women still continues.

The film's effectiveness results not so much from its charming but rather simple stories and its explicit but rather fuzzy political analyses of the role of women in evolving Cuban society. In its individual narratives and its general political philosophy—that it is impossible to be happy in love without also being happy in a just society—the film is certainly no richer or clearer than Griffith's *Intolerance*. But also like the Griffith film, *Lucia* gets its power from the broader intellectual plan that integrates the individual tales and, especially, from the careful visual style, texture, and detail that conveys each of the historical periods. The 1895 sequence is dominated by ultrasharp contrasts of white and black. Solas defines the upper-class Europeanized world of the first Lucia by its extremely sunny whiteness, its brilliant clarity, and the perfectly symmetrical order of everything in Lucia's world—the photographs on the walls, the arrangements of furniture, even the shapes and patterns of trees in her garden. But when Lucia is ripped from her garden world and plunged into her nightmare one, the film stock emphasizes a world that has gone grainy, contrasty, and overblack, the personal experiencing of horror in the visual terms of a

Lucia: *political history as pictorial history. The 1895 Lucia surrounded by the formal elegance and symmetry of her aristocratic world (Raquel Revuelta), the 196 . . . Lucia (Adela Lagra) and her Tomas (Adolfo Llaurado) surrounded by the deep-focus vitality of her peasant world*

cinematic nightmare. The 1932 sequence is dominated by much softer contrasts and by lighting values that produce a slightly sharper focus than the 1895 sections but a much softer one than contemporary fast film stocks. The sequence has the gauzy, overdecorated, Art Deco look of 1930s Hollywood films.

If the film is a history of Cuba from 1895 to 196 . . .—particularly its steady descent of the class ladder, from upper-

Vidas Secas: *the homeless family of "Nordestinos"*

class plantation dwellers to the urban haute bourgeoisie to working-class rural laborers—it is also a history of film lighting, film stocks, and cinematic visual values—from high contrast to soft contrast to deep focus. The final 196 . . . section of the film is indeed shot with fast panchromatic film in deep focus, mirroring the visual values of both contemporary cinema and, not coincidentally, neorealist Italian films of the same period. The film mirrors the problems of contemporary life by capturing the look of contemporary cinema. Although this final section is certainly the most politically conscious in its explicit relevance to contemporary Cuban social life, it is also the most consciously rhetorical and didactic; non-Cubans and non-Marxists may find the psychological subtlety and stylish visual care of the two earlier sections more interesting.

Nelson Pereira dos Santos's *Vidas Secas* is in a very different style and single key—a hard, close, unflinching look at the desperate poverty of a single family of "Nordestinos," the rural peasants of Brazil's Northeast, in 1940. This family— husband, wife, two boys, and faithful dog—roams the barren, burned plains in search of a farm or ranch where they can earn their keep. The couple's

great goal in life is to save enough money for a leather bed—a bed with a sheet of leather to cover the hard bony wooden branches that serve as its "mattress." Fabiano, the very hard-working husband, runs into trouble with a petty government policeman but rather than take the path of rebellion (he gets the opportunity both to join a band of guerillas and to murder this toad in uniform), he remains the hard-working docile slave. The film's setting in the past implies that the man's political docility is a sign of an incompletely evolved political consciousness.

Fabiano's loyalty to the law—despite the law's unworthiness—goes unrewarded, for the family must take to the road again at the end of the film, once more embarking on the desperate search for a place of shelter and survival. Dos Santos depicts the tragic diminution of the family as Fabiano shoots the faithful dog, Baleia, who has brought them food when they were hungry, who has served as guide, companion, and confidant, but who has become too ill to continue the journey. The pathos of this terrible sacrifice, communicated in excruciatingly lengthy and convincing detail, conveys the terrible pathos of such barren, blasted lives. Still another of the film's remarkably effective and communicative devices is its brilliantly cinematic use of available light for both indoor and outdoor sequences. The scorching, blazing power of the sun, the cause of the land's dryness, is also the film's central metaphor and the source of its absolutely authentic depiction of people living in the midst of their genuine surroundings, either outdoors when exposed to its pitiless glare or indoors when trying to escape into the temporary shade and shadow of rooms and houses. Although the film pretends to be set in the past (many Brazilian films, like Glauber Rocha's *Antonio das Mortes,* 1969, must masquerade as apolitical and unconnected to the present), at its conclusion the numerals *1942* appear in the frame, implying that the journey of such people continues, unsolved and unresolved, even into the present.

The Third World political documentaries, like Fernando Solanas's and Octavio Getino's *The Hour of the Furnaces,* have a very different kind of artistic power and political purpose. *Hour of the Furnaces* is a mammoth, three-part, four-hour-and-twenty-minute analysis of the political, economic, and cultural landscape of Argentina, past and present. Part 1 examines Argentinean political-cultural life in the present and the roots of that life in the past—the dependence on foreign investments and capital, the domination by foreign culture and customs, the concentration of wealth in the hands of the few, the political alienation of the working class and the extreme impoverishment of the Indian population. Part 2 examines Peronism, which the film calls the only genuine working-class political movement in Argentinean history—first, the decade of Peron rule, 1945–1955, then the decade of underground Peronist sentiment and activity following the coup that overthrew the Peron regime. Part 3 is a call to arms, urging armed revolution and resistance as the only way to establish a just and equitable government in Argentina. The film's three parts, which might be titled Present, Past, and Future, exhibit the three-part argument of Marxist dialectic —thesis, antithesis, and synthesis.

Hour of the Furnaces is interesting on a number of levels and for a number of reasons. First, like the mammoth political documentaries of Marcel Ophuls (*The Sorrow and the Pity,* 1972; *The Memory of Justice,* 1976), the film shakes its audiences—regardless of their political convictions—with the sense of witnessing and participating in a series of historically important and humanly shattering events. The film presents the country's social chaos and cultural antagonisms so sharply, so clearly, and so comprehensively that audiences from

Hour of the Furnaces: *testament to political oppression and social violence*

more stable, less divided cultures in happier times can only marvel at a spectacle with the intensity of historical fiction but the authenticity of historical fact. Second, the work uses film revealingly as a conscious propagandistic tool. The film adopts the stance of Marxist (rather than Fascist) rhetoric— asking the audience to think about the issues it has presented, to discuss them (indeed there are sections where the film deliberately breaks off and asks the audience to discuss), to formulate questions and to argue about them. This request for conscious and active participation (to which the later Godard films are also painfully and self-consciously devoted) seems antithetical to the Fascist propaganda strategy of hypnotizing viewers by manipulating symbols and metaphors that strike beneath the viewer's threshold of conscious awareness.

But these differences may be only superficial. Plenty of propaganda remains unspoken and implicit in the film. For example, the film—like all South American films—treats the Roman Catholic Church very gingerly (a clear departure from Marxist theory and from Eisenstein's satiric practice), occasionally linking a bishop visually with the forces of governmental repression but never

Memories of Underdevelopment: *the bourgeois intellectual surrounded by books, physical embodiments of his attitudes and values*

accusing the Church as a whole or the "Spirit of Christianity" in general of any role in subjugating "the people." Given the close attachment of the South American working classes to the Church, the film would rather not raise this sensitive issue at all. On the other hand, the soundtrack of the film is a stream of verbal rhetoric that repeats its accusations like a litany, but the film never precisely supports or documents them with pictures. We hear the accusations that the government and economy of Argentina is an "oligarchy," that the oligarchy is supported and controlled by the American CIA, that Argentinean intellectuals and universities are mere servants of decadent European tastes and culture (the film purposely develops an antagonism between workers and intellectuals), but we see no evidence. The film assumes that merely to flash images on the screen of European paintings or of magazine advertisements is in itself an indictment of America, Europe, and Western Civilization as a whole. The film's passionate commitment to its position—a passion that can be so clearly

felt by an audience of whatever political persuasion and that has produced this mammoth cinematic effort in the first place—also leads to the film's less subtle and purely propagandistic handling of complex social issues. The same passionate, historical strengths and ideological, propagandistic weaknesses dominate the two-part, three-hour-ten-minute *The Battle of Chile,* which chronicles the six months of social agitation that led to the coup d'etat against the constitutional government of Salvador Allende in 1973.

Unlike the Marcel Ophuls documentaries, these Third World chronicles are ideologically simplistic and one-sided. The Ophuls films are painfully aware of the complexities and ironies in the commitment to any single political position. Precisely these enriching ironies and complexities have been responsible for the international reputations of these films in countries of whatever ideology. The differences between *The Hour of the Furnaces* and *The Memory of Justice* precisely reveal the problem of Third World filmmakers who wish to achieve a reputation in the first or second world— the need to strike a balance between their own passionate commitments and the conflicting perceptions of audiences in other parts of the world who are not already disposed to agree with them. Eisenstein, Pudovkin, and Vertov achieved this balance in the past by means of the intensity and complexity of their art—the rich visual imagery produced a fullness in the audience's experience of a work that was far denser than the threads of its ideological argument. Two Third World directors, Tomas Gutierrez Alea of Cuba, who received his cinema education at Italy's Centro Sperimentale, and Ousmane Sembene of Senegal, a novelist who was educated in France, reveal many of the broader ironies and complexities of a more international outlook.

Alea's first major work to be seen in

the United States, *Memories of Under-development* (1969), was an extremely ironic portrait of a member of the bourgeoisie who, unlike many other members of his class, remains in Cuba after the fall of Battista. The film carefully and comically reveals the man's difficulty in finding a place for himself in the new Cuban society. His sexual tastes (rather graphically recorded), his cultural tastes (in books, paintings, music) simply do not belong in the new Cuba, and the film simultaneously condemns the man's spiritual emptiness and ironically sympathizes with his isolation. But an even more mature, controlled, and elegant Alea film is *The Last Supper,* perhaps the most careful and visually elegant work of the entire Third World movement, a beautiful costume drama in splendid color. *The Last Supper* is, like the first section of *Lucia,* set in the Cuba of the nineteenth century—on a sugarcane plantation owned by the aristocracy and worked by Black African slaves. As the film's title indicates, the film takes place during Easter week, and the entire work is built on a religious, allegorical foundation. The landowner of the plantation suffers a seizure of aristocratic *weldschmerz*—he knows not why he is living or what the value of life may be. In order to regain his faith, he decides to perform an ideal act of Christian penance and charity; he selects twelve of his own slaves, washes their feet, and invites them to sit at his table as his disciples. The meal they eat together is intended to mirror the ideals of Christian charity and quality—master with slave, all equals in the eye of God.

The lengthy supper sequence (which fills the middle half of the film) becomes a rare moment of both human communion and isolation, emotional togetherness and ideological separation. As the diners consume more and more wine, they feel themselves much closer to one another. (Like Brecht's *Herr Puntila* and Chaplin's *City Lights,* the film uses alcohol as the great eradicator of class barriers.) During the dinner, each of the slaves opens his heart to the master about his past life in Africa, and the master opens his heart to them, espousing the Christian view of life as a mere preparation for salvation and death. During these confessions, each "disciple" moves to sit at the master's right or left in a ritualized reenactment of both sacramental confession and that original Last Supper. The one slave who refuses to be seduced by the master's kindness is Sebastian (with his Christian name ironically evocative of passive, sacrificial martyrdom). Although the master refers to Sebastian as Judas, it remains to be seen who is the true Judas at this table. Only when the master falls asleep does Sebastian tell his own story, a pagan retelling of the Christian "Fall of Man," which sees humankind as a mixture of man and beast—the head of a pig surmounts the heart of a man. Although the master's feelings may be kind, his thoughts, his ideas, his values are those of the pig. The insightful slave accompanies his allegorical tale with a physical remnant of his own African magic: he blows the powder of a magic dust on the master's face. The master awakens from his sleep with a sneeze—and the final section of the film becomes the result of this sneeze, in effect the hangover from this drunken, temporary, and artificial celebration of human communion. The master indeed reveals that his pig's head rules a man's heart.

The next day is Easter Sunday and the slaves—according to the master and the sympathetic plantation priest (another deliberate attempt to attack not the spirit of Christianity but its bastardization)—are to spend the holy day at rest and worship. But the brutal foreman of the plantation can think of nothing but productivity. This foreman represents the hard economic reality beneath the spiritual and philosophical facade of the master, the pig's head above the kind heart, the man who does the ruling class's dirty work. He demands that the slaves get to work. A violent rebellion of slaves results—led by those twelve disciples who sat at the master's table and believed in his commitment to the sanctity of the next day. In the violent struggle, the slaves deliberately kill the vicious foreman (a man who had earlier cut off Sebastian's ear as punishment), accidentally kill his wife, and set fire to the entire plantation. The master's pigheaded answer is the equally violent subduing of the rebellion by armed force and the deliberate murder of every one of the twelve slaves who, the night before, sat with him at table—as an example of the price of revolution.

But Sebastian magically manages to escape—he had predicted during the supper that he would use his magic dust to convert himself into a tree, a rock, a river, a bird. With Sebastian's escape—accomplished by Alea's cross-cutting between the running Sebastian and images of a tree, a rock, a river, a bird—we understand that Sebastian is the film's true Christ and the master himself its betraying Judas. The rebellious spirit of Sebastian is, like the spirit of Christ, an unkillable human force that will be "born again" in later generations of followers. The Black African spirit of Sebastian becomes the film's metaphor for the spirit of the Cuban working-class people—most of them descendants of these African slaves—that will arise and rebel against the shams of Christian social justice in 1959.

Ousmane Sembene has been adapting his own novels into film since 1965 when he made *Black Girl,* a sensitive study of an African girl who feels both stifled and corrupted when brought to the South of France to work as a cleaning lady. One of Sembene's most complex films is his adaptation of his novel, *Xala,* an ironic study of the native African's difficulty in exercising power efficiently and judiciously after having seized it. The

film's prologue is a comic allegory of political change—the native-dressed Black Africans enter a very marble-halled mausoleum-like European-style building, the Chamber of Commerce, and jauntily evict its white occupants and their symbols—busts of European figures, army boots, institutional paintings—spouting rhetoric about "Africa for the Africans" and "Power to the People." But in the very next shot, the African deputies sit in the Chamber's conference room, dressed in very European tuxedoes and tailcoats; in succeeding shots, a white commander, one of those previously expelled from the Chamber, directs a perfect line of metronomically marching Black policemen; two other formerly expelled white deputies present attaché cases stuffed with greenbacks to each of the deputies who sit in perfect symmetrical lines around the conference table; and a procession of Fords and Mercedes Benzes in a perfect line pulls up to the entrance of the Chamber of Commerce to pick up each deputy (Sembene deliberately uses the perfectly straight line and the overperfection of sharp, rectangular compositions as his dominant satiric devices). The prologue's point is clear: a group of Africans have thrown the rascals out of the Chamber of Commerce and become the rascals themselves. The film's prologue poses the question whether it is possible to inhabit the Chamber of Commerce without becoming a practitioner of the same sort of commerce purveyed by the white Western world.

The film's narrative is the story of one of those deputies, a highly respected businessman, whose business, significantly, is importing food. This minister has decided to indulge his sexual appetite by taking a third wife. (Sembene ironically reveals that the sexist Africans have preserved those vestiges of African culture that suit their pleasure under the guise of perpetuating "Africanness.") The wedding party is a curious mixture of

Xala. *Native Africans in the Chamber of Commerce: Westernized clothing and identical, geometrically arranged attaché cases*

African customs (the groom need not even attend the church service) and Western ones (the guests drink cocktails and Coca-Cola; gifts include African ones, like gold and native jewelry, and a Western one, a red-ribboned automobile; a band plays a very terrible and funny pastiche of pop-rock music). This marriage begins the minister's downfall—he sinks steadily into debt, beggary, and social disgrace.

Unfortunately, the minister is mysteriously incapable of sexual arousal with this new young bride he took for sexual purposes. The minister believes that someone has put a curse—a *xala*—on his virility. So he seeks a variety of native magical cures (again Sembene shows that these Westernized Africans become very Africa-conscious when it suits their needs), but his inadequacy is incurable and irreversible. At the end of the film, the minister has fallen lower than the outcast poverty of a group of beggars and cripples who has wandered symbolically

through the film's narrative—beggars who have been swindled out of the food they need to survive by the minister's own economic machinations. The man's true *xala* is that he is a stranger to his own people—not white and not black, not traditional and not modern, not African and not Western. Like all of the hypocritical swindlers and thieves in the outwardly respectable Chamber of Commerce, he is a not.

One of the film's consistent motifs is to draw a contrast between men and women in this society—a sure sign, for Sembene, that the new culture is as stagnant, as immature, as unresponsive to the genuine needs of the African people as the one it replaced. The men in the film all speak French, while the women all speak the native language of Wuluf (the use of different languages in a dialogue film is an interesting use of sound cinema that can be traced to such predecessors as Pabst, Renoir and Satyajit Ray). The men all dress in black-and-white western clothing, while the women dress in colorful native garb. This contrast of neutrality and color (an interesting visual device in a color film) plays a consistent symbolic function in the film. The single colorful object in the conference room of the Chamber of Commerce is the table around which they sit (which is, in effect, their altar); it is green—the traditional color of dollars. The map of Africa in the conference room is black-and-white—like the ministers' Western clothing and like the Western view of the continent's division of races. But in a later conversation between the deputy and his daughter, a university student who represents the new generation and who, although she is an interpreter and translator, uses only Wuluf in everyday conversation, another map of Africa hangs on the wall behind the girl. This map of Africa is dominated by brilliant colors—bright oranges and lavenders—which are identical to the colors of the girl's dress. She is the spirit of a true Africa (just as several of the film's women represent a truer African spirit). The minister's male sexual problem becomes a metaphor for the general sexist and material corruption of the "new" African male, the continent's true *xala*. In *Xala*'s ironic contrasts of Black and White, Old and New, Male and Female, Africa and Europe, Third World and Western World, political justice and political repression, economic freedom and economic dependence, the film brilliantly, maturely, comically, perceptively summarizes all the essential issues of Third World Cinema as a whole.

The New Internationalism

The most striking change in film commerce since the mid-1960s has not been the introduction of individual national traditions but the leveling of national boundaries that has created a truly international market. The extent of international distribution, the extent of American investments in foreign production, the number of international coproductions, the number of international film festivals, and the number of directors working outside their native industries have become more significant than any particularly national statistics. Of course, certain films have always received international distribution, but not until the 1970s did a major American company like Columbia or Warner Brothers distribute a foreign "art film" like *The Emigrants* or *Claire's Knee*. Of course, foreign directors have always worked in America for political or financial reasons, but not since the 1920s have so many worked in the American industry—Antonioni, Forman, Polanski, Malle, et cetera. Of course, there have always been international coproductions, but not since the earliest period of sound have so many international casts and crews worked together: Visconti shot *The Damned* in Italy with Swedish, German, and English stars who spoke English; Ingmar Bergman made *The Touch* with Elliot Gould and, at the last minute, mercifully rejected a plan to remake *The Merry Widow* for MGM with Barbra Streisand and Max von Sydow. And through all this internationalism flows money from American investors (how else can Fellini make a film that costs over $10,000,000?), who need pictures both for their own theatres and the world market, pictures that the American industry can no longer supply exclusively as it did before the Second World War.

Perhaps the precursor of this internationalism is the career of the vagabond director, Luis Buñuel, for forty years a man without a cinematic country, making films in France, Mexico, and only occasionally in his native Spain. Buñuel, a descendant of the surrealism of Paris in the 1920s where he learned his craft from Jean Epstein, has made films in a variety of styles: symbolic-surrealist (*Un Chien andalou*, 1929; *L'Age d'or*, 1930),

documentary (*Los Hurdes,* 1932),
social-realist (*Los Olvidados,* 1950),
psychological case study (*El,* 1952),
religious allegory (*Nazarin,* 1959;
Viridiana, 1961), psychological-surrealist
allegory (*Belle de Jour,* 1967), religious-
surrealist allegory (*The Milky Way,*
1968), political-surrealist erotic drama
(*That Obscure Object of Desire,* 1978),
and social-surrealist allegorical comedy
(*The Discreet Charm of the Bourgeoisie,* 1973;
The Phantom of Liberty, 1974). Through
these differing styles over an amazingly
long career shine the consistent Buñuel
traits: the surrealist's perception of the
insubstantiality of reality coupled with the
surrealist's savage humor (for to smash
the solidity of reality is an act of joy as
well as destruction); the psychologist's
interest in the inner workings of the
human brain (particularly its sexual
fantasies and personal visions of
experience that violate all the norms of
the realists, the professional psychologists,
and the Church); and, finally, his
preoccupation with the Church itself (for
Buñuel, its fundamentally and comically
naïve and false definitions of man). Just
as Ingmar Bergman, the son of a
Lutheran minister, rebelled against his
religious heritage in films that ironically
used the images, the terms, the
metaphors of that religion, Buñuel,
educated by the Jesuits, broke the icons
of his childhood faith and used those
icons as the central artistic metaphors of
his work. But whereas Bergman could
supplement the northern preacher's view
of life as a vale of tears with the notion
that it was also a vale of sunlight, Buñuel
could only supplant the Roman Catholic
cathedral of gold and silk and ruby with
a pile of mortal manure.

The pre-1960 Buñuel films are
strikingly lacking in most of the cinematic
virtues. The stories are loose and clumsy,
the acting overstated and obvious, the
decor inattentive to detail and style. Nor
is Buñuel's work distinguished in either
its cinematography or editing; both his

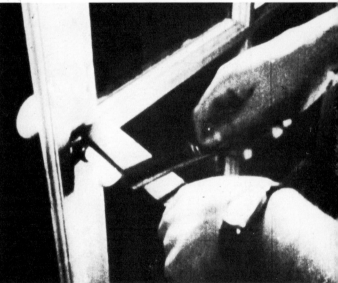

The beginning of Buñuel's film career and of Un
Chien andalou—*the filmmaker sharpens his razor
to assault and alter human vision*

composition and cutting are strictly
functional and quite conventional. The
Buñuel films have two great strengths:
the imaginativeness of the film's abstract
idea and the ferocious energy of its
translation into a concrete fictional
metaphor.

The first event in Buñuel's first film
was a close-up of a razor slicing the
human eyeball. The brutality, the nausea,

the visceral attack of this first action dominate the Buñuel canon. One of the most unflinchingly sadistic and brutal scenes ever filmed is the assault of the juvenile delinquents in *Los Olvidados* on a legless, armless beggar (cripples, dwarfs, blind men, hunchbacks, and other assorted physical freaks are as common in the Buñuel world as priests). The delinquents pull the helpless cripple out of his cart, roll the man over on the ground, kicking the stump of his body, leaving him sprawled on the street like a turtle on its back, after which they gleefully send his cart careening down the street so he can never retrieve it. The vicious hoodlums also murder the film's young innocent boy and later dispose of his body by stuffing it in a wheelbarrow and then dumping it on the slum's garbage heap.

The equation of man and garbage is the central Buñuel theme. The teachings of the Church and the assumptions of social morality infuriate the director, who views man as not only fallen but irretrievable. Buñuel's fury becomes the starting point of a film that intentionally rubs the nose of a naïve innocent in the feces of Buñuel's reality. In the process the audience gets its nose rubbed, too. In *El* a church merely serves as the means for the film's central character, a paranoid lecher, to make a sexual conquest. (The man's paranoia also climaxes in church: an insanely grotesque fantasy that everyone, including the priest, is howling at his cuckoldry.) In *That Obscure Object of Desire,* an unexplained burlap sack weaves metaphorically through the film's narrative of sexual desire and frustration, clearly emblematic of the mortal offal beneath the elegant houses and restaurants in which the characters live, love, and eat. And *Belle de Jour* uses the whorehouse as the ultimate metaphor for genuine sexual passions, whereas marriage, the official social outlet for

sexual passion, is constricting, artificial, and sterile. The result of imposing such artificial behavior on the human beast is perversion, murder, and castration. In fact, in *Belle de Jour,* as in *Los Olvidados* and *El,* such terms are synonymous.

Viridiana is perhaps Buñuel's most even, most whole black-and-white film. It begins in a monastery with the music of Handel's "Messiah"; it ends in the bedroom of a young lecher with rock-and-roll music. The music and the settings mirror the film's journey. The young girl, Viridiana, is a novitiate in a convent on the threshold of taking her final vows. Before taking those vows she makes the customary trip back to the secular world to be sure that she wants to leave it. She visits her rich uncle's estate. He falls under the sexual spell of her beauty. Carried away by his passion, he drugs his niece with the intention of raping her insensate body. But instead of actually committing the rape, he merely tells her that she has been violated, daubing the sheets of her bed with blood to convince her of the physical fact of her sin. The blood of lust on her sheets convinces her that she no longer carries the blood of the lamb in her soul. She decides not to return to the convent.

Rejecting the formal teachings of the Church as a means of saving her soul, Viridiana takes the next step on the film's allegorical path. She turns to natural religion—good works, charity—as a means of helping humankind. Viridiana uses the money and the grounds of her uncle's estate to establish a utopian community for the poor. Viridiana feels her soul strengthened by this Christian-communist colony in which all work together and none go hungry. But one day when Viridiana and the other masters leave on an excursion, the peasants break into the house, set out the fancy linen and china, and begin to devour a banquet of their own. They raucously break furniture and dishes; they drunkenly bloody the white

Viridiana: *Buñuel's beggars and cripples at his parody of "The Last Supper"*

linen with wine. One of the beggars takes a picture of the loathsome group; they pose in the positions of the disciples in da Vinci's "Last Supper"; the beggar woman "snaps the picture" of the gathering by raising her skirt and exposing her naked groin. This lewd burlesque of the sacred scene deflates any hope that this human scum can be improved or helped by any means whatever. Viridiana has failed at both faith and charity. Seeing no hope at all, Viridiana wanders into the bedroom of her sensual cousin were he "plays cards," as he euphemistically puts it. As Viridiana sits down at the card table, her cousin tells her that he has always known she would one day play cards with him. Buñuel's allegory of the vile reality of the human flesh is complete.

Nazarin is also an allegory that develops the gap between the abstract, ideal teachings of Christ and Buñuel's concrete definition of the bestial human animal. *The Discreet Charm of the Bourgeoisie*

develops the gap between the simple concrete reality that the bourgeois expectations assume (the banality of property, success, money, social intercourse, and, especially, eating dinner) and the complex levels of super-realities (wishes, dreams, imaginings, fancies) that actually exist. But one of the funniest, cleverest, and most challenging of the late Buñuel films that combines these two themes is *The Milky Way*, a film named after the route of pilgrimage from Paris to San Sebastian in Spain, where Christian pilgrims of the Middle Ages traveled to view the tomb of St. James. Buñuel's film is more a pilgrimage in time than in space, for as his two modern "pilgrims" (one old, one young; both of them bums, reminiscent of Chaplin or Laurel and Hardy) make the same journey, their "stopping places" are a series of religious heresies that might have existed on or near that route over the past five centuries. Buñuel's film skips among the centuries, making it completely natural for the two twentieth-century pilgrims to meet two young men who continually walk back and forth between events in the seventeenth and twentieth centuries.

The heresies that the two pilgrims visit are magnificently bizarre, all of them based on actual historical testimony, as one would expect from Buñuel. The bizarre authenticity of these "actual" heresies is essential to Buñuel's attempt to show how bizarre are all religious beliefs and to raise the question of what makes heresy heretical. Among the bizarre heretics are a group of worshippers who combine their Latin prayers with sex orgies, continuing to speak in Latin and wear their priestly robes even as the Bacchanalia begins; a convent of nuns who literally re-enact the Crucifixion, driving nails into the palms of the chosen sister (she is so inspired that the nails do not hurt her at all); a swashbuckling duel between two devotees of different sects; a bishop's exhuming the body of one of his predecessors, presumed a saintly cleric, and excommunicating his bones for his now heretical opinions. Even in the posh restaurants and country inns of the present, the waiters and customers seem to have nothing better to discuss than matters of religious controversy, such as transubstantiation and the credibility of miracles.

Buñuel's comic (and serious) point is that today's orthodoxy is tomorrow's heresy: heresy is simply a matter of contemporary opinion. For example, when the pilgrims finally arrive in San Sebastian they discover that no other pilgrims have journeyed there because the Church long ago decided that the presumed bones of St. James that lay entombed there were not the bones of St. James. (The Church can decide whose bones are whose as it pleases, just as it decides whose views are heretical and why.) Buñuel finds it extremely ludicrous that a body of men, calling themselves the Church, can presume to define such

insubstantial matters with such certainty —especially when history (as Buñuel's film shows) reveals the force of that insubstantiality with great clarity.

The cinema is a useful tool for Buñuel to use in making such a point since it is so able to make the solid appear insubstantial and the insubstantial appear solid. The film is capable of showing us historical phantoms in corporeal dress, of showing us supernatural figures (a clairvoyant man with a flowing black cape) in a completely natural guise; even of showing us miracles (the appearance of both the Virgin and of Christ) more concretely than any vision ever appeared to any saint. One of Buñuel's most vigorous (and amusing) demonstrations of the insubstantiality of the concrete and the concreteness of the insubstantial is a sequence in an inn where two men each go to their separate rooms alone. In one of the rooms, however, a beautiful and naked woman miraculously appears in the bed beside one of the men, although he has not opened the door and it is impossible to enter the room in any other way. As he lies in the room next to the tempting woman who cannot possibly be there, a priest begins giving him a lecture on abstinence and chastity (what else?), sitting outside the bedroom door. Except that the priest suddenly appears inside the room, facing the man and woman (who also is not there) while he lectures, although he too cannot possibly have entered the room. But there he is inside the room!

In the same way, the single female object of desire in *Obscure Object* cannot possibly be embodied by two different women, but there the two women concretely are, both of them the single beloved a man would like to possess. The fact that she is two underscores the impossibility of ever fulfilling the desire to *possess* another human being. For Buñuel the cinema has always been the realm of the impossible actual: phenomena, which in the reality of time and space cannot possibly occur, can occur before the viewer's eyes because the cinema is free of reality's time and space. But for Buñuel this feature makes the cinema *more* like life and experience (not less), for reality is composed of thoughts, dreams, ideas, and desires as much as of tangible objects. The heresy that happened in a farmhouse *is there* on that Milky Way just as clearly as that farmhouse is there. The alternating objects of abstract desire—one sweet and virginal, the other fiery and sensual—*are there,* just as clearly as each of those actresses is there. In Buñuel's view, only when people realize the insubstantiality of our supposedly "objective reality" and of our opinions based on it will we be able to avoid doing violence both to reality and to one another.

15 The New Hollywood: 1966–1978

It is not entirely certain when the old American movie became the new American cinema: *Bonnie and Clyde* (1967)? *Who's Afraid of Virginia Woolf?* (1966)? *The Pawnbroker* (1965)? *Dr. Strangelove* (1963)? *Lonely Are the Brave* (1962)? *The Hustler* (1961)? *Psycho* (1960)? The exact film that marked the change is not important and not discoverable, for America slid into its fifth era gradually, just as it slipped into its transitional fourth phase—quite unlike its sudden leap into the second era of the feature film and its third era of synchronized sound. All seven of the above films contain some of the seeds of the period's values: the off-beat antihero protagonist; the sterile society that surrounds him; the explicit treatment of sexual conflicts and psychological perversities; the glorification of the past and the open spaces; the slick but tawdry surfaces of contemporary reality; the mixing of the comic and the serious; the self-conscious use of special cinematic effects (slow motion, quick cutting, ironic juxtaposition of the visual and sound). All seven of the films give evidence of the two clichés that critics used to describe films of the era: sex and

violence. But films have always used sex: whether it was the sexiness of Griffith's Friendless Ones, the sexiness of Marlene Dietrich's veiled face in a key light, or the sexiness of bare breasts and buttocks in a Paris apartment. And films have always been violent—whether it was violent death on a Civil War battlefield in *The Birth of a Nation,* the violent death of a hoodlum on the cathedral steps in *Little Caesar,* or the violent death of the film's protagonists in a slow-motion ballet. The key question about any film style is not whether it uses sex and violence but how it uses them.

This new cinema in America evolved for several reasons; for one, there was a negative cause: the old, steady movie patrons stayed home to watch television. The industry had to find new steady customers, not the ones who would go to a movie four times a year, but those who would go every week.

For another, the new cinema of Europe eventually converted American producers. The innovations of Godard, Truffaut, and Antonioni had already conquered the rising generation of young filmmakers and audiences at the art houses. Even more convincing, Truffaut and Antonioni could make money. The years 1959 and 1960 were as important as any to the future American film. Those were the years of *Breathless, The 400 Blows, Shoot the Piano Player, Hiroshima Mon Amour, L'Avventura,* and *La Dolce Vita.*

Third, though Hollywood repeatedly scoffed at the Underground Cinema, the underground crawled up into Hollywood to enjoy the last laugh. Not only did underground filmmakers succeed by Hollywood's financial standards—for example, Andy Warhol, Robert Downey, and Brian De Palma—but the underground films conditioned a whole generation of young filmgoers (precisely those who became the steady customers for Hollywood films) to understand and accept innovations in cinematic form, visual stimulation, and elliptical construction.

Fourth, the film industry pushed its discovery of the elitism of the new film audience to its limits. Rather than attempt to make all of the films for all of the people, producers and exhibitors realized they must appeal to very special tastes. They could make a few family pictures to serve that special need. They could capitalize on the racial makeup of urban audiences by making "blaxploitation" cops-and-robbers films (*Shaft* and all his descendants). They could make "sexploitation" films for that special audience, catering even further to particular tastes by aiming the films at the specific sexual orientation of the viewers (heterosexual, homosexual, or bisexual) and at their preferred voyeuristic fantasies within those orientations (oral, anal, sado-masochistic, et cetera). *The Devil in Miss Jones* (1973), *Deep Throat* (1972), and *Boys in the Sand* (1971) were probably the three most commercially successful films in their respective "genres." In the same way, the American industry aimed its "art films" (those directed by Arthur Penn, Mike Nichols, Peter Bogdanovich, Robert Altman, and others) at the minority audience that liked those kinds

of films, a group that not only represented a fraction of the American population but also of the film-going public. These films, however, are precisely those that have come to serve as America's best examples of film art and the most important representatives of its fifth era.

And finally, the values of these new American "art films" reflected the sexual and social values of American film audiences in the period. The American college student, the core of this audience, had discovered the sensual pleasures of the body and the joint as two concrete values in a world of conflicting ideals and hypocritical rhetoric. The vision of reality on the screen did not entirely shape its audience; as in the 1930s, the screen still reflected the values of those who sat in front of it. Those values had changed.

Bonnie and Clyde was perhaps the first full statement of the new cinema's values; it has been as influential on the American films that followed it as *Breathless* was in France or *Open City* in Italy. In the years after *Bonnie and Clyde,* the innovations it introduced hardened into obligatory conventions; many of the new "free" films were as impersonal, as subservient to convention and cliché as the Preminger films of the 1950s or the studio films of the 1930s. These conventions of the new cinema can be assembled easily into a list.

First, the protagonists of the films were social misfits, deviates, or outlaws; the villains were the legal, respectable defenders of society. The old bad guys became the good guys; the old good guys, the bad guys. The surprising element in *Bonnie and Clyde* (and *Easy Rider, Cool Hand Luke, Butch Cassidy and the Sundance Kid, Thieves Like Us,* et cetera) was not simply that the protagonists were criminals, for films had depicted their Little Caesars, Scarfaces, and Bonnie Parkers for decades. The surprise was that these new murderers were also charming, warm, loving, compassionate, good-humored. The pursuers with badges

Love, thrills, and bullets. Michael J. Pollard, Faye Dunaway, and Warren Beatty in Bonnie and Clyde

were inevitably the humorless, inhuman ones. Given the outlaw protagonists, the new obligatory ending was the unhappy rather than happy one. The protagonists die; law triumphs over lawlessness. However, good did not triumph over evil, for law and good were antithetical.

The crucial thing about the new antihero heroes was not that they died, since death is inevitable, but that they lived as they did—free, unchained, unswervingly true to themselves. Ironically, despite this reversal of moral values, the American film was still essentially romantic and Manichean, just as it was in the 1920s and 1930s. There were still film characters who lived profoundly beautiful lives and others who lived profoundly vile ones—even if the definitions of beauty and vileness had changed. Even those films that strove for the European ambivalence—*The Last Picture Show, Thieves Like Us, They Shoot Horses, Don't They?, Five Easy Pieces*—still depended upon an idealization of love.

Second, the new American cinema did not ask to be taken as reality but constantly announced that it was artificial. Rather than effacing the film's artfulness, as a Ford or Hawks intentionally did, the new directors threw in as many cinematic

tricks as possible, which both intensified the film's moods and reminded the audience that it was watching a film. Slow motion, freeze-frames, jump-cutting, mixtures of black-and-white and color were all standard, indeed obligatory, tricks of the new trade. This deliberate artificiality had several consequences.

The first was that there was an emotional power in the visual assaults of the medium itself. The viewer responded not just to a story and people but to the physical stimulation of eye and ear for its own sake. One of the advantages that film enjoys over television is that its big screen is more hypnotic, its stereophonic sound more overwhelming. And it is not interrupted by commercials. In McLuhanesque terms, television is much cooler than the films, more distant from its viewers, who necessarily remain more detached. The new American films took even further advantage of their hotness by using color and the wide screen almost exclusively. A second consequence of the film trickery was that the films became emotional metaphors more than literal stories. The quick cutting, the flashes both forward and backward in time (sometimes confusingly interwoven) totally destroyed the definitions of time and space, of now and then, of reality and fantasy, purposely emphasizing emotional continuity at the expense of linear continuity.

Third, the new films played as trickily with sound as they did with images. Gone was the old principle of studio scoring— to underscore a scene with music that increases the action's emotional impact without making the viewer aware of the music's existence. This early principle of film scoring was a clear extension of the piano's function in the nickelodeon. In the new films, there was little of this kind of background music. If there was to be music it had to be either clearly motivated (playing on a radio or record player nearby) or deliberately artificial (a song on the sound track that existed specifically to be noticed and played either in harmony or in counterpoint with the sequence's visuals). In *Butch Cassidy and the Sundance Kid* (1969), the story stops for an idyllic ride on a bicycle accompanied by a pleasant Burt Bacharach rock tune. In *Medium Cool* (1969), the patriotic speeches and songs inside the Democratic Convention hall accompany the riots between students and police in Grant Park. The sound track of *Thieves Like Us* (1973) is a compendium of 1930s radio broadcasts, serving to show how central the radio was to American life in that era, saturating the film with period color, and often commenting ironically on the action (for example, an installment of *Gang Busters* during a bank robbery or a radio version of *Romeo and Juliet* during a love scene).

Some sequences in the new films distorted sound purposely (for example, *The Conversation,* 1974, whose subject is sound recording); others were completely silent, contrasting with the other sequences of song or noise. The new constant of film music was that no longer were scores written by Alfred Newman, Miklos Rozsa, or Max Steiner and performed by the studio's symphony orchestra. Rock and jazz composers wrote the new film scores and the most popular rock groups performed them. The new films used rock music heavily (the scores of *Easy Rider* and *American Graffiti* were samplers of several dozen different rock hits), for rock music was the other artistic and social passion of the young audiences who were supporting the movies.

The new cinema in America became self-consciously concerned with style—with visual texture, a careful attention to the dress, decor, and dialects of the historical era (usually from America's recent past), with a specific use of the camera and sound track to capture and mirror that style authentically. The days of sound-stage shooting had passed; directors preferred the naturalness and authenticity of shooting on location.

Whereas the old Hollywood style was devoted to eliminating the imperfections of reality—graceless rooms, uneven lighting, uncontrollable noise—the new American films required accident and imperfection for their visual style and human credibility. This demand for authenticity was the result of the American cinema's conversion to a uniquely European cinema value—to render the experiential texture of a human event. The new films did not depict action so much as how the action *felt,* so that character rather than plot became the dominant interest. In the manner of Godard's *Breathless* or Truffaut's *Jules and Jim,* the American films captured and developed the feelings of people passing through an event or process. In many ways, the new American films seemed as influenced by the Czechs as the French, for in their attempts to transfer the world of internal sensations to an audience, *Five Easy Pieces* (1971), *Thieves Like Us, The Conversation, The Last Detail* (1974), and *The Deer Hunter* (1978) felt like Czech films. Of course, one of the American film industry's claims was that it now made better "European" pictures than the Europeans, so that American theatres screen fewer and fewer European films each year. On the other hand, the new American films have been losing their devoted European audiences, who seem to prefer the more external, exuberant, and active old American movie.

However Europeanized the fifth American era had become, it still maintained its old inclination toward rigid genres and repetitive cycles. Producers still felt safer with a formula that had succeeded before, and so a series of films about compassionate thieves followed *Bonnie and Clyde,* a series of films about the last assertive gasp of the old frontier followed *The Wild Bunch,* a series of violent police-chase films followed *The French Connection,* a series of Mafia films followed *The Godfather,* a series of sci-fi adventures followed *Star Wars,* et cetera. Despite their new experiential and stylistic commitments, the new films were descendants of the old genres: the western, the gangster, the *policier,* the screwball comedy, and so on. The basic generic division in the new films was between city films and country films. Those two metaphors for American culture—the cement canyons of New York and its other modern cities; the mountain canyons of the Great West—were still the dominant images of the American film.

The city films, which invariably examined the harried and hurried quality of American city life, were dependent on the imagery of the city: hard, close, flat, artificial, cold—stone and neon. Many of the city films developed a thematic opposition between the unnaturalness and brutality of the city and the freedom and openness outside the city. Such new films were clearly descendants of the old *films noirs* of the transitional era (the toughness of living and growing up in the big city), which were themselves descendants of the reporter pictures (tough reporters were indigenous to the big city) of the Studio Era. Close cousins to the city films, thematically as well as geographically, were the suburb films—such as *The Graduate* (1968), *Bob and Carol and Ted and Alice* (1969), and *Goodbye, Columbus* (1969). Appropriately, two of these three films used Los Angeles, that city of suburbs, as setting and metaphor. Even those films that did not assail the inhumanity of the city or suburb took advantage of shooting in Manhattan, using its real settings and gifted actors for the same natural off-beat feeling that the British realist films evoked from London, Manchester, and Birmingham: *A Thousand Clowns* (1965), *A Fine Madness* (1966), *You're a Big Boy Now* (1967), *Up the Down Staircase* (1967), *The Producers* (1968), *The Night They Raided Minsky's* (1968), *Popi* (1969), *The French Connection* (1972), *Taxi Driver* (1974), *Annie Hall* (1977), and *Manhattan* (1979), to name just a few.

The new, "experiential" western—for example, Sam Peckinpah's *The Wild Bunch* (1969), George Roy Hill's *Butch Cassidy and the Sundance Kid* (1969), Robert Altman's *McCabe and Mrs. Miller* (1972)—reveals the internalization and sensualization of a previously external and active genre. For Hawks, the West was a place where a man simultaneously tested his toughness and his ability to retain the humanity that connects him with other human beings; for Ford, the West was a place where man brought civilization and order to savagery and desert. For the new films, the West, the vast plains and deserts, were the last outposts of the free spirit of man and the original pioneer spirit of America. Just as the city films needed the country for contrast, the country films needed the city—the place where sheriffs and policemen and businessmen reside. Both *The Wild Bunch* and *Butch Cassidy* were set in an era when the Old West was crumbling, when the city's values were swallowing the country's. The heroes of both films prefer to remain happy anachronisms rather than surrender to "decency" and the machine. The inevitable sections in slow motion in these new westerns existed to heighten, lyricize, and magnify the moment of death, in effect turning that moment into a prolonged sensual experience. If the new western differed from the old one it was not because it was more violent; plenty of men were shot dead in the old westerns. But in the old western the audience merely saw a man shot dead; the emotional effect came from the suspense before the shooting (who will win the gunfight, when, and how?) and the relief after it. The new western turned the moment of death itself into the emotional experience.

The new gangster film mirrored the same basic generic division between past and present, city and country. The crime films either concerned themselves with rural gangsters of the past or urban gangsters of the present or near-present.

The country-crime genre was essentially a subgenre of the new western. Whereas the protagonists of the western depended on their horses, the central figures of *Bonnie and Clyde, Thieves Like Us,* and *Badlands* (1973) used the automobile as their means of slicing through the open prairies. Contrasted with the happy freedom of Bonnie and Clyde is a nation of economic slaves, the hungry and the poor who are victims of a political system that dwarfs people and undermines their lives with its Depressions. Contrasted with the happy freedom of Bowie, Masefield, and Chickesaw is the boring banality of middle-class drawing rooms and dinner tables, lives that are so tawdry and dull that those corny radio shows serve as their only glimpse of a more exciting existence.

A synthesis of past and present, city and country, gangster and cowboy existed in the idealization of sky, plain, and mountain in *Easy Rider;* the horse had become the motorbike; civilization was personified by the small-town bigots, the county sheriff, institutionalized love (a New Orleans whorehouse), institutionalized fun (Mardi Gras), and institutionalized death (an immense cemetery). But even the free and romantic West is being sullied; a commune of transposed, hip city kids feels as much hostility toward the two easy riders as the "straight" bigots in the towns and city. The only freedom, the only joy is being on the road itself, and even that, as the film's ending shows, can never be enjoyed for long.

Whereas the country-crime films tended toward a softness and slowness, softening human brutality and luxuriating in the luminous beauty of nature, the city-crime films were hard, fast, and cold. If the slow-motion death sequence was obligatory in the western and country-crime film, the breathlessly rapid and assaultive chase was obligatory in the city-crime and police films. The essential technical tool of the city film was editing rather than composition as in the country films, and the basic subjective device was the violent rushing of the traveling or hand-held camera rather than the subjective prolongation of an event in slow motion. Cops in the city-crime films (*Bullitt,* 1968; *The French Connection; The New Centurions,* 1972; *Klute,* 1972; *Serpico,* 1973; *Cruising,* 1979) usually faced two sources of tensions: within themselves (are they just doing their job or are they neurotically driven to violence and sadism?) and within their own departments (the pressures of politicians, bureaucrats, and incompetents). The *film noir* of the transitional era (for example, Lang's *The Big Heat*) was a truly transitional link between the detective films of the Studio Era in which the cop fought crime and of the new era in which a cop fights himself and cops fight each other. The new focus of the gangster city films was less on the push to the top and the inevitable fall (*Little Caesar* or *Scarface*) and more on the mundane problems of living legitimately once the top had been reached (the conflict between the old life of crime and the new respectability in *The Godfather*).

The most obvious link between the New Hollywood and the old was the one "new" genre of the 1970s—what might be called the genre genre. These films parodied the plot structures, stylistic conventions, and movie stars of Hollywood Past, usually by compiling a catalogue of Studio Era clichés—the Neil Simon–Robert Moore comedies (*Murder by Death,* 1976; *The Cheap Detective,* 1978), Dick Richards's *Farewell, My Lovely* (1975), Stanley Donen's *Movie Movie* (1978), some of the early Woody Allen films (*Take the Money and Run,* 1969; *Play It Again, Sam,* 1973), and, of course, almost the entire *oeuvre* of Mel Brooks (*Blazing Saddles,* 1972; *Young Frankenstein,* 1974; *High Anxiety,* 1977).

The new American cinema was not a shift in direction so much as a new use of the traditional themes and images of American literature and American film.

Instead of the indoor, studio-built, glamorized, dialogue-centered films of the first thirty years of sound, the new films preferred to go outdoors, to real locations rather than sets; they emphasized the kinetic effects of film as movement, picture, music, rather than as well-made, logical story. The best new American films were like those that had always been best—a unified blend of story (pared down in the quantity of incident), human insight (carefully textured in the quality of an experience), thematic vision (more ambivalent in its moral positions), and cinematic style (more intrusive and idiosyncratically stylized than ever).

The New American Auteurs

Like the film industries of Europe and Japan, the American cinema has become a directors' cinema, granting proven directors a higher measure of control over the scripting (they, like European directors, are now often listed among the screenwriters), cutting, and production decisions, allowing them more freedom in selecting their projects, and essentially valuing their contribution more than Hollywood ever did in its Studio Era. The American director has become one of the film's stars, and it is significant that many directors of the last decade can make films without any major star at all (*The Last Picture Show, Thieves Like Us, Star Wars, Days of Heaven*), an unheard of practice for major films until 1968 (and Kubrick's *2001*). When François Truffaut in France and Andrew Sarris in America developed the *"auteur* theory" (or *auteur* policy), they did so as a means of distinguishing directorial individuality in the Studio Era, since individuality was often buried beneath the decisions of producers and the scripts of the scenario department. But the new American *auteurs* are film authors in the full sense of a Truffaut, Fellini, Bergman, Forman, or Kurosawa—the ones who control the

responsibility for the entire project so that their own personal visions and visual styles get recorded on film.

The list of these new *auteurs* which follows is necessarily tentative. The American directors who now seem most interesting and most important are all very young; all of them are in mid-career; perhaps none of them has made the masterpiece that fulfills the general promise of his talent and craft (no *Citizen Kane, Breathless,* or *Jules and Jim* among the juvenilia). But all of them have made a cluster of films that reveal both a high level of creativity and imagination as well as a consistency of style and vision.

Woody Allen is the new American comic *auteur* who is most conscious of the older American comic-film tradition that he inherits. His glasses create a "glass character" who clearly resembles Harold Lloyd, his physical clumsiness and unattractiveness parallel Harry Langdon's, and his dryly quiet, offbeat comic ironies suggest the flavor of Buster Keaton. But more than anyone else, Allen resembles Chaplin as an observer and chronicler of the contemporary American social scene. Although his characters wear different names (Fielding Mellish in *Bananas,* 1971; Miles Monroe in *Sleeper,* 1973; Boris Grushenko in *Love and Death,* 1975; Alvie Singer in *Annie Hall,* 1977), a device that parallels Keaton's different names and costumes, Woody Allen's comic persona is a single, familiar, established being, like Charlie, who wanders across the landscape of contemporary urban life, contrasting that persona with the less observant, less sensitive society dwellers who surround him. One might call Woody Allen's entire *oeuvre* "Modern Times," and if the problem for Allen's city dwellers has shifted from the external ones of finding a job and founding a home to the internal one of feeling secure enough to survive between appointments with the analyst, that shift is symptomatic of five decades of change in American life itself. Like Charlie, Woody is terribly out of tune and out of step with the society around him. On the one hand, he is physically, mentally, and emotionally unequipped to accept its norms, values, and definitions. But on the other (also like Charlie), he longs to accept those values and be accepted by them in return, thereby turning his attempts at winning acceptance into monstrous parodies of society's attitudes and rituals themselves.

Allen's comic persona is obviously and deliberately close to Allen's off-screen personality as well—introspective, cynical, neurotic, self-conscious, self-indulgent, hip, flip. His two goals on film seem to be Allen's off-screen goals as well—personal, internal contentment with himself and romantic-sexual fulfillment with another—a parallel emphasized by his off-screen marriages and affairs with the actresses in his films. And so Allen's films come closer to psychoanalysis, to psycho-comedy, than the work of any other American comedian—except, of course, Lenny Bruce, another important (but nonfilmic) Allen ancestor. Allen is obsessed by his relationship with his mother (the re-enacted Passover Seder in *Sleeper;* the contrast of Annie's and Alvie's families in *Annie Hall;* the possession of all three daughters in *Interiors,* 1978, by Eve; and so forth). And he is also haunted by doubts about his own sexual powers and prowess (hence, his lies to Janet Margolin, his first screen romance, in *Take the Money and Run,* 1969; or the subtitled translations of the lies in his first conversation with Annie Hall; or his inability to make up his mind about who or what he wants or loves in *Manhattan,* 1979). Allen's face (freckled and birdlike) and his body (puny and scrawny) emphasize the distance of his persona from the stereotypic romantic ideal (like Charlie in *The Circus* and *City Lights*), thereby reducing these contemporary obsessions with sexual attractiveness and fulfillment to the absurd.

Allen's cinematic technique in his earliest films was, like that of Mack

New American archetypes: the neurotic schlepp and the kooky dame (Diane Keaton and Woody Allen in Annie Hall)

Sennett, truly flip—in two senses of the term. First, it was casual and flippant, taking nothing as serious or sacred (racial and religious stereotypes, political philosophies, politicians, intellectuals, revolutions, conformity, cultural crazes, sexuality, psychology, et cetera), especially the making of the movie itself. He was also flip in that he leapt from gag to gag with astonishing rapidity, often wearing the audience (and his ideas) out before the end of the film and often establishing funny situations that he failed to develop (two dangers of flipping). But Allen's three late 1970s films (*Annie Hall, Interiors, Manhattan*) show far more care and consciousness of cinematic style and "art"—probably because all three were shot by Gordon Willis (cinematographer for both *Godfathers*, *All the President's Men*, and others), the most distinguished cinematographer with whom Allen has collaborated. At the end of *Annie Hall* two young actors attempt to reproduce the farewell scene between Annie and Alvie at the health-food restaurant. That falteringly funny attempt may be taken as a metaphor for Allen's evolution in the use of comedy—the desire to objectify, to concretize personal experiences and private obsessions into comic works that can be publicly performed for others.

Interiors parallels Chaplin's *A Woman of Paris*—a serious study of the artist's concerns (for Allen, family life, the artistic vocation, and sexual fulfillment) that dispenses with the familiar comic persona as a focus and anchor for the study. And *Manhattan* is clearly Allen's *City Lights*—its use of the urban setting, the nostalgic Gershwin music to evoke the 1930s, the equally nostalgic but visually glorious use of black and white (indeed, the film's combination of old-movie monochrome with the new movie's ultra-wide Panavision frame makes the film's visual style a synthesis of past and present). And, of course, *Manhattan* ends with the same kind of agonized unanswered question (and the same close-up of a male face) as did *City Lights*. The difference between Chaplin and Allen, however, may lie in the difference between the two unanswered questions posed by the two endings. The question Chaplin raises—can she possibly love him for what he is rather than for what he *appears* to be—is so much larger than the Allen question—can he possibly wait six months for her return from London.

Does he really love her anyway? Who is she to him? How long is six months? Their relationship seems so much more flippant, more trivial than the relationship between Charlie and the flower seller—upon whom the Tramp's entire being and happiness has come to depend. That gap—between the terrible importance of the final question in *City Lights* and the terrible triviality of the question in *Manhattan*—is Allen's deliberate comment on the difference between life in 1930 and life in 1980, which has become trivialized, ephemeral, superficial, and self-indulgent. The several months that Allen takes for each project—contrasted with the several years that Chaplin invested—also seems a flippancy consistent with the Allen persona, style, and theme.

Robert Altman also makes movies quickly (fifteen feature films in the 1970s). Like Woody Allen he would rather make movies than masterpieces, a large number of attempts rather than a few highly polished gems. As a result, Altman's work is extremely inconsistent, varying from film to film and even from part to part within individual films. Altman's work comes in two narrative sizes. The first is a smaller, closer study of a bizarre central figure or figures who lead very bizarre lives or are possessed by very bizarre dreams—the boy who wants to become a bird and fly in *Brewster McCloud* (1970), the incompetent gun-slinger and the drug-addict dancehall doll in *McCabe and Mrs. Miller* (1971), the picaresque life-style of a hiply updated Philip Marlowe in *The Long Goodbye* (1973), the thieves who want to rob enough banks to settle down to respectable middle-class lives in *Thieves Like Us* (1974), the possessed gambler-friends of *California Split* (1974), the two young water therapists living in the arid desert of *Three Women* (1977). Since these people are possessed by their dreams, it is not surprising that the climaxes of these films—particularly of *McCabe and Mrs. Miller, Brewster McCloud,* and *Three*

Women—fly or float off into some irrational realm of unconscious wish fulfillment.

The second Altman narrative structure requires a much larger canvas. It is a broad sociological and psychological study of a particular American institution, built from a very large number of interwoven human figures, adding up to a cross-sectional view of American life itself. *M*A*S*H* (1970), Altman's first major success, used the activities of a group of American medics in Korea (during the height of America's Vietnam crisis)—as well as many of the familiar antics of American GI movies—to examine American attitudes toward war, particularly those against other races in distant parts of the world. *Nashville* (1975), probably Altman's most solid and respected film, used the American country-and-western recording industry—and all the people it touched or who wanted to be touched by it—to investigate American political and economic structures, as well as the American dreams of fame and success. *Buffalo Bill and the Indians* (1976), perhaps Altman's least successful film, used the wild west show to examine the rape of the American continent and the debasement of the original American pioneer spirit. And *A Wedding* (1978) used a suburban upper-upper-middle-class wedding ceremony to examine the relationship of love and lucre in contemporary American life.

One of the consistent Altman strengths is the compelling spontaneous authenticity of the moments of human interaction—moments of uproarious laughter, sloppy drunkenness, the jocular camaraderie of men and the tender friendship of women, the potential humor and informality in a love scene, the starkness and loneliness of the moment of death. Altman works improvisationally with his actors, and the scenes they build together (between Donald Sutherland and Elliott Gould in *M*A*S*H*, Julie Christie and Warren

Probing beneath the surfaces of American life; apparent domestic tranquility in Nashville *(Lily Tomlin, Ned Beatty, and their deaf-mute child); disguising a vision of American social corruption as a detective thriller or* film noir *in* Chinatown *(Jack Nicholson, Perry Lopez, and Faye Dunaway)*

Beatty in *McCabe and Mrs. Miller*, Keith Carradine and Shelley Duvall in *Thieves Like Us*, Gould and George Segal in *California Split*, Carradine or Lily Tomlin and everybody else in *Nashville*, Duvall and Sissy Spacek in *Three Women*) are hypnotic encounters with acting that feels like life.

The second Altman strength is his perceptive scrutiny of American social institutions, which he explores with haunting and startlingly memorable visual images that stick in the mind long after other details of the narrative have faded. *Brewster McCloud* is dominated by images of the bare, sterile Astrodome, *McCabe and Mrs. Miller* by the icy whiteness and wetness of snow, and *Three Women* by the opposite dryness and dust of a seemingly endless American desert (the contrast of wet and dry, water imagery with arid imagery is as central and clear an issue in the film as any). In *Buffalo Bill* there is the haunting image of the wild west show's master of ceremonies (played by Joel Grey, transported from the same job in the Berlin of *Cabaret*), reflected in the shiny brass prisms of a multihorn megaphone (the juxtaposition of natural human voice with unnatural means of amplification is also central to the film's issues). In *The Long Goodbye* there are fleeting yet repetitive glimpses of the exercising dancers who provide the scenic view from Marlowe's apartment, and in *Three Women* the similarly fleeting yet repetitive glimpses of the perfectly matched twins; in both films these images, which weave through the narrative like musical motifs, are summaries of a purely physical, empty-headed American lifestyle. In *A Wedding* the unforgettable visual splendor of a totally mirrored bathroom converts this place of physical necessity into a gleaming American temple for worship of the shiny, the surface, and the body. The brilliance of Altman's improvised, spontaneous human performances and perceptive, evocative visual imagery frequently overcomes the dreamlike meanderings of his weaker narratives.

Unlike Woody Allen and Robert Altman, Francis Ford Coppola invests much more time (and money) in his film projects, which tend to be either big commercial epics (*Finian's Rainbow*, 1968; *The Godfather* I, 1972, and II, 1974; *Apocalypse Now*, begun in 1976 and finally released in 1979) or smaller, more offbeat style pieces (*You're a Big Boy Now*, 1967; *The Rain People*, 1969; *The Conversation*, 1974). The big projects allow Coppola to exercise his craft, particularly his abilities as a script writer (he has written scripts for films he has not directed, like *Patton*); they also provide him with the money to make the films he wants to make and to run his own American Zoetrope studio in San Francisco. *The Conversation,* with its clever use of sound as both the central subject and the dominant stylistic device of the film, with its furtive and recurring *cinéma vérité* sequences shot in Union Square that are an exact visual equivalent of the sound-recording process, with its effective settings (the modern, barren, absolutely impersonal and Kafkaesque office building; the matter-of-fact detail of the commercial exposition displaying the newest products for snooping and bugging) was perhaps the first of his films to reveal social conscience and intellectual consciousness. Like Polanski's *Chinatown*, the film very effectively exploited the nation's Watergate paranoia. One might see the film's theme as the clash between a person's craft and moral conscience, the pure devotion to artisanship as opposed to the moral responsibilities of engaging in any business that affects the lives of other human beings. One might also see the film as a mirror of Coppola's own dilemma as a film director, one who is always tempted to be more the craftsman than the human being.

The second part of *The Godfather* revealed the epic conception beneath Coppola's adaptation of Mario Puzo's bestseller—not an exploitation of the audience's fascination with Mafia power, privilege, and pervasiveness, but an epic chronicle of debasement and degradation, the dissolution of the American Dream that brought immigrants to this country in the first place. The temporal leaps in Coppola's narrative—late-nineteenth-century Sicily, the arrival of immigrants at Ellis Island, life in New York's Little Italy during the 1910s and 1920s, Battista's corrupt Cuba of the 1950s, Las Vegas of the 1960s—produced a political conversation between the simple hopes of the past and the complex corruption of the present. Like the Ricos and Tony Camontes of Hollywood Past, Michael Corleone (Al Pacino) accumulates wealth and power at the expense of losing everyone close to him—associates, friends, wife, children, brother. Unlike those earlier gangsters, Michael himself does not lose his life but remains—a lonely, stripped, but powerful head of a corporation of crime. He becomes the model for the ultimate American businessman—all business and no man. (The film is not so thematically distant from *The Conversation* after all.) Coppola also pays his dues by helping younger filmmakers—for example, George Lucas made both *THX 1138* (1970) and *American Graffiti* (1973) with the financial backing and filmmaking savvy of Coppola's aid and advice.

Of the younger generation of directors to emerge in the 1970s, Martin Scorsese combines the improvisational acting spontaneity of Altman with the urban, Italian-American sensibility of Coppola. Scorsese seems to succeed most with neorealist psychological portraits of Americans deeply entangled in and by their social environments—New York's Little Italy (*Mean Streets*, 1973), a diner in the arid American Southwest (*Alice Doesn't Live Here Anymore*, 1974), a paranoid hell of New York street life (*Taxi Driver*, 1976). Scorsese is also a capable documentarist (assistant director and editor of *Woodstock*, 1970, as well as director of his own rock documentary, *The Last Waltz*, 1978), but his big Hollywood Musical (*New York, New York*, 1977), originally over four hours long, was finally released in a version half as long that felt twice as long.

Paul Mazursky also specializes in psychological-sociological case histories, usually of city dwellers, but he adds offbeat comic ironies to his very solidly and charmingly acted portraits (*Bob and Carol and Ted and Alice*, 1969; *Harry and Tonto*, 1974; *Next Stop Greenwich Village*, 1976; *An Unmarried Woman*, 1978). Hal

Ashby has also made a string of solidly scripted, subtly acted, wryly comic films (*Harold and Maude*, 1971; *Shampoo*, 1972; *The Last Detail*, 1974; *Coming Home*, 1978; *Being There*, 1979), often about oddballs in conflict with the assumed values of American life. George Lucas weds dazzling visual imagery and spectacularly clever musical tracks to produce style pieces with an authentic and exciting aroma, whether affectionately historical (and autobiographical) recreations of the rock-and-roll past (*American Graffiti*) or flamboyantly energetic creations of a never-never-world future (*Star Wars*, 1977). Part of the success of *Star Wars* must be attributed not only to its dazzling sights and sounds but also to Lucas's clever manipulation of the pure delights of narrative, of storytelling and responding to stories told, stripped of any Moral or Social Significance—an updated *Wizard of Oz*, complete with beribboned, white-dressed Dorothy, several Tin Men, a Cowardly Lion, and an Obi Wan Wizard. Terrence Malick is the potential film poet of this younger generation. Both *Badlands* and *Days of Heaven* (1978) manipulate several complexly contrapuntal lines: both use an ironically immature and imperceptive commentator, a child-woman voice-over narrator, to comment upon intensely personal human emotions of which she is completely unaware; both juxtapose the violent crime of murder (or murders) with the tender human emotion of love; both juxtapose violent narrative events with a spectacularly lush and rhythmically languid series of stunning visual images.

There are several other directors who, not so many years ago, seemed much more interesting than they do today—a further warning about the ephemerality of directorial reputations and the difficulty of assessing artists in mid-career. Peter Bogdanovich was the new American *auteur* who was most influenced by the *auteur* theory and its application to the old Hollywood movie. Like many of the

The imaginative fun of fantastic narrative (Peter Mayhew, Mark Hamill, Alec Guinness, and Harrison Ford in Star Wars); *the haunting evocations of visual poetry (the endless wheat fields of* Days of Heaven)

New Wave French directors, Bogdanovich began as a film critic, his favorite subjects being those lesser known studio directors (Raoul Walsh, Allan Dwan) whose individuality and consistency had not been previously appreciated. Bogdanovich's first film, *Targets* (1968), in many ways his cleverest, is a film buff's film, taking its style from the Roger Corman Technicolor-terror *genre* (of which Bogdanovich is also an advocate and admirer), complete with Boris Karloff as its star. For *The Last Picture Show* (1971) and *Paper Moon* (1973) Bogdanovich re-creates the dry, dusty aridity of America's rural past—of the 1950s and 1930s respectively. He also uses the textures of American films of those decades, in particular his radical decision to use black-and-white. The danger of Bogdanovich's pure universe of art is clear in *What's Up, Doc?* (1972) and *At Long Last Love* (1975), heavy-handed and empty attempts to combine 1930s musical and screwball comedy with contemporary wide-screen, color, and star values. The leaden *Daisy Miller* (1974) and *Nickelodeon* (1976) similarly failed to fulfill the promise of Bogdanovich's earliest films. Unlike the *Cahiers* critics who became filmmakers in France, Bogdanovich seems to have nothing to make movies about except movies themselves.

William Friedkin is the purest and most impersonal technician of the new directors, a man who sees each project as a specific tactical problem to be solved and who then proceeds to solve it in a dazzling way. Among the problems he has posed himself are translating talky stage plays into cinema (*The Birthday Party*, 1968; *The Boys in the Band*, 1969); capturing the texture and flavor of the old burlesque houses, customers, and performers (*The Night They Raided Minsky's*, 1968); translating the violence of urban police life into imagery (*The French Connection*, 1971); bringing the devil to the screen with convincing and terrifying effectiveness (*The Exorcist*, 1973); capturing the social and sexual atmosphere of New York's sado-masochistic homosexual underworld (*Cruising*, 1979). Friedkin's solutions are as eclectic as the problems themselves: developing the human texture of *Boys in the Band;* exercising great care with atmosphere and color textures in *Minsky's;* editing *French Connection* with overwhelming dexterity and virtuosity; employing perhaps the most disturbingly agonizing sound track ever made for *The Exorcist.* Friedkin described his own intention in all his films as that of producing powerful but crude emotional effects—terror, tension, suspense. Unfortunately, two films, *Sorcerer* (1977) and *The Brinks Job* (1979), were crudely

leaden rather than crudely powerful. Even worse for a director who wants to please his bosses and play by the Hollywood rules, both films lost money.

Both Brian De Palma and Steven Spielberg also specialize in violently terrifying, nervously suspenseful entertainments. De Palma began with offbeat projects (*Greetings*, 1968; the film version of the environmental theatre work, *Dionysus in 69*, 1970; *Hi, Mom!*, 1970) and graduated to thrillers that combined Hitchcock psychoses with Roger Corman atrocities (*Obsession*, 1976; *Carrie*, 1976; *The Fury*, 1978; *Dressed to Kill*, 1980). Spielberg's first successful feature, *The Sugarland Express* (1973), a breathlessly ironic, understated chase movie, ballooned into the terrifying *Jaws* (1975) and the mystical *Close Encounters of the Third Kind* (1977), two of the highest grossing films in Hollywood history.

Jaws's success can be traced to its clever combination of a realist social theme (the crusading defender of a money-hungry vacation town), superb acting (by Richard Dreyfuss, Robert Shaw, and Roy Scheider), suspensefully agonized editing (by Verna Fields), a stirring musical score (by John Williams, who has become Hollywood's most prolific and powerful composer), and an emphasis on the people rather than the animal monster, converting the shark into a psychological rather than a physical menace. *Close Encounters*, rather generally condemned by critics, similarly roots its extraterrestrial investigation in the psychological, human earth—the evolution of one ordinary citizen's perception (Richard Dreyfuss again) that those extraterrestrial forces really are there and are coming. As in *Jaws*, Spielberg saves the cinematic pyrotechnics (perhaps too successfully for some) for the climax, which brings the immense rocketship to earth amidst a symphony of song (John Williams again) and a blaze of special visual effects (by Douglas Trumbull, who similarly made the magic for *2001*).

Spielberg's *1941* (1979), however, saves nothing at all. This orgy of pure destruction, of breaking all the toys that Spielberg has lovingly created, has also broken the opposite record that was set by *Jaws: 1941* was the all-time moneyloser at the time—a forty-million dollar disaster.

Of the older generation of Hollywood directors, Mike Nichols (*Who's Afraid of Virginia Woolf?; The Graduate; Catch-22*, 1971; *Carnal Knowledge*, 1972; *The Day of the Dolphin*, 1973), a very successful director of Neil Simon comedies on the stage, made his most important film in 1968 when *The Graduate* seemed to summarize the attitude of the entire younger generation toward the stifling world of bourgeois adulthood. Since that success, Nichols seems to prove with every film that he is very good at observing human beings during comic scenes of off-beat dialogue and very weak at everything else to do with cinema. Arthur Penn is a director of the old school (*The Miracle Worker*, 1962) who came to the films from television dramas and has tried to convert to the new school. His dominant interest seems to be the creation of folk legends out of outlaws or off-beat social rebels (*The Left-Handed Gun*, 1958; *Bonnie and Clyde; Alice's Restaurant*, 1969; *Little Big Man*, 1971), a concern that, like *The Graduate*, made its greatest impact on younger audiences in the antimyth late sixties and early seventies. Penn's dominant weaknesses seem to be a clumsy visual sense (a real liability in the cinematically conscious seventies) and intellectual equipment that is not equal to its aspirations (although many admire Penn's continuing twists of myth and antimyth in *Night Moves*, 1975, and *The Missouri Breaks*, 1976). Sam Peckinpah, who also came to the films from television, is the third director who achieved his greatest success in the antimyth era. Peckinpah's three best films study the crumbling old men (an aged Randolph Scott and Joel McCrea) who

personify the crumbling free spirit of the Old West (*Ride the High Country*, 1962), the inevitability of violence in human experience and the necessity of a man's defining his relation to it (*Straw Dogs*, 1971), or both (*The Wild Bunch*). Peckinpah falls back on a series of predictable mannerisms that show through blatantly in his bad films, which are as bad as the others are good (*Major Dundee*, 1965; *The Ballad of Cable Hogue*, 1970; *Pat Garrett and Billy the Kid*, 1973; *Bring Me the Head of Alfredo Garcia*, 1974; *Cross of Iron*, 1977): plodding, indeed incoherent (dis)continuity; gratuitous slow-motion violence; mannered treatment of existential assertion in the face of cosmic meaninglessness. And Sidney Lumet, who began with little offbeat, New York films in the 1950s (*Twelve Angry Men, The Pawnbroker*), alternates his intimate, realist, New Yorky films (*Serpico*, 1973; *Dog Day Afternoon*, 1975; *Network*, 1976) with grander style pieces displaying different degrees and success of style (*Murder on the Orient Express*, 1974; *Equus*, 1977; *The Wiz*, 1978).

Perhaps the most important American filmmaker of the last two decades is Stanley Kubrick, who is completely detached from the newest fashions of the American cinema because he has detached himself from America. (Like Henry James, Kubrick could be claimed as either an American or English artist. Also like James, but unlike his co-expatriate directors, Richard Lester and Joseph Losey, Kubrick's work remains rooted in American values and culture.) Kubrick had been making "new" movies for years before they became the fashion (which has caught up with him). Kubrick—a perfectionist who, like Welles and Bresson, controls every detail of the film himself, from scripting to cutting—works very slowly. His reputation rests on only seven films: *Paths of Glory* (1957), *Lolita* (1962), *Dr. Strangelove: Or How I Learned to Stop Worrying and Love the Bomb* (1963), *2001: A Space Odyssey* (1968), *A*

Clockwork Orange (1972), *Barry Lyndon* (1975), and *The Shining* (1980). Kubrick's early films, *Fear and Desire* (1953), *Killer's Kiss* (1955), and *The Killing* (1956), are melodramatic potboilers, obvious apprentice work; and on *Spartacus* (1960), Kubrick was more doctor than director, having been brought in by Kirk Douglas to help save an immobile and overstuffed patient.

Kubrick films are unpopular with American critics. In none of the films is there a successful fulfilling love relationship; there is something cold, sterile, and dead about the Kubrick world. Kubrick has also been attacked for being a pure craftsman and a careful imitator of other director's cinematic styles. *Paths of Glory* undeniably recalls the elegant, polite, hypocritical world of Renoir's *Grand Illusion* combined with the Germanic camera movement of Murnau and Pabst. The back-lit, shadowy, up-angle photography of *Dr. Strangelove* irresistibly recalls *Citizen Kane*. But Kubrick's work does not borrow from the work of Renoir and Welles so much as echo it, in the same way that Lester echoes Sennett or Godard echoes the Bogart films. Like Renoir and Welles, Kubrick begins with a deep thematic conviction and a refusal to compromise in developing that conviction.

The essential Kubrick theme is man's love affair with death. Kubrick seems to be a social critic in that his films consistently rip apart the hypocrisies of polite society: the military society of World War I France, the pseudo-intellectual society of suburbia, the political society of the White House and Pentagon, the scientific society that can develop rockets that fly to the moon as well as bombs to annihilate nations, the sterilized banality of a society of the future, the elegant hypocrisies of Europe's eighteenth-century aristocracy. As with Renoir, Kubrick's social evils are human evils; people created society, not the other way around. Human society and humanness are antithetical and yet life is so constituted that human life is paradoxically impossible without human society and impossible with it. Without a society men slaughter each other individually as they do in "The Dawn of Time" sequence in *2001* after the first ape-man discovers how to use a weapon. With society men slaughter each other *en masse* under the pretext of military justice or the necessities of war and national defense.

Kubrick's great cinematic gift is not just his ability to develop this bitterly ironic theme but his gift for finding the perfect ironic tone—part horror, part humor, a mixture of burlesque and Grand Guignol—for developing it. The historical parallel for Kubrick's tone is again Renoir and his bitterly satiric human comedy of manners, *The Rules of the Game*. Few native American directors have been able to handle social satire without turning it into a pie-throwing farce. Although several of Kubrick's characters do indeed throw pies, the cold, hard intellectual edge of Kubrick's satirical knife never lets the sad farce become silly farce. Kubrick's taste is for understatement, and it is understatement that separates satire and farce, a lesson that Kramer, Preminger, Jerry Lewis, Clive Donner, Richard Lester, and Blake Edwards have never learned. An example of the Kubrick touch is in *2001* when Dr. Floyd needs to use the toilet in a space ship. Kubrick gives us a single shot of the man studying an incredibly long list of directions for relieving himself in a nongravity toilet. Another director might have zoomed in to the instructions in close-up or somehow underlined the absurdity of a man needing instructions to perform a natural function. Instead, Kubrick zooms slowly *away* from the instructions, giving us a detached ten-second medium-distance shot, no underlining, no emphasizing. We draw our own ironic conclusions.

Dr. Strangelove is the fullest expression

Dr. Strangelove. *Farcical madmen decide the fate of the world: Merkin Muffley (Peter Sellers), the Russian ambassador (Peter Bull), Dr. Strangelove (Sellers again), General Buck Turgidson (George C. Scott), and company in the "War Room"*

of the Kubrick theme and the Kubrick tone. The film begins with an audacious visual joke. Two jet planes, one refueling the other, look exactly like two human bodies copulating. Kubrick emphasizes the gag by photographing the coupled planes from various "loving" angles and underscoring the planes' passion with a lush romantic version of the syrupy popular tune, "Try a Little Tenderness." The pornographic joke is more than a joke. The whole film synthesizes copulation and murder. The American general, Buck Turgidson (George C. Scott) acts the same in the bedroom with his sweetie as he does in the war room discussing the bomb crisis. The crazed army commander, Jack Ripper, develops his whole theory about the Commies attacking his "precious bodily fluids" with fluoridated water because he cannot make it sexually with women anymore. The American pilots in the atomic bomber work feverishly to drop their bomb on the Rooskies although the plane has been critically damaged. When they finally succeed in dropping it, the plane's commander (Slim Pickens) rides the bomb down to his destruction, whooping like a

cowboy on a bronco, the bomb looking exactly like a surrogate phallus.

The ultimate symbol of man's romance with death is Dr. Strangelove himself, the "converted" Nazi scientist who still delights in the means of mass murder and who, despite his platitudinous respect for American democracy, cannot keep his arm from rising into an instinctive "Sieg heil." The film ends as it began, with a romantic orgy performed by death-dealing machines. The bombs explode in hypnotizingly beautiful rhythms and slow motion; as they explode, the saccharine female voice of Vera Lynn sings her optimistically romantic tune of the 1940s, "We'll Meet Again: don't know where, don't know when." Don't know how.

Kubrick's virtuosity as a stylist tempted him into adapting two essentially unadaptable literary style pieces— Vladimir Nabokov's *Lolita* and Anthony Burgess's *A Clockwork Orange*. Both of the novels are totally dependent on a virtuoso's manipulation of language; Kubrick turned both into films with many remarkable moments and sections, but both films ultimately fail to reproduce the complexity of the original works. And for

the same reason. Both novels use a
first-person narrator; both narrators use
language in a bizarrely abnormal and
idiosyncratic way (Humbert Humbert's
effusive, rhapsodic intellectualizations;
Alex's private argot, Nadsat); and both
novels use such unique language because
this language *is* the mind of the narrator,
the way he sees the world, and that
narrator's mind *is* the subject of the book.
That mind is not Kubrick's subject (or
interest) and in losing the central
intelligence of both novels Kubrick loses
the essence of both original works.

But he makes some interesting
substitutions. In *Lolita* there is Kubrick's
deliciously vicious satire of suburban
pseudo-intellectualism (Shelley Winters's
terrible stabs at French, terrible
pretentions to "Kulchah," and terribly
clumsy and banal sexuality) and the
quirkily hilarious impersonations of Peter
Sellers as Claire Quilty (an almost invisible
character in the novel whose best scene in
the film, a bizarre ping-pong duel with
Humbert Humbert, does not exist in the
novel). In *A Clockwork Orange* there is a
spectacularly balletic violence in the
teenage orgies of destruction and

hilarious satiric comedy in both the
callous reduction of sex to a slapstick
horse race (the brilliantly funny
accelerated-motion seduction scene) and
the tawdriness of Alex's parents' sterile
bourgeois home. Kubrick's dominant
concerns—social violence, social satire,
and social sterility—pull the original
psychological novels in interesting but
more superficial directions.

To some extent, the same is true of
2001: A Space Odyssey, which is really two
films, one mystical, one cynical, which
Kubrick attempts to hold in balance. On
the one hand, Kubrick's astronauts travel
toward the meaning of life itself, the life
force that has specifically planted metal
slabs on the earth at the "dawn of time"
and on the moon to influence human
progress. The mysterious silent slabs are
both beacons and goads. The first slab
provokes the discovery of the first tool, a
discovery that culminates in the invention
of rocket ships and computers, which are
further extensions of human beings
(Kubrick's brilliant dissolve of soaring
bone into floating space ship, as well as
the bony, arm-like extensions of the space
pods, visually establish the connection

between these tools). The second slab provokes the Jupiter Mission, which takes human beings to their next stage of evolution, "beyond the infinite." After some form of education and maturation in a strange room, the life mystery sends the reborn astronaut back to earth in a different kind of space capsule—a womblike bubble. Presumably a new species of human beings will arise from this spacechild messiah. This metaphysical theme necessarily remains fuzzy and elusive in the film; the metal slabs never receive explicit explication, and the force behind the slabs is not developed at all. In fairness to Kubrick, however, the film's narrative premise is that unevolved men are truly incapable of understanding such mysteries, and so for him to explicate them would contradict both the film's narrative logic and its mythical theme.

On the other hand, the film's social and human commentary is quite clear, a satirical study of a race that can improve its machines and weapons but not its mind and instincts. The first tool that the ape-man discovers becomes a weapon. When man travels to the moon, he takes his capitalistic establishments with him— Pan Am, Howard Johnson's, Bell Telephone. The scientist also takes his nationalistic prejudices and loyalties, not being free to discuss scientific problems with his colleagues from other countries. Human beings have "improved" their food into different weakly colored rectangles of textureless goos. (Significantly, the ape-men at the Dawn of Time and the astronaut Beyond the Infinite eat more food-looking food, the latter with silver utensils out of china dishes and crystal glasses; in the middle of the film, between these two poles, everyone eats plastic food in plastic containers.) Kubrick's consistent satiric visual device is to reveal that the essential basis of human progress has been the conversion of the entire environment into perfectly regular, extremely hard-edged rectangles like the cinema screen itself.

When human beings build super machines—the computer, HAL—they build them with human weaknesses. HAL is a superbrain; he also kills because he has been programmed with the human emotion to distrust his associates. Despite the tensions in the film's two quests, *2001* remains one of the most intelligent "big" films ever made: always intriguing, often breathtaking, careful both in attention to detail and to the thematic reason for making the film in the first place. It took Kubrick five years to make it.

The Independent American Cinema

The Independent American Cinema has been called by many names: the American Underground, the American Avant-Garde, The New American Cinema, the Experimental American Cinema among them. By whatever name, another cinema tradition has existed in the United States since the 1940s with a series of assumptions that differ markedly from those of the commercial American cinema. This cinema is highly personal and individual (often one person literally makes the entire film); it has no commercial aspirations or even value (these films rarely play in theatres where one must buy a ticket to see them); and it is necessarily revolutionary in structure, or visual technique, or intellectual attitude, or all three.

There are three conflicting critical attitudes about the Independent Cinema. For many, this cinema represents the narcissistic visual scribblings of the lunatic fringe, whose work is ultimately irrelevant to the development of serious film art (that is, commercial, feature-length "art films"). In support of this position, it is probably true that a vast majority of American filmgoers has never even heard of the most respected Independent filmmakers. A second position finds the Independent Cinema a fertile testing ground for techniques and devices that

The Life and Death of 9413—A Hollywood Extra: *the faceless extra, an unrecognizable black spot, suspended on the limitlessly unconquerable stairway to success*

are later absorbed, refined, and extended by the mainstream (that is, commercial, feature-length "art films") of filmmaking. In support of this position one can point to the influence of the French avant-garde on the later features of Clair, Epstein, Renoir, and Buñuel (all of whom came out of the avant-garde), as well as the fact that many of the stylistic devices and moral attitudes of the new commercial films (their sensuality, the use of slow motion, accelerated motion, shock cutting, split screen) were first seen in Independent films. Yet a third position finds the Independent American Cinema the only significant and serious works of film art in America today. In support of this position, they observe that these are the only films totally free of commercial pressures, totally dependent on the vision of a single artist, and totally aligned with the parallel modernist movements in painting, music, and literature. The business of these Independent films is perception: the way the devices of an art can aid, extend, and complicate a human being's ability to perceive inner and outer realities. That goal might be taken as the

ultimate intention of all the modernist arts.

Rather than engage in this controversy of values, it would be useful simply to trace the history of this movement, to define its principles and principal types, and to mention the accomplishments of its most distinctive filmmakers. The tendency of the earliest avant-garde American films (in the 1920s and 1930s) was to avoid the Hollywood assumptions by making films of pure visual form, films that were, in effect, moving paintings that had no content except the visual content of forms in motion. Although Robert Florey and Slavko Vorkapich's *Life and Death of 9413—A Hollywood Extra* (1928) seems to protest against the facelessness and inhumanity of the modern industrial system (using the movie business as its industry), it is really a series of expressionist paintings made to move, combining the visual settings of the German expressionists (especially *Metropolis*) with the camera trickery of the French surrealists. Ralph Steiner's *H₂O* (1929), which is nothing but a series of images of light reflecting on water, begins

H_2O

with beautiful and recognizable images (say, raindrops splashing in a rippling stream) and steadily becomes more abstract, so that the shots of light and shimmering water cease to look like anything except waving abstractions (a sort of moving Klee or Pollock painting). Among the few early exceptions to this purely formal rule were Joseph Berne's sensitive *Dawn to Dawn* (1934) and Watson and Webber's sexually symbolic *Lot in Sodom* (1933).

The best early films of pure form, movement, rhythm, and (later) music were not made in America, however (except for the early Disney films, which share many of the assumptions of these form-films), but in Europe. In the silent era, Hans Richter and Viking Eggeling excelled in rhythmically moving forms that also manipulated the restrictions of black-and-white. For example, Richter's *Rhythmus 21* (1921) features a variety of kinds of rhythmic movement: rectangular shapes move about the screen; they change their sizes and shapes (expanding and contracting into lines, squares, trapezoids, and so forth); and they change their shades (shifting from white on black to black on white to grey on black, et cetera). In the 1930s, Len Lye in England and Oskar Fischinger in Germany developed the film of pure form and movement to its height by using color and by accompanying the dizzily spinning and changing forms with an appropriate musical background. In effect, these films became dances—the dance of color and shape.

The first important American filmmaker who perceived that a noncommercial, personal film could do something other than make a series of shapes dance around the screen was Maya Deren, a woman who combined her interest in dance, in voodoo, and in subjective, phenomenological psychology in a series of surreal perceptual films. *Meshes of the Afternoon* (1943) and *At Land*

(1944) defy the continuity of space and time, erase the line between dream and reality, turn the entire vision of the film into the streaming consciousness of the filmmaker, who is herself the central performer in the films. She is both the mind behind the film and the body within it. *Meshes of the Afternoon* uses a series of repeating motifs—a shadow walking dreamily down a garden path, a flower, a key, a knife, a telephone receiver, attempts to mount a flight of stairs—that prefigure the use of similarly repeating motifs in *Last Year at Marienbad,* almost two decades later. Deren attacks objective reality by metamorphosizing the knife into the key, the flower into the knife, by making the act of climbing a flight of stairs seem an impossibly difficult and tortuous act (by her use of lenses, camera angles, and slow motion), by combining suggestions of chastity, sexuality, and death without the audience's ever being able to pull the complexly woven themes apart to make solid and coherent sense out of them. The motifs weave together musically rather than rationally, tangling the viewer in a systematic labyrinth of unresolvable resonances. As such, the film serves as a clear bridge between the surrealism of *Chien andalou* and the dream-realities of *Marienbad, Persona, 8 ½,* and *The Milky Way.*

Greatly influenced by Maya Deren, the American avant-garde began building itself into a movement in the mid-1950s —aided by the expanding availability of 8 and 16mm equipment—with the emergence of the work of Stan Brakhage, Robert Breer, Shirley Clarke, Bruce Conner, Kenneth Anger, Gregory Markopoulos, Jonas Mekas, and the Kuchar brothers. Since that time, the Independent Cinema has tended to gravitate toward four vague but recognizable "genres": the formal, the social-satirical, the sexual, and the self-reflexive. As with the avant-garde French films of the 1920s, these categories are neither rigid nor mutually exclusive. A film devoted primarily to the visual effects of imaginatively dancing forms can imply a social and self-reflexive dimension (most notably Robert Breer's *Jamestown Baloos*, 1957, *Horse Over Teakettle*, 1962, and *Fist Fight*, 1964). A sexual film almost invariably satirizes the assumed social values of normality (say, Kenneth Anger's *Scorpio Rising*, 1963). And many of the films devoted to a self-reflexive meditation on the processes of film and filming necessarily devote themselves to dazzling manipulations of visual forms.

The film of pure form, one of the oldest experimental styles of cinema, persisted in the American Underground, much of it influenced by the earlier work of Fischinger and Lye. The outstanding formal dances are the computer films of John Whitney, who, like Fischinger, combines his ceaselessly moving color-forms with appropriate accompanying music (*Catalog*, 1961; *Permutations*, 1968; *Matrix*, 1971). Whitney's films differ from Fischinger's in being more precise and mathematical in their symmetrical visual forms (not surprising since those forms are being spun to symmetrical perfection by a computer) yet looser and freer in their music. (Fischinger used the elegance and precision of classical music—say, Bach's Brandenburg Concerto—while Whitney uses the more improvisatory jazz or Indian raga). Other films in the formal tradition include those of Jordan Belson, who uses his colorfully amorphous evolutions of circular blobs as mandalas, objects of spiritual reflection and contemplation, and some of Robert Breer: *Blazes* (1958), which assaults and smashes the viewer with twenty-four different images per second (more an attack than a "dance"); *69* (1968), another sequence of cleverly evolving forms and colors. Scott Bartlett's *Offon* (1967) succeeds in turning more concrete referents (the eye, eyeball, human forms, a bird, a face) into purely

kaleidoscopic forms in ceaseless motion, accompanied by *musique concrète*. Indeed, this form of modernist "music"—usually a rhythmic assemblage of various abstract sounds such as buzzing, scratching, grinding, whining, and the like—is one of the primary accompaniments of the Underground films, especially the formal and self-reflexive ones.

Bruce Conner is the funniest of the social satirists; he is essentially an editor, and his best films (*A Movie*, 1958; *Cosmic Ray*, 1961; *Report*, 1964; *Marilyn X Five*, 1965) simply splice together existing stock footage to make their satirical point. Conner's point is that men are murderous, violent, destructive, and ultimately suicidal, conducting an assault against their fellow human beings and against nature itself that will eventually kill everyone. Conner supports his view in *A Movie* with pirated film footage of violence and destruction exclusively: planes dropping bombs and then diving to earth in a retributive burst of flames; Indians and cowboys on the warpath; tanks in battle; collisions of racing automobiles; the burning of a zeppelin; the collapse of a bridge; the detonation of the atomic bomb. Conner's movie implies that the business of the movies is to chronicle catastrophe; he splices these catastrophes together with such rhythmic, repetitive, and rapid insistence that the impression of cataclysm is complete. Man is his machines (and the movie is also the product of a machine), and the machines produce death and disaster.

Equally satirical is Stan VanDerBeek's *Breathdeath* (1964), which combines his interest in collage and cartooning with his own apocalyptic vision of a society warring, breathing, and boring itself to death. Tom deWitt's *Atmosfear* (1967) is a satirical view of "pollution": of the air, of the landscapes (with ugly factories and smokestacks and architecture), of the cities (with repressive and restrictive signs), and, ultimately, of the mind. In

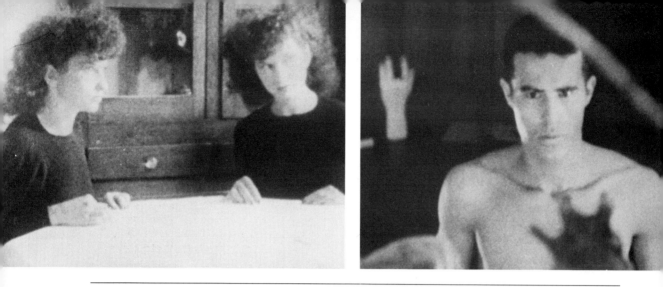

Maya Deren meets herself in Meshes of the Afternoon, *Kenneth Anger seeks to complete himself in* Fireworks

this same satirical tradition are the films of James Broughton (*Mother's Day*, 1948; *Loony Tom, the Happy Lover*, 1951; *The Pleasure Garden*, 1954) and, more recently, Robert Nelson (*Confessions of a Black Mother Succuba*, 1965; *Oh Dem Watermelons*, 1965; *The Great Blondino*, 1967; *Bleu Shut*, 1970).

Yet another kind of satirical Underground film burlesques the business of aboveground movie-making (also an implication of the Bruce Conner films), for society's art mirrors society's values. The comical, usually Camp films in this tradition are those of George and Mike Kuchar (*The Naked and the Nude*, 1957; *I Was a Teenage Rumpot*, 1960; *Pussy on a Hot Tin Roof*, 1961; and their *chef d'oeuvre*, *Sins of the Fleshapoids*, 1964) and some of the early films of Andy Warhol (*Tarzan and Jane Regained . . . Sort of*, 1963; *Harlot*, 1965). Warhol's two opposite interests— the sexual-sociological and the Hollywood Camp—continue to pull his films (including those directed by Paul Morrissey) in opposite directions. His later parody-Camp films are *Lonesome Cowboys*, 1968 (which might be subtitled, "What Cowpokes Really Did When They Slept Together Under the Stars"), *Heat*, 1973

(A "Sunset Boulevard Revisited"), and *Frankenstein*, 1974 (or "What You Always Wanted to See in a 3-D Movie But Never Did Until Now").

As can be seen from the Warhol films, the satirical Independent films are close cousins to the sexual ones, for in his studies of bizarre, "abnormal" sexuality, the Underground filmmaker often comments satirically on society's concepts of normality. The master in the field is Kenneth Anger, the son of a famous Hollywood agent of its Golden Age. The young Anger translated his Hollywood experiences into an outrageously scandalous book about Hollywood sexual practices, *Hollywood Babylon*, which includes such gossipy morsels as the "real" murder weapon in the Virginia Rappe murder case, the "real" reasons for the deaths of Thomas Ince, William Desmond Taylor, and Paul Bern (Jean Harlow's husband), and the various genital sizes of the Hollywood matinee idols. Anger's outrageousness also dominates his films, beginning with his first major work, *Fireworks* (1947), which he made when he was only seventeen. The film is clearly his own adolescent and masochistic fantasy, the symbolic dream journey of a lonely, horny boy (played by Anger himself) who is picked up, beaten, and raped to satiety by sailors, climaxing (literally and figuratively) with the image of a penis metamorphosizing into a Roman candle.

Fetishism and sado-masochism dominate Anger's most important film, *Scorpio Rising*, an examination of the practices, perversions, and paraphernalia of the motorcycle "man," his attachment to costume and symbol (chains, boots, belts, leather, levis, jacket), his idolization of Marlon Brando (in *The Wild One*) and James Dean (another motorcycle freak), his hatred of society's lifeless symbols of goodness (personified by recurring shots of a kitschy Christ in film clips from DeMille's *King of Kings*) and his adoration of cruelty (personified by film clips and stills of Hitler). The motorcycle freak's worship of the macho external is clearly a literal cover-up of his homosexual essence, and Anger uses the sound-track to comment contrapuntally (and comically) on this gap between self and projected self-image. Popular rock-and-roll tunes of the era (in this sense a precursor of *Easy Rider* and *American Graffiti*) dominate the sound track, and at one point, as the cyclist adoringly dons his macho levis, the song goes, "She Wore Blue Velvet." Anger's film is also important in having served as the basis for several of the country's crucial obscenity test cases, first seized and then judged not obscene by the State of New York in 1965.

One of the famous sexual films that has not yet been thus exonerated is Jack Smith's *Flaming Creatures* (1963), an outrageous, funny, and violent attack on sexual definitions, propriety, and normality. Smith's friend, Ken Jacobs (*The Death of P'town,* 1961; *Blonde Cobra,* 1962; *Tom, Tom, the Piper's Son,* 1971), is also in the sexual-social-satirical tradition, as is the later Provincetown-Baltimore filmmaker John Waters (*Mondo Trasho,* 1971; *Multiple Maniacs,* 1971; *Pink Flamingos,* 1972). Some of Warhol's early

work—in particular, *Blow Job* (1964), a thirty-minute reaction shot of the face of a man apparently receiving one—are not only attacks on normal and accepted sexual practices but also Warhol's attack on the normal definition of a movie.

The fourth kind of Independent film, the cinematically self-conscious, self-reflexive one, also attacks the commonly accepted assumptions of what a movie is or ought to be. As the term *self-reflexive* implies, these films are meditations on themselves—as works of film art. As meditations on themselves, these films consciously test the possible definitions of cinema and its processes, revealing the different visual and psychological purposes to which cinema can be put. The underlying commitment of these films is to the act and art of perception itself, to "seeing" (in both senses of sight and insight)—the ways that cinema records the world and the things we can discover both about the world and the cinema as a result. Whereas the purely formal films are dazzling visual shows accompanied by pleasant music (usually lasting less than ten minutes), and the social and sexual films are funny but one-dimensionally iconoclastic, these perceptual films tend to be moodier, quieter, more difficult, and much longer (often over thirty minutes).

Stan Brakhage is the most lyrical, poetic, and romantic of these self-reflexive filmmakers. Brakhage combines a Wordsworthian adoration of nature and child-like innocence with the modernist's meditation on the processes and materials of his art. For Brakhage, the love of film intensifies the love of life and nature, and his films simultaneously celebrate both the world and the remaking of the world with cinema. Brakhage treats celluloid itself as a living, organic substance—growing mold on it (which he calls "a little garden"), baking film in the oven, cutting individual frames of film into pieces and reassembling them as celluloid collages, scratching and etching patterns directly onto the celluloid, assembling an entire "film" (*Mothlight*, 1963) by scattering bits of leaves, flowers, seeds, and moths' wings on pieces of mylar splicing tape and then processing the results (a completely unphotographed film—and a link with Man Ray's scatterings of the 1920s, except that Ray never used organic materials). Brakhage combines these nonphotographic film methods with photographic and montage manipulations like the extreme use of superimposition (up to four images printed in the same frame), radical varying of the focus and exposure settings within individual shots, and elliptical yoking of images that demand mythic and allegorical interpretation.

Brakhage's early films tended to be sexual mood pieces in black and white, clearly influenced by Kenneth Anger's tortured dream-fantasies (*Reflections on Black*, 1955; *Flesh of Morning*, 1956; *Wedlock House: An Intercourse*, 1959). But he converted to color and to the autobiographical recording of his own family and life in 1959 with *Window Water Baby Moving*, in which the filmmaker lovingly observed and captured the birth of his own first child. Brakhage's most important work is *Dog Star Man* (1961–1964), a ninety-minute silent work (no sound, exclusive concentration on the dense visual imagery) in four parts plus a Prelude (a clear Wordsworthian echo). The mythic film combines adoration of nature (mountains, forests, snow, moon, mists, clouds, sun) with the tortuous journey of a man (Brakhage himself) and his dog up a mountainside to create Brakhage's cosmological view of man's relation to the universe, shaped by his ability to translate his visions into works of art.

Bruce Baillie combines Brakhage's romantic consciousness of nature with the social analyst's perception of the corruption of modern life. *Mass for the Dakota Sioux* (1964) and *Quixote* (1965) examine the ways that the pioneer spirit of America—as symbolized by its original inhabitants—has been corrupted by the building of cities, the buying and selling of food, the digging and erecting of edifices by machines. *To Parsifal* (1963) contrasts the natural imagery of woods and water with the modern machines of fishing boat and railroad train. Just as Brakhage recorded his own life in a cinema diary, *Scenes from Under Childhood* (1968), Baillie has constructed his own autobiographical cinema diary, *Quick Billy* (1967–1970).

The films of Hollis Frampton are more logical exercises than romantic quests. *Zorn's Lemma* (1970), a complex, three-part, hour-long film, is probably Frampton's most important—and most difficult—work. In its first section, about four minutes long, the viewer sees a completely black, blank screen during the reading of an alphabetical lesson out of the *Bay State Primer*, one of those early moralistic texts for teaching Puritan children their A B Cs. The second section, about 45 minutes long, is also alphabetical—a silent series of images of New York signs, each one beginning with a different letter of the alphabet. Frampton holds each sign on the screen for exactly one second (24 frames) and he reduces the English alphabet to the Roman one of 24 letters (combining i and j, u and w)—so that the number of letters and the number of frames is identical. Frampton then goes through the entire alphabet with this metronomic, one-second rhythm 108 times—but as he does so, he systematically substitutes a visual image for each letter of the alphabet (a fire replaces x, a shot of waves replaces y, a shot of woods replaces another letter, beans filling up a jar replaces another, and so forth). The second section concludes when, on its 108th cycle, all 24 letters have been converted to 24 visual images, producing, in effect, an entirely new alphabet of purely visual cinema imagery.

The first section of the film used

sounds without images—dominated by blackness; the second, images without sounds—dominated by colors; its third part combines word and image—dominated by whiteness—in a single, apparently unbroken twelve-minute shot (whereas the second part used editing extensively—2,692 images of one-second each). A man, woman, and dog cross a snowy white field (perhaps an allusion to *Dog Star Man*) as a group of female voices recite a visionary text according to a strict, one second, metronomic beat (the aural equivalent of twenty-four frames per second). The point of Frampton's mathematical and alphabetical games is to reveal how insidiously our vision and knowledge is constricted by our methods of seeing and knowing. To create a new alphabet of images is to see the world and the means of recording it differently. The film's thesis, antithesis, and synthesis also charts an optimistic history of American consciousness itself—from the narrow, moralistic beginning of merely hearing, reading, and repeating prepared texts, to the broader but still limited ability to see and use letters for ourselves, to the ultimately liberated ability to see, hear, and feel the world itself.

Perhaps the most celebrated and most controversial of the self-reflexive Independent films is Michael Snow's *Wavelength* (1967), on its surface nothing more than an agonizingly slow forty-five minute zoom shot through a single loft, beginning with a full shot of the entire room and the street outside, ending as an extreme close-up of a portion of a photograph on the far wall of the room. In the course of this inexorable zoom, human figures wander into the space of the frame—two men who move a bookcase, two women who listen to the radio, a drunk or robber who breaks into the loft and collapses on the floor, a young woman who uses the telephone—but all of these humans leave the frame (or the frame leaves them—as it does the man on the floor, when it zooms past his body), never to return again. These people, and whatever pattern of narrative causality has brought them to this particular space at this particular time, are never developed, investigated, or explicated. The usual center of human interest for the usual movie is not at all central to this film.

The central concern of *Wavelength* is the space itself—indeed, space itself. As in Frampton's *Lemma*, the structural logic of the film is rigidly formal and precisely deductive. It begins with a three-dimensional space that might be defined as 12 feet high, 22 feet wide (the usual width of a New York brownstone), and, say, 100 feet deep (the length of the room plus the signs visible outside its windows across the street). The film ends with a two-dimensional space less than 8 inches high and less than 10 inches wide (an 8 by 10 photograph). It also begins as a moving picture in color and ends, in effect, as a still photograph in black and white (and out of focus at that, so that no shape, texture, or depth is discernible at all). The film's structural logic is this implacable narrowing of spatial depth, which is the film's subject as well.

As the lens slides through this space, it attempts to divert us (in both senses of the term) with the differing qualities and characteristics of the space itself. Snow uses different lighting exposures (some of which emphasize the signs outdoors, others of which emphasize the indoors by washing out the outdoors with bright, overexposed whiteness), different color filters, different intensities of printing grain, different times of the night and day, producing different qualities and conditions of light; and, of course, the shifting focal lengths of the zoom lens produce different perceptions of the room and the shapes and textures of its objects. The usual movie chooses to shoot in a particular space, to frame a particular area, because some important human action, necessary for understanding the narrative, takes place in that space. In the usual movie, space is merely the background, the necessary container, for significant human action. But Snow's *Wavelength* takes its chosen space as its most important characteristic (and the most important characteristic of any framed image); what else does a frame frame other than space itself? So for Snow, human actions are only significant when and if they happen to intersect with that framed space—and they are no more important than anything else in that space. When the people leave the frame (or the frame leaves the people), they no longer exist within the space that is the frame's chief concern.

A film like *Wavelength* once again raises the question about the value and significance of the Independent American Cinema. On the one hand, the critic can respond to *Wavelength* with a "So what?" Space that is empty of human significance is truly empty (and very boring). Cinema space is only meaningful if it has been invested with meaning. On the other hand, the critic can respond to *Wavelength* as one of the most perfect expressions of the cinema condition (that movies necessarily frame spaces) as well as one of the most perfect means of educating us about the human condition—that cinema can provoke viewers to perceive the mystery, the expressiveness, the variety, and the "space"ness of the spaces around them, not only in the frame but in the world.

16 A Sixth American Era?

The central historical question about the American cinema of the present and near future is whether America's film art and industry entered a new period of development in the late 1970s. Three criteria have historically marked the transition from one American film era to another. The first is the structure of the film business—the system of marketing and selling films to the public. The Nickelodeon Era evolved out of the period when films were viewed as peep shows in penny arcades or projected as single items on vaudeville bills, by radically changing the marketing procedures—filmmakers no longer sold film strips but rented them. The shifts to feature films, to talking films, to the nonvertically integrated studio films of the Transitional Era, and to the "little films" of the New Hollywood were similarly produced and accompanied by changes in distributing and exhibiting the film product.

The second criterion for defining an historical film period is a major advance or shift in film technology. The change from the Nickelodeon Era to the Feature Film Era in 1915 was partially the result of significant technological progress; films became not only longer but also more fluent, coherent, and complex to sustain their greater narrative length. The introduction of synchronized sound and the wide screen can similarly be seen to have produced or accompanied a new historical period.

The third criterion for defining a period is a shift in film content that mirrors a shift in American cultural values as a whole. Each of the previous eras reflected a dominant cultural value and attitude—the working-class antipretentiousness of the Nickelodeon Era, the middle-class materialism of the Silent Feature Era, the positivism and populism of the post-Depression Studio Era, the retreat from political problems of the post-war Transitional Era, the rebellious, anti-Establishment pessimism of the New Hollywood. The late 1970s have been marked by changes in all three criteria for defining an historical period of American film.

The film business has been converted to what might be termed the "blockbuster mentality." Rather than finance and distribute many modest films that make modest profits, the major American film companies now prefer to finance and distribute a few immense films that will achieve immense box-office grosses. *The Godfather I, American Graffiti, Jaws, Star Wars, The Deep, Grease, Close Encounters of the Third Kind,* and *Superman,* all of them films of the 1970s, are among the top-grossing films of all time. Although *The Birth of a Nation* and *Gone with the Wind* may still be considered more commercially successful than many of the last decade's blockbusters—they made more profit in relation to their cost—the current film industry attitude seems to be to spend a lot of money to make a lot of money. Whereas the most representative films of the New Hollywood, the best American films of the mid-1960s to mid-1970s, were modest "little films" (*Bonnie and Clyde, The Wild Bunch, Easy Rider, Five Easy Pieces, Alice's Restaurant, McCabe and Mrs. Miller, Chinatown, The Conversation, Nashville, One Flew Over the Cuckoo's Nest, Taxi Driver*), the most representative films of the late 1970s seemed to be huge ones. (The obvious exceptions to the previous "little film" rule were the Kubrick projects and *The Godfather*—all of which now appear to have been previews of coming historical attractions.)

What are the reasons for this shift to the blockbuster strategy? One opinion is that American films need European distribution to insure their financial health, but European quotas have increasingly restricted the number of American films that can be shown abroad and the amount of profit they can make there. If only forty American films can be shown in Europe, American film companies need finance only about forty films. A second possible cause is the film industry's discovery of a general axiom of contemporary American corporate business (most effectively understood by the oil industry): the business that can make more profit with less product has achieved the double advantages of doing less and making more. Of course, the Hollywood film companies are now merely corporate branches of the huge conglomerates, which reward their executives for precisely this kind of productive unproductivity. It is also extremely economical to make the same film twice—for example, *The Deep, Jaws II, The Omen II, The French Connection II, Rocky II, The Empire Strikes Back, Superman II,* and, presumably, *Close Encounters of the Fourth, Fifth, and Sixth Kinds*—or to release the same film twice—the frequent rereleases of the hits of two or three years ago. The film industry of the Studio Era never rereleased an old film because it would compete with its new product; today's film industry must rerelease its older films to compensate for a deliberate shortage of new product.

A third possible cause is that many of the smaller, more sociological film projects are now made specifically for television rather than for theatres. The increasing maturity of some made-for-TV movies (*The Autobiography of Miss Jane Pitman* or *The Queen of the Stardust Ballroom*) and the narrative scope and flexibility of the mini-series (*Roots, Holocaust, Rich Man, Poor Man*) have perhaps provided an outlet for the kinds of films that would previously have attracted patrons to theatres.

Many intellectual film critics, upset by the ballooning budgets of the blockbusters, fear that films no longer need to be well made, merely well sold. Media hype seems to have replaced art—or even craft. In truth, several of those films on the all-time highest grossing list seem to have been more blessed in their advertising campaigns than in their making. In response to the critical fear that movies are deader than ever as a meaningful artistic and cultural experience (how often has this cry been repeated in the history of American film during transitions from one film period to the next?), several facts should be recalled. First, there are obvious exceptions to the blockbuster rule. "Little films" continue to be made and continue to do well enough to continue to be made (the Woody Allen films, Altman's, Mazursky's, Ashby's, *Rocky, Julia, Norma Rae, Heaven Can Wait, The China Syndrome, Kramer vs. Kramer,* and so on and on and on).

Second, a big, money-making film is not necessarily uninteresting, unimportant, or unintelligent simply because it is big and makes money. Critics suspect that the best, most artistic films (whatever definition of art the critic has adopted) are inevitably condemned to lose money (the mythic careers of Erich von Stroheim and Orson Welles provoke this suspicion, but in fact *Citizen Kane, Blind Husbands, Foolish Wives,* and *The Merry Widow* all made money). Throughout their history Hollywood films have violated the Romantic and elitist cliché of the inherent contradiction of Art and Commerce. The films of Griffith, Ford, Chaplin, Hawks, Hitchcock, Lubitsch, and so forth prove that this suspicion ain't necessarily so. *The Godfathers* and *Star Wars* may still look like very good films several decades from now when their record grosses will have been forgotten, just as *2001* still looks like a very good film more than a decade after it was a blockbuster hit. Successful film artists have always known how to make artistic virtues of commercial necessities.

A third historical fact is that film fashions roll in waves and spin in cycles. A cycle of "little films" will certainly follow this cycle of blockbusters and blockbuster sequels when the blockbusters cease to make money. The blockbuster period of the mid-1950s to mid-1960s—which began with, say, DeMille's *The Greatest Show on Earth* in 1952—ended with the financial fiasco of *Cleopatra* in 1963, when these big pictures failed to attract big enough audiences to underwrite their big budgets. There is no reason to suppose that this new generation of blockbuster films will not

one day also fall from public favor—particularly when the public tires of the hype and feels cheated by a film that offers nothing but the hype.

The major technological advance of the late 1970s is so subtle that it has passed into common use with much less critical ado than attended the coming of synchronized sound or CinemaScope of the past: the increasing use of soundtracks recorded on magnetic tape, using the Dolby noise-reduction process, rather than optically recorded on celluloid. For fifty years almost all sound tracks have been recorded and reproduced photographically (the recording and reading of light beams alongside the motion picture frames); the new Dolby tracks bond a stripe of magnetic tape to the celluloid. This magnetic recording produces the same degree of aural depth and fidelity (previously available only to the Cinerama process) to which Americans have grown accustomed—and of which they have grown fond—in their home music systems and in discotheques. As in the late 1920s, Americans' listening habits have affected their movie viewing habits. Just as radio made Americans aware that something was missing at the movies, high fidelity stereophonic music systems have produced a similar awareness in the 1970s.

The new magnetic tracks permit film sounds of far greater range, subtlety, depth, power, resonance, and flexibility than was ever possible on optical tracks. Not only do the big blockbusters use the Dolby system as a matter of course (*Star Wars, Superman, Close Encounters,* and such films would be unthinkable and puny without the immense power of their sound tracks) but even poetic or psychological "little films," like *Days of Heaven* and *Invasion of the Body Snatchers,* use the Dolby system as well. True, many of the blockbusters merely exploit the system for its power (especially its loudness—as in the crunchingly,

thumpingly loud LOUD soundtrack of *Superman*). But when has a new cinema invention not merely been exploited for its novelty in its early years, throughout cinema history? The advantage of the Dolby innovation is the same as that of every other technological advance throughout cinema history—it provides a far greater *range* of options and choices for the filmmaker (as proved by the evocative and imaginative sound track of *Days of Heaven*). These new Dolby sound tracks are also belated reminders of

sound's importance to the experience of a film, although most critics and theorists still deafly see film as exclusively or essentially a visual art.

A third indication of historical evolution is that a new cultural attitude seems to have produced and been reflected by a shift in film content. The rebels, misfits, loners, and oddballs that dominated American film from *Bonnie and Clyde* through *Taxi Driver* have been replaced by more ordinary citizens who seek to find a meaningful place for themselves

Views of Vietnam. In The Deer Hunter, *a contrast between here and there (John Cazale, Chuck Aspegren, Robert deNiro, John Savage, Rutanya Alda, Christopher Walken, and Meryl Streep). In* Apocalypse Now, *the grotesque juxtaposition of surfboards, Playboy bunnies, and napalm*

within conventional American society. With the final singing of "God Bless America," the working-class, small-town protagonists of Michael Cimino's *The Deer Hunter* reintegrate themselves, both as individual people and as a whole group, into the fabric of American moral and social life, despite the agony their country forced them to endure. The working-class protagonist of *Saturday Night Fever* also seeks some meaningful place in American social life, other than the escapist dream-dance world of the disco and the

narrow, moral-political provinciality of Bay Ridge. The Dustin Hoffman of *Kramer vs. Kramer* does not want to drop out, as he did in *The Graduate* or *Midnight Cowboy*; he simply wants to live lovingly with his son. The director of *All That Jazz* does not want to make social statements (as he did with *Cabaret* and *Lenny*); he simply wants to create dazzling dances.

And many of these films imply a very clear if cautious optimism about these quests—as opposed to the implacable and irreversible pessimism of the previous era's films. The protagonists of *The Deer Hunter* can share their mutual sympathy (the simultaneously ironic yet touching communal singing of that patriotic song), patch together the shreds of their former life, sadder if not completely wiser. *Saturday Night Fever* implies that Tony Manero (John Travolta) can find a fulfilling future if he expands his narrow, sexist horizons by moving to Manhattan. (This optimistic implication is as facile as anything in the film; how can this clearly defined person ever hope to retain or regain his one ultimate "high"—dancing at the disco?) Interestingly, the film's use of the Big City as a place of spiritual salvation (equally true of *Kramer* and *Jazz*) is a dramatic reversal of a conventional motif of American films as distant as *Mr. Deeds Goes to Town* and *Taxi Driver*—where the Big City is inevitably a moral swamp and emotional prison. Warren Beatty's and Buck Henry's *Heaven Can Wait* is as optimistic a piece of wish-fulfillment as America has produced since Frank Capra's *It's a Wonderful Life* of 1946—a film that simultaneously assures its audience of its immortality, of the computerized order and efficiency of the cosmos, and of the possibility for a human being to achieve athletic prowess, immense wealth, and romantic consummation without forfeiting his humanity, wisdom, kindness, or "soul." As opposed to the tarnished American Dream in *Bonnie and Clyde, Easy Rider,* or *Chinatown, Heaven Can Wait* is a fantasy of the absolute attainment of that Dream— wealth, health, love, and eternal life.

Those recent films that do not optimistically attempt to integrate or reintegrate their protagonists with American social life escape from the social, political, and moral realities of that life altogether. Many American films of the 1970s transported their audiences into nostalgic dreams of the past (*The Way We Were, Summer of 42, Class of 44, Grease, Farewell, My Lovely, Movie Movie,* and all the film parodies of Hollywood Past), into

an amoral, apolitical world of a fantasy present or future (*Star Wars, Superman, Alien*), or into a purely sensual world of chills, thrills, and terror (*The Exorcist, Jaws, Carrie, Dressed to Kill, The Fury*). Film historians of a later generation may look back on these apparently escapist films of this most recent American era (as historians and cultural analysts have done with the apparently escapist and optimistic American films of the 1930s) to reveal that these films successfully raised the most important questions confronting both American personal and public life during the period, but in a more covert, more mythological, and more subconscious way than did the explicit moral and political investigations of what is now the old New Hollywood.

The best American films of the present (and of the future), like those of the past, can and will succeed in transcending their immediate temporal, commercial, technological, and cultural limitations— shaped by the controlling talent and will of a single creator, a perceptive mind, who is able to wed contemporary fashion with the thematic complexity and stylistic fluency that is common to all great art works in any medium at any time. This short history has been a study of these great film minds, those who saw something very clearly and very deeply about human experience and who possessed the art and craft to translate what they saw into something that we could see. This has not been a history of film people—stars, producers, even directors—nor a history of film events— premieres, the founding of studios, the funerals of stars—nor even a history of great individual films. There have been no apocryphal stories of what Dorothy Parker said to Samuel Goldwyn or what Joan Crawford drank for breakfast. The book has studied the themes, the imaginations, the techniques, the visual qualities of those artists who might have become novelists or painters or poets but became filmmakers instead.

In these eighty-five years, most film directors have been typesetters, not poets. To find the artistic individuality, the creative intelligence, the "mind" at the center of most films is an impossible and artificial exercise. For this reason, this short history has also tried to call attention to those facts of film life that turn directors into typesetters. Who is the ultimate creator of a film? the director? the producer? the writer? the photographer? the editor? How independent is the film's creator (whether director or producer or writer) from the demands of the audience on one hand and the demands of the creditors on the other? The shooting of a film is part plan, part accident, and part chaos. Thousands of people may contribute to the final product. The relationship of director to film is vastly different from the relationship of poet to sonnet. The facts of film production would seem to nullify the possibility that any film could achieve a unique and personal spirit and vision. And yet whole canons of films (not just individual accidents) by Griffith, Chaplin, Hawks, Renoir, Bergman, Antonioni, Truffaut and so forth reveal that a single artist's mind can be as clear, as consistent, and as compelling in the film form as in a canon of lyric poems. If one is to discuss the film as a work of art rather than as entertainment, as business,

as societal mirror, or as manufacturer of the twentieth century's new royalty, one must discuss the minds who knew how to create great films and how those minds worked.

This particular kind of film history is itself indicative of present critical and audience opinion about the movies. Never before have audiences been so conscious of the film as art; never have directors been so self-conscious of their work as art. Film study is now a liberal art in American universities. The new film journals (another clear sign of current cinema intellectualism) and film magazines feature interviews with directors as well as with stars. The directors have become stars. This new cinematic self-consciousness will have an impact on the films of the future as more and more people study both the aesthetics of film art and the techniques of film production. Since this self-conscious debt to film tradition has produced exciting films in the past—Vigo's, Clair's, Truffaut's, Godard's, Fassbinder's—it should continue to produce exciting films in the future. The best films of the past have consistently blended an engaging narrative, insightful human relationships, a sincere and convincing intellectual vision, and a functional cinematic style. I expect that the best films of the future will do the same.

Appendix: for Further Reading and Viewing

The books and films below, correlated with each chapter of the text, are intended to give the reader an idea of the extent of available material for further research. Neither the bibliography nor the list of films is exhaustive. In selecting films for the directors, only representative samples of their important work have been listed. Further, only those films that circulate in 16mm prints have been listed. Distributors other than those listed may handle a particular film; the most reliable guide to film distribution is the current catalogue published by each distributor. A list of the major distributors in 16mm with their addresses and telephone numbers follows at the end of the appendix.

1. General Histories of Film and Reference Works

Bawden, Liz-Anne, ed. *Oxford Companion to Film.* New York: Oxford University Press, 1976.

Brownlow, Kevin. *The Parade's Gone By.* New York: Alfred Knopf, 1968.

Crowther, Bosley. *The Lion's Share.* New York: Dutton, 1967.

———. *The Great Films: Fifty Golden Years of Motion Pictures.* New York: G. P. Putnam's Sons, 1967.

Everson, William K. *The American Movie.* New York: Atheneum, 1963.

———. *American Silent Film.* New York: Oxford University Press, 1978.

Griffith, Richard, and Mayer, Arthur. *The Movies.* New York: Simon and Schuster, 1970.

Halliwell, Leslie. *The Filmgoer's Companion.* Fourth Edition. New York: Hill and Wang, 1974.

Haskell, Molly. *From Reverence to Rape: The Treatment of Women in the Movies.* New York: Holt, Rinehart, 1974.

Jacobs, Lewis. *The Rise of the American Film.* New York: Harcourt, Brace, 1939.

Jowett, Garth. *Film: The Democratic Art.* Boston: Little, Brown, 1976.

Knight, Arthur. *The Liveliest Art.* New York: New American Library, 1959.

Macgowan, Kenneth. *Behind the Screen.* New York: Delacorte, 1965.

Pratt, George C. *Spellbound in Darkness.* Rochester: New York Graphic Society, 1966.

Ramsaye, Terry. *A Million and One Nights.* New York: Simon & Schuster, 1964.

Rotha, Paul, and Griffith, Richard. *Film Till Now.* New York: Twayne, 1960.

Sadoul, Georges. *Histoire Générale du Cinéma.* 5 vols. Paris: Éditions Denoël, 1946–54

———. *Dictionnaire des cineastes.* Paris: Seuil, 1977.

———. *Dictionnaire des films.* Paris: Seuil, 1978.

Sarris, Andrew. *The American Cinema: Directors and Directions 1929–1968.* New York: Dutton, 1968.

Sklar, Robert. *Movie-Made America.* New York: Random House, 1975.

Wagenknecht, Edward. *Movies in the Age of Innocence.* Norman: Oklahoma University Press, 1962.

2. Birth (1825–1900)

BOOKS

Dickinson, Thorold. *A Discovery of Cinema.* New York: Oxford University Press, 1971.

Dickson, W. K. L. and Antonia. *A History of the Kinetograph, Kinetoscope, and Kinetophonograph.* New York: Arno Press, 1970.

Marek, K. W. *Archaeology of the Cinema.* New York: Harcourt, Brace, 1965.

Ramsaye, Terry. *A Million and One Nights.* New York: Simon and Schuster, 1964. pp. xxxvii–175.

FILMS

LOUIS AND AUGUSTE LUMIÈRE
The First Programs (1895–1900)—EMG, KIT, MMA
Cinématographe in 1895 (1895–1898)—EMG, MMA

THOMAS EDISON
Films of the 1890s (1895–1899)—MMA
An Edison Album (1896–1907)—KIT
Edison Collection 1, 2 (1895–1903)—EMG

3. Film Narrative (1900–1912)

BOOKS

Arvidson, Linda. *When the Movies Were Young.* Benjamin Blom, 1968.

Balshofer, Fred J., and Miller, Arthur C. *One Reel a Week.* Berkeley and Los Angeles: University of California Press, 1968.

Fell, John. *Film and the Narrative Tradition.* Norman: University of Oklahoma Press, 1974.

Frazer, John. *Artificially Arranged Scenes: The Films of Georges Méliès.* Boston: G. K. Hall, 1980.

Jacobs, Lewis. *The Rise of the American Film.* New York: Harcourt, Brace, 1939, pp. 3–67.

Low, Rachel, and Manvell, Roger. *History of the British Film.* 3 vols. (1896-1918). London: Allen & Unwin, 1948-50.

Ramsaye, Terry. *A Million and One Nights.* New York: Simon & Schuster, 1964, pp. 176-602.

Smith, Albert E., and Koury, P. A. *Two Reels and a Crank.* New York: Doubleday, 1952.

Wagenknecht, Edward. *Movies in the Age of Innocence.* Norman: Oklahoma University Press, 1962, pp. 30-77.

FILMS

GEORGES MÉLIÈS
Georges Méliès Program (1899–1912)—MMA. *The Conjuror, A Trip to the Moon, The Palace of the Arabian Nights, The Doctor's Secret,* and *Conquest of the Pole*
A Trip to the Moon (1902)—EMG, KIT
Various Méliès Programs (1898–1907)—EMG, KIT
Conquest of the Pole (1912)—EMG, KIT

EDWIN S. PORTER
Edwin S. Porter: Five Films (1903–1907)—MMA.
Life of an American Fireman, Uncle Tom's Cabin, The Great Train Robbery, Dream of a Rarebit Fiend, Rescued from an Eagle's Nest
The Life of an American Fireman (1903)—EMG, KIT
The Great Train Robbery (1903)—EMG, KIT
The Dream of a Rarebit Fiend (1906)—EMG, KIT
Rescued from an Eagle's Nest (1907)—EMG, KIT

OTHER FILMS OF THE ERA
Pathé Frères Films (c. 1900)—KIT
Ferdinand Zecca Program (1906–1907)—MMA
Films of Cohl, Feuillade, and Durand (1907–1912)—MMA.
Three Max Linder films (1905–1912)—MMA
A selection of Linder films (1905–1912)—EMG, KIT
The Beginnings of the British film (1901–1911)—MMA.
The Film d'Art (1908–1912)—MMA. *The Assassination of the Duke of Guise* and *Queen Elizabeth*
Fantomas (1913)—MMA
A selection of early British and French films (1900–1913)—EMG

4. Griffith (1908–1931)

BOOKS

Barry, Iris and Bowser, Eileen. *D. W. Griffith: American Film Master.* New York: Museum of Modern Art, 1965.

Gish, Lillian. *The Movies, Mr. Griffith, and Me.* Englewood Cliffs, N. J.: Prentice-Hall, 1969.

Henderson, Robert M. *D. W. Griffith: The Years at Biograph.* New York: Farrar, Straus, 1970.

———. *D. W. Griffith: His Life and Work.* New York: Oxford University Press, 1972.

Huff, Theodore. *Intolerance: Shot-by-Shot Analysis.* New York: Museum of Modern Art, 1966.

Jacobs, Lewis. *The Rise of the American Film.* New York: Harcourt, Brace, 1939, pp. 95–119, 171–201, 384–94.

O'Dell, Paul. With Anthony Slide. *D. W. Griffith and the Rise of Hollywood.* New York: Barnes, 1971.

Wagenknecht, Edward. *The Movies in the Age of Innocence.* Norman: Oklahoma University Press, 1962, pp. 78–137.

FILMS

ONE-REELERS
1776 or *The Hessian Renegades* (1909)—MMA
Griffith Biograph Program (1909–1912)—MMA. *The Lonely Villa, A Corner in Wheat, The Lonedale Operator, The Musketeers of Pig Alley, The New York Hat*
Excellent selection of one-reelers (1908-1912)—EMG, KIT

FOUR-REELERS

The Avenging Conscience (1914)—EMG, KIT, MMA
Home Sweet Home (1914)—MMA
Judith of Bethulia (1914)—EMG, KIT, MED, MMA

FEATURES

The Birth of a Nation (1915)—EMG, KIT, MMA
Intolerance (1916)—EMG, MED, MMA
Hearts of the World (1918)—EMG, KIT
Broken Blossoms (1919)—EMG, KIT, MED, MMA
Way Down East (1920)—EMG, KIT, MED, MMA
Orphans of the Storm (1922)—AUD, MMA
America (1924)—AUD, MMA
Abraham Lincoln (1930)—EMG, KIT, MED
The Struggle (1931)—AUD
(Most of the Griffith program pictures—1916-1927—can be rented from AUD, EMG, KIT, or MMA, e.g., *True Heart Susie, The Idol Dancer, Dream Street, Sorrows of Satan.*)

5. Mack Sennett and Charles Chaplin (1911-1918)

BOOKS

Agee, James. "Comedy's Greatest Era." In *Agee on Film: Reviews and Comments,* pp. 2-19. Boston: Beacon Press, 1964.

Chaplin, Charlie. *My Autobiography.* New York: Simon & Schuster, 1964.

Huff, Theodore. *Charlie Chaplin.* New York: Henry Schuman, 1951.

Lahue, Kalton C., and Brewer, Terry. *Kops and Custard.* Norman: Oklahoma University Press, 1968.

Manvell, Roger. *Chaplin.* Boston: Little, Brown, 1974.

Mast, Gerald. *The Comic Mind: Comedy and the Movies.* 2nd edition. Chicago: University of Chicago Press, 1979, pp. 43–124.

McCabe, John. *Charlie Chaplin.* Garden City, N.Y.: Doubleday, 1978.

Payne, Robert. *The Great God Pan.* New York: Hermitage House, 1952.

Sennett, Mack. *King of Comedy.* New York: Doubleday, 1954.

Tyler, Parker. *Chaplin: Last of the Clowns.* New York: Horizon, 1972.

FILMS

MACK SENNETT (Directed or Supervised)
Mack Sennett Program (1911–1920)—MMA. *Comrades, Mabel's Dramatic Career, The Surf Girl, His Bread and Butter, The Clever Dummy, Astray from the Steerage*
Barney Oldfield's Race for a Life (1913)—EMG, KIT
Teddy at the Throttle (1917)—EMG, KIT, MMA
His Bitter Pill (1916)—MMA
Mickey (1916-1918)—EMG, MMA
Exellent Sennett selection (1912–1924)—EMG, KIT

CHARLES CHAPLIN

Chaplin's Keystone Films (1914)—MMA. *Making a Living, The Knockout, The Masquerader, The Rounders, Getting Acquainted*
Complete selection of Chaplin's one- and two-reel Keystone films—EMG, KIT
Tillie's Punctured Romance (1914)—EMG, KIT
Chaplin's Essanay Films (1915–1916)—MMA. *The Tramp, A Woman, The Bank, Police*
Burlesque on Carmen (1916)—EMG, MED
Complete selection of Essanay comedies (1915–1916)—EMG, KIT
The Mutual two-reelers (1916-1917)—AUD, EMG, KIT. *The Floorwalker, The Fireman, The Vagabond, One A.M., The Count, The Pawnshop, Behind the Screen, The Rink, Easy Street, The Cure, The Immigrant, The Adventurer*
A Dog's Life (1918)—PAR
Shoulder Arms (1918)—PAR
The Idle Class (1921)—PAR
The Kid (1921)—PAR
The Pilgrim (1923)—PAR
A Woman of Paris (1924)—PAR
The Gold Rush (1925)—AUD, EMG, JAN, KIT, MED
The Circus (1928)—PAR
City Lights (1931)—PAR
Modern Times (1936)—PAR
The Great Dictator (1940)—PAR
Monsieur Verdoux (1947)—PAR
Limelight (1952)—PAR
A King in New York (1957)—PAR
A Countess from Hong Kong (1967)—UNI

6. The American Film (1914–1927)

BOOKS

Blesh, Rudi. *Keaton.* New York: Macmillan, 1966.

Curtis, Thomas Quinn. *Von Stroheim.* New York: Farrar, Straus, 1971.

DeMille, Cecil B. *Autobiography.* Englewood Cliffs, N.J.: Prentice-Hall, 1959.

Everson, William K. *The Films of Laurel and Hardy.* New York: Citadel, 1967.

Jacobs, Lewis. *The Rise of the American Film.* New York: Harcourt, Brace, 1939, pp. 81–395.

Keaton, Buster. With Charles Samuels. *My Wonderful World of Slapstick.* New York: Doubleday, 1960.

Kerr, Walter. *The Silent Clowns.* New York: Knopf, 1975.

Lloyd, Harold. *An American Comedy.* New York: Dover, 1971.

Mast, Gerald. *The Comic Mind: Comedy and the Movies.* 2nd edition. Chicago: University of Chicago Press, 1979, pp. 125–196.

Moews, Daniel. *Keaton: The Silent Films Close Up.* Berkeley and Los Angeles: University of California Press, 1977.

O'Leary, Liam. *The Silent Cinema.* New York and London: Dutton/Vista, 1965.

Ramsaye, Terry. *A Million and One Nights.* New York: Simon & Schuster, 1964, pp. 603–834.

Robinson, David. *Buster Keaton.* Bloomington and London: Indiana University Press, 1969.

Rubinstein, E. *Filmguide to The General.* Bloomington and London: Indiana University Press, 1972.

Wagenknecht, Edward. *Movies in the Age of Innocence.* Norman, Okla.: Oklahoma University Press, 1962, pp. 138-256.

Weinberg, Herman G. *The Complete "Greed" of Erich von Stroheim.* New York: Dutton, 1973.

———. *The Complete "Wedding March" of Erich von Stroheim.* Boston: Little, Brown, 1974.

FILMS

ITALIAN SPECTACLE PICTURES
Quo Vadis? (1912)—MMA
Cabiria (1913)—MMA
Anthony and Cleopatra (1914)—EMG, MED
Spartacus (1914)—EMG, MED

CECIL B. DeMILLE
Male and Female (1919)—MMA
King of Kings (1927)—FI, TWY
Sign of the Cross (1932)—UNI
Cleopatra (1934)—UNI
Union Pacific (1939)—UNI
The Greatest Show on Earth (1952)—FI
The Ten Commandments (1956)—FI

DOUGLAS FAIRBANKS
His Picture in the Papers (1916)—EMG, MED
Two Early Films of Douglas Fairbanks (1916–1917)—MMA. *The Mystery of the Leaping Fish* and *Wild and Woolly*
Flirting with Fate (1916)—EMG, MED
Reaching for the Moon (1917)—MMA
The Mark of Zorro (1920)—EMG, MED, MMA
The Mollycoddle (1920)—MMA
The Three Musketeers (1921)—MMA
Robin Hood (1922)—MMA
The Thief of Bagdad (1924)—AUD, KIT, MED, MMA
The Taming of the Shrew (1929)—MMA
Mr. Robinson Crusoe (1932)—EMG, MMA

ROBERT FLAHERTY (silent)
Nanook of the North (1922)—EMG, FI, KIT, MMA
Moana (1926)—MMA

THOMAS INCE (directed or supervised)
The Last of the Line (1914)—MMA
The Taking of Luke McVane (1915)—MMA. With W. S. Hart
Keno Bates, Liar (1915)—MMA. With W. S. Hart
The Coward (1915)—MMA. With Charles Ray
The Deserter (1916)—MMA. With Charles Ray
Civilization (1916)—MMA

BUSTER KEATON
Shorts (1920-1923)—All AUD. *One Week, Convict 13, The Scarecrow, Neighbors, The Haunted House, The Playhouse, The Paleface, Cops, My Wife's Relations, The Blacksmith, The Frozen North, The Electric House, Daydreams, The Balloonatic*
Our Hospitality (1923)—AUD
Sherlock Jr. (1924)—AUD
The Navigator (1924)—AUD
Seven Chances (1925)—AUD
Go West (1925)—AUD
The General (1926)—AUD, EMG, KIT
College (1927)—AUD, EMG, KIT
Steamboat Bill Jr. (1927)—AUD, EMG, KIT
The Cameraman (1928)—FI

HARRY LANGDON
Tramp, Tramp, Tramp (1926)—AUD
The Strong Man (1926)—AUD
Long Pants (1927)—AUD
A selection of Langdon shorts (1924-1926)—AUD, EMG, KIT

LAUREL AND HARDY
Shorts (1927-1932)—AUD, EMG, KIT. *The Finishing Touch, Two Tars, You're Darn Tootin, Leave 'Em Laughing, Bacon Grabbers, Big Business, Double Whoopee, Men O'War, Perfect Day, Below Zero, Brats, The Music Box*
Two Films of Laurel and Hardy (1928–1929)—MMA. *Two Tars, Big Business*
Sons of the Desert (1934)—SWA
Blockheads (1938)—EMG, MED, SWA
A Chump at Oxford (1940)—EMG, MED, SWA

HAROLD LLOYD
High and Dizzy (1921)—MMA
Excellent Selection of Lloyd shorts (1918–1922)—EMG, KIT
Grandma's Boy (1922)—PAR, TIM
Safety Last (1923)—PAR, TIM
The Freshman (1924)—PAR, TIM
For Heaven's Sake (1925)—PAR, TIM
The Kid Brother (1928)—PAR, TIM

ERICH VON STROHEIM
Blind Husbands (1919)—EMG, KIT, MMA, UNI
Foolish Wives (1922)—EMG, KIT, MMA, UNI
Greed (1924)—FI
The Merry Widow (1925)—FI

IMPORTANT FILMS OF THE ERA
Three Vitagraph Comedies (1912–1917)—MMA. *Stenographer Wanted, Goodness Gracious, The Professional Patient*
Two Broncho Billy Westerns (1913–1918)—MMA
A Fool There Was (1915)—EMG, MMA. With Theda Bara (Frank Powell)
Dancin' Fool (1920)—MMA. With Wallace Reid (Sam Wood)

The Toll Gate (1920)—MMA. With W. S. Hart (Lambert Hillyer)

Miss Lulu Bett (1921)—MMA. With Lois Wilson (William C. DeMille)

Tol'able David (1921)—EMG, KIT, MMA. With Richard Barthelmess (Henry King)

Blood and Sand (1922)—AUD, MED, MMA. With Rudolf Valentino (Fred Niblo)

The Hunchback of Notre Dame (1922)—AUD, MED. With Lon Chaney (Wallace Worsley)

Salome (1922)—AUD, EMG, MED. With Alla Nazimova (Charles Bryant)

The Covered Wagon (1923)—KIT (James Cruze)

The White Sister (1925)—FI. With Lillian Gish (Henry King)

The Big Parade (1925)—FI (King Vidor)

Phantom of the Opera (1925)—AUD, MED. With Lon Chaney (Rupert Julian)

Our Dancing Mothers (1926)—AUD, MED. With Clara Bow (Herbert Brenon)

Ben Hur (1926)—FI (Fred Niblo)

The Scarlet Letter (1926)—FI. With Lillian Gish (Victor Sjøstrøm)

Son of the Sheik (1926)—AUD, EMG, KIT. With Valentino (George Fitzmaurice)

What Price Glory? (1926)—EMG, MMA (Raoul Walsh)

Hotel Imperial (1927)—MMA (Mauritz Stiller)

The Wind (1927)—FI. With Lillian Gish (Victor Sjøstrøm)

The Crowd (1928)—FI (King Vidor)

7. *The German Film (1920-1933)*

BOOKS

Armour, Robert A. *Fritz Lang*. Boston: Twayne, 1978.

Barsam, Richard Meran. *Filmguide to Triumph of the Will*. Bloomington and London: Indiana University Press, 1975.

Berg-Pan, Renata. *Leni Riefenstahl*. Boston: Twayne, 1980.

Eisner, Lotte. *The Haunted Screen: Expressionism in the German Cinema*. Berkeley and Los Angeles: University of California Press, 1969.

———. *F. W. Murnau*. Berkeley and Los Angeles: University of California Press, 1973.

———. *Fritz Lang*. New York: Oxford University Press, 1977.

Kracauer, Siegfried. *From Caligari to Hitler*. New York: Noonday, 1959.

Manvell, Roger. With Heinrich Fraenkel. *The German Cinema*. New York: Praeger, 1971.

Prawer, S. S. *Caligari's Children: The Film as Tale of Terror*. New York: Oxford University Press, 1980.

Rotha, Paul, and Griffith, Richard. *Film Till Now*. New York: Twayne, 1960, pp. 252–92.

FILMS

FRITZ LANG

Destiny (Der Müde Tod, 1921)—EMG, KIT, MMA

Doktor Mabuse, Der Spieler (1922)—JAN, MMA

Die Niebelungen (1924)—KIT, MMA

Metropolis (1926)—EMG, JAN, KIT, MMA

Spies (1928)—EMG, KIT, MMA

M (1931)—AUD, EMG, JAN, KIT

F. W. MURNAU

Nosferatu (1922)—EMG, KIT, MMA

The Last Laugh (1924)—EMG, KIT, MMA

Tartuffe (1927)—EMG

Sunrise (1927)—MMA

G. W. PABST

The Joyless Street (1925)—MMA

The Love of Jeanne Ney (1927)—MMA

Westfront 1918 (1930)—JAN, MMA

The Threepenny Opera (1931)—JAN

Kameradschaft (1931)—JAN, AUD

OTHER MAJOR FILMS OF THE ERA

The Cabinet of Doctor Caligari (1920)—AUD, EMG, KIT, MMA (Robert Wiene)

The Golem (1920)—EMG, KIT, MED, MMA (Paul Wegener and Henrik Galeen)

Warning Shadows (1922)—AUD, EMG, KIT, MMA (Arthur Robison)

The Street (1923)—MMA (Karl Grune)

Waxworks (1924)—AUD (Paul Leni)

Variety (1925)—AUD, EMG, KIT, MMA (E. A. Dupont)

Berlin: Symphony of a Great City (1927)—EMG, KIT, MMA (Walther Ruttmann)

Überfall (1929)—KIT, MMA (Erno Metzner)

Kuhle Wampe (1932)—AUD (Slatan Dudow and Bertolt Brecht)

Triumph of the Will (1934)—AUD, KIT, MMA (Leni Riefenstahl)

Olympia (1938)—KIT, MMA (Leni Riefenstahl)

8. *The Soviet Film (1917–1940)*

BOOKS

Barna, Yon. *Eisenstein*. Bloomington: Indiana University Press, 1974.

Dickinson, Thorold, and de la Roche, Catherine, eds. *Soviet Cinema*. London: Falcon Press, 1948.

Eisenstein, S. M. *The Film Sense*. New York: Harcourt, Brace, 1947.

———. *Film Form*. New York: Harcourt, Brace, 1949.

———. *Notes of a Film Director*. London: Lawrence and Wisehart, 1959.

Leyda, Jay. *Kino: History of the Russian and Soviet Film*. New York: Macmillan, 1960.

Nizhny, Vladimir. *Lessons with Eisenstein*. New York: Hill and Wang, 1962.

Pudovkin, V. I. *Film Technique and Film Acting*. London: Vision Press, 1959.

Rotha, Paul and Griffith, Richard. *Film Till Now*. New York: Twayne, 1960, pp. 217–51.

Seton, Marie. *Sergei M. Eisenstein*. New York: Grove Press, 1960.

FILMS

ALEXANDER DOVZHENKO
Zvenigora (1928)—AUD, KIT
Arsenal (1929)—AUD, EMG, KIT, MMA
Earth (1930)—AUD, EMG, KIT
Shors (1939)—AUD

S. M. EISENSTEIN
Strike (1925)—AUD, EMG, KIT, MMA
Potemkin (1925)—AUD, EMG, KIT, MMA
October (1928)—AUD, EMG, KIT, MMA
Old and New or *The General Line* (1929)—AUD, EMG, KIT
Thunder Over Mexico (1933)—MMA
Alexander Nevsky (1938)—AUD, EMG, KIT
Ivan the Terrible I, II (1944–1946)—AUD, EMG, KIT

VSEVLOD I. PUDOVKIN
Chess Fever (1925)—KIT, MMA
Mechanics of the Brain (1926)—AUD
Mother (1926)—AUD, EMG, MMA
The End of St. Petersburg (1927)—AUD, EMG, KIT, MMA
Storm Over Asia (1928)—AUD, EMG, KIT, MMA
The Deserter (1933)—MMA

OTHER FILMS OF THE ERA
Kino-Pravda (1922)—MMA (Dziga-Vertov)
The Cloak (1926)—AUD (Kozintsev and Trauberg)
Bed and Sofa (1927)—AUD, EMG, KIT, MMA (Abram Room)
By the Law (1927)—EMG, KIT, MMA (Lev Kuleshov)
The Man with the Movie Camera (1929)—AUD, EMG, KIT (Dziga-Vertov)
Turksib (1929)—AUD (Victor Turin)
The Road to Life (1931)—AUD, MMA (Nikolai Ekk)
Chapayev (1934)—AUD, MMA (the Vasiliev brothers)
The Youth of Maxim (1935)—AUD, MMA (Kozintsev and Trauberg)
Lenin in October (1937)—AUD (Mikhail Romm)
The Gorky Trilogy (1938–1940)—AUD (Mark Donskoi)

9. The Transition to Sound (1927–1930)

BOOKS

Geduld, Harry M. *The Birth of the Talkies*. Bloomington: Indiana University Press, 1975.

Green, Fitzhugh. *The Film Finds Its Tongue*. New York: Putnam, 1929.

FILMS

ILLUSTRATIVE TRANSITIONAL FILMS
The Coming of Sound (1927-1928)—MMA. *Shaw Talks for Movietone, The Jazz Singer* (excerpts), *The Lights of New York, Steamboat Willie, The Sex Life of the Polyp*
The Jazz Singer (1927)—UA (Alan Crosland)
The Singing Fool (1928)—UA (Lloyd Bacon)
Applause (1929)—UNI (Rouben Mamoulian)
The Broadway Melody (1929)—FI (Harry Beaumont)
Hallelujah (1929)—FI (King Vidor)
The Virginian (1929)—MMA, UNI (Victor Fleming)
All Quiet on the Western Front (1930)—SWA, TWY, UNI (Lewis Milestone)

ERNST LUBITSCH
Passion (1919)—BUD, EMG, KIT, MMA
The Marriage Circle (1924)—BUD, EMG, KIT, MMA
Lady Windermere's Fan (1925)—BUD, EMG
So This Is Paris (1925)—EMG
The Love Parade (1929)—MMA, UNI
Monte Carlo (1930)—UNI
Trouble in Paradise (1932)—MMA, UNI
Design for Living (1933)—UNI
The Merry Widow (1934)—FI
Ninotchka (1939)—FI
The Shop Around the Corner (1940)—FI
To Be or Not to Be (1942)—AUD, BUD, KIT, UFC
Cluny Brown (1946)—FI

10. France Between the Wars (1920–1940)

BOOKS

Bazin, André. *Jean Renoir*, edited by François Truffaut. New York: Simon and Schuster, 1973.

Braudy, Leo. *Jean Renoir*. Garden City, N.Y.: Doubleday, 1972.

Clair, René. *Reflections on the Cinema*. London: Kimber, 1953.

———. *Cinema Yesterday and Today*. New York: Dover, 1972.

Durgnat, Raymond. *Renoir*. Berkeley and Los Angeles: University of California Press, 1973.

Gomes, P. E. Salles. *Jean Vigo*. Berkeley and Los Angeles: University of California Press, 1971.

Leprohon, Pierre. *Jean Renoir*. New York: Crown, 1971.

Mast, Gerald. *The Comic Mind: Comedy and the Movies*. 2nd edition. Chicago: University of Chicago Press, 1979, pp. 224–48, 320–25.

———. *Filmguide to Rules of the Game*. Bloomington: Indiana University Press, 1973.

McGerr, Cecilia. *René Clair*. Boston: Twayne, 1980.

Ray, Man. *Self Portrait*. Boston: Little, Brown, 1963.

Renoir, Jean. *My Life and My Films*. New York: Atheneum, 1974.

Sadoul, Georges. *French Film*. London: Falcon Press, 1953.

Sesonske, Alexander. *Jean Renoir: The French Films.* Cambridge, Mass.: Harvard University Press, 1980.

Welsh, James M. and Kramer, Steven P. *Abel Gance.* Boston: Twayne, 1978.

FILMS

MARCEL CARNÉ
Bizarre, Bizarre (1937)—BUD, KIT
Port of Shadows (1938)—BUD
Le Jour se lève (1939)—BUD, KIT
Les Visiteurs du soir (1942)—JAN
The Children of Paradise (1944–1945)—FI

RENÉ CLAIR
Paris qui dort or *The Crazy Ray* (1923)—EMG, KIT, MMA
Entr'acte (1924)—EMG, KIT, MMA
The Italian Straw Hat (1927)—EMG, KIT
Sous les toits de Paris (1930)—BUD, COR, KIT
Le Million (1931)—BUD, COR, EMG, KIT
À Nous la liberté (1931)—BUD, COR, KIT
The Ghost Goes West (1936)—AUD
I Married a Witch (1942)—BUD
It Happened Tomorrow (1944)—BUD
And Then There Were None (1945)—EMG, KIT, UFC

JULIEN DUVIVIER
Poil de carotte (1933)—BUD
Pepé le Moko (1937)—BUD, KIT
Panique (1948)—KIT

JACQUES FEYDER
Crainquebille (1923)—EMG
Carnival in Flanders (1935)—COR, KIT

MARCEL PAGNOL
Marius (1931)—BUD
Fanny (1932)—BUD
César (1936)—BUD

MAN RAY
Return to Reason (1923)—KIT, MMA
Emak Bakia (1927)—KIT, MMA
Etoile de Mer (1928)—KIT, MMA
Les Mystères du Chateau Dé (1929)—KIT, MMA

JEAN RENOIR
The Little Match Girl (1928)—BUD, EMG, MED, MMA
La Chienne (1931)—AUD
Boudu Saved from Drowning (1932)—BUD, COR, KIT
Toni (1934)—COR
The Crime of M. Lange (1935)—AUD
The Lower Depths (1936)—BUD, EMG, KIT
A Day in the Country (1936)—BUD, KIT
Grand Illusion (1937)—BUD, EMG, JAN, KIT
La Bête humaine (1938)—BUD, KIT
La Marseillaise (1938)—COR
The Rules of the Game (1939)—BUD, EMG, JAN, KIT

The Southerner (1945)—BUD, EMG
The River (1951)—AUD, BUD
French Cancan (1955)—AUD
Picnic on the Grass (1959)—COR

JEAN VIGO
Zéro de conduite (1932)—AUD, BUD, KIT
L'Atalante (1934)—AUD, BUD, EMG, KIT

REPRESENTATIVE SILENT FILMS: SHORTS
Fièvre (1921)—MMA (Louis Delluc)
The Smiling Madame Beudet (1922)—MMA (Germaine Dulac)
Ballet Mécanique (1924)—EMG, KIT, MMA (Fernand Léger)
Menilmontant (1925)—EMG, KIT, MMA (Dimitri Kirsanov)
Anaemic Cinema (1926)—KIT, MMA (Marcel Duchamp)
Rien que les heures (1926)—MMA (Alberto Cavalcanti)
The Seashell and the Clergyman (1928)—EMG, KIT, MMA (Germaine Dulac)

FEATURES
La Roue (1923)—EMG (Abel Gance)
The Late Matthew Pascal (1924–1926)—MMA (Marcel L'Herbier)
Napoléon (1926)—EMG (Abel Gance)
The Fall of the House of Usher (1928)—EMG, MMA (Jean Epstein)
The Passion of Joan of Arc (1928)—AUD, EMG, KIT (Carl-Theodore Dreyer)

11. The American Studio Years (1930–1945)

BOOKS

Adamson, Joe. *Groucho, Harpo, Chico, and Sometimes Zeppo.* New York: Simon and Schuster, 1973.

Agee, James. *Agee on Film: Reviews and Comments.* Boston: Beacon Press, 1964.

Bergman, Andrew. *We're in the Money.* New York: Harper, 1972.

Bogdanovich, Peter, *John Ford.* Berkeley and Los Angeles: University of California Press, 1968.

———. *Allan Dwan: The Last Pioneer.* New York: Praeger, 1971.

Capra, Frank. *The Name Above the Title.* New York: Macmillan, 1971.

Carringer, Robert L. and Sabath, Barry. *Ernst Lubitsch: A Guide to References and Sources.* Boston: G. K. Hall, 1980.

Cowie, Peter. *The Cinema of Orson Welles.* New York: Barnes, 1965.

Crowther, Bosley. *The Lion's Share.* New York: Dutton, 1967, pp. 163–283.

Eyles, Allen. *The Marx Brothers: Their World of Comedy.* New York: Barnes, 1966.

Feild, Robert. *The Art of Walt Disney.* New York: Macmillan, 1943.

Grierson, John. "Directors of the Thirties." In *Film: An Anthology,* edited by Daniel Talbot, pp. 110–29. Berkeley and Los Angeles: University of California Press, 1966.

Gussow, Mel. *Don't Say Yes Until I Finish Talking.* Garden City, N.Y.: Doubleday, 1971.

Higham, Charles. *The Films of Orson Welles.* Berkeley and Los Angeles: University of California Press, 1970.

Huettig, Mae D. *Economic Control of the Motion Picture Industry.* Philadelphia: University of Pennsylvania Press, 1944.

Inglis, Ruth A. *Freedom of the Movies.* Chicago: University of Chicago Press, 1947.

Jacobs, Lewis. *The Rise of the American Film.* New York: Harcourt, Brace, 1939, pp. 419–540.

Kael, Pauline. *The Citizen Kane Book.* Boston: Little, Brown, 1971.

Koszarski, Richard. *Hollywood Directors: 1914–1940.* New York: Oxford University Press, 1976.

Lambert, Gavin. *On Cukor.* New York: Putnam, 1972.

Mast, Gerald. *The Comic Mind: Comedy and the Movies.* 2nd edition. Chicago: University of Chicago Press, 1979, pp. 249–93.

Mayer, Arthur. *Merely Colossal.* New York: Simon and Schuster, 1953.

Naremore, James. *The Magic World of Orson Welles.* New York: Oxford University Press, 1978.

Rosow, Eugene. *Born to Lose: The Gangster Film in America.* New York: Oxford University Press, 1978.

Rosten, Leo C. *Hollywood: The Movie Colony and the Movie Makers.* New York: Harcourt, Brace, 1941.

Sarris, Andrew. *The Films of Josef von Sternberg.* New York: Museum of Modern Art, 1966.

Schickel, Richard. *The Disney Version.* New York: Simon & Schuster, 1968.

Seldes, Gilbert. *The Movies Come from America.* New York: Scribners, 1937.

Spoto, Donald. *The Art of Alfred Hitchcock.* New York: Hopkinson and Blake, 1976.

Taylor, Robert Lewis. *W.C. Fields: His Follies and Fortunes.* Garden City, N.Y.: Doubleday, 1949.

Thomas, Bob. *King Cohn.* New York: G. P. Putnam's Sons, 1967.

———. *Thalberg: Life and Legend.* New York: Doubleday, 1969.

Thorp, Margaret. *America at the Movies.* New Haven, Conn.: Yale University Press, 1939.

Truffaut, François. *Hitchcock.* New York: Simon & Schuster, 1967.

Tyler, Parker. *Magic and Myth of the Movies.* New York: Simon and Schuster, 1970.

———. *The Hollywood Hallucination.* New York: Simon & Schuster, 1970.

Von Sternberg, Josef. *Fun in a Chinese Laundry.* New York: Macmillan, 1965.

Weinberg, Herman G. *Josef von Sternberg.* New York: Dutton, 1967.

———. *The Lubitsch Touch.* New York: Dutton, 1968.

Wood, Robin. *Hitchcock's Films.* New York: Barnes, 1965.

———. *Howard Hawks.* London: Secker and Warburg, 1967.

FILMS

FRANK CAPRA
It Happened One Night (1934)—SWA
Mr. Deeds Goes to Town (1936)—AUD, KIT, TWY
Lost Horizon (1937)—AUD, SWA, TWY
Mr. Smith Goes to Washington (1939)—AUD, KIT, TWY
Meet John Doe (1941)—BUD, EMG, KIT
Arsenic and Old Lace (1944)—UA
It's a Wonderful Life (1946)—AUD, BUD, KIT
State of the Union (1948)—UNI

GEORGE CUKOR
Dinner at Eight (1933)—FI
David Copperfield (1934)—FI
Camille (1936)—FI
Holiday (1938)—AUD
The Philadelphia Story (1940)—FI
Gaslight (1944)—FI
Adam's Rib (1949)—FI
Born Yesterday (1950)—AUD, TWY
Pat and Mike (1952)—FI
A Star Is Born (1954)—TWY
My Fair Lady (1964)—SWA
Travels With My Aunt (1973)—FI

MICHAEL CURTIZ
The Charge of the Light Brigade (1936)—UA
Kid Galahad (1937)—UA
Angels With Dirty Faces (1938)—UA
Dodge City (1939)—UA
Santa Fe Trail (1940)—UA
Casablanca (1942)—UA
Yankee Doodle Dandy (1942)—UA
Mildred Pierce (1945)—UA

WILLIAM DIETERLE
A Midsummer Night's Dream (1935)—UA
The Story of Louis Pasteur (1935)—UA
The Life of Emile Zola (1937)—UA
Juarez (1939)—UA
Dr. Ehrlich's Magic Bullet (1940)—UA

WALT DISNEY
Steamboat Willie (1928)—MMA
The Skeleton Dance (1929)—AUD
A selection of Disney cartoons (1933–1953)—AUD
Pinocchio (1940)—SWA
Dumbo (1941)—FI, SWA
Bambi (1943)—SWA
The Three Caballeros (1944)—FI, SWA, TWY
So Dear to My Heart (1948)—FI, SWA, TWY
Alice in Wonderland (1951)—FI, SWA

W. C. FIELDS
Shorts: *The Barber Shop* (1933), *The Fatal Glass of Beer* (1933), *The Pharamacist* (1933)—AUD, EMG, KIT, MED, TWY
Million Dollar Legs (1932)—MMA, UNI
Tillie and Gus (1933)—UNI
Six of a Kind (1934)—UNI
It's a Gift (1934)—UNI
The Old-Fashioned Way (1935)—UNI
Poppy (1936)—UNI
The Bank Dick (1940)—SWA, TWY, UNI
My Little Chickadee (1940)—SWA, TWY, UNI
Never Give a Sucker an Even Break (1941)—SWA, TWY, UNI

JOHN FORD
The Iron Horse (1924)—FI, MMA
The Lost Patrol (1934)—FI
The Informer (1935)—AUD, FI
The Prisoner of Shark Island (1936)—FI
Stagecoach (1939)—BUD, FI, KIT
The Grapes of Wrath (1940)—FI
The Long Voyage Home (1940)—AUD, FI, KIT
How Green Was My Valley (1941)—FI
My Darling Clementine (1946)—FI
Fort Apache (1948)—AUD
She Wore a Yellow Ribbon (1949)—BUD, TWY, UFC
Wagonmaster (1950)—FI
The Quiet Man (1952)—BUD, KIT
The Searchers (1956)—SWA
The Horse Soldiers (1959)—UA
The Man Who Shot Liberty Valance (1962)—FI

HOWARD HAWKS
The Dawn Patrol (1930)—UA
The Crowd Roars (1932)—UA
Scarface (1932)—UNI
Twentieth Century (1934)—AUD
Bringing Up Baby (1938)—FI
Only Angels Have Wings (1939) AUD
His Girl Friday (1941)—AUD, BUD, EMG, KIT
To Have and Have Not (1944)—UA
The Big Sleep (1946)—UA
Red River (1948)—UA
The Big Sky (1952)—FI
Gentlemen Prefer Blondes (1952)—FI
Rio Bravo (1959)—SWA
El Dorado (1967)—FI

ALFRED HITCHCOCK
The Lodger (1927)—BUD, EMG, KIT, MMA
Blackmail (1929)—BUD, EMG, KIT, MMA
The Man Who Knew Too Much (1934), BUD, EMG, KIT, UNI
The 39 Steps (1935)—BUD, EMG, KIT, UFC
Sabotage (1936)—BUD, EMG, KIT, MMA
The Lady Vanishes (1938)—BUD, EMG, JAN, KIT, UFC
Rebecca (1940)—AUD
Foreign Correspondent (1940)—FI

Suspicion (1941)—FI
Saboteur (1942)—TWY, UNI
Shadow of a Doubt (1943)—TWY, UNI
Lifeboat (1944)—FI
Spellbound (1945)—AUD, BUD
Notorious (1946)—AUD, BUD, TWY
Strangers on a Train (1951)—SWA
To Catch a Thief (1955)—FI
The Wrong Man (1956)—SWA
North by Northwest (1959)—FI
Psycho (1960)—SWA, TWY, UNI
The Birds (1963)—SWA, TWY, UNI
Frenzy (1972)—SWA, TWY, UNI
Family Plot (1976)—SWA, TWY, UNI

FRITZ LANG
Fury (1936)—FI
You Only Live Once (1937)—AUD, BUD, FI
Hangmen Also Die (1943)—BUD
Scarlet Street (1945)—BUD, KIT
Rancho Notorious (1952)—BUD, KIT
The Big Heat (1953)—AUD

THE MARX BROTHERS
The Cocoanuts (1929)—SWA, TWY, UNI
Monkey Business (1931)—SWA, TWY, UNI
Horsefeathers (1932)—SWA, TWY, UNI
Duck Soup (1933)—MMA, SWA, TWY, UNI
A Night at the Opera (1935)—FI
A Day at the Races (1937)—FI
At the Circus (1939)—FI

LEO McCAREY
Ruggles of Red Gap (1935)—MMA, TWY, UNI
The Awful Truth (1937)—AUD
Make Way for Tomorrow (1937)—MMA, UNI
Going My Way (1944)—UNI

JOSEF VON STERNBERG
Underworld (1927)—MMA
The Last Command (1928)—MMA
The Blue Angel (1929)—BUD, JAN, KIT
Morocco (1930)—MMA, TWY, UNI
An American Tragedy (1931)—TWY, UNI
Shanghai Express (1932)—TWY, UNI
The Blonde Venus (1932)—TWY, UNI
The Scarlet Empress (1934)—TWY, UNI
The Devil Is a Woman (1935)—MMA, TWY; UNI

PRESTON STURGES
The Great McGinty (1940)—UNI
The Lady Eve (1941)—UNI
Sullivan's Travels (1941)—UNI
The Palm Beach Story (1942)—UNI
The Miracle of Morgan's Creek (1943)—FI
Hail, the Conquering Hero! (1944)—UNI
Mad Wednesday (1947)—KIT, UNI

RAOUL WALSH
The Roaring Twenties (1939)—UA

They Drive by Night (1940)—UA
High Sierra (1941)—UA
They Died With Their Boots On (1941)—UA
White Heat (1949)—UA

ORSON WELLES
Citizen Kane (1941)—AUD, FI, JAN
The Magnificent Ambersons (1942)—FI
Journey into Fear (1942)—FI
The Lady from Shanghai (1948)—AUD
Macbeth (1948)—AUD, BUD, KIT, TWY
Touch of Evil (1958)—TWY, UNI
Mr. Arkadin (1962)—COR
The Trial (1963)—AUD, BUD

WILLIAM WELLMAN
Wings (1929)—FI
Public Enemy (1931)—UA
Wild Boys of the Road (1933)—UA
The President Vanishes (1934)—MMA
Nothing Sacred (1937)—BUD, KIT
A Star Is Born (1937)—BUD, KIT
The Ox-Bow Incident (1943)—FI
The Story of G.I. Joe (1945)—BUD
Battleground (1949)—FI

MAE WEST
She Done Him Wrong (1933)—MMA, UNI
I'm No Angel (1933)—UNI
Belle of the Nineties (1934)—UNI
Goin' to Town (1935)—UNI

MUSICAL FILMS OF THE ERA
Musicals of the Thirties (1929–1935)—MMA.
    Excerpts from *Rio Rita, Golddiggers of 1933* and
    *1935, 42nd Street, Flying Down to Rio, In
    Caliente,* and *Music in the Air*
Love Me Tonight (1932)—UNI (Rouben Mamoulian)
42nd Street (1933)—UA (Lloyd Bacon/Busby
    Berkeley)
Golddiggers of 1933 (1933)—UA (Mervyn
    LeRoy/Busby Berkeley)
Flying Down to Rio (1933)—FI (Thornton Freeland)
Dames (1934)—UA (Ray Enright/Busby Berkeley)
Footlight Parade (1934)—UA (Lloyd Bacon/Busby
    Berkeley)
The Gay Divorcee (1934)—FI (Mark Sandrich)
Golddiggers of 1935 (1935)—UA (Busby Berkeley)
Top Hat (1935)—FI (Mark Sandrich)
In Caliente (1935)—UA (Busby Berkeley)
Swing Time (1936)—FI (George Stevens)
Shall We Dance? (1937)—FI, MMA (Mark Sandrich)

STUDIO ERA MISCELLANY
Little Caesar (1930)—UA (Mervyn LeRoy)
Dracula (1931)—UNI (Tod Browning)
Frankenstein (1931)—UNI (James Whale)
Freaks (1932)—FI (Tod Browning)
Tarzan, the Ape Man (1932)—FI (W. S. Van Dyke)
Grand Hotel (1932)—FI (Edmund Goulding)

I Am a Fugitive from a Chain Gang (1932)—UA
    (Mervyn LeRoy)
King Kong (1933)—FI, JAN (Cooper and
    Schoedsack)
State Fair (1933)—FI (Henry King)
Our Daily Bread (1934)—JAN, MMA (King Vidor)
The Thin Man (1934)—FI (W. S. Van Dyke)
Imitation of Life (1934)—UNI (John Stahl)
Mutiny on the Bounty (1935)—UNI (Frank Lloyd)
My Man Godfrey (1936)—UNI (Gregory LaCava)
Midnight (1936)—UNI (Mitchell Leisen)
The Petrified Forest (1936)—UA (Archie Mayo)
Easy Living (1937)—MMA, UNI (Mitchell Leisen)
The Good Earth (1937)—FI (Sidney Franklin)
Golden Boy (1938)—AUD (Rouben Mamoulian)
Gone with the Wind (1939)—FI (Victor Fleming)
Jesse James (1939)—UFC (Henry King)
The Wizard of Oz (1939)—FI (Victor Fleming)
Dark Victory (1940)—UA (Edmund Goulding)
Now, Voyager (1940)—UA (Irving Rapper)
Since You Went Away (1944)—BUD (John Cromwell)
Murder, My Sweet (1945)—FI (Edward Dmytryk)
State Fair (1945)—FI (Walter Lang)

12. *Years of Transition (1946–1965)*

BOOKS

Alloway, Lawrence. *Violent America: The Movies* 1946-
    64. New York: The Museum of Modern Art,
    1971.
Battcock, Gregory. *The New American Cinema.* New
    York: Dutton, 1967.
Conant, Michael. *Antitrust in the Motion Picture
    Industry.* Berkeley and Los Angeles: University of
    California Press, 1960.
Dick, Bernard F. *Billy Wilder.* Boston: Twayne, 1980.
Halliday, Jon. *Sirk on Sirk.* New York: Viking, 1969.
Kael, Pauline. "Movies, the Desperate Art." In *Film:
    An Anthology,* edited by Daniel Talbot, pp. 51-71.
    Berkeley and Los Angeles: University of Califor-
    nia Press, 1966.
———."Zeitgeist and Poltergeist; Or, Are Movies
    Going to Pieces?" In *I Lost It at the Movies,* pp.
    3-24. New York: Bantam, 1966.
———."*Hud,* Deep in the Divided Heart of Holly-
    wood." In *I Lost It at the Movies,* pp. 69-83.
Kitses, James. *Horizons West: Mann, Boetticher, Peckin-
    pah.* Bloomington: Indiana University Press, 1969.
Koszarski, Richard. *Hollywood Directors: 1941–76.*
    New York: Oxford University Press, 1977.
Lenihan, John H. *Showdown: Confronting Modern
    America in the Western Film.* Chicago and Cham-
    paign-Urbana: University of Illinois Press, 1979.
MacCann, Richard Dyer. *Hollywood in Transition.*
    Cambridge, Mass.: Houghton, Mifflin, 1962.
Madsen, Axel. *Billy Wilder.* Bloomington: Indiana
    University Press, 1969.
Manvell, Roger. *New Cinema in the USA.* New York
    and London: Dutton/Vista, 1968.

Ross, Lillian. *Picture*. New York: Doubleday, 1962.
Stern, Michael. *Douglas Sirk*. Boston: Twayne, 1979.

FILMS

JULES DASSIN
Brute Force (1947)—IVY
Naked City (1948)—IVY
Thieves' Highway (1949)—FI
Night and the City (1951)—FI
Rififi (1954)—BAU, BUD, KIT
Never on Sunday (1960)—UA
Topkapi (1964)—UA

STANLEY DONEN
On the Town (1949)—FI (co-dir. Gene Kelly)
Singin' in the Rain (1952)—FI (co-dir. Gene Kelly)
Seven Brides for Seven Brothers (1954)—FI
Funny Face (1957)—FI
Two for the Road (1967)—FI
Bedazzled (1968)—FI
Movie Movie (1978)—SWA

JOHN HUSTON
The Maltese Falcon (1941)—UA
The Treasure of the Sierra Madre (1948)—UA
Key Largo (1948)—UA
The Asphalt Jungle (1950)—FI
The Red Badge of Courage (1951)—FI
The African Queen (1951)—AUD, BUD, TWY
Beat the Devil (1954)—AUD
The Misfits (1961)—UA
The Man Who Would Be King (1975)—HUR

ELIA KAZAN
A Tree Grows in Brooklyn (1945)—FI, TWY
Boomerang (1947)—FI
Gentleman's Agreement (1947)—FI
Pinky (1949)—FI
A Streetcar Named Desire (1951)—UA
Viva Zapata! (1952)—FI
On the Waterfront (1954)—AUD, SWA, TWY
East of Eden (1955)—AUD, SWA, TWY
A Face in the Crowd (1957)—FI
Wild River (1960)—FI
Splendor in the Grass (1961)—TWY
The Last Tycoon (1976)—FI

STANLEY KRAMER
The Defiant Ones (1958)—UA
On the Beach (1959)—UA
Inherit the Wind (1960)—UA
Judgment at Nuremberg (1961)—UA
Guess Who's Coming to Dinner (1967)—TWY

SIDNEY LUMET
Twelve Angry Men (1957)—UA
A Long Day's Journey into Night (1962)—KIT, TWY
The Pawnbroker (1965)—AUD
Serpico (1973)—FI
Murder on the Orient Express (1974)—FI
Dog Day Afternoon (1975)—SWA
Network (1976)—UA

JOSEPH L. MANKIEWICZ
The Ghost and Mrs. Muir (1947)—-FI
All About Eve (1950)—FI
Julius Caesar (1953)—FI
The Barefoot Contessa (1954)—UA
Suddenly Last Summer (1959)—TWY

VINCENTE MINNELLI
Cabin in the Sky (1943)—FI
Meet Me in St. Louis (1944)—FI
The Pirate (1948)—FI
An American in Paris (1951)—FI
The Band Wagon (1953)—FI
The Bad and the Beautiful (1953)—FI
Lust for Life (1956)—FI
Designing Woman (1957)—FI
Gigi (1958)—FI
The Reluctant Debutante (1958)—FI
Some Came Running (1959)—FI
Bells Are Ringing (1960)—FI

OTTO PREMINGER
Laura (1944)—FI
The Moon Is Blue (1953)—BUD
The River of No Return (1954)—FI
The Man with the Golden Arm (1955)—BUD
Anatomy of a Murder (1959)—AUD, KIT
Exodus (1960)—UA
Advise and Consent (1962)—AUD, COR, KIT

ROBERT ROSSEN
Johnny O'Clock (1947)—KIT
Body and Soul (1947)—BUD
All the King's Men (1949)—AUD, TWY
The Hustler (1961)—FI
Lilith (1964)—COR

DOUGLAS SIRK
Magnificent Obsession (1954)—UNI
All That Heaven Allows (1956)—UNI
Written on the Wind (1957)—UNI
The Tarnished Angels (1958)—UNI
Imitation of Life (1959)—UNI

GEORGE STEVENS
Alice Adams (1935)—FI
Vivacious Lady (1938)—FI
Gunga Din (1939)—FI
Woman of the Year (1942)—FI
I Remember Mama (1948)—FI
A Place in the Sun (1951)—FI
Shane (1953)—FI
Giant (1956)—AUD, TWY

BILLY WILDER
Double Indemnity (1944)—UNI
The Lost Weekend (1945)—UNI
A Foreign Affair (1948)—UNI

Sunset Boulevard (1950)—FI
Stalag 17 (1953)—FI
Sabrina (1954)—FI
Love in the Afternoon (1957)—HUR
Some Like It Hot (1959)—UA
The Apartment (1960)—UA

WILLIAM WYLER
Dead End (1937)—AUD, BUD, TWY
Wuthering Heights (1939)—AUD, BUD, TWY
The Little Foxes (1941)—AUD, BUD, TWY
The Best Years of Our Lives (1946)—AUD, BUD, TWY
Roman Holiday (1953)—FI
Friendly Persuasion (1956)—HUR
Ben Hur (1959)—FI
Funny Girl (1968)—SWA

FRED ZINNEMANN
The Men (1950)—BUD
High Noon (1952)—BUD, TWY
Member of the Wedding (1952)—AUD
From Here to Eternity (1953)—AUD, TWY
The Nun's Story (1959)—AUD, BUD
A Man for All Seasons (1966)—BUD, SWA
Julia (1977)—FI

TRANSITIONAL ERA MISCELLANY
A Walk in the Sun (1946)—BUD, KIT, MED (Lewis Milestone)
The Killers (1946)—UNI (Robert Siodmak)
Crossfire (1947)—FI (Edward Dmytryk)
Call Northside 777 (1948)—FI (Henry Hathaway)
Easter Parade (1948)—FI (Charles Walters)
Force of Evil (1948)—BUD (Abraham Polonsky)
The Senator Was Indiscreet (1948)—BUD (George S. Kaufman)
I Shot Jesse James (1949)—BUD (Samuel Fuller)
Criss Cross (1949)—UNI (Robert Siodmak)
Winchester 73 (1950)—UNI (Anthony Mann)
The Thing (1951)—FI (Christian Nyby)
Bend of the River (1952)—UNI (Anthony Mann)
Lili (1953)—FI (Charles Walters)
The Wild One (1953)—AUD (Laslo Benedek)
Johnny Guitar (1954)—BUD, KIT (Nicholas Ray)
Bad Day at Black Rock (1955)—FI (John Sturges)
The Big Knife (1955)—UA (Robert Aldrich)
The Blackboard Jungle (1955)—FI (Richard Brooks)
Marty (1955)—UA (Delbert Mann)
Night of the Hunter (1955)—UA (Charles Laughton)
Rebel Without a Cause (1955)—AUD, SWA, TWY (Nicholas Ray)
Invasion of the Body Snatchers (1956)—BUD, KIT (Don Siegel)
Picnic (1956)—AUD, COR (Joshua Logan)
Run of the Arrow (1956)—BUD (Samuel Fuller)
The Goddess (1958)—AUD (John Cromwell)
I Want to Live (1958)—UA (Robert Wise)
The Savage Eye (1959)—AUD (Maddow, Meyers, and Strick)
Elmer Gantry (1960)—UA (Richard Brooks)

The Magnificent Seven (1960)—UA (John Sturges)
A Cold Wind in August (1961)—UA (Alexander Singer)
Breakfast at Tiffany's (1961)—FI (Blake Edwards)
David and Lisa (1962)—AUD, BUD, KIT (Frank Perry)
Lonely Are the Brave (1962)—TWY, UNI (David Miller)
The Manchurian Candidate (1962)—UA (John Frankenheimer)
Experiment in Terror (1962)—TWY (Blake Edwards)
Whatever Happened to Baby Jane? (1962)—SWA (Robert Aldrich)
Shock Corridor (1963)—BUD (Samuel Fuller)
Hud (1963)—FI (Martin Ritt)
The Spy Who Came in from the Cold (1965)—FI (Martin Ritt)
A Thousand Clowns (1965)—UA (Fred Coe)

13. *Postwar Cinema in Italy and France (1945–1980)*

BOOKS

Allen, Don. *Truffaut.* New York: Viking, 1974.
Armes, Roy. *French Cinema Since 1946.* 2 volumes. New York: Barnes, 1966.
———.*The Cinema of Alain Resnais.* New York: Barnes, 1968.
Bazin, André. *What is Cinema?* 2 volumes. Berkeley and Los Angeles: University of California Press, 1967, 1971.
Bondanella, Peter, ed. *Federico Fellini: Essays in Criticism.* New York: Oxford University Press, 1978.
Cameron, Ian, ed. *The Films of Robert Bresson.* New York: Praeger, 1970.
Cameron, Ian and Wood, Robin. *Antonioni.* New York: Praeger, 1968.
Cocteau, Jean. *Cocteau on the Film.* New York: Roy Publishers, 1954.
Cowie, Peter. *Antonioni, Bergman, Resnais.* New York: Thomas Yoseloff, 1964.
Durgnat, Raymond. *Nouvelle Vague: The First Decade.* Essex: Loughton, 1963.
Fellini, Federico. *Fellini on Fellini.* New York: Delacorte, 1976.
Godard, Jean-Luc. *Godard on Godard.* Trans. by Tom Milne. New York: Viking, 1972.
Guarner, José Luis. *Roberto Rossellini.* New York: Praeger, 1970.
Houston, Penelope. *Contemporary Cinema.* Baltimore, Md.: Penguin, 1964.
Insdorf, Annette. *François Truffaut.* Boston: Twayne, 1978.
Jarratt, Vernon. *The Italian Cinema.* New York: Macmillan, 1951.
Kael, Pauline. "The Come-Dressed-as-the-Sick-Soul of Europe Parties: *La Notte, Last Year at Marienbad, La Dolce Vita.*" In *I Lost It at the Movies*, pp. 162-76. New York: Bantam, 1966.

Kreidl, John Francis. *Alain Resnais*. Boston: Twayne, 1979.

Leprohon, Pierre. *Michelangelo Antonioni*. New York: Simon & Schuster, 1963.

Manvell, Roger. *New Cinema in Europe*. New York and London: Dutton/Vista, 1966.

Monaco, James. *The New Wave*. New York: Oxford University Press, 1976.

———. *Alain Resnais*. New York: Oxford University Press, 1978.

Mussman, Toby, ed. *Jean-Luc Godard: A Critical Anthology*. New York: Dutton, 1968.

Petrie, Graham. *The Cinema of François Truffaut*. New York: Barnes, 1970.

Rondi, Gian. *Italian Cinema Today*. New York: Hill & Wang, 1965.

Roud, Richard. *Jean-Luc Godard*. New York: Doubleday, 1968.

Siclier, Jacques. *Nouvelle Vague?* Paris: Editions du Cerf, 1961.

Snyder, Stephen. *Pier Paolo Pasolini*. Boston: Twayne, 1980.

Ward, John. *Alain Resnais, or The Theme of Time*. New York: Doubleday, 1968.

FILMS

ITALY

MICHELANGELO ANTONIONI
Il Grido (1957)—AUD
L'Avventura (1960)—JAN
La Notte (1961)—COR
L'Eclisse (1962)—AUD
The Red Desert (1964)—AUD
Blow Up (1966)—FI
Zabriskie Point (1970)—FI
The Passenger (1975)—FI

BERNARDO BERTOLUCCI
Before the Revolution (1964)—AUD, NYF
The Conformist (1971)—FI
Last Tango in Paris (1973)—UA
1900 (1977)—PAR

VITTORIO DE SICA
Shoeshine (1946)—JAN
The Bicycle Thief (1948)—AUD
Miracle in Milan (1951)—JAN
Umberto D (1952)—JAN
Gold of Naples (1955)—AUD
Two Women (1961)—AUD
The Garden of the Finzi-Contini's (1971)—CIN

FEDERICO FELLINI
Variety Lights (1950)—AUD
The White Sheik (1952)—AUD
La Strada (1954)—JAN
Il Bidone (1955)—AUD
I Vitelloni (1956)—COR
Nights of Cabiria (1957)—AUD

La Dolce Vita (1959)—AUD
8½ (1963)—AUD
Juliet of the Spirits (1965)—AUD
Fellini-Satyricon (1969)—UA
Amarcord (1974)—FI

PIER PAOLO PASOLINI
Accattone! (1961)—AUD
The Gospel According to St. Matthew (1964)—AUD
The Hawks and the Sparrows (1965)—AUD
Teorema (1969)—BUD
The Decameron (1972)—UA
Salo (1977)—UA

ROBERTO ROSSELLINI
Open City (1945)—BUD, EMG, KIT
Paisan (1946)—BUD, EMG, KIT
Germany Year Zero (1947)—AUD
The Miracle (1948)—AUD
Stromboli (1950)—AUD, BUD
General Della Rovere (1959)—AUD, BUD
The Rise to Power of Louis XIV (1965)—AUD

LUCHINO VISCONTI
Ossessione (1942)—AUD
La Terra Trema (1948)—AUD
Senso (1954)—AUD
Rocco and His Brothers (1960)—AUD
The Leopard (1963)—FI
The Damned (1968)—SWA
Death in Venice (1971)—SWA

LINA WERTMÜLLER
Love and Anarchy (1974)—CIN
All Screwed Up (1974)—NEW
The Seduction of Mimi (1974)—NEW
Swept Away (1975)—CIN
Seven Beauties (1976)—CIN

ITALIAN MISCELLANY
Bitter Rice (1949)—AUD (Giuseppi de Santis)
Il Posto (1961)—JAN (Ermanno Olmi)
The Easy Life (1963)—AUD (Dino Risi)
The Fiancés (1963)—JAN (Ermanno Olmi)
The Girl with the Suitcase (1963)—AUD (Valerio Zurlini)
Seduced and Abandoned (1964)—BUD (Pietro Germi)
The Organizer (1964)—BUD (Mario Monicelli)
The 10th Victim (1965)—AUD (Elio Petri)
China is Near (1967)—COR (Marco Bellochio)
Once Upon a Time in the West (1969)—FI (Sergio Leone)
Investigation of a Citizen above Suspicion (1970)—SWA (Elio Petri)
In the Name of the Father (1971)—NYF (Marco Bellochio)

FRANCE

ROBERT BRESSON
Diary of a Country Priest (1951)—AUD
Pickpocket (1959)—NYF

Une Femme douce (1969)—NYF
Lancelot of the Lake (1974)—NYF

CLAUDE CHABROL
The Cousins (1959)—COR
Les Bonnes Femmes (1959)—AUD
Les Biches (1968)—AUD
Le Boucher (1970)—SWA

JEAN COCTEAU
Blood of a Poet (1930)—AUD, BUD, EMG, KIT
Beauty and the Beast (1946)—JAN
Les Parents Terribles (1948)—AUD
Orpheus (1949)—JAN
The Testament of Orpheus (1959)—AUD

JEAN-LUC GODARD
Breathless (1959)—COR
A Woman Is a Woman (1961)—COR
Vivre sa vie (1962)—COR
Les Carabiniers (1963)—FAC
Le Petit Soldat (1963)—COR
Band of Outsiders (1964)—COR
A Married Woman (1964)—SWA
Contempt (1964)—AUD
Alphaville (1965)—COR
Pierrot le fou (1965)—COR
Two or Three Things I Know About Her (1965)—NYF
Masculine/Feminine (1966)—COR
Weekend (1968)—GRO
Le Gai Savoir (1969)—TWY
Tout va bien (1972)—NYF

LOUIS MALLE
Frantic (1958)—AUD, BUD
The Lovers (1958)—NYF
Zazie (1960)—NYF
Viva Maria (1965)—UA
Murmur of the Heart (1971)—BUD
Lacombe, Lucien (1974)—FI
Pretty Baby (1978)—FI

MAX OPHULS
Letter from an Unknown Woman (1948)—BUD
Caught (1949)—BUD
La Ronde (1950)—JAN
The Earrings of Madame de. . .(1953)—COR
Lola Montès (1955)—AUD

ALAIN RESNAIS
Hiroshima Mon Amour (1959)—COR
Last Year at Marienbad (1961)—AUD
Muriel (1963)—COR
La Guerre est finie (1966)—AUD
Stavisky (1974)—CIN
Providence (1977)—CIN

ERIC ROHMER
La Collectioneuse (1967)—COR
My Night at Maud's (1969)—COR

Claire's Knee (1970)—COR
Chloe in the Afternoon (1971)—COR

JACQUES TATI
Mr. Hulot's Holiday (1953)—BUD
Playtime (1968)—BUD
Traffic (1972)—SWA

FRANÇOIS TRUFFAUT
The 400 Blows (1959)—JAN
Shoot the Piano Player (1960)—JAN
Jules and Jim (1961)—JAN
Fahrenheit 451 (1966)—SWA, TWY, UNI
The Bride Wore Black (1968)—UA
Stolen Kisses (1968)—CIN
Bed and Board (1970)—SWA
The Wild Child (1970)—UA
Day for Night (1974)—SWA
The Story of Adele H (1975)—FI
Small Change (1976)—FI
The Man Who Loved Women (1977)—CIN

FRENCH MISCELLANY
Symphonie Pastorale (1947)—AUD (Jean Delannoy)
Les Enfants Terribles (1950)—COR (Jean-Pierre Melville)
Casque d'or (1952)—JAN (Jacques Becker)
Forbidden Games (1952)—JAN (René Clément)
The Wages of Fear (1953)—BUD, KIT (Henri-Georges Clouzot)
Diabolique (1955)—BUD, KIT (Henri-Georges Clouzot)
And God Created Woman (1956)—COR (Roger Vadim)
Purple Noon (1959)—AUD (René Clément)
Paris Belongs to Us (1958–1960)—JAN (Jacques Rivette)
Les Liaisons dangereuses (1959)—AUD (Roger Vadim)
Cleo from Five to Seven (1961)—COR (Agnes Varda)
Sundays and Cybele (1962)—SWA (Serge Bourgignon)
Judex (1963)—BUD, KIT (Georges Franju)
The Umbrellas of Cherbourg (1964)—AUD (Jacques Demy)
Le Bonheur (1965)—JAN (Agnes Varda)
The Battle of Algiers (1966)—AUD (Gillo Pontecorvo)
King of Hearts (1967)—UA (Philippe de Broca)
The Two of Us (1968)—COR (Claude Berri)
L'Amour fou (1968)—NYF (Jacques Rivette)
Z (1969)—CIN (Costa-Gavras)
The Confession (1970)—FI (Costa-Gavras)
La Salamandre (1971)—NYF (Alain Tanner)
The Sorrow and the Pity (1972)—CIN (Marcel Ophuls)
The Mother and the Whore (1973)—NYF (Jean Eustache)
Going Places (1974)—CIN (Bertrand Blier)
Celine and Julie Go Boating (1974)—NYF (Jacques Rivette)
The Wonderful Crook (1975)—NYF (Claude Goretta)
Jonah Who Will Be 25 in the Year 2000 (1976)—NYF (Alain Tanner)
The Lacemaker (1977)—NYF (Claude Goretta)

Get Out Your Handkerchiefs (1978)—NEW (Bertrand Blier)

14. Emerging National Traditions (1945–1980)

BOOKS

Aranda, Francisco. *Luis Buñuel: A Critical Biography.* New York: DaCapo, 1976.

Armes, Roy. *A History of the British Cinema.* New York: Oxford University Press, 1978.

Barnouw, Erik and Krishnaswamy, Subramanyam. *The Indian Film.* New York: Columbia University Press, 1963.

Cowie, Peter. *Swedish Cinema.* New York: Barnes, 1966.

Donner, Jorn. *The Personal Vision of Ingmar Bergman.* Bloomington: Indiana University Press, 1964.

Durgnat, Raymond. *Luis Buñuel.* Berkeley and Los Angeles: University of Calfornia Press, 1968.

Higginbotham, Virginia. *Luis Buñuel.* Boston: Twayne, 1979.

Kaminsky, Stuart, ed. *Ingmar Bergman: Essays in Criticism.* New York: Oxford University Press, 1975.

Kyrou, Ado. *Luis Buñuel: An Introduction.* New York: Simon and Schuster, 1963.

Lauritzen, Einar. *Swedish Film.* Garden City, N.Y.: Doubleday, 1962.

Liehm, Antonin J. *Closely Watched Films: The Czechoslovak Experience.* White Plains, N.Y.: International Arts, 1974.

Mellen, Joan. *The Waves at Genji's Door: Japan Through Its Cinema.* New York: Pantheon, 1976.

——, ed. *Luis Buñuel: Essays in Criticism.* New York: Oxford University Press, 1978.

Richie, Donald. *The Films of Akira Kurosawa.* Berkeley and Los Angeles: University of California Press, 1965.

—— *The Japanese Cinema.* New York: Doubleday, 1971.

—— *Ozu.* Berkeley and Los Angeles: University of California Press, 1973.

—— and Anderson, Joseph. *Japanese Film: Art and Industry.* New York: Grove Press, 1960.

Seton, Marie. *Portrait of a Director: Satyajit Ray.* Bloomington: Indiana University Press 1971.

Simon, John. *Ingmar Bergman Directs.* New York: Harcourt, Brace, 1972.

Stoil, Michael Jon. *Cinema Beyond the Danube.* Metuchen, N.J.: Scarecrow Press, 1974.

FILMS

SWEDEN

INGMAR BERGMAN
Monika (1952)—JAN
The Naked Night (1953)—JAN
Smiles of a Summer Night (1955)—JAN
The Seventh Seal (1957)—JAN
Wild Strawberries (1958)—JAN
The Magician (1959)—JAN
Through a Glass Darkly (1962)—JAN
Winter Light (1963)—JAN
The Silence (1963)—JAN
Persona (1967)—UA
Shame (1969)—UA
The Passion of Anna (1970)—UA
Cries and Whispers (1972)—FI
Scenes from a Marriage (1974)—CIN
The Magic Flute (1975)—FI

SWEDISH MISCELLANY
Miss Julie (1951)—JAN (Alf Sjøberg)
Dear John (1966)—AUD (Lars Magnus Lindgren)
Here's Your Life (1966)—AUD (Jan Troell)
Elvira Madigan (1967)—SWA (Bo Widerberg)
My Sister, My Love (1967)—AUD (Vilgot Sjøman)
I Am Curious (Yellow) (1968)—GRO (Vilgot Sjøman)
Adalen '31 (1969)—FI (Bo Widerberg)
The Emmigrants (1972)—SWA (Jan Troell)

GREAT BRITAIN

LINDSAY ANDERSON
This Sporting Life (1963)—TWY
If. . . (1968)—FI
O Lucky Man! (1973)—SWA

JACK CLAYTON
Room at the Top (1959)—BUD
The Innocents (1961)—FI
The Pumpkin Eater (1964)—AUD

DAVID LEAN
Brief Encounter (1946)—BUD
Great Expectations (1947)—AUD, BUD, TWY
Oliver Twist (1948)—JAN
Summertime (1955)—BUD
The Bridge on the River Kwai (1957)—AUD, COR, SWA, TWY
Lawrence of Arabia (1962)—COR, SWA, TWY
Doctor Zhivago (1965)—FI
Ryan's Daughter (1970)—FI

RICHARD LESTER
A Hard Day's Night (1964)—UA
The Knack (1965)—UA
Help! (1965)—UA
Petulia (1968)—TWY
The Three Musketeers (1974)—FI
The Four Musketeers (1975)—FI
Robin and Marion (1976)—SWA

JOSEPH LOSEY
The Boy with Green Hair (1948)—FI
The Big Night (1951)—UA
The Servant (1963)—JAN

King and Country (1964)—AUD, IVY
Accident (1967)—SWA
The Go-Between (1971)—AUD

LAURENCE OLIVIER
Henry V (1944)—AUD, TWY
Hamlet (1948)—AUD, TWY
Richard III (1955)—JAN

CAROL REED
Odd Man Out (1947)—BUD, JAN
The Fallen Idol (1949)—BUD
The Third Man (1950)—BUD, KIT, TWY
Outcast of the Islands (1952)—BUD, KIT
The Man Between (1953)—BUD
The Key (1958)—AUD, COR
Our Man in Havana (1960)—AUD, COR
Oliver! (1968)—SWA, TWY

TONY RICHARDSON
The Entertainer (1960)—BUD
Sanctuary (1961)—AUD
A Taste of Honey (1962)—TWY
The Loneliness of the Long-Distance Runner (1962)—
   AUD, BUD, TWY
Tom Jones (1963)—UA
Joseph Andrews (1977)—PAR

KEN RUSSELL
Women in Love (1970)—UA
The Music Lovers (1971)—UA
The Devils (1971)—SWA
The Boy Friend (1971)—FI
Tommy (1975)—SWA

JOHN SCHLESINGER
Billy Liar (1963)—BUD, COR, TWY
Darling (1965)—AUD, BUD
Midnight Cowboy (1969)—UA
Sunday, Bloody Sunday (1971)—UA
Day of the Locust (1975)—FI
Marathon Man (1976)—FI

THE BRITISH "LITTLE COMEDIES"
Kind Hearts and Coronets (1949)—JAN (Robert
   Hamer)
Tight Little Island (1949)—JAN (Alexander
   Mackendrick)
The Lavender Hill Mob (1951)—JAN (Charles
   Crichton)
The Man in the White Suit (1952)—JAN (Alexander
   Mackendrick)
The Captain's Paradise (1953)—BUD, TWY (Anthony
   Kimmins)
The Ladykillers (1955)—JAN (Alexander Macken-
   drick)
The Green Man (1957)—AUD (Robert Day)
The Horse's Mouth (1958)—JAN (Ronald Neame)
I'm All Right, Jack (1960)—AUD, COR (John Boult-
   ing)

BRITISH MISCELLANY
The Red Shoes (1948)—TWY (Powell and Press-
   burger)
Tales of Hoffman (1951)—TWY (Powell and Press-
   burger)
The Importance of Being Earnest (1952)—JAN
   (Anthony Asquith)
The Angry Silence (1959)—AUD, COR (Guy Green)
Sons and Lovers (1960)—FI (Jack Cardiff)
Tunes of Glory (1960)—JAN (Ronald Neame)
The Kitchen (1961)—AUD (James Hill)
Saturday Night and Sunday Morning (1961)—COR
   (Karel Reisz)
Whistle Down the Wind (1961)—JAN (Bryan Forbes)
Billy Budd (1962)—HUR (Peter Ustinov)
The Begger's Opera (1963)—TWY (Peter Brook)
Lord of the Flies (1963)—TWY (Peter Brook)
The Girl with Green Eyes (1964)—UA (Desmond
   Davies)
Seance on a Wet Afternoon (1964)—JAN (Bryan
   Forbes)
Morgan! (1966)—SWA (Karel Reisz)
Georgy Girl (1966)—AUD, TWY (Silvio Narizzano)
The Whisperers (1967)—UA (Bryan Forbes)
Marat/Sade (1967)—UA (Peter Brook)
Joanna (1968)—FI (Michael Sarne)
Isadora (1968)—TWY (Karel Reisz)
The Lion in Winter (1968)—AUD (Anthony Harvey)
Romeo and Juliet (1968)—FI (Franco Zeffirelli)
The Prime of Miss Jean Brodie (1969)—FI (Ronald
   Neame)
King Lear (1971)—AUD (Peter Brook)
The Rocky Horror Picture Show (1975)—FI (Jim
   Sharman)

CENTRAL AND EASTERN EUROPE

MILOŠ FORMAN
Black Peter (1963)—AUD
Loves of a Blonde (1965)—AUD
The Firemen's Ball (1967)—CIN
Taking Off (1971)—SWA, TWY, UNI
One Flew Over the Cuckoo's Nest (1976)—UA
Hair (1979)—UA

JAN KADÁR AND ELMAR KLOS
Death is Called Engelchen (1963)—AUD
The Shop on Main Street (1965)—AUD

MIKLOS JANCSO
My Way Home (1964)—AUD
The Round Up (1965)—AUD
The Red and the White (1968)—AUD
Silence and Cry (1968)—AUD

DUŠAN MAKAVEJEV
*Love Affair, or The Case of the Missing Switchboard
   Operator* (1967)—AUD
Innocence Unprotected (1970)—GRO
WR—Mysteries of the Organism (1971)—CIN

ROMAN POLANSKI
Knife in the Water (1962)—BUD, JAN
Repulsion (1965)—SWA
Rosemary's Baby (1968)—FI
Macbeth (1971)—SWA
Chinatown (1974)—FI

ANDREJ WAJDA
A Generation (1955)—JAN
Kanal (1957)—JAN
Ashes and Diamonds (1958)—JAN
Landscape After Battle (1970)—NYF
Everything for Sale (1978)—NYF

MISCELLANY: CZECHOSLOVAKIA, HUNGARY, POLAND, YUGOSLAVIA
The Good Soldier Schweik (1957)—COR (Karel Stekly)
Intimate Lighting (1965)—AUD (Ivan Passer)
Closely Watched Trains (1966)—AUD (Jiři Menzel)
Daisies (1966)—AUD (Veřa Chytilová)
The Fifth Horseman Is Fear (1966)—AUD (Zbyněk Brynych)
A Report on the Party and the Guests (1966)—AUD (Jan Němec)
Salto (1966)—AUD (Tadeusz Konwicki)
I Even Met Happy Gypsies (1967)—AUD (Aleksandar Petrovič)
Capricious Summer (1968)—AUD (Jiři Menzel)
Love (1971)—AUD (Karoly Makk)
Marketa Lazerova (1972)—AUD (František Vlačil)

THE NEW GERMAN CINEMA

RAINER WERNER FASSBINDER
Why Does Herr R. Run Amok? (1969)—NYF
Beware of a Holy Whore (1970)—NYF
The Merchant of the Four Seasons (1972)—NYF
The Bitter Tears of Petra von Kant (1972)—NYF
Ali: Fear Eats the Soul (1974)—NYF
Effi Briest (1974)—NYF
Fox and His Friends (1975)—NYF
Mother Küsters Goes to Heaven (1975)—NYF
Satan's Brew (1976)—NYF
Chinese Roulette (1976)—NYF
Despair (1978)—NEW
The Marriage of Maria Braun (1979)—NYF

WERNER HERZOG
Signs of Life (1968)—NYF
Land of Silence and Darkness (1971)—NYF
Aguirre, The Wrath of God (1973)—NYF
Kaspar Hauser (1975)—CIN
Heart of Glass (1976)—NYF
Stroszek (1977)—NYF
Woyzeck (1979)—NYF

WIM WENDERS
The Goalie's Anxiety at the Penalty Kick (1972)—BAU
Alice in the Cities (1974)—BAU
Kings of the Road (1976)—BAU
The American Friend (1977)—NYF

GERMAN MISCELLANY
The Confessions of Felix Krull (1957)—AUD (Kurt Hoffmann)
The Bridge (1960)—HUR (Bernhard Wicki)
Young Törless (1966)—NYF (Volker Schlöndorff)
The Wild Duck (1976)—NYF (Hans Giessendorfer)
Coup de Grace (1977)—CIN (Volker Schlöndorff)

JAPAN AND INDIA

KON ICHIKAWA
The Harp of Burma (1956)—JAN
Fires on the Plain (1959)—JAN
Odd Obsession (1960)—JAN
Tokyo Olympiad (1964)—AUD

AKIRA KUROSAWA
Drunken Angel (1948)—AUD
Stray Dog (1949)—AUD
Rashomon (1950)—JAN
The Idiot (1951)—NYF
Ikiru (1952)—AUD
Seven Samurai (1954)—AUD
The Lower Depths (1957)—AUD
Throne of Blood (1957)—AUD
Yojimbo (1960)—AUD
Red Beard (1965)—AUD
Dodes' Ka-den (1970)—JAN
Derzu Usala (1975)—FI

KENJI MIZOGUCHI
Sisters of the Gion (1936)—AUD
The Story of the Last Chrysanthemum (1938)—AUD
Utamaro and his Five Women (1946)—NYF
Women of the Night (1948)—AUD
The Life of O'Haru (1952)—NYF
Ugetsu (1953)—JAN
A Geisha (1953)—NYF
The Bailiff (1954)—AUD
Princess Yang Kwei Fei (1955)—NYF
Street of Shame (1956)—JAN

YASUJIRO OZU
I Was Born, But. . . (1932)—NYF
Passing Fancy (1933)—AUD
There Was a Father (1942)—AUD
Late Spring (1949)—NYF
Early Summer (1951)—AUD
The Flavor of Green Tea over Rice (1952)—NYF
Tokyo Story (1953)—NYF
Early Spring (1956)—NYF
Tokyo Twilight (1957)—AUD
Ohayo (1959)—AUD
Floating Weeds (1959)—JAN
Late Autumn (1960)—NYF
End of Summer (1961)—NYF
Autumn Afternoon (1962)—NYF

SATYAJIT RAY
Pather Panchali (1955)—AUD
Aparajito (1956)—AUD

The World of Apu (1958)—AUD
The Music Room (1959)—AUD
Devi (1960)—AUD
Kanchenjungha (1962)—AUD
Mahanagar (1963)—AUD
Days and Nights in the Forest (1970)—COR
Distant Thunder (1973)—CIN
The Chess Players (1978)—JAN

JAPANESE MISCELLANY

Gate of Hell (1953)—JAN, SWA, TWY (Teinosuke Kinugasa)
Samurai (1953)—AUD (Hiroshi Inagaki)
The Rikisha Man (1957)—UNI (Hiroshi Inagaki)
The Human Condition (1959)—AUD (Masaki Kobayashi)
Bad Boys (1960)—AUD (Susumu Hani)
The Island (1961)—AUD (Kaneto Shindo)
She and He (1963)—AUD (Susumu Hani)
Kwaidan (1964)—JAN (Masaki Kobayashi)
Woman in the Dunes (1964)—COR (Hiroshi Teshigahara)
Bwana Toshi (1965)—AUD (Susumu Hani)
Kuroneko (1968)—COR (Kaneto Shindo)
Double Suicide (1969)—AUD (Masahiro Shinoda)
The Man Who Left His Will on Film (1970)—NYF (Nagisa Oshima)
The Ceremony (1971)—NYF (Nagisa Oshima)
Kaseki (1974)—NYF (Masaki Kobayashi)

LUIS BUÑUEL

Un Chien andalou (1929)—AUD, BUD, EMG, KIT, MMA
L'Age d'or (1930)—COR
Los Olvidados (1950)—AUD
El (1952)—AUD
The Adventures of Robinson Crusoe (1952)—AUD
Illusion Travels by Streetcar (1953)—AUD
Nazarin (1958)—AUD
Viridiana (1961)—AUD
The Exterminating Angel (1962)—AUD
Belle de Jour (1966)—AUD
The Milky Way (1969)—SWA
The Discreet Charm of the Bourgeoisie (1972)—FI
That Obscure Object of Desire (1978)—FI

THIRD WORLD CINEMA

CUBA

Memories of Underdevelopment (1968)—UNF (Tomas Guttierez Alea)
Lucia (1969)—UNF (Humberto Solas)
The Man from Maisinicu (1973)—UNF (Manuel Perez)
The Other Francisco (1975)—UNF (Sergio Giral)
Alicia (1976)—UNF (Victor Casaus)
The Last Supper (1977)—UNF (Tomas Guttierez Alea)

SOUTH AMERICA

Vidas Secas (1963)—NYF (Nelson Pereira dos Santos, Brazil)
The Hour of the Furnaces (1968)—UNF (Fernando Solanos and Octavio Getino, Argentina)

The Jackal of Nahueltoro (1969)—UNF (Miguel Littin, Chile)
Blood of the Condor (1969)—UNF (Jorge Sanjines, Bolivia)
Antonio das Mortes (1969)—GRO (Glauber Rocha, Brazil)
The Battle of Chile (1973)—UNF (Patricio Guzman, Chile)
The Promised Land (1973)—UNF (Miguel Littin, Chile)
Rebellion in Patagonia (1974)—UNF (Hector Olivera, Argentina)

AFRICA

Black Girl (1965)—NYF (Ousmane Sembene, Senegal)
Night of Counting the Years (1969)—NYF (Shadi Abdelsalam, Egypt)
Xala (1974)—NYF (Ousmane Sembene, Senegal)
Harvest: 3000 Years (1975)—UNF (Haile Gerima, Ethiopia)
Last Grave at Dimbaza (1975)—UNF (Nana Mahomo, South Africa)
Ceddo (1976)—NYF (Ousmane Sembene, Senegal)
Black and White in Color (1976)—COR (Jean-Jacques Arnaud, Ivory Coast)

15. The American Cinema (1965–1980)

BOOKS

Curtis, David. *Experimental Cinema*. New York: Universe Books, 1971.
Johnson, Robert K. *Francis Ford Coppola*. Boston: Twayne, 1979.
Kael, Pauline, "Commitment and Straitjacket." In *I Lost It at the Movies*, pp. 55–69. New York: Bantam, 1969.
Kolker, Robert Phillip. *A Cinema of Loneliness: Penn, Kubrick, Coppola, Scorsese, Altman*. New York: Oxford University Press, 1980.
Mast, Gerald. *The Comic Mind: Comedy and the Movies*. 2nd edition. Chicago: University of Chicago Press, 1979. pp. 306–19.
McKinney, Doug. *Sam Peckinpah*. Boston: Twayne, 1978.
Monaco, James. *American Film Now*. New York: Oxford University Press, 1979.
Renan, Sheldon. *An Introduction to the American Underground Film*. New York: Dutton, 1967.
Seydor, Paul. *Peckinpah: The Western Films*. Chicago and Champaign-Urbana: University of Illinois Press, 1980.
Sitney, P. Adams. *Visionary Film*. 2nd edition. New York: Oxford University Press, 1979.
Walker, Alexander. *Stanley Kubrick Directs*. New York: Harcourt, Brace, 1971.
Youngblood, Gene. *Expanded Cinema*. New York: Dutton, 1970.

FILMS

WOODY ALLEN
Take the Money and Run (1968)—FI
Bananas (1971)—UA
Everything You Always Wanted to Know About Sex. . .
    (1972)—UA
Sleeper (1973)—UA
Love and Death (1975)—UA
Annie Hall (1977)—UA
Interiors (1978)—UA
Manhattan (1979)—UA

ROBERT ALTMAN
M*A*S*H (1970)—FI
Brewster McCloud (1970)—FI
McCabe and Mrs. Miller (1972)—SWA
Thieves Like Us (1974)—UA
Nashville (1975)—FI
Three Women (1977)—FI

HAL ASHBY
Harold and Maude (1971)—FI
The Last Detail (1973)—SWA
Shampoo (1975)—SWA
Bound for Glory (1976)—UA
Coming Home (1978)—UA
Being There (1979)—UA

PETER BOGDANOVICH
Targets (1968)—FI
The Last Picture Show (1971)—SWA
What's Up, Doc? (1972)—SWA
Paper Moon (1973)—FI

MEL BROOKS
The Producers (1968)—TWY
Blazing Saddles (1972)—SWA
Young Frankenstein (1975)—FI
High Anxiety (1977)—FI

FRANCIS FORD COPPOLA
You're a Big Boy Now (1967)—TWY
The Godfather I (1972)—FI
The Conversation (1974)—FI
The Godfather II (1975)—FI
Apocalypse Now (1979)—UA

GEORGE ROY HILL
The World of Henry Orient (1967)—UA
Thoroughly Modern Millie (1967)—AUD, TWY
Butch Cassidy and the Sundance Kid (1969)—FI
The Sting (1973)—SWA, TWY, UNI
The Great Waldo Pepper (1975)—SWA, TWY, UNI
Slap Shot (1977)—SWA, UNI

STANLEY KUBRICK
Killer's Kiss (1955)—UA
The Killing (1956)—UA
Paths of Glory (1957)—UA
Lolita (1962)—FI
Dr. Strangelove (1963)—SWA
2001: A Space Odyssey (1968)—FI
A Clockwork Orange (1973)—SWA
Barry Lyndon (1975)—SWA

SAM PECKINPAH
Ride the High Country (1962)—FI
The Wild Bunch (1968)—SWA, TWY
The Ballad of Cable Hogue (1970)—TWY
Straw Dogs (1971)—FI
Pat Garrett and Billy the Kid (1973)—FI

ARTHUR PENN
The Left-Handed Gun (1958)—TWY
The Miracle Worker (1962)—UA
Mickey One (1965)—TWY
Bonnie and Clyde (1967)—SWA
Alice's Restaurant (1969)—UA
Little Big Man (1971)—SWA
The Missouri Breaks (1976)—UA

MARTIN SCORSESE
Mean Streets (1973)—SWA
Taxi Driver (1974)—SWA
Alice Doesn't Live Here Anymore (1974)—SWA
New York, New York (1977)—UA

STEVEN SPIELBERG
Sugarland Express (1975)—TWY
Jaws (1976)—SWA, UNI
Close Encounters of the Third Kind (1978)—SWA

AMERICAN MISCELLANY
Who's Afraid of Virginia Woolf? (1966)—SWA (Mike
    Nichols)
A Fine Madness (1966)—AUD (Irvin Kershner)
Cool Hand Luke (1967)—SWA, TWY (Stuart Rosen-
    berg)
In Cold Blood (1967)—SWA (Richard Brooks)
Up the Down Staircase (1967)—TWY (Robert Mulli-
    gan)
In the Heat of the Night (1967)—UA (Norman
    Jewison)
Faces (1968)—BUD (John Cassavetes)
Bullitt (1968)—SWA, TWY (Peter Yates)
The Graduate (1968)—TWY (Mike Nichols)
Night of the Living Dead (1968)—AUD (George A.
    Romero)
Pretty Poison (1968)—FI (Noel Black)
Rachel, Rachel (1968)—AUD, TWY (Paul Newman)
Easy Rider (1969)—SWA (Peter Fonda and Dennis
    Hopper)
They Shoot Horses, Don't They? (1969)—FI (Sidney
    Pollack)
Medium Cool (1969)—FI (Haskell Wexler)
Bob and Carol and Ted and Alice (1969)—AUD (Paul
    Mazursky)
Where's Poppa? (1970)—UA (Carl Reiner)
Patton (1970)—FI (Franklin J. Schaffner)
Five Easy Pieces (1970)—SWA (Bob Rafelson)
Joe (1970)—SWA (John G. Avildsen)

Klute (1971)—SWA (Alan J. Pakula)
The French Connection (1971)—FI (William Friedkin)
THX 1138 (1971)—TWY (George Lucas)
Fritz the Cat (1972)—SWA (Ralph Bakshi)
Deliverance (1972)—SWA, TWY (John Boorman)
Carnal Knowledge (1972)—SWA (Mike Nichols)
Something for Everyone (1972)—SWA (Harold Prince)
Cabaret (1972)—HUR (Bob Fosse)
American Graffiti (1973)—SWA, UNI (George Lucas)
The Exorcist (1974)—SWA (William Friedkin)
Harry and Tonto (1974)—FI (Paul Mazursky)
Lenny (1974)—UA (Bob Fosse)
Badlands (1974)—SWA (Terrence Malick)
All the President's Men (1975)—SWA (Alan J. Pakula)
The Memory of Justice (1976)—FI (Marcel Ophuls)
Carrie (1976)—UA (Brian De Palma)
Rocky (1976)—UA (John G. Avildsen)
The Goodbye Girl (1977)—SWA (Herbert Ross)
Midnight Express (1978)—SWA (Alan Parker)
The Deer Hunter (1978)—SWA (Michael Cimino)
Heaven Can Wait (1978)—FI (Warren Beatty and Buck Henry)
Days of Heaven (1978)—PAR (Terrence Malick)

INDEPENDENT CINEMA MISCELLANY

Rhythmus 21 (1921)—EMG, KIT, MMA (Hans Richter)
Symphonie Diagonale (1921–24)—EMG, KIT, MMA (Viking Eggeling)
The Life and Death of 9413—A Hollywood Extra (1928)—EMG, KIT, MMA (Florey and Vorkapich)
H₂O (1929)—MMA (Ralph Steiner)
Lot in Sodom (1933)—AUD (Watson and Webber)
The Films of Oskar Fischinger (1933–49)—MMA
Colour Box (1935)—MMA (Len Lye)
Swinging the Lambeth Walk (1940)—MMA (Len Lye)
Meshes of the Afternoon (1943)—MMA (Maya Deren)
Fireworks (1947)—CFS, FMC (Kenneth Anger)
Mother's Day (1948)—AUD (James Broughton)
Muscle Beach (1950)—AUD (Joseph Strick)
Loony Tom, the Happy Lover (1951)—AUD, MMA (James Broughton)
The Pleasure Garden (1954)—AUD (James Broughton)
Reflections on Black (1955)—AUD (Stan Brakhage)
The Wonder Ring (1955)—AUD, MMA (Stan Brakhage)
NY, NY (1957)—MMA (Francis Thompson)
Flesh of Morning (1957)—AUD, FMC (Stan Brakhage)
Blazes (1957)—MMA (Robert Breer)
Jamestown Baloos (1957)—MMA (Robert Breer)
A Movie (1958)—AUD, MMA (Bruce Conner)
Anticipation of the Night (1958)—MMA (Stan Brakhage)
Wedlock House: An Intercourse (1959)—AUD, FMC (Stan Brakhage)

Window Water Baby Moving (1959)—FMC, MMA (Stan Brakhage)
The Flower Thief (1960)—FMC (Ron Rice)
Catalog (1961)—MMA (John Whitney)
Cosmic Ray (1961)—AUD, CFS, MMA (Bruce Conner)
Blonde Cobra (1958–63)—FMC (Ken Jacobs)
The Death of P'town (1961)—FMC (Ken Jacobs)
Guns of the Trees (1961)—FMC (Jonas Mekas)
Thanatopsis (1960–62)—FMC (Ed Emshwiller)
Horse Over Teakettle (1962)—FMC, MMA (Robert Breer)
Normal Love (1963)—FMC (Jack Smith)
Dog Star Man (1959–64)—AUD, FMC (Stan Brakhage)
Breathdeath (1963–64)—CFS, FMC (Stan VanDerBeek)
Blow Job (1964)—AND (Andy Warhol)
Scorpio Rising (1962–64)—FMC (Kenneth Anger)
Sins of the Fleshapoids (1964)—FMC (George and Mike Kuchar)
Mass (1963–64)—AUD, MMA (Bruce Baillie)
Fist Fight (1964)—MMA (Robert Breer)
Harlot (1965)—AND (Andy Warhol)
Quixote (1964–65)—AUD, MMA (Bruce Baillie)
My Hustler (1965)—AND (Andy Warhol)
Oh Dem Watermelons (1965)—AUD, FMC, MMA (Robert Nelson)
Report (1965)—AUD (Bruce Conner)
All My Life (1966)—MMA (Bruce Baillie)
The Chelsea Girls (1966)—AND (Andy Warhol)
Castro Street (1966)—AUD, FMC, MMA (Bruce Baillie)
Inauguration of the Pleasure Dome (1954–1966)—FMC (Kenneth Anger)
Relativity (1963–1966)—FMC (Ed Emshwiller)
Wavelength (1967)—MMA (Michael Snow)
The Great Blondino (1967)—MMA (Robert Nelson)
Atmosfear (1967)—MMA (Tom DeWitt)
Offon (1967)—MMA (Scott Bartlett)
Chinese Firedrill (1968)—MMA (Will Hindle)
Permutations (1968)—MMA (John Whitney)
69 (1968)—MMA (Robert Breer)
Trash (1968)—CIN (Andy Warhol and Paul Morrissey)
Scenes from Under Childhood (1968)—AUD, FMC (Stan Brakhage)
The Machine of Eden (1969)—MMA (Stan Brakhage)
Quick Billy (1968–1971)—AUD (Bruce Baillie)
Multiple Maniacs (1970)—FMC (John Waters)
Tom, Tom, the Piper's Son (1971)—MMA (Ken Jacobs)
Zorn's Lemma (1971)—FMC (Hollis Frampton)
Matrix (1971)—MMA (John Whitney)
Deus Ex (1971)—FMC (Stan Brakhage)
Pink Flamingoes (1971)—NEW (John Waters)
The Riddle of Lumen (1972)—FMC (Stan Brakhage)

Distributors

AND
Warhol Films, Inc.
33 Union Square West
New York, N.Y. 10003
(212) 924-4344

AUD
Audio-Brandon Films
34 MacQuesten Parkway South
Mount Vernon, N.Y. 10550
(914) 664-5051

or

1619 N. Cherokee
Los Angeles, Cal. 90028
(213) 463-1131

or

3868 Piedmont Ave.
Oakland, Cal. 94611
(415) 658-9890

or

8400 Brookfield Ave.
Brookfield, Ill. 60513
(312) 485-3925

or

2512 Program Dr.
Dallas, Texas 75220
(214) 357-6494

BAU
Bauer International
119 North Bridge St.
Somerset, N.Y. 08876
(201) 526-5656

BUD
Budget Films
4590 Santa Monica Blvd.
Los Angeles, Cal. 90029
(213) 660-0187

CFS
Creative Film Society
8435 Geyser Ave.
Northridge, Cal. 91324
(213) 786-8277

CIN
Cinema 5 16
595 Madison Ave.
New York, N.Y. 10022
(212) 421-5555

COR
Corinth Films
410 East 62nd St.
New York, N.Y. 10021
(212) 421-4770

EMG
EmGee Film Library
16024 Ventura Blvd.
Encino, Cal. 91436
(213) 981-5506

FAC
FACSEA
922 Fifth Ave.
New York, N.Y. 10021
(212) 737-9700

FI
Films Incorporated
440 Park Avenue South
New York, N.Y. 10016
(212) 889-7910 or (800) 223-6346

or

476 Plasamour Dr. Northeast
Atlanta, Ga. 30324
(404) 873-5101 or (800) 241-5530

or

733 Green Bay Rd.
Wilmette, Ill. 60091
(312) 256-6600 or (800) 323-1406

or

5625 Hollywood Blvd.
Hollywood, Cal. 90028
(213) 466-5481 or (800) 421-0612

FMC
Filmmakers' Cooperative
175 Lexington Ave.
New York, N.Y. 10016
(212) 889-3820

GRO
Grove Press Films
53 East 11th St.
New York, N.Y. 10003
(212) 677-2400

HUR
Hurlock Cine World
13 Arcadia Rd.
Old Greenwich, Conn. 06870
(203) 637-4319

IVY
Ivy Films 16
165 West 46th St.
New York, N.Y. 10036
(212) 765-3940

JAN
Janus Films
now distributed by Films Incorporated
see above

KIT
Kit Parker Films
Carmel Valley, Cal. 93924
(408) 659-3474

MED
Media International
107 North Franklin St.
Madison, Wis. 53703
(608) 255-3184

MMA
Museum of Modern Art
Department of Film
11 West 53rd St.
New York, N.Y. 10019
(212) 956-6100

NEW
New Line Cinema
853 Broadway
New York, N.Y. 10003
(212) 674-7460 or (800) 221-5150

NYF
New Yorker Films
16 West 61st St.
New York, N.Y. 10023
(212) 247-6110

PAR
Paramount Pictures (Nontheatrical)
5451 Marathon Ave.
Hollywood, Cal. 90038
(213) 462-0700 or (800) 421-4432

SWA
Swank Motion Pictures
6762 Forest Lawn Dr.
Hollywood, Cal. 90068
(213) 851-6300

or

220 Forbes Road
Braintree, Mass. 02184
(617) 848-8300

or

201 South Jefferson Ave.
St. Louis, Mo. 63103
(314) 534-6300

or

60 Bethpage Rd.
Hicksville, N.Y. 11801
(516) 931-7500

or

7926 Jones Branch Dr.
McLean, Va. 22102
(703) 821-1040

or

4111 Director's Row
Houston, Texas 77092
(713) 683-8222

or

1200 Roosevelt Rd.
Glen Ellyn, Ill. 60137
(312) 629-9004

TWY
Twyman Films
329 Salem Ave., Box 605
Dayton, Ohio 45401
(513) 222-4014 or (800) 543-9594

or

2321 W. Olive Ave.
Burbank, Cal. 91505
(213) 843-8052

or

175 Fulton Ave., 306
Hempstead, N.Y. 11550
(516) 481-4050

UA
United Artists 16
727 Seventh Ave.
New York, N.Y. 10019
(212) 575-4715

UFC
United Films
1425 South Main St.
Tulsa, Okla. 74119
(918) 583-2681

UNF
Unifilm
1550 Bryant St.
San Francisco, Cal. 94103
(415) 864-7755

or

419 Park Ave. South
New York, N.Y. 10019
(212) 686-9890

UNI
Universal 16
P.O. Box 5000
6060 McDonough Dr.
Norcross, Ga. 30091
(404) 448-0486

or

425 North Michigan Ave.
Chicago, Ill. 60611
(312) 822-0513

or

810 South St. Paul St.
Dallas, Texas 75201
(214) 741-3164

or

8901 Beverly Blvd.
Los Angeles, Cal. 90048
(213) 550-7461

or

445 Park Ave.
New York, N.Y. 10022
(212) 759-7500

Acknowledgments

The author and publisher wish to thank the following for making available photographic stills:

from *Wavelength;* courtesy of Anthology Film Archives.

A Kinetoscope Parlor and *Fred Ott's Sneeze;* reprinted by Arno Press, Inc., 1970.

from the films *Potemkin, Mother, October, Arsenal,* and *The End of St. Petersburg;* courtesy of R. & S. Madell, Russian Film Library.

from the films *Diary of a Country Priest, 8½, Closely Watched Trains, Intimate Lighting, Viridiana, Pather Panchali, Throne of Blood,* and *The Bicycle Thief;* courtesy of Audio-Brandon Films.

from the film *La Strada;* courtesy of Avco-Embassy Films.

from *On the Waterfront;* courtesy of Columbia Pictures Television, a Division of Columbia Pictures Industries, Inc.

from the films *Breathless, Vivre sa vie, The Children of Paradise,* and *À Nous la liberté;* courtesy of Contemporary Films/McGraw-Hill.

from *A Trip to the Moon, The General, The Pawnshop, One A.M., The Last Laugh,* and *Easy Street;* courtesy of Em Gee Film Library.

from *Mr. Hulot's Holiday* and *Playtime,* courtesy of Jacques Tati.

from the films *The 39 Steps, The Rules of the Game, Jules and Jim, The 400 Blows, L'Avventura, Citizen Kane, Ugetsu, Wild Strawberries, The Seventh Seal, The Blue Angel,* and *Grand Illusion;* courtesy of Janus Films.

from *Scorpio Rising;* courtesy of Kenneth Anger.

from *The Passion of Joan of Arc;* courtesy of La Societé Nouvelle des Establishment Gaumont.

from *Lola Montès;* courtesy of Les Films de la Pléade.

from the MGM releases: *Singin' in the Rain,* copyright © 1952 Loew's Inc.; and *Greed,* copyright © 1925 Metro-Goldwyn Pictures Corporation, copyright renewed 1952 by Loew's Inc.

from the films *Seven Years Bad Luck, Rescued by Rover, Queen Elizabeth, The Lonely Villa, The*

New York Hat, The Birth of a Nation, Intolerance, Broken Blossoms, The Surf Girl, High and Dizzy, The Cabinet of Doctor Caligari, The Joyous Microbes, Le Zoetrope, and Muybridge's leaping horse; courtesy of The Museum of Modern Art.

from *The Informer* and *Swing Time;* courtesy of RKO Radio Pictures, a Division of RKO General, Inc.

from *The Red Desert;* courtesy of Rizzoli Editore Corporation.

from *The Gold Rush;* copyright © Roy Export Company Establishment.

from *Metropolis;* courtesy of Standard Film Service.

from *Nosferatu* and *Destiny,* courtesy of Transit Films.

from *Stagecoach;* courtesy of TV Cinema Sales Corporation.

from the films *The Jazz Singer, Golddiggers of 1935, Red River, Persona,* and *Annie Hall;* courtesy of United Artists Corporation.

from the films *Trouble in Paradise, The Scarlet Empress, The Blonde Venus,* and *Foolish Wives;* courtesy of Universal Pictures.

from *Steamboat Willie* and *The Skeleton Dance;* used by permission, copyright © Walt Disney Productions.

from the motion pictures *Rebel Without a Cause,* copyright © 1955; *Day for Night,* copyright © 1974; courtesy of Warner Bros., Inc.

from the films *Lucia, Xala, Memories of Underdevelopment,* and *The Last Supper;* courtesy of Unifilm.

from the films *Vidas Secas, Alice in the Cities, Stroszek, The American Friend, Effi Briest, Ali: Fear Eats the Soul,* and *Aguirre: The Wrath of God;* courtesy of New Yorker Films.

Index

Page numbers in **bold** indicate major entries

Andersson, Harriet, 335
Andrews, Dana, 5
Andy Hardy Gets Spring Fever, 225
Angel, 229
Anger, Kenneth, 180, 438, 439, **440-41**, 442
Angry Silence, The, 348
"Angry Young Man" films, 345, 347, 348
Animation, 10, **30-31, 190-92**, 229, 265, 360-61, 438, 439
   live-action comedy, combined with, 36, 190
Anni Difficili, 285
Annie Hall, 422, 424, 425, 426
Anstey, Edgar, 345
Antimyth era, 432
Antonio-das-Mortes, 406
Antonioni, Michelangelo, 246, 281, **291-96**, 297, 298, 302, 331, 333, 412, 418, 451
Anything Goes, 225
Aparajito, 395, 396, **397-400**
Apartment, The, 275
Apocalypse Now, 428, 449
Applause, **188**
Apu Trilogy. *See Aparajito, Pather Panchali*, and *The World of Apu*.
Arbuckle, Roscoe C. ("Fatty"), 79, 83, 95, **103**, 120, 201
Aristotle, 264
Arletty, 215, 216
Armat, Thomas, 20, 39
Aronson, Max ("Broncho Billy"), 27, 35
L'Arrivé d'un train en gare, 19
L'Arroseur arrosée, 19, **21-22**, 23, 76
Arsenal, **175-77**, 401
"Art" films, 278, 362, 418-19, 436, 437
Artaud, Antonin, 197, 299, 367
Arthur, Jean, 5, 232
Arvidson, Linda, 45
Ashby, Hal, 429, 447
Ashes and Diamonds, **360**
Aspegren, Chuck, 448, 449

Asquith, Anthony, 344, 345
Assassination of the Duke of Guise, The, 43
Astaire, Fred, 221, 222, 224, 275, 276, 277
At Land, 438
At Long Last Love, 431
At the Circus, 233
L'Atalante, **212, 214**
Atmosfear, 439
Atonement of Gosta Berling, The, 323, 334
Attenborough, Richard, 350
August, Joseph, 240, 242
Aurenche, Jean, and Pierre Bost, 313
Austin, Albert, 90
"Auteur theory," 3, 54, 225, 298, 327, 424, 429, 450
Autobiography of Miss Jane Pitman, The, 446
L'Avventura, 246, 292, 293, **294-95**, 400, 419

Bacall, Lauren, 246
Backus, Jim, 272, 273
Bad Day at Black Rock, 272
Baddely, Hermione, 346
Badlands, 423, 429
Baer, Harry, 364
Baillie, Bruce, **442**
Bálázs, Bela, 361
Ballad of a Soldier, 180
Ballad of Cable Hogue, The, 432
Ballet Mécanique, 195, 327
Bananas, 424
Bandits of Orgosolo, The, 297
Banerji, Subir, 398
Bank, The, 88
Bank Dick, The, 234, 235
Bannerjee, Bibhuti, 396
Bara, Theda, **95**
Barbarella, 328
Bardot, Brigitte, 313, 324, 328
Barney Oldfield's Race for a Life, **80-81**, 82
Barrault, Jean-Louis, 215, 216
Barrie, J. M., 108-09
Barrier, 361
Barry Lyndon, 433

Barrymore, John, 245
Barrymore, Lionel, 51, 53, 188, 189, 223
Barthelmess, Richard, 72, 73, 95, 116
Bartlett, Scott, 439
Basehart, Richard, 287
Bates, Alan, 350
Batka, Bedrich, 352
Battle Cry of Peace, The, 129
Battle of Algiers, The, 330, 400
Battle of Chile, The, 402, 408
Bauman, Charles, 42
Bazin, André, 29, 110, 134, 160, 286, 313, 317, 328, 331-32
Beach at Dover, The, 20
Beat the Devil, 270
Beatles, the, 92, 348
Beatty, Ned, 427
Beatty, Warren, 420, 427, 450
Beaumont, Harry, 189
Beauties of the Night, 303
Beautiful Blonde from Bashful Bend, The, 275
Beauty and the Beast, 303, 304
Beauty and the Devil, 302
Beckett, Samuel, 123, 214, 281
Becky Sharp, 265
Bed and Board, 317
Bed and Sofa, 178
Beery, Wallace, 81
Before the Revolution, 298, 300
Being There, 429
Belasco, David, 27, 45, 46, 74
Bellamy, Ralph, 246
Belle de Jour, 413, 414
Belle of the Nineties, 234
Bellochio, Marco, 297
Belmondo, Jean-Paul, 320, 321, 324
Belson, Jordan, 439
Ben Hur, 27, 267
Bend of the River, 272
Benedek, Laslo, 274
Bennett, Alma, 122
Benshi, 378, 398
Bergman, Ingmar, 2, 3, 29, 135, 281, 318, 319, 333,

Nabokov, Vladimir, 434, 435
Naked City, 274
Naked Night, The, 335
Nanook of the North, **117–18,** 124
Napoléon, 196, 263
Nashville, 427, 446
National Board of Censorship (National Board of Review), **42,** 102
Nazarin, 413, 415
Neckár, Václav, 354
Negri, Pola, 131, 187
Neighbor's Wife and Mine, The, 378
Nelson, Robert, 440
Němec, Jan, 352
Neo-Impressionist Painter, The, 31
Neorealism, 277, **283–86,** 291, 297, 298, 345, 348, 353, 361, 396, 406, 429
Network, 432
New Centurions, The, 423
New School, The, 404
"New Wave" ("*Nouvelle Vague*"), 211, **313–30,** 331–32, 350, 353, 430
New York Hat, The, **53,** 54, 57
New York, New York, 429
Newman, Alfred, 421
Newsreels, 100, 167, 178, 183, 253, 255, 315
Next Stop Greenwich Village, 429
Nichols, Dudley, 242, 243
Nichols, Mike, 379, 419, **432**
Nicholson, Jack, 293, 427
Nickelodeon, 431
Nickelodeon, **40,** 41, 101
Niebelungen, Die, 138, 148
Nielsen, Asta, 131, 144
Niepce, Nicéphore, 11
Night and Day, 225
Night and Fog, 325
Night at the Opera, A, 225, 233
Night Moves, 432
Night of Counting the Years, The, 402, 404
Night of the Iguana, 271

Night They Raided Minsky's, The, 422, 431
Nights of Cabiria, 278, **287–88,** 289, 353
Nikkatsu studio, 379
1900, **300,** 301, 404, 405
1941, 432
Ninety in the Shade, 352
Ninotchka, 229
Nordisk, 150
Norma Rae, 447
Normand, Mabel, 78, 80, 81, 82, 83, 103
Norris, Frank, 53, **112–14**
North by Northwest, 250, 271
Nosferatu (1922), **139–41,** 363, 364
Nosferatu (1979), 362
Not as a Stranger, 268
Notorious, 250
Notte, La, 292
Novarro, Ramon, 95
Numero deux, 324
Nykvist, Sven, 339

O, Lucky Man!, 350
Obsession, 431
October, or *Ten Days That Shook the World,* **162–64,** 172, 173, 401
Odd Man Out, 344
Odd Obsession, 394
Of Mice and Men, 225
Offon, 439
Ohayo (Good Morning), **393–94**
Old and New or *The General Line,* **164,** 404
Old-Fashioned Way, The, 235
Oliver!, 344
Oliver Twist, 344
Olivier, Laurence, 266, 305, 344, 347
Olmi, Ermanno, 298
Olvidados, Los, 413, **414**
Olympia, 148
On the Beach, 269
On the Waterfront, 38, 268, 270
Once Upon a Time in the West, 302
One A.M., **88–90**
One Exciting Night, 71
One Flew over the Cuckoo's Nest, 358, 446

One Million B.C., 75
One, Two, Three, 275
Onésime Horloger, 194
L'Onorevole Angelina, 285
Open City (Roma, Città Aperta), **282–83,** 287, 419
Ophuls, Marcel, 407, 408
Ophuls, Max, 215, 217, **304–09,** 319, 363, 365, 366
Organizer, The, 297
Orphans of the Storm, 71
Orphée, 303
Orthochromatic film, 318
Osborne, John, 345, 347
Oshima, Nagisa, 395
Ossessione, 286
O'Toole, Peter, 344
Out in the World, 179
Outlaw and His Wife, The, 334
Owen, Alun, 345
Ox-Bow Incident, The, 226
Oyama, 378
Ozu, Yasujiro, 377, 378, 379, 380, **392–94**

Pabst, G. W., 36, **144–46,** 148, 280, 411, 433
Pacino, Al, 429
Pagnol, Marcel, 211
Paisán, 285, 287
Palace of the Arabian Nights, The, 29
Pallette, Eugene, 204
Panavision, 264, 287, 426
Panchromatic film, 6, 318, 406
Panofsky, Erwin, 134
Paper Moon, 430
Paramount Pictures, 42, 44, 82, **98–99,** 100, 118, 165, 182, 222, **223,** 261, 279
Parents Terribles, Les, 303
Paris, John Ayrton, 9
Paris nous appartiennent, 329
Paris qui dort (The Crazy Ray), **199**
Pasolini, Pier Paolo, **298–300,** 302, 331, 367
Passenger, The, 293
Passer, Ivan, 352, 353, **358–60**